SO-AEE-580

Chicago Public Library

REFERENCE

Form 178 rev. 1-94

Design of
Wood Structures

Donald E. Breyer
*Professor of Civil Engineering
and Engineering Technology
California State Polytechnic University
Pomona, Calif.*

Third Edition

McGraw-Hill, Inc.
New York   San Francisco   Washington, D.C.   Auckland   Bogotá
Caracas   Lisbon   London   Madrid   Mexico City   Milan
Montreal   New Delhi   San Juan   Singapore
Sydney   Tokyo   Toronto

Library of Congress Cataloging-in-Publication Data

Breyer, Donald E.
    Design of wood structures / Donald E. Breyer. — 3rd ed.
        p.   cm.
    Includes bibliographical references and index.
    ISBN 0-07-007678-2
    1. Building, Wooden.   2. Structural engineering.   I. Title.
TH1101.B69 1993
624.1′84—dc20   92-36739
                                                          CIP

Copyright © 1993, 1988, 1980 by McGraw-Hill, Inc. All rights reserved.
Printed in the United States of America. Except as permitted under the
United States Copyright Act of 1976, no part of this publication may be
reproduced or distributed in any form or by any means, or stored in a
data base or retrieval system, without the prior written permission of
the publisher.

    2 3 4 5 6 7 8 9 0   DOC/DOC   9 9 8 7 6 5 4 3

ISBN   0-07-007678-2

*The sponsoring editor for this book was Larry S. Hager, the editing su-
pervisor was Jim Halston, and the production supervisor was Suzanne
W. Babeuf. It was set in Century Schoolbook by McGraw-Hill's
Professional Book Group composition unit.*

Printed and bound by R. R. Donnelley.

Information contained in this work has been obtained by McGraw-
Hill, Inc., from sources believed to be reliable. However, neither
McGraw-Hill nor its authors guarantee the accuracy or complete-
ness of any information published herein, and neither McGraw-
Hill nor its authors shall be responsible for any errors, omissions,
or damages arising out of use of this information. This work is
published with the understanding that McGraw-Hill and its authors are supplying information but are not attempting to render
engineering or other professional services. If such services are required, the assistance of an appropriate professional should be
sought.

BUSINESS/SCIENCE/TECHNOLOGY DIVISION

R00967 27983

Contents

Chapter 6. Beam Design

Chapter 7. Axial Forces and Combined Bending and Axial Forces

Chapter 8. Plywood and Other Structural-Use Panels

Preface

The purpose of this book is to introduce engineers, technologists, and architects to the design of wood strucutres. It is designed to serve either as a text for a course in timber design or as a reference for systematic self-study of the subject.

The book will lead the reader through the complete design of a wood structure (except for the foundation). The sequence of the material follows the same general order that it would in actual design:

1. Vertical design loads and lateral forces
2. Design for vertical loads (beams and columns)
3. Design for lateral forces (horizontal diaphragms and shearwalls)
4. Connection design (including the overall tying together of the vertical- and lateral-force-resisting systems)

The need for such an overall approach to the subject became clear from experience gained in teaching timber design at the undergraduate level.

This text pulls together the design of the various elements into a single reference. A large number of practical design examples are provided throughout the text. Because of their wide usage, buildings naturally form the basis of the majority of these examples. However, the principles of member design and diaphragm design have application to other structures (such as concrete formwork and falsework).

This book relies on practical, current industry literature as the basis for structural design. This includes publications of the National Forest Products Association, the International Conference of Building Officials, and the American Plywood Association.

In the writing of this text, an effort has been made to conform to the spirit and intent of the reference documents. The interpretations are those of the author and are intended to reflect current structural design practice. The material presented is suggested as a guide only, and final design responsibility lies with the structural engineer.

The third edition of this book was promoted by two major developments:

1. Publication of new wood design criteria in the *1991 National Design Specification for Wood Construction (NDS)*

2. Development of new seismic design requirements which are included in the 1988 and 1991 editions of the *Uniform Building Code*

These represent major changes in structural design criteria.

The basic wood design principles in older editions of the NDS remained largely unchanged for many years. However, the 1991 NDS (which became available early in 1992) introduced many substantive changes, including

1. Revised design values for Dimension lumber based on the results of the In-Grade Test Program

2. New design equations for columns, laterally unbraced beams, and beam-columns

3. New connection design principles based on engineering mechanics (known as the yield limit model for dowel-type fasteners)

4. Equation format for wood design criteria

The equation format in the 1991 NDS represents the adoption of a comprehensive set of symbols for the many adjustment factors that may be required in certain design situations. A number of the adjustment factors may drop out of the equations (i.e., the factors default to unity) for frequently encountered conditions. However, the adjustment factors in the equation format are intended to formally remind the user that certain conditions may require an adjustment of allowable stresses. In addition, equations may be used as an alternative to tables, which may be useful in automating certain design calculations.

A table summarizing the possible adjustment factors for the design of wood structural *members* is given inside the front cover of this book, and a similar table for the design of wood *connections* is provided inside the back cover. Again, a number of these factors default to unity in many practical problems, and detailed explanations are given in the text. A large number of practical examples illustrate when the factors are likely to have a significant effect and when they are not.

The new earthquake regulations are the result of work done by the Structural Engineers Association of California (SEAOC). The need to consider irregular features has added a considerable amount to the seismic design requirements, and a new chapter has been added to introduce this subject.

If this book is used as a text for a formal course, an Instructor's Manual is available. Requests on school letterhead should be sent to: Civil Engineering Editor, Professional Book Group, McGraw-Hill Inc., 11 W. 19th Street, New York, NY 10011.

Questions or comments about the text or examples may be addressed to the author in care of California State Polytechnic University, 3801 W. Temple Avenue, Pomona, CA 91786.

Acknowledgment and appreciation for help in writing the third edition are given to David G. Pollock and R. Michael Caldwell of the National Forest Products Association; Russell W. Krivchuk of the International Conference of Building Officials; William A. Baker, Thomas P. Cunningham, Jr., Mike Drorbaugh, John R. Tissell, Ken Walters, and B. J. Yeh of the American Plywood Association; Thomas G. Williamson and Thomas E. Brassell, formerly of the American Institute of Timber Construction; Keven C. K. Cheung and Frank Stewart of the Western Wood Products Association; Lisa Johnson of the Southern Pine Inspection Bureau; Edwin G. Zacher of H. J. Brunnier and Associates; Edward F. Diekmann of GFDS Engineers; Lawrence A. Soltis and Robert Falk of the U.S. Forest Products Laboratory; Don Wood of Wood Engineering; William R. Bloom of STB Structural Engineers; Fredrick C. Pneuman of Pneuman Engineering; Robert M. Powell of Powell, Mika and Associates; Sherm Nelson of Trus Joist MacMillan; Bill McAlpine of Alpine Engineered Products; Karen Colonias of Simpson Strong-Tie; and Ronald L. Carlyle of California State Polytechnic University. Suggestions and information were obtained from many other engineers and suppliers, and their help is gratefully recognized. Thanks again to Cid for typing the first and second editions.

Donald E. Breyer

ABOUT THE AUTHOR

Donald E. Breyer is professor of civil engineering and engineering technology at California State Polytechnic University, Pomona, California. He consults on a wide range of structural engineering projects, especially in the area of wood engineering. Professor Breyer serves on a number of wood industry committees and is the author of all previous editions of *Design of Wood Structures* as well as coeditor of *Classic Wood Structures*, published by the American Society of Civil Engineers.

Nomenclature

Organizations

AITC
American Institute of Timber
Construction
11818 S.E. Mill Plain Blvd.
Suite 407
Vancouver, WA 98684

APA
American Plywood Association
P.O. Box 11700
Tacoma, WA 98411-0700

ATC
Applied Technology Council
2471 E. Bayshore Road
Suite 512
Palo Alto, CA 94303

AWPI
American Wood Preservers
Institute
Tyson's International Building
1945 Old Gallows Rd., Suite 550
Vienna, VA 22182

BOCA
Building Officials and Code
Administrators International, Inc.
17926 South Halsted
Homewood, IL 60430

CABO
Council of American Building
Officials
An organization comprised of the
three major model code groups:
BOCA, ICBO, SBCC.

FPL
U.S. Forest Products Laboratory
One Gifford Pinchot Drive
Madison, WI 53705

ICBO
International Conference of
Building Officials
5360 South Workman Mill Road
Whittier, CA 90601

NFPA
National Forest Products
Association
1250 Connecticut Ave. N.W.
Washington, DC 20036

SBCC
Southern Building Code Congress
International, Inc.
900 Montclair Road
Birmingham, AL 35213

SEAOC
Structural Engineers Association of
 California
2550 Beverly Blvd.
Los Angeles, CA 90057

WWPA
Western Wood Products Association
1500 Yeon Building
Portland, OR 97204

Additional addresses are given in Appendix E, References.

Publications

NDS *National Design Specifications for Wood Construction* (Ref. 2)

PDS "Plywood Design Specification" (Ref. 14.1)

TCM *Timber Construction Manual* (Ref. 3.1)

UBC *Uniform Building Code* (Ref. 1.1)

WWUB *Western Woods Use Book* (Ref. 9.1)

Additional publications are given in Appendix E, References.

Units

ft	foot, feet
ft^2	square foot, square feet
in.	inch, inches
in.^{2}	square inch, square inches
k	1000 lb (kip, kilopound)
ksi	k per square inch (k/in.^{2})
mph	miles per hour
pcf	pounds per cubic foot (lb/ft^3)
plf	pounds per lineal foot (lb/ft)
psf	pounds per square foot (lb/ft^2)
psi	pounds per square inch (lb/in.^{2})
sec	second

Abbreviations

Allow.	allowable
ASD	allowable stress design

B&S	Beams and Stringers
c.-to-c.	center to center
cg	center of gravity
DF-L	Douglas Fir-Larch
DL	dead load (lb, k, lb/ft, k/ft, psf)
Ecc.	eccentric
EMC	equilibrium moisture content
FBD	free-body diagram
FDL	floor dead load (lb, k, lb/ft, k/ft, psf)
FLL	floor live load (lb, k, lb/ft, k/ft, psf)
FS	factor of safety
FSP	fiber saturation point
glulam	structural glued laminated timber
ht	height
IP	inflection point (point of reverse curvature and point of zero moment
J&P	Joists and Planks
lam	lamination
LF	Light Framing
LFRD	load and resistance factor design
LFRS	lateral-force-resisting system
LL	live load (lb, k, lb/ft, k/ft, psf)
LVL	laminated veneer lumber
max.	maximum
MC	moisture content based on oven-dry weight of wood
MDO	medium density overlay (plywood)
MEL	machine evaluated lumber
min.	minimum
MSR	machine stress rated lumber
NA	neutral axis
o.c.	on center
OM	overturning moment
OSB	oriented strand board
℔	plate
P&T	Posts and Timbers
PSL	parallel strand lumber
Q/A	quality assurance
RDL	roof dead load (lb, k, lb/ft, k/ft, psf)

Req'd	required
RLL	roof live load (lb, k, lb/ft, k/ft, psf)
RM	resisting moment
S4S	dressed lumber (surfaced four sides)
Sel. Str.	Select Structural
SCL	structural composite lumber
SJ&P	Structural Joists and Planks
SLF	Structural Light Framing
SL	snow load
Tab.	tabulated
T&G	tongue and groove
TL	total load (lb, k, lb/ft, k/ft, psf)
trib.	tributary
TS	top of sheathing
WSD	working stress design

Symbols

A	area (in.^{2}, ft^2)
a	acceleration
A_g	gross cross-sectional area of a tension or compression member (in.^{2})
A_h	projected area of hole caused by drilling or routing to accommodate bolts or other fasteners at net section (in.^{2})
A_m	gross cross-sectional area of main wood member (in.^{2})
A_n	cross-sectional area of member at a notch (in.^{2})
A_n	net cross-sectional area of a tension or compression member at a connection (in.^{2})
A_s	area of reinforcing steel (in.^{2})
A_s	sum of gross cross-sectional areas of side member(s) (in.^{2})
A_{web}	cross-sectional area of the web of a steel W-shaped beam or wood I joist (in.^{2})
b	length of shearwall parallel to lateral force; distance between chords of shearwall (ft)
b	width of horizontal diaphragm; distance between chords of horizontal diaphragm (ft)
b	width of rectangular beam cross section (in.)

B_t	allowable tension on anchor bolt embedded in concrete or masonry
B_v	allowable shear on anchor bolt embedded in concrete or masonry
C	compression force (lb, k)
C	Code coefficient representing seismic design response spectrum value
c	buckling and crushing interaction factor for columns
c	distance between neutral axis and extreme fiber (in., ft)
C_b	bearing area factor
C_D	load duration factor
C_d	penetration depth factor for connections
C_{di}	diaphragm factor for nail connections
C_e	wind force combined height, exposure, and gust factor coefficient
C_{eg}	end grain factor for connections
C_F	size factor for sawn lumber
C_f	form factor for bending stress
C_{fu}	flat use factor for bending stress
C_g	group action factor for connections
C_H	shear stress adjustment factor
C_L	beam stability factor
C_M	wet service factor for high-moisture conditions
C_P	column stability factor
C_p	seismic response coefficient for determining force on a portion of a structure
C_q	wind pressure coefficient
C_r	repetitive-member factor (bending stress) for Dimension lumber
C_{st}	metal side plate factor for 4-in. shear plate connections
C_T	buckling stiffness factor for 2×4 and smaller Dimension lumber in trusses
C_t	seismic coefficient depending on type of LFRS used to calculate period of vibration T
C_t	temperature factor
C_{tn}	toenail factor for nail connections
C_V	volume factor for glulam
C_Δ	geometry factor for connections
D	diameter (in.)

d	cross-sectional dimension of rectangular column associated with axis of column buckling (in.)
d	depth of rectangular beam cross section (in.)
d	dimension of wood member for shrinkage calculation (in.)
d	pennyweight of nail or spike
d_1	shank diameter of lag bolt (in.)
d_2	pilot hole diameter for the threaded portion of lag bolt (in.)
d_e	effective depth of member at a connection (in.)
d_n	effective depth of member remaining at a notch (in.)
d_x	width of rectangular column parallel to y axis, used to calculate column slenderness ratio about x axis
d_y	width of rectangular column parallel to x axis, used to calculate column slenderness ratio about y axis
E	lateral force due to earthquake (lb, k)
E	length of tapered tip of lag bolt (in.)
e	eccentricity (in., ft)
E, E'	tabulated and allowable modulus of elasticity (psi)
E_{axial}	modulus of elasticity of glulam for axial deformation calculation (psi)
E_m	modulus of elasticity of main member (psi)
E_s	modulus of elasticity of side member (psi)
E_x	modulus of elasticity about x axis (psi)
E_y	modulus of elasticity about y axis (psi)
F	force or load (lb, k)
f_b	actual (computed) bending stress (psi)
F_b, F_b'	tabulated and allowable bending (psi)
F_b^*	tabulated bending stress multiplied by all applicable adjustment factors except C_L (psi)
F_b^{**}	tabulated bending stress multiplied by all applicable adjustment factors except C_V (psi)
F_{bE}	critical buckling (Euler) value for bending member (psi)
f_{bx}	actual (computed) bending stress about strong (x) axis (psi)
F_{bx}, F_{bx}'	tabulated and allowable bending stress about strong (x) axis (psi)
f_{by}	actual (computed) bending stress about weak (y) axis (psi)

F_{by}, F'_{by}	tabulated and allowable bending stress about weak (y) axis (psi)
f_c	actual (computed) compression stress parallel to grain (psi)
F_c, F'_c	tabulated and allowable compression stress parallel to grain (psi)
F_c^*	tabulated compression stress parallel to grain multiplied by all applicable adjustment factors except C_P (psi)
F_{cE}	critical buckling (Euler) value for compression member (psi)
$f_{c\perp}$	actual (computed) compression stress perpendicular to grain (psi)
$F_{c\perp}, F'_{c\perp}$	tabulated and allowable compression stress perpendicular to grain (psi)
$F_{c\perp 0.2}, F'_{c\perp 0.2}$	reduced and allowable compression stress perpendicular to grain at a deformation limit of 0.02 in. (psi)
F_e	dowel bearing strength (psi)
$F_{e\parallel}$	dowel bearing strength parallel to grain for bolt or lag bolt connection (psi)
$F_{e\perp}$	dowel bearing strength perpendicular to grain for bolt or lag bolt connection (psi)
$F_{e\theta}$	dowel bearing strength at angle to grain θ for bolt or lag bolt connection (psi)
F_{em}	dowel bearing strength for main member (psi)
F_{es}	dowel bearing strength for side member (psi)
f_g	actual (computed) bearing stress parallel to grain (psi)
F_g, F'_g	tabulated and allowable bearing stress parallel to grain (psi)
F_p	allowable bearing stress for fastener in steel member (psi, ksi)
F_{px}	seismic story force at level x for designing the horizontal diaphragm (lb, k)
F'_θ	allowable bearing stress at angle to grain θ (psi)
f_s	stress in reinforcing steel (psi, ksi)
F_t	that portion of the seismic base shear V applied to top level in addition to seismic force given by F_x or F_{px} distributions (lb, k)
f_t	actual (computed) tension stress in a member parallel to grain (psi)
F_t, F'_t	tabulated and allowable tension stress parallel to grain (psi)

F_u	ultimate tensile strength for steel (psi, ksi)
F_v	actual (computed) shear stress parallel to grain (horizontal shear) in a beam using full design loads (psi)
f'_v	reduced (computed) shear stress parallel to grain (horizontal shear) in a beam obtained by neglecting the loads within distance d of face of support (psi)
F_v, F'_v	tabulated and allowable shear stress parallel to grain (horizontal shear) in a beam (psi)
F_x	seismic story force at level x for designing vertical elements (shearwalls) in LFRS (lb, k)
F_y	yield strength (psi, ksi)
F_{yb}	bending yield strength of fastener (psi, ksi)
g	acceleration of gravity
h	building height or height of wind pressure zone (ft)
h	height of shearwall (ft)
h_i, h_x	height above base to level i level x (ft)
h_n	height above base to nth or uppermost level in building (ft)
I	importance coefficient for seismic force
I	importance coefficient for wind force
I	moment of inertia (in.^{4}, ft^4)
K	Code multiplier for DL for use in beam deflection calculations to account for creep effects
K	framing coefficient from old seismic base shear formula
K_{bE}	Euler buckling coefficient for beams
K_{cE}	Euler buckling coefficient for columns
K_D	diameter coefficient for nail and spike connections
K_e	effective length factor for column end conditions (buckling length coefficient for columns)
K_f	column stability coefficient for bolt and nail built-up columns
K_L	loading coefficient for evaluating volume effect factor C_V for glulam beams
K_θ	angle to grain coefficient for bolt and lag bolt connections
KS	effective section modulus for plywood (in.^{3})
L	beam span length (ft)
L	length (ft)
l	length (in.)
l	length of bolt in main or side members (in.)

l	length of fastener (in.)
l	unbraced length of column (in.)
l/D	bolt slenderness ratio
l_b	bearing length (in.)
L_c	cantilever length in cantilever beam system (ft)
l_e	effective unbraced length of column (in.)
l_e/d	slenderness ratio of column
$(l_e/d)_x$	slenderness ratio of column for buckling about strong (x) axis
$(l_e/d)y$	slenderness ratio of column for buckling about weak (y) axis
l_e	effective unbraced length of compression side of beam (in.)
l_m	length of bolt in wood main member (in.)
l_s	total length of bolt in wood side members(s) (in.)
l_u	laterally braced length of compression side of beam (in.)
l_x	unbraced length of column considering buckling about strong (x) axis (in.)
l_y	unbraced length of column considering buckling about weak (y) axis (in.)
M	bending moment (in.-lb, in-k, ft-lb, ft-k)
M	mass
M_p	plastic moment capacity (in.-lb, in-k)
M_y	yield moment (in.-lb, in-k)
N	normal reaction (lb, k)
N	number of fasteners in connection
n	number of fasteners in row
n	number of stories (seismic forces)
N, N'	nominal and allowable lateral design value at angle to grain θ for a single split ring or shear plate connector (lb)
P	design wind pressure (psf)
P	total concentrated load or force (lb, k)
p	parallel-to-grain component of lateral force z on one fastener
P	penetration depth of fastener into wood member (in.)
P, P'	nominal and allowable lateral design value parallel to grain for a single split ring or shear plate connector (lb)
P_{lr}	wind pressure on leeward roof (psf)

P_{lw}	wind pressure on leeward wall (psf)
P_u	collapse load (ultimate load capacity)
P_u	vertical wind uplift pressure on horizontal projected area (psf)
P_w	horizontal wind pressure on vertical projected area (psf)
P_{wr}	wind pressure on windward roof (psf)
P_{ww}	wind pressure on windward wall (psf)
Q	static moment of an area about the neutral axis (in.^{3})
q	perpendicular-to-grain component of lateral force z on one fastener
q	soil bearing pressure (psf)
Q, Q'	nominal and allowable lateral design value perpendicular to grain for a single split ring or shear plate connector (lb)
q_a	soil bearing pressure under axial loads (psf)
q_b	bending soil bearing pressure caused by overturning moment (psf)
q_s	wind stagnation pressure (psf)
R	nominal calculated resistance of structure (*see* LRFD)
R	reaction (lb, k)
R	reduction (percent) of roof or floor live load
r	radius of gyration (in.)
R_1	seismic force generated by mass of wall that is parallel to earthquake force being considered
R_B	slenderness ratio of laterally unbraced beam
R_s	reduction in snow load (psf per degree of roof slope over 20 degrees)
R_w	seismic structural system quality factor
S	section modulus (in.^{3})
S	seismic coefficient for soil characteristics for a site
S	shrinkage of wood member (in.)
s	center-to-center spacing between adjacent fasteners in a row (in.)
s	length of unthreaded shank of lag bolt (in.)
SG	specific gravity
SG_m	specific gravity of main member
SG_s	specific gravity of side member
SV	shrinkage value for wood due to 1 percent change in moisture content (in./in.)

T	fundamental period of vibration of structure in direction of seismic force under consideration (sec)
T	tension force (lb., k)
t	thickness (in.)
t_m	thickness of main member (in.)
t_s	thickness of side member (in.)
t_{washer}	thickness of washer (in.)
U	wind uplift resultant force (lb, k)
V	basic wind speed (mph)
V	seismic base shear (lb, k)
V	shear force in a beam, diaphragm, or shearwall (lb, k)
v	unit shear in horizontal diaphragm or shearwall (lb/ft)
V'	reduced shear in beam determined by neglecting load within d from face of supports (lb, k)
v_2	unit shear in second-floor diaphragm (lb/ft)
v_{2r}	unit shear in shearwall between second-floor and roof levels (lb/ft)
v_{12}	unit shear in shearwall between first- and second-floor levels (lb/ft)
v_r	unit shear in roof diaphragm (lb/ft)
W	weight of structure or total seismic dead load (lb, k)
w	tabulated withdrawal design value for single fastener (lb/in. of penetration)
w	uniformly distributed load or force (lb/ft, k/ft, psf, ksf)
W, W'	nominal and allowable withdrawal design value for single fastener (lb)
W_1	DL of 1-ft-wide strip tributary to story level in direction of seismic force (lb/ft, k/ft)
W_2	total DL tributary to second-floor level (lb, k)
W'_2	that portion of W_2 which generates seismic forces in second-floor diaphragm (lb, k)
w_2	uniform load to second-floor horizontal diaphragm (lb/ft, k/ft)
W_{DL}	dead load of structure (lb, k)
W_{foot}	dead load of footing or foundation (lb, k)
w_i, w_x	tributary weight assigned to story level i, level x (lb, k)
W_p	weight of portion of structure (element or component) (lb, k, lb/ft, k/ft, psf)
w_{px}	weight of diaphragm and elements tributary thereto at level x (lb, k, lb/ft, k/ft)

W_r	total DL tributary to roof level (lb, k)
W_r'	that portion of W_r which generates seismic forces in roof diaphragm (lb, k)
w_r	uniform load to roof horizontal diaphragm (lb/ft, k/ft)
x	width of triangular soil bearing pressure diagram (ft)
Z	plastic section modulus (in.^{3})
Z	seismic zone factor
ZIC/R_w	seismic base shear coefficient
z	lateral force on one fastener in wood connection (lb)
Z, Z'	nominal and allowable lateral design value for single fastener in a connection (lb)
Z_α'	allowable resultant design value for lag bolt subjected to combined lateral and withdrawal loading (lb)
$Z_{m\perp}$	nominal lateral design value for single bolt or lag bolt in wood-to-wood connection with main member loaded perpendicular to grain and side member loaded parallel to grain (lb)
$Z_{s\perp}$	nominal lateral design value for single bolt or lag bolt in wood-to-wood connection with main member loaded parallel to grain and side member loaded perpendicular to grain (lb)
$Z_\parallel$	nominal lateral design value for single bolt or lag bolt in connection with all wood members loaded parallel to grain (lb)
$Z_\perp$	nominal lateral design value for single bolt or lag bolt in wood-to-metal connection with wood member(s) loaded perpendicular to grain (lb)
Δ	deflection (in.)
Δ_{MC}	change in moisture content of wood member (percent)
γ	load factor
γ	load/slip modulus for a connection (lb/in.)
ϕ	resistance factor
θ	angle between direction of load and direction of grain (longitudinal axis of member) (degrees)
θ_m	angle of load to grain θ for main member (degrees)
θ_s	angle of load to grain θ for side member (degrees)
μ	coefficient of static friction

1

Wood Buildings and Design Criteria

1.1 Introduction

There are probably more buildings constructed with wood than any other structural material. Many of these buildings are single-family residences, but many larger apartment buildings as well as commercial and industrial buildings also use wood framing.

The widespread use of wood in the construction of buildings has both an economic and an aesthetic basis. The ability to construct wood buildings with a minimal amount of equipment has kept the cost of wood-frame buildings competitive with other types of construction. On the other hand, where architectural considerations are important, the beauty and the warmth of exposed wood are difficult to match with other materials.

Wood-frame construction has evolved from a method used in primitive shelters into a major field of structural design. However, in comparison with the time devoted to steel and reinforced-concrete design, timber design is not given sufficient attention in most colleges and universities.

This book is designed to introduce the subject of timber design as applied to wood-frame building construction. Although the discussion centers on building design, the concepts also apply to the design of other types of wood-frame structures. Final responsibility for the design of a building rests with the structural engineer. However, this book is written to introduce the subject to a broad audience. This includes engineers, engineering technologists, architects, and others concerned with building design. A background in statics and strength of materials is required to adequately follow the text. Most wood-frame buildings are made up of statically determinate members, and the ability to analyze these types of trusses, beams, and frames is also necessary.

1.2   Types of Buildings

There are various types of framing systems that can be used in wood buildings. The most common type of wood-frame construction uses a system of horizontal diaphragms and shearwalls to resist lateral forces, and this book deals specifically with the design of this basic type of building. At one time the building code classified a shearwall building as a *box system,* which was a good physical description of the way in which the structure resists lateral forces. However, the latest building code has dropped this terminology, and most wood-frame shearwall buildings will now be classified as *bearing wall systems.* The distinction between the shearwall and diaphragm system and other systems is explained in Chap. 3.

Other types of wood building systems, such as glulam arches and pole buildings, are beyond the scope of this book. It is felt that the designer should first have a firm understanding of the behavior of basic shearwall buildings and the design procedures that are applied to them. With a background of this nature, the designer can acquire from currently available sources (e.g., Ref. 3.1) the design techniques for other systems.

The basic bearing wall system can be constructed entirely from wood components. See Fig. 1.1. Here the *roof, floors, and walls* use wood framing. The calculations necessary to design these structural elements are illustrated throughout the text in comprehensive examples.

In addition to buildings that use only wood components, another common type of construction makes use of wood components in combination with some other type of structural material. Perhaps the most common mix of structural materials is in buildings that use *wood roof and floor systems* and *concrete tile-up* or *masonry (concrete block or brick) shearwalls.* See Fig. 1.2. This type of construction is very common, especially in one-story commercial and industrial buildings. This construction is economical for small buildings, but its economy increases as the size of the building increases.

Figure 1.1 Two-story wood-frame building. (*Photo by Mike Hausmann.*)

Figure 1.2a *Foreground:* Office portion of wood-frame construction. *Background:* Warehouse with concrete tilt-up walls and wood roof system. (*Photo by Mike Hausmann.*)

Figure 1.2b Building with reinforced-concrete block walls and a wood roof system with plywood sheathing. (*Photo by Mark Williams.*)

Trained crews can erect large areas of *panelized* roof systems in short periods of time.

Design procedures for the wood components used in buildings with concrete or masonry walls are also illustrated throughout this book. The connections between wood and concrete or masonry elements are particularly important and are treated in considerable detail.

This book covers the *complete* design of a wood-frame *box*-type building from the roof level down to the foundation. In a complete building design, *vertical loads and lateral forces* must be considered, and the design procedures for both are covered in detail.

Wind and seismic (earthquake) are the two lateral forces that are normally taken into account in the design of a building. In recent years the design for lateral forces has become a significant portion of the design effort. The reason for this is an increased awareness of the effects of lateral forces. In addition, the building codes have substantially revised the design requirements for both wind and seismic forces. These changes are the result of extensive research in wind engineering and earthquake-resistant design.

1.3 Required and Recommended References

The third edition of this book was prompted by two main developments:

1. Publication of the *1991 National Design Specification for Wood Construction* (Ref. 2)

2. Major revisions to the earthquake design requirements, which were first introduced in the 1988 UBC and are continued in the *1991 Uniform Building Code* (Ref. 1.1)

The *National Design Specification* (NDS) is published by the National Forest Products Association (NFPA) and represents the latest structural design recommendations by the wood industry. The 1991 NDS contains sweeping changes in design values for sawn lumber as a result of the *in-grade testing program* (Chap. 4). In addition there are major changes to the design procedures for wood members and their connections. The address of NFPA is included in the list of organizations in the Nomenclature section of this book and in the references in Appendix E.

All or part of the design recommendations in the NDS will eventually be incorporated into the wood design portions of most building codes. However, the 1991 NDS was not available until early 1992, and the code change process can take considerable time. This book deals specifically with the design provisions of the 1991 NDS, and the designer should verify local building code acceptance before basing the design of a particular wood structure on this criterion.

Because of the subject matter, the reader must have a copy of the *1991 NDS* to properly follow this book. The NDS contains

1. Design specifications for wood members including new column, beam, and combined stress interaction formulas.

2. New methods for connection design using yield limit theory.

3. Tables of design stresses for sawn lumber and structural glued laminated timber (glulam). Values for sawn lumber were revised in the 1991 NDS.

4. Tables of member section properties for both sawn lumber and glulam.

The tables of member properties, allowable stresses, and fastener load capacity are lengthy. Rather than reproducing these tables in this book, it is felt that the reader should be required to have a copy of the basic document for wood design. Having a copy of the NDS and the NDS Supplement for wood design is analogous to having a copy of the AISC *Steel Manual* (Ref. 11) in order to really be familiar with structural steel design.

This book also concentrates heavily on understanding the loads and forces required in the design of a structure. Emphasis is placed on both gravity loads and lateral forces. Toward this goal, the design loads and forces in this book are taken from the 1991 UBC. The UBC is published by the International Conference of Building Officials (ICBO), and it is highly desirable for the reader to have a copy of the 1991 UBC to follow the discussion in this book. However, the UBC is not used in all areas of the country, and a number of the UBC tables that are important to the understanding of this book are reproduced in Appendix C. If a copy of the UBC is not available, the tables in Appendix C will allow the reader to follow the text.

Frequent references are made in this book to the NDS and the UBC. In addition, a number of cross references are made to discussions or examples in this book that may be directly related to a particular subject. The reader should clearly understand the meaning of the following references:

Example reference	Refers to	Where to look
NDS Sec. 15.1	Section 15.1 in 1991 NDS	1991 NDS (required reference)
NDS Supplement Table 4A	Table 4A in 1991 NDS	1991 NDS Supplement (comes with 1991 NDS)
UBC Chap. 23	Chapter 23 in 1991 UBC	1991 UBC (recommended reference)
UBC Table 25-J-1	Table 25-J-1 in 1991 UBC	1991 UBC (recommended reference) or Appendix C of this book
Section 4.15	Section 4.15 of this book	Chapter 4 in this book
Example 9.3	Example 9.3 in this book	Chapter 9 in this book
Figure 5.2	Figure 5.2 in this book	Chapter 5 in this book

A third reference that is often cited in this book is the *Timber Construction Manual* (Ref. 3.1), abbreviated *TCM*. This handbook can be considered the basic reference on structural glued-laminated timber. Although it is a useful reference, it is not necessary to have a copy of the TCM to follow this book. The TCM is currently in the process of being updated, and the fourth edition of the TCM should be available in the near future.

1.4 Building Codes and Design Criteria

Cities and counties across the United States typically adopt a building code to ensure public welfare and safety. Most local governments use one of the three *model codes* as the basic framework for their local building code. The three major model codes are the

1. *Uniform Building Code* (Ref. 1.1)
2. *The BOCA National Building Code/1990* (Ref. 21)
3. *Standard Building Code* (Ref. 22)

The *Building Code Requirements for Minimum Design Loads in Buildings and Other Structures* (Ref. 5.1) is commonly referred to as ASCE 7-88 or simply ASCE 7. It serves as the basis for some of the loading criteria in the model codes and a number of local codes.

Generally speaking, the *Uniform Building Code* is used in the western portion of the United States, *The BOCA National Building Code* in the north, and the *Standard Building Code* in the south. The model codes are revised and updated periodically, usually on a 3-year cycle.

Taken as a group, the model codes set forth the building code requirements for the large majority (roughly 90 percent) of the United States. Certain large cities write their own building codes, and those that use one of the model codes may enact legislation which modifies the model code in some manner.

In writing this design text, it was considered desirable to use one of the model building codes to establish the loading criteria and certain allowable stresses. The *Uniform Building Code* (UBC) is used throughout the text for this purpose. The UBC was selected because it is the most widely used of the three model codes, and, because of its use in the western states, it reflects the most recent seismic design requirements.

The latest UBC emphasizes the need to tie the building together by providing specific detailing requirements to withstand the dynamic motions generated in an earthquake.

Throughout the text reference is made to the *Code* and the *UBC*. As noted in the previous section, when references of this nature are used, the design criteria are taken from the 1991 edition of the *Uniform Building Code*.

Design load and force criteria for this book are taken from the UBC, and these will normally meet or exceed the requirements of other codes. Users of other codes will be able to verify this by referring to UBC tables reproduced in Appendix C. By comparing the design criteria of another code with the information in Appendix C, the designer will be able to determine quickly whether the two are in agreement. Appendix C will also be a helpful cross-reference in checking future editions of the UBC against the values used in this text.

Although the NDS (Ref. 2) is used in this book as the basis for determining the allowable loads for wood members and their connections, note that the Code also has a chapter that deals with these subjects. However, the latest design criteria are typically found in industry-recommended design specifications such as the NDS.

The designer should be aware that the local building code is the legal authority, and the user should verify acceptance by the local code authority before applying new principles. This is consistent with general practice in structural design, which is to follow an approach that is both rational and conservative. The objective is to produce structures which are economical and safe.

In addition to providing design load and force criteria, the UBC is used in this book as the source allowable loads for certain wood elements. For example, the NDS does not cover the design of plywood horizontal diaphragms and shearwalls, and the design values for these and several other items are taken from Chap. 25 of the UBC.

1.5 Organization of the Text

The text has been organized to present the complete design of a wood-frame building in an orderly manner. The subjects covered are presented roughly in the order that they would be encountered in the design of a building.

In a building design, the first items that need to be determined are the design loads. The Code requirements for vertical loads and lateral forces are reviewed in Chap. 2, and the distribution of these in a building with wood framing is described in Chap. 3.

After the distribution of loads and forces, attention is turned to the design of wood elements. As noted previously, there are basically two systems that must be designed, one for *vertical loads* and one for *lateral forces.*

The vertical-load-carrying system is considered first. In a wood-frame building this system is basically composed of beams and columns. Chapters 4 and 5 cover the characteristics and design properties of these wood members. Chapter 6 then outlines the design procedures for beams, and Chap. 7 treats the design methods for columns and members subjected to combined axial and bending.

As one might expect, some parts of the vertical-load-carrying system are also a part of the lateral-force-resisting system. The sheathing for wood roof and floor systems is one such element. The sheathing distributes the vertical loads to the supporting members, and it also serves as the *skin* or *web* of the horizontal diaphragm for resisting lateral forces. The most widely used structural sheathing material in wood-frame construction is plywood. Chapter 8 introduces the grades and properties of plywood (and some of the newer "panel" products) and essentially serves as a transition from the vertical-load- to the lateral-force-resisting system. Chapters 9 and 10 deal specifically with the lateral-force-resisting system. In the typical bearing wall type of buildings covered in this text, the lateral-force-resisting system is made up of a diaphragm that spans horizontally between vertical shear-resisting elements known as shearwalls.

After the design of the main elements in the vertical-load- and lateral-force-resisting systems, attention is turned to the design of the connections. The importance of proper connection design cannot be overstated, and design procedures for various types of wood connections are outlined in Chaps. 11 through 14.

Chapter 15 describes the anchorage requirements between horizontal and vertical diaphragms. Basically anchorage ensures that the horizontal and vertical elements in the building are adequately tied together.

The text concludes with a review of building code requirements for seismicly irregular structures. Chapter 16 also expands the coverage of overturning for shearwalls.

1.6   Structural Calculations

Structural design is at least as much of an *art* as it is a *science*. This book introduces a number of basic structural design principles. These are demonstrated through a large number of practical numerical examples and sample calculations. These should help the reader understand the technical side of the problem, but the application of these tools in the design of wood structures is an art that is developed with experience.

The introduction of the 1991 NDS and the 1991 UBC involves many changes in the technical aspect of wood design. Undoubtedly there are a number of practitioners, already skilled in the art of wood design, who will balk at the added complexity of the design requirements and design equations.

For example, the 1991 NDS includes a new method of obtaining the capacity of a bolt in a wood connection. The new system is based on engineering mechanics. If approached mathematically, evaluation of the strength of a common bolt connection requires the solution of six rather involved yield limit equations. This is in sharp contrast with the previous method of reading the bolt capacity from a table.

Instead of being overly complex, the 1991 NDS can be viewed as bringing wood engineering into the twenty-first century. The new design criteria enable a more accurate method of analysis. In many cases, previous design criteria required the extrapolation of design values. In contrast, the 1991 NDS provides a way to formally account for many variables that occur in different design situations.

For those involved in the design of wood structures on a regular basis, this provides a method to more precisely model structural behavior. On the other hand, the expressions, which are part of a more thorough model, are also more involved. To obtain the full benefit of the new criteria, use of the computer will probably be required. However, advanced programming skills are not required to implement the new design expressions.

A modern *spreadsheet* application program on a microcomputer can be used to create a *template* which can easily generate the solution of the new wood design equations. Using the concept of a template, the design equations need to be entered on a spreadsheet only once. Then they can be used, time after time, to solve similar problems by changing certain variables.

For those not familiar with microcomputer spreadsheets, it should be understood that they are not limited to business applications or bookkeeping operations. A spreadsheet can be used to solve a wide range of engineering problems. It is much easier to solve six engineering equations on a spreadsheet than it is to solve them on a programmable calculator. In addition to being able to solve complex mathematical expressions, spreadsheets have the ability to carry out advanced logical tests and to make decisions. Functions that can be used to perform these operations are built into most spreadsheets.

The modern spreadsheet application relieves the user of many of the tedious programming tasks associated with writing dedicated software. Dedicated computer programs certainly have their place in wood design, just as they do in other areas of structural design. However, the microcomputer spreadsheet has leveled the playing field considerably. Spreadsheet templates can be very simple, or they can be extremely sophisticated. Regardless of programming experience, it should be understood that a very simple spreadsheet template can make the solution of a set of bolt equations easier than looking up a load capacity in a table.

It is highly recommended that the reader become familiar with one of the popular spreadsheet application programs. It is further recommended that a number of the sample problems be solved using the spreadsheet. With very little practice, it is possible to create templates which will solve problems that are repetitive and tedious on a hand-held calculator.

Even with the assurance given about the relatively painless way to implement the new design equations for wood, some people will remain unconvinced. For those who simply refuse to accept or deal with the computer, or for those who have only an occasional need to design a wood structure, the 1991 NDS contains tables that cover a number of common applications. The advantage of the equations is that a wider variety of connection problems can be handled, but the NDS tables can accommodate a number of frequently encountered problems.

Although the NDS tables can handle a number of common situations, some problems will require the solution of the new wood design equations. The form and length of the new equations are such that the solution by hand-held calculator may not be convenient, and the recommended approach is to solve the problem once on a spreadsheet. The "document" thus created can be saved, and it then becomes a *template* for future problems. The template remains intact, and the values for a new problem are input in place of the values for the original problem.

Although the power and convenience of a modern spreadsheet application program should not be overlooked, all the numerical problems and design examples in this book are shown as complete hand solutions. Lap-top computers may eventually replace the hand-held calculator, but the problems in this book are set up for evaluation by calculator.

With this in mind, an expression for a calculation is first given in general terms (i.e., a formula is first stated), then the numerical values are substituted in the expression, and finally the result of the calculation is given. In this way the designer should be able to readily follow the sample calculation.

Note that the conversion from pounds (lb) to kips (k) is often made without a formal notation. This is common practice and should be of no particular concern to the reader. For example, the calculations below illustrate the axial load capacity of a tension member:

$$\text{Allow. } T = F'_t A$$

$$= (1200 \text{ lb/in.}^2)(20 \text{ in.}^2)$$

$$= 24.0 \text{ k}$$

where T = tensile force
F'_t = allowable tensile stress
A = cross-sectional area

The following illustrates the conversion for the above calculations, which is normally done mentally:

$$\text{Allow. } T = F'_t A$$

$$= (1200 \text{ lb/in.}^2)(20 \text{ in.}^2)$$

$$= (24,000 \text{ lb}) \left(\frac{1 \text{ k}}{1000 \text{ lb}} \right)$$

$$= 24.0 \text{ k}$$

The appropriate number of significant figures used in calculations should be considered by the designer. When structural calculations are done on a calculator or computer, there is a tendency to present the results with too many significant figures. Variations in loading and material properties make the use of a large number of significant figures inappropriate. A false degree of *accuracy* is implied when the stress in a wood member is recorded in design calculations with an excessive number of significant figures.

As an example, consider the bending stress in a wood beam. If the calculated stress as shown on the calculator is 1278.356 · · · psi, it is reasonable to report 1280 psi in the design calculations. Rather than representing sloppy work, the latter figure is more realistic in presenting the degree of accuracy of the problem.

Although the calculations for problems in this text were performed on a spreadsheet or calculator, intermediate and final results are generally presented with three or four significant figures.

An attempt has been made to use a consistent set of symbols and abbreviations throughout the text. Comprehensive lists of symbols and abbreviations, and their definitions, follow the Contents. A number of the symbols and abbreviations are unique to this book, but where possible, they are in agreement with those accepted in the industry. The 1991 NDS adopted a comprehensive notation system for many of the factors used in the design calculations for wood structures. This notation system is commonly known as the *equation format* for wood design and is introduced in Chap. 4. The equation format should result in a more consistent application of the adjustment factors in wood design. A summary of the adjustment factors for *wood members* is given inside the front cover of this book, and a summary of the adjustment factors for *wood connections* is found inside the back cover.

The units of measure used in the text are the U.S. Customary System units. The abbreviations for these units are also summarized after the Contents. Factors for converting to SI metric units are included in Appendix D.

1.7 Detailing Conventions

With the large number of examples included in this text, the sketches are necessarily limited in detail. For example, a number of the building plans are shown without doors or windows. However, each sketch is designed to illustrate certain structural design points, and the lack of full details should not detract from the example.

One common practice in drawing wood structural members is to place an X in the cross section of a *continuous* wood member. But a *noncontinuous* wood member is shown with a single diagonal line in cross section. See Fig. 1.3.

1.8 Fire-Resistive Requirements

Building codes place restrictions on the materials of construction based on the occupancy (i.e., what the building will house), area, height, number of occupants, and a number of other factors. The choice of materials affects not only the initial cost of a building, but the recurring cost of fire insurance premiums as well.

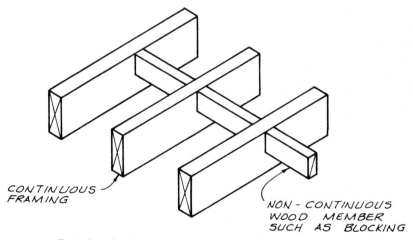

CONTINUOUS FRAMING

NON - CONTINUOUS WOOD MEMBER SUCH AS BLOCKING

Figure 1.3 Typical timber drafting conventions.

The fire-resistive requirements are very important to the building designer. This topic can be a complete subject in itself and is beyond the scope of this book. However, several points that affect the design of wood buildings are mentioned here to alert the designer.

Wood (unlike steel and concrete) is a combustible material, and certain *types of construction* (defined by the Code) do not permit the use of combustible materials. There are arguments for and against this type of restriction, but these limitations do exist.

Generally speaking, the *unrestricted use* of wood is allowed in buildings of limited floor area. In addition, the height of these buildings without automatic fire sprinklers is limited to one, two, or three stories, depending upon the occupancy.

Wood is also used in another type of construction known as *heavy timber*. Experience and fire endurance tests have shown that the tendency of a wood member to ignite in a fire is affected by its cross-sectional dimensions. In a fire, large-size wood members form a protective coating of char which insulates the inner portion of the member. Thus large wood members may continue to support a load in a fire long after an uninsulated steel member has collapsed because of the elevated temperature. This is one of the arguments used against the restrictions placed on "combustible" building materials. (Note that properly insulated steel members can perform adequately in a fire.)

The minimum cross-sectional dimensions required to qualify for the heavy timber fire rating are set forth in building codes. As an example, the UBC states that the minimum cross-sectional dimension for a wood column is 8 in. Different minimum dimensions apply to different types of wood members, and the Code should be consulted for these values. Limits on maximum allowable floor areas are much larger for wood buildings with heavy timber members, compared with buildings without wood members of sufficient size to qualify as heavy timber.

1.9   Industry Organizations

A number of organizations are actively involved in promoting the proper design and use of wood and related products. These include the model building code groups as well as a number of industry-related organizations. The names and addresses of some of these organizations are listed after the Contents. Others are included in the list of references in Appendix E.

2

Design Loads

2.1 Introduction

The calculation of design loads for buildings is covered in this chapter and Chap. 3. Chapter 2 deals primarily with Code-required design loads and forces and how these are calculated and modified for a specific building design. Chapter 3 is concerned with the distribution of these design loads throughout the structure.

In ordinary building design, one normally distinguishes between two major types of design criteria: (1) *vertical (gravity) loads* and (2) *lateral forces*. Although certain members may function only as vertical-load-carrying members or only as lateral-force-carrying members, often members may be subjected to a combination of vertical loads and lateral forces. For example, a member may function as a beam when subjected to vertical loads and as an axial tension or compression member under lateral forces (or vice versa).

Regardless of how a member functions, it is convenient to classify design criteria into these two main categories. Vertical loads offer a natural starting point. Little introduction to gravity loads is required. "Weight" is something with which most people are familiar, and the design for vertical loads is often accomplished first. The reason for starting here is twofold. First, gravity loading is an every-present load, and quite naturally it has been the basic, traditional design concern. Second, in the case of lateral seismic forces, it is necessary to know the magnitude of the vertical loads before the earthquake forces can be estimated.

In the past, the terms *load* and *force* were often used interchangeably. Both were used to refer to a vector quantity with U.S. Customary System units of pounds (lb) or kips (k). There are still not hard-and-fast rules regarding the use of these terms; however, there is a trend to use the term *load* to refer to a gravity or vertical vector and the term *force* to refer to lateral wind or seismic effects. This trend stems from the use of such key phrases in the Code as *dead load, live load,* and *snow load* in referring to gravity loads. On the other hand, terms such as *lateral forces* and *lateral-force-resisting system* refer to wind and seismic considerations. Although there are exceptions to these conventions even in the Code, this pattern of vertical (gravity) loads and lateral (wind and seismic) forces seems to be emerging. To the extent possible, this terminology is used in this book.

Also note that the design of structural framing members usually follows the reverse order in which they are constructed in the field. That is, design starts with the lightest framing member on the top level and proceeds downward, and construction starts at the bottom with the largest members and proceeds upward.

Design loads are the subject of UBC Chap. 23. It is suggested that the reader accompany the remaining portion of this chapter with a review of Chap. 23 of the Code. For convenience, a number of UBC tables are reproduced in Appendix C.

2.2   Vertical Loads—Dead

Vertical loads are classified as either *dead* or *live* loads. Dead loads include the weight of all materials which are permanently attached to the structure. In the case of a wood roof or wood floor system, this would include the weight of the roofing or floor covering, sheathing, framing, insulation, ceiling (if any), and any other permanent materials such as piping or automatic fire sprinklers.

Another dead load which must be included, but one that is easily overlooked (especially on a roof), is the mechanical or air-conditioning equipment. Often this type of load is supported by two or three beams or joists side by side which are the same size as the standard roof or floor framing members. See Fig. 2.1. The alternative is to design special larger (and deeper) beams to carry these isolated equipment loads.

The magnitude of dead loads for various construction materials can be found in a number of references. A fairly complete list of weights is given in Appendix B, and additional tables are given in Refs. 3.1 and 11.1.

Because most building dead loads are estimated as uniform loads in terms of pounds per square foot (psf), it is often convenient to convert the weights of framing members to these units. For example, if the weight per lineal foot of a wood framing member is known, and if the center-to-center spacing of parallel members is also known, the dead load in psf can easily be determined by dividing the weight per lineal foot by the center-to-center spacing. For example, if 2×12 beams weighing 4.3 lb/ft are spaced at 16 in. on center (o.c.), the equivalent uniform load is 4.3 lb/ft $\div$ 1.33 ft = 3.2 psf. A table showing these equivalent uniform loads for typical framing sizes and spacings is given in Appendix A.

It should be pointed out that in a wood structure, the dead load of the *framing members* usually represents a fairly minor portion of the total design load. For this reason a small error in estimating the weights of

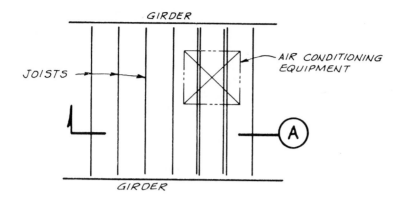

ROOF FRAMING PLAN

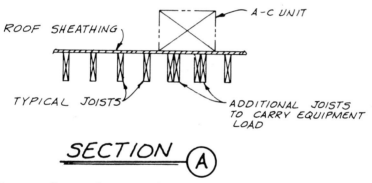

SECTION (A)

Figure 2.1 Support of equipment loads by additional framing.

framing members (either lighter or heavier) typically has a negligible effect on the final member choice. *Slightly* conservative (larger) estimates are usually used for design.

The estimation of the dead load of a structure requires some knowledge of the methods and materials of construction. A "feel" for what the unit dead loads of a wood-frame structure should total is readily developed after exposure to several buildings of this type. The dead load of a typical wood floor or roof system usually ranges between 7 and 20 psf, depending on the materials of construction, span lengths, and whether a ceiling is suspended below the floor or roof. For wood wall systems, values might range between 4 and 20 psf, depending on stud size and spacing and the type of wall sheathings used (for example, ⅜-in. plywood weighs approximately 1 psf whereas ⅞-in. stucco weighs 10 psf of wall surface area). Typical load calculations provide a summary of the makeup of the structure. See Example 2.1.

The dead load of a wood structure that differs substantially from the typical ranges mentioned above should be examined carefully to ensure that the various individual dead load (DL) components are in fact correct. It pays in the long run to stand back several times during the design process and ask, "Does this figure seem reasonable compared with typical values for other similar structures?"

EXAMPLE 2.1   Sample DL Calculation Summary

Roof Dead Loads

Roofing (5-ply with gravel)	= 6.5 psf
Reroofing	= 2.5
½-in. plywood (3 psf × ½ in.)	= 1.5
Framing (estimate 2 × 12 at 16 in. o.c.) =	3.2
Insulation	= 0.5
Suspended ceiling (acoustical tile)	= 2.0
Roof DL	= 16.2
Say RDL	= 17.0 psf

Floor Dead Loads

Floor covering (lightweight concrete 1½ in. at 100 lb/ft³) =	12.5
1⅛-in. plywood (3 psf × 1⅛ in.)	= 3.4
Framing (estimate 4 × 12 at 4 ft-0 in. o.c.)	= 2.5
Ceiling supports (2 × 4 at 24 in. o.c.)	= 0.7
Ceiling (½-in. drywall, 5 psf × ½ in.)	= 2.5
Floor DL	= 21.6 psf
Partition load*	= 20.0
	= 41.6 psf
Say FDL	= 42.0 psf

*Uniform partition loads are required when the location of partitions is unknown or subject to change.

In the summary of roof dead loads in Example 2.1, the load titled "reroofing" is sometimes included to account for the weight of roofing that may be added at some future time. Subject to the approval of the local building official, UBC Appendix Chap. 32 may allow new roofing materials to be applied without the removal of the old roof covering. Depending on the materials (e.g., built-up, asphalt shingle, wood shingle), one or two overlays may be permitted.

Before moving on to another type of loading, the concept of the *tributary area* of a member should be explained. The area that is assumed to load a given member is known as the tributary area. For a beam or girder, this area can be calculated by multiplying the *tributary width* times the span of the member. See Example 2.2.

When the load to a member is uniformly distributed, the load per foot can readily be determined by taking the unit load in psf times the tributary width (lb/ft^2 × ft = lb/ft).

The concept of tributary area will play an important role in the calculation of many types of loads.

EXAMPLE 2.2   Tributary Areas

In many cases a uniform spacing of members is used throughout the framing plan. This example is designed to illustrate the *concept* of tributary area rather than typical framing layouts. See Fig. 2.2.

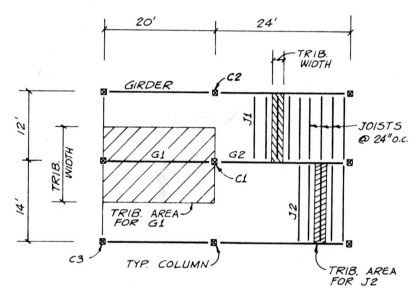

ROOF or *FLOOR   FRAMING PLAN*

Figure 2.2

Tributary Area Calculations

	Trib. A = trib. width × span
Joist J1	Trib. $A = 2 × 12 = 24$ ft^2
Joist J2	Trib. $A = 2 × 14 = 28$ ft^2
Girder G1	Trib. $A = (12/2 + 14/2)20 = 260$ ft^2
Girder G2	Trib. $A = (12/2 + 14/2)24 = 312$ ft^2
Column C1	Trib. $A = (12/2 + 14/2)(20/2 + 24/2) = 286$ ft^2
Exterior column C2	Trib. $A = (12/2)(20/2 + 24/2) = 132$ ft^2
Corner column C3	Trib. $A = (14/2)(20/2) = 70$ ft^2

2.3   Vertical Loads—Live

Vertical live loads are those gravity loads which are not permanently applied, such as people, furniture, construction workers, construction equipment, contents, and so on. Building codes typically specify the minimum roof and floor live loads that must be used in the design of a structure. For example, UBC Table 23-A specifies unit floor live loads in psf for use in the design of floor systems. The Code design requirements are usually thought to represent minimum performance criteria. Thus, if the designer has knowledge that the actual load will exceed these minimum values, the higher values must be used.

In the case of both roof live loads and floor live loads, the *tributary area of the member under design consideration* is taken into account. The idea that the tributary area should be considered in determining the magnitude of the *unit* live load (psf)—not just *total* load—is as follows:

> If a member has a small tributary area, it is likely that a fairly high *unit* live load could be imposed over that relatively small surface area.
>
> On the other hand, as the tributary area becomes large, it is less likely that this large area will be uniformly loaded by the same high unit load considered in the design of a member with a small tributary area.

Therefore the consideration of the tributary area in determining the *unit* live load has to do with the probability that high unit loads are likely to occur over small areas, but that these unit loads will probably not occur over large areas.

The Code considers the tributary area of the *member being designed* when specifying both roof and floor design live loads. The approach, however, is somewhat different. In the case of roof live loads, the Code takes the tributary area directly into account when specifying the live load. For floor live loads, the Code specifies the *basic* unit load depending on the occupancy of the structure (i.e., what it houses). The determination of the floor live load as a function of the tributary area is then left to the designer (the Code, however, provides the method to be used in the determination of this load).

2.4   Roof Live Load

The Code specifies minimum unit live loads that are to be used in the design of a roof system. The live load on a roof is usually applied for a relatively short period of time during the life of a structure. This fact is normally of no concern in the design of structures other than wood. However, as will be shown in subsequent chapters, the length of time for which a load is applied to a *wood structure* does have an effect on the load capacity.

Roof live loads are specified to account for the miscellaneous loads that may occur on a roof. These include loads that are imposed during the construction of the building including the roofing process. Roof live loads that may occur after construction include reroofing operations, air-conditioning and mechanical equipment installation and servicing, and, perhaps, loads caused by fire-fighting equipment. Wind forces and snow loads are not normally classified as live loads, and they are covered separately.

Unit roof live loads can be obtained from UBC Table 23-C. Method 1 in this table gives the unit roof live loads directly by taking into account the tributary area of the member being designed. The larger the tributary area, the lower the unit roof live load. Therefore, each time the design of a new member is undertaken, the first step should be the calculation of the tributary area that the member is assumed to support. The tributary area of a given member is then used to determine the appropriate *unit* roof live load for its design.

Method 2 in UBC Table 23-C is a more recent addition to the Code and allows the designer to *calculate* the unit roof live load for each member as a function of its tributary area. This approach provides a continuous range of live loads, whereas Method 1 provides incremental changes in live loads. These two methods are independent and are not to be combined. Method 2 calculates the percentage reduction in the basic roof live load as the smallest of the following three values:

1. $R = r(A - 150)$

2. $R = 23.1\left(1 + \dfrac{DL}{RLL}\right)$

3. $R = $ maximum permitted reduction given in UBC Table 23-C

where R = reduction in percent
r = rate of reduction (percent per square foot over 150 ft^2) given in UBC Table 23-C
A = tributary area of roof member under consideration
DL = roof dead load
RLL = tabulated roof live load from UBC Table 23-C

A second criterion that UBC Table 23-C uses in establishing roof live loads is the slope or pitch of the roof. Roof slope also relates to the probability of loading. On a roof that is relatively flat, fairly high unit live loads are likely to occur; but on steeply pitched roofs, much smaller unit live loads will be probable.

Both Method 1 and Method 2 take roof slope into account. Example 2.3 illustrates the application of both methods.

EXAMPLE 2.3   Calculation of Roof Live Loads

Determine the uniformly distributed roof loads (including dead load and roof live load) for the members in the building shown in Fig. 2.3. Assume that the roof is flat (except for a minimum slope of $\frac{1}{4}$ in./ft for drainage). Roof DL = 8 psf.

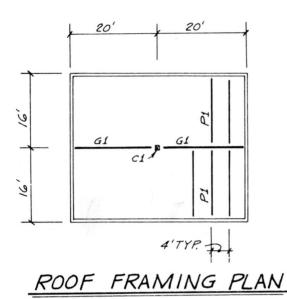

ROOF FRAMING PLAN

Figure 2.3

Tributary Areas

Purlin P1: $A = 4 \times 16 = 64 \text{ ft}^2$

Girder G1: $A = 16 \times 20 = 320$

Column C1: $A = 16 \times 20 = 320$

UBC Table 23-C

METHOD 1

  a. *Purlin.*

$$\text{Trib. } A = 64 \text{ ft}^2 < 200$$

$$\therefore \text{RLL} = 20 \text{ psf}$$

$$w = (\text{DL} + \text{LL})(\text{trib. width})$$

$$= [(8 + 20) \text{ psf}](4 \text{ ft}) = 112 \text{ lb/ft}$$

  b. *Girder.*

$$\text{Trib. } A = 320 \qquad 200 < 320 < 600$$

$$\therefore \text{RLL} = 16 \text{ psf}$$

$$w = [(8 + 16) \text{ psf}](16 \text{ ft}) = 384 \text{ lb/ft}$$

c. Column.

$$\text{Trib. } A = 320 \quad \text{same as girder}$$

$$\therefore \text{RLL} = 16 \text{ psf}$$

$$P = [(8 + 16) \text{ psf}](320 \text{ ft}^2) = 7680 \text{ lb}$$

METHOD 2

Basic roof live load for a flat roof is RLL = 20 psf.

a. Purlin.

$$\text{Trib. } A = 64 \text{ ft}^2 < 150$$

$$\therefore \text{ reduction not allowed}$$

$$w = (DL + LL)(\text{trib. width})$$

$$= [(8 + 20) \text{ psf}](4 \text{ ft}) = 112 \text{ lb/ft}$$

b. Girder.

$$\text{Trib. } A = 320 > 150$$

$$R = r(A - 150)$$

$$= 0.08(320 - 150)$$

$$= 13.6 \text{ percent} \quad \text{(governs)}$$

$$R = 23.1(1 + DL/LL)$$

$$= 23.1(1 + \text{\textonesuperior}\!/_{20}) = 32.3 \text{ percent}$$

$$R = 40 \text{ percent} \quad \text{(UBC Table 23-C)}$$

The smallest of the three values is taken as the reduction of RLL:

$$\text{RLL} = 20(1.00 - 0.136)$$

$$= 17.3 \text{ psf}$$

$$w = [(8 + 17.3) \text{ psf}](16 \text{ ft}) = 404 \text{ lb/ft}$$

c. Column.

$$\text{Trib. } A = 320 \quad \text{same as girder}$$

$$\therefore \text{RLL} = 17.3 \text{ psf}$$

$$P = [(8 + 17.3) \text{ psf}](320 \text{ ft}^2) = 8090 \text{ lb}$$

It should be pointed out that the unit live loads specified in the Code are applied on a horizontal plane. Therefore, roof live loads on a flat roof can be added directly to the roof dead load. In the case of a sloping roof, the dead load would probably be estimated along the sloping roof; the roof live load, however, would be on a horizontal plane. In order to be added together, the roof dead load or live load must be converted to a load along a length consistent with the load to which it is added. Note that both the dead load and the live load are gravity loads, and they both, therefore, are *vertical* (not inclined) vector resultant forces. See Example 2.4.

In certain framing arrangements, unbalanced live loads (or snow loads) can produce a more critical design situation than loads over the entire span. Should this occur, the Code requires that unbalanced loads be considered.

EXAMPLE 2.4   Combined DL + LL on Sloping Roof

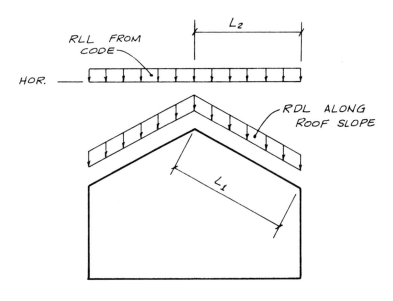

Figure 2.4

The total roof load (DL + LL) can be obtained either as a distributed load along the roof slope or as a load on a horizontal plane. The lengths L_1 and L_2 on which the loads are applied must be considered.

Equivalent total roof loads (DL + LL):

Load on horizontal plane:

$$w_{\text{TL}} = w_{\text{DL}}\left(\frac{L_1}{L_2}\right) + w_{\text{LL}}$$

Load along roof slope:

$$w_{\mathrm{TL}} = w_{\mathrm{DL}} + w_{\mathrm{LL}}\left(\frac{L_2}{L_1}\right)$$

2.5 Snow Load

Snow load is another type of gravity load that primarily affects roof structures. In addition, certain types of floor systems, including balconies and decks, may be subjected to snow loads.

The magnitude of snow loads can vary greatly over a relatively small geographical area. For this reason the UBC simply refers the designer to the local building official for the design snow load.

As an example of how snow loads can vary, the design snow load in a certain mountainous area of southern California is 100 psf, but approximately 5 miles away at the same elevation, the snow load is only 50 psf. This emphasizes the need to be aware of local conditions.

Snow loads can be extremely large. For example, a basic snow load of 240 psf is required in an area near Lake Tahoe. It should be noted that the specified snow loads are on a horizontal plane (similar to roof live loads). Unit snow loads (psf), however, are not subject to the tributary area reductions that can be used for roof live loads.

The slope of the roof has a substantial effect on the magnitude of the design snow load. The Code provides a method by which the basic snow load, obtained from the local building official, may be reduced, depending on the slope of the roof. No reduction is allowed for roofs with slopes less than 20 degrees or for snow loads of 20 psf or less. The UBC provides the following method of reducing the design snow load:

$$R_s = \frac{\mathrm{SL}}{40} - \frac{1}{2}$$

where R_s = reduction in snow load in psf per degree of roof slope over 20 degrees
 SL = total snow load in psf

The use of this reduction and the combination of loads on sloping and horizontal planes is illustrated in Example 2.5. This example also illustrates the effects of using a load on a horizontal plane in design calculations.

EXAMPLE 2.5   Reduction of Snow Loads

Determine the total design dead load plus snow load for the rafters in the building shown in Fig. 2.5a, using the UBC Chap. 23 method for snow load reduction. Determine the design shear and moment for the rafters if they are spaced 4 ft-0 in. o.c. Roof DL has been estimated as 10 psf along the roof, and the basic snow load is given as 75 psf on a horizontal plane.

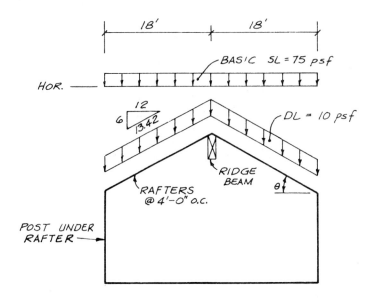

TYPICAL   SECTION

Figure 2.5a

Snow Load

Check reduction:

$$\text{Roof slope} = \theta = \tan^{-1}\frac{6}{12} = 26.6 \text{ degrees} > 20 \text{ degrees}$$

∴ reduction can be used.

$$R_s = \frac{\text{SL}}{40} - \frac{1}{2} = \frac{75}{40} - \frac{1}{2}$$

$$= 1.38 \text{ psf/degree slope over 20 degrees}$$

Reduced snow load:

$$\text{SL} = 75 - 1.38\ (26.6 - 20) \approx 66 \text{ psf}$$

Total Loads

In computing the total load to the rafters in the roof, the different lengths of the dead and snow loads must be taken into account. In addition, the shear and moment in the rafters may be analyzed using the sloping beam method or the horizontal plane method. In the *sloping beam method*, the gravity load is resolved into components that are parallel and perpendicular to the member. The values of shear and moment are based on the normal (perpendicular) component of load and a span length equal to the full length of the rafter. In the *horizontal plane method*, the gravity load is applied to a beam with a span that is taken as the horizontal projection of the rafter. Both methods are illustrated, and the maximum values of shear and moment are compared.

Sloping beam method
(left rafter illustrated)

Horizontal plane method
(right rafter illustrated)

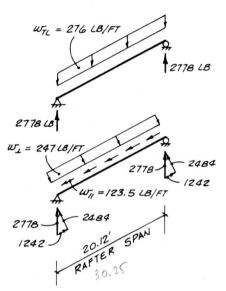

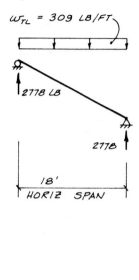

Figure 2.5b Comparison of *sloping beam method* and *horizontal plane method* for determining shears and moments in an inclined beam.

Sloping beam method	Horizontal plane method
TL = DL + SL	TL = DL + SL
$= 10 + 66\left(\dfrac{18}{20.12}\right)$	$= 10\left(\dfrac{20.12}{18}\right) + 66$
= 69 psf	= 77.2 psf
w = 69 psf × 4 ft	w = 77.2 psf × 4 ft
= 276 lb/ft	≈ 309 lb/ft

Use load normal to roof and rafter span parallel to roof.

Use total vertical load and projected horizontal span.

$$V = \frac{wL}{2} = \frac{0.247(20.12)}{2}$$

$$V = \frac{wL}{2} = \frac{0.309(18)}{2}$$

= 2.48 k

= 2.78 k   (conservative)

$$M = \frac{wL^2}{8} = \frac{0.247(20.12)^2}{8}$$

$$M = \frac{wL^2}{8} = \frac{0.309(18)^2}{8}$$

= 12.5 ft-k

= 12.5 ft-k   (same)

NOTE: The horizontal plane method is commonly used in practice to calculate design values for inclined beams such as rafters. This approach is convenient and gives equivalent design moments and conservative values for shear compared with the sloping beam analysis. (By definition *shear* is an internal force *perpendicular* to the longitudinal axis of a beam. Therefore, the calculation of shear for the left rafter in this example is theoretically correct.)

The designer should understand that the snow load provisions given in UBC Chap. 23 have been in the Code for many years, and these requirements represent a simplified approach to design criteria. For example, the Code merely states that the "potential accumulation of snow at valleys, parapets, roof structures and offsets in roofs of uneven configuration shall be considered." However, the method of handling the increased snow load because of this accumulation is not specified, and the procedure is left to the discretion of the designer.

There are more comprehensive snow load criteria available for use in design. ASCE 7-88 (Ref. 5.1) provides a thorough treatment of snow loads which includes, among many other refinements, a method of accounting for the buildup of snow. Steps have been taken to include these more complete snow load provisions in the UBC by allowing the designer to use the Appendix to UBC Chapter 23. This appendix incorporates the essentials of ASCE 7-88 in a somewhat simplified and condensed form. After an appropriate trial use period, it is expected that the material in this appendix will be incorporated into the main body of the UBC. *The BOCA National Building Code* (Ref. 21) and the *Standard Building Code* (Ref. 22) currently use snow load criteria based on ASCE 7-88.

2.6   Floor Live Loads

As noted earlier, floor live loads are specified in UBC Table 23-A. These loads are based on the occupancy or use of the building. Typical *occupancy* or *use* floor live loads range from a minimum of 40 psf for residential structures to much larger values, say 250 psf, for heavy storage facilities.

These Code unit live loads are for members supporting small tributary areas. A small tributary area is defined as an area of 150 ft^2 or less. From the previous discussion of tributary areas, it will be remembered that the magnitude of the *unit* live load can be reduced as the size of the tributary area increases.

It should be pointed out that no reduction is permitted where live loads exceed 100 psf or in areas of public assembly. Reductions are not allowed in these cases because an added measure of safety is desired in these critical structures. In warehouses with high storage loads and in areas of public assembly (especially in emergency situations), it is possible for high unit loads to be distributed over large surface areas.

However, for the majority of wood-frame structures, reductions in floor live loads will be allowed. For these structures, the smallest value of R as

given by the following three criteria represents the percent reduction in
floor live load:

1. $R = r(A - 150)$

2. $R = 23.1\left(1 + \dfrac{\mathrm{DL}}{\mathrm{FLL}}\right)$

3. $R = \begin{cases} 40 \text{ percent maximum for members receiving load from one level} \\ \quad \text{only} \\ 60 \text{ percent maximum for other members} \end{cases}$

where r = reduction rate equal to 0.08 percent per square foot of tributary
           floor area over 150 ft^2
       A = tributary floor area of member under consideration
      DL = floor dead load
     FLL = tabulated floor live load from UBC Table 23-A

The calculation of reduced floor live loads is illustrated in Example 2.6.

EXAMPLE 2.6   Reduction of Floor Live Loads

Determine the total axial force required for the design of the interior column in the floor
framing plan shown in Fig. 2.6. The structure is an apartment building with a floor DL
of 10 psf and, from UBC Table 23-A, a tabulated floor live load of 40 psf. Assume that
roof loads are not part of this problem and the load is received from one level.

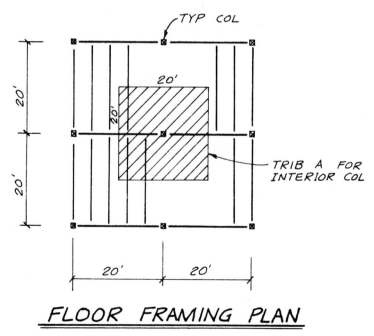

FLOOR FRAMING PLAN

Figure 2.6

Floor Live Load

$$\text{Trib. } A = 20 \times 20 = 400 \text{ ft}^2 > 150$$

$\therefore$ FLL can be reduced:

$$R = r(A - 150) = 0.08(400 - 150)$$

$$= 20 \text{ percent} \quad \text{(governs)}$$

$$R = 23.1\left(1 + \frac{DL}{FLL}\right) = 23.1\left(1 + \frac{10}{40}\right)$$

$$= 28.9 \text{ percent}$$

$$R = 40 \text{ percent} \quad \text{(load from one level only)}$$

The smallest of the three values is taken as the reduction of FLL:

$$\text{FLL} = 40(1.00 - 0.20) = 32 \text{ psf}$$

Total Load

$$\text{TL} = \text{DL} + \text{FLL} = 10 + 32 = 42 \text{ psf}$$

$$P = 42 \times 400 = 16.8 \text{ k}$$

In addition to basic floor unit live loads, UBC Table 23-A provides special alternate concentrated floor loads. Whichever combination of loads, (DL + FLL) or (DL + special concentrated load), produces the more critical situation is the one which is to be used in sizing the framing members.

Concentrated floor loads can be distributed over an area 2½ ft square. Their purpose is to account for miscellaneous nonstationary equipment loads which may occur. In sizing framing members, it will be found that the majority of the designs will be governed by the uniform loads. However, both the concentrated loads and the uniform loads should be checked. For certain wood-framing systems, NDS Sec. 15.1 provides a method of distributing concentrated loads to adjacent parallel beams.

2.7 Deflection Criteria

The above discussion of gravity loads provides a general summary of vertical design load criteria. Certainly any special loads in addition to those mentioned must be taken into account by the designer. Refer to UBC Table 23-B for special loads required by the Code.

The Code establishes deflection limitations for beams, trusses, and similar members that are not to be exceeded under certain gravity loads. The deflection criteria are given in UBC Tables 23-D and 23-E and apply to floor members and roof members that support plastered ceilings. The same limitations apply to both types of members. These deflection limits are intended to ensure user comfort and to prevent excessive cracking of plaster ceilings.

The question of user comfort is tied directly to the confidence that occupants have regarding the safety of a structure. It is possible for a structure to be very safe with respect to satisfying stress limitations, but it may deflect under load to such an extent as to render it unsatisfactory.

Excessive deflections can occur under a variety of loading conditions. For example, user comfort is essentially related to deflection caused by live loads only. The Code therefore requires that the deflection under live load be calculated. This deflection should be less than or equal to the span length divided by 360 ($\Delta_{LL} \leq L/360$).

Another loading condition that relates more to the cracking of plaster and the creation of an unpleasant visual situation is that of total load deflection (i.e., dead load plus live load). For this case, the actual deflection is controlled by the limit of the span divided by 240 ($\Delta_{K\,DL+LL} \leq L/240$).

Notice that in the second criterion above, the calculated deflection is to be under K times the DL plus the LL. In this K is the Code's attempt to reflect the tendency of various structural materials to creep under sustained load. Recall that when a beam or similar member is subjected to a load, there will be an *instantaneous deflection*. For certain materials and under certain conditions, additional deflection may occur under long-term loading, and this added deflection is known as *creep*. In practice, a portion of the live load on a floor may be a long-term or sustained load, but the Code essentially treats the dead load as the only long-term load that must be considered.

Some structural materials are known to undergo creep, and others do not. Furthermore, some materials may creep under certain conditions and not under others. For example, steel members do not creep (at normal temperatures), and therefore K is taken as zero. On the other hand, reinforced concrete will creep, but this behavior is reduced by the presence of compression steel in bending members. Thus, K is defined by an expression for reinforced-concrete beams that is a function of the amount of compression steel in relation to the amount of tension steel in the member.

Finally, the tendency of wood beams to creep is affected by the moisture content (see Chap. 4) of the member. The drier the member, the less the deflection under sustained load. Thus, for seasoned lumber, a K factor of 0.5 is used; for unseasoned wood, K is taken as 1.0. *Seasoned lumber* here is defined as wood having a moisture content of less than 16 percent at the time of construction, and it is further assumed that the wood will be subjected to dry conditions of use (as in most covered structures). Although the K factor is included in the Code, many designers take a conservative approach and simply use the full dead load (that is, $K = 1.0$) in the check for deflection under DL + LL in wood beams. See Example 2.7.

EXAMPLE 2.7   Beam Deflection Limits

The deflection that occurs in a beam can be determined using the principles of strength of materials. For example, the maximum deflection due to bending in a simply supported beam with a uniformly distributed load over the entire span is

$$\Delta = \frac{5wL^4}{384EL}$$

There are several limits on the computed deflection which are not to be exceeded. See Fig. 2.7.

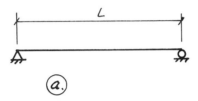

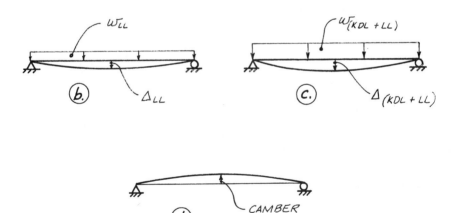

Figure 2.7 *a.* Unloaded beam. *b.* Deflection under live load only. *c.* Deflection under K times dead load plus live load. *d.* Camber is curvature built into fabricated beams that opposes deflection due to gravity loading.

The Code requires that the deflection of floor beams and roof beams that support a rigid ceiling material (such as plaster) be computed and checked against the following criteria:

1. Deflection under live load only shall not exceed the span length divided by 360:

$$\Delta_{LL} \le \frac{L}{360}$$

2. Deflection under K times the dead load plus live load shall not exceed the span length divided by 240:

$$\Delta_{K\,DL+LL} \le \frac{L}{240}$$

The Code values of K may be used:

$$K = \begin{cases} 1.0 & \text{for } \textit{unseasoned} \text{ or green wood} \\ 0.5 & \text{for } \textit{seasoned} \text{ or dry wood} \end{cases}$$

As an alternative, the deflection limit for a wood member under total load (that is, $K = 1.0$) may be conservatively used:

$$\Delta_{TL} \le \frac{L}{240}$$

For members not covered by the Code criteria given above, the designer may choose to use the deflection limits given in Fig. 2.8.

Fabricated wood members, such as glulam beams and wood trusses, may have curvature built into the member at the time of manufacture. This built-in curvature is known as *camber,* and it opposes the deflection under gravity loads to provide a more pleasing visual condition. See Example 6.15 in Sec. 6.6 for additional information. Solid sawn wood beams are not cambered.

Experience has shown that the Code deflection criteria may not provide a sufficiently stiff wood floor system for certain types of buildings. In office buildings and other commercial structures, the designer may choose to use more restrictive deflection criteria than required by the Code. The deflection criteria given in Fig. 2.8 are recommended by AITC. These criteria include limitations for beams under *ordinary usage* (similar to the Code criteria) and limitations for beams where *increased floor stiffness* is desired. These latter criteria depend on the type of beam (joist or girder), span length, and magnitude of floor live load. The added floor stiffness will probably result in increased user comfort and acceptance of wood floor systems.

Other deflection recommendations given in Fig. 2.8 can be used for guidance in the design of members not specifically covered by the Code deflection criteria. For example, the Code does not specify deflection limits for roof members that do not support plastered ceilings, and the AITC recommendations will provide some direction for the designer. In Fig. 2.8, the applied load is live load, snow load, wind load, and so on.

The deflection of members in other possible critical situations should be evaluated by the designer. Members over large glazed areas and members which affect the alignment or operation of special equipment are examples of two such potential problems.

The NDS takes a somewhat different position regarding beam deflection from the Code and the TCM. The NDS does not recommend deflection limits for designing beams or other components, and it essentially leaves these

Recommended Deflection Limitations		
Use classification	Applied load only	Applied load + dead load
Roof beams		
Industrial	$l/180$	$l/120$
Commercial and institutional		
Without plaster ceiling	$l/240$	$l/180$
With plaster ceiling	$l/360$	$l/240$
Floor beams		
Ordinary usage*	$l/360$	$l/240$
Highway bridge stringers	$l/200$ to $l/300$	
Railway bridge stringers	$l/300$ to $l/400$	

* The ordinary usage classification is for floors intended for construction in which walking comfort and minimized plaster cracking are the main considerations. These recommended deflection limits may not eliminate all objections to vibrations such as in long spans approaching the maximum limits or for some office and institutional applications where increased floor stiffness is desired. For these usages the deflection limitations in the following table have been found to provide additional stiffness.

Deflection Limitations for Uses Where Increased Floor Stiffness Is Desired		
Use classification	Applied load only	Applied load + K (dead load)*
Floor beams		
Commercial, office and institutional		
Floor joists, spans to 26 ft†		
LL $\leq$ 60 psf	$l/480$	$l/360$
60 psf $<$ LL $<$ 80 psf	$l/480$	$l/360$
LL $\geq$ 80 psf	$l/420$	$l/300$
Girders, spans to 36 ft†		
LL $\leq$ 60 psf	$l/480$‡	$l/360$
60 psf $<$ LL $<$ 80 psf	$l/420$‡	$l/300$
LL $\geq$ 80 psf	$l/360$‡	$l/240$

* $K = 1.0$ except for seasoned members where $K = 0.5$. Seasoned members for this usage are defined as having a moisture content of less than 16 percent at the time of installation.

† For girder spans greater than 36 ft and joist spans greater than 26 ft, special design considerations may be required such as more restrictive deflection limits and vibration considerations that include the total mass of the floor.

‡ Based on reduction of live load as permitted by the Code.

Figure 2.8 Recommended beam deflection limitations from TCM (Ref. 3.1). (*AITC.*)

serviceability critera to the designer or to the building code. However, the NDS recognizes the tendency of a wood member to creep under sustained loads in NDS Sec. 3.5.2 and NDS Appendix F.

According to the NDS, an unseasoned wood member will creep an amount approximately equal to the deflection under sustained load, and seasoned

wood members will creep about half as much. With this approach the total deflection of a wood member including the effects of creep can be computed.
For green lumber:

$$\Delta_{\text{Total}} = 2.0(\Delta_{\text{long term}}) + \Delta_{\text{short term}}$$

For seasoned lumber and glulam:

$$\Delta_{\text{Total}} = 1.5(\Delta_{\text{long term}}) + \Delta_{\text{short term}}$$

where $\Delta_{\text{long term}}$ = immediate deflection under long-term load. Long-term load is dead load plus an appropriate (long-term) portion of live load. Knowing the type of structure and nature of the live loads, the designer can estimate what portion of live load (if any) will be a long-term load.

$\Delta_{\text{short term}}$ = deflection under short-term portion of design load

The NDS thus provides a convenient method of estimating total deflection including creep. With this information, the designer can then make a judgment about the stiffness of a member. In other words, if the computed deflection is excessive, the design may be revised by selecting a member with a larger moment of inertia.

In recent years, there has been an increasing concern about the failure of roof systems associated with excessive deflections on *flat* roof structures caused by the entrapment of water. This type of failure is known as *ponding* failure, and it represents a progressive collapse caused by the accumulation of water on a flat roof. The initial beam deflection allows water to become trapped. This trapped water, in turn, causes additional deflection. A vicious cycle is generated which can lead to failure if the roof structure is too flexible.

Ponding failures may be prevented by proper design. The first and simplest method is to provide adequate drainage together with a positive slope (even on essentially flat roofs) so that an initial accumulation of water is simply not possible. AITC recommends a minimum roof slope of ¼ in./ft to guard against ponding. This recommendation applies to all members in the roof system. An adequate number and size of roof drains must be provided to carry off this water unless, of course, no obstructions are present. See Ref. 5.1 for additional requirements for roof drains and loads due to rain.

The second method is used in lieu of providing the minimum ¼-in./ft roof slope. Here ponding can be prevented by designing a sufficiently stiff and strong roof structure so that water cannot accumulate in sufficient quantities to cause a progressive failure. This is accomplished by imposing additional deflection criteria for the framing members in the roof structure and by designing these members for increased stresses and deflections. The increased stresses are obtained by multiplying calculated actual stresses under service loads by a magnification factor. The magnification factor is a number greater than 1.0 and is a measure of the sensitivity of a roof structure to accumulate (pond) water. It is a function of the total design roof load (DL + LL) and the weight of ponding water.

Because the first method of preventing ponding is the more direct, positive, and less costly method, it is recommended for most typical designs. Where the minimum slope cannot be provided for drainage, the roof structure should be designed, as described above, for ponding. Because this latter approach is not the more common solution, the specific design criteria are not included here. The designer is referred to Ref. 3.1 for these criteria and a numerical example.

Several methods can be used in obtaining the recommended ¼-in./ft roof slope. The most obvious solution is to place the supports for framing members at different elevations. These support elevations (or the *top-of-sheathing,* abbreviated TS, elevations) should be clearly shown on the roof plan.

A second method which can be used in the case of glulam construction is to provide *additional* camber (see Chap. 5) so that the ¼-in./ft slope is built into supporting members. It should be emphasized that this slope camber is in addition to the camber provided to account for long-term (dead load) deflection.

2.8 Lateral Forces

The subject of lateral forces can easily fill several volumes. Wind and seismic are the two primary lateral forces considered in building design. Each has been the topic of countless research projects, and complete texts deal with the evaluation of these forces. Interest in the design for earthquake effects increased substantially in light of experience obtained in the San Fernando earthquake of 1971 and other recent well-documented earthquakes.

The design criteria included in the Code for wind and seismic forces will be summarized in the remainder of this chapter. The calculation of lateral forces for typical buildings using shearwalls and horizontal diaphragms is covered in Chap. 3.

In dealing with lateral forces, some consideration should be given as to what loads will act concurrently. For example, it is extremely unlikely that the maximum seismic force and the maximum wind force will act simultaneously. Consequently, the Code simply requires that the horizontal seismic force *or* the wind force be used (in combination with other appropriate loads) in design. Of course, the loading which creates the more critical condition is the one which must be used.

Similarly, the UBC does not require that roof live loads (loads which act relatively infrequently) be considered simultaneously with wind or seismic forces. However, in areas subjected to snow loads, all or part (depending on local conditions) of the snow load must be considered simultaneously with lateral forces. For more information on Code-required load and force combinations, see Sec. 2.16.

Before moving on, a final item should be introduced that applies to lateral force design in general. Traditionally the model building codes have permitted an allowable stress increase of one-third (i.e., allowable stresses may be multiplied by 1.33) in designing for lateral forces. For example, UBC Chap. 23 states that allowable stresses "may be increased one-third when considering wind or earthquake forces acting alone or when combined with vertical loads."

This increase in *allowable stress* may be applied to all structural materials including steel, concrete, masonry, wood, and soil-bearing values. On the other hand, if the design is carried out using a "strength method" such as *load and resistance factor design (LRFD),* a reduced load factor is provided for load combinations involving wind or seismic forces. For the design of certain materials, such as structural steel, either allowable stress design *or* load and resistance factor design may be used in practice (Refs. 11.1 and 11.2). However, for wood structures, the LRFD approach is still under development, and current practice is based on *allowable stress design (ASD).*

Another factor that relates to wind and seismic forces applies only to wood design. It is known as the *load duration factor* C_D (Sec. 4.15). Prior editions of the NDS defined $C_D = 1.33$ for wind and seismic stresses. However, the 1991 NDS recommends a change in C_D from 1.33 to 1.6 for these forces.

In the past, the 1.33 allowable stress increase for load combinations involving wind or seismic force (UBC Chap. 23) was viewed by many designers to be the old $C_D = 1.33$ load duration factor for wood (UBC Chap. 25). The fact that both adjustments were numerically the same value led many to this conclusion.

The 1991 NDS indicates that these are really two *different* adjustments based on distinct principles:

1. The *load combination factor* applies to all materials and is the result of a reduced probability that certain design loads will combine with other full design loads.

2. The *load duration factor* is a material property that is unique to wood as a structural material.

The term "load combination factor" does not appear in the UBC, and it is taken from ASCE 7 (Ref. 5.1). In ASCE 7, the load combination factor, which is equivalent to an allowable stress multiplier of 1.33, is stated as a 0.75 multiplier for the design loads. The corresponding load combination involves wind or seismic forces combined with dead load *plus* one or more additional *transient loads* (such as floor live load, roof live load, or snow load). This multiplier recognizes that it is unlikely that all of the *full design loads* will occur simultaneously. The logic behind the allowable stress increase in Chap. 23 of the Code is not as well documented as the load combination factor, but Ref. 1.3 offers a similar explanation.

Although there are some practical differences in application, a *load combination factor* of 0.75 has much the same effect as the general *allowable stress increase* of 1.33 permitted for all materials. In other words, if the design loads are decreased by multiplying by 0.75, or if the allowable stresses are increased by a factor of 1.33, the net result is the same. (*Note:* The inverse of 0.75 is $1/0.75 = 1.33$.)

The 1991 NDS recommends that the material property known as load duration factor C_D be taken as 1.6 for wind and seismic forces. This material property reflects the ability of wood to support higher stresses for short periods (durations) of time. Other materials such as structural steel and reinforced concrete do not have this property.

Because the load combination factor and the load duration factor account for two different principles, the 1991 NDS takes the position that it is appropriate to use both adjustments. The NDS, however, requires that the adjustment for load combination be used *in accordance with the provisions of ASCE 7*. Restated, the load combination factor applies only to combinations involving (1) wind or seismic force plus dead load *and* (2) one or more additional transient loads (floor live load, snow load, etc.). Note that UBC Chap. 23 permits an allowable stress increase of one-third for wind or seismic force plus dead load, which appears to be unconservative from the perspective of a load combination factor.

The concept of a separate *load combination factor* and *load duration factor* C_D fits nicely into an LRFD format. This is, in fact, the approach that is being taken in the development of the LRFD specification for wood. On the other hand, the use of two adjustments for wind and seismic forces in ASD (one involving a new C_D of 1.6) has not yet been addressed by all of the model building code groups.

The code change process can be slow, and each proposed code change is subject to public review and comment. Until the model code groups have taken a position on these points, the designer is advised to carefully consider whether or not to use the two adjustments just described.

In this book, the calculation of code design loads is illustrated, and a load duration factor of 1.6 for wood is used in design examples involving wind or earthquake forces. The designer should verify the acceptance of $C_D = 1.6$ before using it in practice. In addition, because of concern about local code interpretation, the load combination factor is not shown in example problems, and it is left to the designer to *incorporate* or *not incorporate* the adjustment as determined by local practice.

There is one final consideration that affects the traditional one-third increase in allowable stress (UBC Chap. 23) permitted for all materials under lateral earthquake forces. Starting with the 1988 UBC, the earthquake regulations provide some restrictions on the heretofore universal one-third increase in allowable stresses.

The restrictions apply only in areas of *high seismic risk* (i.e., seismic zones 3 and 4) and only to structures with certain forms of *irregularity*. Thus, the designer is now required to selectively apply the one-third increase of allowable stresses (or the 0.75 load combination factor) for earthquake loading.

It will eventually be important to understand the circumstances that limit the application of the allowable stress increase. However, this is a fairly advanced topic, and further details are beyond the scope of this introductory chapter. The limitations on the use of the traditional one-third increase are covered in Chap. 16.

2.9   Wind Forces—Introduction

The 1982 edition of the UBC incorporated major changes to the wind force design criteria of previous codes. Although there have been some changes, the 1991 UBC wind force requirements are based on the provisions introduced in the 1982 UBC.

It should be noted that the simplified wind force requirements used prior to the 1982 Code resulted in adequate designs for the large majority of wood-frame structures. However, the newer wind force criteria have updated the design procedure and brought the Code requirements into agreement with the results of recent research. There are even structures for which the current, more accurate Code criteria are not adequate, and for these structures a more detailed wind force analysis is required. For example, buildings with a height-to-width ratio of 5 or greater may be sensitive to dynamic effects, and a more complete wind analysis is required. The Code draws attention to these and several other situations that require special consideration.

The current wind force requirements in the UBC are based on procedures given in ASCE 7-88 (formerly ANSI A58.1), *Minimum Design Loads in Buildings and Other Structures* (Ref. 5.1). ASCE 7-88 requires the calculation of a number of wind design coefficients. The UBC simplifies the design procedure by combining some of the coefficients and by providing tables for the coefficients rather than requiring computations. A number of the UBC tables for the evaluation of wind forces are included in Appendix C of this book.

After reviewing the very basic wind force examples in this chapter, the reader may likely conclude that even the simplified procedures in the UBC are sufficiently complex that the evaluation of wind forces is best handled on the computer. A modern spreadsheet on a microcomputer can readily be programmed to solve for design wind pressures. Development of a spreadsheet *template* requires an initial investment of time, but once programmed, the computer can evaluate the detailed provisions of the Code automatically.

Although use of the computer is becoming a way of life in design practice, many experienced designers may question the need for such sophistication.

Engineering at one time was an art that reduced complicated physical problems to simple terms which could then be analyzed. The question logically arises as to whether or not the refined wind force criteria in the UBC (or in ASCE 7-88) really lead to structures (at least ordinary structures) that are better designed to resist the action of wind.

The basic Code formula to calculate the design wind pressure P (in psf) is

$$P = C_e C_q q_s I$$

Each of the terms in this expression is defined as follows:

q_s = **wind stagnation pressure.** The stagnation pressure is the starting point for defining the Code wind pressure. It is defined as the theoretical pressure developed by wind impinging upon a vertical surface at sea level.

The wind stagnation pressure is a function of the wind velocity V, which the Code refers to as the *basic wind speed*. The basic wind speed (in miles per hour) can be read from a map of the United States given in UBC Fig. 23-1. This wind speed is based on the "fastest mile," which is defined as the highest recorded velocity averaged over the time it takes a mile of air to pass a given point. Because the basic wind speed is an average value, short-term velocities due to gusts may be much higher. The effects of gusts are handled by one of the other coefficients in the Code wind pressure formula. The wind velocity map shows "special wind regions" which indicate that there may be the need to account for locally higher wind speeds in certain areas.

The basic wind speed is measured at a standard height of 33 ft above ground level with Exposure C (defined below) conditions and is associated with an annual probability of exceedence of 0.02 (mean recurrence interval of 50 years). The minimum velocity to be considered in designing for wind is 70 mph, and a linear interpolation between the wind speed contours in UBC Fig. 23-1 may be used.

Once the designer has determined the basic wind speed from UBC Fig. 23-1 (or from the local building official in special wind regions), the stagnation wind pressure q_s (in psf) can be read from UBC Table 23-F. The values in this table were calculated from the expression $q_s = 0.00256V^2$.

I = **importance factor.** Importance factors are a fairly recent development in the determination of design forces. An importance coefficient was first included in the seismic base shear formula, and more recently one has been incorporated into the wind design expression. The concept behind the importance factor is that certain structures should be designed for higher force levels than ordinary structures. Except for the default value of 1.0, note that the I coefficients for wind and seismic forces are not equal. The 1991

UBC now lists the importance factors for wind and seismic forces in the same table (UBC Table 23-L) for easy comparison and reference.

The I coefficient provides that essential facilities and hazardous facilities be designed to withstand higher wind forces than other structures. *Essential facilities* are those that must remain safe and usable for emergency purposes after a windstorm. Examples of essential facilities include hospitals, fire and police stations, and communications centers. *Hazardous facilities* contain toxic or explosive substances in such quantities as to potentially threaten public safety. For both essential and hazardous facilities the importance factor is $I = 1.15$. This value of I was selected because it represents an approximate conversion of the 50-year wind-speed recurrence interval in UBC Fig. 23-1 to a 100-year recurrence interval.

Buildings that are not classified as essential or hazardous are classified a *special occupancy* or *standard occupancy*. The I coefficient for both special and standard occupancies is the default value of 1.0. The distinction between special and standard occupancies does not affect wind design, but it does affect the inspection requirements for buildings in areas of high seismic risk. See UBC Table 23-K for a complete description of the occupancy classifications for determining I. The I factors for earthquake forces are discussed in Sec. 2.13.

C_e = **combined height, exposure, and gust factor coefficient.** As the name implies, a number of effects have been combined into one coefficient. Values of C_e are obtained from UBC Table 23-G given the height aboveground and the exposure condition of the site.

The wind pressure increases with the height above ground level. A stepped wind pressure diagram may be used on the *windward* side of a building because different values of C_e apply to the heights listed in UBC Table 23-G. See Example 2.8. Note that the value for C_e for 0 to 15 ft applies to the range, and the other values apply to the specific heights (for example, 20 ft, 25 ft).

The simplified stepped wind pressure diagram may be used, but the 1991 UBC allows interpolation between the C_e coefficients for heights above 15 ft. The C_e coefficient for the leeward wall is a constant over the full height, and it is determined using the mean roof height on the leeward side of the building.

EXAMPLE 2.8   Wind Pressure Diagrams on Windward Side

Two possible wind pressure diagrams for the windward side of a building are shown in Fig. 2.9. The stepped pressures on the left in the figure are obtained by applying the values of C_e listed in UBC Table 23-G to *height zones*. The uniformly varying wind pressures on the right are obtained by interpolation between the values of C_e for the specific heights listed. Either type of loading diagram may be used in practice.

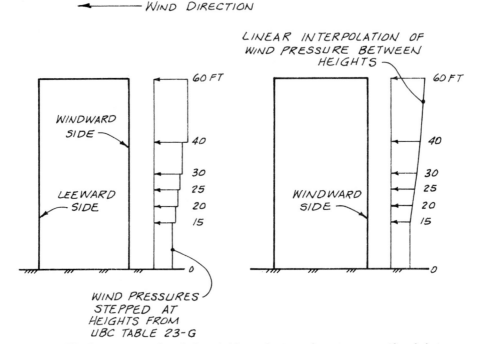

Figure 2.9 Wind pressures on the *windward side* may be stepped or may vary uniformly between specific heights above 15 ft.

Only the pressure on the windward side of the building is shown in Fig. 2.9. Additional wind forces are required that act simultaneously with the pressure on the windward side. These additional forces will include uplift on the roof and may include a suction on the leeward side, depending on which Code method is used to analyze the primary wind-resisting system (Sec. 2.10).

NOTE: Most wood buildings are considerably less than 60 ft high. This example is used to simply illustrate the Code criteria.

Turbulence caused by built-up or rough terrain can cause a substantial reduction in wind speed. ASCE 7-88 defines four types of exposure, which are intended to account for the effects of different types of terrain. However, only three of these (Exposures B, C, and D) have been incorporated into the UBC criteria.

Exposure B includes terrain which has buildings, forests, or surface irregularities 20 ft or more in height covering 20 percent or more of the area extending 1 mile or more from the site. Exposure C has terrain which is flat and generally open, extending ½ mile or more from the site in any full quadrant. Exposure D is the most severe. It has a basic wind speed of 80 mph or greater and has unobstructed flat terrain that faces a large body of water. Exposure D extends inland from the shoreline a distance of ¼ mile or 10 times the building height, whichever is greater.

The Code requires that a particular building site be analyzed and assigned to one of the three exposure categories. The description of Exposure D is quite specific, and the assignment of this exposure should be clear. Exposure B applies to most urban and suburban areas or other terrain which has closely spaced obstructions the size of single-family dwellings or larger. Exposure C is to be used in open country and grasslands which have only scattered obstructions. Exposure A is not currently in the UBC and should be used only with a detailed analysis such as provided in the ASCE 7-88 standard.

C_q = pressure coefficient. Greater wind effects due to gusts tend to be concentrated on smaller tributary areas. Consequently, the C_q coefficient sets forth a number of different multiplying factors, depending on what portion or element of the structure is being designed.

Values of C_q are given in UBC Table 23-H. The first portion of this table gives coefficients to be used in the determination of wind loads on *primary frames and systems* (known as the main wind-force-resisting system in ASCE 7-88). Essentially these coefficients apply when one is considering the structure as a whole in resisting wind forces. The lateral-force-resisting system used in typical wood-frame buildings is described in Chap. 3.

Other portions of UBC Table 23-H provide C_q coefficients for locally higher wind pressures on *elements and components* first *away from discontinuities* and then *at discontinuities*. The term "discontinuity" here refers to a change in geometry (such as the corner of a wall) of the structure that causes locally high wind pressures to develop. The ASCE standard refers to these under the general heading of components and cladding. Examples of wind force determination for the primary system and for a typical component are given in the following sections.

2.10 Wind Forces—Primary Systems

Two methods are given in UBC Table 23-H for determining the design wind forces for the primary lateral-force-resisting system (LFRS). Method 1 is the *normal force method,* and Method 2 is a carryover from earlier codes and is known as the *projected area method.*

Method 1 is a more accurate description of the wind forces, but Method 2 is simpler and produces satisfactory designs for most structures. A problem with the projected area method is that it gives incorrect joint moments in gable rigid frames. Consequently Method 2 is not applied to these types of structures (or to structures greater than 200 ft in height), and Method 1 must be used. Note that many wood-frame structures have a gable profile, but the primary LFRS is usually made up of a system of horizontal diaphragms and shearwalls. Therefore most wood-frame structures do not use gable *rigid frames,* and either Method 1 or Method 2 can be applied. (A gable glulam arch is an example of a wood rigid frame structure which would require Method 1 wind forces.)

In the normal force method, inward pressures are applied to the windward wall, and outward pressures (suction forces) are applied to the leeward wall. The forces on a sloping roof are directed outward on the leeward side, and the force to the windward side will act either inward or outward, depending on the slope of the roof. In the projected area method, horizontal wind forces are applied to the vertical projected area of the building, and a vertically upward pressure (suction force) is applied to the horizontal projected area of the building. See Example 2.9.

Several points should be noted about the wind forces applied to the roof structure. The magnitude of the outward or upward suction values (as given by the pressure coefficient C_q) depends on whether the structure is *enclosed* or *open.* Open structures have much higher outward pressures (see footnote 1 in UBC Table 23-H). Enclosed buildings generally have walls, and wall openings are protected by door and window assemblies.

A building, or a story in a building, is considered to be an open structure if the area of the exterior wall openings on any one side is greater than the sum of the openings in all other exterior walls. This new definition of an *open structure* recognizes the fact that significantly higher internal pressures will not develop unless there are substantially larger openings on one side of the structure. In addition, to be considered open, the area of the openings on one side must exceed 15 percent of the wall area of that side. Doors and windows in exterior walls are considered as openings unless they are protected by assemblies designed to resist the wind forces specified for elements and components (Sec. 2.11). Glazing for windows should meet the requirements of UBC Chap. 54. Obviously structures without walls, such as sheds and carports, are open structures.

In pre-1982 editions of the Code, the uplift wind pressure was considered separately from the horizontal force. However, the current wind force provisions require the two components to be considered simultaneously.

EXAMPLE 2.9   Comparison of Wind Forces Using Methods 1 and 2

Compare the design wind pressures of UBC Methods 1 and 2 for the primary lateral-force-resisting system for the building in Fig. 2.10a. This is a gable structure that does not have a system of rigid frames for resisting lateral forces. The building is a standard occupancy enclosed structure located near Fort Worth, Texas. Exposure C is to be used.

Wind stagnation pressure q_s:

$$V = 70 \text{ mph} \qquad \text{from UBC Fig. 23-1}$$

$$q_s = 12.6 \text{ psf} \qquad \text{from UBC Table 23-F}$$

Importance factor:

$$I = 1.0 \qquad \text{from UBC Table 23-L}$$

Combined height, exposure, and gust coefficient C_e:

The total height of the building is 19 ft, and technically portions of the building are in two height zones. The C_e coefficients are obtained from UBC Table 23-G.

$$C_e = \begin{cases} 1.06 & \text{for 0 to 15 ft} \\ 1.13 & \text{for 20 ft} \end{cases} \quad \text{Use step loading instead of interpolating } C_e.$$

$$\text{Design wind pressure} = P = C_e C_q q_s I$$

Pressure coefficients C_q are obtained from UBC Table 23-H.

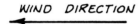

WIND DIRECTION

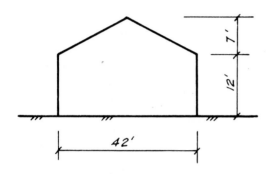

Figure 2.10a

END ELEVATION

METHOD 1 (NORMAL FORCE METHOD)

Windward wall $\qquad\qquad C_q = 0.8$ inward

Wall height is entirely within the 0- to 15-ft-height zone and $C_e = 1.06$.

$$P_{ww} = 1.06(0.8)(12.6)(1.0) = 10.7 \text{ psf inward}$$

Leeward wall $\qquad\qquad C_q = 0.5$ outward

For the leeward wall C_e is a constant and is based on the mean height of the roof.

$$h_{\text{mean}} = \frac{12 + 19}{2} = 15.5 > 15 \text{ ft}$$

C_e could be interpolated, but for simplicity use C_e for 20 ft (conservative).

$$\therefore C_e = 1.13$$

$$P_{lw} = 1.13(0.5)(12.6)(1.0) = 7.1 \text{ psf outward}$$

Windward roof

For the windward roof C_q depends on the slope of the roof. Roof slope is normally given as the rise that occurs in a 12-in. run. Convert a rise of 7 ft in a run of 21 ft to a standard roof slope:

$$\frac{\text{Rise}}{12 \text{ in.}} = \frac{7 \times 12}{21 \times 12}$$

$$\text{Rise} = 4 \text{ in.}$$

$$\therefore \text{Roof slope} = 4:12$$

Roof slope lies in the range $2:12 < 4:12 < 9:12$. For a roof slope in this range, UBC Table 23-H gives two C_q coefficients. One provides an outward force and the other an inward force. The more critical is to be used in design. According to the UBC, wind pressures on roofs are to be based on the mean height of the roof (15.5 ft). Conservatively use $C_e = 1.13$ for a height of 20 ft.

$$C_q = 0.9 \text{ outward}$$

$$P_{wr1} = 1.13(0.9)(12.6)(1.0) = 12.8 \text{ psf} \quad \text{outward}$$

$$C_q = 0.3 \text{ inward}$$

$$P_{wr2} = 1.13(0.3)(12.6)(1.0) = 4.3 \text{ psf} \quad \text{inward}$$

Leeward roof

For the leeward roof C_q is a constant regardless of roof slope.

$$C_q = 0.7 \text{ outward}$$

$$P_{lr} = 1.13(0.7)(12.6)(1.0) = 10.0 \text{ psf} \quad \text{outward}$$

METHOD 2 (PROJECTED AREA METHOD)

Horizontal pressure

$$C_q = 1.3 \text{ any horizontal direction}$$

For structures less than 40 ft in height, this value of C_q is simply the sum of C_q for the windward and leeward walls from Method 1, or $0.8 + 0.5 = 1.3$.

$$P_w = \begin{cases} 1.06(1.3)(12.6)(1.0) = 17.4 \text{ psf} \quad \text{horizontal} \quad\quad 0 \text{ to } 15 \text{ ft} \\ 1.13(1.3)(12.6)(1.0) = 18.5 \text{ psf} \quad \text{horizontal} \quad\quad 15 \text{ to } 20 \text{ ft} \end{cases}$$

Uplift (vertical) pressure

$$C_q = 0.7$$

$$P_u = 1.13(0.7)(12.6)(1.0) = 10.0 \text{ psf} \quad \text{vertical}$$

The wind pressures of Methods 1 and 2 are compared in Fig. 2.10b, and the designer may choose to use one or the other. The selection can be made either for convenience in design or to obtain the most favorable loading. Again, two loadings are obtained with Method 1, and both must be considered.

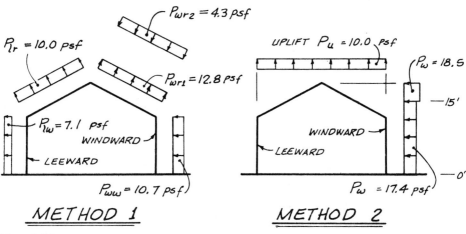

Figure 2.10b

The outward components of roof forces in Method 1 and the upward force in Method 2 are referred to as *uplift* forces. In addition to other considerations, both horizontal and uplift forces must be used in the moment stability analysis (known as a check on *overturning*) of the structure.

Wind uplift requires several considerations. The first could be classified as the direct transfer of the uplift forces from the roof down through the structure. Obviously, if the dead load of the roof structure exceeds the uplift force, little is required in the way of design for uplift. However, for unenclosed structures and structures with light dead loads (these often go hand in hand), design for uplift may affect member sizes.

Connections and footing sizes are the items that typically require special attention even if member sizes are not affected. For example, connections are normally designed for gravity (vertically downward) loads. For large uplift forces, connections may need to be modified to act in tension. It may be necessary to connect a roof beam to a column, or a column to a footing, to transmit the net uplift force from the member on top to the supporting member below. In fact, it may be necessary to size footings to provide an adequate dead load to counter the direct uplift forces.

A second uplift consideration relates to the moment stability of the structure. Depending on how a building is framed, the added requirement for the simultaneous application of the horizontal wind force and uplift wind force could substantially affect the design overturning requirements for a structure.

The net overturning moment OM is the difference between the gross OM and the resisting moment RM. See Example 2.10. The Code requires that $\frac{2}{3}$RM be greater than the OM. In other words, a factor of safety FS of $\frac{3}{2}$, or 1.5, is required for stability for wind. Notice that in this stability check, an overestimation of dead load tends to be unconservative (normally an overestimation of loading is considered conservative). To obtain the design OM, two-thirds of the RM is subtracted from the gross OM. Up to this point, the DL being used in the calculation of RM did not include the weight of the foundation.

Now, if the design OM is a positive value (i.e., the gross OM is more than ⅔RM), the structure will have to be tied to the foundation. The design OM can be replaced by a couple (T and C). The tension force T must be developed by the connection to the foundation. This tension force is also known as the design *uplift* force. If the design OM is negative (i.e., the gross OM is less than or equal to ⅔RM), there will be no uplift problem. Should an uplift problem occur, the DL of the foundation plus the DL of the building must be sufficient to counteract the gross OM.

EXAMPLE 2.10   Overall Moment Stability

Horizontal and vertical wind forces are shown acting on the shearwall in Fig. 2.11. In general, the vertical component may or may not occur, depending on how the roof is

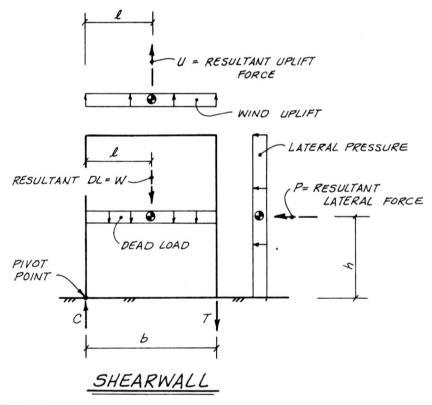

SHEARWALL

Figure 2.11

framed. Roof framing can transmit the uplift force to the wall or some other element in the structure.

In addition to the vertically upward wind pressure, the term *uplift* is sometimes used to refer to the anchorage tie-down force T.

$$\text{Gross overturning moment OM} = P(h) + U(l)$$

$$\text{Resisting moment RM} = W(l)$$

Required factor of safety for overall stability:

$$\text{Req'd FS} = \tfrac{3}{2} = 1.5$$

∴ For no uplift force T the following criterion must be satisfied:

$$\text{Gross OM} \leq \tfrac{2}{3}\text{RM}$$

If this criterion is not satisfied, the net OM is the difference between the gross OM and the RM:

$$\text{Net OM} = \text{gross OM} - \text{RM}$$

The design OM, however, must reflect the required FS and is obtained as follows:

$$\text{Design OM} = \text{gross OM} - \tfrac{2}{3}\text{RM}$$

This moment can then be resolved into a couple (T and C):

$$\text{Uplift force } T = \frac{\text{design OM}}{b}$$

The design uplift force T is to be used for the design of the connection of the shearwall to the foundation. A subsequent stability check which includes the foundation weight in the resisting moment must satisfy the criterion

$$\text{Gross OM} \leq \tfrac{2}{3}\text{RM}$$

The preceding discussion of overturning and the required factor of safety of 1.5 for stability applies to wind forces. A similar analysis is used in earthquake design. However, for lateral seismic forces the UBC requires that the uplift force T be evaluated using 0.85 times the resisting dead load (instead of the two-thirds multiplying factor applied for wind).

There are additional overturning provisions given in the UBC for both wind and seismic forces, but a comprehensive review of these details is beyond the scope of this introductory chapter. See Chap. 16 for a more detailed summary of the design requirements for overturning.

2.11 Wind Forces—Portions of Buildings

The forces to be used in designing the *primary wind-resisting system* are described in Sec. 2.10. These are to be applied to the structure acting as a unit (i.e., to the horizontal diaphragms and shearwalls) in resisting lateral forces. The UBC wind force provisions require that special higher wind pressures be considered in the design of various *elements and components* when considered *individually* (i.e., not part of the primary lateral-force-resisting system). In other words, when a roof beam or wall stud functions as part of the primary LFRS, the design forces will be determined in accordance with Sec. 2.10. However, when the design of these same members is considered independently, the higher wind pressures for elements and components are to be used.

The forces on elements and components are computed using the basic wind pressure formula introduced in Sec. 2.9 ($P = C_e C_q q_s I$). The wind stagnation pressure q_s and the importance factor I will be the same for all wind forces on a given building. The combined height, exposure, and gust factor coefficient C_e is again to be taken from UBC Table 23-G. Suction (outward) forces on elements are to be determined using a constant C_e based on the mean height of the *roof*. Forces acting inward are to be determined using C_e for the actual height of the element.

It is really the larger pressure coefficients C_q that establish the increased wind forces for individual members. In fact, there are *two sets* of wind pressure coefficients given for elements and components. *One set* of coefficients (part 2 of UBC Table 23-H) applies to the design of a general member or element *away from a discontinuity* or significant change in geometry that might produce locally higher wind effects.

These wind pressures are to be applied to the full tributary area of the member or component being designed. The values of C_q for elements and components given in the Code table are conservative, and they apply to small tributary areas (10 ft^2 or less). Footnote 2 to UBC Table 23-H recognizes that the wind pressure on larger areas will be smaller, and it allows the value to C_q to be reduced for the design of members with a tributary wind area greater than 10 ft^2.

Wind tunnel tests and experience have shown that significantly larger forces occur at the edges and corners of a structure. Therefore, the *second set* of pressure coefficients is given (part 3 of UBC Table 23-H) to determine even higher local wind pressures for use in designing similar members and components that are located *near a discontinuity*. The discontinuities to be considered are wall corners, eaves and rakes, and roof ridges.

The areas to which these higher local wind pressures are applied may or may not cover the entire tributary area of a member. The larger forces are to be applied over a distance from the discontinuity of 10 ft or 0.1 times the least width of the structure, whichever is smaller. Wind pressures at discontinuities also apply to tributary areas of 10 ft^2 or less and may be reduced for larger tributary areas.

The pressure coefficients define certain areas that may overlap. The more critical wind pressure condition is to be used in design, but overlapping areas need not be loaded simultaneously by different wind pressures. A number of typical areas for wind forces on elements and components are identified for a simple structure in Example 2.11.

The requirement to consider increased wind pressures on elements and components (both away from and near discontinuities) complicates the design process. A certain amount of engineering judgment is necessary to determine the extent to which these forces need to be considered in the design of a typical wood-frame building. For more information on the UBC wind forces, see Refs. 1.4e to 1.4h. Reference 5.7a provides a detailed analysis of the effects of higher wind pressures required for individual members on a number of conventional wood-frame building components.

EXAMPLE 2.11   Wind Forces—Elements and Components

The basic wind pressure formula $(P = C_e C_q q_s I)$ is used to define two types of forces for designing roof and wall elements and their connections. These pressures are larger than the pressures used to design the primary LFRS. Pressure coefficients are given in UBC Table 23-H for forces on individual member for areas away from discontinuities and at discontinuities. The more critical condition caused by these forces is to be used for design.

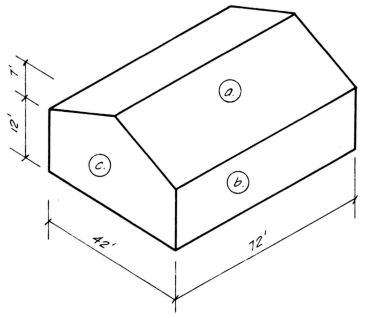

Figure 2.12a General wind force areas for members away from discontinuities.

Wind forces for designing individual elements and components away from discontinuities are obtained with C_q coefficients from part 2 of UBC Table 23-H. Typical locations to be considered are (Fig. 2.12a)

  a. Roof area.
  b. Wall area.
  c. Wall area.

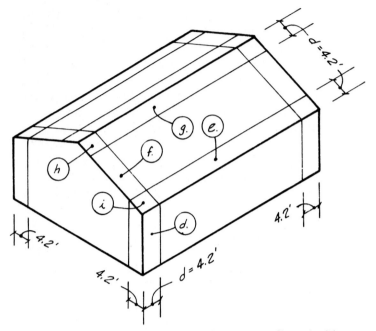

Figure 2.12b   Wind force areas for members at or near discontinuities.

Wind forces for designing individual elements and components at discontinuities are obtained with C_q coefficients from part 3 of UBC Table 23-H. Locations to be considered include (Fig. 2.12b)

  d. Wall corners.
  e. Eave without an overhang.
  f. Rake without an overhang.
  g. Roof ridge.

The force on each area (a to g) is considered separately. The forces on overlapping areas (h and i) do not add. The building in this example does not have a roof overhang. Overhangs at the eaves or rakes represent additional areas that require larger design wind pressures.

Example 2.9 illustrated the computation of wind pressures for designing the *primary wind-force-resisting system* (see the summary in Fig. 2.10b). Wind pressures required for the design of *elements and components* in the same building are evaluated in the remaining portion of this example. The areas considered are those shown in Fig. 2.12a and b. Design conditions (location and exposure condition) are the same as in Example 2.9.

Information from previous example:

q_s = 12.6 psf

I = 1.0

$$C_e = \begin{cases} 1.06 & \text{for 0 to 15 ft} \\ 1.13 & \text{for 15 to 20 ft} \end{cases}$$

Roof slope = 4:12

h_{mean} = 15.5 ft

The structure is an enclosed structure.

Design wind pressure:

$$P = C_e C_q q_s I$$

$$= \begin{cases} 1.06(C_q)(12.6)(1.0) = 13.4C_q & \text{for 0 to 15 ft} \\ 1.13(C_q)(12.6)(1.0) = 14.2C_q & \text{for 15 to 20 ft} \end{cases}$$

Inward pressures are to be based on the height of the element. Wall areas are in the 0- to 15-ft-height zone, and $C_e = 1.06$. *Wind pressures on roofs* and *outward pressures* for all areas are determined by the mean height of the roof. C_e could be interpolated for a mean roof height of 15.5 ft, but for simplicity take $C_e = 1.13$.

All of the wind pressures determined in this example apply to tributary areas of 10 ft^2 or less. For larger tributary areas, these pressures may be reduced in accordance with footnote 2 in UBC Table 23-H.

Elements and Components—Away from Discontinuities

The forces in areas a–c (Fig. 2.12a) are to be applied to the full tributary area of each member considered in design.

Roof forces—area a:
  Enclosed structure with slope *less* than 7:12

$$P = 14.2C_q = 14.2(1.3) = 18.5 \text{ psf}\quad \text{outward}$$

Wall forces—areas b and c:

$$P = 13.4C_q = 13.4(1.2) = 16.0 \text{ psf}\quad \text{inward 0 to 15 ft}$$

$$P = 14.2C_q = 14.2(1.2) = 17.1 \text{ psf}\quad \text{inward 15 to 19 ft}$$

$$P = 17.1 \text{ psf}\quad \text{outward 0 to 19 ft}$$

Elements and Components—At or near Discontinuities

The forces on areas d–g (Fig. 2.12b) are applied to each member considered in the design over width d from the discontinuity. The width d is the smaller of 10 ft or 0.1 times the least width of the structure.

$$\text{Dimension } d = 0.1(42) = 4.2 \text{ ft} < 10 \text{ ft}$$

$$\therefore d = 4.2 \text{ ft}$$

Wall corners—area d (all corners are less than 15 ft in height):

$$P = 13.4C_q = 13.4(1.2) = 16.0 \text{ psf}\quad \text{inward}$$

$$P = 14.2C_q = 14.2(1.5) = 21.4 \text{ psf}\quad \text{outward}$$

Eaves, rakes, and ridges without overhangs—areas e, f, and g:
  Roof slope lies in the range

$$2:12 < 4:12 < 7:12$$

$$P = 14.2C_q = 14.2(2.6) = 37.0 \text{ psf}\quad \text{outward}$$

2.12 Seismic Forces—Introduction

Many designers have a good understanding of the types of loads and forces (gravity and wind) covered thus far. However, the forces that develop during an earthquake may not be as widely understood, and for this reason a fairly complete introduction to seismic forces is given.

The Structural Engineers Association of California (SEAOC) pioneered the work in the area of seismic design forces. Various editions of the SEAOC publication *Recommended Lateral Force Requirements and Commentary* (commonly referred to as the *Blue Book*) have served as the basis for the earthquake design requirements for most building codes. The latest edition of the Blue Book (Ref. 6.1) represents a major change in seismic design format and content, and these provisions are referred to in this book as the *new seismic code*. The provisions of the new seismic code were introduced in the 1988 UBC, and they form the basis of the 1991 UBC earthquake regulations.

The Blue Book has grown immensely in size and complexity. For example, the main body of the Blue Book, titled *Recommended Lateral Force Requirements, 1990 Edition,* is now 60 pages long and the *Commentary* has increased in size to 203 pages.

The designer of a typical wood-frame building could easily be intimidated by the complexity of such a document. However, one should realize that this new seismic code contains many detailed requirements for multistory steel and reinforced-concrete buildings as well as the more common low-rise structures treated in this text.

The remaining portion of Chap. 2 deals with the basic concepts of earthquake engineering, and it is primarily limited to a review of the new seismic code as it applies to structurally *regular* wood-frame buildings. Many of the new requirements in the seismic code deal with added requirements for *irregular* structures. These more advanced topics are covered in later chapters (Chaps. 15 and 16) after the fundamentals of horizontal diaphragms and shearwalls are thoroughly understood.

Courses in structural dynamics and earthquake engineering deal at length with the subject of seismic forces. From structural dynamics it is known that a number of different forces act on a structure during an earthquake. These forces include inertia forces, damping forces, elastic forces, and an equivalent forcing function (mass times ground acceleration). The theoretical solution of the dynamic problem involves the addition of individual responses of a number of *modes of vibration*. Each mode is described by an equation of motion which includes a term reflecting each of the forces mentioned above.

In these types of theoretical studies, ground acceleration records from previous earthquakes are used as input, and the equations of motion are integrated numerically. This technique requires extensive computer time.

A second theoretical method makes use of response spectra which eliminates the extensive numerical integration process.

Both techniques (*integration of the equations of motion* and *response spectra* studies) are forms of a *dynamic analysis*. The new seismic code has expanded the number of structures for which a dynamic analysis is required. For example, *regular* structures over 240 ft in height and *irregular* structures greater than five stories or greater than 65 ft in height must be designed using a dynamic analysis (the Code refers to this as a *dynamic lateral force procedure*).

For buildings which do not require a dynamic analysis, the Code provides a simplified alternative which is known as the *static lateral force procedure*. Most wood-frame buildings fall in the category of being "not more than five stories or 65 feet in height." Consequently, the static lateral force procedure can be applied to the design of practically all wood-frame buildings whether the structure is classified as regular or irregular. The concept involved in this procedure is to design the structure for a set of Code-defined *equivalent static forces*.

Experience has proven that *regular structures* (i.e., symmetric structures and structures without discontinuities) perform much better in an earthquake than irregular structures. Therefore, even if the static lateral force procedure is used in design, the Code penalizes *irregular structures* in areas of high seismic risk with *additional design requirements*. As previously noted, the definition of an irregular structure and a summary of some of the penalties that may be required in the design of an irregular wood building are covered in Chap. 16.

Rather than attempting to define all of the forces acting during an earthquake, the static lateral force procedure given in UBC takes a simplified approach. This empirical method is one that is particularly easy to visualize. The earthquake force is treated as an inertial problem only. Before the start of an earthquake, a building is in static equilibrium (i.e., it is at rest). Suddenly, the ground moves, and the structure attempts to remain stationary. The key to the problem is, of course, the length of time during which the movement takes place. If the ground displacement were to take place very slowly, the structure would simply ride along quite peacefully. However, because the ground movement occurs quickly, the structure lags behind and "seismic" forces are generated. See Example 2.12.

These equivalent static forces are applied at the story levels of the building (i.e., at roof and floor elevations). Note that no such simplified loads are truly "equivalent" to the complicated combination of forces generated during an earthquake. However, it is felt that reasonable building designs are produced when the structure is designed elastically to resist the specified Code forces. The coefficients in the Code forces reflect many of the important dynamic aspects of the problem.

It should be realized that the forces given in the building code are at a *working stress level* and must be multiplied by an appropriate load factor if

EXAMPLE 2.12   Building Subjected to Earthquake

1. Original static position of the building before earthquake
2. Position of building if ground displacement occurs very slowly (i.e., in a static manner)
3. Deflected shape of building because of "dynamic" effects caused by rapid ground displacement

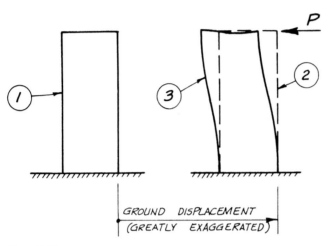

Figure 2.13

The force P in Fig. 2.13 is an "equivalent static" design force provided by the Code and can be used for certain structures in lieu of a more complicated dynamic analysis. This is common practice in wood buildings that make use of horizontal diaphragms and shear-walls.

---

a *strength* approach is used in design. The current practice in wood design is based on a working-stress or allowable-stress design (ASD) concept. However, at some time in the future the design profession will undoubtedly move to a strength design (LRFD) method (see load and resistance factor design in Sec. 4.23). The point of this discussion is to understand that the empirical forces given in the Code static lateral force procedure are considerably lower than would be expected in a major earthquake.

In a working stress approach, the structure is designed to remain *elastic* under the Code static forces. However, it is not expected that a structure will remain elastic in a major earthquake. The key in this philosophy is to *design* and *detail* the structure so that there is sufficient *system ductility* for the building to remain structurally safe when forced into the *inelastic* range in a major earthquake.

Therefore, in areas of high seismic risk, the new seismic code has added *detailing requirements* for all of the principal structural building materials (steel, concrete, masonry, and wood). The term "detailing" here refers to special connection design provisions and to a general tying together of the overall lateral-force-resisting system, so that there is a *continuous path* for the *transfer of lateral forces* from the top of the structure down into the foundation.

Anchorage is another term used to refer to the detailing of a structure so that it is adequately tied together for lateral forces. The basic seismic force requirements are covered in Chaps. 2 and 3, and the detailing and anchorage provisions as they apply to wood-frame structures are addressed in Chaps. 10, 15, and 16.

During an earthquake, vertical ground movement creates vertical forces in addition to the horizontal seismic forces discussed above. However, the vertical components are usually smaller than the horizontal ones, and the structure typically has much more inherent strength vertically than it does horizontally. For these reasons, usual earthquake design practice for buildings is to consider horizontal forces only.

The method used to calculate the Code horizontal story forces is to first calculate the total *base shear* (the total horizontal force acting at the base of the building, V). Once the base shear has been determined, the appropriate percentages of this total force are calculated and assigned to the various story levels throughout the height of the structure. These *story forces* are given the symbol F_x (the force at level x), and a special extra force F_t may be applied at the top level. It should be clear that the sum of the F_x forces and F_t must equal the total base shear V. See Fig. 2.14a. The formulas in the new seismic code for calculating F_x and F_t are the same as those in previous editions of the Code, and they are examined in detail in Sec. 2.14.

Before the Code expressions for these forces are reviewed, it should be noted that the story forces are shown to increase with increasing height above the base of the building. The magnitude of the story forces depends on the mass (dead load) distribution throughout the height of the structure. However, if the dead load is equal at each story level, the distribution provided by the Code formula for F_x will be triangular (i.e., maximum at the roof level and decreasing linearly to zero at the ground level).

The reason for this distribution is that the Code bases its forces on the fundamental mode of vibration of the structure. The fundamental mode is also known as the *first mode* of vibration, and it is the significant mode for most structures.

To develop a feel for the above force distribution, the dynamic model used to theoretically analyze buildings should briefly be discussed. See Fig. 2.14b. In this model, the mass (weight) tributary to each story is assigned to that level. In other words, the weight of the floor and the tributary wall loads halfway between adjacent floors is assumed to be concentrated or "lumped"

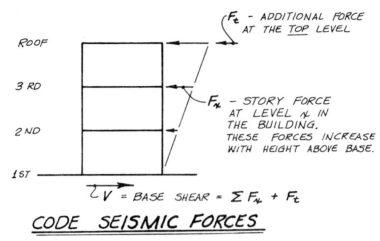

CODE SEISMIC FORCES

Figure 2.14a Code seismic force distribution.

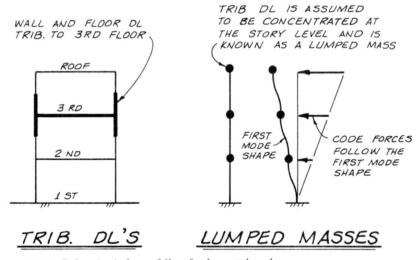

Figure 2.14b Code seismic forces follow fundamental mode.

at the floor level. In analytical studies, this model greatly simplifies the solution of the dynamic problem.

Now, with the term "lumped mass" defined, the concept of a mode shape can be explained. A *mode shape* is a simple displacement pattern that occurs as a structure moves when subjected to a dynamic force. The *first mode shape* is defined as the displacement pattern where all lumped masses are on one side of the reference axis. Higher mode shapes will show masses on both sides of the vertical reference axis. In a dynamic analysis, the complex motion of the complete structure is described by adding together the appropriate percentages of all of the modes of vibration. Again, the Code is essentially based on the first mode.

The point of this discussion is to explain why the F_x story forces increase with increasing height above the base. To summarize, the fundamental or first mode is the critical displacement pattern (deflected shape). The first mode shape shows all masses on one side of the vertical reference axis. Greater displacements and accelerations occur higher in the structure, and the F_x story forces follow this distribution.

2.13   Seismic Force—Base Shear Calculation

The horizontal base shear is calculated from an expression which is essentially inertial in form:

$$F = Ma = \left(\frac{W}{g}\right)a = W\left(\frac{a}{g}\right)$$

where F = inertia force
$\quad M$ = mass
$\quad W$ = weight
$\quad a$ = acceleration
$\quad g$ = acceleration of gravity

The Code form of this expression is somewhat modified. The (a/g) term is replaced by a "seismic base shear coefficient."

The *base shear formula* in the new seismic code is

$$V = \left(\frac{ZIC}{R_w}\right)W$$

compared with the formula from older codes

$$V = (ZIKCS)W$$

Each term in the new base shear formula is defined in the remaining portion of this section. Where appropriate, a comparison between the coefficients in the new and old formulas is made.

V = **base shear.**   The total horizontal seismic force assumed to act at the base of the structure (Fig. 2.14*a*).

W = **weight of structure.**   The total weight of the structure which is assumed to contribute to the development of seismic forces. For most structures, this weight is simply taken as the dead load. However, in structures where a large percentage of the live load is likely to be present at any given time, it is reasonable to include at least a portion of this live load in the value of W. For example, the Code specifies that in storage warehouses W is to include at least 25 percent of the floor live load. Other live loads are not covered specifically by the Code, and the designer must use judgment.

In offices and other buildings where the locations of *partitions* (nonbearing walls) are subject to relocation, UBC Chap. 23 requires that floors be designed for a *dead load of 20 psf.* Use of this partition load was demonstrated in the summary of floor dead loads in Example 2.1 in Sec. 2.2. However, this 20-psf value is to account for localized partition dead loads, and it is intended to be used only for gravity load design. For seismic design it is recognized that the 20-psf loading does not occur at all locations at the same time. Consequently an *average floor DL of 10 psf* may be used for the weight of partitions in determining W for seismic design.

Roof live loads need not be included in the calculation of W, but the Code does require that the snow load be included if it exceeds 30 psf. However, the local building official may allow some reduction in the amount of snow load that is included in W based on the duration of the snow load. This reduction can be as high as 75 percent.

$(ZIC)/R_w$ = seismic base shear coefficient. The product of the three coefficients in the numerator divided by R_w is the new seismic base shear coefficient, and it represents the (a/g) quantity in the basic inertia expression. The five terms in the old base shear coefficient ($ZIKCS$) were all empirical and, to a great extent, were based on judgment. However, the value obtained from the old formula was a base shear that was numerically on the correct order of magnitude. In other words, the base shear given by the old formula was reasonable for use in design.

Even though some of the symbols remain the same, the coefficients in the base shear formula have been assigned new values. The concept in the new seismic code is to place the coefficients that could be rationally or semirationally explained in the numerator of the formula, and to use a single empirical or judgment coefficient (R_w) in the denominator to adjust the final answer to an appropriate magnitude. Hence, the new base shear formula is more rational in form, but the numerical result that it produces does not differ substantially from that obtained using the old formula.

Z = seismic zone factor. UBC Figure 23-2 divides the various regions of the country into six seismic zones: 0, 1, 2A, 2B, 3, and 4. UBC Table 23-I then assigns the following values of Z to the respective zones: 0, 0.075, 0.15, 0.20, 0.30, and 0.40. The larger the Z factor, the larger the seismic force, and seismic zone 4 represents areas of highest seismic risk.

Numerical values of the new Z coefficients represent, in a general sense, the *effective peak ground accelerations* to be used in design for the various seismic zones. Values of effective peak ground acceleration are based on a 10 percent probability of being exceeded in 50 years, which corresponds to a 475-year recurrence interval. The boundaries of the seismic zones were established from geological and seismological studies and with additional input from the design profession, industry, and local building officials.

The effective peak ground acceleration given by Z can be viewed as the horizontal g *factor* applied at the base of a building without being amplified for the dynamic properties of the building or the local site geology. Amplifications for these other effects are taken into account by other coefficients in the base shear formula.

I = occupancy importance factor. An occupancy importance factor was introduced into the seismic base shear formula as a result of failures which occurred in the 1971 San Fernando earthquake. An importance coefficient also appears in the UBC wind pressure formula (Sec. 2.9); however, the I values are different for wind and seismic forces.

The original concept of the importance factor was that certain *essential facilities* should be designed for increased seismic force levels to ensure that they will remain functional for emergency operations following an earthquake. Essential facilities include hospitals, communication centers required for emergency response, fire and police stations, and others. In the old base shear formula, I values ranged from a high of 1.5 for essential facilities to a low of 1.0 for most other structures.

The new seismic code has expanded the occupancy categories to cover four major classes:

I. *Essential facilities*—primarily structures required for emergency and disaster-related operations

$$I = 1.25$$

II. *Hazardous facilities*—structures involved with toxic or explosive substances

$$I = 1.25$$

III. *Special occupancy structures*—certain assembly buildings housing large numbers of people, schools, colleges, power generating stations, and other public utility facilities not classified as essential

$$I = 1.0$$

IV. *Standard occupancy structures*—those not classified as essential, hazardous, or special.

$$I = 1.0$$

A more detailed description of the four occupancy categories for both seismic and wind design can be found in UBC Table 23-K. The numerical values for I are assigned to the four respective occupancy categories in UBC Table 23-L. Future editions of the Code will probably combine the occupancy categories and the I coefficients into one table.

Notice that the importance factor I listed in the new seismic code for essential facilities has *decreased* from $I = 1.5$ in the 1985 UBC (and earlier codes) to $I = 1.25$ in the 1988 and 1991 UBC. This represents a significant change from the recent trend of increased force levels. However, the justification for reducing the I factor is reflected in the basic philosophy of the Blue Book, which recognizes that the design force level represents only a portion of overall seismic performance.

It was noted in Sec. 2.12 that the *detailing* of a structure to form a continuous load path greatly affects its ability to resist earthquake forces. In addition, *inspection* is equally important to ensure that the structure is *constructed* as designed and detailed. The SEAOC Seismology Committee decided that equal or better earthquake performance could be obtained by establishing a *quality assurance* (Q/A) program for certain occupancy importance categories. With a program leading to more reliable designs and constructions, it was reasoned that I could logically be reduced from 1.5 to 1.25.

Consequently, Sec. 1K in the Blue Book (Ref. 6.1) recommends a special quality assurance program for essential, hazardous, and special occupancies in areas of high seismic risk (seismic zones 2, 3, and 4). For these structures the Blue Book recommends

1. *Design review* by an independent structural engineer (separate from the usual building department plan check)

2. Development of an appropriate *testing* and *inspection* program by the structural engineer of record

3. *Construction observation* by the structural engineer of record

Specific details regarding these recommendations are given in the Commentary and the Q/A Appendix of the Blue Book.

Although the 1988 UBC and 1991 UBC are essentially based on the Blue Book, the UBC does not implement all of the Q/A recommendations. UBC Chap. 3 addresses "structural observations" by the responsible engineer or architect. Except for the special case of a structure with *seismic isolation* (UBC Appendix Chap. 23 Division III), the Code is silent on matters such as independent design review. Local agencies and building officials will have to decide if the Q/A provisions in the UBC are adequate when compared to the Blue Book recommendations.

In conclusion, it can be stated that the move to reduce the maximum value of I represents a balanced approach to seismic design. Excessive design force levels cannot compensate for improper structural detailing or improper construction.

C = design response spectrum value.   The Code refers to C as a "numerical coefficient," which may be true, but this terminology fails to convey the fact that C reflects the dynamic properties of the structure. The term "response spectrum value" better describes the purpose of the coefficient C.

It was noted in Sec. 2.12 that a response spectra analysis is one type of *dynamic lateral force procedure* that may be used to analyze a structure. However, the coefficient C is part of the simplified *static lateral force procedure* provided by the Code. In this procedure C accounts for how the building structure and the local site geology amplify the effective peak ground acceleration given by the zone factor Z.

The following discussion will introduce the dynamic properties of a structure and define the general concept of a response spectrum.

The first and most basic dynamic property of a structure is its period of vibration. To define period, first assume that a one-story building has its mass tributary to the roof level, assigned or "lumped" at that level. See Fig. 2.15. The dynamic model then becomes a flexible column with a single concentrated mass at its top. Now, if the mass is given some initial horizontal displacement (point 1) and then released, it will oscillate back and forth (i.e., from 1 to 2 to 3). This movement with no externally applied load is termed *free vibration*. The *period* of vibration T of this structure is defined as the length of time (in seconds) that it takes for one complete cycle of free vibration. The period is a characteristic of the structure (a function of mass and stiffness), and it is a value that can be calculated from dynamic theory.

When the multistory building of Fig. 2.14 was discussed (Sec. 2.12), the concept of the fundamental mode of vibration was defined. Characteristic periods are associated with all the modes of vibration. The *fundamental period* can be defined as the length of time (in seconds) that it takes for the first or fundamental mode (deflected shape) to undergo one cycle of free vibration (Fig. 2.14*b*). The fundamental period can be calculated from theory, or the Code's simple, normally conservative method of estimating T can be used.

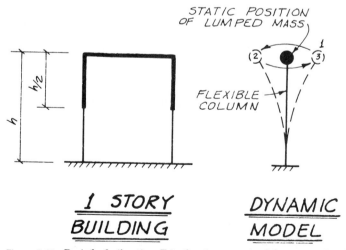

Figure 2.15 Period of vibration T is the time required for one cycle of free vibration. The shaded area represents the tributary wall DL and roof DL, which is assumed to be concentrated at the roof level.

In this latter approach, the UBC provides the following formula for the fundamental period of vibration:

$$T = C_t(h_n)^{3/4}$$

where h_n = height above the base to the nth or top (roof) level, ft

C_t = coefficient depending on a broad classification of the type of lateral-force-resisting system

$$= \begin{cases} 0.035 & \text{for steel moment-resisting frames} \\ 0.030 & \text{for reinforced-concrete moment-resisting frames} \\ & \text{and eccentric braced steel frames} \\ 0.020 & \text{for all other structures} \\ & \text{(including wood-frame buildings)} \end{cases}$$

The Code provides an alternative definition for C_t in buildings with concrete or masonry shearwalls. However, for simplicity $C_t = 0.020$ is used for all buildings in this text. The period of vibration calculated by this simple formula is conservative for most structures. Within limits, a conservative evaluation is one that underestimates the period of the structure.

Damping is another dynamic property of the structure that affects earthquake performance. Damping can be defined as the resistance to motion provided by the internal friction of the building materials. This friction develops as the molecules forming the materials are forced across one another as the structure moves during an earthquake. Damping is a property of the type of building construction and materials used.

With the concept of period of vibration now defined, the idea of a response spectrum can be introduced. In a study of structural dynamics, it has been found that structures which have both the same period and the same amount of damping have essentially the same response to a given earthquake record.

Earthquake records are obtained from strong-motion instruments known as accelerographs which are triggered during an earthquake. Time histories of ground acceleration are obtained and serve as the input for theoretical solutions. The Appendix to UBC Chap. 23 requires that accelerographs be installed in certain buildings over six stories in height and in all buildings over ten stories in height.

Computer solutions of the dynamic problem for a number of buildings with different periods are used to generate a response spectrum. A *response spectrum* is defined as a plot of *maximum response* (acceleration, velocity, displacement, or equivalent static force) versus the period of vibration. See Example 2.13. Once the response spectrum has been generated by the computer, it can be used to determine the effects of an earthquake on other buildings. The information required to obtain values from the response spectrum is simply the period of the structure.

EXAMPLE 2.13   Typical Theoretical Response Spectrum

The term *response spectrum* comes from the fact that *all building periods* are summarized on one graph (for a given earthquake record and a given percentage of critical damping). Figure 2.16 shows the complete *spectrum* of building periods. The curve shifts upward or downward for different amounts of damping.

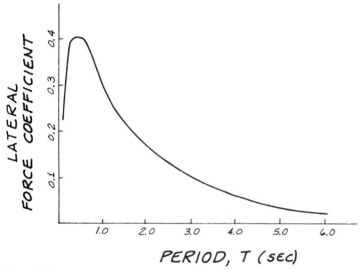

Figure 2.16

The response spectra curve of Fig. 2.16 shows a definite hump or resonance effect that occurs where the period of the structure and the period of the earthquake are close. The Code design curve (Fig. 2.18) makes no attempt to consider a decreased response for a structure with a very short period.

It should be pointed out that a large number of earthquake records are available, and each record can be used to generate a family of theoretical response spectra for buildings with different damping characteristics. However, for a given building site, the Code provides a single design response spectrum curve. The question of damping and the performance of different structural systems is taken into account by the R_w coefficient in the seismic base shear formula.

Now that the basic dynamic properties (period and damping) of a building and the concept of a response spectrum have been introduced, the formula for the response spectrum value C can be reviewed. It should be clear that the coefficient C will depend on the period of vibration T. The Code response spectrum value is computed from the formula

$$C = \frac{1.25S}{T^{2/3}}$$

The value of C need not exceed 2.75, and $C = 2.75$ may be used as a default value under any circumstance.

The coefficient S in the response spectrum formula requires some explanation. Experience in several earthquakes has shown that local soil conditions can have a significant effect on earthquake response. The 1985 Mexico City shock is a prime example of earthquake motions being amplified by local soil conditions. See Example 2.14.

It is perhaps more difficult to visualize, but the soil layers beneath a structure have a period of vibration T_s similar to the period of vibration of a building T. Greater structural damage is likely to occur when the fundamental period of the structure is close to the period of the underlying soil. In these cases a quasi-resonance effect between the structure and the underlying soil develops.

EXAMPLE 2.14   Effect of Local Soil Conditions

Soil-structure resonance is the term used to refer to the amplification of earthquake effects caused by local soil conditions (Fig. 2.17). The soil characteristics associated with a given building site (site-specific) are taken into account by the coefficient S which is incorporated into the definition of C.

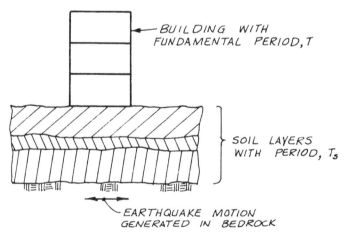

Figure 2.17   Geotechnical profile.

The Code establishes four site profiles (types S_1 through S_4), and a different value of the site coefficient S is assigned to each type (see UBC Table 23-J). If a structure is supported directly on bedrock (soil type S_1), then S is 1.0. However, if the structure rests on a layer of soil, the earthquake motion originating in bedrock may be amplified. In the absence of a geotechnical evaluation, $S = 1.5$ is the default value normally permitted for use in evaluating the response spectrum coefficient C.

An S coefficient appeared directly in the old base shear equation ($V = ZIKCSW$), and a formula was used to define S. However, calculating S from a formula seemed to provide a false sense of understanding of the site-structure interaction problem, and in the new seismic code the S factor is determined in a greatly simplified manner.

The conditions at a specific site are classified into one of four broad soil types. The four basic soil classifications are given the symbols S_1, S_2, S_3, and S_4; and UBC Table 23-J assigns the following values of S to the respective soil types: 1.0, 1.2, 1.5, and 2.0. Without a geotechnical report for a given site, the Code allows soil type S_3 to be assumed, and a corresponding value of $S = 1.5$ may be used. The more critical site factor of $S = 2.0$ is required only if geotechnical information indicates that soil profile S_4 may be present.

The UBC design response spectrum curve is graphed in Fig. 2.18. Although four curves are shown on the graph, only one curve applies to a given building site.

It was noted earlier that in a dynamic analysis, the total response of a structure could be obtained by adding together the appropriate percentages of a number of modes of vibration. However, in the Code static lateral force procedure, the coefficient C represents a *multimode response spectrum envelope*. In other words, the static procedure is based on the fundamental

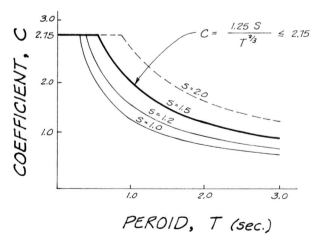

Figure 2.18   UBC design response spectrum. Soil type S_3 may generally be assumed without further geotechnical substantiation, and the curve for C with $S = 1.5$ is the heavier line.

mode, but the response spectrum value C has been increased to account for higher modes of vibration. This is accomplished in the Code formula for C by dividing by $T^{2/3}$ instead of T.

These multimode effects are significant for relatively tall structures which have correspondingly longer periods. However, relatively low-rise structures are characterized by short periods of vibration. Consequently, it should be of little surprise that the default value of $C = 2.75$ will apply to many of the buildings covered in this text. Numerical examples demonstrating this are given in Chap. 3.

R_w = **structural system quality factor.** As noted previously, the terms in the numerator of the seismic base shear coefficient represent rational engineering quantities. Recall that Z represents the effective peak ground acceleration at the base of a structure situated on bedrock. The coefficient C converts this ground acceleration to a lateral force coefficient by evaluating the primary dynamic characteristic of the structure (period of vibration T) *and* the effect of local soil conditions at the site (S factor).

Thus, ZC is a multimode, effective acceleration response spectrum envelope value. When multiplied by the weight W, it represents the horizontal force that is applied to a linear elastic structure subjected to the maximum expected ground motion. The I factor makes further adjustments based on the occupancy importance of the structure.

It was also noted previously that in a major earthquake a structure will not remain *elastic,* and that it will be forced into the *inelastic* range. Inelastic action absorbs significantly more energy from the system. Therefore, if a structure is properly detailed and constructed so that it can perform in a ductile manner (i.e., deform in the inelastic range), it can be designed on a working-stress (elastic) basis for considerably smaller lateral forces (such as those given by the Code static lateral force procedure).

Experience in previous earthquakes indicates that certain types of lateral-force-resisting systems (LFRSs) perform better than others. This better performance can be attributed to the *ductility* (the ability to deform in the inelastic range without fracture) of the system. The *damping* characteristics of the various types of structures also affect seismic performance.

The R_w term in the denominator of the seismic base shear formula is the empirical judgment factor that reduces the lateral seismic forces to an appropriate level for use in conventional working stress design procedures. Numerical values of R_w are assigned to various LFRSs in UBC Table 23-O (R_w factors for nonbuilding structures are given in UBC Table 23-Q).

The four basic structural systems recognized in UBC Table 23-O for conventional buildings are

A. Bearing wall

B. Building frame

C. Moment-resisting frame

D. Dual (combined shearwall and moment-resisting frame)

For these systems R_w values range from 4 to 12. Note that, because R_w appears in the denominator of the base shear coefficient, better performance is expected from systems with larger values of R_w.

In the old seismic code ($V = ZIKCSW$), the performance of the type of LFRS was measured by the K factor. Previous codes referred to buildings with horizontal diaphragms and shearwalls as *box systems*. Box LFRSs were assigned $K = 1.33$, except that all-plywood sheathed systems had $K = 1.0$. The coefficient K in the old seismic code is approximately related to R_w in the new code by the following formula:

$$K = \frac{8}{R_w}$$

In the new seismic code, UBC Table 23-O recognizes (and assigns values of R_w to) many more types of LFRSs than were included in previous codes. Although the term "box system" was very descriptive of the LFRS used in typical wood-frame buildings with horizontal diaphragms and shearwalls, these structures are now classified as either a *bearing wall system* or as a *building frame system*.

It is very common in a wood-frame building to have roof and floor beams resting on load-bearing stud walls. If a load-bearing stud wall is *also* a shearwall, the LFRS will be classified as a *bearing wall system*. For buildings with a bearing wall system the Code assigns the following values of R_w:

Bearing wall system	R_w (new code)	$K = \dfrac{8}{R_w}$ (old code)
1. Light frame shear panels		
a. Plywood sheathing	8	1.0
b. Other than plywood sheathing	6	1.33
2. Shearwalls		
a. Concrete	6	1.33
b. Masonry	6	1.33

The larger value of R_w assigned to buildings three stories or less in height and using *plywood* shearwalls recognizes the good performance of these types of structures in previous earthquakes. Note that the relationship between R_w in the new code and K in the old code is valid for these structural systems.

A *building frame system* may also use horizontal diaphragms and shearwalls to carry lateral forces, but in this case gravity loads are carried by a separate frame. For example, vertical loads could be supported entirely by a wood or steel frame, and lateral forces could be carried by a system of non-load-bearing shearwalls. The term "non-load-bearing" indicates that these walls carry no gravity loads (other than their own dead load). The term "shearwall" indicates that the wall is a lateral-force-resisting element.

The Blue Book Commentary notes that the vertical-load carrying frame in a building frame system need not be designed for any portion of the total lateral force applied to the structure. However, it recommends that the frame be designed for some nominal resistance so that it provides a "second line of defense" against lateral forces.

The distinction between a bearing wall system and a building frame system is essentially this: In a bearing wall system, the walls serve a dual function in that both gravity loads and lateral forces are carried by the same structural element. Here failure of an element in the LFRS during an earthquake could possibly compromise the ability of the system to support gravity loads. On the other hand, because of the separate vertical-load and lateral-force carrying elements in a building frame system, failure of a portion of the LFRS does not necessarily compromise the ability of the system to support gravity loads.

Because of the expected better performance, slightly larger R_w values are assigned to building frame systems than to bearing wall systems:

Building frame system	R_w
1. Light frame shear panels	
a. Plywood sheathing	9
b. Other than plywood sheathing	7
2. Shearwalls	
a. Concrete	8
b. Masonry	8

Building frame systems were not specifically recognized in the old code, and K factors were not assigned. Consequently, a comparison between R_w and K is not given in the above table.

In conclusion, the new seismic base shear formula

$$V = \left(\frac{ZIC}{R_w}\right) W$$

is a more rational expression than the old formula $V = (ZIKCS)W$. The coefficients in the numerator of the new formula have more physical significance, and a single judgment factor R_w is used to adjust the final result to an appropriate force level. In addition, many more types of LFRSs are recognized in the new seismic code.

Each of the coefficients in the base shear formula has been reviewed so the designer should have a good understanding of the terms. For many structures the design force levels given by the new formula are roughly the same as those obtained using the old base shear formula. The significant changes in the new seismic code include the need to consider structural irregularities (Chap. 16) and the added detailing and quality assurance requirements for buildings in areas of high seismic risk.

2.14   Seismic Forces—Primary System

Seismic forces are calculated and distributed throughout the structure in the reverse order used for most other forces. In evaluating wind forces, e.g., the design pressures are calculated first. Later the shear at the base of the structure can be determined by summing forces in the horizontal direction. For earthquake forces the process is just the reverse. The shear at the base of the structure is calculated first, using the base shear formula for V (Sec. 2.13). Then total *story forces* F_x are assigned to the roof and floor levels by distributing the base shear vertically over the height of the structure. Finally, individual story forces are distributed horizontally at each level in accordance with the mass distribution of that level.

The reasoning behind the vertical distribution of seismic forces was given in Sec. 2.12. The general distribution was described, and it was seen that the shape of the first mode of vibration serves as the basis for obtaining the story forces acting on the *primary* lateral-force-resisting system (LFRS). When a part or portion of a building is considered, the seismic force F_p on the individual part may be larger than the seismic forces acting on the primary LFRS. Seismic forces on certain parts and elements of a structure are covered in Sec. 2.15. The methods used to calculate the distributed story forces on the primary lateral-force-resisting system is reviewed in the remaining portion of this section.

The primary LFRS is made up of both horizontal and vertical elements. In most wood-frame buildings, the horizontal elements are roof and floor systems that function as *horizontal diaphragms,* and the vertical elements are wall segments that function as *shearwalls.* A variety of other systems may be used (see Sec. 3.3 for a comparison of several types), but these alternative systems are more common in other kinds of structures (e.g., steel-frame buildings).

Another unique aspect of seismic force evaluation is that there are two different sets of story force distributions for the primary lateral-force-resisting system. One set of story forces is to be used in the design of the vertical elements in the LFRS, and the other set applies to the design of horizontal diaphragms. A different notation system is used to distinguish the two sets of story forces.

The forces for designing the vertical elements (i.e., the shearwalls) are given the symbol F_x, and the forces applied to the design of horizontal diaphragms are given the symbol F_{px}. Both F_x and F_{px} are horizontal *story forces* applied to level x in the structure. Thus, the horizontal forces are assumed to be concentrated at the story levels in much the same manner as the masses tributary to a level are "lumped" or assigned to a particular story height.

Initially it may seem strange that the Code would provide two different distributions (F_x and F_{px}) for designing the *primary LFRS*, but once the reasoning is understood, the concept makes sense. However, the requirement to calculate two sets of seismic story forces is cumbersome at best.

In a multistory structure, the story coefficients given by F_x and F_{px} will be equal at the roof level. At all other story levels, the formulas for F_x and F_{px} will yield seismic forces that are different. Except for the roof level, seismic coefficients given by F_{px} are larger than those given by F_x. It should be clear that the designer must have a good understanding of when each force distribution is to be used.

The rationale behind the F_x and F_{px} distributions has to do with the fact that the forces occurring during an earthquake change rapidly with time. Because of these rapidly changing forces and because of the different modes of vibration, it is likely that the maximum force on an individual horizontal diaphragm will not occur at the same instant in time as the maximum force on another horizontal diaphragm. Hence, the loading given by F_{px} is to account for the possible larger *instantaneous* forces that will occur on individual horizontal diaphragms. Therefore, the F_{px} story force is to be used in the design of individual horizontal diaphragms, diaphragm collectors (drag struts), and related connections. The design of horizontal diaphragms and the definition of terms (such as drag struts) are covered in detail in Chap. 9.

On the other hand, when all of the story forces are considered to be acting on the structure *concurrently*, it is reasonable to use the somewhat smaller distribution of earthquake forces given by F_x. The simultaneous application of all of the F_x story forces does not affect the design of individual horizontal diaphragms. Thus, F_x is used to design the vertical elements (shearwalls) in the primary lateral-force-resisting system. The connections anchoring the shearwall to the foundation, and the foundation system itself, are also to be designed for the accumulated effects of the F_x forces. The design of shearwalls is covered in Chap. 10, and a brief introduction to the foundation design problem for shearwalls is given in Chap. 16.

In practice, the F_x story forces must be determined first because they are then used to evaluate the F_{px} story forces. The formulas for both story force distributions are given in Example 2.15. The F_x *story forces are to be applied simultaneously* to all levels in the primary LFRS for designing the vertical elements in the system. In contrast, the F_{px} *story forces are applied individually* to each level x in the primary LFRS for designing the horizontal diaphragms.

Although the purpose of the F_x forces is to provide the design forces for the shearwalls, the F_x forces are applied to the shearwalls through the horizontal diaphragms. Thus, both F_{px} and F_x are shown as uniform forces on the horizontal diaphragms in Fig. 2.19. To indicate that the diaphragm design forces are applied individually, only *one* of the F_{px} forces is shown with solid lines. In comparison the F_x forces act concurrently and are *all* shown with solid lines.

The formula for F_x will produce a triangular distribution of horizontal story forces if the masses (tributary weights) assigned to the various story levels are all equal (refer to Fig. 2.14a in Sec. 2.12). If the weights are not equal, some variation from the straight-line distribution will result, but the trend will follow the first-mode shape. Accelerations and, correspondingly, inertia forces ($F = Ma$) increase with increasing height above the base.

EXAMPLE 2.15 F_x and F_{px} Story Force Distributions

Two different distributions of seismic forces are used to define earthquake forces on the primary lateral-force-resisting system (Fig. 2.19). The *story forces* for the two major components of the primary LFRS are given by the following distributions.

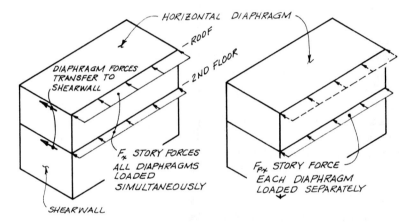

F_x FOR SHEARWALLS   **F_{px} FOR DIAPHRAGMS**

Figure 2.19

F_x Distribution—Vertical Elements
(Shearwalls)

$$F_x = \frac{(V - F_t)\,w_x h_x}{\displaystyle\sum_{i=1}^{n} w_i h_i}$$

where F_x = horizontal force on primary LFRS at story level x for designing vertical
        elements
     V = total base shear

F_t = force applied to top level in addition to F_x
$\quad$ = $(0.07T)V \leq 0.25V$, except that
$\quad$ = 0 $\quad$ when $T \leq 0.7$ sec
w_x, w_i = tributary weights assigned to story level x and i
h_x, h_i = heights above base of building to level x and i, ft

F_{px} Distribution—Horizontal Elements (Diaphragms)

$$F_{px} = \left(\frac{F_t + \sum\limits_{i=x}^{n} F_i}{\sum\limits_{i=x}^{n} w_i} \right) w_{px}$$

where F_{px} = horizontal force on primary LFRS at story level x for designing horizontal elements
$\quad F_i$ = lateral force applied to level i (this is story force determined in accordance with formula for F_x)
$\quad w_{px}$ = weight of diaphragm and elements tributary to diaphragm at level x

Other terms are as defined for F_x.

NOTE: For most low-rise wood-frame buildings, T is less than 0.7 sec and F_t will be zero.

In the formulas for distributing the seismic force over the height of the structure, F_t is a force which is applied at the top level of the structure in addition to the normal story force F_x. The purpose of this force is to account for whip action in tall, slender buildings and to allow for the effects of the higher modes (i.e., other than the first mode) of vibration. When the period of vibration is short (say 0.7 sec or less), there is no whipping effect, and F_t is not used.

It may not be evident at first glance, but the formulas for F_x and F_{px} can be simplified to a form that is similar to the base shear expression. In other words, the earthquake force can be written as the mass (weight) of the structure multiplied by a seismic coefficient. For example,

$$V = (\text{seismic coefficient})W$$

The seismic coefficient in the formula for V is known as the *base shear coefficient*. When all of the terms in the formulas for the story forces (F_x and F_{px}) are evaluated except the dead load w, seismic *story coefficients* are obtained. Obviously, since there are two formulas for story forces, there are two sets of seismic story coefficients.

The story coefficient used to define forces for designing shearwalls is referred to as the F_x *story coefficient.* It is obtained by factoring out the story weight from the formula for F_x:

$$F_x = \frac{(V - F_t)w_x h_x}{\sum\limits_{i=1}^{n} w_i h_i}$$

$$= \left[\frac{(V - F_t)h_x}{\sum\limits_{i=1}^{n} w_i h_i} \right] w_x$$

$$= (F_x \text{ story coefficient}) w_x$$

Likewise, the formula for F_{px} for use in diaphragm design can be viewed in terms of an F_{px} *story coefficient.* The formula for F_{px} is initially expressed in this format:

$$F_{px} = \left(\frac{F_t + \sum\limits_{i=x}^{n} F_i}{\sum\limits_{i=x}^{n} w_i} \right) w_{px}$$

$$= (F_{px} \text{ story coefficient}) w_{px}$$

It should be noted that a one-story building represents a special case for earthquake forces. In a one-story building, the diaphragm loads given by F_x and F_{px} are equal. In fact, the F_x and F_{px} story coefficients are the same as the base shear coefficient. In other words, for a *one-story building:*

Base shear coefficient $= F_x$ story coefficient $= F_{px}$ story coefficient

Having a single seismic coefficient for three forces greatly simplifies the calculation of seismic forces for one-story buildings. *Numerical examples* will greatly help to clarify the evaluation of lateral forces. Several one-story building examples are given in Chap. 3, and a comparison between the F_x and F_{px} force distributions for a two-story building is given in Example 3.9 in Sec. 3.6.

At this point one final concept needs to be introduced concerning the distribution of seismic forces. After the story force has been determined, it is distributed at a given level in proportion to the mass (DL) distribution of that level. See Example 2.16.

The purpose behind this distribution goes back to the idea of an inertial force. If it is visualized that each square foot of dead load has a corresponding inertial force generated by an earthquake, then the loading shown in the sketches becomes clear. If each square foot of area has the same DL, the distributed seismic force is in proportion to the length of the roof or floor that is parallel to the direction of the force. Hence the magnitude of the distributed force is large where the dimension of the floor or roof parallel to the force is large, and it is small where the dimension parallel to the force is small.

EXAMPLE 2.16   Distribution of Seismic Force at Story Level x

Transverse and Longitudinal Directions
Defined

A lateral force applied to a building may be described as being in the transverse or longitudinal direction. These terms are interpreted as follows:

Transverse lateral force is parallel to the short dimension of the building.
Longitudinal lateral force is parallel to the long dimension of the building.

Buildings are designed for seismic forces applied independently in both the transverse and longitudinal directions.

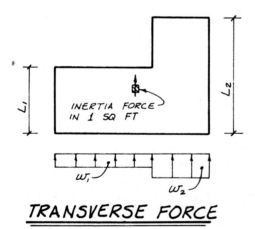

Figure 2.20a Distribution of story force in transverse direction.

Each square foot of DL can be visualized as generating its own inertial force (Fig. 2.20a). If all of the inertial forces generated by these unit areas are summed in the transverse direction, the forces w_1 and w_2 are in proportion to lengths L_1 and L_2, respectively.

The sum of the distributed seismic forces w_1 and w_2 (i.e., the sum of their resultants) equals the transverse story force. For shearwall design the transverse story force is F_x, and for diaphragm design the transverse story force is F_{px}.

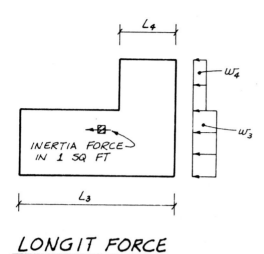

LONGIT FORCE

Figure 2.20*b* Distribution of story force in longitudinal direction.

In the longitudinal direction (Fig. 2.20*b*), L_3 and L_4 are measures of the distributed forces w_3 and w_4. The sum of these distributed seismic forces equals the story force in the longitudinal direction.

NOTE: The distribution of inertial forces generated by the DL of the walls parallel to the direction of the earthquake is illustrated in Chap. 3.

The basic seismic forces acting on the primary lateral-force-resisting system of a *regular* structure have been described in this section. However, one major change introduced in the new seismic code is the requirement to consider the effects of structural *irregularities*. Chapter 23 of the UBC identifies a number of these irregularities. In many cases, increased force levels and reduced stresses are required for the design of an irregular building.

It is important for the designer to be able to identify a structural irregularity and to understand the implications associated with the irregularity. However, a detailed study of these Code provisions is beyond the scope of Chap. 2. In fact, the majority of this book is written as an *introduction* to the basic principles of engineered wood structures. To accomplish this, most of the structures considered are rather simple in nature. Structural irregularities may be common occurrences in daily practice, but they can be viewed as advanced topics at this point in the study of earthquake design.

It is felt the reader should first develop a good understanding of the design requirements for regular structures. Therefore, the provisions for irregular structures are postponed to Chap. 16, after the principles of structural design for regular buildings have been thoroughly covered.

The seismic forces required for the design of elements and components that are not part of the primary LFRS are given in Sec. 2.15.

2.15 Seismic Forces—Portions of Buildings

The seismic forces which have been discussed up to this point are those assumed to be developed in the primary lateral-force-resisting system of a building as it responds to an earthquake. However, when individual elements of the structure are analyzed separately, it may be necessary to consider different seismic effects. One reason for this is that certain elements which are attached to the structure respond dynamically to the motion of the structure rather than to the motion of the ground. Resonance between the structure and the attached element may occur.

The Code provides an "equivalent static" force F_p for various elements (portions) of a structure. By including the F_p forces, the Code takes into account the possible response of an element and the consequences involved if it collapses or fails. The force on a portion of the structure is given by the following formula, which uses two coefficients from the base shear expression:

$$F_p = (ZIC_p)W_p$$

Here (ZIC_p) is the seismic coefficient. The coefficients Z and I have been defined previously (Sec. 2.13); W_p is simply the dead load of the portion of

---

EXAMPLE 2.17   Seismic Forces Normal to Wall

Determine the seismic design force normal to the wall for the building shown in Fig. 2.21. Total wall height is less than 15 ft. The wall spans vertically between the floor and the roof. The wall is constructed of reinforced brick masonry that weighs 90 psf. Known seismic information: $Z = 0.4$ and $I = 1.0$.

Compare the seismic force to the wind force on elements and components away from discontinuities. Known wind information: $q_s = 16.4$ psf, $C_e = 1.06$ (0- to 15-ft-height range), and $I = 1.0$. Note that wind and seismic forces are not considered simultaneously.

Seismic Forces

Forces w_1 and w_2 act normal to the wall in either direction (i.e., inward or outward).

Force to main wall:	*Force to parapet wall:*
$F_p = (ZIC_p)W_p$	$F_p = (ZIC_p)W_p$
$= 0.4(1.0)(0.75)W_p$	$= 0.4(1.0)(2.0)W_p$
$= 0.3W_p$	$= 0.8W_p$

Because W_p is in psf, w can be calculated directly as a uniformly distributed load.

$$w_1 = 0.3W_p = 0.3(90) \qquad w_1 = 0.8W_p = 0.8(90)$$
$$= 27 \text{ psf} \qquad\qquad = 72 \text{ psf}$$

NOTE: The seismic forces w_1 and w_2 are for use in designing the wall elements (i.e., the main portion of the wall below the roof level and the parapet wall). The design of walls with large dead loads (such as concrete and masonry walls) is likely to be governed by seismic forces. Wood-frame walls have small dead loads, and their design will probably be controlled by wind forces.

After the design of the wall elements, it is necessary to determine the magnitude of

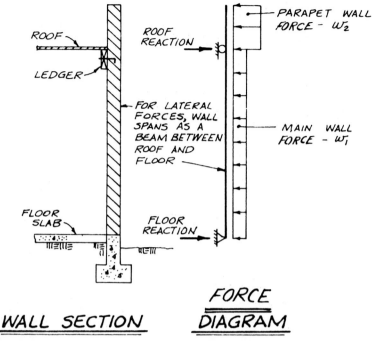

ROOF

ROOF
REACTION

LEDGER

FOR LATERAL
FORCES, WALL
SPANS AS A
BEAM BETWEEN
ROOF AND
FLOOR

FLOOR
SLAB

FLOOR
REACTION

PARAPET WALL
FORCE - W_2

MAIN WALL
FORCE - W_1

WALL SECTION

FORCE DIAGRAM

Figure 2.21

the normal anchorage force at the roof level (the force labeled *roof reaction* in Fig. 2.21). Reference 1.4c states that w_2 is intended for the design of cantilever parapets because of the lack of recovery after these types of elements have undergone yielding. However, when the entire wall section is considered in determining the anchorage force, the smaller load w_1 is to be applied over the full height of the wall including the parapet.

The 1991 UBC has added a new design provision in footnote 3 to UBC Table 23-P. This footnote requires that C_p for determining the *anchorage force* at the horizontal diaphragm (that is, $C_p = 0.75$) be increased 50 percent in the center half of *flexible* diaphragms. The *Blue Book* (Ref. 6.1) Commentary indicates that this increase is to account for the amplified response in the central portion of large flexible diaphragms.

Design procedures for wall anchorage are given in Chap. 15.

Wind Forces

Wind pressure formula:

$$P = C_e C_q q_s I = 1.06(C_q)(16.4)(1.0) = 17.4C_q$$

Values of C_q are given in UBC Table 23-H.

Force to main wall:	*Force to parapet wall:*
$w_1 = 1.2(17.4)$	$w_2 = 1.3(17.4)$
$= 20.9$ psf inward or outward	$= 22.6$ psf inward or outward
Wind < seismic	Wind < seismic
∴ *seismic governs*	∴ *seismic governs*

the structure being considered; C_p is a response coefficient that is given as a constant for various elements (components) of a building. Values of C_p are given in UBC Table 23-P. Example 2.17 demonstrates the calculation of a force on a portion of a building.

At one time the force F_{px} was treated as the force on a portion of the structure. However, the new seismic code now recognizes that force on horizontal diaphragms given by F_{px} is a force on the primary LFRS. See Sec. 2.14 for a discussion of F_{px}.

2.16   Load and Force Combinations

The Code specifies a number of combinations that are to be considered in the design of a structure. These combinations define which loads and forces must be considered simultaneously. Obviously a given combination reflects the probability that various gravity loads and lateral forces will occur concurrently. Some of the probabilities of loading have been mentioned previously.

For example, it is not necessary to consider wind and seismic forces together. In addition, roof live loads are an alternative to snow loads, and so it is not necessary to combine these loads. Roof live loads also occur rather infrequently, and the Code does not require roof live loads to be considered simultaneously with either wind or seismic forces.

However, it is quite possible for a portion of the maximum expected snow load (say, ½ snow) to be present when the full wind force occurs. Likewise, a portion of the design wind force (say, ½ wind) may occur during the maximum snow loading. Thus, several of the combinations required by the UBC provide that a portion of certain loads or forces be considered simultaneously with other full effects. The following general combinations are given in UBC Chap. 23:

1. DL + FLL + RLL (or snow)
2. DL + FLL + wind (or seismic)
3. DL + FLL + wind + ½ snow
4. DL + FLL + snow + ½ wind
5. DL + FLL + snow + seismic

In combination 5, a footnote in the Code indicates that, upon approval of the local building official, snow loads over 30 psf may be reduced 75 percent and snow loads 30 psf or less need not be combined with seismic.

Example 2.10 in Sec. 2.10 introduced the problem of overall moment stability under lateral forces. This is commonly referred to as a check on *overturning*. As the Code requirements for lateral forces (wind and seismic) have become more complex, the general design consideration for the moment stability of a structure has also become more involved.

It is appropriate to at least mention the subject of overturning in this summary of load and force combinations because the Code provides *additional load and force combinations* for use in the moment stability analysis of a structure. These overturning considerations are not directly reflected in the five general combinations listed above. The Code incorporates the additional combinations into the wind and seismic portions of UBC Chap. 23. Example 2.10 illustrated one such combination in evaluating the design overturning moment (i.e., design OM = gross OM − ⅔RM). This load and force combination can be expressed as (wind + ⅔DL).

An extensive review of these types of additional combinations and the corresponding factors of safety for overturning is beyond the scope of Chap. 2. A comprehensive summary of the UBC combinations for overturning and a comparison of wind and seismic provisions are given in Chap. 16.

2.17 Problems

All problems are to be answered in accordance with the 1991 Uniform Building Code (UBC). A number of Code tables are included in Appendix C.

2.1 *Given:* The house framing section shown in Fig. 2.A

Find: *a.* Roof DL in psf on a horizontal plane
        b. Wall DL in psf of wall surface area
        c. Wall DL in lb/ft of wall
        d. Basic (i.e., consider roof slope but not trib. area) unit roof LL in psf
        e. Basic unit roof LL in psf if the slope is changed to ³⁄₁₂

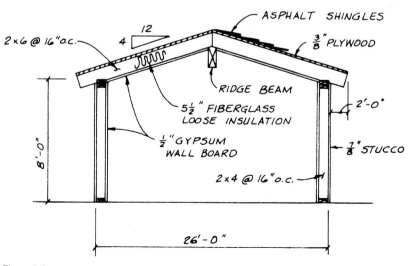

Figure 2.A

2.2 *Given:* The house framing section shown in Fig. 2.B. Note that a roofing square is equal to 100 ft^2.

    Find: *a.* Roof DL in psf on a horizontal plane

                b. Ceiling DL in psf

                c. Basic (i.e., consider roof slope but not trib. area) unit roof LL in psf

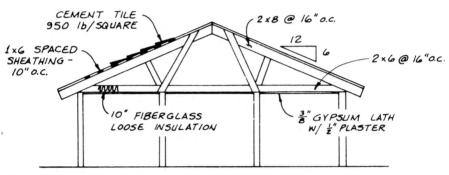

Figure 2.B

2.3 *Given:* The building framing section shown in Fig. 2.C below and on next page.

    Find: *a.* Roof DL in psf

                b. Second-floor DL in psf

                c. Basic (i.e., consider roof slope but not trib. area) unit roof LL in psf

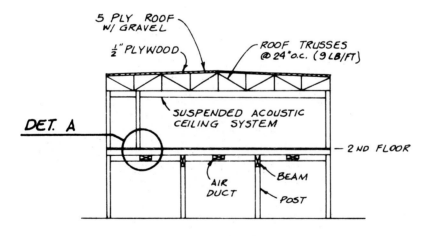

Figure 2.C

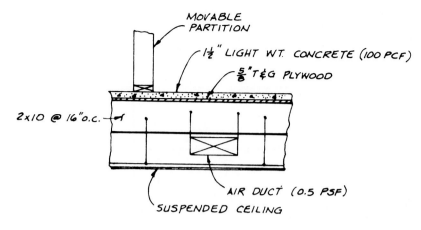

MOVABLE
PARTITION

$1\frac{1}{2}''$ LIGHT W.T. CONCRETE (100 PCF)

$\frac{5}{8}''$ T&G PLYWOOD

2×10 @ 16" o.c.

AIR DUCT (0.5 PSF)

SUSPENDED CEILING

DETAIL A

Figure 2.C *Continued.*

2.4 *Given:* The roof framing plan of the industrial building shown in Fig. 2.D. Roof slope is ¼ in./ft. General construction:

> Roofing—5-ply felt
> Sheathing—$^{15}\!/_{32}$-in. plywood
> Subpurlin—2 × 4 at 24 in. o.c.
> Purlin—4 × 14 at 8 ft-0 in. o.c.
> Girder—6¾ × 33 at 20 ft-0 in. o.c.
> Assume loads are uniformly distributed on supporting members.

Find:
  a. Average DL of entire roof in psf
  b. Tributary DL to subpurlin in lb/ft
  c. Tributary DL to purlin in lb/ft
  d. Tributary DL to girder in lb/ft
  e. Tributary DL to column C1 in k
  f. Basic (i.e., consider roof slope but not trib. area) unit roof LL in psf

2.5 *Given:* Figure 2.A. The ridge beam spans 20 ft-0 in.

Find:
  a. Tributary area to the ridge beam
  b. Roof LL in lb/ft, using UBC Method 1
  c. Roof LL in lb/ft, using UBC Method 2

2.6 *Given:* A roof similar to Fig. 2.A with ³⁄₁₂ roof slope. The ridge beam spans 22 ft-0 in.

Find:
  a. Tributary area to the ridge beam
  b. Roof LL in lb/ft, using UBC Method 1
  c. Roof LL in lb/ft, using UBC Method 2

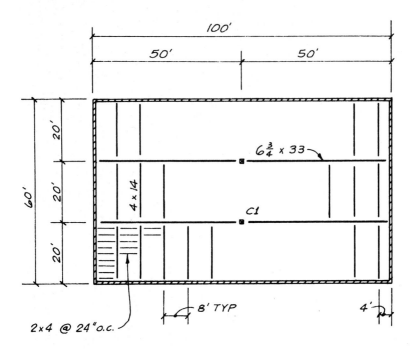

Figure 2.D

2.7 *Given:* Figure 2.B and a basic snow load SL of 70 psf

  Find: Reduced SL in psf on a horizontal plane

2.8 *Given:* A roof similar to Fig. 2.B with 8/12 slope and a basic snow load SL of 90 psf

  Find: Reduced SL in psf on a horizontal plane

2.9 *Given:* The roof structure in Fig. 2.D

  Find: *a.* Unit RLL in psf for
   1. 2 × 4 subpurlin (use Method 1 or 2)
   2. 4 × 14 purlin (use Method 2)
   3. 6¾ × 33 glulam beam (use Methods 1 and 2)
   b. Uniformly distributed LLs in lb/ft for each of the members, using the unit RLLs from (*a*)

2.10 *Given:* The roof structure in Fig. 2.D and a 25-psf snow load

  Find: *a.* Uniformly distributed SL in lb/ft for
   1. 2 × 4 subpurlin
   2. 4 × 14 purlin
   3. 6¾ × 33 glulam bean
   b. Tributary SL to column C1 in k

2.11 *Given:* The building in Fig. 2.C

Find: Second-floor basic (i.e., consider occupancy but not tributary areas) unit LL and concentrated loads for the following uses:
a. Offices
b. Light storage
c. Retail store
d. Apartments
e. Hotel restrooms
f. School classroom

2.12 *Given:* A column supports only loads from the second floor of an office building. The tributary area to the column is 240 ft^2, and the DL is 35 psf.

Find: a. Basic floor LL in psf
b. Reduced FLL in psf
c. Total load to column in k

2.13 *Given:* A beam supports the floor of a classroom in a school building. The beam spans 26 ft, and the trib. width is 16 ft. DL = 20 psf.

Find: a. Basic floor LL in psf
b. Reduced FLL in psf
c. Uniformly distributed total load to the beam in lb/ft
d. Compare the loading in part c with the alternate concentrated load required by the Code. Which loading is more critical for bending, shear, and deflection?

2.14 *Given:* UBC Table 23-A

Find: Four occupancies where the unit floor LL cannot be reduced. List the occupancy and the corresponding unit FLL.

2.15 *Given:* UBC beam deflection criteria

Find: The allowable deflection limits for the following members. Beams are unseasoned wood members
a. Floor beam with 22-ft span
b. Roof rafter that supports a plaster ceiling below. Span = 12 ft

2.16 *Given:* The *Timber Construction Manual* beam deflection recommendations in Fig. 2.8

Find: The allowable limits for the following beams. Beams are seasoned wood members that remain dry in service.
a. Roof rafter in a commercial building that supports a gypsum board ceiling below. Span = 16 ft.
b. Roof girder in an office building supporting an acoustic suspended ceiling. Span = 40 ft.
c. Floor joist in the second floor of a residential building to be designed for "ordinary usage." Span = 20 ft. Tributary width = 4

ft. Floor DL = 16 psf. (Give beam loads in lb/ft for each deflection limit.)

    d. Girder in the second floor of a retail sales building. Increased floor stiffness is desired to avoid public concern about perceived excessive floor deflections. Span = 32 ft. Tributary width = 10 ft. Floor DL = 20 psf. (Give beam loads in lb/ft for each deflection limit.)

2.17 *Given:* The UBC wind force provisions

      Find: *a.* The expression for calculating the design wind pressure
             b. The section in the Code where the terms of the expression are defined
             c. Distinguish between the following wind forces and the areas to which they are applied:
                1. Primary frames and systems
                2. Elements and components away from discontinuities
                3. Elements and components at or near discontinuities
             d. Describe the three wind exposure conditions.

2.18 *Given:* The UBC wind and seismic force provisions

      Find: *a.* The required factor of safety against overturning for a structure subjected to wind forces
             b. The section in the Code where the factor of safety is specified
             c. Does the Code permit the weight of earth superimposed over footings to be included in the dead-load-resisting movement of a structure? Cite Code reference.
             d. What reduction in DL resisting moment is required for moment stability (*uplift*) under seismic forces on a *regular* structure? Cite Code reference. How does this compare to the DL reduction for wind overturning?

2.19 *Given:* The UBC wind force provisions

      Find: *a.* The mean recurrence interval for the wind speeds given in UBC Fig. 23-1.
             b. The approximate mean recurrence interval associated with the wind pressure for essential and hazardous facilities
             c. The height used to determine the combined height, exposure, and gust factor coefficient for the outward pressure on leeward walls

2.20 *Given:* An enclosed building in Tampa, Florida, that is an essential facility. The roof is flat and is 30 ft above grade. Exposure B applies.

      Find: *a.* Basic wind speed
             b. Wind stagnation pressure q_s
             c. Importance factor I
             d. The combined height, exposure, and gust factor coefficient C_e for the roof
             e. The pressure coefficient C_q and the wind pressure P for uplift on

the roof considering the wind force on the primary lateral-force-resisting system. Consider both UBC Method 1 and Method 2.

 f. The pressure coefficient C_q and the wind pressure P for wind uplift on the roof considering the wind force required for designing an element in the roof system away from a discontinuity

2.21 *Given:* The enclosed building in Fig. 2.E is a two-story essential facility located near Denver, Colorado. Wind Exposure C applies.

  Find: The design wind pressures in both principal directions of the building for:
  a. Primary LFRS, using the normal force method
  b. Primary LFRS, using the projected area method
  c. Design of individual structural elements having tributary areas of 20 ft^2 in the wall and roof systems away from discontinuities
  d. Design of individual structural elements in the roof near discontinuities having tributary areas of 50 ft^2. Sketch the wind pressures and show the areas over which they act.

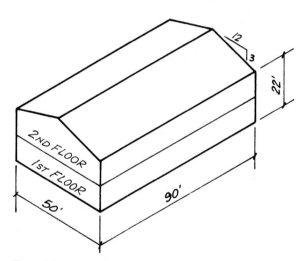

Figure 2.E

2.22 *Given:* UBC seismic design force requirements

  Find: a. The formula for the base shear. Give Code reference.
  b. The maximum value of Z that is used in practice. Cite Code reference. What is the physical significance of Z?
  c. The formula for C and the maximum value of C that is used in practice. Explain the purpose of the C coefficient.
  d. The standard default value for S. Describe the soil profile associated with this value of S.

  Problem continues on p. 86.

   e. Briefly describe the purpose of the R_w coefficient. What value of R_w is used for a building with wood-frame bearing walls that are sheathed with plywood?

2.23   *Given:*   UBC seismic design force requirements

   Find: a. The definition of period of vibration and the Code methods for estimating the fundamental period
   b. How does period of vibration affect seismic forces?
   c. Describe the effects of the interaction of the soil and structure on seismic forces.
   d. What is damping, and how does it affect seismic forces? Do the Code criteria take damping into account?

2.24   *Given:*   UBC seismic design force requirements

   Find: a. Briefly describe the general distribution of seismic forces over the height of a multistory building. What is the physical basis for this distribution?
   b. Give the formulas for F_x and F_{px} and explain why two formulas are required to define story forces on the primary LFRS. Describe the purpose of each. Which formula produces the larger forces?

3

Behavior of Structures under Loads and Forces

3.1 Introduction

The loads and forces required by the Code for designing a building were described in Chap. 2. Chapter 3 deals primarily with the transfer of these from one member to another throughout the structure. The distribution of *vertical loads* in a typical wood-frame building follows the traditional "post-and-beam" concept. This subject is briefly covered at the beginning of the chapter.

The distribution of *lateral forces* may not be as evident as the distribution of vertical loads. The majority of Chap. 3 deals with the transfer of lateral forces from the point of origin, through the building, and into the foundation. This subject is introduced by reviewing the three basic types of lateral-force-resisting systems (LFRSs) used in conventional rectangular-type buildings.

Shearwalls and horizontal diaphragms make up the LFRS used in most wood-frame buildings (or buildings with a combination of wood framing and concrete or masonry walls). The chapter concludes with two detailed examples of lateral force calculations for these types of buildings.

3.2 Structures Subject to Vertical Loads

The behavior of framing systems (post-and-beam type) under vertical loads is relatively straightforward. Sheathing (decking) spans between the most closely spaced beams; these short-span beams are given various names: stiffeners, rafters, joists, subpurlins. The reactions of these members in turn cause loads on the next set of beams in the framing system; these next beams may be referred to as beams, joists, or purlins. Finally, reactions of the second set of beams impose loads on the largest beams in the system. These large beams are known as girders. The girders, in turn, are supported by columns. See Example 3.1.

EXAMPLE 3.1   Typical Post-and-Beam Framing

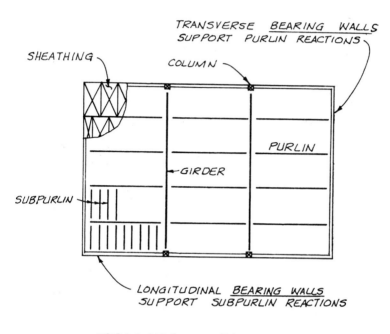

FRAMING   PLAN

Figure 3.1

1. Sheathing spans between subpurlins.
2. Subpurlins span between purlins.
3. Purlins span between girders.
4. Girders span between columns.

Subpurlins and purlins are also supported by bearing walls. *Bearing walls* are defined as walls that support vertical loads in addition to their own weight.

When this framing system is used for a roof, it is often constructed as a *panelized* system. Panelized roofs typically use glulam girders spaced 18 to 40 ft on center, sawn lumber or glulam purlins at 8 ft on center, sawn lumber subpurlins at 24 in. on center, and plywood sheathing. The name of the system comes from the fact that 8-ft-wide roof *panels* are prefabricated

Figure 3.2 Panelized roof system installed with forklift.
(*Photo by Mike Hausmann.*)

and then lifted onto preset girders using forklifts. See Fig. 3.2. The speed of construction and erection makes panelized roof systems very economical. Panelized roofs are widely used on large one-story commercial and industrial buildings. See Ref. 7.5 for more information on panelized roof structures.

Although the loads to successively larger beams are a result of reactions from lighter members, for structural design the loads on beams in this type of system are often assumed to be uniformly distributed. To obtain a feel for whether this approach produces conservative values for shear and moment, it is suggested that a comparison be made between the values of shear and moment obtained by assuming a *uniformly distributed load* and those obtained by assuming *concentrated loads* from lighter beams. The actual loading probably falls somewhere between the two conditions described. See Example 3.2.

Regardless of the type of load distribution used, it should be remembered that it is the *tributary area of the member being designed* (Sec. 2.3) which is used in establishing unit live loads, rather than the tributary area of the lighter members which impose the load. This concept is often confusing when it is first encountered.

EXAMPLE 3.2   Beam Loading Diagrams

Figure 3.3 shows the girder from the building in Fig. 3.1. The load to the girder can be considered as a number of concentrated reaction loads from the purlins. However, a more common design practice is to assume that the load is uniformly distributed. The uniformly distributed load is calculated as the unit load times the tributary width to the girder. As the number of concentrated loads increases, the closer the loading approaches the uniform load case.

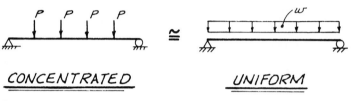

CONCENTRATED   UNIFORM

Figure 3.3

As an example, consider the design load for the girder in Fig. 3.1. Confusion may occur when the *unit* live load for the girder (based on a large tributary area) turns out to be less than the *unit* live load used in the design of the purlin. Obviously, the reaction of the purlin (using the higher live load) must be supported by the girder. Why is the lower live load used for design?

The reasoning is thus: The girder must be capable of supporting *individual* reactions from purlins calculated using the larger unit live load (obtained using the tributary area of the purlin). However, when the entire tributary area of the girder is considered loaded, the smaller unit live load may be used (this was discussed in detail in Chap. 2). Of course, each connection between the purlin and the girder must be designed for the higher unit live load, but not all purlins are subjected to this higher load simultaneously.

The spacing of members and the span lengths depend on the function and purpose of the building. Closer spacing and shorter spans require smaller member sizes, but short spans require closely spaced columns or bearing walls. The need for clear, unobstructed space must be considered when the framing system is first established. Once the layout of the building has been determined, dimensions for framing should be chosen which result in the best utilization of materials. For example, the standard size of a sheet of plywood is 4 ft by 8 ft, and a joist spacing should be chosen which fits this basic module. Spacings of 16, 24, and 48 in. o.c. (o.c. = on center and c.c. = center to center) all provide supports at the edge of a sheet of plywood.

Certainly an unlimited number of framing systems can be used, and the choice of the framing layout should be based on a consideration of the requirements of a particular structure. Several other examples of framing arrangements are shown in Fig. 3.4a, b, and c. These are given to suggest possible arrangements and are not intended to be a comprehensive summary of framing systems.

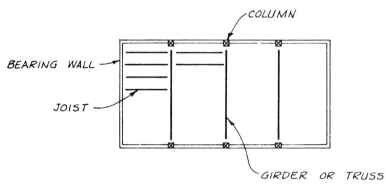

Figure 3.4a Alternate post-and-beam framing.

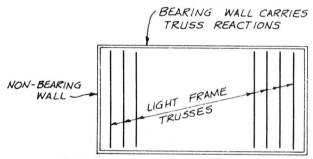

Figure 3.4b Light frame trusses.

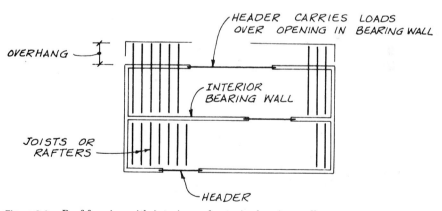

Figure 3.4c Roof framing with interior and exterior bearing walls.

It should be noted that in the framing plans, a break in a member represents a simple end connection. For example, in Fig. 3.4a the lines representing joists are broken at the girder. If a continuous joist is to be shown, a solid line with no break at the girder would be used. This is illustrated in Fig. 3.4c where the joist is continuous at the rear wall overhang. Such points may seem obvious, but a good deal of confusion results if they are not recognized.

3.3 Structures Subject to Lateral Forces

The behavior of structures under lateral forces usually requires some degree of explanation. In covering this subject, the various types of lateral-force-resisting systems (LFRSs) used in ordinary rectangular buildings should be clearly distinguished. See Example 3.3. These LFRSs include

1. Rigid frame
2. Vertical truss (braced frame)
3. Shearwall

EXAMPLE 3.3   Basic Lateral-Force-Resisting Systems

Rigid Frame

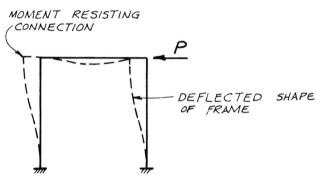

Figure 3.5a

Resistance to lateral forces is provided by *bending* in the column and girders of the rigid frame members.

Vertical Truss (Braced Frame)

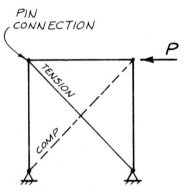

Figure 3.5b

Figure 3.5b

Lateral forces develop *axial* forces in the vertical truss. Slender compression members are typically ignored, and the lateral force is taken by the tension brace.

Shearwall

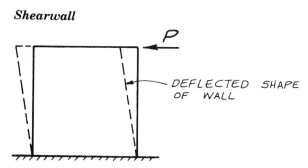

Figure 3.5c

Segments of walls can be designed to function as *shear*-resisting elements in carrying lateral forces. The deflected shape shows shear deformation rather than bending.

Rigid frames, whether statically determinate or indeterminate, resist lateral forces by bending in the frame members. That is, the members have relatively small depths compared with their lengths, and the stresses induced as the structure deforms under lateral forces are essentially flexural. Some axial forces are also developed.

Vertical trusses or braced frames are analyzed in a manner similar to horizontal trusses: connections are assumed to be pinned, and forces are assumed to be applied at the joints. Vertical trusses often take the form of cross or X-bracing. The vertical truss in Fig. 3.5*b* appears to be statically indeterminate. As such, both diagonal members must be designed to function simultaneously (one in tension and the other in compression). Perhaps a more common practice is to ignore the member in compression. This approach has the advantage of not requiring the design of a compression member with a long unbraced length. The resulting truss is statically determinate. The compression member, although ignored, cannot be omitted because it will in turn function as the tension member when the lateral force is applied in the opposite direction.

Steel rods are often used for X-bracing. Obviously such a slender compression member will buckle, and the rod in compression *must* be ignored. The concept of ignoring the member in compression is, however, not limited to rod X-bracing.

Shearwall structures make use of specially designed wall sections to resist lateral forces. A shearwall is essentially a vertical cantilever with the span of the cantilever equal to the height of the wall. The depth of these members (i.e., the length of the wall element parallel to the applied lateral force) is large in comparison with the depth of the structural members in the rigid frame LFRS. For a member with such a large depth compared with its height, *shear* deformation replaces bending as the significant action (hence, the name "shearwall").

It should be mentioned that the LFRSs in Example 3.3 are the *vertical resisting elements* of the system (i.e., the vertical components). Because buildings are three-dimensional structures, some horizontal system must also be provided to carry the lateral forces to the vertical elements. See Example 3.4. A variety of horizontal systems can be employed:

1. Horizontal wall framing
2. Vertical wall framing with horizontal trusses at the story levels
3. Vertical wall framing with horizontal diaphragms at the story levels

---

EXAMPLE 3.4   Horizontal Elements in the LFRS

Horizontal Wall Framing

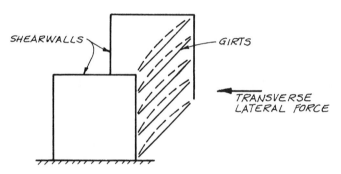

Figure 3.6*a*

Horizontal wall members are known as *girts* and distribute the lateral force to the vertical LFRS. Dashed lines represent the deflected shape of the girts. See Fig. 3.6*a*. The lateral force to the shearwalls is distributed over the height of the wall.

Vertical Wall Framing

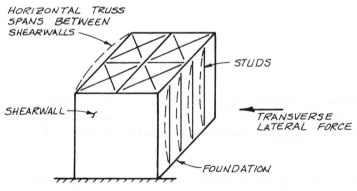

Figure 3.6*b*

Vertical wall members are known as *studs*. The lateral force is carried by the studs to the roof level and the foundation. A horizontal truss in the plane of the roof distributes the lateral force to the transverse shearwalls. The diagonal members in the horizontal truss are often steel rods and are designed to function in tension only (like the vertical truss in Fig. 3.5*b*).

Vertical Wall Framing and Horizontal Diaphragm

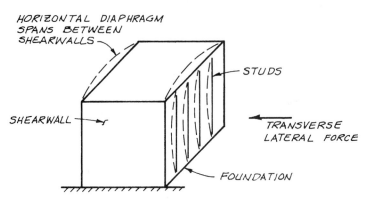

Figure 3.6c

In Fig. 3.6*c* the LFRS is similar to the system in Fig. 3.6*b* except that the horizontal truss in the plane of the roof is replaced with a *horizontal diaphragm*. The use of vertical wall framing and horizontal diaphragms is the most common system in wood-frame buildings because the roof sheathing can be designed economically to function as both a vertical-load- and a lateral-force-carrying element. The horizontal diaphragm is designed as a beam spanning between the shearwalls. The design requirements for horizontal diaphragms and shearwalls are given in Chaps. 9 and 10.

The first two framing systems in Example 3.4 are relatively easy to visualize. The third system is also easy to visualize once the concept of a diaphragm is understood. A diaphragm can be considered to be a large, thin structural element that is loaded in its plane. In Fig. 3.6*c* the vertical wall members develop horizontal reactions at the roof level and at the foundation level (studs are assumed to span as simple beams between these two levels). The reaction of the studs at the roof level provides a force in the plane of the roof. The diaphragm acts as a large horizontal beam.

In wood buildings, or buildings with wood roof and floor systems and concrete or masonry walls, the roof or floor sheathing is designed and connected to the supporting framing members to function as a diaphragm. In buildings with concrete roof and floor slabs, the concrete slabs are designed to function as diaphragms.

The stiffness of a diaphragm refers to the amount of deflection that occurs in the horizontal diaphragm as a result of the in-plane lateral force (Fig.

3.6c shows the deflected shape). Wood diaphragms are not nearly as stiff as concrete slabs, and *wood diaphragms* are referred to as *flexible diaphragms*. *Concrete slabs* are known as *rigid diaphragms*.

In each of the sketches in Example 3.4, the transverse wind force is distributed horizontally to end shearwalls. The same horizontal systems shown in these sketches can be used to distribute lateral forces to the other basic vertical LFRSs (i.e., rigid frames or vertical trusses). Any combination of *horizontal* and *vertical* LFRSs can be incorporated into a given building to resist lateral forces.

The discussion of lateral forces in Example 3.4 was limited to forces in the transverse direction. In addition, a LFRS must be provided for forces in the longitudinal direction. This LFRS will consist of both horizontal and vertical components similar to those used to resist forces in the transverse direction.

Different types of *vertical* elements can be used to resist transverse lateral forces and longitudinal lateral forces in the same building. For example, rigid frames can be used to resist lateral forces in the transverse direction, and shearwalls can be used to resist lateral forces in the other direction. The choice of LFRS in one direction does not necessarily limit the choice for the other direction.

In the case of the *horizontal* LFRS, it is unlikely that the horizontal system used in one direction will be different from the horizontal system used in the other direction. If the sheathing is designed to function as a horizontal diaphragm for lateral forces in one direction, it probably can be designed to function as a diaphragm for forces applied in the other direction. On the other hand, if the roof or floor sheathing is incapable of functioning as a diaphragm, a system of horizontal trusses spanning in both the transverse and longitudinal directions appears to be the likely solution.

The common types of LFRSs for conventional buildings have been summarized as a general introduction and overview. It should be emphasized that the large majority of wood-frame buildings, or buildings with wood roof and floor framing and concrete or masonry walls, use a combination of

1. Horizontal diaphragms

2. Shearwalls

to resist lateral forces. Because of its widespread use, only the design of this type of system is covered in this book.

3.4   Lateral Forces in Buildings with Diaphragms and Shearwalls

The majority of wood structures use the sheathing, normally provided on floors, roofs, and walls, to form horizontal diaphragms and shearwalls that resist lateral wind and seismic forces. To function as a horizontal diaphragm or shearwall, the sheathing must be properly attached to the supporting members. The framing members must also be checked for additional stresses caused by the lateral forces. Furthermore, certain connections must be provided to transfer lateral forces down through the structure. The system must be tied together.

However, the economic advantage is clear. With the added attention to the framing and connection design, the usual sheathing material, which is required in any structure, can also be used to form the lateral-force-resisting system. In this way, one material serves two purposes (i.e., sheathing and lateral force resistance).

The following numerical examples illustrate how lateral forces are calculated and distributed in two different shearwall buildings. The first (Sec. 3.5) demonstrates the procedure for a one-story structure, and the second (Sec. 3.6) expands the system to cover a two-story building. The method used to calculate seismic forces in these two buildings is based on the same criteria, but the solution for the one-story structure is much more direct. It will be recalled from Sec. 2.14 that the seismic base shear and story coefficients are all equal for a one-story building:

$$\text{Base shear coefficient} = F_x \text{ story coefficient} = F_{px} \text{ story coefficient}$$

However, in the case of the two-story building, the general procedure for a multistory structure must be applied. Some individual coefficients may be the same, but in general the base shear and story coefficients are not equal in a multistory building. This requires that the *base shear* be determined first. The *story forces* for designing the shearwalls and horizontal diaphragms are then distributed over the height of the structure.

Wood-frame structures have traditionally been limited to relatively low-rise (one- and two-story) structures, and these are the primary focus of this book. It is interesting to note that there have been an increasing number of three- and four-story (and even taller) wood-frame buildings constructed in recent years. See Fig. 3.7. The method of analysis given for the two-story example can be extended to handle the lateral force evaluation for taller multistory buildings.

3.5 Design Problem: Lateral Forces on One-Story Building

In this section a rectangular one-story building with a wood roof system and masonry walls is analyzed to determine both wind and seismic forces. The building chosen for this example has been purposely simplified so that the basic procedure is demonstrated without "complications." The structure is essentially defined in Fig. 3.8 with a plan view of the horizontal diaphragm and a typical transverse cross section.

Figure 3.7 Four-story wood-frame building with horizontal diaphragms and shearwalls of plywood. (*Photo courtesy of APA.*)

The example is limited to the consideration of the lateral force in the transverse direction. This force is shown in both plan and section views. In the plan view, it is seen as a uniformly distributed force to the horizontal diaphragm, and the diaphragm spans between the shearwalls. In the section view, the lateral force is shown at the point where the walls tie to the horizontal diaphragm. This height is taken as the *reference* location for evaluating the tributary heights to the horizontal diaphragm for both wind and seismic forces.

The critical lateral force for the horizontal diaphragm will be taken as the larger of the two tributary forces: wind or seismic. Although the Code requires the effects of the horizontal and vertical wind pressures to be considered simultaneously, only the horizontal component of the wind force affects the unit shear in the horizontal diaphragm. The possible effects of the vertical wind pressure (uplift) are not addressed in this example.

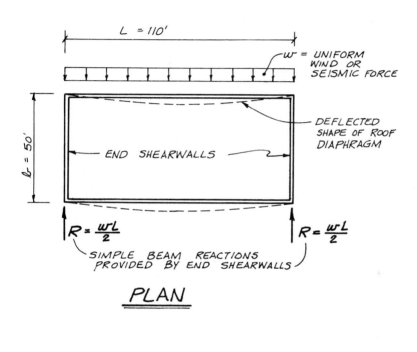

PLAN

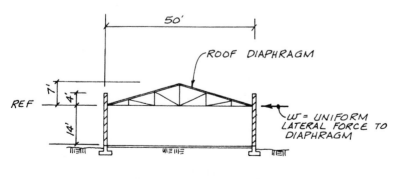

TYP. TRANSVERSE SECTION

Figure 3.8 One-story building subjected to lateral force in transverse direction.

Wind. The wind force in this problem is determined using the projected area method of UBC Table 23-H (Primary systems—Method 2). The uniform force to the roof diaphragm is obtained by multiplying the design wind pressures by the respective heights tributary to the reference point. See Example 3.5. The wall is assumed to span vertically between the roof diaphragm and the foundation. Thus, the tributary height below the diaphragm is simply one-half of the wall height. Above the reference point, the tributary height to the diaphragm is taken as the cantilever height of the parapet wall or the projected height of the roof (whichever is larger).

EXAMPLE 3.5   Wind Force Calculation

Determine the horizontal component of the wind force tributary to the roof diaphragm. The basic wind speed is given as 70 mph. Standard occupancy and Exposure B apply. UBC Method 2 is specified. Selected tables from the UBC are included in Appendix C.

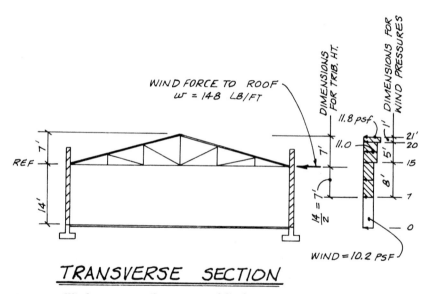

Figure 3.9 Wind pressures tributary to roof diaphragm.

Wind Pressures

Wind pressure formula:

$$P = C_e C_q q_s I$$

$I = 1.0$ (UBC Tables 23-K and 23-L)

$q_s = 12.6$ psf   (UBC Table 23-F)

$C_q = 1.3$ (UBC Table 23-H)

From UBC Table 23-G:

$$C_e = \begin{cases} 0.62 & \text{for 0 to 15 ft} \\ 0.67 & \text{for 20 ft} \\ 0.72 & \text{for 25 ft} \end{cases}$$

For simplicity use step loading for wind pressures (instead of interpolating between height levels to obtain trapezoidal pressure diagrams):

$$P = C_e C_q q_s I = \begin{cases} 0.62(1.3)(12.6)(1.0) = 10.2 \text{ psf} & \text{0 to 15 ft} \\ 0.67(1.3)(12.6)(1.0) = 11.0 \text{ psf} & \text{15 to 20 ft} \\ 0.72(1.3)(12.6)(1.0) = 11.8 \text{ psf} & \text{20 to 21 ft} \end{cases}$$

These wind pressures are shown in the section view in Fig. 3.9.

NOTE: From a practical point of view, a wind pressure of 11.8 psf could reasonably be used over the entire height of the structure without greatly affecting the design of the horizontal diaphragm.

Load to Diaphragm

$$\begin{Bmatrix} \text{Trib. height of} \\ \text{roof diaphragm} \end{Bmatrix} = \begin{Bmatrix} \text{Trib. wall height} \\ \text{below ref. point} \end{Bmatrix} + \begin{Bmatrix} \text{Projected height} \\ \text{above ref. point} \end{Bmatrix}$$

$$\text{Trib. height} = \frac{14}{2} + 7 = 14 \text{ ft}$$

Wind force $w = \Sigma$ (wind pressure $\times$ tributary wind pressure height)

$$= (10.2 \text{ psf} \times 8 \text{ ft}) + (11.0 \text{ psf} \times 5 \text{ ft}) + (11.8 \text{ psf} \times 1 \text{ ft})$$

$$\boxed{w = 148 \text{ lb/ft}}$$

Seismic.   Compared with the seismic analysis for multistory buildings, the calculation of earthquake forces on a one-story (single-degree-of-freedom) structure is greatly simplified. As noted, the primary reason for this is that the base shear coefficient and story coefficients are all equal for a one-story building. This allows the uniform force w to the horizontal diaphragm to be computed directly using the base shear coefficient $(ZIC)/R_w$.

This direct evaluation of the uniform force on the diaphragm requires a clear understanding of the way inertial forces are distributed. To see how the earthquake forces work their way down through the structure, it is helpful to make use of the weight of a 1-ft-wide strip of dead load W_1 taken parallel to the direction of the earthquake being considered. For example, in the case of lateral forces in the transverse direction, the weight of a 1-ft-wide strip of dead load parallel to the short side of the building is used. See the 1-ft strip in Fig. 3.10. Only the dead loads tributary to the roof level are included in W_1.

The weight of this 1-ft-wide strip includes the *roof dead load* and the weight of the *walls* that are *perpendicular* to the direction of the earthquake force being considered. Thus, for seismic forces in the transverse direction, the tributary DL of the longitudinal walls is included in W_1. In the example being considered, there are only two walls perpendicular to the direction of the seismic force. However, if the building had interior longitudinal walls, the weight of these walls tributary to the roof diaphragm would also be included in W_1.

The forces determined in this manner satisfy the Code requirement that the seismic force be applied "in accordance with the mass distribution" of the level. The 1-ft strip of dead load can be viewed as the mass that causes inertial (seismic) forces to develop in the horizontal diaphragm. The weight of the transverse walls does not contribute to the seismic force in the horizontal diaphragm. The forces in the transverse shearwalls are handled in a later part of the example.

The distribution of forces to the primary LFRS in Example 3.6 assumes that the longitudinal walls span between the roof diaphragm and the foundtion. A similar loading for the seismic force on elements and components was shown in Fig. 2.21 (Sec. 2.15).

Example 3.6 demonstrates the method used to compute the seismic coefficient. However, it should be noted that many shearwall buildings have a low height-to-width ratio and are fairly rigid structures. As a result, they tend to have low periods of vibration. For this reason, it is common for low-rise buildings to use the maximum value of C (2.75) in evaluating the seismic coefficient.

For a building of this type in seismic zone 4, the maximum value of C yields a base shear coefficient of 0.183. This is a fairly common value, and it is often used directly without going through the details shown in the example. However, the designer should be aware of the basis for the seismic coefficient so that the proper value can be determined if different conditions are encountered. For example, in a building with a bearing wall LFRS that has both *plywood* horizontal diaphragms and *plywood* shearwalls, the value of R_w is 8 instead of 6. A reduced seismic coefficient will be obtained with an R_w of 8.

The 0.183 seismic coefficient can be interpreted as a loading criterion that requires approximately 18 percent of gravity (g force) to be applied horizontally at the roof level. For an essential or hazardous facility, the g force increases by a factor of 1.25, to approximately 23 percent of gravity.

EXAMPLE 3.6   Seismic Force Calculation

Determine the seismic coefficient and the force to the horizontal diaphragm. See Fig. 3.10. The building is in seismic zone 4. Without a geotechnical study, soil profile S_3 is assumed. The structure is a bearing wall system with masonry shearwalls.

The roof dead load has been determined by prior analysis. The roof DL of 10 psf has been converted to the load on a horizontal plane. The masonry walls are 8-in. medium-weight concrete block units with cells grouted at 16 in. o.c. For this construction the wall DL is 60 psf.

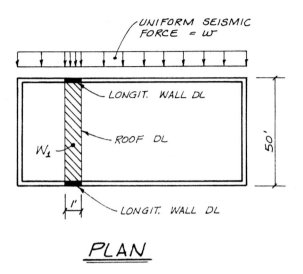

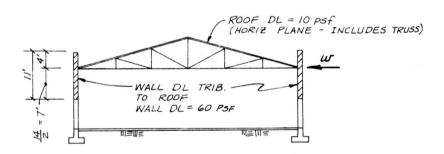

Figure 3.10 Plan view shows a typical 1-ft-wide strip of DL in transverse direction. Weight of this strip W_1 generates a uniform seismic force on the horizontal diaphragm. Section view has mass of walls tributary to roof level indicated by crosshatching. Both views show the force acting on the horizontal diaphragm.

Seismic Coefficient

$$\text{Base shear coefficient} = \text{story coefficients}$$

$$= \frac{ZIC}{R_w}$$

$Z = 0.4$ (UBC Table 23-I for seismic zone 4)

$I = 1.0$ (UBC Tables 23-K and 23-L for standard occupancy)

$S = 1.5$ (UBC Table 23-J for soil profile S_3)

$$T = C_t(h_n)^{3/4}$$

$$= 0.020(14)^{3/4} = 0.145 \text{ sec}$$

$$C = \frac{1.25S}{T^{2/3}} = \frac{1.25(1.5)}{0.145^{2/3}}$$

$$= 6.79 > 2.75$$

$\therefore$ Use $C = 2.75$

$$\frac{ZIC}{R_w} = \frac{0.4(1.0)(2.75)}{6} = 0.183$$

Seismic Force

For a one-story building, the uniform force to the diaphragm can be obtained by multiplying the seismic coefficient by the weight of a 1-ft-wide strip of dead load (W_1) tributary to the roof level.

$$\begin{aligned}
W_1 &= \text{roof DL} = 10 \text{ psf} \times 50 \text{ ft} & = 500 \text{ lb/ft} \\
&+ \text{Wall DL} = 60 \text{ psf} \times 11 \text{ ft} \times 2 \text{ walls} & = 1320 \\
\hline
& & W_1 = 1820 \text{ lb/ft}
\end{aligned}$$

$$w = 0.183 W_1 = 0.183(1820)$$

$$\boxed{w = 334 \text{ lb/ft}}$$

The uniform seismic force of 334 lb/ft greatly exceeds the wind force of 148 lb/ft.

$$\boxed{\therefore \text{ seismic governs}}$$

One of the criteria used to design horizontal diaphragms and shearwalls is the unit shear. Although the design of diaphragms and shearwalls is covered in Chaps. 9 and 10, the calculation of unit shear is illustrated here. See Example 3.7 for the unit shear in the roof diaphragm.

For the building in this example subjected to lateral forces in the transverse direction, the only shearwalls are the exterior end walls. Therefore, the horizontal diaphragm spans as a simple beam between the two transverse end walls. The deflected shape of the roof diaphragm is again shown in Fig. 3.11. The reaction of the diaphragm on the transverse end walls is the reaction of a uniformly loaded simple beam with a span length equal to the distance between shearwalls. The shear diagram for a simple beam shows that the maximum internal shear is equal to the external reaction. The maximum total shear is converted to a unit shear by distributing it along the width of the diaphragm available for resisting the shear.

EXAMPLE 3.7   Unit Shear in Roof Diaphragm

The simple beam loading diagram in Fig. 3.11 is a repeat of the loading on the horizontal diaphragm. The simple beam reactions are shown along with the shear diagram.

The free-body diagram at the bottom of Fig. 3.11 is cut through the diaphragm a small distance away from the transverse shearwalls. The unit shear (lb/ft) is obtained by dividing the maximum total shear from the shear diagram by the width of the diaphragm b.

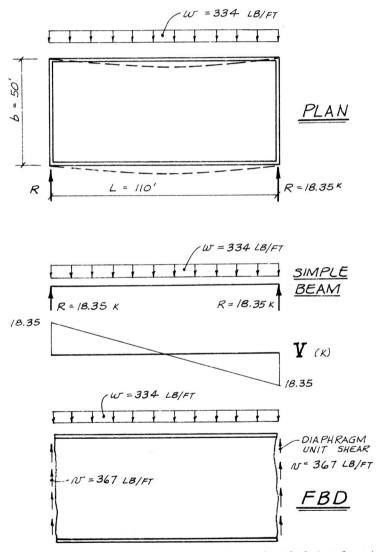

Figure 3.11   Diaphragm unit shear. For simplicity the calculations for unit shear are shown using the nominal length L and diaphragm width b (i.e., wall thickness is ignored).

Diaphragm reaction:

$$R = \frac{wL}{2} = \frac{334(110)}{2} = 18{,}350 \text{ lb} = 18.35 \text{ k}$$

For a simple beam the shear equals the reaction:

$$V = R = 18.35 \text{ k}$$

The unit shear distributes the total shear over the width of the diaphragm. The conventional symbol for *total shear* is V, and the *unit shear* in the diaphragm is assigned the symbol v.

$$v_{\text{roof}} = \frac{V}{b} = \frac{18{,}350}{50} = \boxed{367 \text{ lb/ft}}$$

The forces and shears considered to this point have been those on the horizontal diaphragm. The next step in the lateral force design process is to consider similar quantities in the shearwalls. In determining the uniform force to the horizontal diaphragm, it will be recalled that only the DL of the roof and the longitudinal walls was included in the seismic force. The inertial force generated in the transverse walls was not included in the load to the roof diaphragm. The reason is that the shearwalls carry directly their own seismic force parallel to the wall. These forces do not, therefore, contribute to the force or shear in the horizontal diaphragm.

Several approaches are used by designers to compute wall seismic forces. In the more common method, the unit shear in the shearwall is evaluated at the *midheight* of the wall. See Example 3.8. This convention developed because the length of the shearwall b is often a minimum at this location. For example, any openings in the wall (both doors and windows) are typically intersected by a horizontal line drawn at the midheight of the wall. In addition, this approach is consistent with the lumped-mass seismic model presented in Chap. 2.

The seismic force generated by the top half of the wall is given the symbol R_1. It can be computed as the DL of the top portion of the wall times the seismic coefficient. The total shear at the midheight of the wall is the sum of all forces above this level. For a one-story building, these forces include the reaction from the roof diaphragm R plus the wall seismic force R_1. The unit shear v may be computed once the total shear has been obtained.

EXAMPLE 3.8   Unit Shear in Shearwall

Determine the total shear and unit shear at the midheight of the shearwall in Fig. 3.12. For simplicity, ignore the reduction in wall dead load due to the opening (conservative).

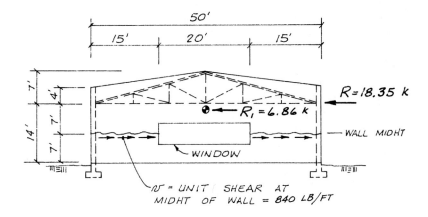

END ELEVATION

Figure 3.12 Shearwall unit shear. Maximum unit shear occurs at midheight of wall.

Wall Seismic Force

Seismic force generated by the top half of the wall:

Wall area $= (11 \times 50) + \frac{1}{2}(3 \times 50) = 625 \text{ ft}^2$

Wall DL $= 625 \text{ ft}^2 \times 60 \text{ psf} = 37.5 \text{ k}$ (neglect window reduction)

$$R_1 = \left(\frac{ZIC}{R_w}\right)W = 0.183(37.5)$$

$$= 6.86 \text{ k}$$

Wall Shear

$$\left\{ \begin{matrix} \text{Total shear at} \\ \text{midheight of wall} \end{matrix} \right\} = \left\{ \begin{matrix} \text{sum of all forces on FBD of} \\ \text{shearwall above midheight} \end{matrix} \right\}$$

$$V = R + R_1 = 18.35 + 6.86$$

$$= 25.21 \text{ k}$$

$$\text{Unit wall shear} = v = \frac{V}{b} = \frac{25,210}{15 + 15}$$

$$\boxed{\dagger v_{\text{wall}} = 840 \text{ lb/ft}}$$

---

†For design of masonry shearwalls in buildings located in seismic zones 3 and 4, this force must be increased by a factor of 1.5 (UBC Chap. 24). For wall openings not symmetrically located, see Sec. 9.6.

As mentioned earlier, the unit shear in the roof diaphragm and in the shearwall constitute one of the main parameters in the design of these elements. There are additional design factors that must be considered, and these are covered in subsequent chapters.

These examples have dealt only with the transverse lateral forces, and a similar analysis is used for the longitudinal direction. Roof diaphragm shears are usually critical in the transverse direction, but both directions should be analyzed. Shearwalls may be critical in either the transverse or longitudinal directions depending on the size of the wall openings.

3.6 Design Problem: Lateral Forces on Two-Story Building

A multistory building has a more involved analysis of seismic forces than a one-story structure. Once the seismic base shear V has been determined, the forces are distributed to the story levels in accordance with the Code formulas for F_x and F_{px}. These seismic forces were reviewed in Secs. 2.13 and 2.14. There it was noted that all three of the seismic forces on the primary LFRS (V, F_x, and F_{px}) could be viewed as a seismic coefficient times the appropriate mass or dead load of the structure. These multiplying factors are referred to as the seismic

Base shear coefficient

F_x story coefficients

F_{px} story coefficients

The purpose of the two-story building problem in Example 3.9 is to compare the maximum wind and seismic forces and to evaluate the unit shears in the horizontal diaphragms and shearwalls. The wind pressures are the same as those in the previous one-story building of Example 3.5, but the forces to the diaphragms are different because of the different tributary heights. Although the final objective of the earthquake analysis is to obtain numerical values of the design forces, it is important to see the overall process. To do this, the calculations emphasize the determination of the various seismic coefficients (g forces). Once the seismic coefficients have been determined, it is a simple matter to obtain the numerical values.

The one-story building example in Sec. 3.5 was divided into a number of separate problems. The two-story structure in Example 3.9 is organized into a single set of design calculations which is more representative of what might be done in practice. However, sufficient explanation is provided to describe the process required for multistory structures.

EXAMPLE 3.9   Two-Story Lateral Force Calculation

Determine the lateral wind and seismic forces in the transverse direction for the two-story office building in Fig. 3.13a. For the critical loading, evaluate the unit shears in the roof and second-floor horizontal diaphragms. Also determine the unit shear in the transverse shearwalls at the midheight of the first- and second-story walls. Assume that there are no openings in the masonry walls.

Wind forces are to be in accordance with UBC Method 2. The basic wind speed is 70 mph. Standard occupancy and Exposure B apply.

The building is located in seismic zone 4, and soil profile S_3 is assumed. The following dead loads have been determined in a prior analysis: roof DL = 20 psf, floor DL = 12 psf, floor DL to account for the weight of interior wall partitions = 10 psf, and exterior wall DL = 60 psf.

NOTE: In buildings where the location of nonbearing walls and partitions is subject to change, the Code requires a partition DL of 20 psf for designing individual floor members for vertical loads. However, for evaluation of seismic design forces, an average floor DL of 10 psf is allowed (UBC Chap. 23).

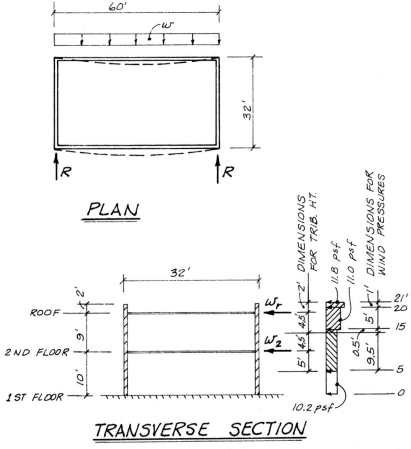

Figure 3.13a Wind pressures and tributary heights to roof and second-floor diaphragms.

Wind Forces

The wind force conditions for this problem are the same as those in Example 3.5. The horizontal wind pressure diagram shown in Fig. 3.13a is taken directly from the previous example (Fig. 3.9), and the pressure calculations are not repeated here. A simple and conservative alternative to the step loading would be to apply the 11.8 psf over the entire height.

Uniformly distributed wind forces to the horizontal diaphragms are determined as follows:

$$\text{Load to diaphragm} = \Sigma \text{ (wind pressure} \times \text{tributary wind pressure height)}$$

Roof:
$$w_r = 11.8 \text{ psf}(1 \text{ ft}) + 11.0 \text{ psf}(5 \text{ ft}) + 10.2 \text{ psf}(0.5 \text{ ft})$$
$$= 72 \text{ lb/ft}$$

Second floor:
$$w_2 = 10.2 \text{ psf}(9.5 \text{ ft})$$
$$= 97 \text{ lb/ft}$$

Seismic Base Shear Coefficient

For the given structure it is expected that the seismic base shear coefficient will be 0.183. Show calculations to verify.

$$\text{Period } T = C_t(h_n^{3/4}) = 0.020(19^{3/4}) = 0.182 \text{ sec} < 0.7$$

$$\therefore F_t = 0$$

$$\text{Site coefficient } S = 1.5$$

$$\text{Response value } C = \frac{1.25S}{T^{2/3}} = \frac{1.25(1.5)}{(0.182)^{2/3}} = 5.84 > 2.75$$

$$\therefore C = 2.75$$

$$\text{Seismic base shear coefficient} = \frac{ZIC}{R_w} = \frac{0.4(1.0)(2.75)}{6}$$

$$= 0.183 \quad \text{as expected}$$

Tributary Roof Dead Loads

The total dead load for the structure is all that is required to compute the base shear V. However, in the process of developing the total dead load, it is beneficial to summarize the tributary loads to the roof diaphragm and second-floor diaphragm using the idea of a 1-ft-wide strip. Recall from Example 3.6 that W_1 represents the mass or weight that will cause a uniform seismic force to be developed in a horizontal diaphragm.

The values of W_1, tributary to the roof and second floor, will eventually be used to determine the distributed story forces. It is recommended that the reader sketch the 1-ft-wide strip on the plan view in Fig. 3.13a. The tributary wall heights are shown on the section view.

Weight of 1-ft-wide strip tributary to roof:

Roof DL	$= (20 \text{ psf})(32 \text{ ft})$	$= 640 \text{ lb/ft}$
+ Wall DL (2 longit. walls)	$= 2(60 \text{ psf})\left(\dfrac{9}{2} + 2\right)$	$= 780$
DL of 1-ft strip at roof	$= W_1$	$= 1420 \text{ lb/ft}$

The mass that generates the entire seismic force in the roof diaphragm is given the symbol W'_r. It is the sum of all the W_1 values at the roof level.

$$W'_r = \Sigma W_1 = 1420 \text{ lb/ft}(60 \text{ ft}) = 85.2 \text{ k}$$

To obtain the total mass tributary to the roof level, the weight of the top half of the transverse shearwalls is added to W'_r. The total DL tributary to the roof level is given the symbol W_r.

$$\text{DL of 2 end walls} = 2(60 \text{ psf})(32)\left(\frac{9}{2} + 2\right) = 25.0 \text{ k}$$

$$\text{Total DL trib. to roof} = W_r = 85.2 + 25.0 = 110.2 \text{ k}$$

Similar quantities are now computed for the second floor.

Tributary Second-Floor Dead Loads

Weight of 1-ft-wide strip tributary to second floor:

Second-floor DL	$= (12 \text{ psf})(32 \text{ ft})$	$= 384 \text{ lb/ft}$
+ Partition DL	$= (10 \text{ psf})(32 \text{ ft})$	$= 320$
+ Wall DL (2 longit. walls)	$= 2(60 \text{ psf})\left(\frac{9}{2} + \frac{10}{2}\right)$	$= 1140$
DL of 1-ft strip at second floor $= W_1$		$= 1844 \text{ lb/ft}$

The mass that generates the entire seismic force in the second floor diaphragm is W'_2.

$$W'_2 = \Sigma W_1 = 1844 \text{ lb/ft}(60 \text{ ft}) = 110.6 \text{ k}$$

The total mass tributary to the second-floor level is the sum of W'_2 and the tributary weight of the transverse shearwalls. The total DL tributary to the second-floor level is given the symbol W_2.

$$\text{DL of 2 end walls} = 2(60 \text{ psf})(32)\left(\frac{9}{2} + \frac{10}{2}\right) = 36.5 \text{ k}$$

$$\text{Total DL trib. to second floor} = W_2 = 110.6 + 36.5 = 147.1 \text{ k}$$

Seismic Table

Calculations of seismic forces for multistory buildings are conveniently carried out in a table. The table is not only convenient for bookkeeping, but columns 5 and 7 provide a comparison of the F_x and F_{px} story coefficients.

The table and the necessary formulas can easily be stored on a microcomputer spreadsheet. Once stored on a spreadsheet, the table serves as a template for future problems. In this way, the computer can be used to handle repetitive calculations and problem formatting (e.g., setting up the table), and the designer can concentrate on the best way to solve the problem at hand. The table can be expanded to take into account taller buildings and to include items such as overturning moments.

The table is shown completely filled out. However, at this point in the solution of the problem, only the first four columns can be completed. Columns 1, 2, and 3 simply list the story levels, heights, and masses (DLs). The values in column 4 are the products of the respective values in columns 2 and 3. The sum of the story masses at the bottom of column 3, Σw_x, is the weight of the structure W to be used in the calculation of base shear.

The steps necessary to complete the remaining columns in the table (columns 5, 6, and 7) are given in the three sections immediately following the table.

Seismic Table

1	2	3	4	5	6	7
Story	h_x	w_x	$w_x h_x$	F_x story force $F_x = (0.01321h_x)w_x$	V_x	F_{px} story force
R	19 ft	110.2 k	2094 ft-k	$F_r = 0.251w_r$ $= 27.7$ k		$F_{pr} = 0.251w_{pr}$
					27.7 k	
2	10 ft	147.1 k	1471 ft-k	$F_2 = 0.132w_2$ $= 19.4$ k		$F_{p2} = 0.183w_{p2}$
					47.1 k	
1	0					
		Σ 257.3 k	Σ 3565 ft-k	$V = \Sigma F_x = 47.1$ k		

Base Shear

The base shear coefficient was determined previously to be 0.183. The total *base shear* for the building is 0.183 times the total weight from column 3.

$$V = \left(\frac{ZIC}{R_w}\right)W = 0.183\,(257.3) = 47.1 \text{ k}$$

The story coefficients for distributing the seismic force over the height of the structure can now be determined. The distribution of forces to the vertical elements in the primary LFRS is given by the Code formula for F_x. A second and generally larger set of seismic forces is used in the design of the horizontal elements (diaphragms). These coefficients come from the Code expression for F_{px}. The F_x story forces must be computed first because they are used in turn to evaluate the F_{px} story forces.

F_x Story Coefficients

In Chap. 2 it was noted that the formula for F_x can be written as an F_x story coefficient times the mass tributary to level x:

$$F_x = (F_x \text{ story coefficient})w_x = \left[\frac{(V - F_t)h_x}{\sum\limits_{i=1}^{n} w_i h_i}\right]w_x$$

The F_x story coefficients will now be evaluated. The base shear V is known, and the force F_t was shown to be zero. The summation term in the denominator is obtained as the last item in column 4 of the seismic table.

$$F_x = \left[\frac{(V - F_t)h_x}{\sum\limits_{i=1}^{n} w_i h_i}\right] w_x = \left[\frac{(47.1 - 0)h_x}{3565}\right] w_x$$

This general formula for F_x is entered at the top of column 5 as

$$F_x = (0.01321h_x)w_x$$

Individual F_x story coefficients follow this entry. At the roof level F_x is given the symbol F_r, and at the second-floor level the symbol is F_2.

Roof:

$$F_r = (0.0132h_r)w_r = (0.0132)(19)w_r = 0.251w_r$$

The numerical value for the seismic force at the roof level is added to column 5 next to the F_x story coefficient:

$$F_r = 0.251w_r = 0.251(110.2 \text{ k}) = 27.7 \text{ k}$$

Second floor:

$$F_2 = (0.0132h_2)w_2 = (0.0132)(10)w_2 = 0.132w_2$$

The numerical value for the seismic force at the second-floor level is also added to column 5.

$$F_2 = 0.132w_2 = 0.132(147.1 \text{ k}) = 19.4 \text{ k}$$

The summation at the bottom of column 5 serves as a check on the numerical values. The *sum* of all the F_x story forces must equal the total base shear.

$$V = \Sigma F_x = F_r + F_2 = 27.7 + 19.4 = 47.1 \text{ k} \qquad OK$$

The values in column 6 of the seismic table represent the total story shears between the various levels in the structure. The story shear can be obtained as the sum of all the F_x story forces above a given section. Because the shear actually occurs *between* story levels, the value for story shear is shown on a line between the story forces in the seismic table.

In a simple structure of this nature, the story shears from column 6 may be used directly in the design of the vertical elements (i.e., the shearwalls). However, as the structure becomes more complicated, a more progressive distribution of seismic forces from the diaphragms to the vertical elements may be necessary. Both approaches are illustrated in this example.

F_{px} Story Coefficients

In Chap. 2 it was noted that the formula for F_{px} can be written as an F_{px} story coefficient times the appropriate mass at level x:

$$F_{px} = (F_{px} \text{ story coefficient})w_{px} = \left(\frac{F_t + \sum\limits_{i=x}^{n} F_i}{\sum\limits_{i=x}^{n} w_i}\right) w_{px}$$

In addition, the Code limits on F_{px} should be checked:

$$(0.35ZI)w_{px} \leq F_{px} \leq (0.75ZI)w_{px}$$

$$0.35(0.4)(1.0)w_{px} \leq F_{px} \leq 0.75(0.4)(1.0)w_{px}$$

$$0.14w_{px} \leq F_{px} \leq 0.30w_{px}$$

The F_{px} story coefficients will be evaluated and the results entered into column 7 in the seismic table. At the roof level F_{px} is given the symbol F_{pr}, and at the second-floor level the symbol F_{p2} is used. In the formula for F_{px}, the force F_t is again zero. The summation of the F_i terms in the numerator is the sum of the F_x story forces (column 5) at and above the level under consideration. The denominator is a similar summation of story weights.

Roof:

$$F_{pr} = \left(\frac{F_r}{w_r}\right)w_{pr} = \left(\frac{27.7}{110.2}\right)w_{pr} = 0.251w_{pr}$$

$$0.14 < 0.251 < 0.30 \quad OK$$

Second floor:

$$F_{p2} = \left(\frac{F_r + F_2}{w_r + w_2}\right)w_{p2} = \left(\frac{27.7 + 19.4}{110.2 + 147.1}\right)w_{p2} = 0.183w_{p2}$$

$$0.14 < 0.183 < 0.30 \quad OK$$

Now that the story coefficients for F_x and F_{px} have been summarized in columns 5 and 7, several observations can be made.

1. The story coefficients for F_x and F_{px} are equal at the roof level.
2. The maximum story coefficients (at the roof level) exceed the magnitude of the base shear coefficient.
3. The minimum value for the F_x story coefficient (at the second-floor level) is less than the base shear coefficient.
4. The minimum value for the F_{px} story coefficient (at the second-floor level) is equal to the magnitude of the seismic base shear coefficient.

These rules are not limited to two-story structures, and they hold true for multistory buildings in general.

With all of the F_{px} and F_x story coefficients determined, the individual distributed forces for designing the horizontal diaphragms and shearwalls can be evaluated. The forces are considered in the following order:

1. Roof diaphragm (using F_{px})
2. Second-floor diaphragm (using F_{px})
3. Shearwalls (using F_x)

The unit shears in the diaphragms and shearwalls are also computed.

Roof Diaphragm (Using F_{px})

Compare the F_{px} seismic force at the roof level with the wind force to determine which is critical. The uniformly distributed seismic force is determined by multiplying the F_{px}

story coefficient at the roof level by the weight of a 1-ft-wide strip of roof DL. The weight W_1 at the roof level was determined earlier in the problem.

$$w_{pr} = 0.251W_1 = 0.251(1420)$$

$$= 356 \text{ lb/ft} > 72 \text{ lb/ft} \quad \text{wind}$$

$$\therefore \text{ seismic governs}$$

The roof diaphragm is treated as a simple beam spanning between transverse end shearwalls. See Fig. 3.13b. For a simple span the shear is equal to the beam reaction. The unit shear in the roof diaphragm is the shear in the diaphragm divided by the width of the diaphragm.

$$V_r = R_r = \frac{w_{pr}L}{2} = \frac{356(60)}{2} = 10.7 \text{ k}$$

$$v_r = \frac{V_r}{b} = \frac{10,700}{32} = \boxed{334 \text{ lb/ft}}$$

This unit shear may be used with the information in Chap. 9 to design the roof diaphragm.

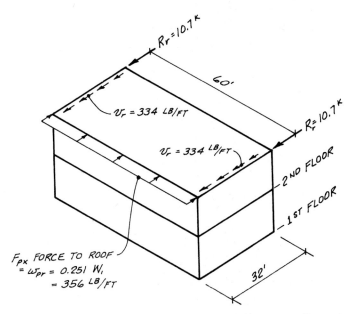

Figure 3.13b   Roof diaphragm design force w_{pr} and the corresponding unit shear in the roof diaphragm v_r.

Second-Floor Diaphragm (Using F_{px})

The second-floor diaphragm is analyzed in a similar manner. See Fig. 3.13c. The seismic force is again obtained by multiplying the F_{px} story coefficient from column 7 by the DL of a 1-ft-wide strip. The weight W_1 comes from the DL summary for the second floor.

$$w_{p2} = 0.183W_1 = 0.183(1844)$$

$$= 337 \text{ lb/ft} > 97 \text{ lb/ft} \quad \text{wind}$$

$$\therefore \text{ seismic governs}$$

$$V_2 = R_2 = \frac{w_{p2}L}{2} = \frac{337(60)}{2} = 10.1 \text{ k}$$

$$v_2 = \frac{V_2}{b} = \frac{10,100}{32} = \boxed{316 \text{ lb/ft}}$$

This unit shear may be used with the information in Chap. 9 to design the second-floor diaphragm.

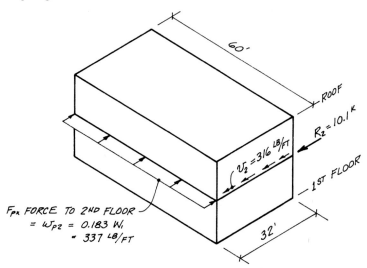

Figure 3.13c Second-floor diaphragm design force w_{p2} and the corresponding unit shear in the second-floor diaphragm v_2.

Uniform Forces to Diaphragms Using F_x Story Coefficients

The uniform forces to the diaphragms in Fig. 3.13*b* and *c* are based on the F_{px} story coefficients and are applied individually to the structure. For shearwall design, the forces to the diaphragms are based on the F_x story coefficients. See Fig. 3.13*d*. These uniformly distributed forces will be used to compute the forces in the shearwalls following the progressive distribution in Method 1 (described later in this example).

Load to roof diaphragm:

It was noted previously that the F_x and F_{px} story coefficients are equal at the roof level. Therefore, the uniform forces given by F_x and F_{px} are equal at the roof level.

$$w_r = w_{pr} = 356 \text{ lb/ft}$$

The reaction of the roof diaphragm on the shearwall is also the same:

$$R_r = 10.7 \text{ k}$$

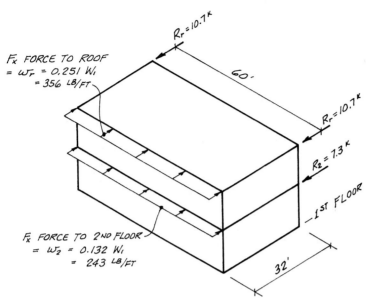

$R_r = 10.7^k$

F_x FORCE TO ROOF
= W_r = 0.251 W_1
      = 356 LB/FT

60·

$R_r = 10.7^k$

$R_2 = 7.3^k$

—1ST FLOOR

F_x FORCE TO 2ND FLOOR
= W_2 = 0.132 W_1
      = 243 LB/FT

32'

Figure 3.13d Seismic forces to roof diaphragm w_r and second-floor diaphragm w_2 are for designing the vertical elements in the LFRS. Concentrated forces on shearwalls are diaphragm reactions R_r and R_2.

Load from second-floor diaphragm:

At the second-floor level the F_x and F_{px} story coefficients are not equal. Therefore, the uniform force on the second-floor diaphragm must be refigured using the F_x story coefficient from column 5.

$$w_2 = 0.132W_1 = 0.132(1844)$$

$$= 243 \text{ lb/ft} > 97 \text{ lb/ft wind}$$

$$\therefore \text{ seismic governs}$$

The reaction of the second-floor diaphragm on the shearwall is

$$R_2 = \frac{w_2L}{2} = \frac{243(60)}{2} = 7.3 \text{ k}$$

Shear at Midheight of Second-Story Walls *(Using F_x Story Forces)*

Two methods for evaluating the shear in the shearwalls are illustrated. The first method demonstrates the progressive distribution of the forces from the horizontal diaphragms to the shearwalls. Understanding Method 1 is essential to the proper use of the F_x story forces for more complicated shearwall arrangements. Method 2 can be applied to simple structures where the distribution of seismic forces to the shearwalls can readily be seen.

METHOD 1

For the shear between the second floor and the roof, the free-body diagram (FBD) of the wall includes two seismic forces. See Fig. 3.13e. One force is the reaction from the roof diaphragm (from Fig. 3.13d), and the other is the inertial force developed by the mass of the top half of the shearwall.

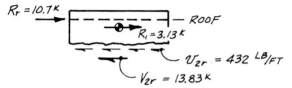

Figure 3.13e   FBD of shearwall cut midway between second-floor and roof levels.

Force from top half of shearwall:

The seismic force generated by the top half of the second-story shearwall is given the symbol R_1. This force is obtained by multiplying the deal load of the wall by the F_x story coefficient for the *roof* level.

$$R_1 = 0.251w = 0.251\left[(60 \text{ psf})\left(\frac{9}{2} + 2\right)(32 \text{ ft})\right]$$

$$= 3.13 \text{ k}$$

The shear in the wall between the second floor and the roof is given the symbol V_{2r}, and it is obtained by summing forces in the x direction.

$$\Sigma F_x = 0$$

$$V_{2r} = R_r + R_1 = 10.7 + 3.13 = 13.83 \text{ k}$$

Unit shear in wall:

$$V_{2r} = \frac{V_{2r}}{b} = \frac{13,830}{32} = \boxed{432 \text{ lb/ft*}}$$

METHOD 2

For this simple rectangular building with two equal-length transverse shearwalls, the shear in one wall V_{2r} can be obtained as one-half of the total story shear from column 6.

$$\text{Wall shear } V_{2r} = \tfrac{1}{2}(\text{story shear } V_{2r})$$

$$= \tfrac{1}{2}(27.7) = 13.85 \text{ k} \quad \text{(same as Method 1)}$$

For other shearwall arrangements, including interior shearwalls, the progressive distribution of forces using Method 1 is required.

Shear at Midheight of First-Story Walls (Using F_x Story Forces)

METHOD 1

The shear in the walls between the first and second floors is obtained from the FBD in Fig. 3.13f. The two forces on the top are the forces from Fig. 3.13e. The load R_2 is the

---

*For the design of masonry shearwalls in buildings located in seismic zones 3 and 4, these design forces must be increased by a factor of 1.5 (UBC Chap. 24). For masonry walls with openings, see Sec. 9.6.

reaction from the second-floor diaphragm (from Fig. 3.13*d*). The final seismic force is the second force labeled R_1. This represents the inertial force generated by the mass of the shearwall tributary to the second floor.

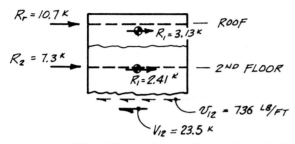

Figure 3.13f FBD of shearwall cut midway between first-floor and second-floor levels.

Force from wall mass tributary to second-floor level:

The R_1 force for the middle portion of the shearwall uses the F_x story coefficient for the second-floor level:

$$R_1 = 0.132w = 0.132\left[(60 \text{ psf})\left(\frac{9}{2} + \frac{10}{2}\right)(32 \text{ ft})\right]$$

$$= 2.41 \text{ k}$$

The shear between the first- and second-floor levels is given the symbol V_{12}. It is obtained by summing forces in the x direction (Fig. 3.13*f*):

$$\Sigma F_x = 0$$

$$V_{12} = R_r + R_1 + R_2 + R_1$$

$$= 10.7 + 3.13 + 7.3 + 2.41$$

$$= 23.5 \text{ k}$$

Unit shear in wall between first and second floor:

$$v_{12} = \frac{V_{12}}{b} = \frac{23,500}{32} = \boxed{736 \text{ lb/ft*}}$$

METHOD 2

Again for a simple rectangular building with two exterior equal-length shearwalls, the total shear in a wall can be determined as one-half of the story shear from column 6.

---

*For the design of masonry shearwalls in buildings located in seismic zones 3 and 4, these design forces must be increased by a factor of 1.5 (UBC Chap. 24). For masonry walls with openings, see Sec. 9.6.

Wall shear V_{12} = ½(story shear V_{12})

$$= ½(47.1) = 23.5 \text{ k} \quad \text{(same as Method 1)}$$

The above analysis is for lateral forces in the transverse direction. A similar analysis is required in the longitudinal direction.

3.7   Problems

All problems are to be answered in accordance with the 1991 Uniform Building Code (UBC). A number of Code tables are included in Appendix C for reference.

3.1   The purpose of this problem is to compare the design values of shear and moment for a girder with different assumed load configurations (see Fig. 3.3 in Example 3.2).

Given: The roof framing plan in Fig. 3.A with girders G1, G2, and G3 supporting loads from purlin P1. Roof DL = 13 psf. Roof LL is to be obtained from UBC Table 23-C, Method 1.

Find: *a.* Draw the shear and moment diagrams for girder G1 (DL + LL), assuming
1. A series of concentrated reaction loads from the purlin P1.
2. A uniformly distributed load over the entire span (unit load times the tributary width).

b. Rework part *a* for girder G2.
c. Rework part *a* for girder G3.

3.2   This problem is the same as Prob. 3.1 except that the roof DL = 23 psf.

3.3   *Given:*   UBC Chap. 23 lateral force requirements

Find: The definition of
a. Building frame system
b. LFRS
c. Shearwall
d. Braced frame
e. Bearing wall system

3.4   *Given:*   The plan and section of the building in Fig. 3.B. The basic wind speed is 80 mph, and exposure B applies. The building is enclosed and has a standard occupancy classification. Roof DL = 15 psf on a horizontal plane. Wind forces to the primary LFRS are to be in accordance with UBC Method 2.

Find: *a.* Uniform wind force on the roof diaphragm in the transverse direction. Draw the loading diagram.
b. The wind force distribution on the roof diaphragm in the longitudinal direction. Draw the loading diagram.

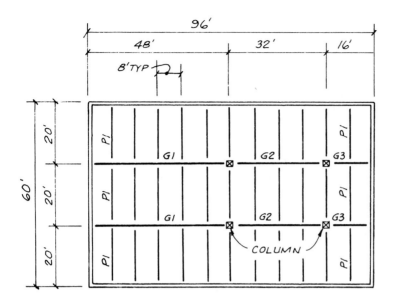

ROOF FRAMING PLAN

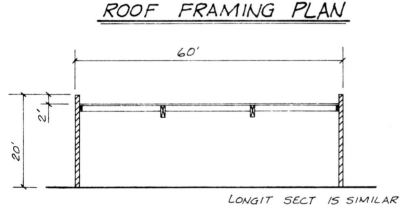

LONGIT SECT IS SIMILAR

TRANSVERSE SECTION

Figure 3.A

    c. The total diaphragm shear and the unit diaphragm shear at line 1

    d. The total diaphragm shear and the unit diaphragm shear at line 4

3.5   *Given:*   The plan and section of the building in Fig. 3.B. Roof DL = 15 psf on a horizontal plane, and wall DL = 12 psf. The seismic base shear coefficient has been calculated as 0.183.

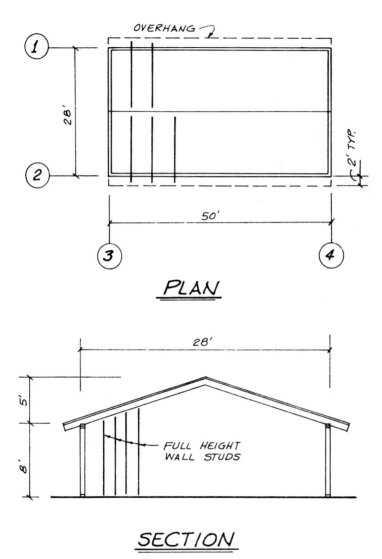

Figure 3.B

Find: *a.* Uniform seismic force on the roof diaphragm in the transverse direction. Draw the loading diagram.

           b. The seismic force distribution on the roof diaphragm in the longitudinal direction. Draw the loading diagram noting the lower force at the overhang.

           c. The total diaphragm shear and the unit diaphragm shear at line 1

           d. The total diaphragm shear and the unit diaphragm shear at line 4

3.6 Repeat Prob. 3.4 except that the wind forces are to be in accordance with UBC Method 1.

3.7 *Given:* The plan and section of the building in Fig. 3.B. Roof DL = 10 psf on a horizontal plane, and wall DL = 8 psf. The seismic base shear coefficient has been calculated as 0.229.

    Find: *a.* Uniform seismic force on the roof diaphragm in the transverse direction. Draw the loading diagram.
        b. The seismic force distribution on the roof diaphragm in the longitudinal direction. Draw the loading diagram, noting the lower force at the overhang.
        c. The total diaphragm shear and the unit diaphragm shear at line 1
        d. The total diaphragm shear and the unit diaphragm shear at line 4

3.8 *Given:* The plan and section of the building in Fig. 3.A. The basic wind speed is 70 mph, and exposure C applies. The building is an enclosed structure with a standard occupancy classification. Roof DL = 13 psf. Wind forces to the primary LFRS are to be in accordance with UBC Method 2.

    Find: *a.* The tributary wind force to the roof diaphragm in lb/ft. Draw the loading diagram
        b. The total diaphragm shear and the unit diaphragm shear at the 60-ft transverse end walls
        c. The total diaphragm shear and the unit diaphragm shear at the 96-ft longitudinal side walls

3.9 Repeat Prob. 3.8 except that the wind forces to the primary LFRS are to be in accordance with UBC Method 1.

3.10 *Given:* The plan and section of the building in Fig. 3.A. The basic wind speed is 70 mph, and exposure C applies. The building is an enclosed structure with an essential occupancy classification. Roof DL = 13 psf.

    Find: *a.* The wind pressure (psf) for designing elements and components in the roof system away from discontinuities
        b. The tributary wind force in lb/ft to a typical purlin using the load from part *a.* Draw the loading diagram
        c. The wind pressure (psf) for designing an element in the roof system near an eave

3.11 *Given:* The plan and section of the building in Fig. 3.A. Roof DL = 10 psf, and the walls are 7½-in.-thick concrete. The building is a bearing wall system located in seismic zone 4. Soil profile S_3 is assumed, and $I = 1.0$.

    Find: For the transverse direction:
        a. The seismic coefficient

      b. The uniform force to the roof diaphragm in lb/ft. Draw the loading diagram

      c. The total diaphragm shear and the unit diaphragm shear adjacent to the transverse walls

      d. The total shear and the unit shear at the midheight of the transverse shearwalls

3.12   Repeat Prob. 3.11 except that the longitudinal direction is to be considered.

3.13   *Given:*   The plan and section of the building in Fig. 3.A. Roof DL = 12 psf, and the walls are 6-in.-thick concrete. The building is located in seismic zone 3. S = 1.5. The building is a bearing wall system and is classified as an essential facility.

       Find: For the transverse direction:
           a. The seismic coefficient
           b. The uniform force to the roof diaphragm in lb/ft. Draw the loading diagram
           c. The total diaphragm shear and the unit diaphragm shear adjacent to the transverse walls
           d. The total shear and the unit shear at the midheight of the transverse shearwalls

3.14   Repeat Prob. 3.13 except that the longitudinal direction is to be considered.

3.15   *Given:*   The elevation of the end shearwall of a building as shown in Fig. 3.C. The force from the roof diaphragm to the shearwall is 10 k. The wall DL = 20 psf, and the seismic coefficient is 0.183.

       Find: The total shear and the unit shear at the midheight of the wall

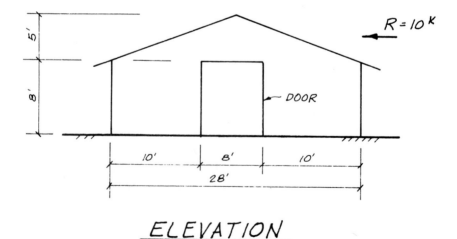

ELEVATION

Figure 3.C

3.16 *Given:* The elevation of the side shearwall of a building as shown in Fig. 3.D. The force from the roof diaphragm to the shearwall is 50 k. The wall DL = 65 psf, and the seismic coefficient is 0.183.

Find: The total shear and the unit shear at the midheight of the wall

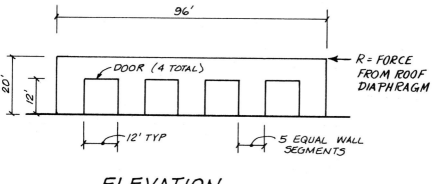

Figure 3.D

3.17 *Given:* The elevation of the side shearwall of a building as shown in Fig. 3.D. The force from the roof diaphragm to the shearwall is 43 k. The wall DL = 75 psf, and the seismic coefficient is 0.229.

Find: The total shear and the unit shear at the midheight of the wall

3.18 *Given:* The plan and section of the building in Fig. 3.E. Roof DL = 15 psf, floor DL = 20 psf (includes an allowance for interior walls), exterior wall DL = 53 psf. Basic wind speed = 80 mph. Exposure C and UBC Method 1 are specified. Enclosed bearing wall structure is classified as an essential facility. The seismic factors are $Z = 0.4$ and $S = 1.5$. Neglect any wall openings.

Find: For the transverse direction:
  a. The unit shear in the roof diaphragm
  b. The unit shear in the floor diaphragm
  c. The unit shear in the second-floor shearwall
  d. The unit shear in the first-floor shearwall

3.19 Repeat Prob. 3.18 except that the longitudinal direction is to be considered.

3.20 *Given:* The plan and section of the building in Fig. 3.E. Roof DL = 10 psf, floor DL = 18 psf plus 10 psf for interior partitions, exterior wall DL = 16 psf. Basic wind speed = 70 mph. Exposure C and UBC Method 2 are specified. Enclosed bearing wall structure has standard occupancy classification. The seismic factors are $Z = 0.4$ and $S = 1.5$. Neglect any wall openings.

Find: For the transverse direction:
  a. The unit shear in the roof diaphragm
  b. The unit shear in the floor diaphragm

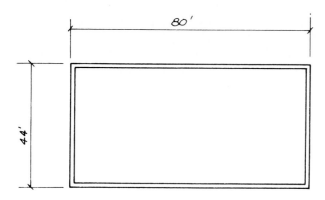

PLAN

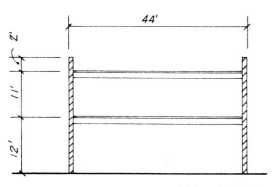

LONGIT SECT IS SIMILAR

TRANSVERSE SECTION

Figure 3.E

  c. The unit shear in the second-floor shearwall
  d. The unit shear in the first-floor shearwall

3.21 Repeat Prob. 3.20 except that the longitudinal direction is to be considered.

3.22 Use a microcomputer spreadsheet to set up the solution of seismic forces for primary lateral-force-resisting system for a multistory building up to four stories.

  The LFRS to be considered consists of horizontal diaphragms and shearwalls. The structural systems may be limited to bearing wall systems with wood-frame roof, floor, and wall construction *or* wood-frame roof and floor construction and masonry or concrete walls. Thus, an R_w of either 6 or 8 (UBC Table 23-O) will apply.

The spreadsheet is to handle structures without "complications." For example, buildings will be limited to structures that are seismically *regular*. In addition, only the exterior walls will be used for shearwalls, and openings in the horizontal diaphragms and shearwalls may be ignored in this assignment. Wind forces are not part of this problem.

The following is to be used for input:

Seismic zone from UBC Fig. 23-2.

Occupancy importance classification from UBC Table 23-K.

Type of bearing wall system (used to establish R_w).

Plan dimensions of rectangular building.

Story heights and parapet wall height (if any).

Roof, floor, and wall dead loads; interior wall dead loads may be handled by increasing the floor dead loads.

The spreadsheet is to do the following:

a. Evaluate the seismic base shear coefficient and numerical value of base shear.
b. Generate the *seismic table* summarizing the F_x and F_{px} story coefficients.
c. Compute the w_x and w_{px} uniformly distributed seismic forces to the horizontal diaphragms.
d. Determine the design unit shears in the horizontal diaphragms.
e. Determine the total shear and unit shear in the exterior shearwalls between each story level.

Properties of Wood and Lumber Grades

4.1 Introduction

The designer should have a basic understanding of the characteristics of wood, especially as they relate to the functioning of structural members. The terms *sawn lumber* and *solid sawn lumber* are often used to refer to wood members that have been manufactured by cutting a member directly from a log. Other structural members may start as lumber which then undergoes additional fabrication processes. For example, small pieces of lumber can be graded into laminating stock then glued and laid up to form larger wood members, known as *glued laminated timbers,* or *glulams.*

Many other wood-based products are available for use in structural applications. Some examples include solid members such as wood poles and timber piles; fabricated components such as trusses, wood I joists, and box beams; and other manufactured products such as structural-use panels (e.g., plywood and oriented strand board), and structural composite lumber (e.g., laminated veneer lumber and parallel strand lumber). A number of these products are recent developments in the wood industry. They are the result of new technology and the economic need to make use of different species and smaller trees that cannot be used to produce solid sawn lumber.

This chapter introduces many of the important physical and mechanical properties of wood. In addition, the sizes and grades of sawn lumber are covered. A number of other wood products are addressed later in this book. For example, glulam is covered in Chap. 5, and the properties and grades of plywood and other structural-use panels are reviewed in Chap. 8. Structural composite lumber and several types of manufactured components are described in Chap. 6.

4.2   Design Specification

The *1991 National Design Specification for Wood Construction* (Ref. 2) is the basic specification in the United States for the structural design of sawn lumber. All or part of the NDS is usually incorporated into the three model building codes.

Traditionally the NDS has been updated on a 3- to 5-year cycle. Although there have been significant changes from time to time, the usual revisions often involved minor changes and the clarification of certain design principles. However, the 1991 NDS represents a significant revision. Major changes in format, allowable stresses, and design principles are introduced in the 1991 NDS.

The reader should have a copy of the 1991 NDS to follow the discussion in this book. Having a copy of the NDS in order to learn timber design is analogous to having a copy of the steel manual in order to learn structural-steel design. One can read about the subject, but it is difficult to really develop a feel for the material without both an appropriate text *and* the basic industry publication. In the case of wood design, the NDS is the basic industry document.

The NDS is divided into two sections:

1. Design section

2. Supplement (design values for lumber)

A third component of the NDS will be the *Commentary*, which is currently under development.

The *design section* covers the basic principles of wood engineering that are applied to *all* species and species groups. The design section is written and published by the National Forest Products Association (NFPA) with input from the wood industry, government agencies and universities, and the structural engineering profession.

Many of the chapters in *this* book deal with the provisions in the design section of the NDS. There are new procedures in the 1991 NDS for beams, columns, members with combined stress, and connections. The study of each of these topics should be accompanied by a review of the corresponding section in the NDS. To facilitate this, a number of sections and tables in the 1991 NDS are referenced throughout the discussion in this book.

The design section of the 1991 NDS has been reorganized and is now presented in "equation format." The term *equation format* simply means that a comprehensive notation system has been introduced for the numerous adjustment factors that may be required for wood design values. Thus, allowable stresses are now presented in equation form.

In previous editions of the NDS, many of the necessary stress adjustments were ignored because the factors were buried in the text or in the footnotes of a table. The notation system introduced in the 1991 NDS makes it much more likely that the designer will take into account the appropriate adjustment factors. Some of the factors are discussed later in this chapter, and others are covered in chapters that deal with specific topics such as beams, columns, and connections.

In addition, many of the empirically based tables for connection design have been replaced in the 1991 NDS with *rationally based equations*. Even if some of the older tables were based on rational principles, the tables in previous editions often covered a very limited set of design conditions. Converting to an equation format allows a much wider variety of design conditions to be handled in practice. Use of the equations can streamline the design process for those designers who use the computer. However, the 1991 NDS also includes an expanded set of design tables (based on the equations) for designers who choose not to use the computer.

The second part of the NDS is known as the *NDS Supplement,* and it contains the numerical values of design stresses for the various species groupings of structural lumber and glued-laminated timber. Although the Supplement is also published by NFPA, the mechanical properties for sawn lumber are obtained from the agencies that write the grading rules for structural lumber. See Fig. 4.1. There are currently seven rules-writing agencies for visually graded lumber that are certified by the American Lumber Standards Committee. The design values in the NDS Supplement are reviewed and approved by the American Lumber Standards Committee.

The NDS Supplement provides *tabulated design values* for the following mechanical properties:

Bending stress F_b

Tension stress parallel to grain F_t

Shear stress F_v

Compression stress parallel to grain F_c

Compression stress perpendicular to grain $F_{c\perp}$

Modulus of elasticity E (some publications use the notation MOE)

---

1. Northeastern Lumber Manufacturers Association (NELMA)
2. Northern Softwood Lumber Bureau (NSLB)
3. Redwood Inspection Service (RIS)
4. Southern Pine Inspection Bureau (SPIB)
5. West Coast Lumber Inspection Bureau (WCLIB)
6. Western Wood Products Association (WWPA)
7. National Lumber Grades Authority (NLGA), a Canadian agency

---

Figure 4.1 List of rules-writing agencies for visually graded structural lumber. The addresses of the American Lumber Standards Committee (ALSC) and the seven rules-writing agencies are listed in the NDS Supplement.

An important part of timber design is being able to locate the proper design value in the tables. The reader is encouraged to verify the numerical values in the examples given throughout this book. As part of this process, it is suggested that tabulated values be checked against the NDS Supplement. Some of the stress adjustments are found in the NDS Supplement, and others are in the NDS design section. An active review of the numerical examples will require use of both.

The material in the *1991 NDS* design section represents the latest in wood design principles. Likewise, the design values in the *1991 NDS Supplement* are the most recent structural properties. It should be understood that the two sections of the NDS are an integrated package. In other words, both parts of the 1991 NDS should be used together, and the user should not mix the design section from one edition with the supplement from another.

However, the reader is cautioned that the NDS represents *recommended* design practice by the wood industry, and it does not have *legal authority* unless it becomes part of a local building code. The code change process can be lengthy, and some codes may not accept all of the industry recommendations. Consequently, it is recommended that the designer verify local code acceptance before using the 1991 NDS.

4.3   Methods of Grading Structural Lumber

The majority of sawn lumber is graded by visual inspection, and material graded in this way is known as *visually graded* structural lumber. As the lumber comes out of the mill, a person familiar with the lumber grading rules examines each piece and assigns a grade by stamping the member. The *grade stamp* includes the grade, the species or species group, and other pertinent information. See Fig. 4.2a. If the lumber grade has recognized mechanical properties for use in structural design, it is referred to as a *stress grade*.

The lumber grading rules establish limits on the size and number of growth (strength-reducing) characteristics that are permitted in the various stress grades. A number of the growth characteristics found in full-size pieces of lumber and their effect on strength are discussed later in this chapter.

The term *resawn lumber* is applied to smaller pieces of wood that are cut from a larger member. The resawing of previously graded structural lumber invalidates the initial grade stamp. The reason for this is that the acceptable size of a defect (e.g., a knot) in the original large member may not be permitted in the same grade for the smaller resawn size. The primary example is the changing of a centerline knot into an edge knot by resawing. Restrictions on edge knots are more severe than those on centerline knots. Thus, if used in a structural application, resawn lumber must be *regraded*.

The designer should be aware that more that one set of grading rules can be used to grade some commercial species groups. For example, Douglas

(a)

Figure 4.2a Typical grade stamps for visually graded lumber. Elements in the grade stamp include (*a*) lumber grading agency (e.g., WWPA), (*b*) mill number (e.g., 12), (*c*) lumber grade (e.g., Select Structural and No. 3), (*d*) commercial lumber species (e.g., Douglas Fir-Larch and Western Woods), (*e*) moisture content at time of surfacing (e.g., S-GRN, and S-DRY). *(WWPA)*

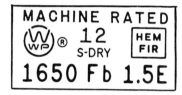

(b)

Figure 4.2b Typical grade stamp for machine stress-rated (MSR) lumber. Elements in the grade stamp include (*a*) MSR marking (e.g., MACHINE RATED), (*b*) lumber grading agency (e.g., WWPA), (*c*) mill number (e.g., 12), (*d*) nominal bending stress (e.g., 1650 psi) and modulus of elasticity (e.g., 1.5×10^6 psi), (*e*) commercial lumber species (e.g., Hem-Fir), (*f*) moisture content at time of surfacing (e.g., S-DRY). *(WWPA)*

Fir-Larch can be graded under Western Wood Products Association (WWPA) rules or under West Coast Lumber Inspection Bureau (WCLIB) rules. There are some differences in allowable stresses between the two sets of rules. The tables of design properties in the NDS Supplement have the grading rules clearly identified (e.g., WWPA and/or WCLIB). The differences in allowable stresses occur only in large-size members known as *Timbers,* and allowable stresses are the same under both sets of grading rules for *Dimension lumber.* The sizes of Timbers and Dimension lumber are covered later in this chapter.

Because the designer usually does not have control over which set of grading rules will be used, the lower allowable stress should be used in design when conflicting values are listed in NDS tables. The higher allowable stress is justified only if a grade stamp associated with the higher design value actually appears on a member. This situation could arise in reviewing the capacity of an existing member.

Although most lumber is visually graded, a small percentage of lumber is *machine stress rated* by subjecting each piece of wood to a nondestructive test. The nondestructive test is highly automated, and the process takes very little time. As lumber comes out of the mill, it passes through a series of rollers. In this process, a bending load is applied about the minor axis of the cross section, and the modulus of elasticity of each piece is measured. In addition to the nondestructive test, machine stress rated lumber is subjected to a visual check. Because of the testing procedure, machine stress rating (MSR) is limited to thin material (2 in. or less in thickness). Lumber graded in this manner is known as *MSR lumber.*

Each piece of MSR lumber is stamped with a grade stamp that allows it to be fully identified, and the grade stamp for MSR lumber differs from the stamp for visually graded lumber. The grade stamp for MSR lumber includes a numerical value of nominal bending stress F_b and modulus of elasticity E. A typical grade stamp for MSR lumber is shown in Fig. 4.2*b*. Tabulated stresses for MSR lumber are given in NDS Supplement Table 4C.

MSR lumber has less variability in mechanical properties than visually graded lumber. Consequently, MSR lumber is often used to fabricate engineered wood products. For example, MSR lumber is used for laminating stock for some glulam beams. Another application is in the production of wood components such as light frame trusses and wood I joists.

A more recent development in the sorting of lumber by measuring its properties is known as *machine evaluated lumber* (MEL). This process will allow a greater mix of F_b/E combinations than is permitted in MSR lumber. Although design values for machine evaluated lumber are listed in the lower part of NDS Supplement Table 4C, MEL is a new process, and lumber graded in this way is currently not available.

4.4 In-Grade Versus Clear-Wood Design Values

Major changes to *tabulated* design values for visually graded structural lumber were introduced in the 1991 NDS Supplement. New adjustments for determining *allowable* stresses have also been incorporated. In previous editions of the NDS, the tabulated stresses were all determined using clear-wood test procedures. However, the tabulated stresses in the 1991 NDS are based in part on *clear-wood test procedures* and in part on the full-size lumber *in-grade test methods.*

There are two broad size classifications of sawn lumber:

1. Dimension lumber

2. Timbers

Dimension lumber are the smaller (thinner) sizes of structural lumber. Dimension lumber usually range in size from 2 × 2 through 4 × 16. In other words, dimension lumber constitutes any material that has a nominal *thickness* of 2 to 4 in. Note that in lumber grading terminology, *thickness* refers to the smaller cross-sectional dimension of a piece of wood, and *width* refers to the larger dimension. The availability of lumber in the wider widths varies with species, and not all sizes are available in all species.

Timbers are the larger sizes and have a 5-in. minimum nominal dimension. Thus, practically speaking, the smallest size timber is a 6 × 6, and any member larger than a 6 × 6 is classified as a timber. There are additional size categories within both Dimension lumber and Timbers, and the further subdivision of sizes is covered later in this chapter.

In 1991 NDS Supplement, the design properties for visually graded sawn lumber are based on two different sets of ASTM standards:

1. *In-grade* procedures (ASTM D 1990), applied to Dimension lumber[*]

2. *Clear-wood* procedures (ASTM D 2555 and D 245), applied to Timbers[*]

The method of establishing design values for visually graded sawn lumber for *Timbers* is based on the *clear-wood strength* of the various species and species combinations. The clear-wood strength is determined by testing small, clear, straight-grained specimens of a given species. For example, the clear-wood bending strength test is conducted on a specimen that measures 2 × 2 × 30 in. The testing methods to be used on small, clear-wood specimens are given in ASTM D 143 (Ref. 13.2). The unit strength (stress) of a small, clear, straight-grained piece of wood is much greater than the unit strength of a full-size member.

After the clear-wood strength properties for the species have been determined, the effects of the natural growth characteristics that are permitted in the different grades of full-size members are taken into account. This is accomplished by multiplying the clear-wood values by a reduction factor known as a *strength ratio*. In other words, the strength ratio takes into account the various strength-reducing defects (e.g., knots) that may be present.

As noted, the procedure for establishing tabulated design values using the clear-wood method is set forth in ASTM Standards D 245 and D 2555 (Refs. 13.3 and 13.6). Briefly, the process involves the following:

1. A statistical analysis is made of a large number of clear-wood strength values for the various commercial species. With the exception of $F_{c\perp}$ and E, the *5 percent exclusion value* serves as the starting point for the development of allowable stresses. The 5 percent exclusion value represents a strength property (e.g., bending strength). Out of 100 clear-wood specimens, 95 could be expected to fail at or above the 5 percent exclusion value, and 5 could be expected to fail below this value.

2. The 5 percent exclusion value for an unseasoned specimen is then increased by an appropriate seasoning adjustment factor to a moisture content of 19 percent or less.

---

[*]See Ref. 13 for the full titles of ASTM standards.

3. Strength ratios are used to adjust the clear-wood values to account for the strength-reducing defects permitted in a given stress grade.

4. The stresses are further reduced by a general adjustment factor which accounts for the duration of the test used to establish the initial clear-wood values, a manufacture and use adjustment, and several other factors.

The combined effect of these adjustments is to provide an average factor of safety on the order of 2.5. Because of the large number of variables in a wood member, the factor of safety for a given member may be considerably larger or smaller than the average. However, for 99 out of 100 pieces, the factor of safety will be greater than 1.25, and for 1 out of 100, the factor of safety will exceed 5. References 9.3, 9.4, and 9.5 give more details on the development of mechanical properties using the clear-wood strength method.

In 1978 a large research project, named the *In-Grade Testing Program,* was undertaken jointly between the lumber industry and the U.S. Forest Products Laboratory (FPL). The purpose of the In-Grade Program was to test full-size Dimension lumber that had been graded in the usual way. The grading rules for the various species did not change, and as the name "In-Grade" implies, the members tested were representative of lumber available in the marketplace. Approximately 73,000 pieces of full-size *Dimension lumber* were tested in bending, tension, and compression parallel to grain in accordance with ASTM D 4761 (Ref. 13.8). Relationships were also developed between mechanical properties and moisture content, grade, and size.

The objective of the In-Grade Program was to verify the published design values that had been determined using the clear-wood strength method. Although some of the values from the In-Grade Testing Program were close, there were enough differences between the In-Grade results and the clear-wood strength values that a new method of determining allowable stress properties was developed. These procedures are given in ASTM Standard D 1990 (Ref. 13.5).*

This brief summary has been given to explain the reasons for the changes in the tabulated design values in the 1991 NDS Supplement. It also explains why the design values for *Dimension lumber* and *Timbers* are published in separate tables in the NDS Supplement. As a practical matter, the designer does not need the ASTM standards to design a wood structure. The ASTM standards simply document the methods used by the rules-writing agencies to develop the tabulated stress properties listed in the NDS Supplement.

---

*ASTM D 1990 does not cover shear and compression perpendicular to grain. Therefore, values of F_v and $F_{c\perp}$ for Dimension lumber are obtained from ASTM D 2555 and D 245.

4.5 Species and Species Groups

A large number of *species* of trees can be used to produce structural lumber. As a general rule, a number of species are grown, harvested, manufactured, and marketed together. From a practical standpoint, the structural designer uses lumber from a commercial *species group* rather than a specific individual species. The same grading rules, tabulated stresses, and grade stamps are applied to all species in the species group. Tabulated stresses for a species group were derived using statistical procedures that ensure conservative values for all species in the group.

In some cases, the mark of one or more *individual* species may be included in the grade stamp. When one or more species from a species *group* are identified in the grade stamp, the allowable stresses for the species group are the appropriate stresses for use in structural design. In other cases, the grade stamp on a piece of lumber may reflect only the name of the *species group,* and the actual species of a given piece will not be known. Special knowledge in wood identification would be required to determine the individual species.

The 1991 NDS Supplement contains a complete list of the species groups along with a summary of the various individual species of trees that may be included in each group. Examples of several commonly used species groups are shown in Fig. 4.3. Individual species as well as the species groups are shown.

It should be noted that there are a number of species groups that have similar names [e.g., Douglas Fir-Larch *and* Douglas Fir-Larch (N). Hem-Fir *and* Hem-Fir (N), and Spruce-Pine-Fir *and* Spruce-Pine-Fir (S)]. It is important to understand that each is a separate and distinct species group, and there are different sets of tabulated stresses for each group. Different properties may be the result of the trees being grown in different geographical locations. However, there may also be different individual species included in combinations with similar names.

One of the new combination groups in the 1991 NDS is Spruce-Pine-Fir (S). Note that Spruce-Pine-Fir was a previously existing Canadian species group. Therefore, when the new U.S. species group was developed, a symbol indicating *south* (S) was added to the name so that the two species groups can be distinguished. In the past, similar reasons account for the suffix *north* (N) being added to a previously existing U.S. species group name, when a new Canadian group was developed.

The choice of species for use in design is typically a matter of economics. For a given location, only a few species groups will be available, and a check with local lumber distributors or a wood products agency will narrow the selection considerably. Although the table in Fig. 4.3 identifies only a small number of the commercial lumber species, those listed account for much of the total volume of structural lumber in North America.

Species Group Name and Group Name Mark that may appear in grade stamp	Individual Species that may be included in the Species Group and Individual Species Mark that may appear in grade stamp	Notes
Douglas Fir-Larch **DOUG. FIR-L**	Douglas Fir (D FIR mark) Western Larch (mark)	Individual species mark for Douglas Fir may also appear as "DOUGLAS FIR" or "D. FIR"
Douglas Fir-Larch (N) **D. FIR(N)**	Douglas Fir[1] Western Larch[1]	(N) - indicates a Canadian species group
Douglas Fir South (D FIR S mark)	Douglas Fir South (D FIR S mark)	South indicates Douglas Fir grown in Arizona, Colorado, Nevada, New Mexico, and Utah
Hem-Fir **HEM FIR**	California Red Fir[1] Grand-Fir[1] Nobel Fir[1] Pacific Silver Fir[1] Western Hemlock **HEM** White Fir[1]	
Hem-Fir (N) **HEM-FIR-N**	Amabilis Fir Western Hemlock	(N) - indicates a Canadian species group
Southern Pine **SYP**	Loblolly Pine[1] Longleaf Pine[1] Shortleaf Pine[1] Slash Pine[1]	Group mark is not used when graded under Southern Pine Inspection Bureau - grade stamp will show: **SPIB**
Spruce-Pine-Fir **S-P-F**	Alpine Fir[1] Balsam Fir[1] Black Spruce[1] Englemann Spruce[1] Jack Pine[1] Lodgepole Pine[1] Red Spruce[1] White Spruce[1]	Canadian species group
Spruce-Pine-Fir (S) **SPF^S**	Balsam Fir[2] Eastern Spruce[2] Englemann Spruce (ES) Jack Pine[1] Lodgepole Pine **LP** Red Pine[2] Sitka Spruce (SS)	(S) - indicates USA species group (established 1991). Eastern Spruce is any combination of Black Spruce, Red Spruce, and White Spruce.

[1] Always use group name mark.

[2] Individual species mark spells out the species.

Figure 4.3 Typical species groups of structural lumber. These and a number of additional species groups are given in the NDS Supplement. The species groups listed here account for a large percentage of the structural lumber sold in the United States. Also shown are the individual species that may be included in a given species group.

The In-Grade Testing Program caused a number of the species groups to be reorganized, and a number of simplifications have been made to the design tables. For example, the number of species groups for western Dimension lumber has decreased from ten in previous editions of the NDS to six in the 1991 NDS. A number of allowable stresses also changed. Some design values changed substantially from previously published values, and others were relatively unaffected. The trend of changes varies with the member size and type of stress. For example, the In-Grade results have decreased the tabulated bending strength for some lumber in the wider widths. On the other hand, values for compression parallel to grain have generally increased.

The changes brought about by the In-Grade Testing Program therefore vary with the type of member. Some beams will have considerably reduced moment capacities, but these same members, if loaded as a column, may have increased compressive strengths. Thus, if a member is subjected to combined bending and compressive loading, it may have interaction components that offset each other.

The 1991 NDS has new design equations for beams, columns, and members subjected to combined stresses. Therefore, an overall assessment of the changes in wood design criteria will have to take into account the effects of both the new design equations *and* the changes in design stresses for the various species groups. With the limited experience available at this time, the overall impact is unknown.

The species of trees used for structural lumber are classified as hardwoods and softwoods. These terms are not necessarily a description of the physical properties of the wood, but are rather classifications of trees. *Hardwoods* are broadleafed deciduous trees. *Softwoods,* on the other hand, have narrow, needlelike leaves and are generally evergreen and are known as conifers. By far the large majority of structural lumber comes from the softwood category.

For example, Douglas Fir-Larch and Southern Pine are two species groups that are widely used in structural applications. Although these contain species that are all classified as softwoods, they are relatively dense and have structural properties that exceed those of many hardwoods.

It has been noted that the lumber grading rules establish the limits on the strength-reducing characteristics permitted in the various lumber grades. Before discussing the various stress grades, a number of the natural growth characteristics found in lumber will be described.

4.6 Cellular Makeup

As a biological material, wood represents a unique structural material because its supply can be renewed by growing new trees in forests which have been harvested. Proper forest management is necessary to ensure a continuing supply of lumber.

Wood is composed of elongated, round, or rectangular tubelike cells. These cells are much longer than they are wide, and the length of the cells is essentially parallel with the length of the tree. The cell walls are made up of *cellulose,* and the cells are bound together by material known as *lignin.*

If the cross section of a log is examined, concentric rings are seen. One ring represents the amount of wood material which is deposited on the outside of the tree during one growing season. One ring then is termed an *annual ring.* See Fig. 4.4.

The annual rings develop because of differences in the wood cells that are formed in the early portion of the growing season compared with those formed toward the end of the growing season. Large, thin-walled cells are formed at the beginning of the growing season. These are known as *early-wood* or *springwood* cells. The cells deposited on the outside of the annual ring toward the end of the growing season are smaller, have thicker walls, and are known as *latewood* or *summerwood* cells. It should be noted that annual rings occur only in trees that are located in climate zones which have distinct growing seasons. In tropical zones, trees produce wood cells which are essentially uniform throughout the entire year.

Because summerwood is denser than springwood, it is stronger (the more solid material per unit volume, the greater the strength of the wood). The annual rings, therefore, provide one of the *visual* means by which the strength of a piece of wood may be evaluated. The more summerwood in relation to the amount of springwood (other factors being equal), the stronger the piece of lumber. This comparison is normally made by counting the number of growth rings per inch.

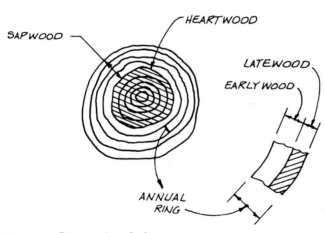

Figure 4.4 Cross section of a log.

In addition to annual rings, two different colors of wood may be noticed in the cross section of the log. The darker center portion of the log is known as *heartwood*. The lighter portion of the wood near the exterior of the log is known as *sapwood*. The relative amount of heartwood compared with sapwood varies with the species of tree. Heartwood, because it occurs at the center of the tree, is obviously much older than sapwood, and, in fact, heartwood represents wood cells which are inactive. These cells, however, provide strength and support to the tree. Sapwood, on the other hand, represents both living and inactive wood cells. Sapwood is used to store food and transport water. The strength of heartwood and sapwood is essentially the same. Heartwood is somewhat more decay-resistant than sapwood, but sapwood more readily accepts penetration by wood-preserving chemicals.

4.7 Moisture Content and Shrinkage

The *solid* portion of wood is made of a complex cellulose-lignin compound. The cellulose comprises the framework of the cell walls, and the lignin cements and binds the cells together.

In addition to the solid material, wood contains moisture. The moisture content (MC) is measured as the percentage of water to the oven dry weight of the wood:

$$\text{MC} = \frac{\text{moist weight} - \text{oven dry weight}}{\text{oven dry weight}} \times 100 \text{ percent}$$

The moisture content in a living tree can be as high as 200 percent (i.e., in some species the weight of water contained in the tree can be 2 times the weight of the solid material in the tree). However, the moisture content of structural lumber in service is much less. The average moisture content that lumber assumes in service is known as the *equilibrium moisture content* (EMC). Depending on atmospheric conditions, the EMC of structural framing lumber in a covered structure (dry conditions) will range somewhere between 7 and 14 percent. In most cases, the MC at the time of construction will be higher than the EMC of a building (perhaps 2 times higher). See Example 4.1.

Moisture is held within wood in two ways. Water contained in the cell cavity is known as *free water*. Water contained within the cell walls is known as *bound water*. As wood dries, the first water to be driven off is the free water. The moisture content that corresponds to a complete loss of free water (with 100 percent of the bound water remaining) is known as the *fiber saturation point* (FSP). No loss of bound water occurs as lumber dries above the fiber saturation point. In addition, no volume changes or changes in other structural properties are associated with changes in moisture content above the fiber saturation point.

EXAMPLE 4.1   Bar Chart Showing Different MC Conditions

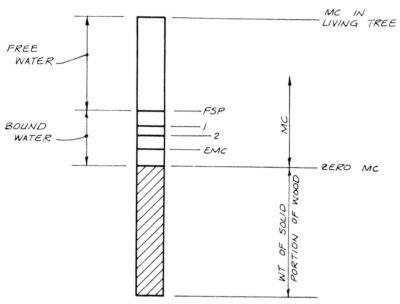

Figure 4.5

Figure 4.5 shows the moisture content in lumber in comparison with its solid weight. The values indicate that the lumber was manufactured (point 1) at an MC below the fiber saturation point. Some additional drying occurred before the lumber was used in construction (point 2). The EMC is shown to be less than the MC at the time of construction. This is typical for most buildings.

However, with moisture content changes below the fiber saturation point, bound water is lost and volume changes occur. If moisture is lost, wood shrinks; if moisture is gained, wood swells. Decreases in moisture content below the fiber saturation point are accompanied by increases in strength properties. Prior to the In-Grade Testing Program, it is generally believed that the more lumber dried, the greater would be the increase in strength. However, results from the In-Grade Program show that strength properties peak at around 10 to 15 percent MC. For a moisture content below this, member strength capacities remain about constant.

The fiber saturation point varies with species, but the *Wood Handbook*

(Ref. 4.1) indicates that 30 percent is average. Individual species may differ from the average. The drying of lumber in order to increase its structural properties is known as *seasoning*. As noted, the MC of lumber in a building typically decreases after construction until the EMC is reached. Although this drying in service can be called seasoning, the term *seasoning* often refers to a controlled drying process. Controlled drying can be performed by air or kiln drying (k.d.), and both increase the cost of lumber.

From this discussion it can be seen that there are opposing forces occurring as wood dries below the fiber saturation point. On one hand, shrinkage decreases the size of the cross section with a corresponding reduction in section properties. On the other hand, a reduction in MC down to approximately 15 percent increases most structural properties. The net effect of a decrease in moisture content in the 10 to 30 percent range is beneficial.

Shrinkage can also cause cracks to form in lumber. As lumber dries, the material near the surface of the member loses moisture and shrinks before the wood at the inner core. Longitudinal cracks, known as *seasoning checks*, may occur near the neutral axis (middle of wide dimension) of the member as a result of this nonuniform drying process. See Fig. 4.6a in Example 4.2. Cracking of this nature causes a reduction in shear strength which is taken into account in the lumber grading rules and tabulated design values. This type of behavior is more common in thicker members.

Another point should be noted about the volume changes associated with shrinkage. The dimensional changes as the result of drying are not uniform. Greater shrinkage occurs parallel (tangent) to the annual ring than normal (radial) to it. See Fig. 4.6b. These nonuniform dimensional changes may cause radial checks.

In practice, the orientation of growth rings in a member will be arbitrary. In other words, the case shown in Fig. 4.6c is a rather unique situation with the annual rings essentially parallel and perpendicular to the sides of the member. Annual rings can be at any angle with respect to the sides of the member.

It is occasionally necessary for the designer to estimate the amount of shrinkage or swelling that may occur in a structure. The more common case involves shrinkage of lumber as it dries in service. Several approaches may be used to estimate shrinkage.

One method comes from the *Wood Handbook* (Ref. 4.1). Values of tangential, radial, and volumetric shrinkage from clear-wood samples are listed for many individual species. The shrinkage percentages are assumed to take place from no shrinkage at a nominal FSP of 30 percent to full shrinkage at zero MC. A linear interpolation is used for shrinkage at intermediate MC values. See Fig. 4.6c. The maximum shrinkage can be estimated using the tangential shrinkage, and the minimum can be evaluated with the radial value. Thus, the method from the *Wood Handbook* can be used to bracket the probable shrinkage.

EXAMPLE 4.2   Shrinkage of Lumber

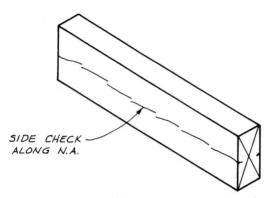

SIDE CHECK
ALONG N.A.

Figure 4.6a Seasoning checks may occur in the wide side of a member at or near the neutral axis. These cracks form because wood near the surface dries and shrinks first. In larger pieces of lumber, the inner core of the member loses moisture and shrinks much slower. Checking relieves the stresses caused by non-uniform drying.

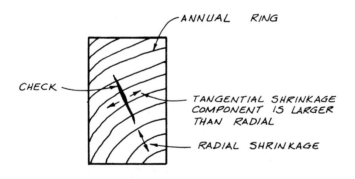

ANNUAL   RING

CHECK

TANGENTIAL SHRINKAGE COMPONENT IS LARGER THAN RADIAL

RADIAL SHRINKAGE

LUMBER   SECTION

Figure 4.6b Tangential shrinkage is greater than radial shrinkage. This promotes the formation of radial cracks known as *end checks*.

The *Wood Handbook* lists average clear-wood shrinkage percentages for many individual species of wood. Tangential shrinkage is greatest. Radial shrinkage is on the order of one-half of the tangential value, but is still significant. Longitudinal shrinkage is very small and is usually disregarded.

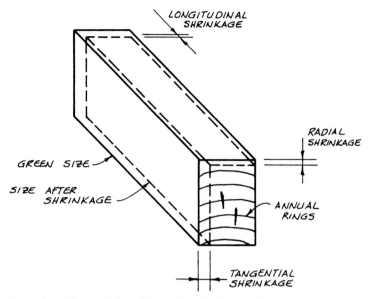

Figure 4.6c Tangential, radial, and longitudinal shrinkage.

A second approach to shrinkage calculations is given in Ref. 4.6. It provides formulas for calculating the percentage of shrinkage for the *width* and *thickness* of a piece of lumber. This method was used for shrinkage adjustments for the In-Grade Test data and is included in the appendix to ASTM D 1990 (Ref. 13.5).

In structural design, there are several reasons why it may be more appropriate to apply a simpler method for estimating the shrinkage than either of the two methods just described:

1. Shrinkage is a variable property. The shrinkage that occurs in a given member may be considerably different from those values obtained using the published *average* radial and tangential values.

2. Orientation of the annual rings in a real piece of lumber is unknown. The sides of a member are probably not parallel or perpendicular to the growth rings.

3. The designer will probably know only the *species group,* and the *individual species* of a member will probably not be known.

For these and perhaps other reasons, a very simple method of estimating shrinkage in structural lumber is recommended in Ref. 20. In this third approach, a constant shrinkage value of 6 percent is used for both the width and the thickness of a member. The shrinkage is taken as zero at a FSP of 30 percent, and the full 6 percent shrinkage is assumed to occur at a MC of zero. A linear relationship is used for MC values between 30 and 0. See Example 4.3.

Although Ref. 20 specifically deals with western species lumber, the recommend general shrinkage coefficient should give reasonable estimates of shrinkage in most species.

EXAMPLE 4.3   Simplified Method of Estimating Shrinkage

Estimate the shrinkage that will occur in a four-story wood-frame wall that uses Hem-Fir framing lumber. Consider a decrease in moisture content from 15 to 8 percent.

Framing is typical platform construction with 2 × 12 floor joists resting on bearing walls. Wall framing is conventional 2 × studs with a typical single 2 × bottom plate and double 2 × top plates. See Fig. 4.7.

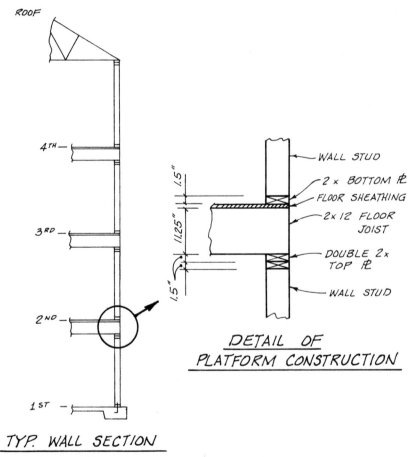

Figure 4.7 Details for estimating shrinkage in four-story building.

The species group of Hem-Fir is given. The list in Fig. 4.3 indicates that any one of six species may be grade-marked with the group name of Hem-Fir. If the individual species is known, the shrinkage coefficients from *Wood Handbook* (Ref. 4.1) could be used to bracket the total shrinkage, using tangential and radial values. However, for practical design purposes, the simplified approach from Ref. 20 is used to develop a design estimate of the shrinkage.

A shrinkage of 6 percent of the member dimension is assumed to occur between MC = 30 percent and MC = 0 percent. Linear interpolation allows the shrinkage value (SV) per degree change in moisture content to be calculated as

$$\text{Shrinkage value SV} = \tfrac{6}{30} = 0.2 \text{ percent per 1 percent change in MC}$$

$$= 0.002 \text{ in./in. per 1 percent change in MC}$$

The shrinkage S that occurs in the dimension d of a piece is calculated as the shrinkage value times the dimension times the change in moisture content:

$$\text{Shrinkage } S = \text{SV} \times d \times \Delta_{MC}$$

$$= 0.002 \times d \times \Delta_{MC}$$

Shrinkage in the depth of one 2×12 floor joist:

$$S_{\text{floor}} = 0.002 \times d \times \Delta_{MC}$$

$$= 0.002 \times 11.25 \times (15 - 8) = 0.158 \text{ in.}$$

Shrinkage in the thickness* of one $2 \times$ wall plate.

$$S_{\text{plate}} = 0.002 \times d \times \Delta_{MC}$$

$$= 0.002 \times 1.5 \times (15 - 8) = 0.021 \text{ in.}$$

Shrinkage in the length of a stud: The longitudinal shrinkage of a piece of lumber is small.

$$S_{\text{stud}} \approx 0$$

The first floor is a concrete slab. The second, third, and fourth floors each use 2×12 floor joists (three total). There is a $2 \times$ bottom plate on the first, second, third, and fourth floors (four total). There is a double $2 \times$ plate on top of the first-, second-, third-, and fourth-floor wall studs (a total of eight $2 \times$ top plates).

$$\text{Total } S = \sum S = 3(S_{\text{floor}}) + 12(S_{\text{plate}})$$

$$= 3(0.158) + (4 + 8)(0.021)$$

$$\boxed{\text{Total } S = 0.725 \text{ in.} \approx \tfrac{3}{4} \text{ in.}}$$

---

*In lumber terminology, the larger cross-sectional dimension of a piece of wood is known as the width, and the smaller is the thickness.

To carry out the type of shrinkage estimate illustrated in Example 4.3, the designer must be able to establish reasonable values for the initial and final moisture content for the lumber. The *initial moisture content* is defined to some extent by the specification for the lumber for a particular job. The general MC range at the time of manufacture is shown in the grade stamp, and this value needs to be reflected in the lumber specification for a job.

The *grade stamp* on a piece of lumber will contain one of three MC designations, which indicates the condition of the lumber at the time of manufacture. *Dry lumber* is defined as lumber having a moisture content of 19 percent or less. Material with a moisture content of over 19 percent is defined as *unseasoned* or *green lumber*.

When unseasoned lumber is grade-stamped, the term "S-GRN" (surfaced green) will appear. "S-DRY" (surfaced dry) indicates that the lumber was manufactured with a moisture content of 19 percent or less. Refer to the sample grade stamps in Fig. 4.2*a* for examples of these markings. Some smaller lumber sizes may be seasoned to 15 percent or less in moisture content and marked "MC 15." It should be understood that larger-size wood members (i.e., Timbers) are not produced in a dry condition. The large cross-sectional dimensions of these members would require an excessive amount of time for seasoning.

In addition to the MC range reflected in the grade stamp, the initial moisture content of lumber in place in a structure is affected by a number of variables including the size of the members, time in transit to the job site, construction delays, and time for construction. Reference 20 recommends that in practical situations the following assumptions can reasonably be made:

Moisture designation in grade stamp	Initial moisture content assumed in service
S-GRN (MC greater than 19 percent at time of manufacture)	19 percent
S-DRY (MC of 19 percent or less at time of manufacture)	15 percent

It should be noted that these recommendations are appropriate for relatively thin material (e.g., the 2 × floor joists and wall plates in Example 4.3). However, larger-size members will dry slower. The designer should take this and other possible factors into consideration when estimating the initial moisture content for shrinkage calculations.

The *final moisture content* can be taken as the equilibrium moisture content (EMC) of the wood. Various surveys of the moisture content in existing buildings have been conducted, and it was previously noted that the EMC in most buildings ranges between 7 and 14 percent.

Reference 5.6 gives typical EMC values of several broad atmospheric zones. The average EMC for framing lumber in the "dry southwestern states" (eastern California, Nevada, southern Oregon, southwest Idaho, Utah, and western Arizona) is given as 9 percent. The MC in most covered structures in this area is expected to range between 7 and 12 percent. For the remainder of the United States, the average EMC is given as 12 percent with an expected range of 9 to 14 percent. These values basically agree with the 8 to 12 percent MC suggested in Ref. 20.

The average values and the MC ranges can be used to estimate the EMC for typical buildings. Special conditions must be analyzed individually. As an alternative, the moisture content of wood in an existing structure can be measured with a portable, hand-held moisture meter.

The discussion of moisture content and shrinkage again leads to an important conclusion that was mentioned earlier: Wood is a unique structural material, and its behavior must be understood if it is to be used successfully. Wood is not a static material, and significant changes in dimensions can result because of atmospheric conditions.

Even if shrinkage calculations are not performed, the designer should allow for the movement (shrinkage or swelling) that may occur. This may be necessary in a number of cases. A primary concern in structural design is the potential splitting of wood members.

Wood is very weak in tension perpendicular to grain. The majority of shrinkage occurs across the grain, and connection details must accommodate this movement. If a connection does not allow lumber to shrink freely, tension stresses perpendicular to grain may develop. Splitting of the member will be the likely result. The proper detailing of connections to avoid built-in stresses due to changes in moisture content is covered in Chaps. 13 and 14.

In addition to the structural failures that may result from cross-grain tension, there are a number of other practical shrinkage considerations. Although these may not affect structural safety, they may be crucial to the proper functioning of a building. Consider the shrinkage evaluated in the multistory structure in Example 4.3. Several types of problems could occur.

For example, consider the effect of ceiling joists, trusses, or roof beams supported by a four-story wood-frame wall on one end *and* a concrete or masonry wall on the other end. Shrinkage will occur in the wood wall but not in the concrete or masonry. Thus, one end of the member in the top level will eventually be ¾ in. lower than the other end. This problem occurs as the result of *differential* movement.

Even greater differential movement problems can occur. Consider an all-wood-frame building again, of the type in Example 4.3. In all-wood construction, the shrinkage will be uniform throughout. However, consider the effect of adding a short-length concrete block wall (say, a stair tower enclosure) in the middle of one of the wood-frame walls. The differential movement between the wood-frame wall and the masonry wall now takes place in a very short distance. Distress of ceiling, floor, and wall sheathing will likely develop.

Other potential problems include the possible buckling of finish wall siding. Even if the shrinkage is uniform throughout a wall, there must be sufficient clearance in wall covering details to accommodate the movement. This may require slip-type architectural details (for example, Z flashing). In addition, plumbing, piping, and electrical and mechanical systems must allow for the movement due to shrinkage. This can be accomplished by providing adequate clearance or by making the utilities flexible enough to accommodate the movement without distress. See Ref. 20 for additional information.

4.8 Effect of Moisture Content on Lumber Sizes

The moisture content of a piece of lumber obviously affects the cross-sectional dimensions. The width and depth of a member are used to calculate the section properties used in structural design. These include area A, moment of inertia I, and section modulus S.

Fortunately for the designer, it is not necessary to compute section properties based on a consideration of the initial MC and EMC and the resulting shrinkage (or swelling) that occurs in the member. Grading practices for *Dimension lumber* have established the *dry* size (MC $\leq$ 19 percent) of a member as the basis for structural calculations. This means that only one set of cross-sectional properties needs to be considered in design.

This is made possible by manufacturing lumber to different cross-sectional dimensions based on the moisture content of the wood at the time of manufacture. Therefore, lumber which is produced from green wood will be somewhat larger at the time of manufacture. However, when this wood reaches a dry moisture content condition, the cross-sectional dimensions will closely coincide with those for lumber produced in the dry condition. Again, this discussion has been based on the manufacturing practices for dimension lumber.

Because of their large cross-sectional dimensions, *Timbers* are not produced in a dry condition since an excessive amount of time would be required to season these members. For this reason, cross-sectional dimensions that correspond to a *green* (MC $>$ 19 percent) condition have been established as the basis for design calculations for these members. In addition, tabulated stresses have been adjusted to account for the higher moisture content of timbers.

4.9 Durability of Wood and the Need for Pressure Treatment

The discussion of the moisture content of lumber often leads to concerns about the durability of wood structures and the potential for decay. However, the record is clear. If wood is used properly, it can be a permanent building material. If wood is used incorrectly, major problems can develop, sometimes very rapidly. Again, understanding the material is the key to its proper use. The performance of many classic wood structures (Ref. 5.8) is testimony to the durability of wood in properly designed structures.

Generally, if it is protected (i.e., not exposed to the weather or not in contact with the ground) and is used at a relatively low moisture content (as in most covered structures), wood performs satisfactorily without chemical treatment. Wood is also durable when *continuously* submerged in *fresh* water. However, if the moisture content is high and varies with time, or if wood is in contact with the ground, the use of an appropriate preservative treatment should be considered.

High MC values can occur in wood roof systems over swimming pools and in processing plants with high-humidity conditions. *High* moisture content is generally defined as exceeding 19 percent in sawn lumber and as being 16 percent or greater in glulam. Problems involving high moisture content can also occur in geographic locations with high humidity.

In some cases, moisture can become entrapped in roof systems that have *below-roof insulation*. This type of insulation can create dead-air spaces, and moisture from condensation or other sources may lead to decay. Moisture-related problems have occurred in some flat or nearly flat roofs. To create air movement, a minimum roof slope of ½ in./ft is now recommended for panelized roofs that use below-roof insulation. A number of other recommendations have been developed by the industry to minimize these types of problems. See Refs. 3.9, 7.6, and 14.16.

When required for new construction, chemicals can be impregnated into the lumber and other wood products by a pressure-treating process. The chemical preservatives prevent or effectively retard the destruction of wood. Pressure treating usually takes place in a large steel cylinder. The wood to be treated is transported into the cylinder on a tram, and the cylinder is closed and filled with a preservative. The cylinder is then subjected to pressure which forces the chemical into the wood.

The chemical does not saturate the complete cross section of the member. Therefore, field cutting and drilling of holes for connections after treating should be minimized. It is desirable to carry out as much fabrication of structural members as possible before the members are treated. The depth of penetration is known as the *treated zone*. The retention of the chemical treatment is measured in lb/ft^3 *in the treated zone*. The required retention amounts vary with the end use and type of treatment.

Rather than focusing only on moisture content, a more complete overview of the question of long-term performance and durability recognizes that several instruments can destroy wood. The major ones are

1. Decay

2. Termites

3. Marine borers

4. Fire

Each of these is addressed briefly in this section, but a comprehensive review of these subjects is beyond the scope of this book. Detailed information is available in Refs. 4.1, 9.5, and 26. In the case of an existing wood structure that has been exposed to some form of destruction, guidelines are available for its evaluation, maintenance, and upgrading (Ref. 5.3).

Decay is caused by fungi which feed on the cellulose or lignin of the wood. These fungi must have food, moisture (MC greater than approximately 20 percent), air, and favorable temperatures. All of these items are required for decay to occur (even so-called dry rot requires moisture).

If any of the requirements is not present, decay will not occur. Thus, untreated wood that is continuously dry (MC < 20 percent, as in most covered structures), or continuously wet (submerged in fresh water—no air), will not decay. Exposure to the weather (alternate wetting and drying) can set up the conditions necessary for decay to develop. Pressure treatment introduces chemicals that poison the food supply of the fungi.

Termites can be found in most areas of the United States, but they are more of a problem in the warmer-climate areas. Subterranean termites are the most common, but drywood and dampwood species also exist. Subterranean termites nest in the ground and enter wood which is near or in contact with damp ground. The cellulose forms the food supply for termites.

The UBC requires a minimum clearance of 18 in. between the bottom of unprotected floor joists (12 in. for girders) and grade. Good ventilation of crawl spaces and proper drainage also aid in preventing termite attack. Lumber which is near or in contact with the ground, and wall plates on concrete ground-floor slabs and footings, must be pressure-treated to prevent termite attack. (Foundation-grade redwood has a natural resistance and can be used for wall plates.) The same pressure treatments provide protection against decay and termites.

Marine borers are found in salt waters, and they present a problem in the design of marine piles. Pressure-treated piles have an extensive record in resisting attack by marine borers.

A brief introduction to the fire-resistive requirements for buildings was given in Chap. 1. Where necessary to meet building code requirements, or where the designer decides that an extra measure of fire protection is desirable, *fire-retardant-treated wood* may be used. This type of treatment involves the use of chemicals in formulations that have fire-retardant properties. Some of the types of chemicals used are preservatives and thus also provide decay and termite protection. Fire-retardant treatment, however, requires higher concentrations of chemicals in the treated zone than normal preservative treatments.

The tabulated design values in the NDS Supplement apply to both untreated and pressure-preservative-treated lumber. In other words, there is no required stress modification for preservative treatments. *Preservative treatments* are those that guard against decay, termites, and marine borers. The high concentrations of chemicals used in fire-retardant treated lumber will probably require that allowable design values be reduced. However, the reduction coefficients vary with the treating process, and the *NDS refers the designer to the company providing the fire-retardant treatment and re-drying service for the appropriate factors.*

The three basic types of pressure preservatives are

1. Creosote and creosote solutions

2. Oilborne treatments (pentachlorophenol and others dissolved in one of four hydrocarbon solvents)

3. Waterborne oxides

There are a number of variations in each of these categories. The choice of the preservative treatment and the required retentions depend on the application. Detailed information on pressure treatments and their uses can be obtained from the American Wood Preservers Institute (AWPI). For the address of AWPI, see the list of organizations in the Nomenclature section.

An introduction to pressure treatments is given in Ref. 5.6. This reference covers fire-resistive requirements and fire hazards as well as preservative and fire-retardant treatments. Reference 3.5 provides a concise summary of preservative treatments. See Ref. 26 for additional information on the use of wood in adverse environments.

4.10 Growth Characteristics of Wood

Some of the more important growth characteristics that affect the structural properties of wood are density, moisture content, knots, checks, shakes, splits, slope of grain, reaction wood, and decay. The effects of density, and how it can be measured visually by the annual rings, were described previously. Likewise, moisture content and its effects have been discussed at some length. The remaining natural growth characteristics also affect the strength of lumber, and limits are placed on the size and number of these structural defects permitted in a given stress grade. These items are briefly discussed here.

Knots constitute that portion of a branch or limb that has been incorporated into the main body of the tree. See Fig. 4.8. In lumber, knots are classified by form, size, quality, and occurrence. Knots decrease the mechanical properties of the wood because the knot displaces *clear wood* and because the slope of the grain is forced to deviate around the knot. In addition, stress concentrations occur because the knot interrupts wood fibers. Checking also may occur around the knot in the drying process. Knots have an effect on both tension and compression capacity, but the effect in the tension zone is greater. Lumber grading rules for different species of wood

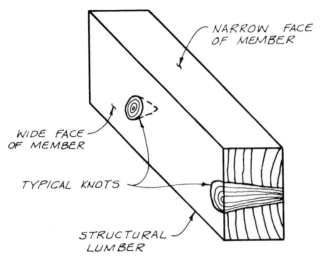

Figure 4.8 Examples of knots. Lumber grading rules for the commercial species have different limits for knots occurring in the wide and narrow faces of the member.

describe the size, type, and distribution (i.e., location and number) of knots allowed in each stress grade.

Checks, shakes, and *splits* all constitute separations of wood fibers. See Fig. 4.9. Checks have been discussed earlier and are radial cracks caused by nonuniform volume changes as the moisture content of wood decreases (Sec. 4.7). Recall that the outer portion of a member shrinks first, which may cause longitudinal cracks. In addition, more shrinkage occurs tangentially to the annual ring than radially. Checks therefore are seasoning defects. Shakes, on the other hand, are cracks which are usually parallel to the annual ring and develop in the standing tree. Splits represent complete separations of the wood fibers throughout the thickness of a member. A split may result from a shake or seasoning or both. Splits are measured as the penetration of the split from the end of the member parallel to its length. Again, lumber grading rules provide limits on these types of defects.

The term *slope of grain* is used to describe the deviation of the wood fibers from a line that is parallel to the edge of a piece of lumber. Slope of grain is expressed as a ratio (for example, 1 in 8, 1 in 15, etc.). See Fig. 4.10. In structural lumber, the slope of grain is measured over a sufficient length and area to be representative of the general slope of wood fibers. Local deviations, such as around knots, are disregarded in the general slope measurement. Slope of grain has a marked effect on the structural capacity of a wood member. Lumber grading rules provide limits on the slope of grain that can be tolerated in the various stress grades.

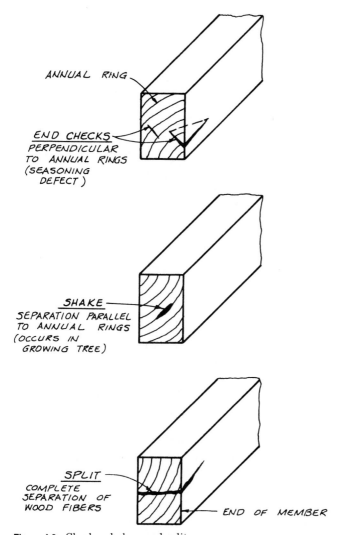

ANNUAL RING

END CHECKS
PERPENDICULAR
TO ANNUAL RINGS
(SEASONING
DEFECT)

SHAKE
SEPARATION PARALLEL
TO ANNUAL RINGS
(OCCURS IN
GROWING TREE)

SPLIT
COMPLETE
SEPARATION OF
WOOD FIBERS

END OF MEMBER

Figure 4.9 Checks, shakes, and splits.

Reaction wood (known as compression wood in softwood species) is abnormal wood that forms on the underside of leaning and crooked trees. It is hard and brittle, and its presence denotes an unbalanced structure in the wood. Compression wood is not permitted in readily identifiable and damaging form in stress grades of lumber.

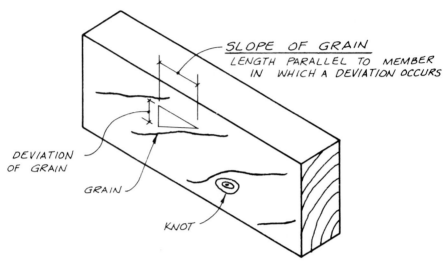

Figure 4.10 Slope of grain.

Decay is a degradation of the wood caused by the action of fungi. Grading rules establish limits on the decay allowed in stress-graded lumber. Section 4.9 describes the methods of preserving lumber against decay attack.

4.11   Sizes of Structural Lumber

Structural calculations are based on the *standard net size* of a piece of lumber. The effects of moisture content on the size of lumber are discussed in Sec. 4.8. The designer may have to allow for shrinkage when detailing connections, but standard dimensions are accepted for stress calculations.

Most structural lumber is *dressed lumber*. In other words, the lumber is *surfaced* to the standard net size, which is less than the *nominal* (stated) size. See Example 4.4. Lumber is dressed on a planing machine for the purpose of obtaining smooth surfaces and uniform sizes. Typically lumber will be S4S (surfaced four sides), but other finishes can be obtained (for example, S2S1E indicates surfaced two sides and one edge).

Dressed lumber is used in many structural applications, but large timbers are commonly *rough sawn* to dimensions that are close to the standard net sizes. The textured surface of rough-sawn lumber may be desired for architectural purposes and may be specially ordered in smaller sizes. The cross-sectional dimensions of rough-sawn lumber are approximately ⅛ in. larger than the standard dressed size. A less common method of obtaining a rough surface is to specify *full-sawn* lumber. In this case, the actual size of the lumber should be the same as the specified size. Cross-sectional properties

EXAMPLE 4.4   Dressed, Rough-Sawn, and Full-Sawn Lumber

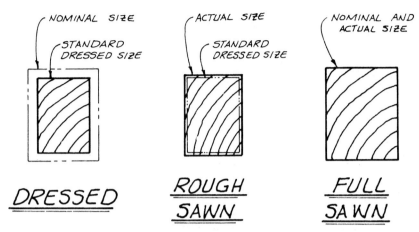

Figure 4.11

Consider an 8 × 12 member (nominal size = 8 in. × 12 in.).

1. *Dressed lumber.* Standard net size = 7½ in. × 11½ in. Refer to NDS Supplement Tables 1A and 1B for dressed lumber sizes.
2. *Rough-sawn lumber.* Approximate size = 7⅝ in. × 11⅝ in. Rough size is approximately ⅛ in. larger than the dressed size.
3. *Full-sawn lumber.* Minimum size 8 in. × 12 in. Full-sawn lumber is not generally available.

for rough-sawn and full-sawn lumber are not included in the NDS because of their relatively infrequent use.

The terminology in the wood industry that is applied to the dimensions of a piece of lumber differs from the terminology normally used in structural calculations. The grading rules refer to the thickness and width of a piece of lumber. It was previously stated that the *thickness* is the smaller cross-sectional dimension, and the *width* is the larger.

However, in the familiar case of a beam, design calculations usually refer to the *width* and *depth* of a member. The width is parallel to the neutral axis of the cross section, and the depth is perpendicular. In most beam problems, the member is loaded about the strong or *x* axis of the cross section. Therefore, the width of a beam is usually the smaller cross-sectional dimension, and the depth is the larger. Naturally, the strong axis has larger values of section modulus and moment of inertia. Loading a beam about the strong axis is also described as having the *load applied to the narrow face of the beam.*

Another type of beam loading is less common. If the bending stress is about the weak axis or *y* axis, the section modulus and moment of inertia are much smaller. *Decking* is an obvious application where a beam will have the *load applied to the wide face of the member.* In this case the width is the larger cross-sectional dimension, and the depth is the smaller. As with all structural materials, the objective is to make the most efficient use of materials. Thus, a wood beam is used in bending about the strong axis whenever possible.

The dimensions of sawn lumber are given in the 1991 NDS Supplement Table 1A, *Nominal and Minimum Dressed Sizes of Sawn Lumber.* However, a more useful table for design is the list of cross-sectional properties in the NDS Supplement Table 1B, *Section Properties of Standard Dressed (S4S) Sawn Lumber.* The properties include nominal and dressed dimensions, area, and section modulus and moment of inertia for both the *x* and *y* axes. The section properties for a typical sawn lumber member are verified in Example 4.5. The weight per linear foot for various densities of wood is also given in Table 1B.

EXAMPLE 4.5   Section Properties for Dressed Lumber

Show calculations for the section properties of a 2 × 8 sawn lumber member. Use standard net sizes for dressed (S4S) lumber, and verify the section properties in NDS Table 1B.

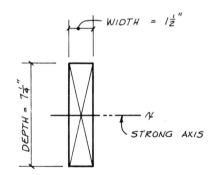

2 × 8   SECTION

Figure 4.12a Dimensions for section properties about strong *x* axis of 2 × 8.

Section Properties for x Axis

$$A = bd = 1\tfrac{1}{2} \times 7\tfrac{1}{4} = 10.875 \text{ in.}^2$$

$$S_x = \frac{bd^2}{6} = \frac{1.5(7.25)^2}{6} = 13.14 \text{ in.}^3$$

$$I_x = \frac{bd^3}{12} = \frac{1.5(7.25)^3}{12} = 47.63 \text{ in.}^4$$

The section properties for the x axis agree with those listed in the NDS Supplement.

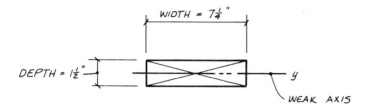

Figure 4.12b Dimensions for section properties about weak y axis of 2×8.

Section Properties for y Axis

$$S_y = \frac{bd^2}{6} = \frac{7.25(1.5)^2}{6} = 2.719 \text{ in.}^3$$

$$I_y = \frac{bd^3}{12} = \frac{7.25(1.5)^3}{12} = 2.039 \text{ in.}^4$$

The section properties for the y axis agree with those listed in the NDS Supplement.

4.12 Size Categories and Stress Grades

The lumber grading rules which establish allowable stresses for use in structural design have been developed over many years. In this development process, the relative size of a piece of wood was used as a guide in anticipating the application or "use" that a member would receive in the field. For example, pieces of lumber with rectangular cross sections make more efficient beams than members with square (or approximately square) cross sections. Thus, if the final application of a piece of wood were known, the stress-grading rules would take into account the primary function (e.g., axial strength or bending strength) of the member. See Example 4.6.

EXAMPLE 4.6   Size and Use Categories

There are three main *size categories* of lumber. The categories and nominal size ranges are:

Boards	1 to 1½ in. thick
	2 in. and wider
Dimension lumber	2 to 4 in. thick
	2 in. and wider
Timbers	5 in. and thicker
	5 in. and wider

A number of additional subdivisions are available within the main size categories. Each represents a size and use category in the lumber grading rules. The primary *size and use categories* for stress-graded (structural) lumber are as follows:

Boards
  Stress-Rated Board (SRB)

Dimension lumber
  Structural Light Framing (SLF)
  Light Framing (LF)
  Studs
  Structural Joists and Planks (SJ&P)
  Decking

Timbers
  Beams and Stringers (B&S)
  Posts and Timbers (P&T)

Stress-Rated Boards may be used in structural applications. However, because they are relatively thin pieces of lumber, Stress-Rated Boards are not commonly used for structural framing. Therefore, the remaining discussion is limited to a consideration of Dimension lumber and Timbers. Sizes in the seven basic subcategories of structural lumber are summarized in the following table.

Symbol	Name	Nominal dimensions		Examples of sizes
		Thickness	Width	
LF SLF	Light Framing and Structural Light Framing	2 to 4 in.	2 to 4 in.	2 × 2, 2 × 4, 4 × 4
SJ&P	Structural Joist and Plank	2 to 4 in.	5 in. and wider	2 × 6, 2 × 14, 4 × 10
	Stud	2 to 4 in.	2 to 6 in.	2 × 4, 2 × 6, 4 × 6 (lengths limited to 10 ft and shorter)
	Decking*	2 to 4 in.	4 in. and wider	2 × 4, 2 × 8, 4 × 6
B&S	Beams and Stringers	5 in. and thicker	More than 2 in. greater than thickness	6 × 10, 6 × 14, 12 × 16
P&T	Posts and Timbers	5 in. and thicker	Not more than 2 in. greater than thickness	6 × 6, 6 × 8, 12 × 14

*Decking is normally stressed about its minor axis. In this book, all other bending members are assumed to be stressed about the major axis of the cross section, unless otherwise noted.

It has been noted that size and use are related. However, in the process of determining the allowable stresses for a member, the structural designer needs to place emphasis on understanding the *size* classifications. The reason is that *different allowable stresses* apply to the *same stress grade name* in the *different size categories*. For example, Select Structural (a stress grade) is available in SLF, SJ&P, B&S, and P&T size categories. Allowable stresses for a given commercial species of lumber are generally different for Select Structural in all of these size categories. See Example 4.7.

EXAMPLE 4.7   Stress Grades

Typical stress grades vary within the various size and use categories. The stress grades shown are for Douglas Fir-Larch.

1. *Structural Light Framing* (SLF)
   Select Structural
   No. 1 and Better
   No. 1
   No. 2
   No. 3
2. *Light Framing* (LF)
   Construction
   Standard
   Utility
3. *Structural Joist and Plank* (SJ&P)
   Select Structural
   No. 1 and Better
   No. 1
   No. 2
   No. 3

4. *Stud*
   Stud
5. *Decking*
   Selected Decking
   Commercial Decking
6. *Beams and Stringers* (B&S)
   Dense Select Structural
   Dense No. 1
   No. 1
   No. 2
7. *Posts and Timbers* (P&T)
   Dense Select Structural
   Dense No. 1
   No. 1
   No. 2

NOTE: The stress grades listed are intended to be representative, and they are not available in all species groups. For example, *No. 1 and Better* is available only in DF-L and Hem-Fir. Southern Pine has a number of additional *dense* and *nondense* stress grades.

Several important points should be made about the *size and use categories* given in Example 4.6 *and* the *stress grades* listed in Example 4.7:

1. *Decking* is normally stressed in bending about the minor axis of the cross section, and allowable stresses for Decking are listed in a separate table. See NDS Supplement Table 4E, *Design Values for Visually Graded Decking*.

2. Allowable stresses for Dimension lumber (except Decking) are given in a number of separate tables. In these tables the stress grades are grouped together regardless of the size and use subcategory. This represents a simplification of the stress tables compared with previous editions of the NDS. The simplification was made possible by results of the In-Grade Testing Program.

Allowable stresses for *Dimension lumber* are listed in the following tables in the 1991 NDS Supplement:

Table 4A.   *Base Design Values for Visually Graded Dimension Lumber (All Species except Southern Pine)*

Table 4B.   *Design Values for Visually Graded Southern Pine Dimension Lumber*

Table 4C.   *Design Values for Mechanically Graded Dimension Lumber*

The simplification of the allowable stresses in Tables 4A and 4B requires the use of several revised adjustment factors (Sec. 4.13).

3. Allowable stresses for Beams and Stringers (B&S) and Posts and Timbers (P&T) are given in NDS Supplement Table 4D, *Design Values for Visually Graded Timbers (5 × 5 and Larger)*. Table 4D covers all species groups including Southern Pine.

Allowable stresses for B&S are generally different from the allowable stresses for P&T. This requires a complete listing of values for all of the stress grades for both of these size categories. Furthermore, it should be noted that there are two sets of design values for both B&S and P&T in three species groups: Douglas Fir-Larch, Hem-Fir, and Western Cedars. This is the result of differences in grading rules from two agencies.

As noted, the lumber grading rules reflect the *anticipated use* of a wood member based on its size, but no such restriction exists for the *actual use* of the member by the designer. In other words, lumber that falls into the B&S size category was originally anticipated to be used as a bending member. As a rectangular member, a B&S bending about its strong axis is a more efficient beam (because of its larger section modulus) than a square (or essentially square) member such as a P&T. However, allowable stresses are tabulated for tension, compression, and bending for *all size categories*. The designer may, therefore, use a B&S in any of these applications.

Although size and use are related, it must be emphasized again that the *allowable stresses depend on the size* of a member rather than its *use*. Thus, a member in the P&T size category is always graded as a P&T even though it could possibly be used as a beam. Therefore, if a 6 × 8 is used as a beam, the allowable bending stress for a P&T applies. Similarly, if a 6 × 10 is used as a column, the compression value for a B&S must be used.

The general notation used in the design of wood structures is introduced in the next section. This is followed by a review of a number of the adjustment factors required in wood design.

4.13   Notation for ASD

The design of wood structures under the 1991 NDS follows the principles known as *allowable stress design* (ASD). A *load and resistance factor design*

(LRFD) specification for engineered wood construction is in the final development stages (Sec. 4.23). It is expected that ASD will continue to be the primary method used in the near future. This will be followed by a transition period when both methods may be applied in design practice. It is expected that eventually the LRFD method will become the primary design technique.

The notation system for stress calculations in ASD for wood structures is very similar to that used in the design of steel structures according to the ASD steel manual (Ref. 11.1). However, wood is a unique structural material, and its proper use may require a number of adjustment factors. Although the basic concepts of timber design are very straightforward, the many possible adjustment factors can make wood design cumbersome in the beginning. The conversion of the NDS to an *equation format* has provided much better organization of this material.

In allowable stress design, actual stresses in a member are computed as the structure is subjected to a set of Code-required loads. Generally speaking, the forces and stresses in wood structures are computed according to the principles of engineering mechanics and strength of materials. The same basic linear elastic theory is applied in the design of wood beams as is applied to the design of steel members in ASD. The unique properties of wood members and the differences in behavior are usually taken into account with adjustment factors.

For consistency, it is highly recommended that the adjustment factors for wood design be kept as multiplying factors for allowable stresses. An alternative approach of using the stress adjustments to modify design loads can lead to confusion. The modification of design loads with wood design adjustment factors is not recommended. The general notation system for use in ASD for wood structures is summarized in Example 4.8.

EXAMPLE 4.8   Symbols for Stresses and Adjustment Factors

Symbols for use in wood design have been standardized in the 1991 NDS.

Actual Stresses

Actual stresses are calculated from known loads and member sizes. These stresses are given the symbol of lowercase f, and a subscript is added to indicate the type of stress. For example, the axial tension stress in a member is calculated as the force divided by the cross-sectional area. The notation is

$$f_t = \frac{P}{A}$$

Tabulated Stresses

The stresses listed in the tables in the NDS Supplement are referred to as *tabulated stresses* or *tabulated design values*. All the tabulated stresses (except modulus of elasticity) include reductions for safety. The values of modulus of elasticity listed in the tables are average values and do not include reductions for safety. Tabulated stresses are given the symbol of an uppercase F, and a subscript is added to indicate the type of stress. For example, F_t represents the tabulated tension stress parallel to grain. The modulus of elasticity is assigned the traditional symbol E.

Allowable Stresses

Tabulated stresses for wood simply represent a starting point in the determination of the allowable stress for a particular design. *Allowable stresses* are determined by multiplying the tabulated stresses by the appropriate adjustment factors. The term "allowable design *value*" is perhaps more general than "allowable *stress*" in that it can properly be applied to quantities that do not have a factor of safety (such as modulus of elasticity) as well as to those that do.

It is highly desirable to have a notation system that permits the designer to readily determine whether a design value in a set of calculations is a *tabulated* or an *allowable* property. A prime is simply added to the symbol for the tabulated stress to indicate that the necessary adjustments have been applied to obtain the allowable stress. For example, the allowable tension stress is obtained by multiplying the tabulated value for tension by the appropriate modification factors:

$$F_t' = F_t \times (\text{product of adjustment factors})$$

For a design to be acceptable, the actual stress must be less than or equal to the allowable stress:

$$f_t \leq F_t'$$

On the other hand, if the actual stress exceeds the allowable stress, the design needs to be revised.

The following design values are included in the NDS Supplement:

Design value	Symbol for tabulated design value	Symbol for allowable (adjusted) design value
Bending stress	F_b	F_b'
Tension stress parallel to grain	F_t	F_t'
Shear stress parallel to grain	F_v	F_v'
Compression stress perpendicular to grain	$F_{c\perp}$	$F_{c\perp}'$
Compression stress parallel to grain	F_c	F_c'
Modulus of elasticity	E	E'

Adjustment Factors

The adjustment factors in wood design are usually given the symbol of an uppercase C, and one or more subscripts are added to indicate the purpose of the adjustment. Some of the subscripts are uppercase letters, and others are lowercase. Therefore, it is important to pay close attention to the form of the subscript, because simply changing from an uppercase to a lowercase subscript can change the meaning of the adjustment factor. Some of the possible adjustment factors for use in determining allowable design values are

$$C_D = \text{load duration factor}$$

$$C_M = \text{wet service factor (previously known as moisture content factor)}$$

C_F = size factor

C_{fu} = flat use factor

C_f = form factor

C_t = temperature factor

C_r = repetitive member factor

C_H = shear stress factor

These adjustment factors do not apply to all tabulated design values. In addition, other adjustments may be necessary in certain types of problems. For example, the column stability factor C_P is required in the design of wood columns. The factors listed here are simply representative, and the additional adjustment factors are covered in the chapters where they are needed.

The large number of factors is an attempt to remind the designer to not overlook something that can affect the performance of a structure. However, in many practical design situations, a number of adjustment factors may have a value of 1.0. In such a case, the adjustment is said to *default to unity*. Thus, in many common designs, the problem will not be as complex as the long list of adjustment factors would make it appear.

A comprehensive summary of the modification factors for design values for *wood members* is given in NDS Table 2.3.1, *Applicability of Adjustment Factors*. A similar table is provided inside the front cover of this book for quick reference. A summary of the factors for use in the design of mechanical fasteners is given in NDS Table 7.3.1, *Applicability of Adjustment Factors for Connections*. A similar table for the types of *wood connections* covered in this book is provided inside the back cover for convenience.

Some of the adjustment factors will cause the tabulated stress to decrease, and others will cause the stress to increase. When factors that reduce strength are considered, a larger member size will be required to support a given load. On the other hand, when circumstances exist which produce increased strength, smaller, more economical members can result if these factors are taken into consideration. The point here is that a number of items can affect the strength of wood. These items *must* be considered in design when they result in a reduction of member capacity. Factors which increase the calculated strength of a member *may* be considered in the design.

This discussion emphasizes that a *conservative* approach (i.e., in the direction of greater safety) in structural design is the general rule. Factors which cause member sizes to increase *must* be considered. Factors which cause them to decrease *may* be considered or ignored. The question of whether the latter *can* be ignored has to do with economics. It may not be practical to ignore reductions in member sizes that result from a beneficial set of conditions.

Most adjustments for wood design are handled as a string of multiplying factors that are used to convert tabulated stresses to allowable stresses for a given set of design circumstances. However, to avoid an excessive number of coefficients, often only those coefficients which have an effect on the final design are shown in calculations. In other words, if an adjustment has no effect on a stress value (i.e., it defaults to $C = 1.0$), the factor is often omitted from design calculations.

On the other hand, it should be noted that a number of adjustment factors have been in the NDS for many years. Until the equation format was introduced in the 1991 NDS, these factors were not given a mathematical notation, and many designers omitted them from structural calculations even though the adjustments should have been used. In this book the adjustment factors will generally be shown, including those with values of unity. A general summary of adjustment factors is usually part of a computer evaluation of allowable stresses. The tables inside the front and back covers of this book provide a convenient summary of adjustment factors for allowable stresses in wood members and allowable loads on wood connections.

The adjustment factors mentioned in Example 4.8 are described in the remainder of this chapter. Others are covered in the chapters that deal with specific problems.

4.14   Wet Service Factor C_M

The moisture content of wood and its relationship to strength were described in Sec. 4.7. Tabulated design stresses in NDS Supplement generally apply to wood that is used in a *dry condition,* as in most covered structures.

For sawn lumber, the tabulated values apply to members with an equilibrium moisture content (EMC) of 19 percent or less. Values apply whether the lumber is manufactured S-DRY or S-GRN. If the moisture content in service will exceed 19 percent for an extended period of time, the tabulated values are to be multiplied by an appropriate *wet service factor* C_M. Note that the subscript M refers to moisture.

For *member stresses in sawn lumber,* the appropriate values of C_M are obtained from the summary of *Adjustment Factors* at the beginning of each table in the NDS Supplement (i.e., at the beginning of Tables 4A to 4E). In most cases, C_M is less than 1.0 when the moisture content exceeds 19 percent. The exceptions are noted in the tables for C_M. For lumber used at a moisture content of 19 percent or less, the default value of $C_M = 1.0$ applies.

In the past, lumber grade marked MC15 was permitted use of a C_M greater than 1.0, but as a result of the In-Grade Program, this has been deleted from the 1991 NDS. For some grades of Southern Pine the wet service factor has been incorporated into the tabulated values, and for these cases the use of an additional C_M is not appropriate.

For *connection design,* the moisture content at the time of fabrication of the connection *and* the moisture content in service are both used to evaluate C_M. Values of C_M for connection design are summarized in NDS Table 7.3.3.

For *glulam members* (Chap. 5), tabulated stresses apply to MC values of less than 16 percent (that is, $C_M = 1.0$). For a MC of 16 percent or greater, use of C_M less than 1.0 is required. Values of C_M for glulam members are given in the summary of *Adjustment Factors* preceding NDS Supplement Tables 5A and 5B.

4.15 Load Duration Factor C_D

Wood has a unique structural property. It can support higher stresses if the loads are applied for a short period of time. This is particularly significant when one realizes that if an overload occurs, it is probably the result of a temporary load.

All tabulated design stresses and nominal fastener design values for connections apply to *normal* duration loading. In fact, the tables in the NDS generally remind the designer that the published values apply to "normal load duration and dry service conditions." This, together with the equation format of the 1991 NDS, should highlight the need for the designer to account for other conditions. The load duration factor C_D is the adjustment factor used to convert *tabulated* stresses and nominal fastener values to *allowable* values based on the time of loading.

In other words, C_D converts values for normal duration to design values for other durations of loading. Normal duration is taken as 10 years, and floor live loads are conservatively associated with this time of loading. Because tabulated stresses apply directly to floor live loads, $C_D = 1.0$ for this type of loading. For other loads, the duration factor lies in the range $0.9 \leq C_D \leq 2.0$. It should be noted that C_D applies to all tabulated design values except compression perpendicular to grain $F_{c\perp}$ and modulus of elasticity E.

The historical basis for the load duration factor is the curve shown in Fig. 4.13. See Example 4.9. The load duration factor is plotted on the vertical axis versus the accumulated duration of load on the horizontal axis. This graph appears in the *Wood Handbook* (Ref. 4.1), the TCM, and in the NDS Appendix B. Over the years this plot has become known as the *Madison Curve* (the FPL is located in Madison, Wisconsin), and its use has been integrated into design practice since the 1940s. The durations associated with the various design loads are shown on the graph and in the summary below the graph.

The term "duration of load" refers to the total *accumulated* length of time that a load is applied during the life of a structure. Furthermore, in considering duration, it is the *full design load* that is of concern, and not the length of time over which a portion of the load may be applied. For example, it is obvious that some wind or air movement is almost always present. However, in assigning C_D for wind, the duration is taken as the total length of time over which the design *maximum* wind force will occur.

A major change was introduced in the 1991 NDS regarding the load duration factor assigned to *wind and seismic* forces (NDS Sec. 2.3.2). In the past a 1-day duration was conservatively assumed for wind and seismic forces, and a corresponding duration factor of $C_D = 1.33$ was the traditional value. The possible confusion about the *load duration factor* of 1.33 for these lateral forces *and* the *load combination factor* of the same magnitude is discussed in Secs. 2.8 and 16.2.

Wind forces in the UBC and in the other model building codes are now based on the wind force provisions in ASCE 7-88 (Ref. 5.1). Research indicates that the peak wind forces in ASCE 7 have a cumulative duration of a few seconds. In addition, strong-motion earthquake effects are typically less than a minute in duration. Because of these duration studies, the 1991 NDS has adopted an accumulated duration of 10 minutes for wind and seismic forces. This shifts the load duration factor for wind and seismic forces to $C_D = 1.6$ on the Madison Curve. See Ref. 7.1 for additional background on the change of C_D from 1.33 to 1.6.

The designer is again cautioned to verify local acceptance of $C_D = 1.6$ before using it in practice. Values of C_D for other loads have not changed from those that have been used for many years.

EXAMPLE 4.9   Load Duration Factor

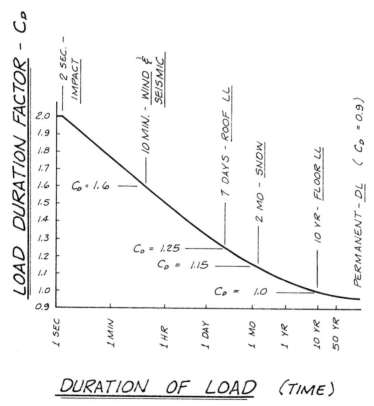

Figure 4.13   Madison curve.

Shortest-duration load in combination	C_D
Dead load	0.9
Floor live load	1.0
Snow load	1.15
Roof live load	1.25
Wind or seismic force	1.6
Impact	2.0

NOTES: 1. Check all Code-required load and force combinations. 2. The C_D associated with the shortest-duration load or force in a given combination is used to adjust the tabulated stress. 3. The critical combination of loads and forces is the one that requires the largest-size structural member.

It was previously recommended that adjustment factors, including C_D, be applied as multiplying factors for adjusting tabulated stresses. Modifications of actual stresses or modifications of applied loads should not be used to account for duration of load. A consistent approach in the application of C_D to the tabulated stress will avoid confusion.

The stresses that occur in a structure are usually not the result of a single applied load (see Sec. 2.16 for a discussion of Code-required load combinations). Quite to the contrary, they are normally caused by a combination of loads and forces that act simultaneously. The question then arises about which load duration factor should be applied when checking a stress caused by a given combination. It should be noted that the load duration factor applies to the *entire combination of loads* and not just to that portion of the stress caused by a load of a particular duration. The C_D to be used is the one associated with the *shortest*-duration load or force in a given combination.

For example, consider the possible load combinations on a floor beam that also carries a column load from the roof. What are the appropriate load duration factors for the various load combinations? If stresses under the DL alone are checked, $C_D = 0.9$. If stresses under (DL + FLL) are checked, the shortest-duration load in the combination is FLL, and $C_D = 1.0$. For (DL + FLL + snow), $C_D = 1.15$. If the structure is located in an area where snow loads do not occur, the last combination becomes (DL + FLL + RLL), and $C_D = 1.25$.

In this manner, it is possible for a smaller load of longer duration (with a small C_D) to be more critical than a larger load of shorter duration (with a large C_D). Whichever combination of loads, together with the appropriate load duration factor, produces the largest member size is the one that must be used in the design of the structure. It may be necessary, therefore, to check several different combinations of loads to determine which combination governs the design. With some practice, the designer can often tell by inspection which combinations need to be checked. In many cases, only one or possibly two combinations need be checked. See Example 4.10.

EXAMPLE 4.10   Comparison of Load Combinations

Determine the design loads and the critical load combination for the beam in Fig. 4.14. The tributary width to the beam and the design unit loads are given.

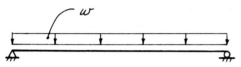

Figure 4.14

$$\text{Tributary width} = 10 \text{ ft}$$

$$\text{Roof DL} = 20 \text{ psf}$$

$$\text{Roof LL} = 16 \text{ psf}$$

Part a

Load combination 1 (DL alone):

$$w_{DL} = 20 \times 10 = 200 \text{ lb/ft}$$

$$C_D = 0.90$$

Load combination 2 (DL + RLL):

$$w_{TL} = (20 + 16)10 = 360 \text{ lb/ft}$$

$$C_D = 1.25$$

The tabulated stress for the beam is to be multiplied by 0.90 for load combination 1 and 1.25 for load combination 2. Theoretically both load combinations must be considered. However, with some practice, the designer will be able to tell from the relative magnitude of the loads which combination is critical. For example, 360 lb/ft is so large in comparison with 200 lb/ft that load combination 2 will be critical. Therefore, calculations for load combination 1 are not required. If it cannot be determined by inspection which loading is critical, calculations for both load cases should be performed.

In some cases calculations for two or more cases *must* be performed. Often this occurs in members with combined axial and bending loads. These types of problems are considered in Chap. 7.

Part b

Show calculations which verify the critical load case for the beam in part *a* without complete stress calculations. Remove "duration" by dividing the design loads by the appropriate C_D factors.*

Load combination 1:

$$\frac{w_{\text{DL}}}{C_D} = \frac{200}{0.9} = 222 \text{ lb/ft}†$$

Load combination 2:

$$\frac{w_{\text{TL}}}{C_D} = \frac{360}{1.25} = 288 \text{ lb/ft}†$$

$$222 < 288$$

$$\therefore \text{ load combination 2 governs}$$

When designers first encounter the adjustment for duration of load, they like to have a *system* for determining the critical loading combination. See Example 4.10, part *b*. Essentially the system involves removing the question of load duration from the problem. If the sum of the loads in a given combination is divided by the C_D for the combination, duration is removed from the load. If this is done for each required load combination, the resulting loads can be compared. The largest modified load represents the critical combination.

This method is not foolproof. The C_D has full effect for short columns and no effect for very long columns. Thus, the method is accurate for short columns, and it becomes less appropriate as the length increases. A similar caution applies to laterally unsupported beams.

There is a second objection to the system just described. It runs counter to the recommendation that modification factors be applied to the tabulated stress and not to the design loads. Thus, if this analysis is used, the calculations should be done separately (perhaps on scrap paper). Once the critical combination is known, the actual design loads (not modified) can be used in formal calculations, and C_D can be applied to the tabulated stresses in the usual manner.

---

*This method is appropriate for short columns and beams with full lateral support. The effect of C_D decreases as the unbraced length of these members increases. When Euler-type buckling governs, the loads should be compared without dividing by C_D.

†These modified loads are used to determine the critical load combination only. Actual design loads (for example, $w = 360$ lb/ft should be used in calculations, and $C_D = 1.25$ should be applied to tabulated stresses.

4.16   Size Factor C_F

It has been known for some time that the size of a wood member has an *effect* on its *unit* strength (stress). This behavior is taken into account by the *size factor* C_F (NDS Sec. 4.3.2). In previous editions of the NDS, a size factor was applied only to allowable bending stress in larger-size members (i.e., Timbers and glulams) that had depths greater than 12 in. The 1991 NDS has an expanded number of size-effect factors. Size factors now apply to both *Dimension lumber* and *Timbers*.

Visually graded Dimension lumber.   It was previously noted that the tables of design stresses for visually graded dimension lumber have been simplified in the 1991 NDS. However, the In-Grade Testing Program led to a conclusion that there is a size effect in Dimension lumber, and this effect occurs in a number of design properties. The goal of simplifying the stress tables *and* including the expanded size effects was made possible by the introduction of a number of *size factors* for Dimension lumber. The 1991 NDS Supplement provides a size-effect factor C_F for tension stress parallel to grain, compression stress parallel to grain, and bending stress.

The size factors C_F for most species of visually graded Dimension lumber are summarized in the *Adjustment Factor* section that precedes NDS Supplement Table 4A. The size factors for F_b, F_t, and F_c are given in a table which depends on the stress *grade* and the *width* (depth) of the piece of lumber. For bending stress, the *thickness* of the member also affects the size factor.

Tabulated stresses for use with these expanded size factors are termed "*base* design values" in the title of NDS Supplement Table 4A. In other words, the allowable stresses for a given piece of Dimension lumber are obtained by multiplying *base values* by the appropriate size factors. The concept of base design values lends itself to the evaluation of allowable stresses in a computer program or microcomputer spreadsheet template.

The size factors for Southern Pine Dimension lumber are handled somewhat differently. For Southern Pine, a number of the size factors have been incorporated into the tabulated values given in NDS Supplement Table 4B. Thus, the tabulated values for Southern Pine are said to be "size-specific," and the concept of base design values is not included in the table for Southern Pine.

Unfortunately, the size-specific tables for Southern Pine do not completely avoid the use of a C_F multiplier. Bending values in Table 4B apply to lumber that has a nominal thickness of 2 in. A size factor of $C_F = 1.1$ is provided for F_b if the lumber being considered has a nominal thickness of 4 in. instead of 2 in. In addition, a size factor of $C_F = 0.9$ is provided for F_b, F_t, and F_c for Dimension lumber that has a width greater than 12 in.

Refer to NDS Supplement Tables 4A and 4B for values of C_F for Dimension lumber and for a comparison of base design values with size-specific design values.

Timbers. The size factor for Timbers remains unchanged from that used in previous editions of the NDS. The C_F for Timbers applies only to F_b. Essentially the size factor reflects the fact that as the *depth* of a beam increases, the *unit strength* (and correspondingly the allowable stress) decreases. When the depth d of a timber exceeds 12 in., the size factor is defined by the expression

$$C_F = \left(\frac{12}{d}\right)^{1/9}$$

For members that are less than 12 in. deep, the size factor defaults to unity: $C_F = 1.0$.

At one time this size factor was also used for glulam beams. However, the size factor for glulams has been replaced with the volume-effect factor C_V (Chap. 5).

4.17 Repetitive Member Factor C_r

Many wood structures have a series of closely spaced parallel members. The members are often connected together by sheathing or decking. In this arrangement, the performance of the *system* does not depend solely on the capacity of an individual member. This can be contrasted to an engineered wood structure with relatively large structural members spaced a greater distance apart. The failure of one large member would essentially be a failure of the system.

The system performance of a series of small, closely spaced wood members is recognized in the 1991 NDS by providing a 15 percent increase in the tabulated bending stress F_b. This increase is provided by the *repetitive-member factor C_r* (NDS Sec. 4.3.4). It applies only to F_b and only to Dimension lumber used in a repetitive system. A *repetitive-member system* is defined as one that has

1. Three or more parallel members of Dimension lumber

2. Members spaced not more than 24 in. on center

3. Members connected together by a load-distributing element such as roof, floor, or wall sheathing

For a repetitive-member system, the tabulated F_b may be multiplied by $C_r = 1.15$. For all other framing systems and stresses $C_r = 1.0$.

The repetitive-member factor recognizes system performance. If one member should become overloaded, parallel members come into play. The load is distributed by sheathing to adjacent members, and the load is shared by a number of beams. The repetitive-member factor is not applied to the larger sizes of wood members (i.e., Timbers and glulams) because these large members are not normally spaced closely enough together to qualify as a repetitive member.

When a concentrated load is supported by a deck which distributes the load to parallel beams, the entire concentrated load need not be assumed to be supported by one member. NDS Sec. 15.1 provides a method for the *Lateral Distribution of a Concentrated Load* to adjacent parallel beams. According to Ref. 9.2, the single-member bending stress (that is, $C_r = 1.0$) applies if the load distribution in NDS Sec. 15.1 is used.

4.18 Flat Use Factor C_{fu}

Except for decking, tabulated bending stresses for Dimension lumber apply to wood members that are stressed in flexure about the strong axis of the cross section. The NDS refers to this conventional type of beam loading as *edgewise* use or *load applied to narrow face* of the member.

In a limited number of situations, Dimension lumber may be loaded in bending about the minor axis of the cross section. The terms *flatwise use* and *load applied to wide face* describe this application. When members are loaded in bending about the weak axis, the tabulated bending stresses F_b may be increased by multiplying by the *flat-use factor* C_{fu} (NDS Sec. 4.3.3). Numerical values for C_{fu} are given in the *Adjustment Factor* sections of NDS Supplement Tables 4A to 4C.

Tabulated bending stresses for Beams and Stringers also apply to the usual case of bending about the x axis of the cross section. The 1991 NDS does not provide a flat-use factor for bending about the y axis. It is recommended that the designer contact the appropriate rules-writing agency for assistance if this situation is encountered.

The tabulated bending stress for a glulam beam that is stressed in bending about the weak axis is given the symbol F_{by}. Values of F_{by} apply to glulams that have a cross-sectional dimension *parallel to the wide face of the laminations* of 12 in. For beams that are less than 12 in. wide, the value of F_{by} may be increased by a flat-use factor. For values of C_{fu} for glulams, see NDS Supplement Tables 5A and 5B.

4.19 Shear Stress Factor C_H

The presence of splits, checks, and shakes reduces the flexural shear capacity of a wood member. Although the actual vertical shear stress and the actual horizontal shear stress in a beam are equal, the shear strength of a wood beam is much less parallel to the grain than across the grain. For this reason, the term *horizontal shear* is often used to refer to the flexural shear stress that is parallel to the grain.

Tabulated values of shear stress F_v for sawn lumber reflect the assumption that the member may be split along its full length. The conservative values for F_v may be increased when the amount of splitting in a member is known *and* when no increase in splitting is expected in service. Generally the amount of splitting will be known when an existing member can be inspected. Estimates about anticipated splitting can be made by evaluating the service conditions (e.g., dry use *or* exposed to the weather).

The increase in shear capacity for reduced splitting is provided by multiplying the tabulated shear stress by the *shear stress factor* C_H. Values of C_H are given in the *Adjustment Factor* section of NDS Supplement Tables 4A to 4D.

4.20 Temperature Factor C_t

The strength of a member is affected by the temperature of the wood in service. Strength is increased as the temperature cools below the normal temperature range found in most buildings. On the other hand, the strength decreases as temperatures are increased. The *temperature factor* C_t is the multiplier that is used to reduce tabulated stresses if higher than normal temperatures are encountered in a design situation.

Tabulated design values apply to wood used in the ordinary temperature range and perhaps *occasionally* heated up to 150°F. Prolonged exposure to temperatures above 150°F may result in a *permanent* loss of strength. Reductions in strength caused by heating below 150°F are generally reversible. In other words, strength is recovered as the temperature is reduced to the normal range.

Values of C_t are given NDS Sec. 2.3.4. The first temperature range that requires a reduction in design values is $100°F < T < 125°F$. At first this seems to be a rather low temperature range. After all, temperatures in many of the warmer areas of the country often exceed 100°F. In these locations, is it necessary to reduce the tabulated design stresses for members in a wood roof system? The answer is that it is generally *not* considered necessary. Members in roof structures subjected to *temporarily* elevated temperatures are not usually subjected to the *full* design load under these conditions. For example, snow loads will not be present at these elevated temperatures, and roof live loads occur infrequently. Furthermore, any loss in strength should be regained when the temperature returns to normal.

For these and other reasons, $C_t = 1.0$ is normally used in the design of ordinary wood-frame buildings. However, in an industrial plant there may be operations that cause temperatures to be consistently elevated. Structural members in these types of situations may require use of a temperature factor less than 1. Additional information is given in NDS Appendix C.

4.21 Form Factor C_f

The form factor C_f has been in the specification for wood design for many years, but its use is very limited. The purpose of the form factor is to adjust the tabulated bending stress F_b for certain nonrectangular cross sections. The 1991 NDS provides two form factors (NDS Sec. 2.3.8): one for circular cross sections, and one for a square beam loaded in the plane of the diagonal (i.e., a beam with a diamond cross section).

Circular cross sections are common in wood design in the case of round timber piles and poles. Timber piles are used for foundation structures, and the most common application of poles is for utility structures. Poles are also used as the supporting frame for both vertical loads and lateral forces in *pole buildings.*

Pole buildings originated in farm applications such as sheds. Other uses of pole buildings include elevated housing in coastal areas that are subject to flooding. The framing for the lower floor level in this type of housing is chosen to be above high-water level during storm conditions. The floor and roof framing is attached to vertical poles that are embedded in earth.

Another use of pole framing for housing is on property with a fairly steep slope. Again, floor and roof framing is attached to vertical poles. In this case, the advantage of pole construction is that it does not require extensive grading of the property and the construction of retaining walls.

Timber piles and poles usually involve wood that is in contact with soil or concrete. Consequently these members are usually treated with a pressure preservative (Sec. 4.9). Properties for treated round timber piles are given in NDS Table 6A *Design Values for Treated Round Timber Piles.* It should be noted that the bending stresses in NDS Table 6A already have the form factor C_f included (NDS Sec. 6.3.9). Therefore, the designer should not apply $C_f = 1.18$ for circular cross sections to the values of F_b given in NDS Table 6A. For untreated piles see NDS Sec. 6.3.5.

The design of round timber poles and piles is beyond the scope of this book. Information can be obtained from the American Wood Preservers Institute (AWPI). See the list of addresses in the Nomenclature section of this book for the address of AWPI.

4.22   Design Problem: Allowable Stresses

If one examines NDS Table 2.3.1, *Applicability of Adjustment Factors* (see the inside front cover of this book), it will be noticed that the temperature factor C_t applies to all design values. However, it should be realized that this table shows what adjustments *may* be required under certain conditions. It simply serves as a reminder to the designer to not overlook a necessary adjustment. The table says nothing about the *frequency of use* of an adjustment factor.

It was observed in Sec. 4.20 that the temperatures in most wood buildings do not require a reduction in design values. Thus, C_t is a factor that is rarely used in the design of typical wood buildings, and the default value of $C_t = 1.0$ often applies. On the other hand, the load duration factor C_D is a common adjustment factor that is used in the design of practically all wood structures. In this case, $C_D = 1.0$ only when the floor live load controls the design.

Several examples are given to illustrate the use of the NDS tables and the required adjustment factors. Complete design problems are given later in this book, and the current examples simply emphasize obtaining the correct *allowable* stress. The first requirement is to obtain the correct *tabulated* value from the NDS Supplement for the given size, grade, and species group. The second step is to apply the appropriate *adjustment* factors.

Example 4.11 deals with four different sizes of the same stress grade (No. 1) in a single species group (Douglas Fir-Larch). Dimensions are obtained from NDS Supplement Tables 1A and 1B. The example clearly shows the effect of a number of variables. Several different loading conditions and stress adjustment factors are illustrated. The reader is encouraged to verify the tabulated design values and the adjustment factors in the NDS.

Some stress adjustment factors in NDS Table 2.3.1 are not shown in this example. These factors do not apply to the given problem. Other factors may have a default value of unity and are shown for information purposes. Note that C_D does not apply to $F_{c\perp}$ or E.

EXAMPLE 4.11   Determination of Allowable Stresses

Determine the *allowable* design stresses for the four members given below. All members are No. 1 DF-L. Bending loads will be about the strong axis of the cross section (load applied to narrow face). Bracing conditions are such that buckling is not a concern. Consider dry-service conditions (EMC ≤ 19 percent) unless otherwise indicated. Normal temperature conditions apply.

For each member a *single* load duration factor C_D will be used to adjust the design values for the given load combination. In practice, a number of loading conditions must be checked, and each load case will have an appropriate C_D. Limiting each member to a single-load case is done for simplicity in this example.

Part a

Roof rafters are 2 × 8 at 24 in. o.c., and they directly support the roof sheathing. Loads are (DL + RLL).

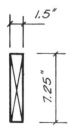

Figure 4.15a A 2 × 8 is a Dimension lumber size.

Tabulated design values of visually graded DF-L *Dimension lumber* are obtained from NDS Supplement Table 4A. The framing arrangement qualifies for the 15 percent increase in bending stress for repetitive members. The load duration factor is 1.25 for the combination of (DL + RLL). Dimension lumber requires a size-effect factor for F_b, F_t, and F_c.

$$F'_b = F_b(C_D \times C_M \times C_t \times C_F \times C_r)$$

$$= 1000(1.25 \times 1.0 \times 1.0 \times 1.2 \times 1.15)$$

$$= 1725 \text{ psi}$$

$$F'_t = F_t(C_D \times C_M \times C_t \times C_F)$$

$$= 675(1.25 \times 1.0 \times 1.0 \times 1.2) = 1012 \text{ psi}$$

$$F'_v = F_v(C_D \times C_M \times C_t)$$

$$= 95(1.25 \times 1.0 \times 1.0) = 119 \text{ psi}$$

$$F'_{c\perp} = F_{c\perp}(C_M \times C_t) = 625(1.0 \times 1.0) = 625 \text{ psi}$$

$$F'_c = F_c(C_D \times C_M \times C_t \times C_F)$$

$$= 1450(1.25 \times 1.0 \times 1.0 \times 1.05) = 1903 \text{ psi}$$

$$E' = E(C_M \times C_t)$$

$$= 1,700,000(1.0 \times 1.0) = 1,700,000 \text{ psi}$$

Part b

Roof beams are 4 × 10 at 4 ft-0 in. o.c. Loads are (DL + SL).

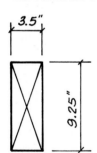

Figure 4.15b A 4 × 10 is a Dimension lumber size.

Design values for visually graded DF-L *Dimension lumber* are again obtained from NDS Supplement Table 4A. A 4-ft framing module exceeds the 24-in. spacing limit for repetitive members, and $C_r = 1.0$. The load duration factor is 1.15 for the combination of (DL + SL).

$$F'_b = F_b(C_D \times C_M \times C_t \times C_F \times C_r)$$

$$= 1000(1.15 \times 1.0 \times 1.0 \times 1.2 \times 1.0) = 1380 \text{ psi}$$

$$F'_t = F_t(C_D \times C_M \times C_t \times C_F)$$

$$= 675(1.15 \times 1.0 \times 1.0 \times 1.1) = 854 \text{ psi}$$

$$F'_v = F_v(C_D \times C_M \times C_t)$$

$$= 95(1.15 \times 1.0 \times 1.0) = 109 \text{ psi}$$

$$F'_{c\perp} = F_{c\perp}(C_M \times C_t) = 625(1.0 \times 1.0) = 625 \text{ psi}$$

$$F'_c = F_c(C_D \times C_M \times C_t \times C_F)$$

$$= 1450(1.15 \times 1.0 \times 1.0 \times 1.0) = 1667 \text{ psi}$$

$$E' = E(C_M \times C_t)$$

$$= 1,700,000(1.0 \times 1.0) = 1,700,000 \text{ psi}$$

Part c

A 6 × 16 floor beam supports loads from both the floor and the roof. Several load combinations have been studied, and the critical loading is (DL + FLL + RLL).

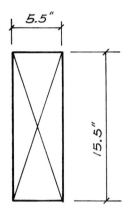

5.5″

15.5″

Figure 4.15c A 6 × 16 is a Beams and Stringers size.

A B&S has a minimum cross-sectional dimension of 5 in., and the cross section is *more* than 2 in. out of square. *Beams and Stringers* sizes are described in Example 4.6 (Sec. 4.12). Tabulated stresses are obtained from NDS Supplement Table 4D. To be conservative, take the smaller tabulated stresses listed for the two sets of grading rules (WCLIB and WWPA). In this problem the values are the same for both.

The load duration factor for the combination of loads is based on the shortest-duration load in the combination. Therefore, $C_D = 1.25$. Unlike Dimension lumber, large members have one size factor, and it applies to bending stress only. When the depth of a Timber exceeds 12 in., the size factor is given by the following expression

$$C_F = \left(\frac{12}{d}\right)^{1/9} = \left(\frac{12}{15.5}\right)^{1/9} = 0.972$$

$$F'_b = F_b(C_D \times C_M \times C_t \times C_F)$$

$$= 1350(1.25 \times 1.0 \times 1.0 \times 0.972) = 1640 \text{ psi}$$

$$F'_t = F_t(C_D \times C_M \times C_t)$$

$$= 675(1.25 \times 1.0 \times 1.0) = 844 \text{ psi}$$

$$F'_v = F_v(C_D \times C_M \times C_t)$$

$$= 85(1.25 \times 1.0 \times 1.0) = 106 \text{ psi}$$

$$F'_{c\perp} = F_{c\perp}(C_M \times C_t) = 625(1.0 \times 1.0) = 625 \text{ psi}$$

$$F_c' = F_c(C_D \times C_M \times C_t)$$

$$= 925(1.25 \times 1.0 \times 1.0) = 1156 \text{ psi}$$

$$E' = E(C_M \times C_t)$$

$$= 1,600,000(1.0 \times 1.0) = 1,600,000 \text{ psi}$$

Part d

A 6 × 8 is used as a column to support a roof. It also supports tributary wind forces, and the critical loading condition has been determined to be (DL + FLL + wind). High-humidity conditions exist, and the moisture content of this member may exceed 19 percent.

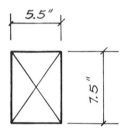

Figure 4.15d A 6 × 8 is a Posts and Timbers size.

A P&T has a minimum cross-sectional dimension of 5 in., and the section is *not more than* 2 in. out of square. *Posts and Timbers* sizes are described in Example 4.6 (Sec. 4.12). Tabulated stresses are obtained from NDS Supplement Table 4D. To be conservative, take the smaller tabulated stresses listed for the two sets of grading rules (WCLIB and WWPA). In this problem the values are the same for both.

The load duration factor for the combination of loads is based on the shortest-duration load in the combination. Therefore, $C_D = 1.6.$* The depth of this member is less than 12 in., and C_F defaults to unity. Recall that for Timbers the size factor applies only to F_b.

$$F_b' = F_b(C_D \times C_M \times C_t \times C_F)$$

$$= 1200(1.6 \times 1.0 \times 1.0 \times 1.0) = 1920 \text{ psi}$$

$$F_t' = F_t(C_D \times C_M \times C_t)$$

$$= 825(1.6 \times 1.0 \times 1.0) = 1320 \text{ psi}$$

$$F_v' = F_v(C_D \times C_M \times C_t)$$

$$= 85(1.6 \times 1.0 \times 1.0) = 136 \text{ psi}$$

$$F_{c\perp}' = F_{c\perp}(C_M \times C_t) = 625(0.67 \times 1.0) = 419 \text{ psi}$$

$$F_c' = F_c(C_D \times C_M \times C_t)$$

$$= 1000(1.6 \times 0.91 \times 1.0) = 1456 \text{ psi}$$

$$E' = E(C_M \times C_t)$$

$$= 1,600,000(1.0 \times 1.0) = 1,600,000 \text{ psi}$$

*Verify local code acceptance before using $C_D = 1.6$ in practice.

4.23   Future Directions in Wood Design

One thing should be clear after the introduction to lumber and the properties of wood given in this chapter. The wood industry is not a static business. If there is a better way of doing something, a better way of doing it will be found. In this book the question of "better" generally refers to developing more accurate methods of structural design, but there is an underlying economic force that drives the system.

It was noted at the beginning of Chap. 4 that many wood-based products that are in widespread use today were unavailable only a few years ago. These include a number of structural-use panels, wood I joists, resawn glulam beams, laminated veneer lumber (LVL), and more recently parallel strand lumber (PSL). A number of these developments, especially in the area of reconstituted wood products, are the result of new technology, and they represent an economic response to environmental concerns. With these products the move is plainly in the direction of *engineered* wood construction.

The design profession is caught in the middle of this development spiral. Anyone who is at all familiar with previous editions of the NDS will testify to the broad changes to the wood design criteria in the 1991 NDS. Changes include new lumber values originating from the In-Grade Test Program, new column and laterally unbraced beam formulas, new interaction equation for members with combined stresses, and an engineering mechanics approach to the design of wood connections. The design equations may be more cumbersome to solve by hand, but this is one of the prices in the move to engineered wood construction. The designer who has to deal with the newer, more involved procedures can get relief through the use of a modern microcomputer. The 1991 NDS is a much better-organized tool and is user-friendly in spite of the somewhat more complicated equations.

The 1991 NDS is based on a deterministic method known as *allowable stress design* (ASD). Some argue that the method should be referred to more appropriately as the *working stress design* (WSD) because the stresses that are computed are based on working or service loads. Both names have been used in the past, but ASD seems to be the term most widely used today.

Another approach to design is based on reliability theory. As with ASD, various terms are used to refer to this alternative system. These include *reliability-based design, probability-based design, limit states design,* and *load and resistance factor design* (LRFD). Of these, *load and resistance factor design* is the approach that is generally agreed upon by the profession as the appropriate technique for use in structural design.

Reinforced concrete has operated under this general design philosophy in the "strength" method for quite some time. The structural-steel industry currently recognizes both ASD and LRFD formats (Refs. 11.1 and 11.2). A fairly recent study indicated that the ASD method for steel design is still the more widely used approach. However, as experience is gained, it is expected that the LRFD will eventually become the accepted design method for structural steel.

The wood industry is also in the process of moving to an LRFD format, but it is a number of years behind the structural-steel industry in making this transition. In mid-1991 the wood industry completed a 3-year project to develop an *LRFD Specification for Engineered Wood Construction.* The document is an effort to produce an industrywide design specification. The LRFD specification was developed by a team from the wood industry, university faculty, and the design profession. It has been subjected to trial use by professionals who are knowledgeable in the area of timber design. The LRFD specification is currently (early 1993) in the hands of an American Society of Civil Engineers (ASCE) committee charged with developing it as a national standard (joint ASCE/ANSI).

Given that the LRFD specification is in the process of being developed, a logical question arises about the need for the sweeping changes in the 1991 NDS. How soon will the 1991 NDS be out of date? Would it make sense to simply wait for the final LRFD specification? To answer these questions, it should be understood that many of the *changes in the 1991 NDS* were introduced *in preparation* for the *LRFD specification.* For example, the yield limit theory for connection design was introduced in the 1991 NDS because it will also be the basis for connection design in the LRFD specification.

The 1991 NDS has undergone many improvements in organization, and it can stand on its own as a modern tool for the design of engineered wood structures based on ASD principles. In addition, the 1991 NDS can be viewed as a useful tool in the transition to an LRFD specification for wood. Although there will be changes in format, many of the formulas in the LRFD specification will be familiar to the designer who has worked with the 1991 NDS.

A brief description about the differences between ASD and LRFD is given now. In ASD, actual stresses are checked to be less than or equal to allowable stresses:

$$\text{Actual stress} \leq \text{allowable stress}$$

It has been noted that a 5 percent exclusion value is the basis for most allowable stresses. Although this approach generally produces safe designs, the reliability differs with each structure. Some wood-based products are highly variable, and others are much less variable. Two examples from this chapter are visually graded sawn lumber and MSR lumber. Visually graded lumber is more variable than MSR lumber, and many other examples can be cited. In addition, current design practice assumes that dead loads, live loads, and lateral forces are known with equal reliability. Obviously this is not the case, because it is possible to predict some loads (e.g., dead loads) much more accurately than others. These differences are not reflected directly in ASD.

The title "load and resistance factor design" is a good description of the reliability-based design procedure. As the name implies, service loads (loads expected under normal service conditions) are multiplied by appropriate *load factors,* and the nominal resistance of the structure (such as the calculated moment or shear capacity of a member) is multiplied by appropriate strength-reduction factors *(resistance factors).*

For a structure to be useful, the resistance offered by the structure must equal or exceed the load effects:

$$\phi R \geq \sum \gamma Q \dagger$$

where ϕ = resistance factor
R = nominal calculated resistance of the structure (such as shear or moment capacity)
γ = load factor
Q = effects of service loads (such as the shear or moment in a member)

Resistance factors ϕ are numerically less than unity and are designed to reduce the calculated nominal resistance (strength) of a structure. The purpose of this reduction in calculated strength is to account for resistance uncertainties such as material properties and variability. On the other side of the equation, load factors γ are values greater than unity and are intended to account for the uncertainties of loading. Thus the load factor for dead load is smaller than the load factor for live loads. In addition, load factors can be used to account for the importance of a structure. Designers who are familiar with the strength design of reinforced concrete should have a feel for load and resistance factors.

For additional information on reliability-based design in wood, see Refs. 9.4 and 25.

4.24 Problems

Design values and adjustment factors in the following problems are to be taken from the 1991 NDS. Assume wood will be used in dry-service conditions and at normal temperatures unless otherwise noted.

4.1 *a.* Describe softwoods.
   b. Describe hardwoods.
   c. What types of trees are used for most structural lumber?

---

†In practice, service loads are multiplied by the appropriate load factors, and the factored loads, in turn, increase the *effect* of the applied loads.

4.2   Sketch the cross section of a log. Label and define the following items:
a. Annual ring
b. The two types of wood cells
c. Heartwood and sapwood

4.3   Define the following terms:
a. Moisture content
b. Fiber saturation point
c. Equilibrium moisture content

4.4   Give the moisture content ranges for:
a. Dry lumber
b. Green lumber

4.5   What is the average EMC for an enclosed building in southern California? Cite reference.

4.6   Determine the dressed size, area, moment of inertia, and section modulus for the following members. Give values for both axes. Tables may be used (cite reference).
a. 2 × 4
b. 8 × 8
c. 4 × 10
d. 6 × 16

4.7   a. Give the range of sizes of lumber in Dimension lumber.
b. Give the range of sizes of lumber in Timbers.
c. Briefly summarize why the design values in the NDS Supplement for members in these broad categories are given in separate tables. What tables apply to Dimension lumber and what tables apply to Timbers?

4.8   Give the range of sizes for the following size and use subcategories. In addition, indicate whether these categories are under the general classification of *Dimension lumber* or *Timbers*.
a. Beams and Stringers
b. Structural Light Framing
c. Decking
d. Structural Joists and Planks
e. Posts and Timbers
f. Light Framing
g. Stud

4.9   Briefly describe what is meant by the terms "visually graded sawn lumber" and "machine stress-rated (MSR) lumber." What tables in the NDS Supplement give design values for each? Are there any size distinctions? Explain.

4.10   Assume that the following members are visually graded lumber from a species group other than Southern Pine. Indicate whether the members are a size of Dimension lumber, Beams and Stringers (B&S), or Posts and Timbers

(P&T). Also give the appropriate table in the NDS Supplement for obtaining design values. The list does not include material that is graded as Decking.

a. 10 × 12   e. 2 × 12
b. 14 × 14   f. 6 × 12
c. 4 × 8   g. 8 × 12
d. 4 × 4   h. 8 × 10

4.11 Repeat Prob. 4.10 except the material is Southern Pine.

4.12 What stress grades are listed in the NDS Supplement for visually graded Hem-Fir in the following size categories? Give table reference.

a. Dimension lumber
b. Beams and Stringers (B&S)
c. Posts and Timbers (P&T)

4.13 What stress grades are listed in the NDS Supplement for visually graded Southern Pine in the following size categories? Give table reference.

a. Dimension lumber
b. Beams and Stringers (B&S)
c. Posts and Timbers (P&T)

4.14 Give the tabulated design values for No. 1 DF-L for the following sizes. List values for F_b, F_t, F_v, $F_{c\perp}$, F_c, and E. Give table reference.

a. 10 × 10   e. 2 × 10
b. 12 × 14   f. 6 × 12
c. 4 × 16   g. 6 × 8
d. 4 × 4   h. 10 × 14

4.15 Give the notation for the following stress adjustment factors. In addition, list the design properties (that is, F_b, F_t, F_v, $F_{c\perp}$, F_c, or E) that may require adjustment (NDS Table 2.3.1) by the respective factors.

a. Size factor   e. Temperature factor
b. Form factor   f. Wet service factor
c. Load duration factor   g. Shear stress factor
d. Repetitive member factor h. Flat use factor

4.16 Briefly describe the following adjustments. To what design values do they apply? Give NDS reference for numerical values of adjustment factors.

a. Load duration factor
b. Wet service factor
c. Size factor
d. Repetitive member factor

4.17 What change to the load duration factor C_D was introduced in the 1991 NDS? Briefly explain.

4.18 Regarding wind and seismic forces, distinguish between the terms *load duration factor* and *load combination factor*. Refer to Sec. 2.8 to help answer this question.

4.19 Give the load duration factor C_D associated with the following loads:
  a. Snow
  b. Wind
  c. Floor live load
  d. Roof live load
  e. Dead load

4.20 What tabulated design values for wood, if any, are not subject to adjustment for duration of loading?

4.21 Under what conditions is a *reduction* in tabulated values for wood design required based on duration of loading?

4.22 Above what moisture content is it necessary to reduce the allowable stresses for most species of (*a*) sawn lumber and (*b*) glulam?

4.23 Under what conditions is it necessary to adjust the allowable stresses in wood design for temperature effects? Cite NDS reference for the temperature modification factors.

4.24 Distinguish between pressure-preservative-treated wood and fire-retardant-treated wood. Under what conditions is it necessary to adjust allowable stresses in wood design for the effects of pressure-impregnated chemicals? Where are adjustment factors obtained?

4.25 Should lumber be pressure-treated if it is to be used in an application where it will be continuously submerged in fresh water? Salt water? Explain.

4.26 *Given:* A column in a building is subjected to several different loads, including roof DL = 3 k; roof LL = 5 k; floor DL = 6 k; floor LL = 10 k; and wind force = 10 k (resulting from overturning forces on the lateral-force-resisting system). Assume that the column is a short column, and, therefore, the load duration factor C_D applies. Consider the load combinations described in Sec. 2.16.

  Find: The critical combination of loads.

4.27 *Given:* A column in a building is subjected to several different loads, including roof DL = 10 k; roof LL = 2 k; floor DL = 8 k; floor LL = 10 k; and wind force = 6 k (resulting from overturning forces on the lateral-force-resisting system). Assume that the column is a short column, and, therefore, the load duration factor C_D applies. Consider the load combinations described in Sec. 2.16.

  Find: The critical combination of loads.

4.28 *Given:* A column in a building is subjected to several different loads, including roof DL = 5 k; roof LL = 7 k; floor DL = 6 k; floor LL = 15 k; snow load = 18 k; and wind force = 10 k and seismic force = 12 k (resulting from overturning forces on the lateral-force-resisting system). Assume that the column is a short column, and, therefore, the load duration factor C_D applies. Consider the load combinations described in Sec. 2.16.

Find: The critical combination of loads.

4.29 A column in a structure supports a water tank. The axial load from the tank plus water is P_w, and the axial load resulting from the lateral overturning force is P_l. Because the contents of the tank are present much of the time, the load P_w is considered a permanent load.

Find: The critical load combination for each of the following loadings. Assume that the column is a short column range, and, therefore, the load duration factor C_D applies.
   a. $P_w = 60$ k; $P_l = 10.5$ k
   b. $P_w = 60$ k; $P_l = 40.3$ k
   c. $P_w = 60$ k; $P_l = 55.1$ k

4.30 Determine the tabulated and allowable design values for the following members and loading conditions. All members are No. 2 Hem-Fir. Bending occurs about the strong axis.
   a. Roof joists are 2 × 10 at 16 in. o.c. which directly support the roof sheathing. Loads are (DL + SL).
   b. A 6 × 14 carries an equipment load that can be considered a permanent load.
   c. Purlins in a roof are 4 × 14 at 8 ft o.c. Loads are (DL + RLL).
   d. Floor beams are 4 × 6 at 4 ft o.c. Loads are (DL + FLL). High-humidity conditions exist, and the moisture content may exceed 19 percent.

4.31 Determine the tabulated and allowable design values for the following members and loading conditions. All members are Select Structural Southern Pine. Bending occurs about the strong axis.
   a. Roof joists are 2 × 6 at 24 in. o.c. which directly support the roof sheathing. Loads are (DL + SL).
   b. A 4 × 12 supports (DL + FLL + RLL).
   c. Purlins in a roof are 2 × 10 at 4 ft o.c. Loads are (DL + RLL).
   d. Floor beams are 4 × 10 at 4 ft o.c. Loads are (DL + FLL + wind).

4.32 Estimate the amount of shrinkage that will occur in the depth of the beam in Fig. 4.A. Use the simplified shrinkage approach recommended in Ref. 20. Assume an initial moisture content of 19 percent and a final moisture content of 10 percent.

   NOTE: The top of the wood beams should be set higher than the top of the girder by an amount equal to the estimated shrinkage. After shrinkage, the roof sheathing will be supported by beams and girders that are all at the same elevation. Without this allowance for shrinkage, a wave or bump may be created in the sheathing where it passes over the girder.

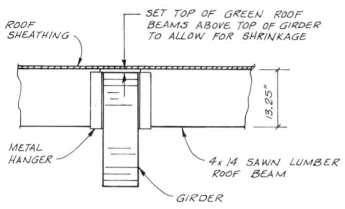

Figure 4.A   Top of roof beams set higher for shrinkage.

4.33   Estimate the total shrinkage that will occur in a four-story building similar to the one in Example 4.3. Floor joists are 2 × 10's instead of 2 × 12's. The initial moisture content can be taken as 19 percent, and the final moisture content is assumed to be 9 percent. All other information is the same as in Example 4.3.

4.34   Use a microcomputer spreadsheet or a database to input the tabulated design values for one or more species (as assigned) of sawn lumber. Include values for both Dimension lumber, Beams-and-Stringers, and Posts-and-Timbers sizes.

   The purpose of the spreadsheet is to list *tabulated* design values (F_b, F_t, F_v, $F_{c\perp}$, F_c, or E) as output for a specific problem with the following input being provided by the user:
   a. Species (if values for more than one species are in spreadsheet or database)
   b. Stress grade of lumber (e.g., Select Structural, No. 1, etc.)
   c. Nominal size of member (for example, 2 × 4, 6 × 12, 6 × 6, etc.)

4.35   Expand or modify the spreadsheet from Prob. 4.34 to develop *allowable* design values. The spreadsheet should be capable of applying all the adjustment factors introduced in Chap. 4 except C_{fu}, C_H, and C_t. The input should be expanded to provide sufficient information to the spreadsheet template so that the appropriate adjustment factors can be computed or drawn from a database or table.

   Output should include a summary of the adjustment factors and the final design values F'_b, F'_t, F'_v, $F'_{c\perp}$, F'_c, or E'. Default values of unity may be listed for any adjustment factor that does not apply.

Structural
Glued Laminated
Timber

5.1 Introduction

Sawn lumber is manufactured in a large number of sizes and grades (Chap. 4) and is used for a wide variety of structural members. However, the cross-sectional dimensions and lengths of these members are limited by the size of the trees available to produce this type of lumber.

When the span becomes long or when the loads become large, the use of sawn lumber may become impractical. In these circumstances (and possibly for architectural reasons) structural glued laminated timber *(glulam)* can be used.

Glulam members are fabricated from relatively thin laminations (nominal 1 and 2 in.) of wood. These laminations can be end-jointed and glued together in such a way to produce wood members of practically any size and length. Lengths of glulam members are limited by handling systems and length restrictions imposed by highway transportation systems rather than by the size of the tree.

This chapter provides an introduction to glulam timber and its design characteristics. The similarities and differences of glulam and sawn wood members are also noted.

5.2 Sizes of Glulam Members

The specifications for glulam permit the fabrication of a member of any width and any depth. However, standard practice has resulted in commonly accepted widths and thicknesses of laminations (see Ref. 3.11). The generally accepted dimensions for glulams fabricated from the Western Species are slightly different from those for Southern Pine glulams. See Fig. 5.1. Because of surfacing requirements, Southern Pine laminations are usually thinner and narrower, although they can be manufactured to the same net sizes as Western Species if necessary. The dimensions given in Fig. 5.1 are net sizes, and the total depth of a member will be a multiple of the lamination thickness.

Straight or slightly curved glulams will be fabricated with 1½-in. (or 1⅜-in.) laminations. If a member is sharply curved, thinner (¾-in.) laminations should be used in the fabrication because smaller built-in stresses will result.

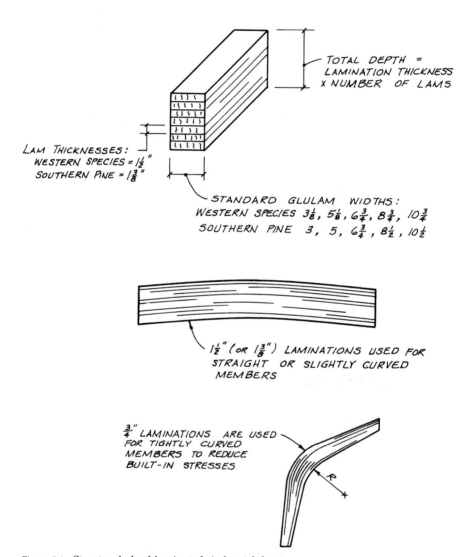

Figure 5.1 Structural glued laminated timber (glulam).

These thinner laminations are not used for straight or slightly curved glulams because cost is heavily influenced by the number of glue lines in a member. Only the design of straight and slightly curved rectangular members is included in this text. The design of tapered members and curved members (including arches) is covered in the TCM (Ref. 3.1).

The sizes of glulam members are called out on plans by giving their net dimensions (unlike sawn lumber which uses "nominal" sizes). Cross-sectional properties for glulams are listed in the *1991 NDS Supplement Table 1C, Section Properties of Glued Laminated Timber.* This table provides section properties for both Southern Pine glulam sizes and Western Species glulam sizes. Section properties include

1. Cross-sectional area A (in.^{2})
2. Section modulus about the strong axis S_x (in.^{3})
3. Moment of inertia about the strong axis I_x (in.^{4})
4. Section modulus about the weak axis S_y (in.^{3})
5. Moment of inertia about the weak axis I_y (in.^{4})

Section properties for glulam are determined using the same basic principles illustrated in Example 4.5 (Sec. 4.11). The approximate weight per linear foot for a given size glulam can be obtained by converting the cross-sectional area in NDS Supplement Table 1C from in.^{2} to ft^2 and multiplying by the following unit weights:

Type of glulam	Unit weight
Southern Pine	36 pcf
Western Species	
Douglas Fir-Larch	35 pcf
Hem-Fir and California Redwood	27 pcf

5.3 Resawn Glulam

In addition to the standard sizes of glulams shown in Fig. 5.1, NDS Supplement Table 1C gives section properties for a narrower width Western Species glulam. Glulams that are 2½ in. wide are obtained by ripping a glulam manufactured from nominal 2 × 6 laminations into two pieces. The relatively narrow beams that are produced in this way are known as *resawn glulams.* See Fig. 5.2. Although section properties are listed only for 2½ in.-wide beams, wider resawn members can be produced from glulams manufactured from wider laminations.

The resawing of a glulam to produce two narrower members introduces some additional manufacturing controls that are not required on the production of a normal-width member which is not going to be resawn. For example, certain strength-reducing characteristics (such as knot size or location) may be permitted in a 5⅛-in. glulam that is not going to be resawn.

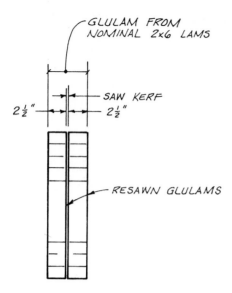

Figure 5.2 Resawn glulams are obtained by longitudinally cutting standard-width glulams to form narrower members. For example, a 2½-in.-wide member is obtained by resawing a glulam manufactured from nominal 2 × 6 laminations. A resawn glulam is essentially an industrial-use (i.e., not architectural) beam because three sides of the members are finished and one side is sawn.

If the member is going to be resawn, a more restrictive set of limitations may apply.

Resawn glulams are a fairly recent development in the glulam industry. These members can have large depths. With a narrow width and a large depth, resawn glulams produce beams with very efficient cross sections. In other words, the section modulus and moment of inertia for the strong axis (that is, S_x and I_x) are large for the amount of material used in the production of the member. On the negative side, very narrow members are weak about the minor axis (that is, S_y and I_y are small). The relatively thin nature of these members requires that they be handled properly in the field to ensure that they are not damaged during construction. In addition, it is especially important that a deep, narrow beam be properly braced so that the member does not buckle when a load is applied.

Resawn glulams are used as an alternative to certain sizes of sawn lumber. They also provide an option to wood I joists in some applications. Resawn beams are normally used where appearance is not a major concern.

5.4   Fabrication of Glulams

Specifications covering the design and fabrication of glulam members (Refs. 3.2 and 3.3) are published by the American Institute of Timber Construction (AITC). AITC is a technical trade association of the structural glued laminated timber industry. AITC also publishes the *Timber Construction Manual* (TCM, Ref. 3.1), which was introduced in Chap. 1 and is referenced throughout this book. The TCM is a wood engineering handbook that can be considered the basic reference on glulam (for convenience, it also includes information on other structural wood products such as sawn lumber).

Most structural glulam members are produced using Douglas Fir or Southern Pine. Hem-Fir and several other species can also be used. Quality control standards ensure the production of a reliable product. In fact, the structural properties of glulam members in most cases exceed the structural properties of sawn lumber.

The reason that the structural properties for glulam are so high is that the material included in the member can be selected from relatively high-quality laminating stock. The growth characteristics that limit the structural capacity of a large solid sawn wood member can simply be excluded in the fabrication of a glulam member.

In addition, laminating optimizes material by dispersing the strength-reducing defects in the laminating material throughout the member. For example, consider the laminations that are produced from a sawn member with a knot that completely penetrates the member at one section. See Fig. 5.3. If this member is used to produce laminating stock which is later reassembled in a glulam member, it is unlikely that the knot defect will be reassembled in all the laminations at exactly the same location in the glulam member. Therefore, the reduction in cross-sectional properties at any section

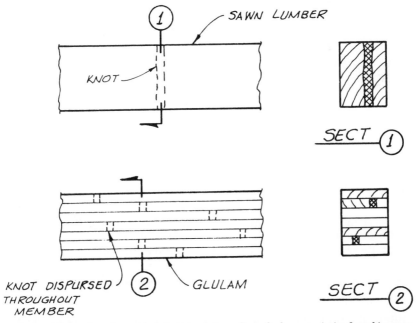

Figure 5.3 Dispersion of growth defects in glulam. Growth characteristics found in sawn lumber can be eliminated or (as shown in this sketch) dispersed throughout the member to reduce the effect at a given cross section.

consists only of a portion of the original knot. The remainder of the knot is distributed to other locations in the member.

Besides dispersing strength-reducing characteristics, the fabrication of glulam members makes efficient use of available structural materials in another way. High-quality laminations are located in the portions of the cross section which are more highly stressed. For example, in a beam, wood of superior quality is located in the outer tension and compression zones. This coincides with the location of maximum bending stresses. See Example 5.1. Although the maximum bending compressive and tensile stresses are equal, research has demonstrated that the outer laminations in the tension zone are the most critical laminations in a beam. For this reason, additional grading requirements are used for the outer tension laminations.

EXAMPLE 5.1   Distribution of Laminations in Glulam Beams

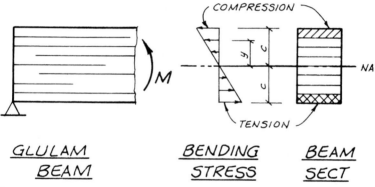

GLULAM   BENDING   BEAM
BEAM   STRESS   SECT

Figure 5.4

Bending stress calculation:

$$\text{Arbitrary point} \qquad f_b = \frac{My}{I}$$

$$\text{Maximum stress} \qquad f_b = \frac{Mc}{I}$$

In glulam beams, high-quality laminations are located in areas of high stress (i.e., near the top and bottom of the beam). Lower-quality wood is placed near the neutral axis where the stresses are lower. The outer tension laminations are critical and require the highest-grade stock.

The different grades of laminations over the depth of the cross section really make a glulam a composite beam. Recall from strength of materials that a composite member is one that is made up of more than one material with different values of modulus of elasticity. Composite members are analyzed using the transformed section method. The most obvious example of a composite member in building construction is a reinforced-concrete beam, but a glulam is also a composite member because the different grades of laminations have different E's.

However, from a designer's point of view, a glulam beam can be treated as a homogeneous material with a rectangular cross section. Allowable stresses have been determined in accordance with ASTM D 3737 (Ref. 13.7) using transformed sections. Thus, except for differences in design values and section properties, a glulam design is carried out in much the same manner as the design of a solid sawn beam.

Glulam beams are usually loaded in bending about the strong axis of the cross section. Large section properties and the distribution of laminations over the depth of the cross section make this an efficient use of materials. This is the loading condition assumed in Example 5.1, and bending about the strong axis should be assumed unless otherwise noted. In the tables for glulam design values, bending about the *strong axis* is described as the transverse load being applied *perpendicular to the wide face of the laminations*. See Example 5.2. Loading about the minor axis is also possible, but it is much less common. Different tabulated stresses apply to members loaded about the x and y axes.

EXAMPLE 5.2   Bending of Glulams

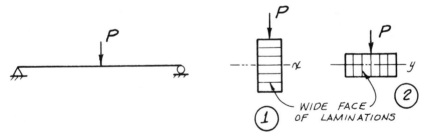

Figure 5.5

Bending can occur about either the x or y axis of a glulam. In section 1 the load is perpendicular to the wide faces of the laminations, and bending occurs about the major axis of the member. This is the more common situation. In section 2 the load is parallel to the wide faces of the laminations, and bending occurs about the weak or minor axis of the member.

Laminations are selected and dried to a moisture content of less than 16 percent before gluing. Differences in moisture content for the laminations in a member should not exceed 5 percent in order to minimize internal stresses and checking. Because of the relatively low moisture content (MC) of glulam members at the time of fabrication, the change in moisture content in service (i.e., the initial MC minus the EMC) is generally much smaller for glulam than it is for sawn lumber. Thus glulams are viewed as being more dimensionally stable. Even though the percent change in MC is normally less, the depth of a glulam is usually much larger than that of a sawn member. Thus the possible effects of shrinkage need to be considered in glulam design. See Sec. 4.7 for more discussion of shrinkage and Chap. 14 for recommendations about how to avoid shrinkage-related problems in connections.

Two types of glue are permitted in the fabrication of glulam members: (1) dry-use adhesives (casein glue) and (2) wet-use adhesives (usually phenol-resorcinol-base, resorcinol-base, or melamine-base adhesives). Both types of glue are capable of producing joints which have horizontal shear capabilities in excess of the capacity of the wood itself.

Although both types of glue are permitted by industry standards, currently the wet-use adhesives are used almost exclusively. This became common practice when room-temperature-setting glues were developed for exterior use. Wet-use adhesives, as the name implies, can withstand severe conditions of exposure.

The laminations run parallel to the length of a glulam member. The efficient use of materials and the long length of many glulam members require that effective end splices be developed in a given lamination. Several different configurations of lamination *end-joint* splices are possible including *finger* and *scarf* joints. See Fig. 5.6.

Finger joints produce high-strength joints when the fingers have relatively flat slopes. The fingers have very small blunt tips to permit glue squeeze-out. Finger joints also make efficient use of laminating stock because the lengths of the fingers are usually short in comparison with the lengths of scarf joints. With scarf joints, the flatter the slope of the joint, the greater the strength of the connection. Scarf slopes of 1 in 5 or flatter for compression and 1 in 10 or flatter for tension are recommended (Ref. 4.2).

If the width of the laminating stock is insufficient to produce the required width of glulam, more than one piece of stock can be used for a lamination. The *edge joints* in a lamination can be glued; or they can be staggered in adjacent laminations, and a reduced shear stress can be used in design.

Although one should be aware of the basic fabrication procedures and concepts outlined in this section, the building designer does not have to be concerned about designing the individual laminations, splices, and so on. In fact AITC has separated its laminating specification into two parts. One gives structural engineering properties and is titled *Design* (Ref. 3.2), and the other deals with the fabrication requirements for glulam and is titled *Manufacturing* (Ref. 3.3). The design values from Ref. 3.2 are reproduced in the NDS Supplement for convenience, and problems in this book refer to

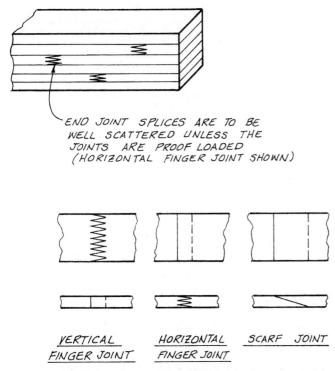

END JOINT SPLICES ARE TO BE
WELL SCATTERED UNLESS THE
JOINTS ARE PROOF LOADED
(HORIZONTAL FINGER JOINT SHOWN)

VERTICAL   HORIZONTAL   SCARF JOINT
FINGER JOINT   FINGER JOINT

Figure 5.6 End-joint splices in laminating stock. Most glulam fabricators use either the vertical or horizontal finger joints for end-joint splices. In addition, proof loading of joints is common, and in this case the location of end joints is not restricted.

the NDS tables. In practice, designers involved with glulam on a regular basis should obtain copies of Refs. 3.2 and 3.3 as well as a number of other AITC publications.

The manufacturing standards for glulam are based on ANSI A190.1, *Structural Glued Laminated Timber,* and implementation is ensured through a quality control system. Quality assurance involves the inspection and testing of glulam production by a qualified agency. The majority of glulam produced in the United States is inspected by two agencies: AITC Inspection Bureau and American Wood Systems (AWS), a related corporation of the American Plywood Association (APA). Each glulam is grade-stamped for identification purposes. See Fig. 5.7. In addition, because of the importance of the tension laminations, the top of a glulam bending member is also marked with a stamp. This identification allows construction personnel in the field to orient the member properly in the structure (i.e., get it right side up). If a glulam were inadvertently turned upside down, the compression laminations would be stressed in tension and the strength of

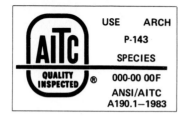

Figure 5.7 Typical grade stamps for glulam.

the member could be greatly reduced. Some of the items in the grade stamp include

1. Quality control agency (e.g., American Institute of Timber Construction or American Wood Systems)
2. Structural use (possible symbols: *B*, simple span bending member; *C*, compression member; *T*, tension member; and CB, continuous or cantilever bending member)
3. Plant of mill number (for example, 143 and 0000 shown)
4. Standard for structural glued laminated timber (i.e., ANSI A190.1-1983)
5. Laminating specification and combination symbol (for example, 117-88 24F-V4)

5.5 Grades of Glulam Members

For strength, grades of glulam members are given as combinations of laminations. The two main types are *bending combinations* and *axial combinations*. In addition to grading for strength, glulam members are graded for appearance. One of the three appearance grades (Industrial, Architectural, and Premium) should be specified along with the strength requirements to ensure that the member furnished is appropriate for the intended use. It is important to understand that the selection of an appearance grade does not affect the strength of a glulam (see Ref. 3.6 for additional information).

Members that are stressed principally in bending and loaded in the normal manner (i.e., with the applied load perpendicular to the wide faces of the laminations) are produced from the bending combinations. Bending combinations are defined by a *combination symbol* and the *species* of the laminating stock. The combination symbol is made up of two parts. The first is the allowable bending stress for the grade in hundreds of psi followed by the letter F. For example, 24F indicates a bending combination with a tabulated bending stress of 2400 psi for normal duration of loading and dry-service conditions. Bending combinations that are available include 16F, 20F, 22F, 24F, and 26F flexural stress levels.

It should be noted that a number of combinations of laminations can be used to produce a given bending stress level. Therefore, there is an abbreviation that follows the bending stress level which gives the distribution of laminating stock to be used in the fabrication of a member. Two basic abbreviations are used in defining the combinations: one is for visually graded laminating stock (for example, 24F-V3), and the other is for laminating stock that is graded for stiffness (for example, 22F-E5). Machine-stress-rated (MSR) lumber is an example of E-rated laminating stock.

In addition to the combination symbol, the species of wood is required to define the grade. The symbols for the species are DF for Douglas Fir-Larch, DFS for Douglas Fir South, HF for Hem-Fir, WW for Western Woods, and SP for Southern Pine. Section 5.4 indicated that higher-quality laminating stock is located at the outer faces of a glulam bending combination, and lower-quality stock is used for the less highly stressed inner zone. In a similar manner, the laminating specifications allow the mixing of more than one species of wood in certain combinations. The idea is again to make efficient use of raw materials by allowing the use of a strong species for the outer laminations and a weaker species for the center core.

If more than one species of wood is used in a member, both species are specified (for example, DF/HF indicates DF outer laminations and HF inner core laminations). If only one species is used throughout the member, the species symbol is repeated (for example, DF/DF). Although the laminating specification allows the mixing of more than one species, most glulam production currently uses laminating stock from only one species of wood for a given member.

Members which are principally axial-load-carrying members are identified with a numbered combination symbol such as 1, 2, 3, and so on. Because axial load members are assumed to be uniformly stressed throughout the cross section, the distribution of lamination grades is uniform across the member section, compared with the distribution of lamination quality used for beams.

Glulam combinations are, in one respect, similar to the "use" categories of sawn lumber. The *bending combinations* anticipate that the member will be used as a beam, and the *axial combinations* assume that the member will be loaded axially.

Bending combinations are fabricated with higher-quality laminating stock at the outer fibers, and consequently they make efficient beams. This fact, however, does not mean that a bending combination cannot be loaded axially. Likewise, an axial combination can be designed for a bending moment. The combinations, then, have to do with efficiency, but they do not limit the use of a member. The ultimate use is determined by stress calculations.

Design values for glulams are listed in the following tables in the 1991 NDS Supplement:

Table 5A   *Design Values for Structural Glued Laminated Softwood Timber (Members stressed primarily in bending)*. These are the bending combinations.

Table 5B   *Design Values for Structural Glued Laminated Softwood Timber (Members stressed primarily in axial tension and compression)*. These are the axial load combinations.

Tabulated design values for glulam did not change as part of the revision in the 1991 NDS. Therefore, design values are available in a number of other publications including Refs. 3.1 and 3.2 and UBC Chap. 25. The tables include the following properties:

Bending stress F_b

Tension stress parallel to grain F_t

Shear stress parallel to grain F_v

Compression stress parallel to grain F_c

Compression stress perpendicular to grain $F_{c\perp}$

Modulus of elasticity E

Tabulated design values for glulam are the same basic stresses that are listed for solid sawn lumber, but the glulam tables are more complex. The reason for this is the way glulams are manufactured with different grades of laminations. As a result, different design properties apply for bending loads about both axes, and a third set is provided for axial loading. It is suggested that the reader accompany this summary with a review of NDS Supplement Tables 5A and 5B.

The stresses for the more common application of a glulam member are listed first in the tables. For example, a *bending combination* will normally be used as a beam loaded about the strong axis, and design values for loading about the x axis are the first values given in NDS Table 5A. These are followed by values for loading about the y axis and for axial loading.

For loading about the x axis, two values of F_{bx} are listed. The first value represents the more efficient use of a glulam, and consequently it is the more frequently used stress in design. F_{bx} *tension/tension* indicates that the high-quality tension laminations are stressed in tension (i.e., tension zone stressed in tension). If, for example, a glulam were installed upside down, the second value of F_{bx} would apply. In other words, F_{bx} *compression/tension* indicates that the lower-quality compression laminations are stressed in tension (i.e., compression zone stressed in tension).

The real purpose for listing F_{bx} *compression/tension* is not to analyze beams that are installed improperly (although that is one possible use). An application of this stress in a beam that is properly installed is given in Chap. 6. The reason for mentioning the case of a beam being installed upside down is to simply illustrate why the two values for F_{bx} can be so different.

Three values of modulus of elasticity are given in Table 5A: E_x, E_y, and E_{axial}. Values of E_x and E_y are for use in beam deflection calculations about the x and y axes, respectively. They are also used in stability calculations for columns and laterally unbraced beams. On the other hand, E_{axial} is to be used for deformation calculations in members subjected to axial loads, such as the shortening of a column or the elongation of a tension member.

Two design values for compression perpendicular to grain $F_{c\perp}$ are listed in NDS Table 5A. One value applies to bearing on the face of the outer tension lamination, and the other applies to bearing on the compression face. The allowable bearing stress may be larger for the tension face because of the higher-quality laminations in the tension zone.

Design values listed in NDS Table 5B are for *axial combinations* of glulams, and, therefore, the properties for axial loading are the first given in the table. The distribution of laminations for the axial combinations does not follow the distribution for beams given in Example 5.1. Consequently, values for F_{bx} *tension/tension* and F_{bx} *compression/tension* do not apply to axial combinations. The design stresses for a glulam from an axial combination depend on the number of laminations in a particular member.

Both of the tables for glulam have an extensive set of footnotes which should be consulted for possible modification of design values.

It was noted in Sec. 5.4 that the different grades of laminations in a combination may have different properties (strength and stiffness). However, the tabulated design values and conventional cross-sectional properties are used in practice on the assumption that the member has uniform properties throughout.

Two basic methods can be used by the designer to specify a glulam. The traditional approach is a carryover from designing with other materials (e.g., structural steel or sawn lumber). Here the designer specifies the *size* and *grade* of member required for a given structural application. For example, in steel design a wide-flange beam could be specified as a W24 × 76 of A36 steel. Likewise in wood design a sawn beam could be designated as a 6 × 16 Select Structural Douglas Fir-Larch.

However, in glulam design the method of specifying by size and grade can cause a problem. A review of the glulam tables reveals a large number of bending and axial combinations. Unless the designer is aware of what combinations are readily available, specifying by size and grade (combination) could be uneconomical or could result in delays. Hence, if a designer specifies a glulam in this manner, the availability should be verified in advance.

A second method of specifying glulam is recommended by the glulam industry. In this alternative the designer specifies the required member *size* and the *minimum design values* (such as the minimum required F_b, F_v, and

E). It is then the responsibility of the glulam manufacturer to furnish a member that has properties that equal or exceed the values specified. The idea is to provide an adequate member while allowing the producer as much flexibility as possible in the fabrication and use of raw materials.

In spite of the effort to promote specifying by stress, the majority of glulam members continue to be specified by size and grade. Additional information on ordering and specifying glulam members can be obtained from AITC.

5.6   Stress Adjustments for Glulam

The notation for tabulated stresses, adjustment factors, and allowable stresses is essentially the same for glulam and for sawn lumber. Refer to Sec. 4.13 for a review of the notation used in wood design. The basic system involves the determination of an allowable stress by multiplying the tabulated stress by a series of adjustment factors

$$F' = F \times (\text{product of } C \text{ factors})$$

The tabulated design values for glulams are generally larger than similar properties for sawn lumber. This is essentially a result of the selective placement of laminations and the dispersion of imperfections. However, glulams are a wood product, and they are subject to many of the stress adjustments described in Chap. 4 for sawn lumber. Some of the adjustment factors are numerically the same for glulam and sawn lumber, and others are different. In addition, some adjustments apply only to sawn lumber, and several other factors are unique to glulam design.

The general summary of adjustment factors for use in wood design is given in the 1991 NDS Table 2.3.1, *Applicability of Adjustment Factors*. See the inside front cover of this book for a simplified version of this table. Several adjustment factors for glulam were previously described for sawn lumber. A brief description of the similarities and differences for glulam and sawn lumber is given here. Where appropriate the reader is referred to Chap. 4 for further information.

Wet service factor (C_M)

Tabulated design values for glulam are for dry conditions of service. For glulam, dry is defined as MC < 16 percent. For moisture contents of 16 percent or greater, tabulated stresses are multiplied by C_M. Values of C_M for glulam are given in the Adjustment Factors section preceding NDS Supplement Tables 5A and 5B. With high moisture content, the need for pressure treatment (Sec. 4.9) should be considered.

Load duration factor (C_D)

Tabulated design values for glulam are for normal duration of load. Normal duration is defined as 10 years and is associated with floor live loads. Loads and load combinations of other durations are taken into account by multiplying by C_D. The same load duration factors are used for both glulam and sawn lumber. See Sec. 4.15 for a complete discussion.

Flat use factor (C_{fu})

The flat use factor is somewhat different for sawn lumber and for glulam. For sawn lumber, tabulated values for F_b apply to bending about the x axis. When bending occurs about the y axis, tabulated values of F_b are multiplied by C_{fu} (Sec. 4.18) to convert the value to a property for the y axis.

On the other hand, glulam members have tabulated bending values for both the x and y axes (that is, F_{bx} and F_{by} are both listed). When the depth of the member for bending about the y axis (i.e., the cross-sectional dimension parallel to the wide faces of the laminations) is less than 12 in., the tabulated value of F_{by} may be increased by multiplying by C_{fu}. Values of C_{fu} for glulam are found in the Adjustment Factors section preceding NDS Supplement Tables 5A and 5B.

Because most beams are stressed about the strong axis and not about the y axis, the flat use factor is not a commonly applied adjustment factor. In addition, C_{fu} exceeds unity, and it can conservatively be ignored.

Temperature factor (C_t)

Tabulated design values for glulam are for use at normal temperatures. Section 4.20 discussed design values for other temperature ranges.

Volume factor (C_v)

It has been noted that the allowable stress in a wood member is affected by the relative size of the member. This general behavior is termed *size effect*. In sawn lumber, the size effect is taken into account by size factor C_F.

In the past, the same size factor was applied to F_b for glulam that is currently applied to the F_b for sawn lumber in the Timber sizes, namely,

$$C_F = \left(\frac{12}{d}\right)^{1/9}$$

This formula no longer applies to glulam, because the expression is a function of the depth of the member only. Recent research indicates that the size effect in glulam is related to the *volume* of the member rather than to only its depth.

Therefore, the volume factor C_V replaces the size factor C_F for use in glulam design; C_V applies only to bending stress. Tabulated values of F_b apply to a standard-size glulam beam with the following base dimensions: width = $5\frac{1}{8}$ in., depth = 12 in., length = 21 ft. The volume-effect factor C_V is used to obtain the allowable bending stress for other sizes of glulams.

See Example 5.3. It has been shown that the volume effect is less significant for Southern pine than for other species, and the volume-effect factor is thus species-dependent.

EXAMPLE 5.3   Volume Factor C_V for Glulam

Tabulated values of F_b apply to a glulam with the dimensions shown in Fig. 5.8.

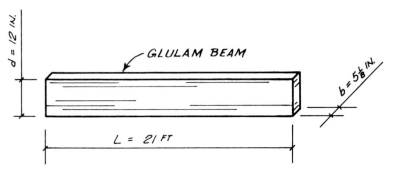

Figure 5.8 *Base dimensions* for bending stress in glulam.

The allowable bending stress for a glulam of another size is obtained by multiplying the tabulated stress (and other adjustments) by the volume-effect factor.

$$F_b' = F_b \times C_V \times \dots$$

For Western Species glulam

$$C_V = K_L \left(\frac{21}{L}\right)^{1/10} \left(\frac{12}{d}\right)^{1/10} \left(\frac{5.125}{b}\right)^{1/10} \le 1.0$$

For Southern Pine glulam

$$C_V = K_L \left(\frac{21}{L}\right)^{1/20} \left(\frac{12}{d}\right)^{1/20} \left(\frac{5.125}{b}\right)^{1/20} \le 1.0$$

where L = length of beam between points of zero moment, ft
d = depth of beam, in.
b = width of beam, in. *Note:* For laminations that consist of more than one piece, b is width of widest piece in layup.
K_L = loading condition coefficient

Loading condition	K_L
Single-span beam	
Uniformly distributed load	1.0
Concentrated load at midspan	1.09
Two equal concentrated loads at one-third points of span	0.96
Continuous beam or cantilever beam	
All loading conditions	1.0

The application of the volume-effect factor is shown in Sec. 5.7. Other modification factors for glulam design are introduced as they are needed.

5.7 Design Problem: Allowable Stresses

The allowable stresses for a glulam member are evaluated in Example 5.4. As with sawn lumber, the first step is to obtain the correct tabulated design values from the NDS Supplement. The second step is to apply the appropriate adjustment factors. A primary difference between a glulam problem and a sawn lumber problem is the use of the volume factor instead of the size factor.

In this example, a single load combination is given and one load duration factor C_D is used to adjust all allowable stresses. It is recognized that in practice a number of different loading combinations must be considered (Sec. 2.16), and the same load duration factor may not apply to all design properties. Appropriate loading combinations are considered in more complete problems later in this book. A single C_D is used in Example 5.4 for simplicity.

EXAMPLE 5.4   Determination of Allowable Design Values for a Glulam

A glulam beam is shown in Fig. 5.9. The member is Douglas Fir-Larch with a combination symbol of 24F-V3. From the sketch the bending load is about the x axis of the cross section. Loads are (DL + SL + wind). Use a single C_D based on the shortest duration in the combination. Bracing conditions are such that buckling is not a concern. Consider dry-service application (EMC < 16 percent). Normal temperature conditions apply.

Determine the following allowable stresses:

Bending stress about the strong axis F'_{bx}
Tension stress parallel to grain F'_t
Compression stress parallel to grain F'_c
Compression stress perpendicular to grain under concentrated load $F'_{c\perp}$ on compression face
Compression stress perpendicular to grain at support reactions $F'_{c\perp}$ on tension face
Shear stress parallel to grain F'_v
Modulus of elasticity for deflection calculations (beam loaded about strong axis) E'_x

Douglas Fir is a Western Species glulam. The combination 24F-V3 is recognized as a *bending combination* that is fabricated from *visually graded* laminating stock. Tabulated properties are taken from NDS Supplement Table 5A. Bending is about the strong axis of the member. The member is properly installed (top side up), and the tension laminations are on the bottom of the beam. The moment diagram is positive throughout, and bending tension stresses are on the bottom of the member. It is thus confirmed that the normally used bending stress is appropriate (that is, F_{bx} tension zone stressed in tension applies to the problem at hand).

The shortest duration load in the combination is wind, and $C_D = 1.6$. The designer is advised to verify local code acceptance of $C_D = 1.6$ before using in practice. Any stress adjustment factors in NDS Table 2.3.1 that are not shown in this example do not apply

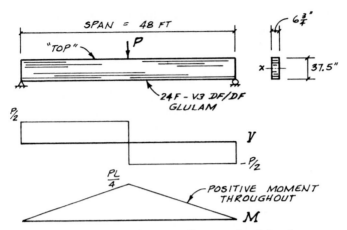

Figure 5.9 Load, shear, and moment diagrams for glulam beam.

to the given problem or have a default value of unity. Recall that C_D does not apply to $F_{c\perp}$ or to E.

Volume Factor C_V

The dimensions of the given member do not agree with the base dimensions for the standard-size glulam in Example 5.3. Therefore the bending stress will be multiplied by C_V. The length L in the formula is the distance between points of zero moment, which in this case is the span length of 48 ft.

$$C_V = K_L\left(\frac{21}{L}\right)^{1/10}\left(\frac{12}{d}\right)^{1/10}\left(\frac{5.125}{b}\right)^{1/10}$$

$$= 1.09\left(\frac{21}{48}\right)^{0.1}\left(\frac{12}{37.5}\right)^{0.1}\left(\frac{5.125}{6.75}\right)^{0.1} = 0.871$$

Allowable Design Values

$$F'_{bx} = F_{bx}(C_D \times C_M \times C_t \times C_V) = 2400(1.6 \times 1.0 \times 1.0 \times 0.871)$$

$$= 3345 \text{ psi tension/tension}$$

$$F'_t = F_t(C_D \times C_M \times C_t) = 1100(1.6 \times 1.0 \times 1.0) = 1760 \text{ psi}$$

$$F'_c = F_c(C_D \times C_M \times C_t) = 1600(1.6 \times 1.0 \times 1.0) = 2560 \text{ psi}$$

$$F'_{c\perp} = F_{c\perp}(C_M \times C_t) = 560\ (1.0 \times 1.0)$$

$$= 560 \text{ psi on compression face (at concentrated load)}$$

$$F'_{c\perp} = F_{c\perp}(C_M \times C_t) = 650(1.0 \times 1.0)$$

$$= 650 \text{ psi on tension face (at support reactions)}$$

$$F'_v = F_v(C_D \times C_M \times C_t) = 165(1.6 \times 1.0 \times 1.0) = 264 \text{ psi}$$

$$E'_x = E(C_M \times C_t) = 1,800,000(1.0 \times 1.0) = 1,800,000 \text{ psi}$$

5.8 Problems

Design values and adjustment factors in the following problems are to be taken from the 1991 NDS. Assume that glulams will be used in dry-service conditions and at normal temperatures unless otherwise noted.

5.1 What is the usual thickness of laminations used to fabricate glulam members from
a. Western Species?
b. Southern Pine?
c. Under what conditions would thinner laminations be used?

5.2 What are the usual widths of glulam members fabricated from:
a. Western Species
b. Southern Pine

5.3 How are the *strength grades* denoted for a glulam that is
a. Primarily a bending member fabricated with visually graded laminations?
b. Primarily a bending member fabricated with *E*-rated laminations?
c. Primarily an axial-load-carrying member?
d. What are the *appearance grades* of glulam members, and how do they affect the grading for strength?

5.4 Briefly describe what is meant by resawn glulam. What range of sizes is listed in NDS Supplement Table 1C for resawn glulam?

5.5 What is the most common type of lamination end-joint splice used in glulam members? Sketch the splice.

5.6 If the width of a lamination in a glulam beam is made up of more than one piece of wood, must the edge joint between the pieces be glued?

5.7 Describe the distribution of laminations used in the fabrication of a glulam to be used principally as an axial load member.

5.8 Describe the distribution of laminations used in the fabrication of a glulam member that is used principally as a bending member.

5.9 Briefly describe the meaning of the following glulam designations:
a. Combination 20F-V4 DF/DF
b. Combination 24F-V5 DF/HF

Problem continues on next page.

     c. Combination 24F-E2 HF/HF
     d. Combination 22F-V2 SP/SP
     e. Combination 5 DF
     f. Combination 48 SP

5.10 Tabulated values of F_{bx} for a bending combination apply to a glulam of a "standard" size. What are the dimensions of this hypothetical beam? Describe the adjustment that is required if a member of another size is used.

5.11 *Given:* A $5\frac{1}{8} \times 28.5$ 24F-V4 Douglas Fir-Larch glulam is used to span 32 ft, carrying a load of (DL + SL). The load is a uniform load over a simple span, and the beam is supported so that buckling is prevented.

     Find: *a.* Sketch the beam and the cross section. Show calculations to verify the section properties S_x and I_x for the member, and compare with values in NDS Supplement Table 1C.
          b. Determine the allowable stresses associated with the section properties in part *a.* These include F'_{bx} tension/tension, $F'_{c\perp x}$, F'_{vx}, and E'_x.
          c. Repeat part *b* except the moisture content of the member may exceed 16 percent.

5.12 *Given:* Assume that the member in Prob. 5.11 may also be loaded about the minor axis.

     Find: *a.* Show calculations to verify the section properties S_y and I_y for the member. Compare with values in NDS Supplement Table 1C.
          b. Determine the allowable stresses associated with the section properties in part *a.* These include F'_{by}, $F'_{c\perp y}$, F'_{vy}, and E'_y.
          c. Repeat part *b*, except the moisture content of the member may exceed 16 percent.

5.13 *Given:* Assume that the member in Problem 5.11 may also be subjected to an axial tension or compression load.

     Find: *a.* Show calculations to verify the cross-sectional area A for the member. Compare with the value in NDS Supplement Table 1C.
          b. Determine the allowable stresses associated with the section properties in part *a.* These include F'_t, F'_c, and E'_{axial}.
          c. Repeat part *b*, except the moisture content of the member may exceed 16 percent.

5.14 Repeat Prob. 5.11 except the member is a 5×33 24F-V3 Southern Pine glulam.

5.15 Explain why the allowable stress tables for glulam bending combinations list two values of compression perpendicular to grain for loads normal to the x axis ($F_{c\perp x}$).

5.16 Explain why the allowable stress tables for glulam bending combinations list two values of horizontal shear stress about the y axis (F_{vy}).

5.17   List the load duration factors C_D associated with the design of glulam members for the following loads:
   a. Dead load
   b. Snow
   c. Wind
   d. Floor live load
   e. Seismic
   f. Roof live load

5.18   Over what moisture content are the tabulated stresses in glulam to be reduced by a wet-service factor C_M?

5.19   List the wet-service factors C_M to be used for designing glulam beams with high moisture contents.

6

Beam Design

6.1 Introduction

The design of rectangular sawn wood beams and straight or slightly curved rectangular glulam beams is covered in this chapter. Glulam members may be somewhat more complicated than sawn lumber beams, and the special design procedures that apply only to glulam design are noted. Where no distinction is made, it may be assumed that essentially the same procedures apply to both sawn lumber and glulam design.

Glulam beams are sometimes tapered and/or curved for architectural considerations, to improve roof drainage, or to lower wall heights. The design of these types of members requires additional considerations beyond the information presented in this book. For the additional design considerations for these advanced subjects, see the TCM (Ref. 3.1).

The design of wood beams follows the same basic overall procedure used in the design of beams of other structural materials. The factors that need to be considered are

1. Bending (including lateral stability)
2. Shear
3. Deflection
4. Bearing

The first three items can govern the size of a wood member. The fourth item must be considered in the design of the supports. In many beams the bending stress is the critical design item. For this reason, a trial size is often obtained from bending stress calculations. The remaining items are then simply checked using the trial size. If the trial size proves inadequate in any of the checks, the design is revised.

Computer solutions to these problems can greatly speed up the design process, and with the use of the computer, much more thorough beam deflection studies are possible. However, the basic design process needs to be understood.

Designers are cautioned about using canned programs in a *blackbox* approach. Any program used should be adequately documented, and sufficient output should be available so that results can be verified by hand solutions. The emphasis throughout this book is on understanding the design criteria. A modern microcomputer spreadsheet can be an effective tool in design. With such an application program the user can tailor the solution to meet a variety of goals. With very little computer training, the designer can develop a *template* to solve a basic problem on a spreadsheet. A basic template can serve as the starting point for more sophisticated spreadsheet solutions.

6.2   Bending

In discussing the strength of a wood beam, it is important to understand that the bending stresses are parallel to the length of the member and are thus parallel to the grain of the wood. This is the common beam design problem (Fig. 6.1*a*), and it is the general subject of this section. See Example 6.1.

Occasionally, however, bending stresses across the grain (Fig. 6.1*b*) are developed, and the designer needs to recognize this situation. It has been noted previously that wood is relatively weak in *tension perpendicular to grain*. This is true whether the cross-grain tension stress is caused by a direct tension force perpendicular to grain or by loading that causes cross-grain bending. Cross-grain tension should generally be avoided.

EXAMPLE 6.1   Bending in Wood Members

Longitudinal Bending Stresses—(Parallel to Grain)

Ordinarily, the bending stress in a wood beam is parallel to the grain. The free-body diagram (FBD) in Fig. 6.1*a* shows a *typical beam* cut at an arbitrary point. The internal forces *V* and *M* are required for equilibrium. The bending stress diagram indicates that the stresses developed by the moment are longitudinal stresses, and they are, therefore, *parallel to grain*. Bending is shown about the strong or *x* axis of the member.

Cross-Grain Bending—Not Allowed

Section 1 in Fig. 6.1*b* shows a concrete wall connected to a wood horizontal diaphragm. The lateral force is shown to be transferred from the wall through the *wood ledger* by means of anchor bolts and nailing.

Section 2 indicates that the ledger cantilevers from the anchor bolt to the diaphragm level. Section 3 is an FBD showing the internal forces at the anchor bolt and the bending stresses that are developed in the ledger. The bending stresses in the ledger are *across the grain* (as opposed to being parallel to the grain). Wood is very weak in cross-grain

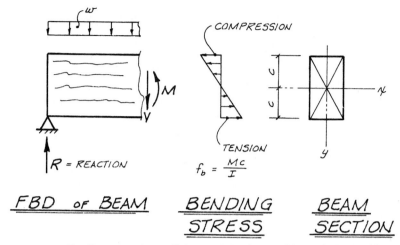

$$f_b = \frac{Mc}{I}$$

__FBD__ OF __BEAM__   __BENDING STRESS__   __BEAM SECTION__

Figure 6.1a Bending stress is parallel to grain in the usual beam design problem.

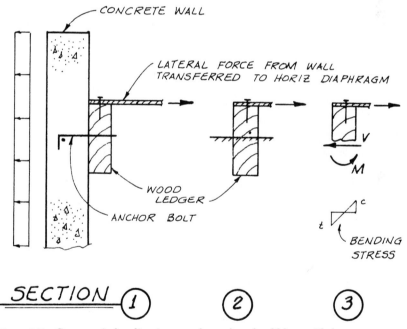

__SECTION__ ①   ②   ③

Figure 6.1b Cross-grain bending in a wood member should be avoided.

bending and tension. This connection is introduced at this point to define the cross-grain bending problem. Tabulated bending stresses for wood design apply to longitudinal bending stresses only.

Because of failures in some ledger connections of this type, cross-grain bending and cross-grain tension are not permitted by the Code for the anchorage of seismic forces.

Even for other loading conditions, designs should generally avoid stressing wood in bending or tension across the grain.

It should be noted that the use of a wood ledger in a building with concrete or masonry walls is still a very common connection. However, additional anchorage hardware is required to prevent the ledger from being stressed across the grain. Anchorage for this type of connection is covered in detail in Chap. 15.

The design moment in a wood beam is obtained using ordinary elastic theory. Most examples in this book use the nominal span length for evaluating the shear and moment in a beam. This is done to simplify the design calculations. However, in some problems it may be advantageous to take into account the technical definition of span length given in NDS Sec. 3.2.1.

Practically speaking, the span length is usually taken as the distance from the center of one support to the center of the other support. However, in most cases the *furnished* bearing length at a support will exceed the *required* bearing length. Thus, the NDS permits the designer to consider the span to be the *clear* distance between supports *plus* one-half of the *required* bearing length at each end. The required bearing length is a function of compression perpendicular to grain $F_{c\perp}$ (Sec. 6.8).

The critical location for shear in a wood beam is at a distance d from the face of the beam support (a similar practice is followed in reinforced-concrete design). The span length for bending and the critical loading condition for shear are shown later in this chapter in Fig. 6.13 (Sec. 6.5). Again, for hand calculations the shear and moment in a beam are often determined using a nominal span length. The added effort to obtain the more technical definition of span length is normally justified only in cases where the member appears to be overstressed using the nominal center-to-center span length.

The check for bending stresses in a wood beam uses the familiar formula from strength of materials

$$f_b = \frac{Mc}{I} = \frac{M}{S} \leq F'_b$$

where f_b = actual (computed) bending stress
M = moment in beam
c = distance from neutral axis to extreme fibers
I = moment of inertia of beam cross section about axis of bending
$S = \dfrac{I}{c}$
    = section modulus of beam cross section about axis of bending
F'_b = allowable bending stress

According to allowable stress design (ASD) principles, this formula says that the *actual* (computed) bending stress must be less than or equal to the *allowable* bending stress. The allowable stress takes into account the necessary adjustment factors to tabulated stresses that may be required for a wood member.

Most wood beams are used in an efficient manner. In other words, the *moment* is *applied about the strong axis (x axis) of the cross section.* From an engineering point of view, this seems to be the most appropriate description of the common loading situation. However, other terms are also used in the wood industry to refer to bending about the strong axis. For *solid sawn* lumber of rectangular cross section, the terms *loaded edgewise, edgewise bending,* and *load applied to the narrow face* of the member all refer to bending about the x axis. For *glulam* beams, the term *load applied perpendicular to the wide face* of the laminations is commonly used.

As wood structures become more highly engineered, there is a need to generalize the design expressions to handle a greater variety of situations. In a general approach to beam design, the moment can occur about either the x or y axis of the beam cross section. See Example 6.2. For sawn lumber, the case of bending about the weak axis (y axis) is described as *loaded flatwise, flatwise bending,* and *load applied to the wide face of the member.* For glulam, it is referred to as *load applied parallel to the wide face of the laminations.* In engineering terms, *weak-axis bending* and *bending about the y axis* are probably better descriptions.

Throughout this book the common case of bending about the strong axis is assumed, unless otherwise noted. Therefore, the symbols f_b and F'_b imply bending about the x axis and thus represent the values f_{bx} and F'_{bx}. Where needed, the more complete notation of f_{bx} and F'_{bx} is used for clarity. (An exception to the general rule of bending about the strong axis is Decking, which is normally stressed about the y axis.)

EXAMPLE 6.2   Strong- and Weak-Axis Bending

The large majority of wood beams are rectangular in cross section and are loaded as efficient bending members. See Fig. 6.2a. This common condition is assumed, unless otherwise noted.

The bending stress in a beam loaded about the strong axis (Fig. 6.2a) is

$$f_{bx} = \frac{M_x}{S_x} = \frac{M_x}{bd^2/6} \le F'_{bx}$$

A less efficient (and therefore less common) type of loading is to stress the member in bending about the minor axis. See Fig. 6.2b. Although it is not common, a structural member may occasionally be loaded in this manner.

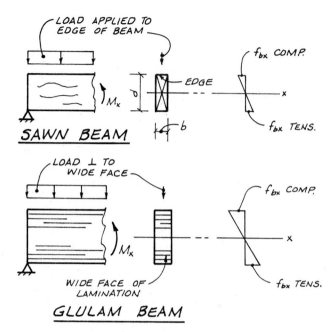

Figure 6.2a Most wood beams have bending about the strong axis. For sawn lumber, *loaded edgewise*. For glulam, *load perpendicular to wide face of laminations*.

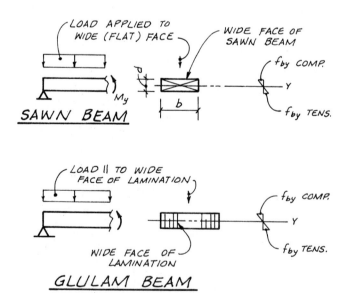

Figure 6.2b Occasionally beams have bending about weak axis. For sawn lumber, *loaded flatwise*. For glulam, *load parallel to wide face of laminations*.

The bending stress in a beam loaded about the weak axis (Fig. 6.2b) is

$$f_{by} = \frac{M_y}{S_y} = \frac{M_y}{bd^2/6} \leq F'_{by}$$

The designer must be able to recognize and handle either bending application.

The formula from engineering mechanics for bending stress f_b was developed for an ideal material. Such a material is defined as a solid, homogeneous, isotropic (having the same properties in all directions) material. In addition, plane sections before bending are assumed to remain plane during bending, and stress is assumed to be linearly proportional to strain.

From the discussion of some of the properties of wood in Chap. 4, it should be clear that wood does not fully satisfy these assumptions. Wood is made up of hollow cells which generally run parallel to the length of a member. In addition, there are a number of growth characteristics such as annual rings, knots, slope of grain, and moisture content. However, adequate beam designs are obtained by applying the ordinary bending formula and adjusting the allowable stress to account for the unique characteristics of wood beams.

The starting point is to obtain the correct *tabulated* bending stress for the appropriate species and grade of member. Values of F_b are listed in NDS Supplement Tables 4A to 4D for sawn lumber and NDS Supplement Tables 5A to 5C for glulam. NDS Table 2.3.1, *Applicability of Adjustment Factors*, then provides a string of multiplying factors to obtain the *allowable* bending stress once the tabulated stress is known. See the inside front cover of this book for a similar table. The *allowable bending stress* is defined as

$$F'_b = F_b(C_D)(C_M)(C_t)(C_L)(C_F)(C_V)(C_{fu})(C_r)(C_c)(C_f)$$

where F'_b = allowable bending stress
$\quad\quad F_b$ = tabulated bending stress
$\quad\quad C_D$ = load duration factor (Sec. 4.15)
$\quad\quad C_M$ = wet-service factor (Sec. 4.14—note that subscript M stands for moisture)
$\quad\quad C_t$ = temperature factor (Sec. 4.20)
$\quad\quad C_L$ = beam stability factor (consider when lateral support to compression side of beam may permit beam to buckle laterally—Sec. 6.3)
$\quad\quad C_F$ = size factor (Sec. 4.16)
$\quad\quad C_V$ = volume factor (Sec. 5.6)
$\quad\quad C_{fu}$ = flat use factor (Sec. 4.18)
$\quad\quad C_r$ = repetitive member factor (Sec. 4.17)

C_c = curvature factor [Apply only to curved glulam beams; C_c = 1.0 for straight and cambered (slightly curved) glulams. The design of curved beams is beyond the scope of this book.]

C_f = form factor (Sec. 4.21)

The reader is referred to the appropriate sections in Chaps. 4 and 5 for background on the adjustment factors discussed previously. Lateral stability is an important consideration in the design of a beam. The beam stability factor C_L is an adjustment factor that takes into account a reduced moment capacity if lateral torsional buckling can occur. Initially it is assumed that buckling is prevented, and C_L defaults to unity. See Example 6.3.

It should be realized that the long list of adjustment factors for determining F'_b is basically provided as a reminder that a number of special conditions may require an adjustment of the tabulated value. However, in many practical design situations, a number of the possible adjustment factors will default to 1.0. In addition, not all of the possible adjustments apply to all types of wood beams. Section 6.4 shows how the string of adjustment factors can be greatly reduced for practical beam design.

EXAMPLE 6.3   Full Lateral Support of a Beam

The analysis of bending stresses is usually introduced by assuming that lateral torsional buckling of the beam is prevented. Continuous support of the compression side of a beam essentially prevents the member from buckling (Fig. 6.3a).

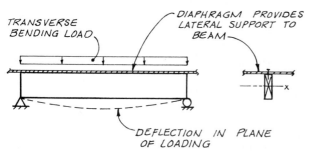

Figure 6.3a   Direct attachment of a roof or floor diaphragm provides full lateral support to top side of a beam. When subjected to transverse loads, a beam with full lateral support is stable, and it will deflect only in its plane of loading.

A beam with positive moment everywhere has *compressive* bending stresses on the top side of the member throughout its length. An effective connection (proper nailing) of a roof or floor diaphragm to the top side of such a beam reduces the unbraced length to zero (l_u = 0). Technically the unbraced length is the *spacing of the nails* through the sheathing and into the compression side of the beam. For most practical diaphragm construction and most practical beam sizes, the unbraced length can be taken as zero.

Many practical wood structures have *full* or *continuous* lateral support as part of their normal construction. See Fig. 6.3b. Closely spaced beams in a repetitive framing ar-

Figure 6.3b When plywood sheathing is properly attached to framing, a diaphragm is formed that provides stability to beams. *(Photo courtesy APA.)*

rangement are shown. However, a roof or floor diaphragm can also be used to provide lateral support to larger beams and girders, and the concept is not limited to closely spaced members.

With an unbraced length of zero, lateral buckling is eliminated, and the beam stability factor C_L defaults to unity. For other conditions of lateral support, C_L may be less than 1.0. The stability of laterally unbraced beams is covered in detail in Sec. 6.3.

Several points should be mentioned concerning the tabulated bending stress for different kinds of wood beams. Unlike glulam, the tables for sawn lumber do not list separate design properties for bending about the x and y axes. Therefore, it is important to understand which axis is associated with the tabulated values.

Tabulated bending stresses F_b for *visually graded sawn lumber* apply to both the x and y axes *except* for Beams and Stringers and Decking. Because Decking is graded with the intent that the member will be used flatwise (i.e., weak-axis bending), the tabulated value in the NDS Supplement is F_{by}. A flat-use factor C_{fu} has already been incorporated into the tabulated value, and the designer should not apply C_{fu} to Decking. The use of Decking is mentioned only briefly, and it is not a major subject in this book.

For members in the B&S size category, the tabulated bending stress applies to the x axis only (i.e., $F_b = F_{bx}$). However, for other members including Dimension lumber and Posts and Timbers sizes, the tabulated bending stress applies to both axes (i.e., $F_b = F_{bx} = F_{by}$). To obtain the allowable bending stress for the y axis, F_b must be multiplied by the appropriate flat-use factor C_{fu}.

In the infrequent case that a member in the B&S size category is loaded in bending about the minor axis, the designer should contact the appropriate rules-writing agency for assistance in determining the tabulated bending stress for the y axis. To determine F_{by} for a B&S, one must be familiar with the lumber grading rules for the species involved and with ASTM D 245 (Ref. 13.3). The use of F_{bx} and F_{by} for a B&S is demonstrated in Example 7.17 (Sec. 7.17). Addresses of the lumber rules-writing agencies are given in the NDS Supplement.

Another point needs to be understood about the allowable bending stresses in the B&S size category. ASTM D 245 allows the application of a less restrictive set of grading criteria to the outer thirds of the member length. This practice anticipates that the member will be used in a *simple beam* application. It further assumes that the length of the member will not be reduced substantially by sawing the member into shorter lengths.

Therefore, if a B&S is used in some other application where the maximum bending stress does not occur in the middle third of the original member length (e.g., a cantilever beam or a continuous beam), the designer should specify that the grading provisions applicable to the middle third of the length shall be applied to the entire length. See Example 6.4.

EXAMPLE 6.4   Allowable Bending Stresses for Beams and Stringers

Tabulated bending stresses for B&S sizes are for bending about the x axis of the cross section. Lumber grading agencies may apply less restrictive grading rules to the outer

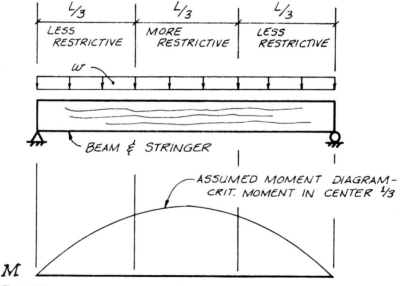

Figure 6.4

thirds of the member length. This assumes that the maximum moment will be located in the middle third of the member length. The common uniformly loaded simply supported beam is the type of loading anticipated by this grading practice.

If the loading or support conditions result in a moment diagram which does not agree with the assumed distribution, the designer should specify that the grading rules normally applied to the middle third shall be applied to the entire length.

A similar problem develops if a long B&S member is ordered and then cut into shorter lengths (see NDS Sec. 4.1.7). A note on the plans should prohibit cutting beams of this type, *or* full-length grading should be specified.

NOTE: A way to reduce the length of a B&S without affecting its stress grade is to cut approximately equal lengths from *both* ends.

A brief introduction to tabulated bending stresses for glulams was given in Chap. 5. Recall that *two* values of F_{bx} are listed for the glulam bending combinations in NDS Supplement Table 5A along with a value of F_{by}. It should be clear that F_{by} is for the case of bending about the weak axis of the member, but the two values for F_{bx} require further explanation. Although the computed bending stresses in a rectangular beam are equal at the extreme fibers, tests have shown the outer *tension laminations* are critical. Therefore, high-grade tension laminations are placed in the outer tension zone of the beam. The *top* of a glulam beam is marked in the laminating plant so that the member can be identified at the job site and oriented properly in the structure.

If the beam is loaded so that the tension laminations are stressed in tension, the appropriate bending stress is F_{bx} *tension zone stressed in tension*. In this book the following notation is used to indicate this value: $F_{bx\ t/t}$. In most cases a glulam beam is used in an efficient manner, and F_{bx} is normally $F_{bx\ t/t}$. In other words, F_{bx} is assumed to be $F_{bx\ t/t}$ unless otherwise indicated. On the other hand, if the member is loaded in such a way that the compression laminations are stressed in bending tension, the tabulated value known as F_{bx} *compression zone stressed in tension* $(F_{bx\ c/t})$ is the corresponding tabulated bending stress.

A review of NDS Supplement for glulam shows that the two tabulated stresses for F_{bx} just described can vary by a factor of 2. Accordingly, depending on the combination, the calculated bending strength of a member could be 50 percent less than expected if the beam were inadvertently installed upside down. Thus, it is important that the member be installed properly in the field.

Simply supported beams under gravity loads have positive moment throughout, and bending tensile stresses are everywhere on the bottom side of the member. Here the designer is just concerned with F_{bx} *tension zone stressed in tension*. See Example 6.5.

In the design of beams with both positive and negative moments, both values of F_{bx} need to be considered. In areas of negative moment (tension on the top side of the beam), the value of F_{bx} *compression zone stressed in tension* applies. When the negative moment is small, the reduced allowable bending stress for the compression zone stressed in tension may be satisfactory. Small negative moments may occur, for example, in beams with relatively small cantilever spans.

EXAMPLE 6.5 F_{bx} in Glulam Bending Combinations

Some glulam beams are fabricated so that the allowable bending tensile stress is the same for both faces of the member. Others are laid up in such a manner that the allowable bending tensile stresses are not the same for both faces of the beam. Two different allowable bending stresses are listed in the glulam tables:

1. F_{bx} tension zone stressed in tension $F_{bx\ t/t}$
2. F_{bx} compression zone stressed in tension $F_{bx\ c/t}$ (this value never exceeds $F_{bx\ t/t}$, and it may be much less)

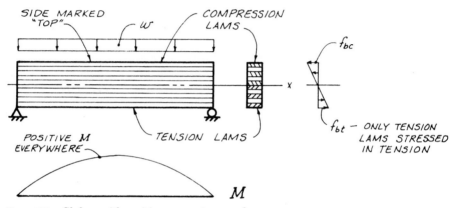

Figure 6.5a Glulam with positive moment everywhere.

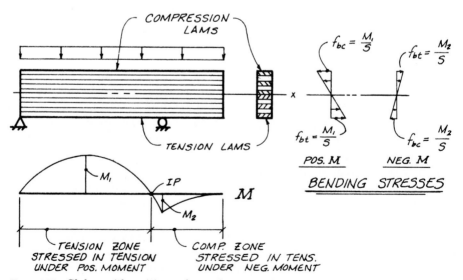

Figure 6.5b Glulam with positive and negative moments.

In Fig. 6.5a the designer needs to consider only $F_{bx\ t/t}$ because there is tension everywhere on the bottom side of the beam.

However, when positive and negative moments occur (Fig. 6.5b), both values of F_{bx} need to be considered.

In Figure 6.5b $F_{bx\ t/t}$ applies to M_1, and $F_{bx\ c/t}$ is used for M_2. If M_1 and M_2 are equal, a bending combination can be used which has equal values for the two F_{bx} stresses.

Figure 6.5c Large glulam beam in manufacturing plant undergoing finishing operation. A stamp is applied to the "top" of a glulam so that field crews will install the member right side up. *(Photo courtesy FPL.)*

On the other hand, when the negative moment is large, the designer is not limited to a small value of $F_{bx\ c/t}$. The designer can specify that tension zone grade requirements, including end-joint spacing, must be applied to both sides of the member. In this case the higher allowable bending stress $F_{bx\ t/t}$ may be used to design for both positive and negative moments. Large negative moments often occur in cantilever beam systems (Sec. 6.16). For additional information regarding F_{bx} tension zone stressed in tension and F_{bx} compression zone stressed in tension, see Refs. 3.1 and 3.2.

A final general point should be made about the strength of a wood beam. The *notching of structural members* to accommodate piping or mechanical systems is the subject of considerable concern in the wood industry. The notching and cutting of members in residential construction is fairly common practice. Although this may not be a major concern for members in repetitive systems which are lightly loaded, it can cause serious problems in other situations. Therefore, a note on the building plans should prohibit the cutting or notching of any structural member unless it is specifically detailed on the structural plans.

The effects of notching in areas of *bending stresses* are often addressed separately from the effects of notching on the *shear capacity* at the end of a beam. The discussion in the remaining portion of this section deals primarily with the effects of a notch where a bending moment exists. For shear considerations see Sec. 6.5.

The effect of a notch on the bending strength of a beam is not fully understood, and convenient methods of analyzing the bending stress at a notch are not currently available. However, it is known that the critical location of a notch is in the bending tension zone of a beam. Besides reducing the depth available for resisting the moment, stress concentrations are developed. Stress concentrations are especially large for the typical square-cut notch.

To limit the effect, the NDS says that the maximum depth of a notch shall not exceed one-sixth the depth of the member and that the notch shall not be located in the middle third of the member. Although not stated, it is apparent that this latter criterion applies to simply supported beams because of the high bending stresses in this area. Except for notches at the ends of a member, the NDS prohibits the notching of the tension side of beams when the nominal width of the member is 4 in. or greater.

Notches are especially critical in glulams because of the high-quality laminations at the outer fibers. Again, the tension laminations are the most critical and are located on the bottom of a beam that is subjected to a positive moment. For glulam beams the TCM recommends that notching in the tension face be avoided. Even at the ends of a beam (where the moment is theoretically zero), the TCM limits the depth of a notch to one-tenth the depth of the beam.

These negative statements about the use of notches in wood beams should serve as a warning about the potential hazard that can be created by stress concentrations due to reentrant corners. Failures have occurred in beams with notches located some distance from the point of maximum bending and at a load considerably less than the design load.

The problem is best handled by avoiding notches. In the case of an existing notch, some strengthening of the member at the notch may be advisable.

Recent research has been conducted on the effect of notches, and Ref. 27 summarizes proposed design criteria for notched wood beams. The goal is to develop an engineering approach to handling notches in wood members that will eventually be incorporated into design codes and specifications. Until formal criteria become available, the designer is limited to the general rules and recommendations mentioned above.

6.3 Lateral Stability

When a member functions as a beam, a portion of the cross section is stressed in compression and the remaining portion is stressed in tension. If the compression zone of the beam is not braced to prevent lateral movement, the member may buckle at a bending stress that is less than the allowable stress defined in Sec. 6.2. The allowable bending stress described in Sec. 6.2 assumed that lateral torsional buckling was prevented by the presence of adequate bracing.

The bending compressive stress can be thought of as creating an equivalent column buckling problem in the compressive half of the cross section. Buckling in the plane of loading is prevented by the presence of the stable tension portion of the cross section. Therefore, if buckling of the compression side occurs, movement will take place *laterally* between points of lateral support. See Example 6.6.

EXAMPLE 6.6   Lateral Buckling of Bending Member

Unlike the beam in Example 6.3, the girder in Fig. 6.6 does not have full lateral support.

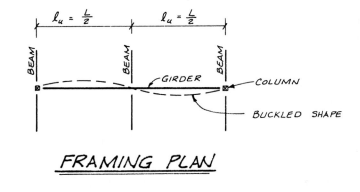

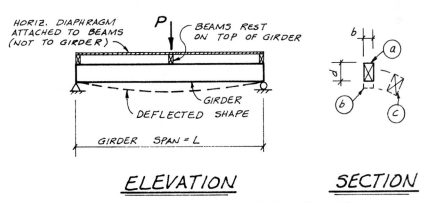

Figure 6.6   Bending member with span length L and unbraced length l_u.

1. The distance between points of lateral support to the compression side of a bending member is known as the *unbraced length* l_u of the beam. The beams that frame into the girder in Fig. 6.6 provide lateral support to the compression (top) side of the girder at a spacing of $l_u = L/2$.

2. It is important to realize that the *span* of a beam and the *unbraced length* of a beam are two different items. They may be equal, but they may also be quite different. The span is used to calculate stresses and deflections. The unbraced length, together with the cross-sectional dimensions, is used to analyze the stability of a bending member.

In other words, the span L gives the actual bending stress f_b, and the unbraced length l_u defines the allowable stress F'_{bx}.

3. The section view in Fig. 6.6 shows several possible conditions:
   a. The unloaded position of the girder.
   b. The deflected position of the girder under a vertical load with no instability. Vertical deflection occurs if the girder remains stable.
   c. The buckled position. If the unbraced length is excessive, the compression side of the member may buckle laterally in a manner similar to a slender column. Buckling takes place between points of lateral support. This buckled position is also shown in the plan view.

4. When the top of a beam is always in compression (positive moment everywhere) and when roof or floor sheathing is effectively connected directly to the beam, the unbraced length approaches zero. Such a member is said to have full lateral support. When lateral buckling is prevented, the strength of the beam depends on the bending strength of the material and not on stability considerations.

In many practical situations, the question of lateral instability is simply eliminated by providing lateral support to the compression side of the beam at close intervals. It has been noted that an effective connection (proper nailing) of a roof or floor *diaphragm* to the compression side of a beam causes the unbraced length to approach zero ($l_u = 0$), and lateral instability is prevented by *full* or *continuous* lateral support.

In the case of laterally unbraced *steel beams* (W shapes), the problem of stability is amplified because cross-sectional dimensions are such that relatively *slender* elements are stressed in compression. Slender elements have large width-to-thickness (b/t) ratios, and these elements are particularly susceptible to buckling.

In the case of rectangular *wood beams*, the dimensions of the cross section are such that the depth-to-thickness ratios (d/b) are relatively small. Common framing conditions and cross-sectional dimensions cause large reductions in allowable bending stresses to be the exception rather than the rule. Procedures are available, however, for taking lateral stability into account, and these are outlined in the remainder of this section.

Two methods of handling the lateral stability of beams are currently in use. One method is based on *rules of thumb* that have developed over time. These rules are applied to the design of sawn lumber beams. In this approach the required type of lateral support is specified on the basis of the depth-to-thickness ratio d/b of the member.

These rules are outlined in NDS Sec. 4.4.1, *Stability of Bending Members,* and in UBC Chap. 25. As an example, the rules state that if $d/b = 6$, bridging or full-depth solid blocking is required at intervals of 8 ft-0 in. maximum.

These can be omitted *if* both edges are held in line or *if* the compression edge is adequately supported laterally by sheathing *and* the beam is supported at bearing points so that rotation is prevented. See Example 6.7.

EXAMPLE 6.7 **Lateral Support of Beams—Approximate Method**

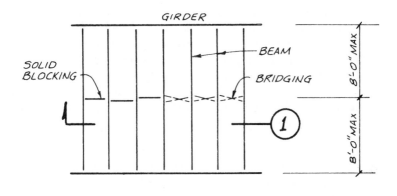

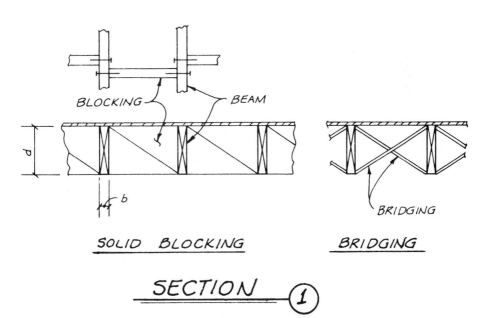

Figure 6.7 Solid (full depth) blocking or bridging for lateral stability based on traditional rules involving (d/b) ratio of beam.

When $d/b = 6$, lateral support can be provided by full-depth solid blocking or by bridging spaced at 8 ft-0 in. maximum. *Solid blocking* must be the same depth as the beams. Adjacent blocks may be staggered to facilitate construction (i.e., end nailing through beam). *Bridging* is cross-bracing made from wood (typically 1×3 or 1×4) or light-gauge steel (available prefabricated from manufacturers of hardware for wood construction).

These requirements for lateral support are *approximate* because only the proportions of the cross section (i.e., the b/d ratio) are considered. The second, more accurate method of accounting for lateral stability uses the *slenderness* ratio R_B of the beam. See Example 6.8. The slenderness ratio considers the unbraced length (distance between points of lateral support to the compression side of the beam) in addition to the dimensions of the cross section. This method was developed for large, important glulam beams, but it applies equally well to sawn beams.

EXAMPLE 6.8   Slenderness Ratio for Bending Members

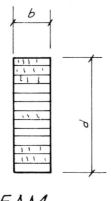

BEAM
SECTION

Figure 6.8

The *slenderness ratio* for a beam measures the tendency of the member to buckle laterally between points of lateral support to the *compression side* of the beam. Dimensions are in inches.

$$R_B = \sqrt{\frac{l_e d}{b^2}}$$

where R_B = slenderness ratio for a bending member
  b = beam width
  d = beam depth

l_u = unbraced length of beam (distance between points of lateral support as in Fig. 6.6)

l_e = effective unbraced length

The effective unbraced length is a function of the type of span, loading condition, and l_u/d ratio of the member. Several definitions of l_u are given here for common beam configurations. NDS Table 3.3.3, *Effective Length, l_e, for Bending Members,* summarizes these and a number of additional loading conditions involving multiple concentrated loads.

Cantilever Beam		
Type of load	When $l_u/d < 7$	When $l_u/d \geq 7$
Uniformly distributed load	$l_e = 1.33 l_u$	$l_e = 0.90 l_u + 3d$
Concentrated load at free end	$l_e = 1.87 l_u$	$l_e = 1.44 l_u + 3d$
Single-Span Beam		
Type of load	When $l_u/d < 7$	When $l_u/d \geq 7$
Uniformly distributed load	$l_e = 2.06 l_u$	$l_e = 1.63 l_u + 3d$
Concentrated load at midspan with no lateral support at center	$l_e = 1.80 l_u$	$l_e = 1.37 l_u + 3d$
Concentrated load at center with lateral support at center	$l_e = 1.11 l_u$	
Two equal concentrated loads at one-third points and lateral support at one-third points	$l_e = 1.68 l_u$	

NOTE: For a cantilever or single-span beam with any loading, the following values of l_u may conservatively be used:

$$l_e = \begin{cases} 2.06 \, l_u & \text{when } l_u/d < 7 \\ 1.63 \, l_u + 3d & \text{when } 7 \leq l_u/d \leq 14.3 \\ 1.84 \, l_u & \text{when } l_u/d > 14.3 \end{cases}$$

In calculating the beam slenderness ratio R_B, the effective unbraced length is defined in a manner similar to the effective length of a column (Chap. 7). For a beam, the effective length l_e depends on the end conditions (span type) and type of loading. In addition the ratio of the unbraced length to the beam depth l_u/d may affect the definition of effective length.

Once the slenderness ratio of a beam is known, the effect of lateral stability on the allowable bending stress may be determined. For large slenderness ratios, the allowable bending stress is reduced greatly, and for small slenderness ratios, lateral stability has little effect. At a slenderness ratio of zero, the beam can be considered to have full lateral support, and the allowable bending stress is as defined in Sec. 6.2 with $C_L = 1.0$.

The maximum beam slenderness ratio permitted by the NDS is 50. Thus, the range for beam slenderness is $0 \leq R_B \leq 50$. The effect of lateral stability on the bending strength of a beam is best described on a graph of the allowable bending stress F'_{bx} plotted against the beam slenderness ratio R_B. See Example 6.9. The 1991 NDS has a new formula for evaluating the effect of lateral stability on beam capacity. The new expression gives a continuous curve for F'_{bx} over the entire range of beam slenderness ratios, and it replaces the old three-segment curve (short, intermediate, and long ranges of beam slenderness) that was used in previous specifications.

The new formula for lateral stability is similar in format to the Ylinen column formula introduced in Chap. 7. The Ylinen-based formula for allowable bending stress may be cumbersome to apply by hand, but it is easy to evaluate on a programmable calculator or microcomputer spreadsheet.

EXAMPLE 6.9   Allowable Bending Stress Considering Lateral Stability

The 1991 NDS has a continuous curve for evaluating the effects of lateral torsional buckling on the bending strength of a beam. See Fig. 6.9a. Lateral torsional buckling may occur between points of lateral support to the compression side of a beam as the member is stressed in bending about the x axis of the cross section.

The tendency for a beam to buckle is eliminated if the moment occurs about the weak axis of the member. Therefore, the allowable stress reduction given by the curve in Fig. 6.9a is limited to bending about the x axis, and the bending stress is labeled F'_{bx}. However, the x subscript is often omitted, and it is understood that the reduced allowable bending stress is about the x axis (that is, $F'_b = F'_{bx}$).

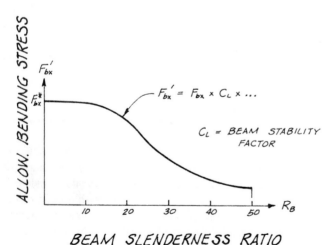

Figure 6.9a Typical plot of allowable bending stress about the x axis F'_{bx} versus beam slenderness ratio R_B.

Allowable Bending Stress

The allowable bending stress curve in Fig. 6.9*a* is obtained by multiplying the tabulated bending stress by the beam stability factor C_L *and* all other appropriate adjustment factors.

$$F'_{bx} = F_{bx}(C_L) \times \cdots$$

where F'_{bx} = allowable bending stress for x axis
F_{bx} = tabulated bending stress for x axis
C_L = beam stability factor (defined below)
$\times \cdots$ = product of other appropriate adjustment factors

Beam Stability Factor C_L

$$C_L = \frac{1 + F_{bE}/F^*_{bx}}{1.9} - \sqrt{\left(\frac{1 + F_{bE}/F^*_{bx}}{1.9}\right)^2 - \frac{F_{bE}/F^*_{bx}}{0.95}}$$

where F_{bE} = Euler-based critical buckling stress for bending members
$$= \frac{K_{bE}E'_y}{R_B^2}$$
F^*_{bx} = tabulated bending stress for x axis multiplied by certain adjustment factors
$= F_{bx} \times$ (product of all adjustment factors except C_{fu}, C_V, and C_L)
K_{bE} = 0.438 for visually graded lumber
   = 0.609 for material with less variability such as MSR lumber and glulam. See NDS Appendices D and F.2 for additional information.
E'_y = modulus of elasticity associated with lateral torsional buckling
   = modulus of elasticity about y axis multiplied by all appropriate adjustment factors. Recall that C_D does not apply to E. For sawn lumber, $E_y = E_x$. For glulam, E_x and E_y may be different.
   = $E_y(C_M)(C_t)$
R_B = slenderness ratio for bending member (Example 6.8)

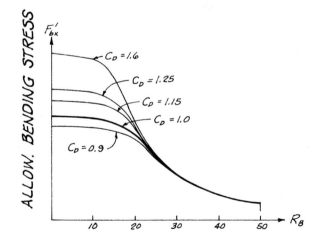

BEAM SLENDERNESS RATIO

Figure 6.9*b*   Effect of load duration factor on F'_{bx} governed by lateral stability.

In lateral torsional buckling, the bending stress is about the x axis. With this mode of buckling, instability is related to the y axis, and E_y is used to evaluate F_{bE}.

The load duration factor C_D has full effect on allowable bending stress in a beam that has full lateral support. On the other hand, C_D has no influence on the allowable bending stress when instability predominates. A transition between C_D having full effect at a slenderness ratio of 0 and C_D having no effect at a slenderness of 50 is automatically provided in the definition of C_L. This relationship is demonstrated in Fig. 6.9b.

The form of the expression for the *beam stability factor* C_L is the same as the form of the *column stability factor* C_P. The column stability factor is introduced in Sec. 7.4 on column design. Both expressions serve to reduce the allowable stress based on the tendency of the member to buckle. For a beam, C_L measures the effects of lateral torsional buckling, and for a member subjected to axial compression, C_P evaluates column buckling.

The formulas to evaluate C_L and C_P are new to the 1991 NDS, and they replace the short, intermediate, and long beam and column buckling formulas that were included in previous editions of the NDS. The general form of the expressions is the result of column studies by Ylinen. They were confirmed by work done at the Forest Products Laboratory (FPL) as part of a unified treatment of combined axial and bending loads for wood members (Ref. 5.2). The beam stability factor and the column stability factor provide a continuous curve for allowable stresses.

The expressions for C_L and C_P both make use of an elastic buckling stress divided by a factor of safety (FS). The Euler critical buckling stress is the basis of the elastic buckling stress

$$F_{\text{Euler}} = F_E = \frac{\pi^2 E}{(\text{slenderness ratio})^2 \times \text{FS}}$$

Recall that values of modulus of elasticity listed in the NDS Supplement are average values. The factor of safety in the F_E formula includes an adjustment which converts the average modulus of elasticity to a 5 percent exclusion value on pure bending modulus of elasticity.

For beam design, the elastic buckling stress is stated as

$$F_{bE} = \frac{K_{bE}E_y'}{R_B^2}$$

When a value of $K_{bE} = 0.438$ is used in this expression, the allowable bending stress F_{bx}' for *visually graded sawn lumber* includes a factor of safety of 1.66. Visually graded sawn lumber is generally more variable than other wood products that are used as beams (e.g., MSR lumber and glulam). For these latter materials, a factor of safety of 1.66 is maintained when $K_{bE} = 0.609$ is used to compute F_{bE}. Use of $K_{bE} = 0.438$ for glulam and MSR lumber would represent less than a 0.01 percent lower exclusion value with a factor of safety of 1.66. (See NDS Appendices D and F.)

In the lateral torsional analysis of beams, the bending stress about the x axis is the concern. However, instability with this mode of buckling is associated with the y axis (see the section view in Fig. 6.6), and E_y is used to compute F_E. For glulams, the values of E_x and E_y may not be equal, and the designer should use E_y from the glulam tables to evaluate the Euler stress for beam buckling.

For the beam and column stability factors, the elastic buckling value F_E is divided by a materials strength property to form a ratio that is used repeatedly in the formulas for C_L and C_P. For beams the material strength property is given the notation F_b^*. In this book subscript x is sometimes added to this notation. This is a reminder that F_b^* is the tabulated bending stress for *the x axis* F_{bx} multiplied by certain adjustment factors. Again, the ratio F_{bE}/F_b^* is used a number of times in the Ylinen formula.

From strength of materials it is known that the Euler formula defines the critical buckling stress in long slender members. The effect of beam and column stablity factors (C_L and C_P) is to define an allowable stress curve that converges on the Euler curve for large slenderness ratios.

Several numerical examples are given later in this chapter that demonstrate the application of C_L for laterally unbraced beams. Section 6.4 summarizes the adjustments for allowable bending stress for different types of beam problems.

6.4 Allowable Bending Stress Summary

The comprehensive listing of adjustment factors given in Sec. 6.2 for determining F_b' is a general summary, and not all of the factors apply to all beams. The purpose of this section is to identify the adjustment factors required for specific applications. In addition, a number of the adjustment factors that frequently default to unity are noted. This simplification of allowable bending stress is also included inside the front cover of this book in the "Expand Table of Adjustment Factors for Bending Stress."

Some repetition of material naturally occurs in a summary of this nature. The basic goal, however, is to simplify the long list of possible adjustment factors and to provide a concise summary of the factors relevant to a particular type of beam problem. The objective is to have a complete outline of the design criteria, without making the problem appear overly complicated. Knowing what adjustment factors default to unity for frequently encountered design problems should help in this process.

The allowable bending stresses for sawn lumber are given in Example 6.10. The example covers *visually graded sawn lumber,* and bending stresses apply to all size categories except Decking. The grading rules for Decking presume that loading will be about the minor axis, and published values are F_{by}. The flat use factor C_{fu} has already been applied to the tabulated F_b for Decking.

EXAMPLE 6.10   Allowable Bending Stress—Visually Graded Sawn Lumber

The allowable bending stresses for sawn lumber beams of rectangular cross section are summarized in this example. The common case of bending about the strong axis is covered first. See Fig. 6.10a. The appropriate adjustment factors are listed, and a brief comment is given as reminder about each factor. Certain common default values are suggested (e.g., dry-service conditions and normal temperatures, as found in most covered structures).

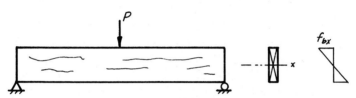

Figure 6.10a   Sawn lumber beam with moment about strong axis.

Allowable Bending Stress for Strong Axis

$$F'_{bx} = F_{bx}(C_D)(C_M)(C_t)(C_L)(C_F)(C_r)$$

where F'_{bx} = allowable bending stress about x axis

   $F_{bx} = F_b$ = tabulated bending stress. Recall that for sawn lumber, tabulated values of bending stress apply to x axis (except Decking). Values are listed in NDS Supplement Tables 4A and 4B for Dimension lumber and in Table 4D for Timbers.

   C_D = load duration factor (Sec. 4.15)

   C_M = wet service factor (Sec. 4.14)

      = 1.0 for MC ≤ 19 percent (as in most covered structures)

   C_t = temperature factor (Sec. 4.20)

      = 1.0 for normal temperature conditions

   C_L = beam stability factor

      = 1.0 for continuous lateral support of compression face of beam. For other conditions compute C_L in accordance with Sec. 6.3.

   C_F = size factor (Sec. 4.16). Obtain values from Adjustment Factors section of NDS Supplement Tables 4A and 4B for Dimension lumber and in Table 4D for Timbers.

   C_r = repetitive member factor (Sec. 4.17)

      = 1.15 for Dimension lumber applications that meet the definition of a repetitive member

      = 1.0 for all other conditions

Although bending about the strong axis is the common bending application, the designer should also be able to handle problems when the loading is about the weak axis. See Fig. 6.10b.

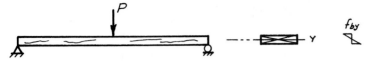

Figure 6.10b Sawn lumber beam with moment about weak axis.

Allowable Bending Stress for Weak Axis

$$F'_{by} = F_{by}(C_D)(C_M)(C_t)(C_F)(C_{fu})$$

where F'_{by} = allowable bending stress about y axis

$F_{by} = F_b$ = tabulated bending stress. Recall that tabulated values of bending stress apply to y axis for all sizes of sawn lumber except Beams and Stringers. Values of F_b are listed in NDS Supplement Tables 4A and 4B for Dimension lumber and in Table 4D for Timbers. For F_{by} in a B&S size, the lumber rules-writing agency should be contacted.

C_D = load duration factor (Sec. 4.15)

C_M = wet-service factor (Sec. 4.14)

= 1.0 for MC ≤ 19 percent (as in most covered structures)

C_t = temperature factor (Sec. 4.20)

= 1.0 for normal temperature conditions

C_F = size factor (Sec. 4.16). Obtain values from Adjustment Factors section of NDS Supplement Tables 4A and 4B for Dimension lumber and in Table 4D for Timbers.

C_{fu} = flat-use factor (Sec. 4.18). Obtain values from Adjustment Factors section of NDS Supplement Tables 4A and 4B for Dimension lumber. Contact appropriate lumber rules-writing agency to obtain C_{fu} for a B&S.

A summary of the appropriate adjustment factors for a glulam beam is given in Example 6.11. Note that the size factor C_F that is used for sawn lumber beams is replaced by the volume factor C_V in glulams. However, in glulams the volume factor C_V is not applied simultaneously with the beam stability factor C_L. The industry position is that volume factor C_V is a bending stress coefficient that adjusts for strength in the tension zone of a beam. Therefore, it is not applied concurrently with the beam stability factor C_L, which is an adjustment related to the bending strength in the compression zone of the beam.

EXAMPLE 6.11 Allowable Bending Stress—Glulam

The allowable bending stresses for straight or slightly curved glulam beams of rectangular cross section are summarized in this example. The common case of bending about the strong axis with the tension laminations stressed in tension is covered first. See Fig. 6.11a. This summary is then revised to cover the case of the compression laminations stressed in tension. As with the sawn lumber example, the appropriate adjustment factors are listed along with a brief comment.

Figure 6.11a Glulam beam with moment about strong axis.

Allowable Bending Stress for Strong Axis

A glulam beam *bending combination* is normally stressed about the x axis. The usual case is with the tension laminations stressed in tension. The notation F_{bx} typically refers to this loading situation. The allowable bending stress is taken as the smaller of the following two values:

$$F'_{bx} = F'_{bx\,t/t} = F_{bx\,t/t}(C_D)(C_M)(C_t)(C_L)$$

and

$$F'_{bx} = F'_{bx\,t/t} = F_{bx\,t/t}(C_D)(C_M)(C_t)(C_V)$$

where $F'_{bx} = F'_{bx\,t/t}$ = allowable bending stress about x axis with high-quality tension laminations stressed in tension

$F_{bx} = F_{bx\,t/t}$ = tabulated bending stress about x axis tension zone stressed in tension. Values are listed in NDS Supplement Table 5A.

C_D = load duration factor (Sec. 4.15)

C_M = wet service factor (Sec. 4.14)

= 1.0 for MC < 16 percent (as in most covered structures)

C_t = temperature factor (Sec. 4.20)

= 1.0 for normal temperature conditions

C_L = beam stability factor

= 1.0 for continuous lateral support of compression face of beam. For other conditions of lateral support C_L is evaluated in accordance with Sec. 6.3.

C_V = volume factor (Sec. 5.6)

Glulam beams are sometimes loaded in bending about the x axis with the compression laminations stressed in tension. The typical application for this case is in a beam with a relatively short cantilever (Fig. 6.5b). The allowable bending stress is taken as the smaller of the following two values:

$$F'_{bx\,c/t} = F_{bx\,c/t}(C_D)(C_M)(C_t)(C_L)$$

and

$$F'_{bx\,c/t} = F_{bx\,c/t}(C_D)(C_M)(C_t)(C_V)$$

where $F'_{bx\,c/t}$ = allowable bending stress about x axis with compression laminations stressed in tension

$F_{bx\,c/t}$ = tabulated bending stress about x axis with compression zone stressed in tension. Values are listed in NDS Supplement Table 5A.

Other terms are as defined above.

Although loading about the strong axis is the common application for a bending combination, the designer may occasionally be required to handle problems with bending about the weak axis. See Fig. 6.11b.

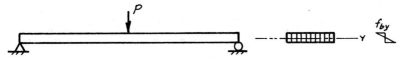

Figure 6.11b Glulam beam with moment about weak axis.

Allowable Bending Stress for Weak Axis

$$F'_{by} = F_{by}(C_D)(C_M)(C_t)(C_{\text{fu}})$$

where F'_{by} = allowable bending stress about y axis
    F_{by} = tabulated bending stress about y axis. Values are listed in NDS Supplement Table 5A.
    C_D = load duration factor (Sec. 4.15)
    C_M = wet service factor (Sec. 4.14)
       = 1.0 for MC < 16 percent (as in most covered structures)
    C_t = temperature factor (Sec. 4.20)
       = 1.0 for normal temperature conditions
    C_{fu} = flat use factor (Sec. 4.18). Obtain values from Adjustment Factors section of NDS Supplement Table 5A. Flat use factor may conservatively be taken equal to 1.0.

Example 6.11 deals with the most common type of glulam which is a bending combination. A glulam constructed from an axial load combination does not have the distribution of laminations that is used in a bending combination. Therefore, only one value of F_{bx} is tabulated for axial combination glulams, and the distinction between $F_{bx\,t/t}$ and $F_{bx\,c/t}$ is not required. Other considerations for the allowable bending stress in an axial combination glulam are similar to those in Example 6.11. Tabulated values and adjustment factors for axial combination glulams are given in NDS Supplement Table 5B.

The designer should not be overwhelmed by the fairly extensive summary of allowable bending stresses. Most sawn lumber and glulam beam applications involve bending about the strong axis, and most glulams have the tension zone stressed in tension. The other definitions of allowable bending stress are simply provided to complete the summary and to serve as a reference in the cases when they may be needed.

Numerical examples later in this chapter will demonstrate the evaluation of allowable bending stresses for both visually graded sawn lumber and glulams.

6.5 Shear

The shear stress in a beam is often referred to as *horizontal* shear. From strength of materials it will be recalled that the shear stress at any point in the cross section of a beam can be computed by the formula

$$f_v = \frac{VQ}{Ib}$$

Recall also that the horizontal and vertical shear stresses at a given point are equal. The shear strength of wood parallel to the grain is much less than the shear strength across the grain, and in a wood beam the grain is parallel with the longitudinal axis. In the typical horizontal beam, then, the horizontal shear is critical.

It may be helpful to compare the shear stress distribution given by VQ/Ib for a typical steel beam and a typical wood beam. See Example 6.12. Theoretically the formula applies to the calculation of shear stresses in both types of members. However, in design practice the shear stress in a steel W shape is approximated by a nominal (average web) shear calculation.

The average shear stress calculation gives reasonable results in typical steel beams, but it does not apply to rectangular wood beams. The maximum shear in a rectangular beam is 1.5 times the average shear stress. This difference is significant and cannot be disregarded.

EXAMPLE 6.12   Horizontal Shear Stress Distribution

Steel Beam

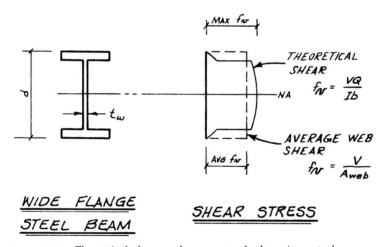

Figure 6.12a Theoretical shear and average web shear in a steel beam.

For a steel W shape, a nominal check on shear is made by dividing the total shear by the cross-sectional area of the web:

$$\text{Avg. } f_v = \frac{V}{A_{\text{web}}} = \frac{V}{dt_w} \approx \text{max. } f_v$$

Wood Beam

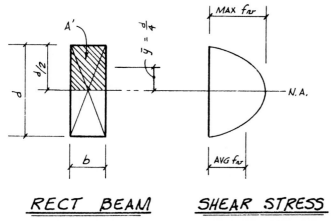

RECT BEAM   SHEAR STRESS

Figure 6.12b Shear stress distribution in a typical wood beam (rectangular section).

For rectangular beams the theoretical *maximum* "horizontal" shear *must* be used. The following development shows that the maximum shear is 1.5 times the average:

$$\text{Avg. } f_v = \frac{V}{A}$$

$$\text{Max. } f_v = \frac{VQ}{Ib} = \frac{VA'\bar{y}}{Ib} = \frac{V(bd/2)(d/4)}{(bd^3/12) \times b}$$

$$= \frac{3V}{2bd} = 1.5\frac{V}{A} = 1.5 \text{ (avg. } f_v)$$

A convenient formula for horizontal shear stresses in a rectangular beam is developed in Example 6.12. For wood cross sections of other configurations, the distribution of shear stresses will be different, and it will be necessary to use the basic shear stress formula or some other appropriate check, depending on the type of member involved. The check on shear for a rectangular wood beam is

$$f_v = \frac{1.5V}{A} \leq F'_v$$

where f_v = actual (computed) shear stress in beam

V = maximum design shear in beam

A = cross-sectional area of beam

F'_v = allowable shear stress

$= F_v(C_D)(C_M)(C_t)(C_H)$

F_v = tabulated shear stress

The terms used to evaluate the allowable shear stress were introduced in Chap. 4. The adjustment factors and typical values for frequently encountered conditions are

C_D = load duration factor (Sec. 4.15)

C_M = wet service factor (Sec. 4.14)

= 1.0 for dry-service conditions, as in most covered structures. Dry-service conditions are defined as

MC $\leq$ 19 percent for sawn lumber

MC $<$ 16 percent for glulam

C_t = temperature factor (Sec. 4.20)

= 1.0 for normal temperature conditions

C_H = shear stress factor (Sec. 4.19)

= 1.0 is conservative for sawn lumber

= 1.0 always for glulam

The presence of splits, checks, and shakes in a wood member will reduce the horizontal shear capacity. Tabulated values of shear stress for sawn lumber assume that a member will have extensive splitting, and published values of F_v are conservative. This can be seen by comparing values of F_v in the NDS tables for sawn lumber and glulam of the same species. The extensive splitting possible in solid sawn lumber does not occur in a manufactured product such as glulam.

When the length of a split or shake at the end of a sawn lumber member is known, and it is judged that the length will not increase, values of C_H greater than 1.0 may be obtained from the Adjustment Factors section of NDS Supplement Tables 4A, 4B, 4C, and 4D. Because the tables already recognize that less splitting occurs in glulam, C_H defaults to unity for glulam beams.

In beams that are likely not to be critical in shear, the value of V used in the shear stress formula is often taken as the maximum shear from the shear diagram. However, the NDS permits the maximum design shear to be reduced in stress calculations. To take this reduction into account, the load must be applied to one face of the beam, and the support reactions are on the other face. This is the usual type of loading. The reduction does not apply, for example, to the case where the loads are hung or suspended from the bottom face of the beam.

The reduction in shear is accomplished by neglecting or removing all loads (both distributed and concentrated) within a distance d (equal to the depth of the beam) from the face of the beam supports. See Example 6.13. In the case of a single moving concentrated load, a reduced shear may be obtained by locating the moving load at a distance d from the support (rather than placing it directly at the support). These reductions in computed shear stress can be applied in the design of both glulam and sawn lumber beams.

EXAMPLE 6.13   Reduction in Loads for Horizontal Shear Calculations

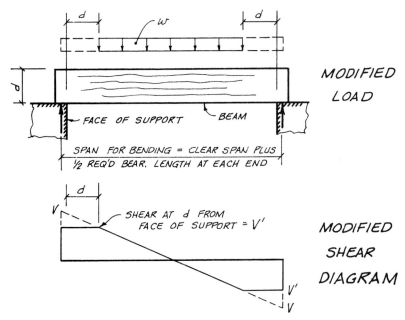

Figure 6.13 Permitted reduction in shear for calculating f_v.

1. The maximum design shear may be reduced by omitting the loads within a distance d (the depth of the beam) from the face of the support. This procedure applies to concentrated loads as well as uniformly distributed loads.
2. The modified loads are *only* for *horizontal shear stress* calculations in wood (sawn and glulam) beams. The full design loads must be used for other design criteria.
3. The concept of omitting loads within d from the support is based on an assumption that the loads are applied to one side of the beam (usually the top) and the member is supported by bearing on the opposite side (usually the bottom). In this way the

omitted loads are transmitted to the supports by diagonal compression. A similar type of adjustment for shear is used in reinforced-concrete design.

The *span length for bending* is defined in Sec. 6.2 and is shown in Fig. 6.13 for information. It is taken as the clear span plus one-half of the required bearing length at each end. Although this definition is permitted, it is probably more common (and conservative) in practice to use the distance between the centers of bearing. The span for bending is normally the length used to construct the shear and moment diagrams.

When the details of the beam support conditions are fully known, the designer may choose to calculate the shear stress at a distance d from the *face* of the support. However, in this book many of the examples do not have the support details completely defined. Consequently, if the reduction for shear is used in an example, the loads are conservatively omitted within a distance d from the reaction point in the "span for bending." The designer should realize that the point of reference is technically the face of the support and a somewhat greater reduction in calculated shear may be obtained.

Since a higher actual shear stress will be calculated without this modification, it is conservative not to apply it. It is convenient in calculations to adopt a notation which indicates whether the reduced shear from Example 6.13 is being used. Here V represents a shear which is not modified, and V' is used in this book to indicate a shear which has been reduced. Correspondingly, f_v is the shear stress calculated using V, and f_v' is the shear based on V'.

$$f_v' = \frac{1.5V'}{A} \le F_v'$$

Other terms are as previously defined. The modified load diagram is to be used for horizontal shear stress calculations only. Reactions and moments are to be calculated using the full design loads.

The *basic procedure* for checking shear stresses in a beam has been described above, and this basic procedure is applied in the design of most wood beams. The NDS provides additional shear stress procedures which are beyond the scope of this book. These additional procedures may be used to justify a *sawn lumber* beam that appears to be overstressed according to the basic procedure. This system is described in NDS Secs. 3.4.3.2 and 4.4.2 and NDS Appendix E.

It was noted earlier that bending stresses often govern the size of a beam, but secondary items, such as shear, *can* control the size under certain circumstances. It will be helpful if the designer can learn to recognize the type of beam in which shear is critical. As a general guide, shear is critical on relatively *short, heavily loaded spans*. With some experience, the designer will be able to identify by inspection what probably constitutes a "short, heavily loaded" beam. In such a case the design would start by obtaining a trial beam size which satisfies the horizontal shear formula. Other items, such as bending and deflection, would then be checked.

If a beam is notched at a free end, the shear at the notch must be checked. To do this, the theoretical formula for horizontal shear is applied with the actual depth at the notch d_n used in place of the total beam depth d. See Example 6.14. For square-cut notches in the tension face, the calculated stress must be increased by a stress concentration factor which is taken as the ratio of the total beam depth to the net depth at the notch (d/d_n). Notches of other configurations which tend to relieve stress concentrations will have lower stress concentration factors. *The notching of a beam in areas of bending tensile stresses is not recommended* (see Sec. 6.2 for additional comments).

EXAMPLE 6.14 Shear in Notched Beams

NOTCHED BEAM
- WIDTH = b
d
d_n
SUPPORTING
MEMBER

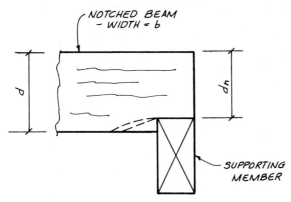

Figure 6.14*a* Notch at supported end.

For square-cut notches at the *end* of a beam on the tension side, the shear stress is increased by a stress concentration factor d/d_n:

$$f_v = \frac{1.5V}{bd_n}\left(\frac{d}{d_n}\right) \leq F'_v$$

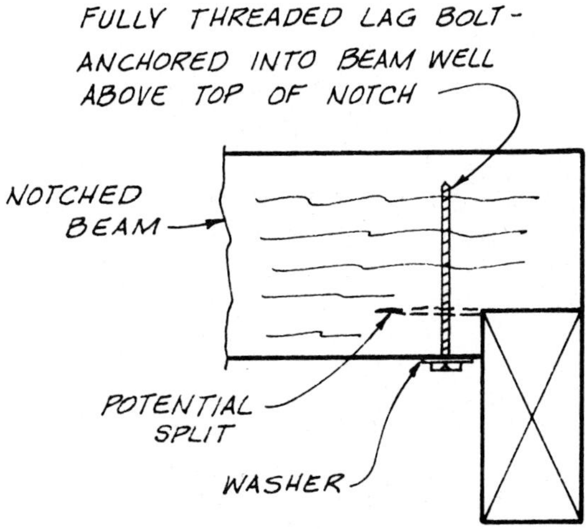

FULLY THREADED LAG BOLT -
ANCHORED INTO BEAM WELL
ABOVE TOP OF NOTCH
NOTCHED
BEAM
POTENTIAL
SPLIT
WASHER

Figure 6.14*b* Mechanical reinforcement at notched end.

Notches in the tension face of a beam induce tension perpendicular to the grain. These interact with horizontal shear to cause a splitting tendency at the notch. Tapered notches can be used to relieve stress concentrations (dashed lines in Fig. 6.14a).

Mechanical reinforcement such as the fully threaded lag bolt in Fig. 6.14b can be used to resist splitting.

Stress concentrations at notches and design procedures for the mechanical reinforcement of notches with lag bolts are currently under investigation. See Ref. 27 for a proposed design criteria.

Notches at the end of a beam in the compression face are less critical than notches in the tension side. The TCM (Ref. 3.1) provides a method for analyzing the effects of reduced stress concentrations for notches in the compression side. Additional provisions for horizontal shear at bolted connections in beams are covered in Sec. 13.7.

6.6   Deflection

The deflection limits for wood beams required by the Code and the additional deflection limits recommended by AITC are discussed in Sec. 2.7. Actual deflections for a trial beam size are calculated for a known span length, support conditions, and applied loads. Deflections may be determined from a traditional deflection analysis, from standard beam formulas, or from a computer analysis. The actual (calculated) deflections should be less than or equal to the allowable deflections given in Chap. 2. See Example 6.15.

EXAMPLE 6.15   Beam Deflection Criteria and Camber

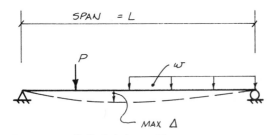

Figure 6.15a Deflected shape of beam.

Actual Deflection

The maximum deflection is a function of the loads, type of span, moment of inertia, and modulus of elasticity:

$$\text{Max. } \Delta = f\left(\frac{P, w, L}{I, E'}\right)$$

where E' = allowable (i.e., adjusted) modulus of elasticity

$\quad\quad$ = $E(C_M)(C_t)(C_T)$

Other terms for beam deflection analysis are as normally otherwise defined.

The adjustment factors for evaluating the allowable (i.e., adjusted) modulus of elasticity are introduced in Chap. 4. The factors and typical values for frequently encountered conditions are

$\quad E$ = tabulated modulus of elasticity

$\quad\quad$ = E_x for usual case of bending about strong axis

$\quad C_M$ = wet-service factor (Sec. 4.14)

$\quad\quad$ = 1.0 for dry-service conditions as in most covered structures. Dry-service conditions are defined as

$\quad\quad\quad$ MC $\leq$ 19 percent for sawn lumber

$\quad\quad\quad$ MC $<$ 16 percent for glulam

$\quad C_t$ = temperature factor (Sec. 4.20)

$\quad\quad$ = 1.0 for normal temperature conditions

$\quad C_T$ = buckling stiffness factor

$\quad\quad$ = 1.0 for beam deflection calculations. (*Note:* A buckling stiffness factor other than unity may be applied to E for column stability calculations in certain light wood truss applications. See NDS Sec. 4.4.3.)

Deflections are often checked under live load alone Δ_{LL} and under total load Δ_{TL} (dead load plus live load). Recall that in the total load deflection check, the dead load may be multiplied by a factor K (UBC Table 23-E). See Sec. 2.7 for additional information.

Deflection Criteria

$$\text{Max. } \Delta_{LL} \leq \text{allow. } \Delta_{LL}$$

$$\text{Max. } \Delta_{TL} \leq \text{allow. } \Delta_{TL}$$

If these criteria are not satisfied, a new trial beam size is selected using the moment of inertia and the allowable deflection as a guide.

Camber

Camber is initial curvature built into a member which is opposite to the deflection under gravity loads.

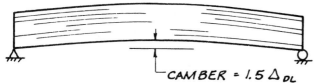

Figure 6.15b Typical camber built into glulam beam is 1.5 times dead load deflection.

The material property that is used to evaluate beam deflection is the adjusted modulus of elasticity E'. The NDS refers to this as the allowable modulus of elasticity. The modulus of elasticity has relatively few adjustment factors. The few adjustments that technically apply to E default to unity for many common beam applications. Note that the load duration factor C_D does not apply to modulus of elasticity (Sec. 4.15).

It will be recalled that the tabulated modulus of elasticity is an average value. It is common design practice to evaluate deflections using the average E. However, in certain cases deflection may be a critical consideration, and NDS Appendix F may be used to convert the average E to a lower-percentile modulus of elasticity. Depending on the required need, the average modulus of elasticity can be converted to a value that will be exceeded by either 84 percent or 95 percent of the individual pieces. These values are given the symbols $E_{0.16}$ and $E_{0.05}$ and are known as the 16 percent and 5 percent lower exclusion values, respectively. See NDS Appendix F for additional information.

In the design of glulam beams and wood trusses, it is common practice to call for a certain amount of camber to be built into the member. Camber is defined as an initial curvature or reverse deflection which is built into the member when it is fabricated. In glulam design, the typical camber is 1.5 Δ_{DL}. This amount of camber should produce a nearly level member under long-term deflection, including creep. Additional camber may be required to improve appearance or to obtain adequate roof slope to prevent ponding. See Chap. 2 for more information on deflection.

6.7 Design Summary

One of the three design criteria discussed in the previous sections (bending, shear, and deflection) will determine the required size of a wood beam. In addition, consideration must be given to the type of lateral support that will be provided to prevent lateral instability. If necessary, the bending stress analysis will be expanded to take the question of lateral stability into account. With some practice, the structural designer may be able to tell which of the criteria will be critical by inspection.

The sequence of the calculations used to design a beam has been described in the above sections. It is repeated here in summary.

For many beams the bending stress is the critical design item. Therefore, a trial beam size is often developed from the bending stress formula

$$\text{Req'd } S = \frac{M}{F_b'}$$

A trial member is chosen which provides a furnished section modulus S that is greater than the required value. Because the magnitude of the size factor C_F or the volume factor C_V is not definitely known until the size of the beam has been chosen, it may be helpful to summarize the actual versus allowable bending stresses after a size has been established:

$$f_b = \frac{M}{S} \leq F_b'$$

After a trial size has been established, the remaining items (shear and deflection) should be checked. For a rectangular beam, the shear is checked by the expression

$$f_v = \frac{1.5V}{A} \leq F_v'$$

In this calculation a reduced shear V' can be substituted for V, and f_v' becomes the computed shear in place of f_v. If this check proves unsatisfactory, the size of the trial beam is revised to provide a sufficient area A so that the shear is adequate.

The deflection is checked by calculating the actual deflection using the moment of inertia for the trial beam. The actual deflection is then compared with the allowable deflection:

$$\Delta \leq \text{allow. } \Delta$$

If this check proves unsatisfactory, the size of the trial beam is revised to provide a sufficient moment of inertia I so that the deflection criteria are satisfied.

It is possible to develop a trial member size by starting with something other than bending stress. For example, for a beam with a short, heavily loaded span, it is reasonable to establish a trial size using the shear calculation

$$\text{Req'd } A = \frac{1.5V}{F_v'}$$

The trial member should provide an area A which is greater than the required area.

If the structural properties of wood are compared with the properties of other materials, it is noted that the modulus of elasticity for wood is relatively low. For this reason, in fairly long span members, deflection can be the critical item. Obviously, if this case is recognized, or if more restrictive deflection criteria are being used in design, the trial member size should be based on satisfying deflection limits. Then the remaining criteria of bending and shear can be checked.

The section properties such as section modulus and moment of inertia increase rapidly with an increase in depth. Consequently, narrow and deep cross sections are more efficient beams.

In lieu of other criteria, the most economical beam for a given grade of lumber is the one that satisfies all stress and deflection criteria with the minimum cross-sectional area. Sawn lumber is purchased by the board foot (a board foot is a volume of wood based on nominal dimensions that corresponds to a 1 × 12 piece of wood 1 ft long). The number of board feet for a given member is obviously directly proportional to the cross-sectional area of a member.

A number of factors besides minimum cross-sectional area can affect the final choice of a member size. First, there are detailing considerations in which a member size must be chosen which fits in the structure and accommodates other members and their connections. Second, a member size may be selected that is uniform with the size of members used elsewhere in the structure. This may be convenient from a structural detailing point of view, and it also can simplify material ordering and construction. Third, the availability of lumber sizes and grades must also be considered. However, these other factors can be considered only with knowledge about a specific job, and the general practice in this book is to select the beam with the least cross-sectional area.

The design summary given above is essentially an outline of the process that may be used in a hand solution. Computer solutions can be used to automate the process. Generally computer designs will be more direct in that the required section properties for bending, shear, and deflection (that is, S, A, and I) will be computed directly with less work done by trial and error. However, even with computer solutions, wood design often involves iteration to some extent in order to obtain a final design.

The designer is encouraged to start using the computer by developing simple microcomputer spreadsheet templates for beam design calculations. If a dedicated computer program is used, the designer should ensure that sufficient output and documentation are available that the results can be verified by hand.

6.8   Bearing Stresses

Bearing stresses perpendicular to the grain of wood occur at beam supports or where loads from other members frame into the beam. See Example 6.16. The actual bearing stress is calculated by dividing the load or reaction by the contact area between the members or between the member and the connection bearing plate. The actual stress must be less than the allowable bearing stress

$$f_{c\perp} = \frac{P}{A} \leq F'_{c\perp}$$

The allowable compressive stress perpendicular to grain is obtained by multiplying the tabulated value by a series of adjustment factors

$$F'_{c\perp} = F_{c\perp}(C_M)(C_t)(C_b)$$

where $F'_{c\perp}$ = allowable compressive (bearing) stress perpendicular to grain

$F_{c\perp}$ = tabulated compressive (bearing) stress perpendicular to grain

C_M = wet service factor (Sec. 4.14)

= 1.0 for dry-service conditions, as in most covered structures. Dry-service conditions are defined as

MC $\leq$ 19 percent for sawn lumber

MC $<$ 16 percent for glulam

C_t = temperature factor (Sec. 4.20)

= 1.0 for normal temperature conditions

C_b = bearing area factor (defined below)

= 1.0 is conservative for all cases

For *sawn lumber* a single value of $F_{c\perp}$ is listed for individual stress grades in the NDS Supplement. For *glulams* a number of different tabulated values of $F_{c\perp}$ are listed. For a glulam bending combination stressed about the x axis, the value of $F_{c\perp x}$ to be used depends on whether the bearing occurs on the *compression* laminations or on the higher-quality *tension* laminations. For the common case of a beam with a positive moment, the compression laminations are on the top side of the member, and the tension laminations are on the bottom.

The bearing area factor C_b is used to account for an effective increase in bearing length. The bearing length l_b (in.) is defined as the dimension of the contact area measured *parallel* to the grain. Bearing area factor C_b may be used to account for additional wood fibers beyond the actual bearing length l_b that develop normal resisting force components. Under the conditions shown in Fig. 6.16b, a value of C_b greater than 1.0 is obtained by adding $3/8$ in. to the actual bearing length.

Note that C_b is always greater than or equal to 1.0. It is, therefore, conservative to disregard the bearing area factor (i.e., use a default value of unity). Values of C_b may be read from NDS Table 2.3.10, or they may be calculated as illustrated in Example 6.16.

Compression perpendicular to grain is generally not considered to be a matter of life safety. Instead, it relates to the amount of deformation that is acceptable in a structure. Currently published values of bearing perpendicular to grain $F_{c\perp}$ are *average* values which are based on a *deformation limit* of 0.04 in. when tested in accordance with ASTM D 143 (contained in Ref. 13). This deformation limit has been found to provide adequate service in typical wood-frame construction.

One of the most frequently used adjustment factors in wood design is the load duration factor C_D (Sec. 4.15), and it should be noted that C_D is not applied to the current definition of compression perpendicular to grain. In addition, tabulated values of $F_{c\perp}$ are generally lower for glulam than for sawn lumber of the same deformation limit (for a discussion of these differences see Ref. 3.1).

EXAMPLE 6.16 Bearing Perpendicular to Grain

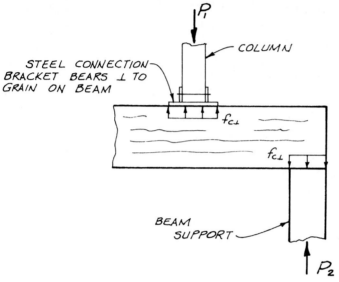

Figure 6.16a Compression perpendicular to grain.

Bearing stress calculation:

$$f_{c\perp} = \frac{P}{A} \leq F'_{c\perp}$$

where $f_{c\perp}$ = actual (computed) bearing stress perpendicular to grain
  P = applied load or reaction (force P_1 or P_2 in Fig. 6.16a)
  A = contact area
  $F'_{c\perp}$ = allowable bearing stress perpendicular to grain

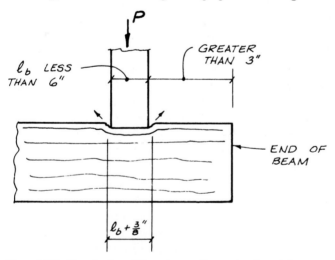

Figure 6.16b Required conditions to use C_b greater than 1.0.

Adjustment Based on Bearing Length

When the bearing length l_b (Fig. 6.16b) is less than 6 in. *and* when the distance from the end of the beam to the contact area is more than 3 in., the allowable bearing stress may be increased (multiplied) by the bearing area factor C_b.

Essentially, C_b increases the effective bearing length by $3/8$ in. This accounts for the additional wood fibers that resist the applied load after the beam becomes slightly indented.

Bearing area factor:

$$C_b = \frac{l_b + 0.375}{l_b}$$

In design applications where deformation may be critical, a reduced value of $F_{c\perp}$ may be appropriate. The following expressions are recommended when a deformation limit of 0.02 in. (one-half of the limit associated with the tabulated value) is desired.

For sawn lumber

$$F_{c\perp 0.02} = 0.73F_{c\perp} + 5.60$$

For glulam (Ref. 3.1)

$$F_{c\perp 0.02} = 0.73F_{c\perp}$$

where $F_{c\perp 0.02}$ = reduced compressive stress perpendicular to grain value at deformation limit of 0.02 in.

$F_{c\perp}$ = tabulated compressive stress perpendicular to grain (deformation limit of 0.04 in.)

The other adjustments described previously for $F_{c\perp}$ also apply to $F_{c\perp 0.02}$.

The bearing stress discussed thus far has been perpendicular to the grain in the wood member. A second type of bearing stress is known as the bearing stress parallel to grain. It applies to the bearing that occurs on the end of a member, and it is not to be confused with the compressive stress parallel to the grain that occurs away from the end (e.g., column stress in Sec. 7.4). The bearing stress parallel to the grain assumes that the member is adequately braced and that buckling does not occur. The actual bearing stress parallel to the grain is not to exceed the allowable stress

$$f_g = \frac{P}{A} \le F'_g$$

where f_g = actual (computed) bearing stress parallel to grain on *end* of member

P = load parallel to grain on end of wood member

A = net bearing area

F'_g = allowable compressive (bearing) stress parallel to grain on end of wood member

= $F_g(C_D)(C_t)$

F_g = tabulated compressive (bearing) stress parallel to grain on end of wood member. Obtain values from NDS Supplement Table 2A.

C_D = load duration factor (Sec. 4.15)

C_t = temperature factor (Sec. 4.20)

= 1.0 for normal temperature conditions

The tabulated value of F_g is a constant for a given species group and is independent of the stress grade. Note that F_g is subject to only two adjustments and that C_M is not required in the formula for F'_g because Table 2A takes moisture service condition into account directly.

Bearing parallel to grain applies to two wood members bearing end to end as well as end bearing on other surfaces. Member ends are assumed to be accurately cut square. When f_g exceeds $0.75F'_g$, bearing is to be on a steel plate or other appropriate rigid bearing surface. When required for end-to-end bearing of two wood members, the rigid insert shall be at least a 20-gage metal plate with a snug fit between abutting ends.

A comparison of the tabulated bearing stresses parallel to grain F_g and perpendicular to grain $F_{c\perp}$ shows that the values differ substantially. To make this comparison, refer to NDS Supplement Tables 2A and 4A to 4D.

It is also possible for bearing stresses in wood members to occur at some angle other than 0 or 90 degrees with respect to the direction of the grain. In this case, an allowable bearing stress somewhere between F'_g and $F'_{c\perp}$ is determined from the Hankinson formula. See Example 6.17.

EXAMPLE 6.17   Bearing at an Angle to Grain

Bearing at some angle to grain (Fig. 6.17) other than 0 or 90 degrees:

$$f_\theta = \frac{P}{A} \leq F'_\theta$$

where f_θ = actual bearing stress at angle to grain θ

P = applied load or reaction

A = contact area

F'_θ = allowable bearing stress at angle to grain θ

Hankinson Formula

The allowable stress at angle to grain θ is given by the Hankinson formula

$$F'_\theta = \frac{F'_g F'_{c\perp}}{F'_g \sin^2 \theta + F'_{c\perp} \cos^2 \theta}$$

where F'_g = allowable bearing stress parallel to grain

$F'_{c\perp}$ = allowable bearing stress perpendicular to grain

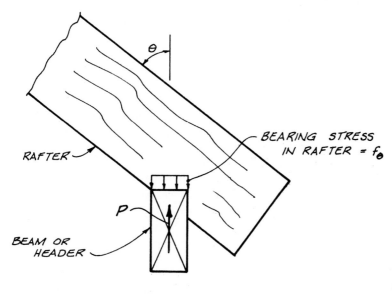

RAFTER CONNECTION

Figure 6.17 Bearing stress in two wood members. Bearing in rafter is at an angle to grain θ. Bearing in the supporting beam or header is perpendicular to grain.

This formula can probably best be solved mathematically, but the graphical solution in NDS Appendix J, *Solution of Hankinson Formula,* may be useful in visualizing the effects of angle of load to grain.

NOTE: The connection in Fig. 6.17 is given to illustrate bearing at an angle θ. For the condition shown, bearing stresses may be governed by compression perpendicular to the grain $f_{c\perp}$ in the beam supporting the rafter, rather than by f_θ in the rafter. If $f_{c\perp}$ in the beam is excessive, a bearing plate between the rafter and the beam can be used to reduce the bearing stress in the beam. The bearing stress in the rafter would not be relieved by use of a bearing plate.

As indicated in Example 6.17, the allowable stress adjustments are applied individually to F_g and $F_{c\perp}$ *before* F'_θ is computed using the Hankinson formula.

A number of examples are now given to illustrate the design procedures for beams. A variety of sawn lumber and glulam beams are considered with different support conditions and types of loading.

6.9 Design Problem: Sawn Beam

In this beam example and those that follow, the span lengths for bending and shear are, for simplicity, taken to be the same length. However, the designer may choose to determine the *design moment* based on the clear span plus one-half the required bearing length at each end (Sec. 6.2) and the *design shear* at a distance d from the support (Sec. 6.5). These different span length considerations are described in Example 6.13 (Sec. 6.5) for a simply supported beam.

In Example 6.18 a typical sawn lumber beam is designed for a roof that is essentially flat. Minimum slope is provided to prevent ponding. An initial trial beam size is determined from bending stress calculations. The extensive list of possible adjustment factors for bending stress is reduced to six for the case for a visually graded sawn lumber beam with bending about the strong axis (see Example 6.10 in Sec. 6.4 and inside front cover of this book).

The beam in this problem is used in dry-service conditions and at normal temperatures, and C_M and C_t both default to unity. In addition, the roof sheathing provides continuous lateral support to the compression side of the beam. Consequently, there is no reduction in moment capacity due to lateral stability, and C_L is unity. Therefore, the potential number of adjustment factors for allowable bending stress is reduced to three in this typical problem. The allowable bending stress is affected by the load duration factor C_D, the size factor for Dimension lumber C_F, and the repetitive-member factor C_r.

After selection of a trial size, shear and deflection are checked. The shear stress is not critical, but the second deflection check indicates that deflection under (DL + RLL) is slightly over the recommended allowable deflection. The decision of whether to accept this deflection is a matter of judgment. In this case it was decided to accept the deflection, and the trial size was retained for the final design.

EXAMPLE 6.18   Sawn Beam Design

Design the roof beam in Fig. 6.18 to support the given loads. Beams are spaced 16 in. o.c. (1.33 ft), and sufficient roof slope is provided to prevent ponding. The ceiling is gypsum wallboard. Plywood roof sheathing prevents lateral buckling. Material is No. 1 Douglas Fir-Larch (DF-L).

Roof DL = 14 psf, and roof LL = 20 psf. The MC ≤ 19 percent, and normal temperature conditions apply. Tabulated stresses and section properties are to be taken from the 1991 NDS.

Loads

Uniform loads are obtained by multiplying the given design loads by the tributary width.

$$w_{DL} = 14 \text{ psf} \times 1.33 \text{ ft} = 18.67 \text{ lb/ft}$$

$$\underline{w_{LL} = 20 \times 1.33 \qquad\qquad = 26.67}$$

$$\text{Total load } w_{TL} = 45.33 \text{ lb/ft}$$

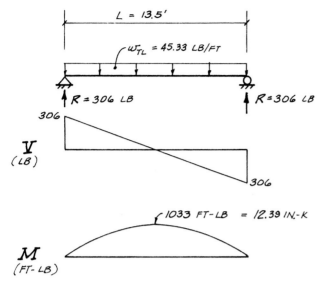

Figure 6.18 Trial size from bending calculations is 2 × 6 (Dimension lumber size).

The required load combinations are DL alone with $C_D = 0.9$, and (DL + RLL) with $C_D = 1.25$. By a comparison of the loads and the load duration factors (Example 4.10 in Sec. 4.15), it is determined that the critical load combination is DL + RLL (i.e., total load governs).

Determine a trial size based on bending, and then check other criteria.

Bending

The span length and load for this beam are fairly small. It is assumed that the required beam size is from the range of sizes known as Dimension lumber. Tabulated stresses are found in NDS Supplement Table 4A. The beam qualifies for the repetitive-member stress increase of 15 percent. A size factor of $C_F = 1.2$ is initially assumed, and the true size factor is confirmed after a trial beam is developed. C_M, C_t, and C_L default to 1.0.

$$F'_b = F'_{bx} = F_{bx}(C_D)(C_M)(C_t)(C_L)(C_F)(C_r)$$

$$= 1000(1.25)(1.0)(1.0)(1.0)(1.2)(1.15)$$

$$= 1725 \text{ psi}$$

$$\text{Req'd } S = \frac{M}{F'_b} = \frac{12,390}{1725} = 7.18 \text{ in.}^3$$

A trial beam size is obtained by reviewing the available sizes in NDS Supplement Table 1B. The general objective is to choose the member with the least area that furnishes a section modulus greater than the required. However, certain realities must also be considered. For example, a 1-in. nominal board would not be used for this type of beam application.

$$\text{Try } 2 \times 6 \quad S = 7.56 \text{ in.}^3 \quad > \quad 7.18 \quad OK$$

The trial size of a 2×6 was determined using an assumed value for C_F. The size factor can now be verified in the Adjustment Factors section of NDS Supplement Table 4A:

$$C_F = 1.3 > 1.2 \quad OK$$

At this point the member has been shown to be adequate for bending stresses. However, it is often convenient to compare the actual stress and the allowable stress in a summary.

$$f_b = \frac{M}{S} = \frac{12,390}{7.56} = 1640 \text{ psi}$$

$$F'_b = F_b(C_D)(C_M)(C_t)(C_L)(C_F)(C_r)$$

$$= 1000(1.25)(1.0)(1.0)(1.0)(1.3)(1.15)$$

$$= 1870 \text{ psi} > 1640$$

$$\therefore \quad \text{Bending} \quad OK$$

NOTE: A 2×5 can be checked with $C_F = 1.4$, but the reduced section modulus causes f_b to exceed F'_b. Furthermore, 2×5's may not be readily available.

Shear

Because it is judged that the shear stress for this beam is likely not to be critical, the maximum shear from the shear diagram is used without modification. C_M, C_t, and C_H are all set equal to 1.0.

$$f_v = \frac{1.5V}{A} = \frac{1.5(306)}{8.25} = 55.6 \text{ psi}$$

$$F'_v = F_v(C_D)(C_M)(C_t)(C_H)$$

$$= 95(1.25)(1.0)(1.0)(1.0)$$

$$= 119 \text{ psi} > 55.6$$

$$\therefore \quad \text{Shear} \quad OK$$

Deflection

The Code does not specify deflection criteria for roof beams that do not support plastered ceilings. The calculations below use the recommended deflection criteria from Ref. 3.1 for roof beams in a commercial building (see Fig. 2.8 in Sec. 2.7).

Recall that the modulus of elasticity for a wood member is not subject to adjustment for duration, and the buckling stiffness factor C_T does not apply to deflection calculations. The adjustment factors for E in this problem all default to unity.

$$E' = E(C_M)(C_t)$$

$$= 1,700,000(1.0)(1.0) = 1,700,000 \text{ psi}$$

$$\Delta_{LL} = \frac{5w_{LL}L^4}{384E'I} = \frac{5(26.7)(13.5)^4(1728 \text{ in.}^3/\text{ft}^3)}{384(1,700,000)(20.8)} = 0.56 \text{ in.}$$

$$\text{Allow. } \Delta_{LL} = \frac{L}{240} = \frac{13.5 \times 12}{240} = 0.67 \text{ in.} > 0.56 \quad OK$$

Deflection under total load can be calculated using the same beam deflection formula, or it can be figured by proportion.

$$\Delta_{LL} = \Delta_{TL}\left(\frac{w_{TL}}{w_{LL}}\right) = 0.56\left(\frac{45.3}{26.7}\right) = 0.95 \text{ in.}$$

$$\text{Allow. } \Delta = \frac{L}{180} = \frac{13.5 \times 12}{180} = 0.90 \text{ in.} < 0.95$$

In the second deflection check, the actual deflection is slightly over the allowable. The decision whether to accept or reject the trial beam is a matter of judgment:

1. The deflection calculation for this beam was performed as a *guide* only, and it is not a Code requirement for this building.
2. The possible detrimental effects of this deflection must be weighed against the economics of using a larger beam throughout the structure.

After a consideration of the facts concerning this particular building, assume that it is decided to accept the trial size.

> *Use* 2 × 6 No. 1 DF-L
> MC ≤ 19 percent

Bearing

Evaluation of bearing stresses requires knowledge of the support conditions. Without such information, the minimum bearing length will simply be determined. Recall that C_D does not apply to $F_{c\perp}$.

$$F'_{c\perp} = F_{c\perp}(C_M)(C_t)(C_b) = 625(1.0)(1.0)(1.0) = 625 \text{ psi}$$

$$\text{Req'd } A = \frac{R}{F'_{c\perp}} = \frac{306}{625} = 0.49 \text{ in.}^2$$

$$\text{Req'd } l_b = \frac{A}{b} = \frac{0.49}{1.5} = 0.33 \text{ in.}$$

All practical support conditions provide bearing lengths in excess of this minimum value.

6.10 Design Problem: Rough-Sawn Beam

In this example, a large rough-sawn beam with a fairly short span is analyzed. The cross-sectional properties for dressed lumber (S4S) are smaller than those for rough-sawn lumber, and it would be conservative to use S4S section properties for this problem. However, the larger section properties obtained using the rough-sawn dimensions are used in this example. Refer to Sec. 4.11 for information on lumber sizes.

Because the load (and the corresponding beam size) is relatively large in comparison to the span length, it is likely that shear will be the critical design item. For this reason the shear capacity is checked first. In this problem the basic shear adjustment of neglecting any loads within a distance d from the support is used. See Example 6.19.

The importance of understanding the size categories for sawn lumber is again emphasized. The member in this problem is a Beams and Stringers size, and tabulated design values are taken from NDS Supplement Table 4D.

EXAMPLE 6.19   Rough-Sawn Beam

Determine if the 6 × 18 rough-sawn beam in Fig. 6.19*a* is adequate to support the given loads. The member is Select Structural DF-L. The load is a combination of (DL + FLL). Lateral buckling is prevented. The beam is used in dry-service conditions (MC ≤ 19 percent) and at normal temperatures. Allowable stresses are to be taken from the 1991 NDS.

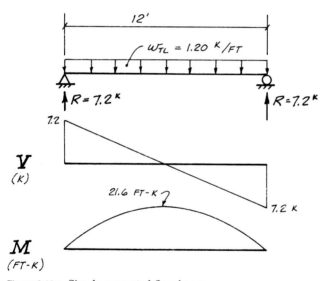

Figure 6.19a   Simply supported floor beam

Section Properties

The dimensions of rough-sawn members are approximately ⅛ in. larger than standard dressed sizes.

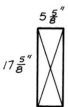

Figure 6.19b   Rough-sawn 6 × 18. For a member in the *Beams and Stringers* size category, the smaller cross-sectional dimension (i.e., the thickness) is 5 in. or larger, and the width is more than 2 in. greater than the thickness.

$$A = bd = (5\tfrac{5}{8})(17\tfrac{5}{8}) = 99.14 \text{ in}^2$$

$$S = \frac{bd^2}{6} = \frac{(5\tfrac{5}{8})(17\tfrac{5}{8})^2}{6} = 291.2 \text{ in.}^3$$

$$I = \frac{bd^3}{12} = \frac{(5\tfrac{5}{8})(17\tfrac{5}{8})^3}{12} = 2566 \text{ in.}^4$$

Shear

Start with the modified shear (the modified load diagram applies to shear calculations *only*).

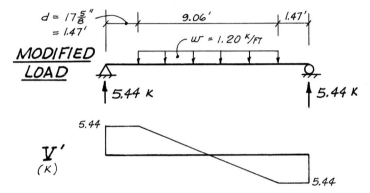

Figure 6.19c   Modified shear V' used to compute reduced shear f_v'.

$$f_v' = \frac{1.5V'}{A} = \frac{1.5(5440)}{99.14} = 82.3 \text{ psi}$$

$$F_v' = F_v(C_D)(C_M)(C_t)(C_H)$$

$$= 85(1.0)(1.0)(1.0)(1.0)$$

$$= 85 \text{ psi} > 82.3 \qquad OK$$

Bending

$$M = 21.6 \times 12 = 259 \text{ in.-k}$$

$$f_b = \frac{M}{S} = \frac{259{,}000}{291.2} = 890 \text{ psi}$$

The size factor for a sawn member in the Beams and Stringers category is given by the formula

$$C_F = \left(\frac{12}{d}\right)^{1/9} = \left(\frac{12}{17.625}\right)^{1/9} = 0.958$$

The load duration factor for the combination of (DL + FLL) is 1.0. All of the adjustment factors for allowable bending stress default to unity except C_F.

$$F'_b = F_b(C_D)(C_M)(C_t)(C_L)(C_F)(C_r)$$

$$= 1600(1.0)(1.0)(1.0)(1.0)(0.958)(1.0)$$

$$= 1535 \text{ psi} > 890 \quad OK$$

Deflection

Because the percentages of DL and FLL were not given, only the total load deflection is calculated.

$$E' = E(C_M)(C_t)$$

$$= 1,600,000(1.0)(1.0) = 1,600,000 \text{ psi}$$

$$\Delta_{\text{TL}} = \frac{5w_{\text{TL}}L^4}{384E'I} = \frac{5(1200)(12)^4(12 \text{ in./ft})^3}{384(1,600,000)(2566)} = 0.14 \text{ in.}$$

$$\text{Allow. } \Delta_{\text{TL}} = \frac{L}{240} = \frac{12(12)}{240} = 0.60 > 0.14 \quad OK$$

Bearing

$$F'_{c\perp} = F_{c\perp}(C_M)(C_t)(C_b) = 625(1.0)(1.0)(1.0) = 625 \text{ psi}$$

$$\text{Req'd } A_b = \frac{R}{F'_{c\perp}} = \frac{7200}{625} = 11.52 \text{ in.}^2$$

$$\text{Req'd } l_b = \frac{A}{b} = \frac{11.52}{5.625} = 2.05 \text{ in. min.}$$

> 6 × 18 rough-sawn
> Sel. Str. DF-L beam is   *OK*

NOTE: A lower stress grade could be used for this beam.

Bending and deflection are seen to be not critical. In fact, the stress grade for this beam could be reduced from Select Structural to No. 1, and the given size would still be acceptable. The reason for this is that the allowable shear stress is the same for all stress grades in the Beams and Stringers size category. The lower grade of No. 1 DF-L has an allowable bending stress that is greater than the actual:

$$F'_b = F_b \times C_F \times \cdots$$

$$= 1350 \times 0.958$$

$$= 1295 \text{ psi}$$

$$f_b = 890 < 1295 \quad OK$$

The deflection check would remain unchanged because the modulus of elasticity is the same for Select Structural and No. 1. A more economical beam would be obtained with the lower stress grade.

The importance of understanding the size categories of sawn lumber can be seen by comparing the allowable stresses shown above for No. 1 DF-L Beams and Stringers (B&S) with those in Example 6.18 for No. 1 DF-L Dimension lumber. For a given grade, the allowable stresses depend on the size category.

6.11 Design Problem: Sawn-Beam Analysis

The two previous examples have involved beams in the Dimension lumber and Beams and Stringers size categories. Example 6.20 is provided to give additional practice in determining allowable stresses. The member is again Dimension lumber, but the load duration factor, the wet service factor, and the size factor are all different from those in previous problems. Wet service factors and the size factor are obtained from the Adjustment Factors section in the NDS Supplement.

EXAMPLE 6.20   Sawn-Beam Analysis

Determine if the 4 × 16 beam given in Fig. 6.20 is adequate for a DL of 70 lb/ft and a snow load of 180 lb/ft. Lumber is stress grade No. 1 and Better, and the species group is Hem-Fir. Adequate bracing is provided, so that lateral stability is not a concern.

This beam is used in a factory where the EMC will exceed 19 percent,[*] but temperatures are in the normal range. Beams are 4 ft-0 in. o.c. The minimum roof slope for drainage

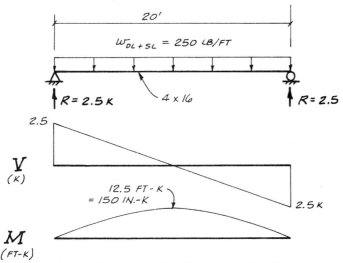

Figure 6.20 A 4 × 16 beam is in the *Dimension lumber* size category.

---

[*]The need for pressure-treated lumber to prevent decay should be considered (Sec. 4.9).

is provided so that ponding need not be considered. Arbitrary allowable deflection limits for this design are $L/360$ for snow load and $L/240$ for total load.

Allowable stresses and section properties are to be in accordance with the 1991 NDS.

Bending

Section properties for a 4 × 16 are listed in NDS Supplement Table 1B.

$$f_b = \frac{M}{S} = \frac{150{,}000}{135.7} = 1105 \text{ psi}$$

The load duration factor is $C_D = 1.15$ for the load combination of (DL + SL). Beam spacing does not qualify for the repetitive-member stress increase, and $C_r = 1.0$. Lateral stability is given to not be a consideration, and $C_L = 1.0$.

For a 4 × 16 the size factor is read from Table 4A:

$$C_F = 1.0$$

Also from Table 4A the wet-service factor for bending is given as

$$C_M = 0.85$$

Except that, when $F_b(C_F) \le 1150$ psi, $C_M = 1.0$.

In the case of 4 × 16 No. 1 & Btr Hem-Fir:

$$F_b(C_F) = 1050(1.0) < 1150$$

$$\therefore C_M = 1.0$$

The coefficients for determining F'_{bx} for a sawn lumber beam are obtained from the summary in Example 6.10 in Sec. 6.4 (see also inside front cover of this book). In the bending stress summary given below, most of the adjustment factors default to unity. However, it is important for the designer to follow the steps leading to this conclusion.

$$F'_b = F_b(C_D)(C_M)(C_t)(C_L)(C_F)(C_r)$$

$$= 1050(1.15)(1.0)(1.0)(1.0)(1.0)(1.0)$$

$$= 1205 \text{ psi} > 1105 \quad OK$$

Shear

$$f_v = \frac{1.5V}{A} = \frac{1.5(2500)}{53.375} = 70.3 \text{ psi}$$

$$F'_v = F_v(C_D)(C_M)(C_t)(C_H)$$

$$= 75(1.15)(0.97)(1.0)(1.0)$$

$$= 83.7 \text{ psi} > 70.3 \text{ psi\dagger} \quad OK$$

---

†If f_v had exceeded F'_v, the design shear could have been reduced in accordance with Sec. 6.5.

Deflection

$$E' = E(C_M)(C_t) = 1,500,000(0.9)(1.0) = 1,350,000 \text{ psi}$$

$$\Delta_{SL} = \frac{5wL^4}{384E'I}$$

$$= \frac{5(180)(20)^4(1728)}{384(1,350,000)(1034)} = 0.46 \text{ in.}$$

$$\text{Allow. } \Delta_{SL} = \frac{L}{360} = \frac{20 \times 12}{360} = 0.67 > 0.46 \quad OK$$

By proportion,

$$\Delta_{TL} = \left(\frac{250}{180}\right)0.46 = 0.64 \text{ in.}$$

$$\text{Allow. } \Delta_{TL} = \frac{L}{240} = \frac{20 \times 12}{240} = 1.00 > 0.64 \quad OK$$

| 4 × 16 No. 1 & Btr |
| Hem-Fir beam   *OK* |

6.12 Design Problem: Glulam Beam with Full Lateral Support

The examples in Secs. 6.12, 6.13, and 6.14 all deal with the design of the same glulam beam, but different conditions of lateral support for the beam are considered in each problem. The first example deals with the design of a beam that has *full lateral support* to the compression side of the member, and lateral stability is simply not a concern. See Example 6.21.

EXAMPLE 6.21   Glulam Beam—Full Lateral Support

Determine the required size of 24F-V3 DF glulam for the simple-span beam shown in Fig. 6.21. Assume dry-service conditions and normal temperature range. Roof DL = 200 lb/ft, and snow load = 800 lb/ft. Use the AITC-recommended deflection limits for a roof beam in a commercial building without a plaster ceiling (see Fig. 2.8 in Sec. 2.7). By inspection the critical load combination is

$$TL = DL + SL = 200 + 800 = 1000 \text{ lb/ft}$$

A number of adjustment factors for determining allowable stresses can be determined directly from the problem statement. For example, the load duration factor is $C_D = 1.15$ for the combination of (DL + SL). In addition, the wet-service factor is $C_M = 1.0$ for a glulam with MC < 16 percent, and the temperature factor is $C_t = 1.0$ for members used at normal temperatures.

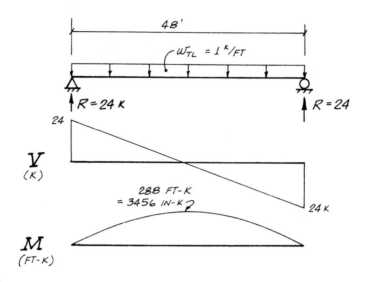

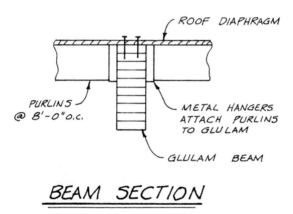

BEAM SECTION

Figure 6.21 Glulam beam with span of 48 ft and full lateral support to the compression side of the member provided by roof diaphragm.

Bending

The glulam beam will be loaded such that the tension laminations will be stressed in tension, and the tabulated stress $F_{bx\,t/t}$ applies. The summary for glulam beams in Example 6.11 in Sec. 6.4 (and inside the front cover) indicates that there are two possible definitions of allowable bending stress. One considers the effects of lateral stability as measured by the beam stability factor C_L. The other evaluates the effect of beam width, depth, and length as given by the volume factor C_V.

Lateral stability:
$$F'_{bx} = F_{bx}(C_D)(C_M)(C_t)(C_L)$$

Volume effect:
$$F'_{bx} = F_{bx}(C_D)(C_M)(C_t)(C_V)$$

The sketch of the beam cross section shows that the compression side of the beam (positive moment places the top side in compression) is restrained from lateral movement by an effective connection to the roof diaphragm. The unbraced length is zero, and the beam slenderness ratio is zero. Lateral buckling is thus prevented, and the beam stability factor $C_L = 1.0$. In this case, only the allowable bending stress using the volume factor needs to be considered.

Before the volume factor can be evaluated, a trial beam size must be established. This is done by assuming a value for C_V which will be later verified. Assume $C_V = 0.82$. Tabulated stresses are obtained from NDS Supplement Table 5A.

$$F'_{bx} = F_{bx}(C_D)(C_M)(C_t)(C_V)$$

$$= 2400(1.15)(1.0)(1.0)(0.82)$$

$$= 2263 \text{ psi}$$

$$\text{Req'd } S = \frac{M}{F'_b} = \frac{3,456,000}{2263} = 1527 \text{ in.}^3$$

As in most beam designs, the objective is to select the member with the least cross-sectional area that provides a section modulus greater than the required. This can be done using the S_x column for Western Species glulams in NDS Supplement Table 1C.

$$Try \; 6\tfrac{3}{4} \times 37\tfrac{1}{2} \text{ (twenty-five } 1\tfrac{1}{2}\text{-in. lams)}$$

$$A = 253.1 \text{ in.}^2$$

$$S = 1582 \text{ in.}^3 > 1527 \quad OK$$

$$I = 29,660 \text{ in.}^4$$

The trial size was based on an assumed volume factor. Determine the actual C_V (see Sec. 5.6 for a review of C_V), and revise the trial size if necessary.

$$C_V = K_L \left(\frac{21}{L}\right)^{1/10} \left(\frac{12}{d}\right)^{1/10} \left(\frac{5.125}{b}\right)^{1/10}$$

$$= 1.0 \left(\frac{21}{48}\right)^{0.1} \left(\frac{12}{37.5}\right)^{0.1} \left(\frac{5.125}{6.75}\right)^{0.1}$$

$$= 0.799 < 0.82$$

Because the assumed value of C_V was not conservative, the actual and allowable stresses will be compared in order to determine if the trial size is adequate.

$$f_b = \frac{M}{S} = \frac{3,456,000}{1582} = 2185 \text{ psi}$$

$$F'_b = F_b(C_D)(C_M)(C_t)(C_V)$$

$$= 2400(1.15)(1.0)(1.0)(0.799)$$

$$= 2205 \text{ psi} > 2185 \quad OK$$

Shear

Ignore the reduction of shear given by V' (conservative). The factor C_H applies only to sawn lumber and defaults to 1.0 for glulam.

$$f_v = \frac{1.5V}{A} = \frac{1.5(24{,}000)}{253.1} = 142 \text{ psi}$$

$$F_v' = F_v(C_D)(C_M)(C_t)(C_H) = 165(1.15)(1.0)(1.0)$$

$$= 190 > 142 \quad OK$$

Deflection

$$E_x' = E_x(C_M)(C_t)$$

$$= 1{,}800{,}000(1.0)(1.0)$$

$$= 1{,}800{,}000 \text{ psi}$$

$$\Delta_{\text{TL}} = \frac{5w_{\text{TL}}L^4}{384E'I} = \frac{5(1000)(48)^4(12 \text{ in.}/\text{ft})^3}{384(1{,}800{,}000)(29{,}660)} = 2.24 \text{ in.}$$

$$\frac{\Delta_{\text{TL}}}{L} = \frac{2.24}{48 \times 12} = \frac{1}{257} < \frac{1}{180} \quad OK$$

By proportion,

$$\Delta_{\text{SL}} = \left(\frac{800}{1000}\right)\Delta_{\text{TL}} = 0.8(2.24) = 1.79 \text{ in.}$$

$$\frac{\Delta_{\text{SL}}}{L} = \frac{1.79}{48 \times 12} = \frac{1}{321} < \frac{1}{240} \quad OK$$

$$\text{Camber} = 1.5\Delta_{\text{DL}} = 1.5\left(\frac{200}{1000}\right)(2.24) = 0.67 \text{ in.}$$

Bearing

The support conditions are unknown, and so the required bearing length will simply be determined. Use $F_{c\perp}'$ for bearing on the tension face of a glulam bending about the x axis. Recall that C_D does not apply to $F_{c\perp}$.

$$F_{c\perp}' = F_{c\perp}(C_M)(C_t)(C_b)$$

$$= 650(1.0)(1.0)(1.0) = 650 \text{ psi}$$

$$\text{Req'd } A = \frac{R}{F_{c\perp}'} = \frac{24{,}000}{650} = 36.9 \text{ in.}^2$$

$$\text{Req'd } l_b = \frac{36.9}{6.75} = 5.47 \qquad \text{Say } l_b = 5\tfrac{1}{2} \text{ in. min.}$$

> *Use*   6¾ × 37½ (twenty-five 1½-in. lams)
>   24F-V3 DF glulam—camber 0.67 in.

In Sec. 6.13 this example is reworked with lateral supports at 8 ft-0 in. o.c. This spacing is obtained when the purlins rest on top of the glulam. With this arrangement the sheathing is separated from the beam, and the distance between points of lateral support becomes the spacing of the purlins.

In Sec. 6.14, the beam is analyzed for an unbraced length of 48 ft-0 in. In other words, only the ends of the beam are stayed against translation and rotation. This condition would exist if no diaphragm action developed in the sheathing (i.e., the sheathing for some reason was not capable of functioning as a diaphragm), or if no sheathing or effective bracing is present along the beam. Fortunately, this situation is not common in ordinary building design.

6.13   Design Problem: Glulam Beam with Lateral Support at 8 ft-0 in.

In order to design a beam with an unbraced compression zone, it is necessary to check both *lateral stability* and *volume effect*. To check lateral stability, a trial beam size is required so that the beam slenderness ratio R_B can be computed. This is similar to column design, where a trial size is required before the column slenderness ratio and the strength of the column can be evaluated.

All criteria except unbraced length are the same for this example and the previous problem. Therefore, initial trial beam size is taken from Example 6.21. The 6¾ × 37½ trial represents minimum beam size based on the volume-effect criterion. Because all other factors are the same, only the lateral stability criteria are considered in this example. See Example 6.22. The calculations for C_L indicate that lateral stability is less critical than the volume effect for this problem. The trial size, then, is adequate.

EXAMPLE 6.22   Glulam Beam—Lateral Support at 8 ft-0 in.

Rework Example 6.21, using the modified lateral support condition shown in the beam section view in Fig. 6.22. All other criteria are the same. See Fig. 6.21 for the load, shear, and moment diagrams.

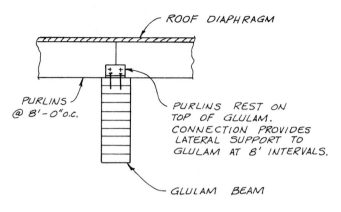

<u>BEAM SECTION</u>

Figure 6.22 Beam from Example 6.21 with revised lateral support conditions.

Bending

The allowable stresses for a glulam beam bending about the x axis are summarized in Example 6.11 and inside the front cover of this book. Separate allowable stresses are provided for lateral stability and volume effect:

Lateral stability: $F'_{bx} = F_{bx}(C_D)(C_M)(C_t)(C_L)$

Volume effect: $F'_{bx} = F_{bx}(C_D)(C_M)(C_t)(C_V)$

   See Example 6.21 for the development of a trial size based on the volume effect. This trial size will now be analyzed for the effects of lateral stability using an unbraced length of 8 ft-0 in.

Try $6\frac{3}{4} \times 37\frac{1}{2}$ 24F-V3 DF glulam

Slenderness ratio for bending member R_B

Unbraced length $l_u = 8$ ft $= 96$ in.

Effective unbraced lengths are given in Example 6.8 and in NDS Table 3.3.3. For a single-span beam with a uniformly distributed load, the definition of l_e depends on the l_u/d ratio

$$\frac{l_u}{d} = \frac{96}{37.5} = 2.56 < 7$$

$$\therefore l_e = 2.06 l_u = 2.06(96) = 198 \text{ in.}$$

$$R_B = \sqrt{\frac{l_e d}{b^2}} = \sqrt{\frac{198(37.5)}{(6.75)^2}} = 12.76$$

Coefficients for computing beam stability factor C_L

A beam subject to lateral torsional buckling is governed by stability about the y axis, and the modulus of elasticity for use in determining the beam stability factor is E'_y.

The Euler critical buckling stress for a glulam beam uses the coefficient $K_{bE} = 0.609$.

$$E'_y = E_y(C_M)(C_t) = 1,600,000(1.0)(1.0)$$

$$= 1,600,000 \text{ psi}$$

$$F_{bE} = \frac{K_{bE}E'_y}{R_B^2} = \frac{0.609(1,600,000)}{12.76^2} = 5987 \text{ psi}$$

The tabulated bending stress about the x axis modified by all factors except C_V and C_L is given the notation F_b^*

$$F_{bx}^* = F_{bx}(C_D)(C_M)(C_t)$$

$$= 2400(1.15)(1.0)(1.0) = 2760 \text{ psi}$$

$$\frac{F_{bE}}{F_{bx}^*} = \frac{5987}{2760} = 2.169$$

$$\frac{1 + F_{bE}/F_{bx}^*}{1.9} = \frac{1 + 2.169}{1.9} = 1.668$$

Beam stability factor

$$C_L = \frac{1 + F_{bE}/F_{bx}^*}{1.9} - \sqrt{\left(\frac{1 + F_{bE}/F_{bx}^*}{1.9}\right)^2 - \frac{F_{bE}/F_{bx}^*}{0.95}}$$

$$= 1.668 - \sqrt{1.668^2 - 2.169/0.95}$$

$$= 0.962$$

From Example 6.21, the volume factor for this beam is

$$C_V = 0.799 \quad < \quad C_L$$

$\therefore$ Volume effect governs over lateral stability.

The allowable bending stress for the beam with lateral support to the compression side at 8 ft-0 in. is the same as that for the beam in Example 6.21:

$$F'_b = 2205 \text{ psi} > 2185 \quad \text{OK}$$

> *Use* 6¾ × 37½
> 24F-V3 DF glulam

The beam in Example 6.22 is seen to be unaffected by an unbraced length of 8 ft. The beam slenderness ratio R_B is the principal measure of lateral stability, and R_B is a function of the unbraced length, beam depth, and beam width. The slenderness ratio is especially sensitive to beam *width* because of the square in the denominator.

A large slenderness ratio is obtained in Example 6.23 by increasing the unbraced length from 8 to 48 ft.

6.14   Design Problem: Glulam Beam with Lateral Support at 48 ft-0 in.

The purpose of this brief example is to illustrate the impact of a very long unbraced length and a correspondingly large beam slenderness ratio. See Example 6.23. As with the previous example, the initial trial size is taken from Example 6.21 because a trial size is required in order to calculate the beam slenderness ratio.

This example illustrates why it is desirable to have at least some intermediate lateral bracing. The very long unbraced length causes the trial size to be considerably overstressed, and a new trial beam size is required.

The problem is not carried beyond the point of checking the initial trial beam because the purpose of the example is simply to demonstrate the effect of lateral buckling. A larger trial size would be evaluated in a similar manner.

EXAMPLE 6.23   Glulam Beam—Lateral Support at 48 ft-0 in.

Rework the beam design problem in Examples 6.21 and 6.22 with lateral supports at the ends of the span only. See Fig. 6.21 for the load, shear, and moment diagrams.

Bending

The allowable stresses for a glulam beam are

$$\text{Lateral stability:} \qquad F'_{bx} = F_{bx}(C_D)(C_M)(C_t)(C_L)$$

$$\text{Volume effect:} \qquad F'_{bx} = F_{bx}(C_D)(C_M)(C_t)(C_V)$$

The size in Example 6.21 was based on the volume factor C_V. This member will now be checked for the effects of lateral stability with an unbraced length of 48 ft-0 in.

$$\textit{Try} \quad 6\tfrac{3}{4} \times 37\tfrac{1}{2} \quad 24F\text{-}V3 \quad DF \text{ glulam}$$

Slenderness ratio for bending member R_B

$$\text{Unbraced length } l_u = 48 \text{ ft} = 576 \text{ in.}$$

Effective unbraced lengths are given in Example 6.8 and in NDS Table 3.3.3. For a single-span beam with a uniformly distributed load, the definition of l_e depends on the l_u/d ratio

$$\frac{l_u}{d} = \frac{576}{37.5} = 15.36 > 7$$

$$\therefore l_e = 1.63 l_u + 3d = 1.63(576) + 3(37.5) = 1051 \text{ in.}$$

$$R_B = \sqrt{\frac{l_e d}{b^2}} = \sqrt{\frac{1051(37.5)}{(6.75)^2}} = 29.42$$

Coefficients for computing beam stability factor C_L

$$F_{bE} = \frac{K_{bE}E'_y}{R_B^2} = \frac{0.609(1,600,000)}{(29.42)^2} = 1126 \text{ psi}$$

$$F_{bx}^* = F_{bx}(C_D)(C_M)(C_t)$$

$$= 2400(1.15)(1.0)(1.0) = 2760 \text{ psi}$$

$$\frac{F_{bE}}{F_{bx}^*} = \frac{1126}{2760} = 0.408$$

$$\frac{1 + F_{bE}/F_{bx}^*}{1.9} = \frac{1 + 0.408}{1.9} = 0.741$$

Beam stability factor

$$C_L = \frac{1 + F_{bE}/F_{bx}^*}{1.9} - \sqrt{\left(\frac{1 + F_{bE}/F_{bx}^*}{1.9}\right)^2 - \frac{F_{bE}/F_{bx}^*}{0.95}}$$

$$= 0.741 - \sqrt{0.741^2 - 0.408/0.95}$$

$$= 0.395$$

From Example 6.21, the volume factor for this beam is

$$C_V = 0.799 > C_L$$

∴ Lateral stability governs over the volume factor.

The allowable bending stress for the beam with lateral support to the compression side at 48 ft-0 in. is

$$F'_b = F_b(C_D)(C_M)(C_t)(C_L)$$

$$= 2400(1.15)(1.0)(1.0)(0.395)$$

$$= 1090 \text{ psi}$$

$$f_b = 2185 \text{ psi} > 1090 \qquad \text{NG}$$

The trial size of a 6¾ × 37½ is considerably overstressed in bending and is no good (NG). A revised trial size is thus required and is left as an exercise for the reader.

6.15   Design Problem: Glulam with Compression Zone Stressed in Tension

Some glulam beams have *balanced* combinations of laminations. These have the same allowable bending stress on the top and bottom faces of the member. Other combinations have tension lamination requirements only on one side of the beam. For this latter case there are two different values of allowable bending stress:

1. F_{bx} *tension zone stressed in tension* $(F_{bx\ t/t})$

2. F_{bx} *compression zone stressed in tension* $(F_{bx\ c/t})$

The member in this example involves a combination that is not balanced. See Example 6.24.

The beam in this problem has a large positive moment and a small negative moment. The beam is first designed for the large positive moment using $F_{bx\ t/t}$. The bending stress that results from the negative moment is then checked against the smaller allowable bending stress $F_{bx\ c/t}$. The cantilever beam system in Example 6.28 uses a balanced bending combination.

EXAMPLE 6.24   Compression Zone Stressed in Tension

The roof beam in Fig. 6.23 is a 24F-V3 DF glulam. The design load includes a concentrated load and a uniformly distributed load. Loads are a combination of (DL + RLL). Lateral support is provided to the top face of the beam by the roof diaphragm. However, the bottom face is laterally unsupported in the area of negative moment except at the reaction point. The beam is used in dry-service conditions and at normal temperatures. The min-

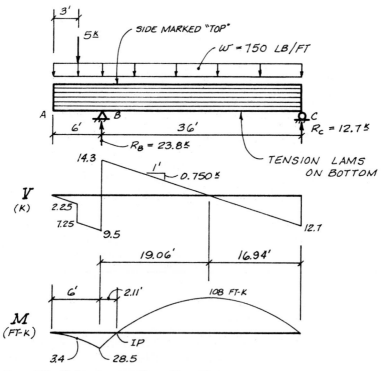

Figure 6.23 Glulam beam with small cantilever.

imum roof slope is provided so that ponding need not be considered. For this problem consider bending stresses only.

Positive Moment (Tension Zone Stressed in Tension)

In the area of positive bending moment, the allowable bending stress is $F_{bx\,t/t}$. Allowable stresses for a glulam beam are

Lateral stability: $\qquad F_b' = F_{bx\,t/t}' = F_{bx\,t/t}(C_D)(C_M)(C_t)(C_L)$

Volume effect: $\qquad F_b' = F_{bx\,t/t}' = F_{bx\,t/t}(C_D)(C_M)(C_t)(C_V)$

Also in the area of positive bending moment, the unbraced length is $l_u = 0$ because continuous lateral support is provided to the top side of the beam by the roof diaphragm. Therefore C_L defaults to unity, and lateral stability *does not govern* (DNG).

Develop a trial beam size, using an assumed value for the volume factor, and check the actual C_V later. The load duration factor is $C_D = 1.25$ for the combination of (DL + RLL). Both C_M and C_t default to unity. Tabulated stress are given in NDS Supplement Table 5A.

Assume $C_V = 0.90$:

$$F_b' = F_{bx\,t/t}' = F_{bx\,t/t}(C_D)(C_M)(C_t)(C_V)$$

$$= 2400(1.25)(1.0)(1.0)(0.90) = 2700 \text{ psi}$$

$$\text{Max. } M = 108 \text{ ft-k} = 1295 \text{ in.-k (from Fig. 6.23)}$$

$$\text{Req'd } S = \frac{M}{F_b'} = \frac{1{,}295{,}000}{2700} = 480 \text{ in.}^3$$

Refer to NDS Supplement Table 1C, and choose the smallest Western species glulam size that furnishes a section modulus greater than the required.

$$\textit{Try } 5\tfrac{1}{8} \times 24 \quad 24\text{F-V3} \quad \text{DF glulam}$$

$$S = 492 \text{ in.}^3 > 480 \qquad \textit{OK}$$

Verify C_V.

The volume factor is a function of the length, depth, and width of a beam. The length is to be taken as the distance between points of zero moment in Fig. 6.23 ($L = 36 - 2.11 = 33.89$ ft). However, it is simple and conservative to use the full span length of 36 ft.

$$C_V = K_L \left(\frac{21}{L}\right)^{1/10} \left(\frac{12}{d}\right)^{1/10} \left(\frac{5.125}{b}\right)^{1/10} \leq 1.0$$

$$= 1.0 \left(\frac{21}{36}\right)^{0.1} \left(\frac{12}{24}\right)^{0.1} \left(\frac{5.125}{5.125}\right)^{0.1}$$

$$= 0.884 < 1.0$$

The assumed value of $C_V = 0.90$ was not conservative. Therefore, compare the actual and allowable bending stresses in a summary:

$$f_b = \frac{M}{S} = \frac{1{,}295{,}000}{492} = 2630 \text{ psi}$$

$$F'_b = F'_{bx\,t/t} = F_{bx\,t/t}(C_D)(C_M)(C_t)(C_V)$$

$$= 2400(1.25)(1.0)(1.0)(0.884)$$

$$= 2650 \text{ psi} > 2630$$

$$\therefore \text{ Positive moment} \quad OK$$

Negative Moment (Compression Zone Stressed in Tension)

The trial beam size remains the same, and the computed bending stress is

$$\text{Neg. } M = 28.5 \text{ ft-k} = 342 \text{ in.-k}$$

$$f_b = \frac{M}{S} = \frac{342,000}{492} = 695 \text{ psi}$$

In the area of negative bending moment, the tabulated bending stress is $F_{bx\,c/t} = 1200$ psi. The allowable stress is the smaller value determined from the two criteria

Lateral stability: $\qquad F'_b = F'_{bx\,c/t} = F_{bx\,c/t}(C_D)(C_M)(C_t)(C_L)$

Volume effect: $\qquad F'_b = F'_{bx\,c/t} = F_{bx\,c/t}(C_D)(C_M)(C_t)(C_V)$

Lateral stability

The possibility of lateral buckling needs to be considered because the bottom side of the beam does not have continuous lateral support.

Slenderness ratio for beam R_B:

To the left of the support:

$$l_u = 6 \text{ ft} = 72 \text{ in.}$$

To the right of the support to the inflection point (IP):

$$l_u = 2.11 \text{ ft} = 25.3 \text{ in.} \quad \text{(not critical)}$$

Effective unbraced lengths are given in Example 6.8 (Sec. 6.3) and in NDS Table 3.3.3. For a cantilever beam with any loading, the definition of l_e depends on the l_u/d ratio

$$\frac{l_u}{d} = \frac{72}{24} = 3.0 < 7$$

$$\therefore l_e = 2.06l_e = 2.06(72) = 148 \text{ in.}$$

$$R_B = \sqrt{\frac{l_e d}{b^2}} = \sqrt{\frac{148(24)}{(5.125)^2}} = 11.64$$

Coefficients for computing beam stability factor C_L:

$$E'_y = E_y(C_M)(C_t) = 1,600,000(1.0)(1.0)$$

$$= 1,600,000 \text{ psi}$$

$$F_{bE} = \frac{K_{bE}E'_y}{R_B^2} = \frac{0.609(1,600,000)}{11.64^2} = 7190 \text{ psi}$$

$$F^*_{bx} = F_{bx}(C_D)(C_M)(C_t)$$

$$= 1200(1.25)(1.0)(1.0) = 1500 \text{ psi}$$

$$\frac{F_{bE}}{F^*_{bx}} = \frac{7190}{1500} = 4.793$$

$$\frac{1 + F_{bE}/F^*_{bx}}{1.9} = \frac{1 + 4.793}{1.9} = 3.049$$

Beam stability factor

$$C_L = \frac{1 + F_{bE}/F^*_{bx}}{1.9} - \sqrt{\left(\frac{1 + F_{bE}/F^*_{bx}}{1.9}\right)^2 - \frac{F_{bE}/F^*_{bx}}{0.95}}$$

$$= 3.049 - \sqrt{3.049^2 - 4.793/0.95}$$

$$= 0.987$$

Volume effect

The length to compute the volume factor is defined as the distance between points of zero moment ($L = 6 + 2.11 = 8.11$ ft).

$$C_V = K_L \left(\frac{21}{L}\right)^{1/10} \left(\frac{12}{d}\right)^{1/10} \left(\frac{5.125}{b}\right)^{1/10} \leq 1.0$$

$$= 1.0\left(\frac{21}{8.11}\right)^{0.1} \left(\frac{12}{24}\right)^{0.1} \left(\frac{5.125}{5.125}\right)^{0.1}$$

$$= 1.026 > 1.0$$

$$\therefore C_V = 1.0$$

The lateral stability factor governs over the volume factor.

$$F'_b = F'_{bx\,c/t} = F_{bx\,c/t}(C_D)(C_M)(C_t)(C_L)$$

$$= 1200(1.25)(1.0)(1.0)(0.987)$$

$$= 1480 \text{ psi}$$

$$f_b = 695 \text{ psi} < 1480 \quad OK$$

$5\frac{1}{8} \times 24$ 24F-V3 DF glulam OK for bending

6.16 Cantilever Beam Systems

Cantilever beam systems have an internal hinge connection are often used in glulam construction. The reason for this is that a smaller-size beam can generally be used with a cantilever system compared with a series of simply supported beams. The cantilever length L_c in the cantilever beam system is an important variable. See Example 6.25. A cantilever length can be established for which an optimum beam size can be obtained.

EXAMPLE 6.25   Cantilever Beam Systems

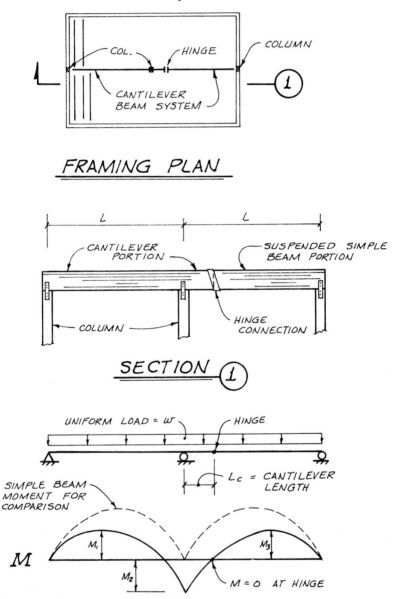

Figure 6.24 Two span cantilever beam system.

The *bending strength* of a cantilever beam system can be optimized by choosing the cantilever length L_c so that the local maximum moments M_1, M_2, and M_3 will all be equal. For the two-equal-span cantilever system shown in Fig. 6.24, with a constant uniform load on both spans, the cantilever length

$$L_c = 0.172L$$

gives equal local maximum moments

$$M_1 = M_2 = M_3 = 0.086wL^2$$

This maximum moment is considerably less than the maximum moment for a uniformly loaded simple beam:

$$M = \frac{wL^2}{8} = 0.125wL^2$$

Recommended cantilever lengths for a number of cantilever beam systems are given in the TCM (Ref. 3.1). These are found in the table and chart titled *Cantilever Beam Coefficients*. Both balanced and unbalanced loading conditions are considered.

Cantilever beam systems are not recommended for floors. Proper cambering is difficult, and cantilever beam systems in floors may transmit vibrations from one span to another. AITC recommends the use of simply supported beams for floors.

For the design of roofs, UBC Chap. 23 requires that if the RLL is less than 20 psf, the case of DL on all spans plus RLL on alternate spans (unbalanced RLL) must be considered in addition to full (DL + RLL) on all spans. For floor beams, the case of (DL + full FLL) and (DL + unbalanced FLL) must be considered regardless of the magnitude of the FLL. See Example 6.26.

EXAMPLE 6.26   Load Cases for a Two-Span Cantilever Beam System

Load Case 1: (DL + LL on All Spans)

This load constitutes the maximum total load and can produce the critical design moment, shear, and deflection. See Fig. 6.25.

Load Case 2: (DL + Unbalanced LL on Left Span)

When unbalanced LL is required, this load will produce the critical positive moment in the left span.

Load Case 3: (DL + Unbalanced LL on Right Span)

This load case will produce the same maximum negative moment as load case 1. It will also produce the maximum length from the interior support to the inflection point on the moment diagram for the left span. Depending on bracing conditions this length could be

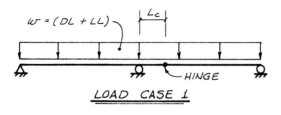

$$w = (DL + LL)$$

LOAD CASE 1

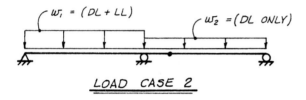

$w_1 = (DL + LL)$ $w_2 = (DL \ ONLY)$

LOAD CASE 2

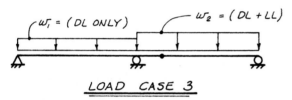

$w_1 = (DL \ ONLY)$ $w_2 = (DL + LL)$

LOAD CASE 3

Figure 6.25 When RLL < 20 psf, *full* and *unbalanced* LL are required.

critical for lateral stability. In addition, this load case will produce the minimum reaction at the left support. For a large LL and a long cantilever length, it is possible to develop an uplift reaction at this support.

The case of unbalanced live loads can complicate the design of cantilever beam systems. This is particularly true if deflections are considered. When unbalanced live loads are required, the optimum cantilever span length L_c will be different from those established for the same uniform load on all spans.

In a cantilever system the compression side of the member is not always on the top of the beam. This will require a *lateral stability* analysis of bending stresses even though the top of the girder may be connected to the horizontal diaphragm. See Example 6.27.

EXAMPLE 6.27   Lateral Stability of Cantilever Systems

Moment diagram sign convention:

Positive moment = compression on top of beam

Negative moment = compression on bottom of beam

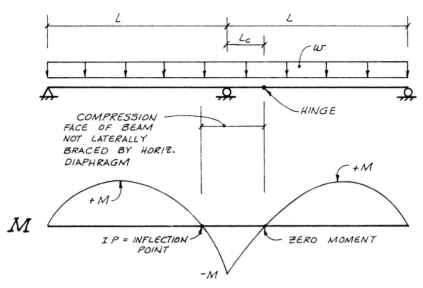

Figure 6.26a Unbraced length considerations for negative moment.

In areas of negative moment (Fig. 6.26a), the horizontal diaphragm is connected to the tension side of the beam, and this does not provide lateral support to the compression side of the member. If the lower face of the beam is braced (Fig. 6.26b) at the interior

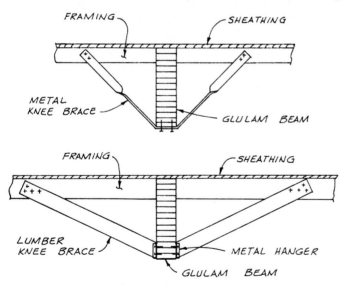

TYP. BRACES FOR
NEGATIVE MOMENT

Figure 6.26b Methods of bracing bottom side of beam.

column, the unbraced length l_u for evaluating lateral stability is the cantilever length L_c, or it is the distance from the column to the inflection point (IP). For the given beam these unbraced lengths are equal (Fig. 6.26a) under balanced loading. If lateral stability considerations cause a large reduction in the allowable bending stress, additional diagonal braces from the diaphragm to the bottom face of the beam may be required.

Several types of knee braces can be used to brace the bottom side of the beam. A *prefabricated metal knee brace* and a *lumber knee brace* are shown in Fig. 6.26b. The distance between knee braces, or the distance between a brace and a point of zero moment, is the unbraced length. For additional information on unbraced lengths, see Ref. 3.1.

In order to avoid the use of diagonal braces for aesthetic reasons, some designers use a beam-to-column connection which is designed to provide lateral support to the bottom face of the beam. Considerable care and engineering judgment must be exercised in the design of this type of connection to ensure effective lateral restraint.

6.17 Design Problem: Cantilever Beam System

In this example a cantilever beam system with two equal 50-ft spans is designed. See Example 6.28. The initial step is to determine the cantilever length L_c.

The girder is designed for a reduced roof live load, and this requires that both full and unbalanced loading be considered. For this loading, L_c is taken as $0.2L$. Two different beam sizes are developed because the three local maximum moments are not equal for the required load cases. The larger beam is required for the cantilever beam member AD, and the smaller size is for the suspended beam member DF.

For the cantilever member AD, it is necessary to check lateral stability for the portion of the member where negative moment occurs (compression on the bottom of the beam).

The final part of the example considers the camber provisions for the girder. Hand calculations are shown for the deflection analysis under dead loads. However, this is done for illustration purposes only, and it is recognized that deflection calculations will normally be done by computer.

In cambering members, most glulam manufacturers are able to set jigs at 4-ft intervals. However, the designer in most cases does not have to specify the camber settings at these close intervals. Typically the required camber would be specified at the midspans, at the internal hinge points, and perhaps at the point of inflection. The manufacturer, then, would establish the camber at various points along the span, using a parabolic or circular curve. Camber tolerance is roughly $\pm\frac{1}{4}$ in.

EXAMPLE 6.28   Cantilever Beam System

Design a cantilever roof beam system, using UBC roof design loads. Determine the optimum location of the hinge. Use 22F-V8 Douglas Fir glulam. Tributary width to the girder is 20 ft. Roof DL = 14 psf, including an estimated 2 psf (40 lb/ft) for the weight of the girder. There is no snow load, and the beam does not support a plastered ceiling. The member is used in a dry-service condition ($C_M = 1.0$) and at normal temperatures

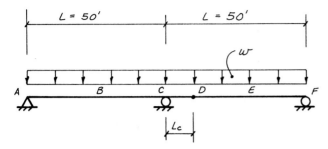

Figure 6.27a

$(C_t = 1.0)$. Allowable stresses and section properties are obtained from the NDS Supplement.

Loads

As noted in Sec. 6.16, the Code requires that unbalanced roof LL be considered unless the live load is 20 psf or greater. Thus, one possible design approach is to use a 20-psf RLL on all spans.

$$w_{DL} = 14 \times 20 = 280 \text{ lb/ft}$$

$$\underline{w_{LL} = 20 \times 20 = 400}$$

$$w_{TL} = 680 \text{ lb/ft}$$

An alternate design can be made using a reduced roof LL, considering (DL + LL) on all spans or (DL + unbalanced LL), whichever is critical.

$$\text{Trib } A > 600 \text{ ft}^2 \qquad \therefore \text{RLL} = 12 \text{ psf}$$

$$w_{DL} = 14 \times 20 = 280 \text{ lb/ft}$$

$$\underline{w_{LL} = 12 \times 20 = 240 \cdot}$$

$$w_{TL} = 520 \text{ lb/ft}$$

A smaller section will be obtained with the reduced live load.
    In Example 6.25 a cantilever length of

$$L_c = 0.172L$$

was recommended for a two-span cantilever system with a constant uniform load on both spans. When unbalanced live load is also considered, a different cantilever length will give approximately equal positive and negative moments for the cantilever segment. This length is

$$L_c = 0.2L = 0.2(50) = 10 \text{ ft}$$

With the cantilever length known, the shear and moment diagrams for the three loading conditions can be drawn (see Fig. 6.27*b*, *c*, and *d*).

Load Case 1: (DL + RLL on All Spans)

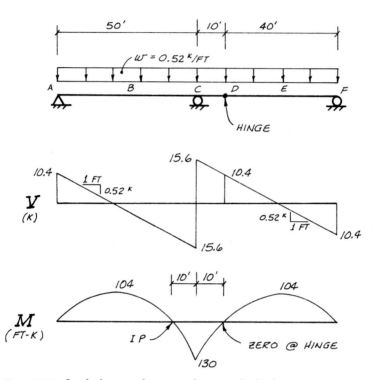

Figure 6.27b   Load, shear, and moment diagrams for load case 1.

Member AD

BENDING:

The glulam combination 22-V8 DF is "balanced" to provide equal positive and negative moment capacity. In other words, F_{bx} *tension zone stressed in tension* and F_{bx} *compression zone stressed in tension* are equal for this combination.

Maximum moments from load cases 1, 2, and 3:

$$\text{Max.} + M \approx \text{max.} - M = 130 \text{ ft-k} = 1560 \text{ in.-k}$$

NOTE: For comparison, the moment for a simple beam is

$$M = \frac{wL^2}{8} = \frac{0.52(50)^2}{8} = 162 \text{ ft-k} \gg 130$$

Load Case 2: (DL + Unbalanced RLL on Left Span)

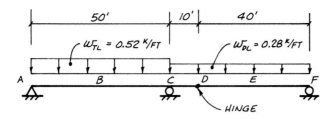

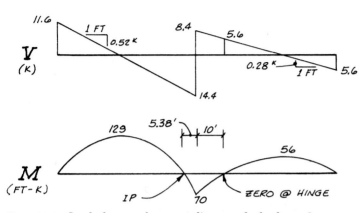

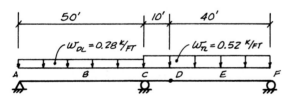

Figure 6.27c Load, shear, and moment diagrams for load case 2.

Load Case 3: (DL + Unbalanced RLL on Right Span)

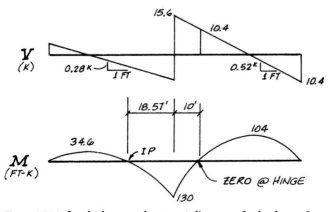

Figure 6.27d Load, shear, and moment diagrams for load case 3.

The maximum positive and negative moments in member AD are seen to be equal. It will be recalled that the allowable bending stress in a glulam is the smaller value given by two criteria

Volume effect: $$F_b' = F_{bx}(C_D)(C_M)(C_t)(C_V)$$

Lateral stability: $$F_b' = F_{bx}(C_D)(C_M)(C_t)(C_L)$$

A trial beam size will be developed using the volume factor. This size will then serve as the basis for the check on lateral stability.

Volume effect

Start by assuming a value for C_V, and verify it later. The load duration factor is $C_D = 1.25$ for the combination of (DL + RLL). Both C_M and C_t default to unity. Tabulated stresses are given in NDS Supplement Table 5A.
    Assume $C_V = 0.90$:

$$F_b' = F_{bx}(C_D)(C_M)(C_t)(C_V)$$

$$= 2200(1.25)(1.0)(1.0)(0.90) = 2475 \text{ psi}$$

$$\text{Req'd } S = \frac{M}{F_b'} = \frac{1{,}560{,}000}{2475} = 630 \text{ in.}^3$$

Refer to NDS Supplement Table 1C, and choose the glulam (Western Species) with the smallest area that furnishes a section modulus greater than the required.

$$\textit{Try} \quad 5\tfrac{1}{8} \times 28\tfrac{1}{2} \quad 22\text{F-V8} \quad \text{DF glulam}$$

$$S = 693.8 \text{ in.}^3 > 630 \quad \textit{OK}$$

Verify C_V.
    The volume factor is a function of the length, depth, and width. The length is to be taken as the distance between points of zero moment. The distance between points of zero moment for member AD is summarized for the three load cases:

Load case	Positive moment	Negative moment
1 (Fig. 6.27b)	$L = 50 - 10 = 40$ ft	$L = 10 + 10 = 20$ ft
2 (Fig. 6.27c)	$L = 50 - 5.38 = 44.62$ ft	$L = 5.38 + 10 = 15.38$ ft
3 (Fig. 6.27d)	$L = 50 - 18.57 = 31.43$ ft	$L = 18.57 + 10 = 28.57$ ft

The maximum distance between points of zero moment is 44.62 ft. (Note that $L = 50$ ft could conservatively be used.)

$$C_V = K_L \left(\frac{21}{L}\right)^{1/10} \left(\frac{12}{d}\right)^{1/10} \left(\frac{5.125}{b}\right)^{1/10} \leq 1.0$$

$$= 1.0 \left(\frac{21}{44.62}\right)^{0.1} \left(\frac{12}{28.5}\right)^{0.1} \left(\frac{5.125}{5.125}\right)^{0.1}$$

$$= 0.851 < 1.0$$

The assumed value of $C_V = 0.90$ was not conservative. Therefore, verify trial size by comparing the actual and allowable bending stresses:

$$f_b = \frac{M}{S} = \frac{1,560,000}{693.8} = 2250 \text{ psi}$$

$$F'_b = F_{bx}(C_D)(C_M)(C_t)(C_V)$$

$$= 2200(1.25)(1.0)(1.0)(0.851)$$

$$= 2340 \text{ psi} > 2250$$

∴ Bending stress for trial beam size as defined by volume factor is *OK*.

Lateral stability

In the area of positive bending moment, the roof diaphragm will be continuously attached to the top side of the girder. Thus, there is full lateral support where there is positive moment, and lateral stability is not a consideration.

However, in the area of negative bending moment, the compression (bottom) side of the member is laterally unsupported between the hinge and the column and between the column and the inflection point. The distance between points of lateral support for member *AD* is summarized for the three load cases:

Load case	Negative moment
1 (Fig. 6.27*b*)	$l_{u \text{ max}} = 10 \text{ ft}$
2 (Fig. 6.27*c*)	$l_{u \text{ max}} = 10 \text{ ft}$
3 (Fig. 6.27*d*)	$l_{u \text{ max}} = 18.57 \text{ ft}$

The maximum unbraced length is 18.57 ft. An evaluation of the lateral stability factor C_L for an unbraced length of 18.57 ft was done separately and is not shown. The lateral stability factor for $l_u = 18.57$ ft causes the allowable bending stress F'_b to be reduced substantially below the actual bending stress f_b. To solve this problem, an additional diagonal brace (Fig. 6.26*b*) will be provided between the column and the inflection point. Locate this intermediate brace so that l_u to the left of the column is 10 ft or less. Therefore, the maximum unbraced length to the left and right of the column is 10 ft.

Show calculations to determine the effect of an unbraced length of 10 ft on allowable bending stress.

$$l_u = 10 \text{ ft} = 120 \text{ in.}$$

Slenderness ratio for beam R_B:

Effective unbraced lengths are given in Example 6.8 (Sec. 6.3) and in NDS Table 3.3.3. For a cantilever or single-span beam with any loading, the definition of l_e depends on the l_u/d ratio.

$$\frac{l_u}{d} = \frac{120}{28.5} = 4.21 < 7$$

$$\therefore l_e = 2.06 l_e = 2.06(120) = 247 \text{ in.}$$

$$R_B = \sqrt{\frac{l_e d}{b^2}} = \sqrt{\frac{247(28.5)}{(5.125)^2}} = 16.38$$

Coefficients for computing beam stability factor C_L

$$E'_y = E_y(C_M)(C_t) = 1,600,000(1.0)(1.0)$$

$$= 1,600,000 \text{ psi}$$

$$F_{bE} = \frac{K_{bE}E'_y}{R_B^2} = \frac{0.609(1,600,000)}{16.38^2} = 3630 \text{ psi}$$

$$F_b^* = F_{bx}(C_D)(C_M)(C_t)$$

$$= 2200(1.25)(1.0)(1.0) = 2750 \text{ psi}$$

$$\frac{F_{bE}}{F_b^*} = \frac{3630}{2750} = 1.321$$

$$\frac{1 + F_{bE}/F_b^*}{1.9} = \frac{1 + 1.321}{1.9} = 1.222$$

Beam stability factor

$$C_L = \frac{1 + F_{bE}/F_b^*}{1.9} - \sqrt{\left(\frac{1 + F_{bE}/F_b^*}{1.9}\right)^2 - \frac{F_{bE}/F_b^*}{0.95}}$$

$$= 1.222 - \sqrt{1.222^2 - 1.321/0.95}$$

$$= 0.903$$

Allowable bending stress

$$F'_b = F_{bx}(C_D)(C_M)(C_t)(C_L)$$

$$= 2200(1.25)(1.0)(1.0)(0.903)$$

$$= 2480 \text{ psi} > f_b = 2250 \qquad OK$$

$\therefore$ The allowable bending stress given by volume factor *and* lateral stability factor are both satisfactory.

SHEAR:

Max. $V = 15.6$ k   Neglect reduced shear V' (conservative).

$$f_v = \frac{1.5V}{A} = \frac{1.5(15,600)}{146.1} = 160 \text{ psi}$$

$$F'_v = F_V(C_D)(C_M)(C_t)(C_H)$$

$$= 165(1.25)(1.0)(1.0)(1.0)$$

$$= 206 \text{ psi} > 160 \qquad OK$$

Member *AD* trial size 5⅛ × 28½ is adequate for bending and shear.

Member DF

BENDING:

Member *DF* has positive moment everywhere, and the compression side of the member has continuous lateral support. Therefore, $l_u = 0$, and lateral stability need not be considered. Determine a trial size, using the volume factor.

$$\text{Max. } M = 104 \text{ ft-k} = 1248 \text{ in.-k}$$

Assume $C_V = 0.87$:

$$F'_b = F_{bx}(C_D)(C_M)(C_t)(C_V)$$

$$= 2200(1.25)(1.0)(1.0)(0.87) = 2390 \text{ psi}$$

$$\text{Req'd } S = \frac{M}{F'_b} = \frac{1,248,000}{2390} = 522 \text{ in.}^3$$

Select a 5⅛ in. wide trial size glulam from NDS Supplement Table 1C.

$$\textit{Try} \quad 5\tfrac{1}{8} \times 25\tfrac{1}{2} \quad 22\text{F-V8} \quad \text{DF glulam}$$

$$S = 555.4 \text{ in.}^3 > 522 \quad \textit{OK}$$

Verify C_V.

$$C_V = K_L \left(\frac{21}{L}\right)^{1/10} \left(\frac{12}{d}\right)^{1/10} \left(\frac{5.125}{b}\right)^{1/10} \leq 1.0$$

$$= 1.0\left(\frac{21}{40}\right)^{0.1} \left(\frac{12}{25.5}\right)^{0.1} \left(\frac{5.125}{5.125}\right)^{0.1}$$

$$= 0.870 < 1.0$$

The actual value and the assumed value of C_V are equal, and the trial size for bending is adequate. Show a comparison of actual and allowable bending stresses anyway:

$$f_b = \frac{M}{S} = \frac{1,248,000}{555.4} = 2245 \text{ psi}$$

$$F'_b = F_{bx}(C_D)(C_M)(C_t)(C_V)$$

$$= 2200(1.25)(1.0)(1.0)(0.870)$$

$$= 2390 \text{ psi} > 2245 \quad \textit{OK}$$

SHEAR:

$$\text{Max. } V = 10.4 \text{ k} \qquad \text{Neglect reduction.}$$

$$f_v = \frac{1.5V}{A} = \frac{1.5(10,400)}{130.7} = 119 \text{ psi}$$

$$F'_v = F_V(C_D)(C_M)(C_t)(C_H)$$

$$= 165(1.25)(1.0)(1.0)(1.0)$$

$$= 206 \text{ psi} > 119 \quad OK$$

Member DF trial size $5\frac{1}{8} \times 25\frac{1}{2}$ is adequate for bending and shear.

Deflection and Camber

Trial sizes for members AD and DF have been determined considering bending and shear stresses. Attention is now turned to deflections.

If done by hand, a comprehensive deflection analysis for a cantilever beam system can be a cumbersome calculation. This is especially true if unbalanced loads are involved. Some designers choose to perform a complete deflection analysis, and others do not. This is really at the discretion of the designer because the Code does not provide deflection criteria for roofs (except for those that support a plastered ceiling). Computer solutions can greatly reduce the design effort in analyzing deflections.

To simplify this example, only the dead load deflection calculation is illustrated. This is required in order to determine the camber for the beam (camber $= 1.5\Delta_{DL}$).

Various methods of calculating deflection can be used. Here the dead load deflection is calculated by the superposition of handbook deflection formulas (Refs. 3.1 and 11.1). The deflection is evaluated at three points:

At the center of span AC (point B)

At the hinge (point D)

At the midspan of the suspended beam (point E)

Bending is about the x axis, and the modulus of elasticity for deflection calculations is

$$E'_x = E_x(C_M)(C_t)$$

$$= 1,700,000(1.0)(1.0) = 1,700,000 \text{ psi}$$

Section properties:

Member AD: $I_x = 9887 \text{ in.}^4$

Member DF: $I_x = 7082 \text{ in.}^4$

NOTE: The camber provisions included in this example are for long-term deflection. A minimum roof slope of $\frac{1}{4}$ in./ft (in addition to long-term DL deflection considerations) is required to provide drainage and avoid ponding.

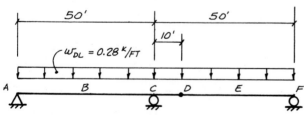

Figure 6.27e Loading for camber.

CAMBER AT B:

Deflection at B due to uniform load on member AD:

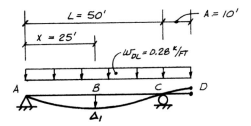

Figure 6.27f

$$\Delta_1 = \frac{wX}{24E'IL} (L^4 - 2L^2X^2 + LX^3 - 2A^2L^2 + 2A^2X^2)$$

$$= \frac{(0.28)(25)(12 \text{ in./ft})^3}{24(1700)(9887)(50)} [(50)^4 - 2(50)^2(25)^2 + 50(25)^3$$

$$- 2(10)^2(50)^2 + 2(10)^2(25)^2]$$

$$= 2.12 \text{ in. down}$$

Deflection at B due to load on DF:

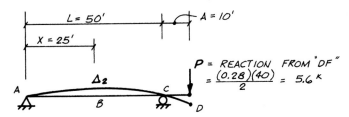

Figure 6.27g

$$\Delta_2 = \frac{PAX}{6E'IL} (L^2 - X^2)$$

$$= \frac{(5.6)(10)(25)(12)^3}{6(1700)(9887)(50)} [(50)^2 - (25)^2]$$

$$= 0.90 \text{ in. up}$$

$$\Delta_{DL} = \Delta_1 + \Delta_2 = 2.12 - 0.90 = 1.22 \text{ in. down}$$

$$\text{Camber at } B = 1.5\Delta_{DL} = 1.5(1.22) = 1.83 \approx 1\tfrac{7}{8} \text{ in. up}$$

CAMBER AT HINGE D:

Deflection at D due to uniform load on AD:

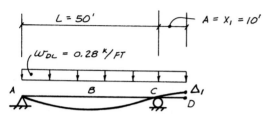

Figure 6.27h

$$\Delta_1 = \frac{wX_1}{24E'I}(4A^2L - L^3 + 6A^2X_1 - 4AX_1^2 + X_1^3)$$

$$= \frac{(0.28)(10)(12\ \text{in.}/\text{ft})^3}{24(1700)(9887)}[(4)(10)^2(50) - (50)^3 + 6(10)^2(10) - 4(10)(10)^2 + (10)^3]$$

$$= 1.22\ \text{in.}\quad \text{up}$$

Deflection at D due to load on DF:

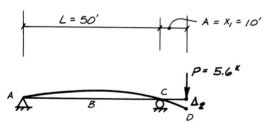

Figure 6.27i

$$\Delta_2 = \frac{PX_1}{6E'I}(2AL + 3AX_1 - X_1^2)$$

$$= \frac{(5.6)(10)(12)^3}{6(1700)(9887)}[(2)(10)(50) + 3(10)(10) - (10)^2]$$

$$= 1.15\ \text{in.}\quad \text{down}$$

$$\Delta_{\text{DL}} = \Delta_1 + \Delta_2 = -1.22 + 1.15 = -0.07\ \text{in.}\quad\text{very small}$$

Specify *no camber* at hinge D.

CAMBER AT E:

The left support of member DF (i.e., the hinge) has been found to have a very small deflection. The dead load deflection calculation for point E is a simple beam deflection calculation.

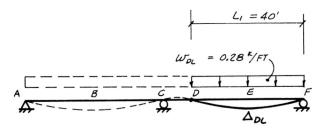

Figure 6.27j

$$\Delta_{DL} = \frac{5wL_1^4}{384E'I} = \frac{5(0.28)(40)^4(12)^3}{384(1700)(7082)} = 1.34 \text{ in. down}$$

$$\text{Camber at } E = 1.5\Delta_{DL} = 1.5 \times 1.34 \approx 2 \text{ in.} \quad \text{up}$$

> *Use* 5⅛ × 28½ for member AD
>   5⅛ × 25½ for member DF
>   22F-V8   DF glulam
>
>   Camber: 1⅞ in. up at point B
>   Zero camber at hinge D
>   2 in. up at point E

6.18   Lumber Roof and Floor Decking

Lumber sheathing (1-in. nominal thickness) can be used to span between closely spaced roof or floor beams. However, plywood and other structural-use panels are often used for this application. Plywood and other panel products are covered in Chap. 8.

Timber decking is used for longer spans. It is available as *solid decking* or *laminated decking*. Solid decking is made from dry lumber and is available in several grades in a number of commercial wood species. Common sizes are 2 × 6, 3 × 6, and 4 × 6 (nominal sizes). Various types of edge configurations are available, but tongue-and-groove (T&G) edges are probably the most common. See Fig. 6.28. A single T&G is used on 2-in.-nominal decking, and a double T&G is used on the larger thicknesses.

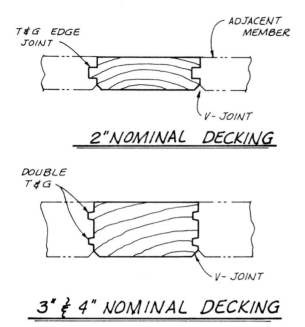

T&G EDGE JOINT

ADJACENT MEMBER

V-JOINT

2" NOMINAL DECKING

DOUBLE T&G

V-JOINT

3" & 4" NOMINAL DECKING

Figure 6.28 Solid lumber decking. Decking can be obtained with various surface patterns if the bottom side of the decking is architecturally exposed. These sketches show a V-joint pattern.

Glued laminated decking is fabricated from three or more individual laminations. Laminated decking also has T&G edge patterns.

Decking essentially functions as a series of parallel beams that span between the roof or floor framing. Bending stresses or deflection criteria usually govern the allowable loads on decking. Spans range from 3 to 20 ft and more depending on the load, span type, grade, and thickness of decking. The *layup* of decking affects the load capacity. See Example 6.29. It has been noted elsewhere that Decking is graded for bending about the minor axis of the cross section.

EXAMPLE 6.29   Layup of Decking

Layup refers to the arrangement of end joints in decking. Five different layups are defined in Ref. 3.1, and three of these are shown in Fig. 6.29. Controlled random layup is economical and simply requires that end joints in adjacent courses be well staggered. Minimum end-joint spacing is 2 ft for 2-in. nominal decking and 4 ft for 3- and 4-in. nominal decking. In addition, end joints that occur on the same transverse line must be separated by at least two courses. End joints may be mechanically interlocked by matched T&G

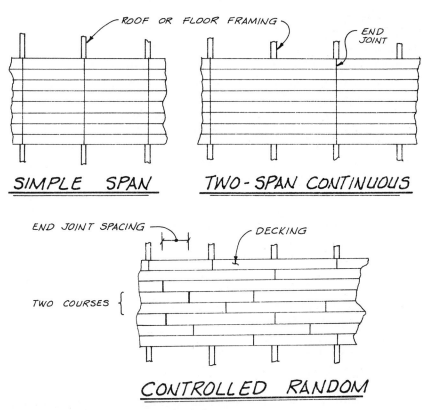

Figure 6.29 Three forms of layup for decking.

ends or by wood or metal splines to aid in load transfer. For other requirements see Ref. 3.1.

The TCM gives bending and deflection coefficients for the various types of layups. These can be used to calculate the required thickness of decking. However, the designer can often refer to allowable span and load tables for decking requirements. UBC Table 25-U gives the allowable span for 2-in. T&G decking. Reference 3.1 includes allowable load tables for simple span and controlled random layups for a variety of thicknesses.

6.19 Fabricated Wood Components

Several fabricated wood products are covered in considerable detail in this book. These include glulam (Chap. 5) and plywood and other structural-use panel products (Chap. 8). In addition to these, a number of other fabricated wood elements can be used as beams in a roof or floor system. Many of these components are produced as proprietary products, and consequently design criteria and material properties may vary from manufacturer to manufacturer.

The purpose of this section is simply to describe some of the wood components that may be used in typical wood-frame buildings. The structural design of some of these products may be performed by the manufacturer. For example, the design engineer for a building may decide to use a certain system in a roof application. After the spacing of the members has been established and the loading has been determined, the engineering staff of the supplier may design the component to perform in the specified manner.

For other components the project engineer may use certain information supplied by the manufacturer to determine the size of the required structural member. The information provided by the manufacturer can take the form of load/span tables or allowable stresses and effective section properties. Cooperation between the designer and the supplier is recommended in the early planning stages. The designer should also verify local building code recognition of the product and the corresponding design criteria.

The fabricated wood components covered in this section are

1. Structural composite lumber (SCL)
   a. Laminated veneer lumber (LVL)
   b. Parallel strand lumber (PSL)
2. Prefabricated wood I joists
3. Light-frame wood trusses

Structural composite lumber refers to engineered lumber that is produced in a manufacturing plant. Although glulam was described in Chap. 5 as a composite material, the term *structural composite lumber* generally refers to a reconstituted wood product made from much smaller pieces of wood. It is fabricated by gluing together thin pieces of wood that are dried to a low moisture content. The glue is a waterproof adhesive. As a result of the manufacturing process, SCL is dimensionally stable and has less variability than sawn lumber.

The allowable stresses for glulams are generally higher than those for solid sawn lumber, and allowable stresses for structural composite lumber are higher than those for glulam. Tabulated bending stresses F_b for SCL range from 2300 to 3200 psi, and tabulated shear stresses F_v range from 150 to 290 psi (Ref. 31). Current practice involves production of two general types of SCL which are known as laminated veneer lumber *and* parallel strand lumber.

Laminated veneer lumber (LVL) is similar in certain respects to glulam and plywood. It is fabricated from veneer similar to that used in plywood. The veneer typically ranges in thickness between $\frac{1}{10}$ and $\frac{1}{6}$ in. and is obtained from the rotary cutting process illustrated Fig. 8.3. Laminated veneer lumber generally makes use of the same species of wood used in the production of structural plywood (i.e., Douglas Fir-Larch and Southern Pine).

Unlike plywood which is cross-laminated, the veneers in LVL are laid up with the wood fibers all running in one direction (i.e., parallel to the length of the member). The parallel orientation of the wood fiber is one reason for the high allowable stresses in SCL. Selective grading of veneer and the dispersion of defects as part of the manufacturing process (similar to the dispersion of defects in glulam, see Fig. 5.3) are additional reasons for the higher stress values. The layup of veneer for LVL can also follow a specific pattern similar to glulam to meet strength requirements.

LVL is produced in either a continuous-length manufacturing operation or in fixed lengths. Fixed lengths are a function of the press size in a manufacturing plant. However, any desired length can be obtained by end jointing members of fixed lengths. Laminated veneer lumber is produced in boards or billets that can range from ¾ to 3½ in. thick and may be 4 ft wide and 80 ft long. A billet is then sawn into sizes as required for specific applications. See Example 6.30.

EXAMPLE 6.30   Laminated Veneer Lumber

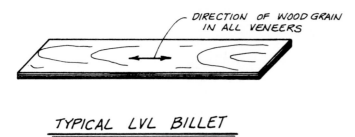

DIRECTION OF WOOD GRAIN IN ALL VENEERS

TYPICAL LVL BILLET

Figure 6.30a Billet of laminated veneer lumber.

Laminated veneer lumber is fabricated from sheets of veneer that are glued into panels called billets. Unlike the cross-lamination of veneers in plywood (Sec. 8.3), LVL has the direction of the wood grain in all veneers running parallel with the length of the billet. Pieces of LVL are trimmed from the billet for use in a variety of applications. See Fig. 6.30b.

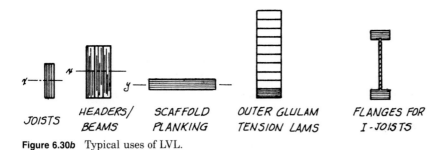

| JOISTS | HEADERS/ BEAMS | SCAFFOLD PLANKING | OUTER GLULAM TENSION LAMS | FLANGES FOR I-JOISTS |

Figure 6.30b Typical uses of LVL.

Uses of laminated veneer lumber include beams, joists, headers, and scaffold planking. Beams and headers may require multiple thicknesses of LVL to obtain the necessary member width. LVL can also be used for the higher-quality tension laminations in glulams. Additional applications include flanges of prefabricated wood I joists and chords of trusses. Two LVL beams are shown in Fig. 6.30c.

Figure 6.30c Laminated veneer lumber beams. *(Trus Joist MacMillan)*

The use of LVL is economical where the added expense of the material is offset by its increased strength and greater reliability.

There are two types of *parallel strand lumber* (PSL) currently in production. One type is made from the same species of wood used for plywood (i.e., Douglas Fir-Larch and Southern Pine). It starts with a sheet of veneer, which is clipped into narrow *strands* that are approximately ½ in. wide and 8 ft long. The strands are dried, coated with a waterproof adhesive, and bonded together under pressure and heat. The strands are aligned so that the wood grain is parallel to the length of the member (hence the name).

The second type of PSL is made from small-diameter trees of Aspen that previously could not be used in structural applications because of size. Flaking machines are used for small-diameter logs (instead of veneer peelers) to produce wood flakes that are approximately ½ in. wide, 0.03 in. thick, and 1 ft long. The flakes are also glued and bonded together under pressure and heat.

Both forms of parallel strand lumber (i.e., the type made from 8-ft-long *strands* and the type produced from 1-ft-long *flakes*) result in a final piece called a billet. Billets of PSL are similar to those of LVL (Fig. 6.30a), but the sizes are different. Billets of PSL can be as large as 12 in. wide, 17 in. deep, and 60 ft long. Again, final sizes for field applications are obtained by sawing the billet. Parallel strand lumber may be used alone as high-grade structural lumber for beams and columns. See Example 6.31. It may also be used in the fabrication of other structural components similar to the LVL applications in Example 6.30.

EXAMPLE 6.31   Parallel Strand Lumber

Figure 6.31a Parallel strand lumber. *(Trus Joist MacMillan)*

Parallel strand lumber is manufactured from strands or flakes of wood with the grain parallel to the length of the member. High-quality wood members in large sizes are possible with this form of SCL. See Fig. 6.31a. Applications include beams and columns which can be left architecturally exposed. See Fig. 6.31b.

Figure 6.31*b* Beams and columns of PSL. *(Trus Joist MacMillan)*

The use of *prefabricated wood components* has increased substantially in recent years. The most widely used form of these composite members is the wood *I joist,* but *box beams* are also used. See Example 6.32. Wood I joists are efficient bending members for two reasons. First, the cross section is an efficient shape. The most popular steel beams (W shapes and S shapes) have a similar configuration. The large flange areas are located away from the neutral axis of the cross section, thus increasing the moment of inertia and section modulus. In other words, the shape is efficient because the flanges are placed at the point in the cross section where the material does the most good: At the point of maximum flexural stress. The relatively thin web is satisfactory as long as it has adequate shear strength.

Second, wood I joists are efficient from a material usage standpoint. The flanges are stressed primarily in tension and compression as the result of the flexural stresses in the member. The material used for the flanges in wood I joists has high tensile and compressive strengths. Some manufacturers use sawn lumber flanges, but laminated veneer lumber flanges are common.

Although the bending moment is primarily carried by the flanges, it will be recalled that the shear in the I beam is essentially carried by the web. Wood I joists also gain efficiency by using web materials that are strong in shear. Plywood and oriented strand board panels are used in other high shear applications such as horizontal diaphragms (Chap. 9) and shearwalls (Chap. 10), in addition to being used as the web material in fabricated wood beams.

EXAMPLE 6.32   Prefabricated Wood I Joists

Figure 6.32a Typical prefabricated wood I joists. *(Louisiana-Pacific Corporation)*

(a)

Initially, prefabricated wood I joists were constructed with solid sawn lumber flanges and plywood webs. However, more recently I joists are produced from some of the newer wood products. For example, laminated veneer lumber (LVL) may be used for flanges and oriented strand board (OSB) for web material (Fig. 6.32a).

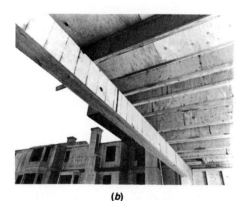

Figure 6.32b Wood I joists supported on LVL header. *(Trus Joist MacMillan)*

(b)

Prefabricated wood I joists have gained wide acceptance in certain areas of the country for repetitive framing applications (Fig. 6.32b and c). Web stiffeners for wood I joists may be required to transfer concentrated loads or reactions in bearing through the flange and into the web. Prefabricated metal hardware is available for a variety of connection applications. Because of the slender cross section of I joists, particular attention must be paid to stabilizing the members against translation and rotation. The manufacturer's recommendations for bracing and blocking should be followed in providing stability for these members.

Figure 6.32c Wood I joists as part of a wood roof system in a building with masonry walls. *(Trus Joist MacMillan)*

(c)

Wood I joists make efficient use of materials, and because of this they are relatively lightweight and easy to handle by crews in the field. In addition to strength, the depth of the cross section provides members that are relatively stiff for the amount of material used. Wood I joists can be used to span up to 40 or 50 ft, but many applications are for shorter spans. Wood I joists can be deep and slender, and care should be taken in the installation of these members to ensure adequate stability. Information on the design of lumber and plywood beams is available in Refs. 14.1 and 14.2. Additional information on the design and installation of wood I joists is available from manufacturers (e.g., Refs. 30 and 31).

Wood trusses represent another common type of fabricated wood component. Heavy wood trusses have a long history of performance, but light wood trusses are more popular today. The majority of residential wood structures, and many commercial and industrial buildings, use some form of closely spaced light wood trusses in roof and floor systems. Common spans for these trusses range up to 75 ft, but larger spans are possible. The spacing of trusses is on the order of 16 to 24 in. o.c. for floors and up to 8 ft o.c. in roof systems.

Some manufacturers produce trusses that have wood top and bottom chords and steel web members. However, the majority of truss manufacturers use light-gage toothed metal plates to connect wood chords and wood web members. See Example 6.33. The metal plates have teeth which are produced by stamping the metal plates. The metal plates are placed over the members to be connected together and the teeth are pressed into the wood.

EXAMPLE 6.33 Light-Frame Wood Trusses

Figure 6.33a Wood trusses with tubular steel webs. Trusses in the foreground are supported on a wood member attached to a steel W shape beam. In the background, trusses rest on glulam. *(Trus Joist MacMillan)*

Figure 6.33b Metal plate connected trusses being placed in roof system supported on masonry walls. *(Alpine Engineered Products, Inc.)*

Trusses can be manufactured with sawn lumber or LVL chords and steel web members (Fig. 6.33a). Trusses can be supported in a variety of ways. The top or bottom chord of a truss can bear on wood walls or beams, on steel beams, or on top of concrete or masonry walls. Another method is to suspend the truss from a ledger attached to a concrete or masonry wall.

Metal-plate-connected trusses (Fig. 6.33b) use toothed or barbed plates to connect the truss members. See Fig. 11.3 in Sec. 11.2 for a photograph of metal plate connectors. Typically the metal plates are assigned a unit load capacity (lb/in.² of contact area). Thus the required plate size is determined by dividing the forces to be transferred through the connection by the unit load capacity of the metal plate.

Light wood trusses are rather limber elements perpendicular to their intended plane of loading. Because of this flexibility, proper handling procedures are required in the field to avoid damage to the truss during erection. The use of strongbacks with a sufficient number of pickup points for lifting the trusses into place will avoid buckling of the truss about its weak axis during installation. Once a truss is properly positioned, it must be braced temporarily until the sheathing and permanent bracing are in place (Ref. 5.7b). Trusses which are not adequately braced can easily buckle or rotate. However, once the bracing is in place, the trusses provide a strong, stiff, and economical wood framing system.

The Truss Plate Institute (TPI) is the technical trade association of the metal plate truss industry. TPI publishes the "Design Specification for Metal Plate Connected Trusses" (Ref. 23.1), which provides detailed design requirements for these trusses. Among other considerations, this specification requires that the continuity of the chords at the joints in the truss be taken into account. In addition to its design specification, TPI publishes other pertinent literature such as the "Commentary and Recommendations for Bracing Wood Trusses" (Ref. 23.2). Additional information on wood trusses and bracing can be obtained from truss manufacturers (e.g., Refs. 28, 29, and 31).

6.20 Problems

Allowable stresses and section properties for the following problems are to be in accordance with the 1991 NDS. Dry-service conditions, normal temperatures, and bending about the strong axis apply unless otherwise indicated.

Some problems require the use of a *microcomputer spreadsheet*. Problems that are solved on a spreadsheet can be saved and used as a *template* for other similar problems. Templates can have many degrees of sophistication. Initially, a template may only be a hand (i.e., calculator) solution worked on a spreadsheet. In a simple template of this nature, the user will be required to provide many of the "lookup" functions for such items as

Tabulated stresses

Lumber dimensions

Load duration factor

Wet service factor

Size factor

Volume factor

As the user gains experience with spreadsheets, the template can be expanded to perform lookup and decision-making functions that were previously done manually.

Advanced computer programming skills are not required to create effective spreadsheet templates. Valuable templates can be created by designers who normally do only hand solutions. However, some programming techniques are helpful in automating *lookup* and *decision-making* steps.

The first requirement is that a spreadsheet operate correctly (i.e., calculate correct values). Another major consideration is that the input and output be structured in an orderly manner. A sufficient number of intermediate answers should be displayed and labeled so that the solution can be verified by hand.

6.1 *Given:* The beam in Fig. 6.A with the following information:

Load:	$P = 2\,\text{k}$
Load combination:	DL + RLL
Span:	$L = 8\,\text{ft}$
Member size:	4×8
Stress grade and species:	No. 1 DF-L
Unbraced length:	$l_u = 0$
Moisture content:	MC $\leq$ 19 percent
Deflection limit:	Allow. $\Delta \leq l/360$

  Find: a. Size category (Dimension lumber, B&S, or P&T)
  b. Tabulated stresses: F_b, F_v, and E
  c. Allowable stresses: F_b', F_v', and E'
  d. Actual stresses and deflection: f_b, f_v, and Δ
  e. Compare the actual and allowable design values, and determine if the member is adequate.

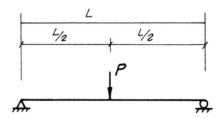

Figure 6.A

6.2 Repeat Prob. 6.1 except the moisture content exceeds 19 percent.

6.3 Repeat Prob. 6.1 except the unbraced length is $l_u = L/2 = 4\,\text{ft}$. $C_M = 1.0$.

6.4   Use the hand solution to Probs. 6.1 and 6.3 as a guide to develop a micro-computer spreadsheet template to solve similar problems.
   a. Consider only the specific criteria given in Probs. 6.1 and 6.3.
   b. Expand the template to handle any

> Span length L
> Magnitude load P
> Unbraced length l_u
> Sawn lumber trial member size

   The spreadsheet is to include a list (i.e., database) of tabulated stresses for all size categories (Dimension lumber, B&S, P&T) of No. 1 DF-L.
   c. Expand the database in part b to include all stress grades of DF-L from No. 2 through Select Structural.

6.5   Repeat Prob. 6.1 except the unbraced length is $l_u = L = 8$ ft.

6.6   *Given:*   The beam in Fig. 6.A with the following information:

Load:	$P = 1.5$ k
Load combination:	DL + SL
Span:	$L = 24$ ft
Member size:	$3\frac{1}{8} \times 21$
Bending combination glulam:	24F-V4 DF
Unbraced length:	$l_u = 0$
Moisture content:	MC < 16 percent
Deflection limit:	Allow. $\Delta \le l/240$

   Find: a. Tabulated stresses: F_b, F_v, E_x, and E_y
      b. Allowable stresses: F'_b, F'_v, E'_x, and E'_y
      c. Actual stresses and deflection: f_b, f_v, and Δ
      d. Compare the actual and allowable design values and determine if the member is adequate. How much camber should be provided if the dead load on the beam is 35 percent of the given total load?

6.7   Repeat Prob. 6.6 except the moisture content exceeds 16 percent.

6.8   Repeat Prob. 6.6 except the unbraced length is $l_u = L/2 = 12$ ft. $C_M = 1.0$.

6.9   Use the hand solution to Probs. 6.6 and 6.8 as a guide to develop a micro-computer spreadsheet template to solve similar problems.
   a. Consider only the specific criteria given in Probs. 6.6 and 6.8.
   b. Expand the template to handle any

> Span length L
> Magnitude load P
> Unbraced length l_u
> Size Western Species bending combination glulam

   The spreadsheet is to include a list (i.e., database) of tabulated stresses for glulam bending combinations 20F-V4, 22F-V4, and 24F-V4 DF-L.

6.10 *Given:* The beam in Fig. 6.B with the following information:

Load:

$w_{DL} = 200$ lb/ft
$w_{RLL} = 250$ lb/ft
$w_{TL} = 450$ lb/ft

Load combination:	DL + RLL
Span:	$L = 10$ ft
Member size:	4×10
Stress grade and species:	Sel. Str. Hem-Fir
Unbraced length:	$l_u = 0$
Moisture content:	MC $\leq$ 19 percent
Deflection limit:	Allow. $\Delta_{RLL} \leq l/360$
	Allow. $\Delta_{(KDL+RLL)} \leq l/240$

Find: *a.* Size category (Dimension lumber, B&S, or P&T)
   b. Tabulated stresses: F_b, F_v, and E
   c. Allowable stresses: F'_b, F'_v, and E'
   d. Actual stresses and deflection: f_b, f_v, f'_v, and Δ
   e. Compare the actual and allowable design values, and determine
      if the member is adequate.

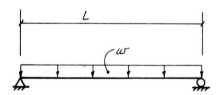

Figure 6.B

6.11 Repeat Prob. 6.10 except the moisture content exceeds 19 percent.

6.12 Repeat Prob. 6.10 except the unbraced length is $l_u = L/2 = 5$ ft.

6.13 Use the hand solution to Probs. 6.10 and 6.12 as a guide to develop a microcomputer spreadsheet template to solve similar problems.
   a. Consider only the specific criteria given in Probs. 6.10 and 6.12.
   b. Expand the template to handle any

   Span length L
   Magnitude load w
   Unbraced length l_u
   Sawn lumber trial member size

   The spreadsheet is to include a list (i.e., database) of tabulated stresses
   for all size categories (Dimension lumber, B&S, P&T) of Sel. Str. Hem-
   Fir.
   c. Expand the database in part *b* to include all stress grades of Hem-Fir from
   No. 2 through Select Structural.

6.14   *Given:*   The beam in Fig. 6.B with the following information:

Load:	$w_{DL} = 200$ lb/ft
	$w_{SL} = 300$ lb/ft
	$w_{TL} = 500$ lb/ft
Load combination:	DL + SL
Span:	$L = 20$ ft
Member size:	$5 \times 19\frac{1}{4}$
Glulam bending combination:	24F-V1 SP
Unbraced length	$l_u = 0$
Moisture content:	MC < 16 percent
Deflection limit:	Allow. $\Delta_{SL} \leq l/360$
	Allow. $\Delta_{(KDL+SL)} \leq l/240$

Find: a. Tabulated stresses: F_b, F_v, E_x, and E_y
b. Allowable stresses: F'_b, F'_v, E'_x, and E'_y
c. Actual stresses and deflection: f_b, f_v, f'_v, and Δ
d. Compare the actual and allowable design values, and determine if the member is adequate. How much camber should be provided?

6.15   Repeat Prob. 6.14 except the moisture content exceeds 16 percent.

6.16   Repeat Prob. 6.14 except the unbraced length is $l_u = L/2 = 10$ ft. $C_M = 1.0$.

6.17   Use the hand solution to Probs. 6.14 and 6.16 as a guide to develop a microcomputer spreadsheet template to solve similar problems.
a. Consider only the specific criteria given in Probs. 6.14 and 6.16.
b. Expand the template to handle any

Span length L
Magnitude load w
Unbraced length l_u
Size Southern Pine bending combination glulam

The spreadsheet is to include a list (i.e., database) of tabulated stresses for glulam bending combinations 16F-V1, 20F-V1, 22F-V1, and 24F-V1 SP.

6.18   *Given:*   The beam in Fig. 6.C with the following information:

Load:	$P = 2$ k
Load combination:	DL + FLL
Span:	$L_1 = 8$ ft
	$L_2 = 4$ ft
Member size:	4×12
Stress grade and species:	Sel. Str. SP
Unbraced length:	$l_u = 0$
Moisture content:	MC ≤ 19 percent
Deflection limit:	Allow. $\Delta_{\text{free end}} \leq 2(L_2/360)$
	Allow. $\Delta_{\text{between supports}} \leq L_1/360$

Find: a. Size category (Dimension lumber, B&S, or P&T)
   b. Tabulated stresses: F_b, F_v, and E
   c. Allowable stresses: F_b', F_v', and E'
   d. Actual stresses and deflection: f_b, f_v, and Δ
   e. Compare the actual and allowable design values, and determine if the member is adequate.

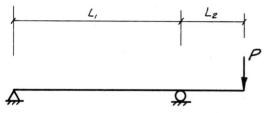

Figure 6.C

6.19   Repeat Prob. 6.18 except the moisture content exceeds 19 percent.

6.20   Repeat Prob. 6.18 except lateral support is provided at the vertical supports and at the free end.

6.21   Use the hand solution to Probs. 6.18 and 6.20 as a guide to develop a micro-computer spreadsheet template to solve similar problems.
   a. Consider only the specific criteria given in Probs. 6.18 and 6.20.
   b. Expand the template to handle any

Span lengths L_1 and L_2
Magnitude load P
Unbraced length l_u
Sawn lumber trial member size

The spreadsheet is to include a list (i.e., database) of tabulated stresses for all size categories (Dimension lumber, B&S, P&T) of Sel. Str. SP.
   c. Expand the database in part *b* to include the stress grades of No. 2, No. 1, and Select Structural Southern Pine.

6.22   *Given:*   A series of closely spaced floor beams is to be designed. Loading is similar to Fig. 6.B. The following information is known:

Load:	w_{DL} = 18 psf
	w_{FLL} = 50 psf
Load combination:	DL + FLL
Span:	L = 14 ft
Member spacing:	Trib. width = b = 16 in. o.c.
Stress grade and species:	No. 1 Hem-Fir
Unbraced length:	l_u = 0
Moisture content:	MC ≤ 19 percent
Deflection limit:	Allow. $\Delta_{FLL} \leq l/360$
	Allow. $\Delta_{(KDL+FLL)} \leq l/240$

Find: Minimum beam size. As part of the solution also give
  a. Size category (Dimension lumber, B&S, or P&T)
  b. Tabulated stresses: F_b, F_v, and E
  c. Allowable stresses: F_b', F_v', and E'
  d. Actual stresses and deflection: f_b, f_v, f_v', and Δ

6.23   *Given:*   The roof rafters in Fig. 6.D are 24 in o.c. Roof DL is 12 psf along
  the roof, and roof LL is in accordance with UBC Table 23-C, Method
  1. Calculate design shear and moment, using the horizontal plane
  method of Example 2.5 (see Fig. 2.5*b*). Lumber is No. 2 DF-L. Lateral
  stability is not a problem. Disregard deflection. $C_M = 1.0$ and $C_t =$
  1.0.

Find: Minimum rafter size. As part of the solution also give
  a. Size category (Dimension lumber, B&S, or P&T)
  b. Tabulated stresses: F_b and F_v
  c. Allowable stresses: F_b' and F_v'
  d. Actual stresses: f_b and f_v

6.24   Repeat Prob. 6.23 except that the rafers are spaced 6 ft-0 in. o.c.

6.25   *Given:*   The roof rafters in Fig. 6.D are 24 in. o.c. The roof DL is 15 psf along
  the roof, and the design snow load is 50 psf. Calculate the design
  shear and moment, using the horizontal plane method of Example
  2.5 (see Fig. 2.5*b*). Disregard deflection. Lateral stability is not a
  problem. Lumber is No. 1 DF-L. $C_M = 1.0$ and $C_t = 1.0$.

Find: The minimum rafter size. As part of the solution also give
  a. Size category (Dimension lumber, B&S, or P&T)
  b. Tabulated stresses: F_b and F_v
  c. Allowable stresses: F_b' and F_v'
  d. Actual stresses: f_b and f_v

6.26   *Given:*   The beam in Fig. 6.E is supported laterally at the ends only. The
  span length is $L = 25$ ft. The member is a 6 × 14 DF-L Select
  Structural. The load is a combination of (DL + FLL). $C_M = 1.0$ and
  $C_t = 1.0$.

Find: The allowable bending moment in ft-k and the corresponding allowable load P in k.

6.27   *Given:*   The beam in Fig. 6.E has the compression side of the member supported laterally at the ends and midspan only. The span length is
  $L = 25$ ft. The member is a 3⅛ × 18 DF glulam combination 24F-
  V4. The load is a combination of (DL + RLL). $C_M = 1.0$ and $C_t =$
  1.0.

Find: The allowable bending moment in ft-k and the corresponding allowable load P in k.

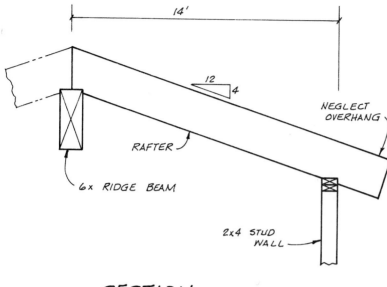

SECTION

Figure 6.D

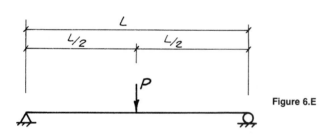

Figure 6.E

6.28 *Given:* The beam in Fig. 6.E has the compression side of the member supported laterally at the ends and the quarter points. The span length
is $L = 24$ ft. The member is a resawn glulam $2\frac{1}{2} \times 19\frac{1}{2}$ DF 24F-
V4. The load is a combination of (DL + RLL). $C_M = 1.0$ and $C_t =$
1.0.

Find: The allowable bending moment in ft-k and the corresponding allowable load P in k.

6.29 Repeat Prob. 6.27 except that the member is a $3 \times 17\frac{7}{8}$ Southern Pine glulam
combination 24F-V3, and the load is a combination of (DL + SL).

6.30 *Given:* The rafter connection in Fig. 6.F. The load is a combination of roof
(DL + SL). Lumber is No. 1 Spruce-Pine-Fir (South). $C_M = 1.0$ and
$C_t = 1.0$.

Find: a. The actual bearing stress in the rafter and in the top plate of the wall.
            b. The allowable bearing stress in the top plate.
            c. The allowable bearing stress in the rafter.

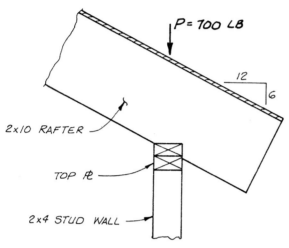

Figure 6.F

6.31   *Given:*   The rafter connection in Fig. 6.F with the slope changed to $^{12}/_{12}$. The load is a combination of (DL + RLL). Lumber is No. 2 DF-L that is used in a high-moisture-content condition (MC > 19 percent). $C_t = 1.0$.

            Find: a. The actual bearing stress in the rafter and in the top plate of the wall.
                         b. The allowable bearing stress in the top plate.
                         c. The allowable bearing stress in the rafter.

6.32   *Given:*   The beam-to-column connection in Fig. 6.G. The gravity reaction from the simply supported beam is transferred to the column by bearing (not by the bolts). Assume the column and the metal bracket have adequate strength to carry the load. $C_t = 1.0$.

            Find: The maximum allowable beam reaction governed by bearing stresses for the following conditions:
                         a. The beam is a 4 × 12 No. 1 DF-L. MC ≤ 19 percent, and the dimensions are $A = 12$ in. and $B = 5$ in. Loads are (DL + SL).
                         b. The beam is a 5⅛ × 33 DF glulam Combination 24F-V3. MC = 18 percent, and the dimensions are $A = 0$ and $B = 12$ in. Loads are (DL + SL).
                         c. The beam is a 6 × 16 No. 1 DF-L. MC = 20 percent, and the dimensions are $A = 8$ in. and $B = 10$ in. Loads are (DL + RLL).
                         d. What deformation limit is associated with the bearing stresses used in parts *a* to *c*?

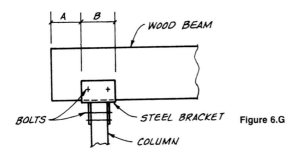

Figure 6.G

6.33 Repeat Prob. 6.32 except a deformation limit of 0.02 in. is to be used.

6.34 *Given:* The beam in Fig. 6.H is a 5⅛ × 19.5 DF glulam combination 16F-V3. The load is (DL + SL). MC < 16 percent. Lateral support is provided to the top side of the member by a roof diaphragm. C_t = 1.0.

Find: Check the given member for bending and shear stresses.

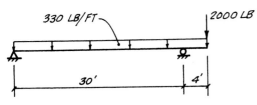

Figure 6.H

6.35 *Given:* The roof framing plan of the commercial building in Fig. 6.I. There is no ceiling. The *total* dead loads to the members are

Subpurlin (2 × 4 at 24 in. o.c.) = 7.0 psf

Purlins (4 × 14 at 8 ft-0 in. o.c.) = 8.5

Girder = 10.0

The roof is flat except for a minimum slope of ¼ in./ft to prevent ponding. Roof live loads are to be in accordance with UBC Table 23-C, Method 1. The roof diaphragm provides continuous lateral support to the top side of all beams. C_M = 1.0 and C_t = 1.0.

Find: *a.* Check the subpurlins, using No. 1 & Btr DF-L. Are the AITC-recommended deflection criteria satisfied?
b. Check the purlins, using No. 1 & Btr DF-L. Are the AITC deflection limits met?
c. Design the girder, using 24F-V4 DF glulam. Determine the minimum size, considering both strength and stiffness.

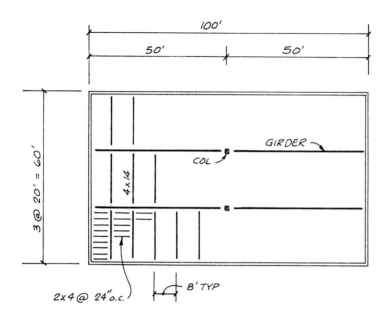

ROOF FRAMING PLAN

Figure 6.I

6.36   *Given:*   The girder in the roof framing plan in Fig. 6.J is to be designed using the optimum cantilever length L_c. The girder is 20F-V7 DF glulam. RDL = 16 psf. The top of the girder is laterally supported

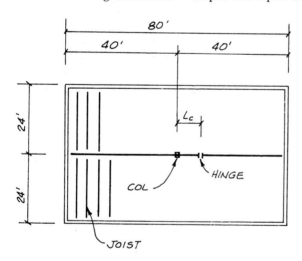

ROOF FRAMING PLAN

Figure 6.J

by the roof diaphragm. Deflection need not be checked, but camber requirements are to be determined. The roof is flat except for a minimum slope of ¼ in./ft to prevent ponding. $C_M = 1.0$ and $C_t = 1.0$.

Find: *a.* The minimum required beam size if the girder is designed for a 20-psf roof LL with no reduction for tributary area.

         b. The minimum required beam size if the girder is designed for a basic 20-psf roof LL that is to be adjusted for tributary area. Roof LL is to be determined in accordance with UBC Table 23-C, Method 1. For the roof LL reduction, consider the tributary area of the suspended portion of the cantilever system.

7

Axial Forces and Combined Bending and Axial Forces

7.1 Introduction

An axial force member has the load applied parallel to the longitudinal axis through the centroid of the cross section. The axial force may be either tension or compression. Because of the need to carry vertical gravity loads down through the structure into the foundation, columns are more often encountered than tension members. Both types of members, however, see widespread use in structural design in such items as trusses and diaphragms.

In addition to the design of axial force members, this chapter covers the design of members with a more complicated loading condition. These include members with bending (beam action) occurring simultaneously with axial forces (tension or compression). This type of member is often referred to as a *combined stress* member. A combination of loadings is definitely more critical than the case of the same forces being applied individually. The case of compression combined with bending is probably encountered more often than tension plus bending, but both types of members are found in typical wood-frame buildings.

To summarize, the design of the following types of members is covered in this chapter:

1. Axial tension
2. Axial compression
3. Combined bending and tension
4. Combined bending and compression

The design of axial force tension members is relatively straightforward, and the required size of a member can be solved for directly. For the other three types of members, however, a trial-and-error solution is the typical design approach. Trial-and-error solutions may seem awkward in the beginning. However, with a little practice the designer will be able to pick an initial trial size which will be relatively close to the required size. The final selection can often be made with very few trials. Several examples will illustrate the procedure used in design.

As noted, the most common axial load member is probably the column, and the most common combined stress member is the beam-column (combined bending and compression). See Fig. 7.1. In this example an axial load is assumed to be applied to the interior column by the girder. For the exterior column there is both a lateral force that causes bending and a vertical load that causes axial compression.

The magnitude of the lateral force (wind or seismic) to the column depends on the unit design force and how the wall is framed. The wall may be framed horizontally to span between columns, or it may be framed vertically to span between story levels (Example 3.4 in Sec. 3.3).

Numerous other examples of axial force members and combined load members can be cited. However, the examples given here are representative, and they adequately define the type of members and loadings that are considered in this chapter.

7.2   Axial Tension Members

Wood members are stressed in tension in a number of structural applications. For example, trusses have numerous axial force members, and roughly half of these are in tension. It should be noted that unless the loads frame directly into the joints in the truss and unless the joints are pinned, bending stresses will be developed in addition to the axial stresses obtained in the standard truss analysis.

Axial tension members also occur in the chords of horizontal and vertical diaphragms. In addition, tension members are used in diaphragm design when the length of the horizontal diaphragm is greater than the length of the shearwall to which it is attached. This type of member is known as a drag strut, and it is considered in Chap. 9.

The check for the axial tension stress in a member of known size uses the formula

$$f_t = \frac{P}{A_n} \leq F_t'$$

where f_t = actual (computed) tension stress parallel to grain
   P = axial tension force in member
   A_n = net cross-sectional area
      = $A_g - \Sigma A_h$

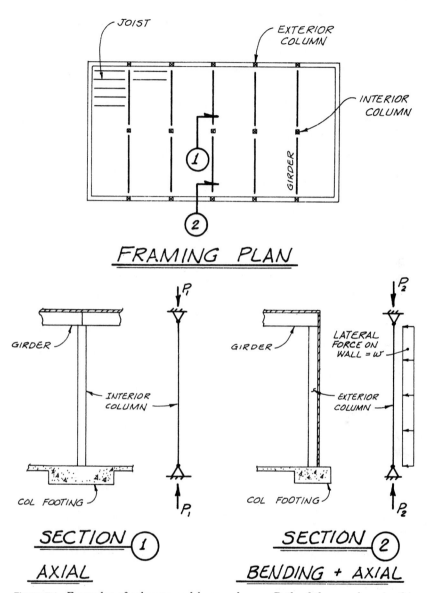

Figure 7.1 Examples of columns and beam-columns. Both of the members in this example are vertical, but horizontal or inclined members with this type of loading are also common.

$$A_g = \text{gross cross-sectional area}$$
$$\Sigma A_h = \text{sum of projected area of holes at critical section}$$
$$F'_t = \text{allowable tension stress parallel to grain (defined below)}$$

The formula for comparing the actual stress in a member with the allowable stress is usually referred to as an analysis expression. In other words, an *analysis* problem involves *checking* the adequacy of a member of known size. In a *design* situation, the size of the member is unknown, and the usual objective is to establish the minimum required member size.

In a tension member design, the axial stress formula can be rewritten to solve for the required area by dividing the load by the allowable tension stress. Although certain assumptions may be involved, this can be described as a *direct solution*. The member size determined in this way is usually something close to the final solution.

It was previously noted that the design of axial tension members is the only type of problem covered in Chap. 7 that can be accomplished by direct solution. Columns, for example, involve design by trial and error because the allowable stress depends on the column slenderness ratio. The slenderness ratio, in turn, depends on the size of the column, and it is necessary to first establish a trial size. The adequacy of the trial size is evaluated by performing an analysis. Depending on the results of the analysis, the trial size is accepted or adjusted up or down. Members with combined stresses are handled in a similar way.

It should be emphasized that the tension stress problems addressed in this chapter are for parallel-to-grain loading. The weak nature of wood in tension perpendicular to grain is noted throughout this book, and the general recommendation is again to avoid stressing wood in tension across the grain.

There are a variety of fasteners that can be used to connect wood members. The projected area of holes or grooves for the installation of fasteners is to be deducted from the *gross area* to obtain the *net area*. Some frequently used fasteners in wood connections include nails, bolts, lag bolts, split rings, and shear plates, and the design procedures for these are covered in Chaps. 11 through 13.

In determining the net area of a tension member, the projected area for nails is usually disregarded. The projected area of a bolt hole is a rectangle. A split ring or shear plate connector involves a dap or groove cut in the face of the wood member plus the projected area of the hole for the bolt (or lag bolt) that holds the assembly together. See Example 7.1. The projected area removed from the cross section for the installation of a lag bolt is determined by the shank diameter and the diameter of the lead or pilot hole for the threads.

EXAMPLE 7.1   Net Areas at Connections

The gross area of a wood member is the width of the member times its depth:

$$A_g = b \times d$$

The standard net dimensions and the gross cross-sectional areas for sawn lumber are given in NDS Supplement Table 1B. Similar properties for glulam members are listed in NDS Supplement Table 1C.

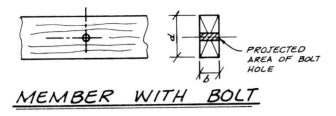

MEMBER WITH BOLT

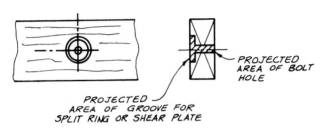

MEMBER WITH CONNECTOR IN ONE FACE

Figure 7.2 *Net section* through two wood members. One member is shown cut at a bolt hole. The other is at a joint with a split ring or shear plate connector in one face plus the projected area of a bolt. The bolt is required to hold the entire assembly (wood members and connectors) together. Photographs of split ring and shear plate connectors are included in Chap. 13 (Fig. 13.23*a* and *b*).

The projected areas for fasteners to be deducted from the gross area are as follows:

Nail holes—disregarded.

Bolt holes—computed as the hole diameter times the width of the wood member. The hole diameter is between $\frac{1}{32}$ and $\frac{1}{16}$ in. larger than the bolt diameter (NDS Sec. 8.1.2). In this book the bolt hole, for strength calculation purposes, is conservatively taken as the bolt diameter plus $\frac{1}{8}$ in.

Lag bolt holes—a function of the connection details. See NDS Appendix L for lag bolt dimensions. Drill diameters for lead holes and shank holes are given in NDS Sec. 9.1.2.

Split ring and shear plate connectors—a function of the connection details. See NDS Appendix K for the projected areas of split rings and shear plates.

If more than one fastener is used, the sum of the projected areas of all the fasteners *at the critical section* is subtracted from the gross area. For staggered fastener pattern, see NDS Sec. 3.1.2.

Perhaps the most common situation that requires a reduction of area for tension member design is a bolted connection. The 1991 NDS requires that the hole diameter be $\frac{1}{32}$ to $\frac{1}{16}$ in. larger than the bolt diameter. It also recommends against tight-fitting installations that require forcible driving of the bolt. In *ideal* conditions it is appropriate to take the hole diameter for calculation purposes equal to the actual hole diameter.

In practice, ideal installation procedures are often viewed as goals. There are many field conditions that may cause the actual installation to be less than perfect. For example, a common bolt connection is through two steel side plates with the wood member between the two metal plates. Holes in the steel plates are usually punched in the shop, and holes in the wood member are drilled in the field.

It is difficult to accurately drill the hole in the wood member from one side (through a hole in one of the steel plates) and have it align perfectly with the hole in the steel plate on the opposite side. The hole will probably be drilled partially from both sides with some misalignment where they meet. Some oversizing of the bolt hole typically occurs as the two holes are reamed to correct alignment for the installation of the bolt. This is one example of a practical field problem, and a number of others can be cited.

In this book the hole diameter for net-area calculations will arbitrarily be taken as the bolt diameter plus $\frac{1}{8}$ in. Although this is not a Code requirement in wood design, in some small way it recognizes the fact that field conditions seldom meet laboratory standards. Computing the net area of a member in this manner is more conservative than required. However, this design practice is not intended to account for poor workmanship in the installation of fasteners. See Chap. 13 for more information on bolted connections.

The allowable tension stress in a wood member is determined by multiplying the tabulated tension stress by the appropriate adjustment factors:

$$F'_t = F_t(C_D)(C_M)(C_t)(C_F)$$

where F'_t = allowable tension stress parallel to grain

$\quad\quad F_t$ = tabulated tension stress parallel to grain

$\quad\quad C_D$ = load duration factor (Sec. 4.15)

$\quad\quad C_M$ = wet service factor (Sec. 4.14)

$\quad\quad\quad$ = 1.0 for dry service conditions (as in most covered structures). Dry service is defined as

$\quad\quad\quad\quad$ MC $\leq$ 19 percent for sawn lumber

$\quad\quad\quad\quad$ MC $<$ 16 percent for glulam

$\quad\quad C_t$ = temperature factor (Sec. 4.20)

$\quad\quad\quad$ = 1.0 for normal temperature conditions

$\quad\quad C_F$ = size factor (Sec. 4.16) for tension. Obtain values for visually graded Dimension lumber from the Adjustment Factors section of NDS Supplement Tables 4A and 4B.

$\quad\quad\quad$ = 1.0 for sawn lumber in B&S and P&T sizes and MSR lumber

$\quad\quad\quad$ = 1.0 for glulam

It can be seen that the usual adjustment factors for load duration, moisture content, temperature, and size effect apply to tension stresses parallel to grain. Numerical values for the load duration factor depend on the shortest-duration load in a given combination of loads. Values of C_M and C_t frequently default to unity, but the designer should be aware of conditions that may require an adjustment. The size factor for tension applies to visually graded Dimension lumber only, and values are obtained from NDS Tables 4A and 4B.

7.3 Design Problem: Tension Member

In this example the required size for the lower chord of a truss is determined. The loads are assumed to be applied to the top chord of the truss only. See Example 7.2.

To determine the axial forces in the truss members, it is necessary to have the loads applied to the joints. Loads for the truss analysis are obtained by taking the tributary width to one joint times the uniform load. Because the actual loads are applied uniformly to the top chord, these members will have combined stresses. Other members in the truss will have axial forces only if the joints are pinned.

The tension force in the bottom chord is obtained through a standard truss analysis (method of joints). The member size is determined by calculating the required net area and adding to it the area removed by the bolt hole.

EXAMPLE 7.2   Tension Chord

Determine the required size of the lower (tension) chord in the truss in Fig. 7.3a. The loads are (DL + SL), and the effects of roof slope on the magnitude of the snow load have already been taken into account. Joints are assumed to be pinned.

Connections will be made with a single row of ¾-in.-diameter bolts. Trusses are 4 ft-0 in. o.c. Lumber is No. 1 Spruce-Pine-Fir (South) [abbreviated S-P-F(S)]. MC ≤ 19 percent, and normal temperatures apply. Allowable stresses and cross-sectional properties are to be taken from the 1991 NDS.

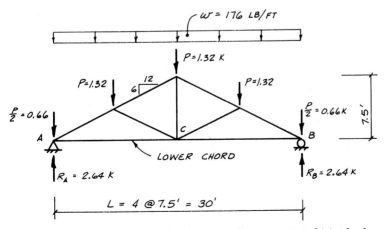

Figure 7.3a Uniform load on top chord converted to concentrated joint loads.

Loads

$$\text{RDL} = 14 \text{ psf} \quad \text{horizontal plane}$$

$$\underline{\text{Reduced SL} = 30}$$

$$\text{TL} = 44 \text{ psf}$$

$$w_{\text{TL}} = 44 \times 4 = 176 \text{ lb/ft}$$

For truss analysis (load to joint),

$$P = 176 \times 7.5 = 1320 \text{ lb}$$

Force in Lower Chord

Use method of joints.

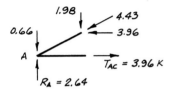

Figure 7.3b   Free body diagram of joint A.

Determine Required Size of Tension Member

The relatively small tension force will require a Dimension lumber member size. The allowable tension stress is obtained from NDS Supplement Table 4A for S-P-F(S), which was a new United States species group in 1991. A value for the size factor for tension stress parallel to grain will be assumed and checked later.

Assume $C_F = 1.3$.

$$F'_t = F_t(C_D)(C_M)(C_t)(C_F)$$

$$= 400(1.15)(1.0)(1.0)(1.3) = 598 \text{ psi}$$

$$\text{Req'd } A_n = \frac{P}{F'_t} = \frac{3960}{598} = 6.62 \text{ in.}^2$$

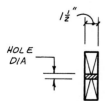

Figure 7.3c   Net section of tension member.

The actual hole diameter is to be $\frac{1}{32}$ to $\frac{1}{16}$ in. larger than the bolt size. For net-area calculations, arbitrarily assume that the bolt hole is $\frac{1}{8}$ in. larger than the bolt (for stress calculations only). Select a trial size from NDS Supplement Table 1B.

$$\text{Req'd } A_g = A_n + A_h$$

$$= 6.62 + 1.5(\frac{3}{4} + \frac{1}{8}) = 7.93 \text{ in.}^2$$

Try 2 × 6:

$$A = 8.25 > 7.93 \quad OK$$

Verify the size factor for tension in NDS Supplement Table 4A for a 6-in. nominal width:

$$C_F = 1.3 \quad \text{(same as assumed)} \quad OK$$

> *Use* 2 × 6 No. 1 S-P-F(S)

NOTE: The simplified truss analysis used in this example applies only to trusses with pinned joints. If some form of toothed steel gusset is used for the connections, the design should conform to Ref. 23.1 or applicable building code standard.

7.4 Columns

In addition to being a compression member, a *column* generally is suffi-ciently long that the possibility of buckling needs to be considered. On the other hand, the term *short column* usually implies that a compression mem-ber will not buckle, and its strength is related to the crushing capacity of the material.

In order to evaluate the tendency of a column to buckle, it is necessary to know the size of the member. Thus in a design situation, a trial size is first established. With a known size or a trial size, it is possible to compare the actual stress with the allowable stress. Based on this comparison, the member size will be accepted or rejected.

The check on the capacity of an axially loaded wood column of known size uses the formula

$$f_c = \frac{P}{A} \leq F'_c$$

where f_c = actual (computed) compressive stress parallel to grain
P = axial compressive force in member
A = cross-sectional area
F'_c = allowable compressive stress parallel to grain as defined later in this section

In the calculation of actual stress f_c, the cross-sectional area to be used will be either the gross area A_g of the column or the net area A_n at some hole in the member. The area to be used depends on the location of the hole along the length of the member and the tendency of the member at that point to buckle laterally. If the hole is located at a point which is braced, the gross area of the member may be used in the check for column stability between brace locations. Another check of f_c at the reduced cross section (using the net area) should be compared with the allowable compressive stress for a short column with no reduction for stability at the braced location. See Example 7.3. The other possibility is that some reduction of column area occurs in the laterally unbraced portion of the column. In the latter case, the net area is used directly in the stability check.

EXAMPLE 7.3   Actual Stresses in a Column

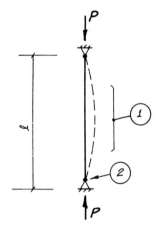

Figure 7.4 Pinned end column.

Actual Stresses

In Fig. 7.4 it is assumed that there are no holes in the column except at the supports (connections). Check the following column stresses:

1. Away from the supports

$$f_c = \frac{P}{A_g} \le F_c' \quad \text{as determined by column stability (using } C_P)$$

2. At the connection where buckling is not a factor

$$f_c = \frac{P}{A_n} \le F_c' \quad \text{as determined for a } \textit{short} \text{ column (without } C_P)$$

The allowable stress in a column reflects many of the familiar adjustment factors in addition to column stability:

$$F'_c = F_c(C_D)(C_M)(C_t)(C_F)(C_P)$$

where F'_c = allowable compressive stress parallel to grain
$\quad\ \ F_c$ = tabulated compressive stress parallel to grain
$\quad\ C_D$ = load duration factor (Sec. 4.15)
$\quad C_M$ = wet service factor (Sec. 4.14)
$\qquad$ = 1.0 for dry service conditions as in most covered structures. Dry service conditions are defined as
$\qquad$ MC $\leq$ 19 percent for sawn lumber
$\qquad$ MC $<$ 16 percent for glulam
$\quad\ \ C_t$ = temperature factor (Sec. 4.20)
$\qquad$ = 1.0 for normal temperature conditions
$\quad\ C_F$ = size factor (Sec. 4.16). Obtain values for visually graded Dimension lumber from Adjustment Factors section of NDS Supplement Tables 4A and 4B.
$\qquad$ = 1.0 for Timbers
$\qquad$ = 1.0 for MSR lumber
$\qquad$ = 1.0 for glulam
$\quad\ C_P$ = column stability factor
$\qquad$ = 1.0 for fully supported column

The size factor for compression applies only to Dimension lumber sizes, and C_F defaults to 1.0 for other members. The column stability factor takes buckling into account, and the slenderness ratio is the primary measure of buckling. The column slenderness ratio and C_P are the subjects of the remainder of this section.

In its traditional form, the slenderness ratio is expressed as the effective unbraced length of a column divided by the least radius of gyration, l_e/r. For the design of rectangular wood columns, however, the slenderness ratio is modified to a form that is somewhat easier to apply. Here the slenderness ratio is the effective unbraced length of the column divided by the least dimension of the cross section, l_e/d.

Use of this modified slenderness ratio is possible because the radius of gyration r can be expressed as a direct function of the width of a rectangular column. See Example 7.4. The constant in the conversion of the modified slenderness ratio is simply incorporated into the allowable stress column design formulas.

Most wood columns have rectangular cross sections, and the allowable stress formula given in this chapter is for this common type of column. However, a column of nonrectangular cross section may be analyzed by substituting $r\sqrt{12}$ in place of d in the formula for rectangular columns. For round columns see NDS Sec. 3.7.3. A much more detailed analysis of the slenderness ratio for columns is given in the next section.

EXAMPLE 7.4   Column Slenderness Ratio—Introduction

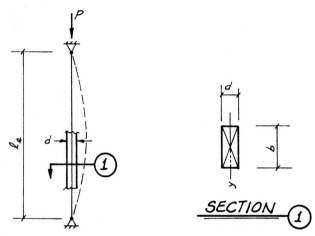

Figure 7.5 Typical wood column with rectangular cross section.

Column stability is measured by the slenderness ratio.

$$\text{General slenderness ratio} = \frac{l_e}{r}$$

where l_e = effective unbraced length of column
$\quad r = r_y$ = least radius of gyration of column cross section

$$\text{Slenderness ratio for } \textit{rectangular columns} = \frac{l_e}{d}$$

where l_e = effective unbraced length of column
$\quad d$ = least cross-sectional dimension of column*

For a rectangular cross section, the dimension d is directly proportional to the radius of gyration.

$$r_y = \sqrt{\frac{I_y}{A}} = \sqrt{\frac{bd^3/12}{bd}} = \sqrt{\frac{d^2}{12}} = d\sqrt{\frac{1}{12}}$$

$$\therefore \quad r \propto d$$

A more complete review of column slenderness ratio is given in Sec. 7.5.

---

*In beam design, d is normally associated with the strong axis.

The column stability factor C_P was shown previously as an adjustment factor for obtaining the allowable compressive stress in a column. The treatment of C_P as another multiplying factor is convenient from an organizational or bookkeeping point of view. However, the expression for C_P times F_c essentially defines the *column curve* or *column equation* for wood design. The other coefficients in the expression for F_c' are more in keeping with the general concept of adjustment factors, and the column equation as given by $F_c \times C_P$ is probably more basic to column behavior than the term *adjustment factor* implies.

The column equation in the 1991 NDS provides a continuous curve over the full range of slenderness ratios. See Example 7.5. This continuous function replaces the short, intermediate, and long column ranges that were used in previous editions of the NDS. The column expression in the 1991 NDS was originally developed by Ylinen and was verified by studies at the Forest Products Laboratory. The Ylinen formula also serves as the basis for the expression used for laterally unsupported beams in Sec. 6.3.

Zahn (Ref. 7.4) explained that the *behavior of wood columns* as given by the Ylinen formula is the result of the *interaction* of two modes of failure: *buckling* and *crushing*. Pure *buckling* is defined by the Euler critical buckling stress

$$F_{\text{cr}} = \frac{\pi^2 E}{(l_e/d)^2}$$

For use in allowable stress design (ASD) the Euler stress is divided by an appropriate factor of safety and is expressed in the NDS as

$$F_{cE} = \frac{K_{cE}E'}{(l_e/d)^2}$$

The K_{cE} term incorporates π^2 divided by the factor of safety. The Euler column stress F_{cE} is graphed in Fig. 7.6a, and it will be noted that the Ylinen formula converges to the Euler-based formula for columns with large slenderness ratios.

The second mode of failure is crushing of the wood fibers. When a compression member fails by pure crushing, there is no column buckling. Therefore in ASD, *crushing* is measured by the tabulated compressive stress parallel to grain multiplied by all applicable adjustment factors except C_P. This value is given the symbol F_c^* and is defined mathematically as

$$F_c^* = F_c(C_D)(C_M)(C_t)(C_F)$$

The value of F_c^* is the limiting value of allowable column stress at a zero slenderness ratio.

Again, column behavior is defined by the *interaction* of the buckling and crushing modes of failure, and the ratio F_{cE}/F_c^* appears several times in the

Ylinen formula. The coefficient c in the Ylinen formula is viewed by Zahn as a generalized interaction parameter. The value of c lies in the range

$$0 \le c \le 1.0$$

A value of $c = 1.0$ is an upper bound of column behavior and can only be met by an ideal material, loaded under ideal conditions. Because practical columns do not satisfy these idealizations, the value of c for wood compression members is less than one. The more a wood column deviates from the ideal situation, the smaller c becomes. Glulam members are generally thought to be straighter and more homogeneous than sawn lumber, and consequently glulam is assigned a larger value for c. The value of $c = 0.9$ for glulam was selected as an interim value, and it is in the process of being confirmed by tests at the FPL. Depending on the results of this research, the value of c for glulam may be revised in the future. The effects of different values of c are shown in Fig. 7.6b.

As the slenderness ratio increases, the column expression makes a transition from an allowable stress based on the crushing strength of wood (at a zero slenderness ratio) to an allowable stress based on the Euler curve (for large slenderness ratios). The Ylinen column curve more closely fits the results of column tests. Compared with previously used column formulas, the Ylinen equation gives slightly more conservative values of allowable compressive stress for members with intermediate slenderness ratios.

EXAMPLE 7.5   Ylinen Column Equation

The 1991 NDS uses a continuous curve for evaluating the effects of column buckling. The allowable column stress given by the Ylinen equation is plotted versus column slenderness ratio in Fig. 7.6a.

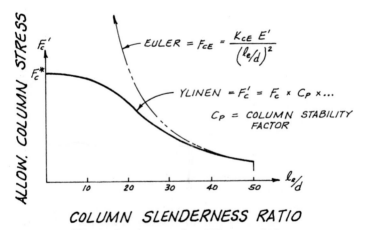

Figure 7.6a Ylinen column curve: plot of F'_c versus l_e/d.

Allowable Column Stress

The allowable column stress curve in Fig. 7.6a is obtained by multiplying the tabulated compressive stress parallel to grain F_c by the column stability factor C_P and all other appropriate factors.

$$F'_c = F_c(C_P) \times \cdots$$

where F'_c = allowable compressive stress in a column
$ F_c$ = tabulated compressive stress parallel to grain
$ C_P$ = column stability factor (defined below)
$ \times \cdots$ = product of other appropriate adjustment factors

Column Stability Factor

$$C_P = \frac{1 + F_{cE}/F^*_c}{2c} - \sqrt{\left(\frac{1 + F_{cE}/F^*_c}{2c}\right) - \frac{F_{cE}/F^*_c}{c}}$$

where F_{cE} = Euler critical buckling stress for columns
$\phantom{where F_{cE}} = \dfrac{K_{cE}E'}{(l_e/d)^2}$
$ F^*_c$ = limiting compressive stress in column at zero slenderness ratio
$ =$ tabulated compressive stress parallel to grain multiplied by all adjustment factors except C_P
$ = F_c(C_D)(C_M)(C_t)(C_F)$
$ K_{cE}$ = 0.3 for visually graded lumber
$\phantom{where K_{cE}} =$ 0.418 for material with less variability such as MSR lumber and glulam. See NDS Appendix F.2 for additional information.
$ E'$ = modulus of elasticity associated with the axis of column buckling (see Sec. 7.4). Recall that C_D does not apply to E. For sawn lumber, $E_x = E_y$. For glulam, E_x and E_y may be different.
$ = E(C_M)(C_t)(C_T)$
$ c$ = buckling and crushing interaction factor for columns
$ =$ 0.9 for glulam columns
$ =$ 0.8 for sawn lumber columns
$ C_T$ = buckling stiffness factor for 2 × 4 *and smaller compression chords in trusses* with plywood nailed to narrow face of member
$ =$ 1.0 for all other members
$ C_F$ = size factor (Sec. 4.16) for compression. Obtain values for visually graded Dimension lumber from the Adjustment Factors section of NDS Supplement Tables 4A and 4B.
$ =$ 1.0 for sawn lumber in B&S and P&T sizes and MSR lumber
$ =$ 1.0 for glulam

Other factors are as previously defined.

The interaction between column buckling and crushing of wood fibers in a compression member is measured by parameter c. The effect of several different values of c is illustrated in Fig. 7.6b.

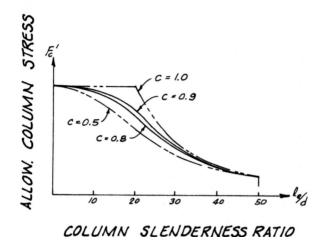

COLUMN SLENDERNESS RATIO

Figure 7.6b Plot of F_c' versus l_e/d showing the effect of different values of c. The parameter c measures the interaction between crushing and buckling in wood columns.

A value of $c = 1.0$ applies to idealized column conditions. Practical wood columns have $c < 1.0$:

For sawn lumber: $c = 0.8$

For glulam: $c = 0.9$

The effect of the load duration factor varies depending on the mode of column failure that predominates. See Fig. 7.6c.

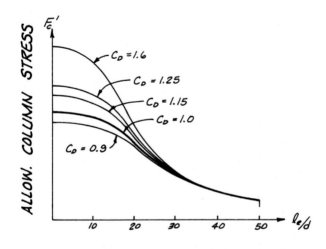

COLUMN SLENDERNESS RATIO

Figure 7.6c Plot of F_c' versus l_e/d showing the effect of load duration on allowable column stress.

The load duration factor C_D has full effect on allowable column stress when crushing controls (i.e., at a zero slenderness ratio). On the other hand, C_D has no influence on the allowable column stress when instability predominates. A transition between C_D having full effect at $l_e/d = 0$, and C_D having no effect at the maximum slenderness ratio of 50, is automatically provided in the definition of C_P.

The designer should have some understanding about the factor of safety provided by the column formula. It was noted in an earlier chapter that the values of modulus of elasticity listed in the NDS Supplement are average values. Furthermore, the tabulated values have been modified to account for shear deformation.

The pure bending modulus of elasticity is obtained by multiplying the value of E listed in NDS Supplement Table 4A by a factor of 1.03. In addition, the formula for F_{cE} includes an adjustment which converts the average modulus of elasticity to a 5 percent exclusion value. When a value of $K_{cE} = 0.3$ is used for *sawn lumber,* the allowable column stress F_c' includes a *factor of safety* of 1.66 at an approximate 5 percent lower exclusion value.

MSR lumber and glulam are less variable than sawn lumber. For these less variable materials, a factor of safety of 1.66 is maintained at a 5 percent lower exclusion value when $K_{cE} = 0.418$ is used to compute F_{cE}. If a value of $K_{cE} = 0.3$ is retained for glulam and MSR lumber, the corresponding allowable stress represents less than a 0.01 percent lower exclusion value with a factor of safety of 1.66 (see NDS Appendices F and H).

The design of a glulam column follows essentially the same procedure as that used for a sawn column. In addition to the values of c and K_{cE} in the expressions for C_P, the basic difference for glulam is in the tabulated design values. Recall that glulam is available in either bending or axial combinations. Although pure columns are axial force members, bending combinations may also be loaded in compression. For these members the designer will have to select the appropriate value(s) of modulus of elasticity (E_x and/or E_y) for column analysis from the glulam tables. This is demonstrated in Example 7.7 in Sec. 7.7.

7.5 Detailed Analysis of Slenderness Ratio

The concept of the slenderness ratio was briefly introduced in Sec. 7.4. There it was stated that the *least* radius of gyration is used in the l_e/r ratio and that the *least* dimension of the column cross section is used in the l_e/d ratio.

These statements assume that the unbraced length of the column is the same for both the x and the y axes. In this case the column, if loaded to failure, would buckle about the weak y axis. See Fig. 7.7a. Note that if buckling occurs about the y axis, the column moves in the x direction. Figure 7.7a illustrates this straightforward case of column buckling. Only the slenderness ratio about the weak axis needs to be calculated.

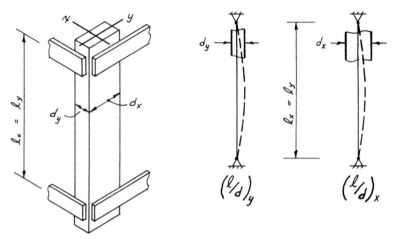

Figure 7.7a By inspection the slenderness ratio about the *y* axis is larger and is therefore critical.

Although this concept of column buckling applies in many situations, the designer should have a deeper insight into the concept of the slenderness ratio. Conditions can exist under which the column may actually buckle about the *strong* axis of the cross section rather than the weak axis.

In this more general sense, the column can be viewed as having two slenderness ratios. One slenderness ratio would evaluate the tendency of the column to buckle about the *strong* axis of the cross section. The other would measure the tendency of buckling about the *weak* axis. For a rectangular column these slenderness ratios would be written

$$\left(\frac{l_e}{d}\right)_x$$ for buckling about strong *x* axis (column movement in *y* direction)

$$\left(\frac{l_e}{d}\right)_y$$ for buckling about weak *y* axis (column movement in *x* direction)

If the column is loaded to failure, buckling will occur about the axis that has the larger slenderness ratio. In design, the larger slenderness ratio is used to calculate the allowable compressive stress. (Note that it is conceivable in a glulam column with different values for E_x and E_y that a slightly smaller l_e/d could produce the critical F'_c.)

The reason that the strong axis can be critical can be understood from a consideration of the *bracing* and *end conditions* of the column. The *effective unbraced length* is the length to be used in the calculation of the slenderness ratio. It is possible to have a column with different unbraced lengths for the *x* and *y* axes. See Fig. 7.7b. In this example the unbraced length for the *x* axis is twice as long as the unbraced length for the *y* axis. In practice,

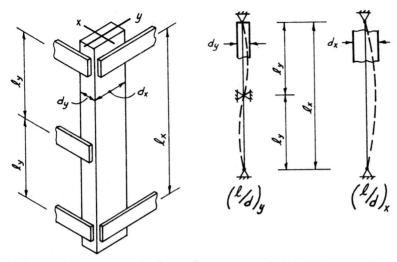

Figure 7.7b Different unbraced lengths for both axes. Because of the intermediate bracing for the y axis, the critical slenderness ratio cannot be determined by inspection. Both slenderness ratios must be calculated, and the larger value is used to determine F_c'.

bracing can occur at any interval. The effect of column end conditions is explained below.

Another case where the unbraced lengths for the x and y axes are different occurs when sheathing is attached to a column. If the sheathing is attached to the column with an effective connection, buckling about an axis that is perpendicular to the sheathing is prevented. See Fig. 7.8. The most common example of this type of column is a stud in a bearing wall. The wall sheathing

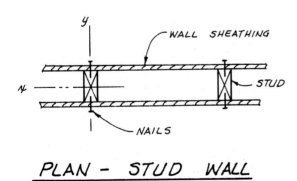

PLAN - STUD WALL

Figure 7.8 Column braced by sheathing. Sheathing attached to stud prevents column buckling about the weak (y) axis of the stud. Therefore, consider buckling about the x axis only.

can prevent column buckling about the weak axis of the stud, and only the slenderness ratio about the strong axis of the member needs to be evaluated.

The final item regarding the slenderness ratio is the effect of column *end conditions.* The length *l* used in the slenderness ratio is theoretically the unbraced length of a *pinned-end* column. For columns with other end conditions, the length is taken as the distance between inflection points (IPs) on a sketch of the buckled column. An inflection point corresponds to a point of reverse curvature on the deflected shape of the column and represents a point of zero moment. For this reason the inflection point is considered as a pinned end for purposes of column analysis. The *effective unbraced length* is taken as the distance between inflection points. When only one inflection point is on the sketch of the buckled column, the mirror image of the column is drawn to give a second inflection point.

Typically six "ideal" column end conditions are identified in various fields of structural design. See Fig. 7.9a. The recommended effective length factors for use in the design of wood columns are given in Fig. 7.9b. The effective unbraced length can be determined by multiplying the effective length factor K_e times the actual unbraced length.

$$\text{Effective length} = \text{distance between inflection points}$$

$$= \text{effective length factor} \times \text{unbraced length}$$

$$l_e = K_e \times l$$

The effective lengths shown on the column sketches in Fig. 7.9a are *theoretical* effective lengths, and practical field column end conditions can only approximate the ideal pinned and fixed column end conditions. The recommended *design* effective length factors from NDS Appendix G are to be used for practical field end conditions.

In practice, the designer must determine which "ideal" column most closely approximates the actual end conditions for a given column. Some degree of judgment is required for this evaluation, but several key items should be considered in making this comparison.

First, note that three of the ideal columns undergo sidesway, and the other three do not. *Sidesway* means that the top of the column is relatively free to displace laterally with respect to the bottom of the column. The designer must be able to identify which columns will undergo sidesway and, on the other hand, what consitutes restraint against sidesway. In general, the answer to this depends on the type of lateral-force-resisting system (LFRS) used (Sec. 3.3).

Usually, if the column is part of a system in which lateral forces are resisted by *bracing* or by *shearwalls,* sidesway will be prevented. These types of LFRSs are relatively rigid, and the movement of one end of the column with respect to the other end is restricted. If an overload occurs in this case, column buckling will be symmetric. See Fig. 7.10. However, if the column

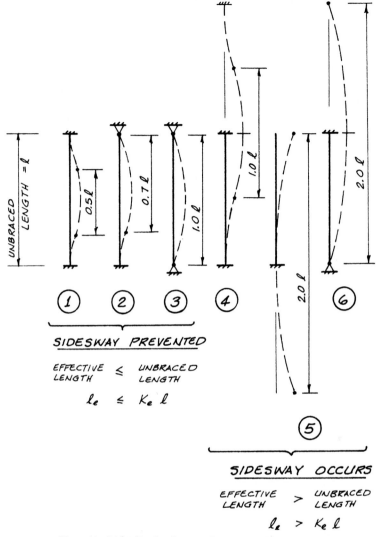

Figure 7.9a Six typical idealized columns showing buckled shapes and theoretical effective lengths.

Column No.	1	2	3	4	5	6
Theoretical effective length factors	0.5	0.7	1.0	1.0	2.0	2.0
Recommended design K_e	0.65	0.8	1.0	1.2	2.1	2.4

Figure 7.9b Table of theoretical and recommended effective length factors K_e. Values of recommended K_e are from NDS Appendix G.

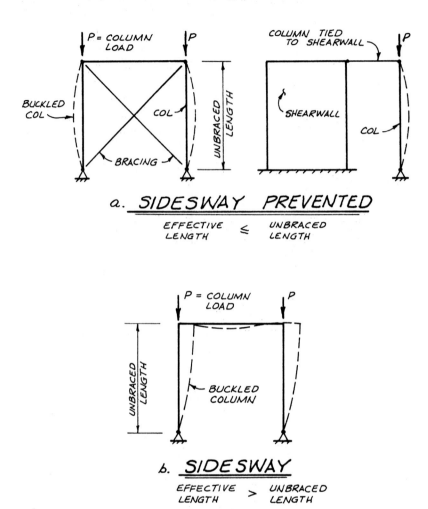

Figure 7.10 Columns with and without sidesway. (*a*) Braced frames or buildings with shearwalls limit the displacement of the top end of the column so that sidesway does not occur. (*b*) Columns in rigid frames (without bracing) will undergo sidesway if the columns buckle.

is part of a *rigid frame* type of LFRS, the system is relatively flexible, and sidesway can occur. Typical columns for the types of buildings considered in this text will have sidesway prevented.

It should also be noted that columns with *sidesway prevented* have an effective length which is *less than or equal to* the actual unbraced length ($K_e \leq 1.0$). A common and conservative practice is to consider the effective length equal to the unbraced length for these columns ($K_e = 1.0$).

For columns where *sidesway* can occur, the effective length is *greater than* the actual unbraced length ($K_e > 1.0$). For these types of columns, the larger slenderness ratio causes the allowable axial load to be considerably less than the allowable load on a column with both ends pinned and braced against sidesway.

In addition to answering the question of sidesway, the comparison of an actual column to an ideal column should evaluate the effectiveness of the column connections. Practically all wood columns have *square-cut ends*. For structural design purposes, this type of column end condition is normally assumed to be pinned. Square-cut column ends do offer some restraint against column end rotation. However, most practical column ends are not exactly square, and some *accidental eccentricity* may be present due to non-uniform bearing. These effects are often assumed to be compensating. Therefore, columns in a typical wood-frame building with shearwalls are usually assumed to be type 3 in Fig. 7.9*a*, and the effective length factor is taken to be unity.

It is possible to design moment-resisting connections in wood members, but they are the exception rather than the rule. As noted, the majority of connections in ordinary wood buildings are "simple" connections, and it is generally conservative to take the effective length equal to the unbraced length. However, the designer should examine the actual *bracing conditions* and *end conditions* for a given column and determine whether or not a larger effective length should be used.

7.6 Design Problem: Axially Loaded Column

The design of a column is a trial-and-error process because, in order to determine the allowable column stress F'_c, it is first necessary to know the slenderness ratio l_e/d. In the following example, only two trials are required to determine the size of the column. See Example 7.6.

Several items in the solution should be emphasized. First, the importance of the size category should be noted. The initial trial is a Dimension lumber size, and the second trial is a Posts and Timbers size. Tabulated stresses are different for these two size categories.

The second item concerns the load duration factor. This example involves (DL + RLL). It will be remembered that roof live load is an arbitrary minimum load required by the Code, and C_D for this combination is 1.25. For many areas of the country the design load for a roof will be (DL + SL), and the corresponding C_D for snow would be 1.15.

EXAMPLE 7.6   Sawn Lumber Column

Design the column in Fig. 7.11*a*, using No. 1 Douglas Fir-Larch. Bracing conditions are the same for buckling about both the x and y axes. The load is combined dead load and roof live load. MC $\leq$ 19 percent ($C_M = 1.0$), and normal temperatures apply ($C_t = 1.0$). Allowable stresses are to be in accordance with the 1991 NDS.

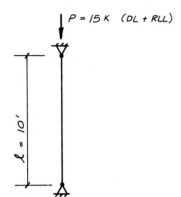

$P = 15\,K \quad (DL + RLL)$

$\ell = 10'$

Figure 7.11a Elevation view of column.

Trial 1

Try 4 × 6 (Dimension lumber size category). From NDS Supplement Table 4A

$$F_c = 1450 \text{ psi}$$

$$C_F = 1.1 \qquad \text{size factor for compression}$$

$$E = 1,700,000 \text{ psi}$$

$$A = 19.25 \text{ in.}^2$$

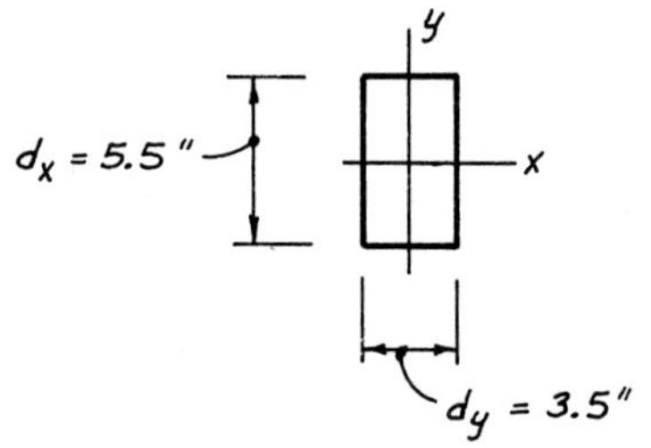

$d_x = 5.5\,''$

$d_y = 3.5\,''$

Figure 7.11b Cross section of 4 × 6 trial column.

Determine capacity using Ylinen column equation (Example 7.5):

$$\left(\frac{l_e}{d}\right)_{max} = \left(\frac{K_e l}{d}\right)_y = \frac{1 \times 10 \text{ ft} \times 12 \text{ in./ft}}{3.5 \text{ in.}} = 34.3$$

$$E' = E(C_M)(C_t)(C_T) = 1,700,000(1.0)(1.0)(1.0)$$

$$= 1,700,000 \text{ psi}$$

For visually graded sawn lumber,

$$K_{cE} = 0.3$$

$$c = 0.8$$

$$F_{cE} = \frac{K_{cE}E'}{(l_e/d)^2} = \frac{0.3(1,700,000)}{(34.3)^2} = 434 \text{ psi}$$

$$F_c^* = F_c(C_D)(C_M)(C_t)(C_F)$$

$$= 1450(1.25)(1.0)(1.0)(1.1) = 1994 \text{ psi}$$

$$\frac{F_{cE}}{F_c^*} = \frac{434}{1994} = 0.218$$

$$\frac{1 + F_{cE}/F_c^*}{2c} = \frac{1 + 0.218}{2(0.8)} = 0.761$$

$$C_P = \frac{1 + F_{cE}/F_c^*}{2c} - \sqrt{\left(\frac{1 + F_{cE}/F_c^*}{2c}\right)^2 - \frac{F_{cE}/F_c^*}{c}}$$

$$= 0.761 - \sqrt{(0.761)^2 - 0.218/0.8} = 0.207$$

$$F_c' = F_c(C_D)(C_M)(C_t)(C_F)(C_P)$$

$$= 1450(1.25)(1.0)(1.0)(1.1)(0.207)$$

$$= 412 \text{ psi}$$

Allow. $P = F_c'A = 0.412(19.25) = 7.94 \text{ k} < 15$ *NG*

Trial 2

Try 6×6 (P&T size category). Values from NDS Supplement Table 4D:

$F_c = 1000$ psi
$E = 1,600,000$ psi
Size factor for compression defaults to unity for all sizes except Dimension lumber ($C_F = 1.0$).
$d_x = d_y = 5.5$ in.
$A = 30.25$ in.²

Determine column capacity and compare with the given design load.

$$\left(\frac{l_e}{d}\right)_{max} = \frac{1.0(10 \text{ ft} \times 12 \text{ in./ft})}{5.5 \text{ in.}} = 21.8$$

$$E' = E(C_M)(C_t) = 1,600,000(1.0)(1.0)$$

$$= 1,600,000 \text{ psi}$$

$$K_{cE} = 0.3$$

$$c = 0.8$$

$$F_{cE} = \frac{K_{cE}E'}{(l_e/d)^2} = \frac{0.3(1,600,000)}{(21.8)^2} = 1008 \text{ psi}$$

$$F_c^* = F_c(C_D)(C_M)(C_t)(C_F)$$

$$= 1000(1.25)(1.0)(1.0)(1.0) = 1250 \text{ psi}$$

$$\frac{F_{cE}}{F_c^*} = \frac{1008}{1250} = 0.807$$

$$\frac{1 + F_{cE}/F_c^*}{2c} = \frac{1 + 0.807}{2(0.8)} = 1.129$$

$$C_P = \frac{1 + F_{cE}/F_c^*}{2c} - \sqrt{\left(\frac{1 + F_{cE}/F_c^*}{2c}\right)^2 - \frac{F_{cE}/F_c^*}{c}}$$

$$= 1.129 - \sqrt{(1.129)^2 - 0.807/0.8} = 0.613$$

$$F_c' = F_c(C_D)(C_M)(C_t)(C_F)(C_P)$$

$$= 1000(1.25)(1.0)(1.0)(1.0)(0.613)$$

$$= 766 \text{ psi}$$

Allow. $P = F_c'A = 0.766(30.25) = 23.2 \text{ k} > 15 \qquad OK$

> *Use*   6 × 6 column   No. 1   DF-L

7.7   Design Problem: Capacity of a Glulam Column

This example determines the axial load capacity of a glulam column that is fabricated from a bending combination. See Example 7.7. Usually if a glulam member has an axial force only, an axial combination (rather than a bending combination) will be used. However, this example demonstrates the proper selection of E_x and E_y in the evaluation of a column. (Note that for an axial combination $E_x = E_y = E_{\text{axial}}$ and the proper selection of modulus of elasticity is automatic.)

To make the use of a glulam bending combination a practical problem, one might consider the given loading to be one possible load case. Another load case could involve the *axial* force *plus* a transverse *bending* load. This second load case would require a combined stress analysis (Sec. 7.12). Two different unbraced lengths are involved in this problem, and the designer must determine the slenderness ratio for the x and y axes.

EXAMPLE 7.7   Capacity of a Glulam Column

Determine the axial compression load capacity of the glulam column in Fig. 7.12. The column is a 6¾ × 11 22F-V3 Southern Pine glulam. It is used in an industrial plant where the MC will exceed 16 percent. Normal temperatures apply. Loads are (DL + SL).
Glulam properties are from the 1991 NDS Supplement.

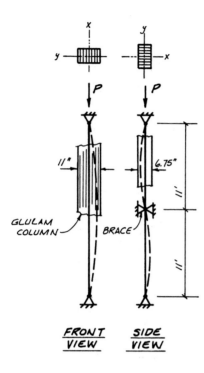

x

y —[[[[]]]—
y

y

—[[]]—x

P

P

11"

6.75"

GLULAM
COLUMN

BRACE

Figure 7.12 Front and side elevation views of glulam column
showing different bracing conditions for column buckling
about x and y axes. Also shown
are section views above the respective elevations.

FRONT
VIEW

SIDE
VIEW

Tabulated stresses from NDS Supplement Table 5A:

When the moisture content of glulam is 16 percent or greater, a wet use factor C_M less than one is required and the need for pressure treatment should be considered.

$$F_c = 1500 \text{ psi} \qquad C_M = 0.73$$

$$E_x = 1{,}600{,}000 \text{ psi} \qquad C_M = 0.833$$

$$E_y = 1{,}400{,}000 \text{ psi} \qquad C_M = 0.833$$

$$E_{\text{axial}} = 1{,}400{,}000 \text{ psi} \qquad C_M = 0.833$$

NOTE: E_x and E_y are used in beam deflection calculations and for stability analysis, and E_{axial} is used for axial deformation computations. However, a conservative column analysis could be obtained using 1,400,000 psi for both E_x and E_y.

In this problem there are different unbraced lengths about the x and y axes. Therefore, the effects of column buckling about both axes of the cross section are evaluated. In a member with E_x equal to E_y, this analysis would simply require the comparison of the slenderness ratios for the x and y axes [that is, $(l_e/d)_x$ and $(l_e/d)_y$]. The load capacity of the column would then be evaluated using the larger slenderness ratio $(l_e/d)_{\text{max}}$. However, in the current example there are different material properties for the x and y axes, and a full evaluation of the column stability factor is given for both axes.

Analyze Column Buckling About x Axis

$$\left(\frac{l_e}{d}\right)_x = \frac{1.0(22 \text{ ft} \times 12 \text{ in./ft})}{11 \text{ in.}} = 24.0$$

Use E_x to analyze buckling about the x axis.

$$E'_x = E_x(C_M)(C_t) = 1,600,000(0.833)(1.0)$$

$$= 1,333,000 \text{ psi}$$

Column stability factor x axis:

$$K_{cE} = 0.418 \qquad \text{for glulam}$$

$$c = 0.9$$

$$F_{cE} = \frac{K_{cE}E'_x}{[(l_e/d)_x]^2} = \frac{0.418(1,333,000)}{(24.0)^2} = 967 \text{ psi}$$

$$F^*_c = F_c(C_D)(C_M)(C_t)(C_F)$$

$$= 1500(1.15)(0.73)(1.0)(1.0) = 1259 \text{ psi}$$

$$\frac{F_{cE}}{F^*_c} = \frac{967}{1259} = 0.768$$

$$\frac{1 + F_{cE}/F^*_c}{2c} = \frac{1 + 0.768}{2(0.9)} = 0.982$$

For x axis $\quad C_P = \dfrac{1 + F_{cE}/F^*_c}{2c} - \sqrt{\left(\dfrac{1 + F_{cE}/F^*_c}{2c}\right)^2 - \dfrac{F_{cE}/F^*_c}{c}}$

$$= 0.982 - \sqrt{(0.982)^2 - 0.768/0.9} = \boxed{0.648}$$

Analyze Column Buckling About y Axis

$$\left(\frac{l_e}{d}\right)_y = \frac{1.0(11 \text{ ft} \times 12 \text{ in./ft})}{6.75 \text{ in.}} = 19.6$$

Use E_y to analyze buckling about the y axis.

$$E'_y = E_y(C_M)(C_t) = 1,400,000(0.833)(1.0)$$

$$= 1,166,000 \text{ psi}$$

$$F_{cE} = \frac{K_{cE}E'_y}{[(l_e/d)_y]^2} = \frac{0.418(1,166,000)}{(19.6)^2} = 1275 \text{ psi}$$

$$F^*_c = F_c(C_D)(C_M)(C_t)(C_F)$$

$$= 1500(1.15)(0.73)(1.0)(1.0) = 1259 \text{ psi}$$

$$\frac{F_{cE}}{F_c^*} = \frac{1275}{1259} = 1.012$$

$$\frac{1 + F_{cE}/F_c^*}{2c} = \frac{1 + 1.012}{2(0.9)} = 1.118$$

For y axis $C_P = \dfrac{1 + F_{cE}/F_c^*}{2c} - \sqrt{\left(\dfrac{1 + F_{cE}/F_c^*}{2c}\right)^2 - \dfrac{F_{cE}/F_c^*}{c}}$

$$= 1.118 - \sqrt{(1.118)^2 - 1.012/0.9} = \boxed{0.764}$$

The x axis produces the smaller value of the column stability factor, and the x axis is critical for column buckling.

$$F_c' = F_c(C_D)(C_M)(C_t)(C_F)(C_P)$$

$$= 1500(1.15)(0.73)(1.0)(1.0)(0.648)$$

$$= 817 \text{ psi}$$

Allow. $P = F_c'A = 0.817(74.25) = 60.6$ k

$$\boxed{\text{Allow. } P = 60.6 \text{ k}}$$

7.8 Design Problem: Capacity of a Bearing Wall

An axial compressive load may be applied to a wood-frame wall. For example, an interior bearing wall may support the reactions of floor or roof joists (Fig. 3.4c). Exterior bearing walls also carry reactions from joists and rafters, but, in addition, exterior walls usually must be designed to carry lateral wind forces. (The UBC requires a minimum 5-psf lateral force on interior walls. Theoretically both interior and exterior walls must be designed to carry lateral seismic forces perpendicular to the wall surface. However, for typical wood-frame walls, the dead load of the wall is so small that the seismic force is often not critical—especially when a C_D of 1.6 is considered.)

In Example 7.8 the vertical load capacity of a wood-frame wall is determined. Two main factors should be noted about this problem. The first relates to the column capacity of a stud in a wood-frame wall. Because sheathing is attached to the stud throughout its height, continuous lateral support is provided in the x direction. Therefore, the possibility of buckling about the weak y axis is prevented. The column capacity is evaluated by the slenderness ratio about the strong axis of the stud, $(l_e/d)_x$.

The second factor to consider is the bearing capacity of the top and bottom wall plates. It is possible that the vertical load capacity of a bearing wall may be governed by compression perpendicular to the grain on the wall plates rather than by the column capacity of the studs. This is typically not a problem with major columns in a building because steel bearing plates can be used to distribute the load perpendicular to the grain on supporting members. However, in a standard wood-frame wall, the stud bears *directly* on the horizontal wall plates.

EXAMPLE 7.8   Capacity of a Stud Wall

Determine the vertical load capacity of the stud shown in Fig. 7.13a. There is no bending. Express the allowable load in pounds per lineal foot of wall. Lumber is Standard-grade Hem-Fir. Load is (DL + SL). $C_M = 1.0$ and $C_t = 1.0$.

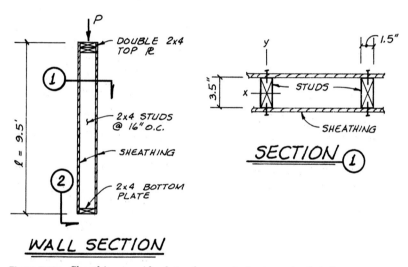

Figure 7.13a   Sheathing provides lateral support about y axis of stud.

Wall studs are 2×4 (Dimension lumber size category). Values from NDS Supplement Table 4A:

$$F_c = 1300 \text{ psi}$$

$$C_F = 1.0 \quad \text{for compression}$$

$$E = 1{,}200{,}000 \text{ psi}$$

Bearing capacity of wall plate: $F_{c\perp} = 405 \text{ psi}$

Column Capacity of Stud

Buckling about the weak axis of the stud is prevented by the sheathing, and the only slenderness ratio required is for the x axis.

$$\left(\frac{l_e}{d}\right)_y = \frac{0}{1.5 \text{ in.}} = 0$$

$$\left(\frac{l_e}{d}\right)_x = \frac{1.0(9.5 \text{ ft} \times 12 \text{ in./ft})}{3.5 \text{ in.}} = 32.6$$

$$E' = E(C_M)(C_t)(C_T) = 1,200,000(1.0)(1.0)(1.0)$$

$$= 1,200,000 \text{ psi}$$

For visually graded sawn lumber

$$K_{cE} = 0.3$$

$$c = 0.8$$

$$F_{cE} = \frac{K_{cE}E'}{[(l_e/d)_x]^2} = \frac{0.3(1,200,000)}{(32.6)^2} = 339 \text{ psi}$$

$$F_c^* = F_c(C_D)(C_M)(C_t)(C_F)$$

$$= 1300(1.15)(1.0)(1.0)(1.0) = 1495 \text{ psi}$$

$$\frac{F_{cE}}{F_c^*} = \frac{339}{1495} = 0.227$$

$$\frac{1 + F_{cE}/F_c^*}{2c} = \frac{1 + 0.227}{2(0.8)} = 0.767$$

$$C_P = \frac{1 + F_{cE}/F_c^*}{2c} - \sqrt{\left(\frac{1 + F_{cE}/F_c^*}{2c}\right)^2 - \frac{F_{cE}/F_c^*}{c}}$$

$$= 0.767 - \sqrt{(0.767)^2 - 0.227/0.8} = 0.215$$

$$F_c' = F_c(C_D)(C_M)(C_t)(C_F)(C_P)$$

$$= 1300(1.15)(1.0)(1.0)(1.0)(0.215)$$

$$= 322 \text{ psi}$$

$$\text{Allow. } P = F_c'A = 322(5.25) = 1690 \text{ lb}$$

$$\text{Allow. } w = \frac{1690 \text{ lb}}{1.33 \text{ ft}} = \boxed{1270 \text{ lb/ft*}}$$

---

*The effect of the minimum code lateral force of 5 psf normal to the surface of interior walls should also be considered. This load case will involve combined axial and bending stresses.

Bearing Capacity of Wall Plates

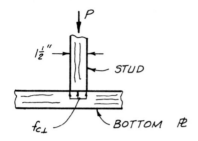

Figure 7.13b Bearing on bottom
wall plate.

The conditions necessary to apply the bearing area factor are summarized in Fig. 6.16b (Sec. 6.8). A typical stud is located more than 3 in. from the end of the wall plate, and the bearing length of 1½ in. is less than the 6-in. limit. Therefore, the bearing area factor can be used to adjust $F_{c\perp}$. Recall that C_D does not apply to $F_{c\perp}$.

$$F'_{c\perp} = F_{c\perp}(C_M)(C_t)(C_b)$$

$$= 405(1.0)(1.0)\left(\frac{1½ + 3/8}{1½}\right)$$

$$= 506 \text{ psi} > 322$$

$$F'_{c\perp} > F'_c$$

∴ column capacity governs over bearing perpendicular to the grain.

7.9 Built-up Columns

A *built-up* column is constructed from several parallel wood members which are nailed or bolted together to function as a composite column. These are to be distinguished from *spaced columns,* which have specially designed timber connectors to transfer shear between the separate parallel members.

The NDS includes criteria for designing spaced columns (NDS Sec. 15.2). Spaced columns can be used to increase the allowable load in compression members in heavy wood trusses. They are, however, relatively expensive to fabricate and are not often used in ordinary wood buildings. For this reason spaced columns are not covered in this text.

Built-up columns see wider use because they are fairly easy to fabricate, and their design is briefly covered here. The combination of several members in a built-up column results in a member with a larger cross-sectional dimension d and, correspondingly, a smaller slenderness ratio l_e/d.

With a smaller slenderness ratio, a larger allowable column stress can be used. Therefore, the allowable load on a built-up column is larger than the allowable load for the same members used individually. However, the fasteners connecting the members do not fully transfer the shear between the various pieces, and the capacity of a *built-up* column is less than the capacity of a *solid* sawn or glulam column of the same size and grade.

The capacity of a built-up column is determined by first calculating the column capacity of an equivalent solid column. This value is then reduced by an adjustment factor K_f that depends on whether the built-up column is fabricated with nails or bolts. This procedure is demonstrated in Example 7.9.

Recall that, in general, a column has two slenderness ratios: one for possible buckling about the x axis, and another for buckling about the y axis. In the typical problem, the allowable column stress is simply evaluated using the larger of the two slenderness ratios.

For a built-up column this may or may not be the controlling condition. Because the reduction factor K_f measures the effectiveness of the shear transfer between the individual laminations, the K_f factor applies only to the column slenderness ratio for the axis *parallel to the weak axis of individual laminations*. In other words, the column slenderness ratio parallel to the strong axis of the individual laminations does not require the K_f reduction. Depending on the relative magnitude of $(l_e/d)_x$ and $(l_e/d)_y$, the evaluation of *one* or possibly *two* allowable column stresses may be required.

The design of built-up columns is covered in NDS Sec. 15.3. The procedure applies to columns that are fabricated from two to five full-length parallel members that are nailed or bolted together. Details for the nailing or bolting of the members in order to qualify as a built-up column are given in the NDS.

Work has been done at the Forest Products Laboratory (Ref. 4.7) on the effect of built-up columns fabricated with members that are not continuous over the full length of the column. Information regarding design recommendations for nail-laminated posts with butt joints may be obtained from the FPL.

EXAMPLE 7.9   Strength of Built-up Column

Determine the allowable axial load on the built-up column in Fig. 7.14. Lumber is No. 1 DF-L. Column length is 13 ft-0 in. $C_D = 1.0$, $C_M = 1.0$, and $C_t = 1.0$.

The 2 × 6s comprising the built-up column are in the Dimension lumber size category. Design values are obtained from NDS Supplement Table 4A:

$$F_c = 1450 \text{ psi}$$

$$C_F = 1.1 \quad \text{for compression}$$

$$E = 1,700,000 \text{ psi}$$

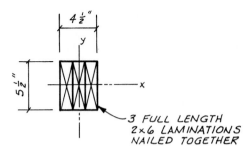

-3 FULL LENGTH
2×6 LAMINATIONS
NAILED TOGETHER

Figure 7.14 Cross section of nailed built-up column. For nailing requirements see NDS Sec. 15.3.3.

BUILT-UP COLUMN

Column Capacity

$$\left(\frac{l_e}{d}\right)_x = \frac{1.0(13.0 \text{ ft} \times 12 \text{ in./ft})}{5.5} = 28.4$$

$$\left(\frac{l_e}{d}\right)_y = \frac{1.0(13.0 \text{ ft} \times 12 \text{ in./ft})}{4.5 \text{ in.}} = 34.7$$

$$\left(\frac{l_e}{d}\right)_{max} = \left(\frac{l_e}{d}\right)_y$$

The adjustment factor K_f applies to the allowable stress for the column axis that is parallel to the weak axis of the individual laminations. Therefore, K_f applies to the column stress based on $(l_e/d)_y$. In this problem the y axis is critical for both column buckling as well as the reduction for built-up columns, and only one allowable column stress needs to be evaluated.

$$E' = E(C_M)(C_t)(C_T) = 1,700,000(1.0)(1.0)(1.0)$$

$$= 1,700,000 \text{ psi}$$

For visually graded sawn lumber

$$K_{cE} = 0.3$$

$$c = 0.8$$

$$F_{cE} = \frac{K_{cE}E'}{(l_e/d)^2} = \frac{0.3(1,700,000)}{(34.7)^2} = 424 \text{ psi}$$

$$F_c^* = F_c(C_D)(C_M)(C_t)(C_F)$$

$$= 1450(1.0)(1.0)(1.0)(1.1) = 1595 \text{ psi}$$

$$\frac{F_{cE}}{F_c^*} = \frac{424}{1595} = 0.266$$

$$\frac{1 + F_{cE}/F_c^*}{2c} = \frac{1 + 0.266}{2(0.8)} = 0.791$$

For nailed built-up columns

$$K_f = 0.6$$

$$C_P = \left[K_f \frac{1 + F_{cE}/F_c^*}{2c} - \sqrt{\left(\frac{1 + F_{cE}/F_c^*}{2c}\right)^2 - \frac{F_{cE}/F_c^*}{c}} \right]$$

$$= 0.6[0.791 - \sqrt{(0.791)^2 - 0.266/0.8}]$$

$$= 0.6(0.249) = 0.149$$

$$F_c' = F_c(C_D)(C_M)(C_t)(C_F)(C_P)$$

$$= 1450(1.0)(1.0)(1.0)(1.1)(0.149)$$

$$= 238 \text{ psi}$$

Capacity of a nailed built-up (three 2 × 6's) column:

$$\text{Allow. } P = F_c'A = 0.238(3 \times 8.25 \text{ in.}^2)$$

$$\boxed{\text{Allow. } P = 5.88 \text{ k}}$$

For the nailing requirements of a mechanically laminated built-up column, see NDS Sec. 15.3.3.

In Example 7.9, the y axis gave the maximum slenderness ratio, and the y axis also required the use of the reduction factor K_f. In such a problem, only one allowable column stress needs to be evaluated. However, another situation could require the evaluation of a second allowable column stress. For example, if an additional lamination is added to the column in Fig. 7.14, the maximum slenderness ratio would become $(l_e/d)_x$, and an allowable column stress would be determined using $(l_e/d)_x$ *without* K_f. Another allowable stress would be evaluated using $(l_e/d)_y$ *with* K_f. The smaller of the two allowable stresses would then govern the capacity of the built-up member.

7.10 Combined Bending and Tension

When a bending moment occurs simultaneously with an axial tension force, the effects of combined stresses must be taken into account. The distribution of axial tensile stresses and bending stresses can be plotted over the depth of the cross section of a member. See Example 7.10.

From the plots of combined stress it can be seen that on one side of the member the axial tensile stresses and the bending tensile stresses add. On the opposite face, the axial tensile stresses and bending compressive stresses cancel. Depending on the magnitude of the stresses involved, the resultant stress on this face can be *either* tension or compression.

Therefore, the capacity of a wood member with this type of combined loading can be governed by either a combined *tension* criterion or a net *compression* criterion. These criteria are given in NDS Sec. 3.9.1, *Bending and Axial Tension*.

Combined axial tension and bending tension

First, the combined *tensile* stresses are analyzed in an *interaction equation*. In this case the interaction equation is a straight-line expression (Fig. 7.15b) which is made up of two terms known as *stress ratios*. The first term measures the effects of axial tension, and the second term evaluates the effects of bending. In each case the actual stress is divided by the corresponding allowable stress. The allowable stresses in the denominators are determined in the usual way with one exception. Because the actual bending stress is the *bending tensile* stress, the allowable bending stress does not include the lateral stability factor C_L. In other words, F_b^* is F_b' determined with C_L set equal to unity.

It may be convenient to think of the stress ratios in the interaction equation as percentages or fractions of total member capacity. For example, the ratio of actual tension stress to allowable tension stress, f_t/F_t', can be viewed as the fraction of total member capacity that is used to resist axial tension. The ratio of actual bending stress to allowable bending stress f_b/F_b^* then represents the fraction of total member capacity used to resist bending. The sum of these fractions must be less than the total member capacity, 1.0.

Net compressive stress

Second, the combined stresses on the opposite face of the member are analyzed. If the sense of the combined stress on this face is tension, no additional work is required. However, if the combined stress at this point is *compressive*, a bending analysis is required. The allowable bending stress in the denominator of the second combined stress check must reflect the lateral stability of the compression side of the member. This is done by including the lateral stability factor C_L in evaluating F_b'. Refer to Sec. 6.3 for information on C_L.

EXAMPLE 7.10   Criteria for Combined Bending and Tension

The axial tensile stress and bending stress distributions are shown in Fig. 7.15a. If the individual stresses are added algebraically, one of two possible combined stress distri-

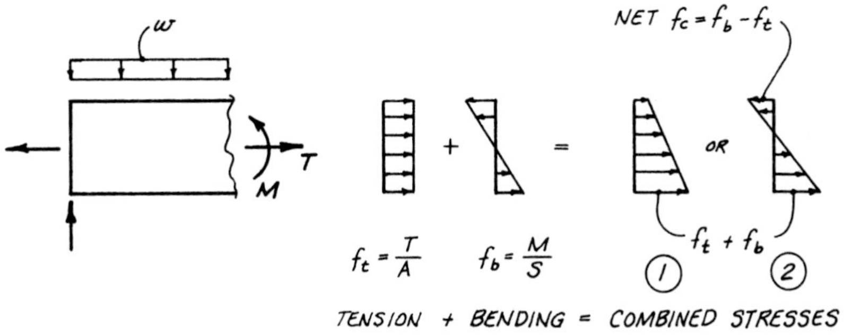

Figure 7.15a   Combined bending and axial tension stresses.

butions will result. If the axial tensile stress is larger than the bending stress, a *trapezoidal* combined stress diagram results in tension everywhere throughout the depth of the member (combined stress diagram 1). If the axial tensile stress is smaller than the bending stress, the resultant combined stress diagram is *triangular* (combined stress diagram 2).

Theoretically the following stresses in Fig. 7.15a are to be analyzed:

1. *Combined axial tension and bending tension stress.* This is done by using the straight-line interaction equation described below. These combined stresses are shown at the bottom face of the member in stress diagrams 1 and 2.
2. *Net compressive stress.* This stress is shown on the top surface of the member in stress diagram 2.

Combined Axial Tension and Bending Tension

The basic straight-line interaction equation is used for combined axial tensile and bending tensile stresses (NDS equation 3.9-1). The two stress ratios define a point on the graph in Fig. 7.15b. If the point lies on or below the line representing 100 percent of member strength, the interaction equation is satisfied.

INTERACTION EQUATION

$$\frac{f_t}{F'_t} + \frac{f_b}{F^*_b} \leq 1.0$$

where f_t = actual (computed) tensile stress parallel to grain
   = T/A
   F'_t = allowable tensile stress (Sec. 7.2)
   = $F_t(C_D)(C_M)(C_t)(C_F)$
   f_b = actual (computed) bending tensile stress. For usual case of bending about x axis, this is f_{bx}.
   = M/S
   F^*_b = F'_b allowable bending *tensile* stress without the adjustment for lateral stability. For the usual case of bending about the x axis of a rectangular cross section, the allowable bending stress is
   = $F_b(C_D)(C_M)(C_t)(C_F)(C_r)$ for sawn lumber
   = $F_b(C_D)(C_M)(C_t)(C_V)$ for glulam

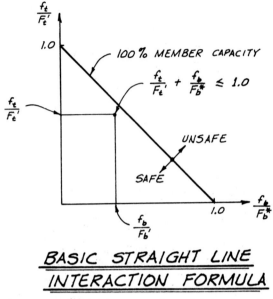

BASIC STRAIGHT LINE INTERACTION FORMULA

Figure 7.15b Interaction curve for axial tension plus bending tension.

Net Compressive Stress

When the bending compressive stress exceeds the axial tensile stress, the following stability check is given by NDS equation 3.9-2.

$$\frac{Net\ f_c}{F'_b} = \frac{f_b - f_t}{F_b^{**}} \le 1.0$$

where net f_c = net compressive stress

f_b = actual (computed) bending *compressive* stress. For usual case of bending about x axis, this is f_{bx}.

= M/S

f_t = actual (computed) axial tensile stress parallel to grain

= T/A

F_b^{**} = F'_b allowable bending *compressive* stress (Sec. 6.3). The beam stability factor C_L applies, but the volume factor C_V does not. For usual case of bending about x axis of rectangular cross section, allowable bending stress is

= $F_b(C_D)(C_M)(C_t)(C_L)(C_F)(C_r)$ for sawn lumber

= $F_b(C_D)(C_M)(C_t)(C_L)$ for glulam

The designer should use a certain degree of caution in applying the criterion for the *net compressive stress*. Often, combined stresses of this nature are the result of different loadings, and the maximum bending compressive stress may occur *with* or *without* the axial tensile stress.

For example, the bottom chord of the truss in Fig. 7.16a will always have the DL moment present regardless of the loads applied to the top chord. Thus f_b is a constant in this example. However, the tension force in the member varies depending on the load applied to the top chord. The tensile stress f_t will be small if DL alone is considered, and it will be much larger under DL plus snow load. To properly check the net compressive stress, the designer must determine the *minimum* f_t that will occur simultaneously with the bending stress f_b.

On the other hand, a simple and conservative approach for evaluating bending compressive stresses is to ignore the reduction in bending stress provided by the axial tensile stress. In this case the compressive stress ratio becomes

$$\frac{\text{Gross } f_c}{F'_b} = \frac{f_b}{F^{**}_b} \le 1.0$$

This check on the *gross* bending compressive stress can be rewritten as

$$f_b \le F'_b = F^{**}_b$$

where $F'_b = F^{**}_b$ is the allowable bending stress considering the effects of lateral stability and other applicable adjustments. This more conservative approach is used for the examples in this book. Under certain circumstances, the designer may wish to consider the *net* compressive stress.

It should be noted that NDS Sec. 3.9.1 introduces special notation for F'_b for use in the combined bending plus axial tension interaction equations. The symbols F^*_b and F^{**}_b are allowable bending stress values obtained with certain adjustment factors deleted. These are noted in Example 7.10 and are summarized inside the front cover of this book.

The design expressions given in Example 7.10 are adequate for most combined bending and axial tension problems. However, as wood structures become more highly engineered, there may be the need to handle problems involving axial tension plus bending about both the x and y axes. In this case the expanded criteria in Example 7.11 may be used.

EXAMPLE 7.11   Generalized Criteria for Combined Bending and Tension

The problem of biaxial bending plus axial tension has not been studied extensively. However, the following interaction equations are extensions of the NDS criteria for the general axial tension plus bending problem.

Combined Axial Tension and Bending
Tension

$$\frac{f_t}{F'_t} + \frac{f_{bx}}{F'_{bx}} + \frac{f_{by}}{F'_{by}} \le 1.0$$

The three terms all have the same sign. The allowable stresses include applicable adjustments (the adjustment for lateral stability C_L does not apply to bending tension).

Net Compressive Stress

For the check on *net* bending compressive stress the tension term is negative:

$$-\frac{f_t}{F'_t} + \frac{f_{bx}}{F'_{bx}} + \frac{f_{by}}{F'_{by}} \leq 1.0$$

Depending on the magnitude of the stresses involved, or reasons of simplicity, the designer may prefer to omit the negative term in this expression.

An even more conservative approach is to apply the general interaction formula for the net compressive stress in Example 7.14 (Sec. 7.12) with the axial component of the expression set equal to zero. This provides a more conservative biaxial bending (i.e., bending about the x and y axes) interaction formula. The allowable bending stress terms in the biaxial bending interaction equation would include all appropriate adjustment factors. Because the focus is on compression, the effect of lateral torsional buckling is to be taken into account with the beam stability factor C_L, but the volume factor C_V does not apply.

7.11   Design Problem: Combined Bending and Tension

The truss in Example 7.12 is similar to the truss in Example 7.2. The difference is that in the current example, an additional load is applied to the bottom chord. This load is uniformly distributed and represents the weight of a ceiling supported by the bottom chord of the truss.

The first part of the example deals with the calculation of the axial force in member AC. In order to analyze a truss, it is necessary for the loads to be resolved into joint loads. The tributary width to the three joints along the top chord is 7.5 ft, and the tributary width to the joint at the midspan of the truss on the bottom chord is 15 ft. The remaining loads (both top and bottom chord loads) are tributary to the joints at each support.

The design of a combined stress member is a trial-and-error procedure. In this example, a 2×8 bottom chord is the initial trial, and it proves satisfactory. *Independent* checks on the tension and bending stresses are first completed. The independent check on the bending stress automatically satisfies the check on the *gross* bending compression discussed in Sec. 7.10. Finally, the combined effects of tension and bending are evaluated.

It should be noted that the load duration factor used for the independent check for axial tension is $C_D = 1.15$ for combined (DL + SL). Dead load plus snow causes the axial force of 4.44 k. The independent check of bending uses $C_D = 0.9$ for DL, because only the DL of the ceiling causes the bending moment of 10.8 in.-k.

In the combined stress check, however, $C_D = 1.15$ applies to *both* the axial and the bending portions of the interaction formula. Recall that the C_D to be used in checking stresses caused by a *combination* of loads is the one associated with the shortest-duration load in the combination. For combined stresses, then, the same C_D applies to both terms.

EXAMPLE 7.12   Combined Bending and Tension

Design the lower chord of the truss in Fig. 7.16a. Use No. 1 and Better Hem-Fir. MC ≤ 19 percent, and normal temperature conditions apply. Connections will be made with a single row of ¾-in.-diameter bolts. Connections are assumed to be pinned. Trusses are 4 ft-0 in. o.c. Loads are applied to both the top and bottom chords. Assume that lateral buckling is prevented by the ceiling. Allowable stresses are from the 1991 NDS.

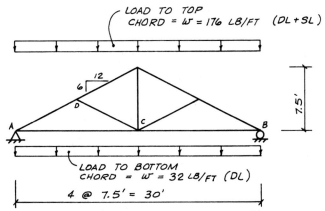

Figure 7.16a Loading diagram for truss. The uniformly distributed loads between the truss joints cause bending stresses in top and bottom chords, in addition to axial truss forces. Bottom chord has combined bending and axial tension.

Loads

TOP CHORD:

$$RDL = 14 \text{ psf} \quad \text{(horizontal plane)}$$

$$\underline{Snow = 30 \text{ psf}} \quad \text{(reduced snow load based on roof slope)}$$

$$TL = 44 \text{ psf}$$

$$w_{TL} = 44 \times 4 = 176 \text{ lb/ft to truss}$$

Load to joint for truss analysis:

$$P_T = 176 \times 7.5 = 1320 \text{ lb/joint}$$

BOTTOM CHORD:

$$\text{Ceiling DL} = 8 \text{ psf}$$

$$w_{DL} = 8 \times 4 = 32 \text{ lb/ft}$$

Load to joint for truss analysis:

$$P_B = 32 \times 15 = 480 \text{ lb/joint}$$

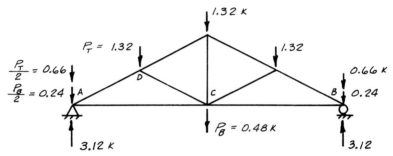

Figure 7.16b Loading diagram for truss. The distributed loads to the top and bottom chords are converted to concentrated joint forces for conventional truss analysis.

Force in lower chord (method of joints):

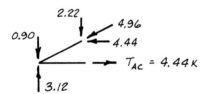

Figure 7.16c Free body diagram of joint A.

Load diagram for tension chord AC:

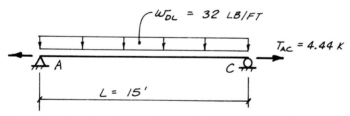

Figure 7.16d Loading diagram for member AC. The tension force is obtained from the truss analysis, and the bending moment is the result of the transverse load applied between joints A and C.

Member Design

Try 2 × 8 No. 1 & Btr Hem-Fir (Dimension lumber size category).
Values from NDS Supplement Table 4A:

$$F_b = 1050 \text{ psi}$$

$$F_t = 700 \text{ psi}$$

Size factors:

$$C_F = 1.2 \text{ for bending}$$

$$C_F = 1.2 \text{ for tension}$$

Section properties:

$$A_g = 10.875 \text{ in.}^2$$

$$S = 13.14 \text{ in.}^3$$

AXIAL TENSION:

1. Check axial tension at the net section. Because this truss is assumed to have pinned connections, the bending moment is theoretically zero at this point. Arbitrarily assume the hole diameter is ⅛ in. larger than the bolt diameter (for stress calculations only).

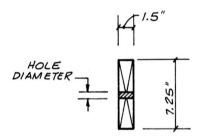

HOLE DIAMETER

Figure 7.16e Net section for tension member.

$$A_n = 1.5[7.25 - (0.75 + 0.125)] = 9.56 \text{ in.}^2$$

$$f_t = \frac{T}{A_n} = \frac{4440}{9.56} = 464 \text{ psi}$$

$$F'_t = F_t(C_D)(C_M)(C_t)(C_F)$$

$$= 700(1.15)(1.0)(1.0)(1.2) = 966 \text{ psi}$$

$$966 > 464 \text{ psi} \quad OK$$

2. Determine tension stress at the point of maximum bending stress (midspan) for use in the interaction formula.

$$f_t = \frac{T}{A_g} = \frac{4440}{10.875} = 408 \text{ psi} < 966 \quad OK$$

BENDING:

For a simple beam with a uniform load,

$$M = \frac{wL^2}{8} = \frac{32(15)^2}{8} = 900 \text{ ft-lb} = 10,800 \text{ in.-lb}$$

$$f_b = \frac{M}{S} = \frac{10,800}{13.14} = 822 \text{ psi}$$

The problem statement indicates that lateral buckling is prevented. In addition, the truss spacing exceeds the limit for repetitive members. Therefore, the beam stability factor C_L and the repetitive-member factor C_r are both 1.0.

The bending stress of 822 psi is caused by DL alone. Therefore, use $C_D = 0.9$ for an independent check on bending. Later use $C_D = 1.15$ for the combined stress check in the interaction formula.

$$F_b' = F_b(C_D)(C_M)(C_t)(C_L)(C_F)(C_r)$$

$$= 1050(0.9)(1.0)(1.0)(1.0)(1.2)(1.0)$$

$$= 1134 \text{ psi} > 822 \qquad OK$$

In terms of NDS notation, this value of F_b' is F_b^{**}.

COMBINED STRESSES:

1. Axial tension plus bending tension:

$$F_b^* = F_b' = F_b(C_D)(C_M)(C_t)(C_F)(C_r)$$

$$= 1050(1.15)(1.0)(1.0)(1.2)(1.0)$$

$$= 1449 \text{ psi}$$

$$\frac{f_t}{F_t'} + \frac{f_{bx}}{F_{bx}'} = \frac{408}{966} + \frac{822}{1449} = 0.99$$

$$0.99 < 1.0 \qquad OK$$

2. Net bending compressive stress. The *gross* bending compressive stress was shown to be not critical in the independent check on bending ($f_b = 822$ psi $< F_b' = 1134$). Therefore, the *net* bending compressive stress is automatically *OK*. The simpler, more conservative check on compression is recommended in this book.

The 2 × 8 No. 1 & Btr Hem-Fir member is seen to pass the combined stress check. The combined stress ratio of 0.99 indicates that the member is roughly overdesigned by 1 percent (1.0 corresponds to full member capacity or 100 percent of member strength).

$$(1.0 - 0.99)100 = 1\% \text{ overdesign}$$

Because of the inaccuracy involved in estimating design loads and because of variations in material properties, a calculated overstress of 1 or 2 percent (i.e., combined stress ratio of 1.01 or 1.02) is considered by many designers to still be within the "spirit" of the design specifications. Judgments of this nature must be made individually with knowledge of the factors relating to a particular problem. However, in this problem the combined stress ratio is less than 1.0, and the trial member size is acceptable.

> *Use* 2 × 8 No. 1 & Btr Hem-Fir

NOTE: The simplified analysis used in this example applies only to trusses with pinned joints. For a truss connected with toothed steel gussets, a design approach should be used which takes the continuity of the joints into account (Ref. 23.1).

7.12 Combined Bending and Compression

Structural members that are stressed simultaneously in bending and compression are known as *beam-columns*. These members occur frequently in wood buildings, and the designer should have the ability to handle these types of problems. In order to do this, it is first necessary to have a working knowledge of laterally unsupported beams (Sec. 6.3) and axially loaded columns (Secs. 7.4 and 7.5). The interaction formulas presented in this section can then be used to handle the combination of these stresses.

The straight-line interaction equation was introduced in Fig. 7.15b (Sec. 7.10) for combined bending and axial tension. At one time a similar straight-line equation was also used for the analysis of beam-columns. More recent editions of the NDS used a modified version of the basic equation.

There are many variables that affect the strength of a beam-column. The 1991 NDS has a new interaction equation for the analysis of beam-columns that was developed by Zahn (Ref. 5.2). It represents a unified treatment of

1. Column buckling

2. Lateral torsional buckling of beams

3. Beam-column interaction

The Ylinen buckling formula was introduced in Sec. 7.4 for column buckling and in Sec. 6.3 for the lateral buckling of beams. The allowable stresses F'_c and F'_{bx} determined in accordance with these previous sections are used in the Zahn interaction formula to account for the first two items. The added considerations for the *simultaneous* application of beam and column loading can be described as beam-column interaction. These factors are addressed in this section.

When a bending moment occurs simultaneously with an axial force, a more critical combined stress problem exists in comparison with combined bending and tension. In a beam-column, an additional bending stress is created which is known as the P-Δ *effect*. The P-Δ effect can be described in this way. First consider a member without an axial load. The bending moment developed by the *transverse* loading causes a deflection Δ. When the axial force P is then applied to the member, an *additional* bending moment of $P \times \Delta$ is generated. See Example 7.13. The P-Δ moment is known as a *second-order effect* because the added bending stress is not calculated directly. Instead, it is taken into account by *amplifying* the computed bending stress in the interaction equation.

The most common beam-column problem involves axial compression combined with a bending moment about the *strong* axis of the cross section. In this case, the actual bending stress f_{bx} is multiplied by an amplification factor that reflects the magnitude of the load P and the deflection Δ. This concept should be familiar to designers who also do structural steel design. The amplification factor in the 1991 NDS is similar to the one used for beam-columns in the AISC steel specification (Ref. 11.1).

The amplification factor is a number greater than 1.0 given by the following expression:

$$\text{Amplification factor for } f_{bx} = \left(\frac{1}{1 - f_c/F_{cEx}} \right)$$

This amplification factor is made up of two terms that measure the P-Δ effect for a bending moment about the strong x axis. The intent is to have the amplification factor increase as

1. Axial force P increases.

2. Deflection Δ due to bending about the x axis increases.

Obviously the compressive stress $f_c = P/A$ increases as the load P increases. As f_c becomes larger, the amplification factor will increase.

The increase in the amplification factor due to an increase in Δ may not be quite as clear. The increase for Δ is accomplished by the term F_{cE}. F_{cE} is defined as the value obtained from the Euler buckling stress formula evaluated using the column slenderness ratio for the axis about which the bending moment is applied. Thus, if the transverse loads cause a moment about the x axis, the *slenderness ratio about the x axis* is used to determine F_{cE}. The notation used in this book for this quantity is F_{cEx}.

Figure 7.6a (Sec. 7.4) shows both the Ylinen column equation and the Euler equation. For purposes of beam-column analysis, it should be understood that the allowable column stress F_c' is defined by the Ylinen formula, but the amplification factor for P-Δ makes use of the Euler formula. For use in the amplification factor, the value given by the expression for F_{cEx} is applied over the entire range of slenderness ratios. In other words, F_{cEx} goes to ∞ as the slenderness ratio becomes small, and F_{cEx} approaches 0 as $(l_e/d)_x$ becomes large.

The logic in using F_{cEx} in the amplification factor for P-Δ is that the deflection will be large for members with a large slenderness ratio. Likewise, Δ will be small as the slenderness ratio decreases. Thus, F_{cEx} produces the desired effect on the amplification factor.

It is necessary for the designer to clearly understand the reasoning behind the amplification factor. In a general problem there are two slenderness ratios: one for the x axis $(l_e/d)_x$ and one for the y axis $(l_e/d)_y$. In order to analyze combined stresses, the following convention should be applied:

1. Column buckling is governed by the larger slenderness ratio, $(l_e/d)_x$ or $(l_e/d)_y$, and the allowable column stress F'_c is given by the Ylinen formula.

2. When the bending moment is about the x axis, the value of F_{cE} for use in the amplification factor is to be based on $(l_e/d)_x$.

EXAMPLE 7.13   Interaction Equation for Beam-Column with Moment about x Axis

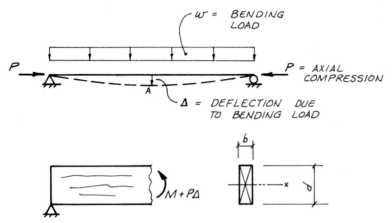

Figure 7.17a   Deflected shape of beam showing P-Δ moment. The computed bending stress f_b is based on the moment M from the moment diagram. The moment diagram considers the effects of the transverse load w, but does not include the secondary moment $P \times \Delta$. The P-Δ effect is taken into account by amplifying the computed bending stress f_b.

By cutting the beam-column in Fig. 7.17a and summing moments at point A, it can be seen that a moment of $P \times \Delta$ is created which *adds* to the moment M caused by the transverse load. In a beam with an axial tension force, this moment *subtracts* from the normal bending moment, and it is conservatively ignored.

The general interaction formula (Eq. 3.9-3 in the 1991 NDS) reduces to the following form for the common case of an axial compressive force combined with a bending moment about the x axis:

$$\left(\frac{f_c}{F'_c}\right)^2 + \left(\frac{1}{1 - f_c/F_{cEx}}\right)\frac{f_{bx}}{F'_{bx}} \leq 1.0$$

where f_c = actual (computed) compressive stress
     = P/A

    F'_c = allowable column stress as given by Ylinen formula (Secs. 7.4 and 7.5). Consider critical slenderness ratio $(l_e/d)_x$ or $(l_e/d)_y$. The critical slenderness ratio produces the smaller value of F'_c.
     = $F_c(C_D)(C_M)(C_t)(C_F)(C_P)$

f_{bx} = actual (computed) blending stress about x axis

  = M_x/S_x

F'_{bx} = allowable bending stress about x axis considering effects of lateral torsional buckling (Sec. 6.3)

For sawn lumber:

F'_{bx} = $F_b(C_D)(C_M)(C_t)(C_F)(C_L)$

For glulam the smaller of following bending stress values should be used:

F'_{bx} = $F_b(C_D)(C_M)(C_t)(C_L)$

F'_{bx} = $F_b(C_D)(C_M)(C_t)(C_V)$

F_{cEx} = Euler-based elastic buckling stress. Because transverse loads cause a bending moment about x axis, F_{cE} is based on slenderness ratio for x axis, i.e., $(l_e/d)_x$.

  = $\dfrac{K_{cE}E'_x}{[(l_e/d)_x]^2}$

The interaction formula for a beam-column takes into account a number of factors, including column buckling, lateral torsional buckling, and the P-Δ effect. It is difficult to show on a graph, or even a series of graphs, all of the different variables in a beam-column problem. However, the interaction plots in Fig. 7.17b are helpful in visualizing

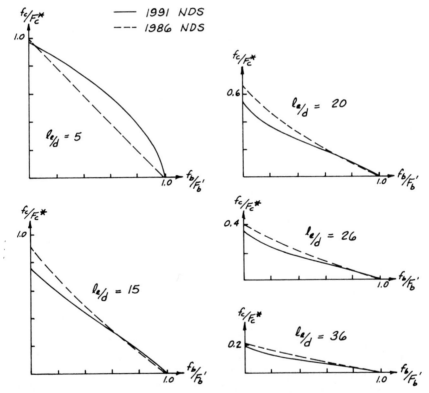

Figure 7.17b   Five interaction curves for beam-columns with different slenderness ratios. The curves show the comparison of the Zahn equation from the 1991 NDS compared with the interaction formula from the 1986 NDS. For small slenderness ratios (for example, l_e/d = 5) the 1991 NDS is more liberal. However, for larger slenderness ratios the 1991 NDS is more conservative.

some of the patterns. The five interaction graphs show the differences between the results obtained with the 1991 NDS interaction equation and those from previous editions. The graphs are representative only, and results vary with specific problems. The ordinate on the vertical axis shows the effect of different slenderness ratios in that the ratio of f_c/F_c^* decreases as the slenderness ratio increases. Recall that F_c^* includes all of the adjustments to the tabulated compressive stress except C_P.

For very small slenderness ratios, the Zahn interaction formula is more liberal than the older formula. However, as the slenderness ratio increases, the newer formula is more conservative. In each case, the Zahn formula more closely fits test results.

The interaction formula in Example 7.13 covers the common problem of axial compression with a bending moment about the strong axis. This can be viewed as a special case of the Zahn general interaction equation. The general formula has a third term which provides for consideration of a bending moment about the y axis. See Example 7.14.

The concept of a general interaction equation can be carried one step further. The problems considered up to this point have involved axial compression plus bending caused by transverse loads. Although this is a very comprehensive design expression, Zahn's expanded equation permits the compressive force in the column to be applied with an eccentricity. Thus in the general case, the bending moments about the x and y axes can be the result of transverse bending loads *and* an eccentrically applied column force.

The general loading condition is summarized as follows:

1. Compressive force in member $= P$
2. Bending moment about x axis
   a. Moment due to transverse loads $= M_x$
   b. Moment due to eccentricity about x axis $= P \times e_x$
3. Bending moment about y axis
   a. Moment due to transverse loads $= M_y$
   b. Moment due to eccentricity about y axis $= P \times e_y$

A distinction is made between the moments caused by transverse loads and the moments from an eccentrically applied column force. This distinction is necessary because the bending stresses that develop as a result of the eccentric load are subject to an *additional P-Δ* amplification factor. The general interaction formula may appear overly complicated at first glance, but taken term by term, it is straightforward and logical. The reader should keep in mind that greatly simplified versions of the interaction formula apply to most practical loading conditions (e.g., the version in Example 7.13). The simplified expression is obtained by setting the appropriate stress terms in the general interaction equation equal to zero.

EXAMPLE 7.14   General Interaction Formula for Combined Compression and Bending

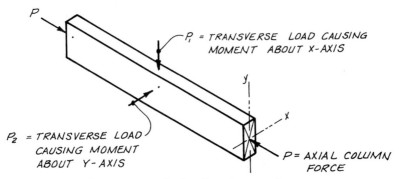

Figure 7.18a Axial compression plus bending about x and y axes.

The member in Fig. 7.18a has an *axial* compression load, a transverse load causing a moment about the x axis, and a transverse load causing a moment about the y axis. The following interaction formula from the 1991 NDS (NDS Sec. 3.9.2) is used to check this member:

$$\left(\frac{f_c}{F'_c}\right)^2 + \frac{f_{bx}}{F'_{bx}(1 - f_c/F_{cEx})} + \frac{f_{by}}{F'_{by}[1 - f_c/F_{cEy} - (f_{bx}/F_{bE})^2]} \leq 1.0$$

where f_{by} = actual (computed) bending stress about y axis
$\quad\quad = M_y/S_y$
$\quad F'_{by}$ = allowable bending stress about y axis (Sec. 6.4)
$\quad F_{cEy}$ = Euler elastic buckling stress based on slenderness ratio for y axis $(l_e/d)_y$
$$\quad\quad = \frac{K_{cE}E'_y}{[(l_e/d)_y]^2}$$
$\quad F_{bE}$ = elastic buckling stress considering lateral torsional buckling of beam; F_{bE} based on beam slenderness factor R_B (Sec. 6.3)
$$\quad\quad = \frac{K_{bE}E'_y}{R_B^2}$$

Other terms are as previously defined.

If one or more of the loads in Fig. 7.18a do not exist, the corresponding terms in the interaction formula are set equal to zero. For example, if there is no load causing a moment about the y axis, f_{by} is zero and the third term in the interaction formula drops out. With $f_{by} = 0$, the interaction formula reduces to the form given in Example 7.13.

On the other hand, if the axial column force does not exist, f_c becomes zero, and the general formula becomes an interaction formula for biaxial bending (i.e., simultaneous bending about the x and y axes).

In the interaction problems considered thus far, the bending stresses have been caused only by transverse applied loads. In some cases, bending stresses may be the result of an eccentric column force. See Fig. 7.18b. The development of a generalized interaction formula for beam-columns with transverse *and* eccentric bending stresses is shown below. In the general formula, the amplification for P-Δ effect introduced in Example 7.13 is applied the same way. However, the bending stresses caused by the *eccentric* column force are subject to an *additional* P-Δ amplification.

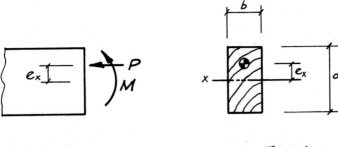

BEAM-COLUMN   SECTION

Figure 7.18b Bending moment M due to transverse loads plus eccentric column force $P \times e$. Note that the eccentric moment $P \times e$ is a computed (first-order) bending moment, and it should not be confused with the second-order P-Δ moment. The eccentric moment in Fig. 7.18b causes a bending stress about the x axis.

Cross-Sectional Properties

$$A = bd$$

$$S = \frac{bd^2}{6}$$

Bending Stresses

$$\text{Total moment} = \text{transverse load } M + \text{eccentric load } M$$

$$= M + Pe$$

Bending stress due to transverse bending loads:

$$f_b = \frac{M}{S}$$

Bending stress due to eccentrically applied column force:
Computed stress:

$$\frac{Pe}{S} = \frac{Pe}{bd^2/6} = f_c\left(\frac{6e}{d}\right)$$

Amplified eccentric bending stress:

$$f_c\left(\frac{6e}{d}\right) \times (\text{amplification factor}) = f_c\left(\frac{6e}{d}\right)\left[1 + 0.234\left(\frac{f_c}{F_{cE}}\right)\right]$$

Bending stress due to transverse loads + amplified eccentric bending stress

$$= f_b + f_c\left(\frac{6e}{d}\right)\left[1 + 0.234\left(\frac{f_c}{F_{cE}}\right)\right]$$

General Interaction Formula

The interaction formula is expanded here to include the effects of eccentric bending stresses. Subscripts are added to the eccentric terms to indicate the axis about which the eccentricity occurs. This general form of the interaction formula is given in NDS Sec. 15.4.

$$\left(\frac{f_c}{F_c'}\right)^2 + \frac{f_{bx} + f_c(6e_x/d_x)[1 + 0.234(f_c/F_{cEx})]}{F_{bx}'(1 - f_c/F_{cEx})}$$

$$+ \frac{f_{by} + f_c(6e_y/d_y)[1 + 0.234(f_c/F_{cEy})]}{F_{by}'[1 - f_c/F_{cEy} - (f_{bx}/F_{bE})^2]} \le 1.0$$

In the general interaction formula in Example 7.14, it is assumed that the eccentric load is applied at the *end* of the column. In some cases an eccentric compression force may be applied through a *side bracket* at some point between the ends of the column. The reader is referred to NDS Sec. 15.4.2 for an approximate method of handling beam-columns with side brackets.

Several examples of beam-column problems are given in the remaining portion of this chapter.

7.13 Design Problem: Beam-Column

In this first example, the top chord of the truss analyzed in Example 7.12 is considered. The top chord is subjected to bending loads caused by (DL + SL) being applied along the member, rather than framing directly into the joints. The top chord is also subjected to axial compression, which is obtained from a truss analysis using tributary loads to the truss joints.

A 2 × 8 is selected as the trial size. In a beam-column problem, it is often convenient to divide the stress calculations into three subproblems. In this approach, somewhat independent checks on axial, bending, and combined stresses are performed. See Example 7.15.

The first check is on *axial* stresses. Because the top chord of the truss is attached directly to the roof sheathing, lateral buckling about the weak axis of the cross section is prevented. Bracing for the strong axis is provided at the truss joints by the members that frame into the top chord.

The compressive stress is calculated at two different locations along the length of the member. First, the allowable column stress F_c' adjusted for column stability is checked away from the joints, using the gross area in the calculation of f_c. The second calculation involves the stress at the net section at a joint compared with the allowable stress F_c' without the reduction for stability.

In the *bending* stress calculation, the moment is determined by use of the horizontal span of the top chord and the load on a horizontal plane. It was shown in Example 2.5 (Sec. 2.5) that the moment obtained using the *horizontal plane method* is the same as the moment obtained using the inclined span length and the normal component of the load.

The final step is the analysis of *combined* stresses. The top chord has axial compression plus bending about the strong axis, and the simple interaction formula from Example 7.13 applies. The trial member is found to be acceptable.

EXAMPLE 7.15   Beam-Column Design

Design the top chord of the truss shown in Fig. 7.16a in Example 7.12. The axial force and bending loads are reproduced in Fig. 7.19a. Use No. 1 Southern Pine. MC ≤ 19 percent, and normal temperatures apply.

Connections will be made with a single row of ¾-in.-diameter bolts. The top chord is stayed laterally throughout its length by the roof sheathing. Trusses are 4 ft.-0 in. o.c. Allowable stresses and section properties are to be obtained from the 1991 NDS.

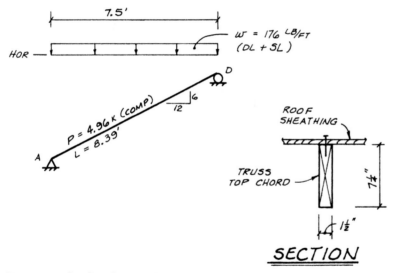

Figure 7.19a   Loading diagram for top chord of truss. Section view shows lateral support by roof sheathing.

Try 2 × 8. Tabulated stresses in NDS Supplement Table 4B for Southern Pine in the Dimension lumber size category are size-specific:

$$F_c = 1650 \text{ psi}$$

$$F_b = 1500 \text{ psi}$$

$$E = 1{,}700{,}000 \text{ psi}$$

Because the tabulated values are size-specific, most stress grades of Southern Pine have the appropriate size factors already incorporated into the published values. For these grades, the size factors can be viewed as defaulting to unity:

$$C_F = 1.0 \text{ for compression parallel to grain}$$

$$C_F = 1.0 \text{ for bending}$$

Some grades of Southern Pine, however, require size factors other than unity. Section properties:

$$A = 10.875 \text{ in.}^2$$

$$S = 13.141 \text{ in.}^3$$

Axial

1. *Stability* check. Column buckling occurs away from truss joints. Use gross area.

$$f_c = \frac{P}{A} = \frac{4960}{10.875} = 456 \text{ psi}$$

$(l_e/d)_y = 0$ because of lateral support provided by roof diaphragm

$$\left(\frac{l_e}{d}\right)_x = \frac{8.39 \text{ ft} \times 12 \text{ in./ft}}{7.25 \text{ in.}} = 13.9$$

$$E' = E(C_M)(C_t) = 1{,}700{,}000(1.0)(1.0)$$

$$= 1{,}700{,}000 \text{ psi}$$

For visually graded sawn lumber:

$$K_{cE} = 0.3$$

$$c = 0.8$$

$$F_{cE} = \frac{K_{cE}E'}{[(l_e/d)_{\max}]^2} = \frac{0.3(1{,}700{,}000)}{(13.9)^2} = 2645 \text{ psi}$$

$$F_c^* = F_c(C_D)(C_M)(C_t)(C_F)$$

$$= 1650(1.15)(1.0)(1.0)(1.0) = 1898 \text{ psi}$$

$$\frac{F_{cE}}{F_c^*} = \frac{2645}{1898} = 1.394$$

$$\frac{1 + F_{cE}/F_c^*}{2c} = \frac{1 + 1.394}{2(0.8)} = 1.496$$

$$C_P = \frac{1 + F_{cE}/F_c^*}{2c} - \sqrt{\left(\frac{1 + F_{cE}/F_c^*}{2c}\right)^2 - \frac{F_{cE}/F_c^*}{c}}$$

$$= 1.496 - \sqrt{(1.496)^2 - 1.394/0.8} = 0.792$$

$$F'_c = F_c(C_D)(C_M)(C_t)(C_F)(C_P)$$

$$= 1650(1.15)(1.0)(1.0)(1.0)(0.792)$$

$$= 1502 \text{ psi} > 456 \quad OK$$

2. *Net section check.* Arbitrarily assume the hole diameter is ⅛ in. larger than the bolt (for stress calculations only).

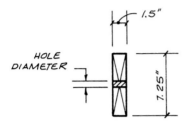

Figure 7.19b Net section of top chord at connection.

$$A_n = 1.5(7.25 - 0.875) = 9.56 \text{ in.}^2$$

$$f_c = \frac{P}{A_n} = \frac{4960}{9.56} = 518 \text{ psi}$$

At braced location there is no reduction for stability.

$$F'_c = F_c^* = F_c(C_D)(C_M)(C_t)(C_F)$$

$$= 1650(1.15)(1.0)(1.0)(1.0)$$

$$= 1898 \text{ psi} > 518 \quad OK$$

Bending

Assume simple span (no end restraint). Take span and load on horizontal plane (refer to Example 2.5 in Sec. 2.5).

$$M = \frac{wL^2}{8} = \frac{0.176(7.5)^2}{8} = 1.24 \text{ ft-k} = 14.85 \text{ in.-k}$$

$$f_b = \frac{M}{S} = \frac{14,850}{13.14} = 1130 \text{ psi}$$

The beam has full lateral support. Therefore l_u and R_B are zero, and the lateral stability factor is $C_L = 1.0$. In addition, the spacing of the trusses is 4 ft o.c., and the allowable bending stress does not qualify for the repetitive-member increase, and $C_r = 1.0$.

$$F'_b = F_b(C_D)(C_M)(C_t)(C_L)(C_F)(C_r)$$

$$= 1500(1.15)(1.0)(1.0)(1.0)(1.0)(1.0)$$

$$= 1725 \text{ psi} > 1130 \quad OK$$

Combined Stresses

There is no bending stress about the y axis, and $f_{by} = 0$. Furthermore, the column force is concentric, and the general interaction formula reduces to

$$\left(\frac{f_c}{F'_c}\right)^2 + \frac{f_{bx}}{F'_{bx}(1 - f_c/F_{cEx})} \leq 1.0$$

The load duration factor C_D for use in the interaction formula is based on the shortest-duration load in the combination, which in this case is snow load. A C_D of 1.15 for snow was used in the individual checks on the axial stress and bending stress. Therefore, the previously determined values of F'_c and F'_b are appropriate for use in the interaction formula.

In addition to the allowable stresses, the combined stress check requires the elastic buckling stress F_{cE} for use in evaluating the amplification factor. The bending moment is about the strong axis of the cross section, and the P-Δ effect is measured by the slenderness ratio about the x axis [that is, $(l_e/d)_x = 13.9$].

The value of F_{cE} determined earlier in the example was for the column buckling portion of the problem. Column buckling is based on $(l_e/d)_{max}$. The fact that $(l_e/d)_{max}$ and $(l_e/d)_x$ are equal, is a coincidence in this problem. In other words, F_{cE} for the column portion of the problem is based on $(l_e/d)_{max}$, and F_{cE} for the P-Δ analysis is based on the axis about which the bending moment occurs, $(l_e/d)_x$. In this example, the two values of F_{cE} are equal, but in general they could be different.

$$F_{cEx} = F_{cE} = 2645 \text{ psi}$$

$$\left(\frac{f_c}{F'_c}\right)^2 + \left(\frac{1}{1 - f_c/F_{cEx}}\right)\frac{f_{bx}}{F'_{bx}} = \left(\frac{456}{1502}\right)^2 + \left(\frac{1}{1 - 456/2645}\right)\frac{1130}{1725}$$

$$(0.304)^2 + 1.21(0.655) = 0.884 < 1.0 \quad OK$$

$$\boxed{Use \ \ 2 \times 8 \ \ No. \ 1 \ \ SP}$$

NOTE: The simplified analysis used in this example applies only to trusses with pinned joints. For a truss connected with toothed steel gussets, a design approach should be used which takes the continuity of the joints into account (Ref. 23.1).

It should be noted that all stress calculations in this example are for loads caused by the design load of (DL + SL). For this reason the load duration factor for snow (1.15) is applied to each *individual* stress calculation as well as to the *combined* stress check.

In some cases of combined loading, the *individual* stresses (axial and bending) may not both be caused by the same load. In this situation, the respective C_D values are used in evaluating the individual stresses. However, in the *combined* stress calculation, the same C_D is used for all components. Recall that the C_D for the *shortest*-duration load applies to the entire combination. The appropriate rules for applying C_D should be followed in checking both individual and combined stresses. The application of different C_D's in the individual stress calculations is illustrated in some of the following examples.

7.14 Design Problem: Beam-Column Action in a Stud Wall

A common occurrence of beam-column action is found in an exterior bearing wall. Axial column stresses are developed in the wall studs by vertical gravity loads. Bending stresses are caused by lateral wind or seismic forces.

The wind force used in this example is the outward pressure for an element in a wall near a corner discontinuity (Sec. 2.11). A wind stagnation pressure of 16.4 psf is given, and wind Exposure C applies. The building is a Standard-occupancy structure, and $I = 1.0$ for both wind and seismic forces. The building is located in seismic zone 4, and the seismic force normal to the surface of a wall is given by the Code expression for F_p (Sec. 2.15). For this loading, C_p is 0.75, and the seismic coefficient is 0.3.

For typical wood-frame walls, the wall DL is so small that the design wind force usually exceeds the seismic force F_p. This applies to the normal wall force only, and seismic may be critical for parallel-to-wall (i.e., shear-wall) forces. In buildings with large wall dead loads, the F_p seismic force can exceed the wind force. Large wall dead loads usually occur in concrete and masonry (brick and concrete block) buildings.

In the two-story building of Example 7.16, the studs carry a number of axial compressive loads including dead, roof live, and floor live loads. In *load case 1*, the various possible combinations of gravity loads are considered.

In Example 4.10 part *b* (Sec. 4.15), a "system" was introduced to determine the critical load combination. This system breaks down in the analysis of certain members because of the effect of the load duration factor. Figure 7.6c, earlier in this chapter, shows that C_D has a varied effect on F_c' depending on the slenderness ratio of the column. Therefore, the idea of dividing out the load duration factor is inappropriate except for *short* columns.

As a result, each vertical load combination should theoretically be checked using the appropriate C_D. In this example, the load case of (DL alone) can be eliminated by inspection. The results of the other two vertical loadings are close, and the critical combination can be determined by evaluating the ratio f_c/F_c' for each combination. The loading with the larger stress ratio is critical. Only the calculations for the critical combination of (DL + RLL + FLL) are shown in the example for load case 1.

Load case 2 involves both vertical loads and lateral forces. According to the UBC, roof live load need not be considered simultaneously with lateral forces (Sec. 2.16). Thus, for the combined stress check, the vertical load effects are recalculated for (DL + FLL). The reduction of f_c from 123 to 97.3 psi has a relatively minor effect on the final outcome of this problem. However, for larger axial forces, the difference could be important. If snow load had occurred in this problem instead of RLL, the SL would be considered simultaneously with lateral forces, although some reduction may be possible.

Notice that C_D for wind (the shortest-duration load in the combination) applies to both components of stress in the interaction formula.

EXAMPLE 7.16   Combined Bending and Compression in a Stud Wall

Check the 2 × 6 stud in the first-floor bearing wall in the building shown in Fig. 7.20a. Consider the given vertical loads and lateral forces. Lumber is No. 2 DF-L. MC ≤ 19 percent, and normal temperatures apply (C_M = 1.0 and C_t = 1.0). Allowable stresses are to be in accordance with the 1991 NDS.

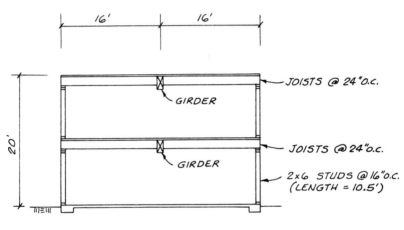

TRANSVERSE   SECTION

Figure 7.20a Transverse section showing exterior bearing walls.

The following gravity loads are given:

$$\text{Roof DL} = 10 \text{ psf}$$

$$\text{Roof LL} = 20 \text{ psf}$$

$$\text{Wall DL} = 7 \text{ psf}$$

$$\text{Floor DL} = 8 \text{ psf}$$

$$\text{Floor LL} = 40 \text{ psf}$$

The following lateral forces are also given:
  Outward *wind* pressure on a typical stud near a wall corner (wind force on element in area of discontinuity)

$$P = C_e C_q q_s I = 1.06(1.5)(16.4 \text{ psf})(1.0)$$

$$= 26.1 \text{ psf horizontal}$$

Seismic force normal to wall (seismic force on elements or portions of a structure)

$$F_p = ZIC_pW_p = 0.4(1.0)(0.75)W_p = 0.3W_p$$

$$= 0.3(7 \text{ psf}) = 2.1 \text{ psf} < 26.1$$

$$\therefore \text{ Wind governs.}$$

NOTE: The lateral wind and seismic forces are applied in this book without the *load combination factor* discussed in Sec. 2.8. Local code interpretations may vary regarding the load combination factor, especially when the load duration factor C_D is applied. The designer should verify that its use is acceptable before applying it in practice. The load combination factor is not shown in this example (conservative). Recall that Ref. 5.1 requires at least *two* transient loads in order to apply the load combination factor.

Try 2 × 6 No. 2 DF-L (Dimension lumber size):

Values from NDS Supplement Table 4A:

$$F_b = 875 \text{ psi}$$

$$F_c = 1300 \text{ psi}$$

$$F_{c\perp} = 625 \text{ psi}$$

$$E = 1{,}600{,}000 \text{ psi}$$

Size factors:

$$C_F = 1.3 \quad \text{for bending}$$

$$C_F = 1.1 \quad \text{for compression parallel to grain}$$

Section properties:

$$A = 8.25 \text{ in.}^2$$

$$S = 7.56 \text{ in.}^3$$

Load Case 1: Gravity Loads Only

Tributary width of roof and floor framing to the exterior bearing wall is 8 ft.

Dead loads:

$$\text{Roof DL} = 10 \text{ psf} \times 8 \text{ ft} = 80 \text{ lb/ft}$$

$$\text{Wall DL} = 7 \text{ psf} \times 20 \text{ ft} = 140 \text{ lb/lft}$$

$$\underline{\text{Floor DL} = 8 \text{ psf} \times 8 \text{ ft} = 64 \text{ lb/ft}}$$

$$w_{\text{DL}} = 284 \text{ lb/ft}$$

Live loads:

$$\text{Roof LL} = 20 \text{ psf} \times 8 \text{ ft} = 160 \text{ lb/ft}$$

$$\text{Floor LL} = 40 \text{ psf} \times 8 \text{ ft} = 320 \text{ lb/ft}$$

LOAD COMBINATIONS:

Calculate the axial load on a typical stud:

$$\text{DL alone} = (284 \text{ lb/ft})(1.33 \text{ ft}) = 378 \text{ lb} \qquad C_D = 0.9$$

$$\text{DL + FLL} = (284 + 320)1.33 = 803 \text{ lb} \qquad C_D = 1.0$$

$$\text{DL + FLL + RLL} = (284 + 320 + 160)1.33 = 1016 \text{ lb} \qquad C_D = 1.25$$

The combination of DL alone can be eliminated by inspection. When the C_D's are considered for the second two combinations, the net effects are roughly the same. However, (DL + FLL + RLL) is the critical vertical loading, and stress calculations for this combination only are shown. The axial stress in the stud and the bearing stress on the wall plate are equal.

$$f_c = f_{c\perp} = \frac{P}{A} = \frac{1016}{8.25} = 123 \text{ psi}$$

COLUMN CAPACITY:

Sheathing provides lateral support about the weak axis of the stud. Therefore, check column buckling about the x axis only ($L = 10.5$ ft and $d_x = 5.5$ in.):

$$\left(\frac{l_e}{d}\right)_y = 0 \qquad \text{because of sheathing}$$

$$\left(\frac{l_e}{d}\right)_{max} = \left(\frac{l_e}{d}\right)_x = \frac{10.5 \text{ ft} \times 12 \text{ in./ft}}{5.5 \text{ in.}} = 22.9$$

$$E' = E(C_M)(C_t) = 1,600,000(1.0)(1.0)$$

$$= 1,600,000 \text{ psi}$$

For visually graded sawn lumber:

$$K_{cE} = 0.3$$

$$c = 0.8$$

$$F_{cE} = \frac{K_{cE}E'}{(l_e/d)^2} = \frac{0.3(1,600,000)}{(22.9)^2} = 915 \text{ psi}$$

$$F_c^* = F_c(C_D)(C_M)(C_t)(C_F)$$

$$= 1300(1.25)(1.0)(1.0)(1.1) = 1788 \text{ psi}$$

$$\frac{F_{cE}}{F_c^*} = \frac{915}{1788} = 0.512$$

$$\frac{1 + F_{cE}/F_c^*}{2c} = \frac{1 + 0.512}{2(0.8)} = 0.945$$

$$C_P = \frac{1 + F_{cE}/F_c^*}{2c} - \sqrt{\left(\frac{1 + F_{cE}/F_c^*}{2c}\right)^2 - \frac{F_{cE}/F_c^*}{c}}$$

$$= 0.945 - \sqrt{(0.945)^2 - 0.512/0.8} = 0.442$$

$$F_c' = F_c(C_D)(C_M)(C_t)(C_F)(C_P)$$

$$= 1300(1.25)(1.0)(1.0)(1.1)(0.442)$$

$$= 790 \text{ psi} > 123 \quad OK$$

BEARING OF STUD ON WALL PLATES:

For a bearing length of 1½ in. on a stud more than 3 in. from the end of the wall plate:

$$C_b = \frac{l_b + 0.375}{l_b} = \frac{1.5 + 0.375}{1.5} = 1.25$$

$$F_{c\perp}' = F_{c\perp}(C_M)(C_t)(C_b) = 625(1.0)(1.0)(1.25)$$

$$= 781 \text{ psi} > 123 \quad OK$$

$$f_c < F_c' \quad \text{and} \quad f_c < F_{c\perp}'$$

$$\therefore \text{Vertical loads} \quad OK$$

Load Case 2:   Gravity Loads + Lateral Forces

BENDING:

Wind governs over seismic. Force to one stud:

$$\text{Wind} = 26.1 \text{ psf}$$

$$w = 26.1 \text{ psf} \times 1.33 \text{ ft} = 34.8 \text{ lb/ft}$$

$$M = \frac{wL^2}{8} = \frac{34.8(10.5)^2}{8} = 480 \text{ ft-lb} = 5755 \text{ in.-lb}$$

$$f_b = \frac{M}{S} = \frac{5755}{7.56} = 761 \text{ psi}$$

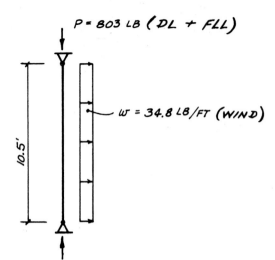

Figure 7.20b Loading for beam-column analysis.

The stud has full lateral support provided by sheathing. Therefore, l_u and R_B are zero, and the lateral stability factor is $C_L = 1.0$. The load duration factor for wind is $C_D = 1.6$, and the repetitive-member factor is 1.15.

$$F'_b = F_b(C_D)(C_M)(C_t)(C_L)(C_F)(C_r)$$

$$= 875(1.6)(1.0)(1.0)(1.0)(1.3)(1.15)$$

$$= 2093 \text{ psi} > 761 \quad OK$$

NOTE: The load duration factor recommended by the 1991 NDS for wind and seismic forces (Sec. 2.8) is $C_D = 1.6$. In the past, $C_D = 1.33$ was used for these loads. The designer should verify local code acceptance before using $C_D = 1.6$.

AXIAL:

According to the UBC, roof live load need not be considered simultaneously with lateral forces. Therefore, use (DL + FLL) for combined stresses.

$$f_c = \frac{P}{A} = \frac{803}{8.25} = 97.3 \text{ psi}$$

In load case 1, it was noted that (DL + FLL + RLL) is the critical combination for gravity loads. Therefore, a separate allowable axial stress for (DL + FLL) alone (i.e., using $C_D = 1.0$) is not shown. In the combined stress calculation, a single C_D is used throughout. Hence, F'_c is determined here using $C_D = 1.6$.

Again, the slenderness ratio about the y axis is zero because of the continuous support provided by the sheathing. The column slenderness ratio and the elastic buckling stress that were determined previously apply to the problem at hand:

$$\left(\frac{l_e}{d}\right)_{max} = \left(\frac{l_e}{d}\right)_x = 22.9$$

$$F_{cE} = 915 \text{ psi}$$

$$F_c^* = F_c(C_D)(C_M)(C_t)(C_F)$$

$$= 1300(1.6)(1.0)(1.0)(1.1) = 2288 \text{ psi}$$

$$\frac{F_{cE}}{F_c^*} = \frac{915}{2288} = 0.400$$

$$\frac{1 + F_{cE}/F_c^*}{2c} = \frac{1 + 0.400}{2(0.8)} = 0.875$$

$$C_p = \frac{1 + F_{cE}/F_c^*}{2c} - \sqrt{\left(\frac{1 + F_{cE}/F_c^*}{2c}\right)^2 - \frac{F_{cE}/F_c^*}{c}}$$

$$= 0.875 - \sqrt{(0.875)^2 - 0.400/0.8} = 0.359$$

$$F_c' = F_c(C_D)(C_M)(C_t)(C_F)(C_P)$$

$$= 1300(1.6)(1.0)(1.0)(1.1)(0.359)$$

$$F_c' = 822 \text{ psi} > 97.3 \quad OK$$

COMBINED STRESS:

The simplified interaction formula from Example 7.13 (Sec. 7.12) applies:

$$\left(\frac{f_c}{F_c'}\right)^2 + \frac{f_{bx}}{F_{bx}'(1 - f_c/F_{cEx})} \leq 1.0$$

Recall that the allowable column stress F_c' is determined using the maximum slenderness ratio for the column $(l_e/d)_{max}$, and the Euler buckling stress F_{cEx} for use in evaluating the P-Δ effect is based on the slenderness ratio for the axis with the bending moment. In this problem the bending moment is about the strong axis of the cross section, and $(l_e/d)_x$, coincidentally, controls both F_c' and F_{cEx}. In general, one slenderness ratio does not necessarily define these two quantities.

The value of F_{cE} determined earlier in the example using $(l_e/d)_x$ is also F_{cEx}:

$$F_{cEx} = F_{cE} = 915 \text{ psi}$$

$$\left(\frac{f_c}{F_c'}\right)^2 + \left(\frac{1}{1 - f_c/F_{cEx}}\right)\frac{f_{bx}}{F_{bx}'} = \left(\frac{97.3}{822}\right)^2 + \left(\frac{1}{1 - 97.3/915}\right)\frac{761}{2093}$$

$$(0.118)^2 + 1.12(0.364) = 0.421 < 1.0 \quad OK$$

2 × 6   No. 2   DF-L   exterior bearing wall   *OK*

Although several load cases were considered, the primary purpose of Example 7.15 is to illustrate the application of the interaction formula for beam-columns applied to a stud wall. The reader should understand that other load cases, including uplift due to wind, may be required in the analysis of a bearing wall subject to lateral forces.

7.15 Design Problem: Glulam Beam-Column

In this example a somewhat more complicated bracing condition is considered. The column is a glulam that supports both roof dead and live loads as well as lateral wind forces. See Example 7.17.

In load case 1 the vertical loads are considered, and (DL + RLL) is the critical loading. The interesting aspect of this problem is that there are different unbraced lengths for the x and y axes. Lateral support for the strong axis is provided at the ends only. However, for the weak axis the unbraced length is the height of the window.

In load case 2 the vertical DL and lateral wind force are considered. Bending takes place about the strong axis of the member. The bending analysis includes a check of lateral stability using the window height as the unbraced length. In checking combined stresses, a C_D of 1.6 for wind is applied to all components of the interaction formula. Note that C_D appears several times in the development of the allowable column stress, and F'_c must be reevaluated for use in the interaction formula.

The example makes use of a member that is an axial-load glulam combination. Calculations show that the bending stress is more significant than the axial stress, and it would probably be a more efficient design to choose a member from the glulam bending combinations instead of an axial combination. However, with a combined stress ratio of 0.632, the given member is considerably understressed.

EXAMPLE 7.17   Glulam Beam-Column

Check the column in the building shown in Fig. 7.21a for the given loads. The column is an axial combination 2 DF glulam (combination symbol 2) with tension laminations (F_{bx} = 2000 psi). The member supports the tributary DL, RLL, and lateral wind force. The wind force is transferred to the column by the window framing in the wall.

The lateral force is the inward or outward wind pressure on a wall element away from a discontinuity. The basic wind speed is 80 mph, and Exposure C applies. For simplicity, use a uniform wind pressure over the full 16-ft height. The building is a Standard-occupancy structure. Wind pressure is

$$P = C_e C_q q_s I = 1.06(1.2)(16.4)(1.0) = 20.9 \text{ psf}$$

The seismic force is not critical. Tabulated glulam design values are to be taken from the 1991 NDS Supplement Table 5B. C_M = 1.0, and C_t = 1.0.

NOTE: The lateral wind and seismic forces are applied in this book without the *load combination factor* (discussed in Sec. 2.8). Local code interpretations may vary regarding the load combination factor, especially when the load duration factor C_D is applied. The designer should verify that its use is acceptable before applying it in practice. The load combination factor is not shown in this example (conservative). Recall that Ref. 5.1 requires at least *two* transient loads in order to apply the load combination factor.

Glulam Column

$5\frac{1}{8} \times 7\frac{1}{2}$ *Axial combination 2 DF glulam:*

$A = 38.4$ in.^{2} $F_c = 1900$ psi

$S_x = 48$ in.^{3} $F_{bx} = 2000$ psi   (requires tension laminations)

$E_x = E_y = 1,700,000$ psi

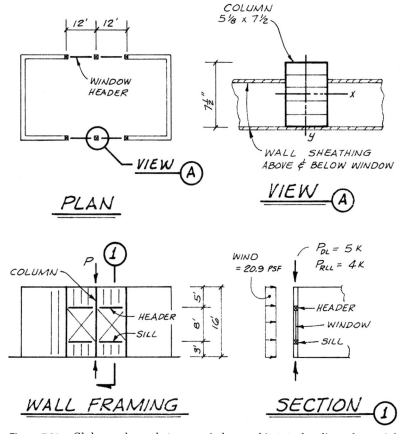

Figure 7.21a Glulam column between windows subject to bending plus axial compression.

Load Case 1:   Gravity Loads

$$DL = 5 \text{ k}$$

$$DL + RLL = 5 + 4 = 9 \text{ k}$$

By inspection (DL + RLL) is the critical vertical loading condition, and the load duration factor for the combination is $C_D = 1.25$.

$$f_c = \frac{P}{A} = \frac{9000}{38.4} = 234 \text{ psi}$$

Neglect the column end restraint offered by wall sheathing for column buckling about the y axis. Assume an effective length factor (Fig. 7.9) of $K_e = 1.0$ for both the x and y axes.

$$\left(\frac{l_e}{d}\right)_x = \frac{1(16 \text{ ft} \times 12 \text{ in./ft})}{7.5 \text{ in.}} = 25.6$$

$$\left(\frac{l_e}{d}\right)_y = \frac{1(8 \text{ ft} \times 12 \text{ in./ft})}{5.125 \text{ in.}} = 18.7 < 25.6$$

The larger slenderness ratio governs the allowable column stress. Therefore, the strong axis of column is critical, and $(l_e/d)_x$ is used to determine F'_c.

$$E_x = E_y = 1,700,000 \text{ psi}$$

$$E' = E(C_M)(C_t) = 1,700,000(1.0)(1.0)$$

$$= 1,700,000 \text{ psi}$$

For glulam:

$$K_{cE} = 0.418$$

$$c = 0.9$$

$$F_{cE} = \frac{K_{cE}E'}{[(l_e/d)_{\max}]^2} = \frac{0.418(1,700,000)}{(25.6)^2} = 1084 \text{ psi}$$

$$F^*_c = F_c(C_D)(C_M)(C_t)$$

$$= 1900(1.25)(1.0)(1.0) = 2375 \text{ psi}$$

$$\frac{F_{cE}}{F^*_c} = \frac{1084}{2375} = 0.457$$

$$\frac{1 + F_{cE}/F^*_c}{2c} = \frac{1 + 0.457}{2(0.9)} = 0.809$$

$$C_P = \frac{1 + F_{cE}/F^*_c}{2c} - \sqrt{\left(\frac{1 + F_{cE}/F^*_c}{2c}\right)^2 - \frac{F_{cE}/F^*_c}{c}}$$

$$= 0.809 - \sqrt{(0.809)^2 - 0.457/0.9} = 0.425$$

$$F'_c = F_c(C_D)(C_M)(C_t)(C_P)$$

$$= 1900(1.25)(1.0)(1.0)(0.425)$$

$$= 1010 \text{ psi} > 234 \quad OK$$

The member is adequate for vertical loads.

Load Case 2: DL + Wind

RLL need not be considered simultaneously with wind. (If snow load occurs in place of roof live load, it must be considered along with one-half the wind load. In addition, one-half the snow load must be considered simultaneously with the full wind load.) The load duration factor for (DL + wind) is taken as 1.6 throughout the check for combined stresses. The designer should verify local building code acceptance of $C_D = 1.6$ before using in practice.

AXIAL (DL):

$$f_c = \frac{P}{A} = \frac{5000}{38.4} = 130 \text{ psi}$$

From load case 1:

$$\left(\frac{l_e}{d}\right)_{max} = \left(\frac{l_e}{d}\right)_x = 25.6$$

$$F_{cE} = \frac{K_{cE}E'}{[(l_e/d)_{max}]^2} = 1084 \text{ psi}$$

$$F^*_c = F_c(C_D)(C_M)(C_t)$$

$$= 1900(1.6)(1.0)(1.0) = 3040 \text{ psi}$$

$$\frac{F_{cE}}{F^*_c} = \frac{1084}{3040} = 0.357$$

$$\frac{1 + F_{cE}/F^*_c}{2c} = \frac{1 + 0.357}{2(0.9)} = 0.754$$

$$C_P = \frac{1 + F_{cE}/F^*_c}{2c} - \sqrt{\left(\frac{1 + F_{cE}/F^*_c}{2c}\right)^2 - \frac{F_{cE}/F^*_c}{c}}$$

$$= 0.754 - \sqrt{(0.754)^2 - 0.357/0.9} = 0.339$$

$$F'_c = F_c(C_D)(C_M)(C_t)(C_P)$$

$$= 1900(1.6)(1.0)(1.0)(0.339)$$

$$= 1031 \text{ psi}$$

$$\text{Axial stress ratio} = \frac{f_c}{F'_c} = \frac{130}{1031} = 0.126$$

BENDING (WIND):

The window headers and sills span horizontally between columns. Uniformly distributed wind forces to a typical header and sill are calculated using a 1-ft section of wall and the tributary heights shown in Fig. 7.21b.

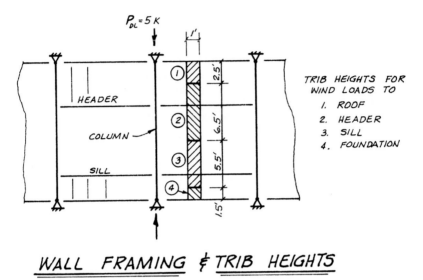

Figure 7.21b Wall framing showing tributary wind pressure heights of 6.5 ft and 5.5 ft to window header and sill, respectively.

Wind on header = w_1 = (20.9 psf)(6.5 ft) = 136 lb/ft

Horizontal reaction of two headers on center column (Fig. 7.21c):

$$P_1 = (136 \text{ lb/ft})(12 \text{ ft}) = 1627 \text{ lb}$$

Wind on sill = w_2 = (20.9 psf)(5.5 ft) = 115 lb/ft

Horizontal reaction of two sills on center column:

$$P_2 = (115 \text{ lb/ft})(12 \text{ ft}) = 1377 \text{ lb}$$

From the moment diagram in Fig. 7.21c,

$$M_x = 6884 \text{ ft-lb} = 82.6 \text{ in.-k}$$

$$f_b = \frac{M}{S} = \frac{82,610}{48} = 1720 \text{ psi}$$

Bending is about the strong axis of the cross section. The allowable bending stress for a glulam is governed by the smaller of two criteria: volume effect or lateral stability (see Example 6.11 in Sec. 6.4, and the bending stress summary inside the front cover of this book). The wind pressure can act either inward or outward, and tension laminations are required on both faces of the glulam.

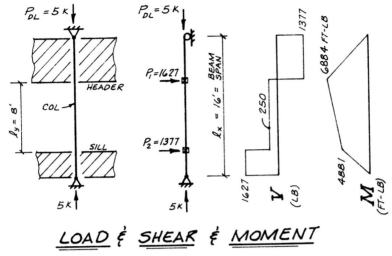

LOAD & SHEAR & MOMENT

Figure 7.21c Load, shear, and moment diagrams for center column subject to lateral wind forces. Concentrated forces are header and sill reactions from window framing.

Allowable stress criteria:

$$F'_b = F_b(C_D)(C_M)(C_t)(C_L)$$

$$F'_b = F_b(C_D)(C_M)(C_t)(C_V)$$

Compare C_L and C_V to determine the critical design criteria.

Beam stability factor C_L

If the beam-column fails in lateral torsional buckling as a beam, the cross section will move in the plane of the wall between the window sill and header. Thus, the unbraced length for beam stability is the height of the window.

$$l_u = 8 \text{ ft} = 96 \text{ in.}$$

The loading condition for this member does not match any of the conditions in NDS Table 3.3.3. However, the effective length given in the footnote to this table may be conservatively used for any loading.

$$\frac{l_u}{d} = \frac{96}{7.5} = 12.8$$

$$7 \le 12.8 \le 14.3$$

$$\therefore \quad l_e = 1.63l_u + 3d$$

$$= 1.63(96) + 3(7.5) = 179 \text{ in.}$$

$$R_B = \sqrt{\frac{l_e d}{b^2}} = \sqrt{\frac{179(7.5)}{(5.125)^2}} = 7.15$$

$$K_{bE} = 0.609 \qquad \text{for glulam}$$

$$F_{bE} = \frac{K_{bE}E'_y}{R_B^2} = \frac{0.609(1,700,000)}{(7.15)^2} = 20{,}260 \text{ psi}$$

$$F_b^* = F_b(C_D)(C_M)(C_t)$$

$$= 2000(1.6)(1.0)(1.0) = 3200 \text{ psi}$$

$$\frac{F_{bE}}{F_b^*} = \frac{20{,}260}{3200} = 6.33$$

$$\frac{1 + F_{bE}/F_b^*}{1.9} = \frac{1 + 6.33}{1.9} = 3.86$$

$$C_L = \frac{1 + F_{bE}/F_b^*}{1.9} - \sqrt{\left(\frac{1 + F_{bE}/F_b^*}{1.9}\right)^2 - \frac{F_{bE}/F_b^*}{0.95}}$$

$$= 3.86 - \sqrt{(3.86)^2 - 6.33/0.95} = 0.991$$

Volume factor C_V

The loading condition of two unequal concentrated loads does not match the load cases in NDS Table 5.3.2. $K_L = 1.0$ appears to be reasonable. For DF glulam, $x = 10$.

$$C_V = K_L\left(\frac{21}{L}\right)^{1/x}\left(\frac{12}{d}\right)^{1/x}\left(\frac{5.125}{b}\right)^{1/x} \leq 1.0$$

$$= 1.0\left(\frac{21}{16}\right)^{0.1}\left(\frac{12}{7.5}\right)^{0.1}\left(\frac{5.125}{5.125}\right)^{0.1}$$

$$= 1.077 > 1.0$$

$$\therefore \quad C_V = 1.0$$

Neither beam stability nor volume effect has a significant impact on this problem. However, the smaller value of C_L and C_V indicates that stability governs over volume effect.

$$C_L = 0.991$$

$$F'_b = F_b(C_D)(C_M)(C_t)(C_L)$$

$$= 2000(1.6)(1.0)(1.0)(0.991)$$

$$= 3170 \text{ psi}$$

$$\text{Bending stress ratio} = \frac{f_b}{F'_b} = \frac{1720}{3170} = 0.542$$

COMBINED STRESSES:

The bending moment is about the strong axis of the cross section, and the amplification for P-Δ is measured by the column slenderness ratio about the x axis. *Note:* It is a coincidence that the allowable column stress F'_c and the amplification factor for the P-Δ

effect are both controlled by $(l_e/d)_x$ in this problem. Recall that F'_c is governed by $(l_e/d)_{max}$, and the P-Δ effect is controlled by the slenderness ratio for the axis about which the bending moment is applied.

$$\left(\frac{l_e}{d}\right)_{\substack{bending \\ moment}} = \left(\frac{l_e}{d}\right)_x = 25.6$$

$$F_{cEx} = \frac{K_{cE}E'}{[(l_e/d)_x]^2} = \frac{0.418(1,700,000)}{(25.6)^2} = 1084 \text{ psi}$$

$$\text{Amplification factor} = \frac{1}{1 - f_c/F_{cEx}} = \frac{1}{1 - 130/1084} = 1.14$$

$$\left(\frac{f_c}{F'_c}\right)^2 + \left(\frac{1}{1 - f_c/F_{cEx}}\right)\frac{f_b}{F'_b} = (0.126)^2 + 1.14(0.542)$$

$$= 0.632 < 1.0 \quad OK$$

> $5\frac{1}{8} \times 7\frac{1}{2}$ axial combination 2 DF glulam with
> tension laminations ($F_{bx} = 2000$ psi) is *OK* for
> combined bending and compression.

7.16 Design for Minimum Eccentricity

The design procedures for a column with an axial load were covered in detail in Secs. 7.4 and 7.5. A large number of interior columns and some exterior columns qualify as axial-load-carrying members. That is, the applied load is *assumed* to pass directly through the centroid of the column cross section, and, in addition, no transverse bending loads are involved.

Although many columns can theoretically be classified as axial load members, there may be some question about whether the load in practical columns is truly an axial load. In actual construction there may be some misalignment or nonuniform bearing in connections that causes the load to be applied eccentrically.

Some eccentric moment probably develops in columns which are thought to support axial loads only. The magnitude of the eccentric moment, however, is unknown. Many designers simply ignore the possible eccentric moment and design for axial stresses only. This practice may be justified because practical columns typically have square-cut ends. In addition, the ends are attached with connection hardware such that the column end conditions do not exactly resemble the end conditions of an "ideal" pinned-end column. With the restraint provided by practical end conditions, the effective column length is somewhat less than the actual unbraced length. Thus the possible effect of an accidental eccentricity may be compensated by normal field end conditions.

However, Ref. 9.2 states that the possible eccentric moment should not be ignored, and it suggests that columns should be designed for some minimum eccentricity. The minimum eccentricity recommended is similar to the minimum eccentricity formerly required in the design of axially loaded reinforced-concrete columns. In this approach, the moment is taken as the compressive load times an eccentricity of 1 in. or one-tenth the width of the column $(0.1d)$, whichever is larger. The moment is considered independently about both principal axes.

In the design of wood columns, there is no Code requirement to design for a minimum eccentric moment. The suggestion that some designers may provide for an eccentric moment in their column calculations is presented here for information only. Including an eccentric moment in the design column is definitely a more conservative design approach. Whether or not eccentricity should be included is left to the judgment of the designer.

7.17 Design Problem: Column with Eccentric Load

Example 7.18 demonstrates the use of the interaction formula for eccentric loads. The load is theoretically an axial load, but the calculations are expanded to include a check for the minimum eccentricity discussed in Sec. 7.16. The same interaction formula would be used in the case of a known eccentricity.

The problem illustrates the significant effect of an eccentricity. Without the eccentricity, the member capacity is simply evaluated by the axial stress ratio of 0.690. However, the combined stress ratio is 0.899 for an eccentricity about the x axis and 0.917 for an eccentricity about the y axis. The combined stress ratios are much closer to the full member capacity, which is associated with a value of 1.0.

This example also demonstrates that F_{by} for a member in the Beams and Stringers size category does not equal F_{bx}. The reduction factor for F_{by} varies with grade. Assistance in obtaining the value of F_{by} *for a B&S* can be obtained from the appropriate lumber rules-writing agency.

EXAMPLE 7.18   Column Design for Minimum Eccentricity

The column in Fig. 7.22a is an interior column in a large auditorium. The design roof DL + SL are theoretically axial loads on the column. Because of the importance of the column, it is desired to provide a conservative design with a minimum eccentricity of $1.0d$ or 1 in. Bracing conditions are shown. Lumber is Select Structural DF-L, and C_M and C_t both equal 1.0.

$$DL = 20 \text{ k}$$

$$\underline{SL = 50 \text{ k}}$$

$$P_{TL} = 70 \text{ k} \qquad \text{(total load governs over DL alone)}$$

A load duration factor of $C_D = 1.15$ applies throughout the problem.

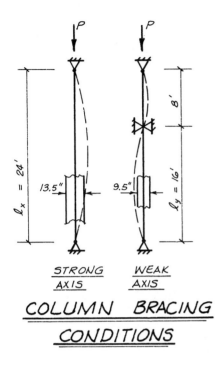

COLUMN BRACING

CONDITIONS

Figure 7.22a Sawn lumber column with different bracing conditions for x and y axes.

Try 10×14 Sel. Str. DF-L.

The trial size is in the B&S size category. Recall that a member in the Beams and Stringers size category has cross-sectional dimensions of 5 in. or greater and a width that exceeds the thickness by more than 2 in. Design values are obtained from NDS Supplement Table 4D:

DF-L in this size category may be graded under two different sets of lumber grading rules. If any tabulated stresses conflict, use the smaller value (conservative):

$$F_c = 1100 \text{ psi}$$

$$F_{bx} = 1600 \text{ psi*}$$

$$E_x = 1,600,000 \text{ psi}$$

---

*Tabulated values of allowable bending stress for members in the B&S size category are for bending about the x axis. The flat-use factor C_{fu} is the adjustment factor that converts the allowable bending stress to the y axis (that is, $F_{by} = F_{bx} \times C_{fu}$). However, values of C_{fu} are not currently published for the sizes covered in NDS Supplement Table 4D (Timbers). The value of $C_{fu} = 0.88$ for use in this example applies to Select Structural. It is recommended that the designer contact the appropriate lumber rules-writing agency to obtain values about the y axis for Beams and Stringers.

Section properties:

$$b = 9.5 \text{ in.}$$

$$d = 13.5 \text{ in.}$$

$$A = 128.25 \text{ in.}^2$$

$$S_x = 288.6 \text{ in.}^3$$

$$S_y = 203.1 \text{ in.}^3$$

Axial

$$f_c = \frac{P}{A} = \frac{70,000}{128.25} = 546 \text{ psi}$$

$$\left(\frac{l_e}{d}\right)_x = \frac{24 \text{ ft} \times 12 \text{ in./ft}}{13.5 \text{ in.}} = 21.3$$

$$\left(\frac{l_e}{d}\right)_y = \frac{16 \text{ ft} \times 12 \text{ in./ft}}{9.5 \text{ in.}} = 20.2$$

$E_x = E_y$, and the larger slenderness ratio governs the allowable column stress. Therefore, the strong axis is critical.

$$E' = E(C_M)(C_t) = 1,600,000(1.0)(1.0)$$

$$= 1,600,000 \text{ psi}$$

For visually graded sawn lumber:

$$K_{cE} = 0.3$$

$$c = 0.8$$

Determine allowable column stress:

$$F_{cE} = \frac{K_{cE}E'}{[(l_e/d)_{\max}]^2} = \frac{0.3(1,600,000)}{(21.3)^2} = 1055 \text{ psi}$$

The size factor for compression parallel to grain applies only to Dimension lumber, and C_F defaults to unity for a B&S.

$$F_c^* = F_c(C_D)(C_M)(C_t)(C_F)$$

$$= 1100(1.15)(1.0)(1.0)(1.0) = 1265 \text{ psi}$$

$$\frac{F_{cE}}{F_c^*} = \frac{1055}{1265} = 0.834$$

$$\frac{1 + F_{cE}/F_c^*}{2c} = \frac{1 + 0.834}{2(0.8)} = 1.146$$

$$C_P = \frac{1 + F_{cE}/F_c^*}{2c} - \sqrt{\left(\frac{1 + F_{cE}/F_c^*}{2c}\right)^2 - \frac{F_{cE}/F_c^*}{c}}$$

$$= 1.146 - \sqrt{(1.146)^2 - 0.834/0.8} = 0.625$$

$$F_c' = F_c(C_D)(C_M)(C_t)(C_P)$$

$$= 1100(1.15)(1.0)(1.0)(0.625)$$

$$F_c' = 791 \text{ psi} > 546 \qquad OK$$

Alternatively, the axial stress ratio is shown to be less than 1.0:

$$\frac{f_c}{F_c'} = \frac{546}{791} = 0.690 < 1.0$$

The member is adequate for the axial load.

Eccentric Load about Strong Axis

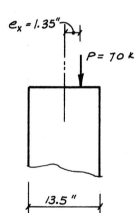

$e_x = 1.35''$

$P = 70\,k$

$13.5''$

Figure 7.22b Column load applied with eccentricity about x axis.

AXIAL

The axial stress check is unchanged for this load case.

BENDING:

There are no transverse loads, and the only bending stress is due to the eccentric column force.

$$e_x = 0.1d = 0.1(13.5) = 1.35 \text{ in.} > 1.0$$

$$\text{Ecc. } f_{bx} = \frac{Pe_x}{S_x} = f_c\left(\frac{6e_x}{d_x}\right) = 546\left(\frac{6 \times 1.35}{13.5}\right) = 327 \text{ psi}$$

Size factor

$$C_F = \left(\frac{12}{d}\right)^{1/9} = \left(\frac{12}{13.5}\right)^{1/9} = 0.987$$

Lateral stability

The eccentric moment is about the strong axis of the cross section. Lateral torsional buckling may occur in a plane perpendicular to the plane of bending. Therefore, the unbraced length for lateral stability is 16 ft. Determine l_e in accordance with footnote 1 to NDS Table 3.3.3.

$$l_u = 16 \text{ ft} = 192 \text{ in.}$$

$$\frac{l_u}{d} = \frac{192}{13.5} = 14.2$$

$$7.0 \le 14.2 \le 14.3$$

$$\therefore \quad l_e = 1.63 l_u + 3d$$

$$= 1.63(192) + 3(13.5) = 353 \text{ in.}$$

$$R_B = \sqrt{\frac{l_e d}{b^2}} = \sqrt{\frac{353(13.5)}{(9.5)^2}} = 7.27$$

$$K_{bE} = 0.438 \qquad \text{for visually graded sawn lumber}$$

$$F_{bE} = \frac{K_{bE} E_y'}{R_B^2} = \frac{0.438(1,600,000)}{(7.27)^2} = 13,255 \text{ psi}$$

$$F_b^* = F_b(C_D)(C_M)(C_t)(C_F)$$

$$= 1600(1.15)(1.0)(1.0)(0.987) = 1816 \text{ psi}$$

$$\frac{F_{bE}}{F_b^*} = \frac{13,255}{1816} = 7.299$$

$$\frac{1 + F_{bE}/F_b^*}{1.9} = \frac{1 + 7.299}{1.9} = 4.368$$

$$C_L = \frac{1 + F_{bE}/F_b^*}{1.9} - \sqrt{\left(\frac{1 + F_{bE}/F_b^*}{1.9}\right)^2 - \frac{F_{bE}/F_b^*}{0.95}}$$

$$= 4.368 - \sqrt{(4.368)^2 - 7.299/0.95} = 0.992$$

$$F_{bx}' = F_b(C_D)(C_M)(C_t)(C_L)(C_F)(C_r)$$

$$= 1600(1.15)(1.0)(1.0)(0.992)(0.987)(1.0)$$

$$= 1802 \text{ psi} > 327 \qquad OK$$

COMBINED STRESSES:

There are two amplification factors for combined stresses when all or part of the bending stress is due to an eccentric load.

Amplification factor for eccentric bending stress

The current check on eccentric bending moment is about the x axis, and the amplification factor is a function of the slenderness ratio for the x axis.

$$\left(\frac{l_e}{d}\right)_x = 21.3$$

The Euler elastic buckling stress was evaluated previously using this slenderness ratio in the axial stress portion of the problem.

$$F_{cEx} = F_{cE} = 1055 \text{ psi}$$

$$\frac{f_c}{F_{cEx}} = \frac{546}{1055} = 0.518$$

$$(\text{Amp Fac})_{ecc} = 1 + 0.234\left(\frac{f_c}{F_{cEx}}\right) = 1 + 0.234(0.518) = 1.121$$

General P-Δ amplification factor

$$\text{Amp Fac} = \frac{1}{1 - f_c/F_{cEx}} = \frac{1}{1 - 546/1055} = 2.073$$

$$\left(\frac{f_c}{F'_c}\right)^2 + \left(\frac{1}{1 - f_c/F_{cEx}}\right)\frac{f_b + f_c(6e_x/d_x)[1 + 0.234(f_c/F_{cEx})]}{F'_{bx}}$$

$$= (0.690)^2 + (2.073)\left[\frac{0 + 327(1.121)}{1802}\right]$$

$$= 0.899 < 1.0$$

Eccentric load is OK for bending about x axis.

Eccentric Load about Weak Axis

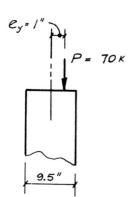

$e_y = 1''$

$P = 70\text{k}$

$9.5''$

Figure 7.22c Column load applied with eccentricity about y axis.

AXIAL:

The axial stress check remains the same.

BENDING:

The only bending stress is due to the eccentric column force.

$$e_y = 0.1d = 0.1(9.5) = 0.95 \text{ in.} < 1.0$$

$$\therefore e_y = 1.0 \text{ in.}$$

$$\text{Ecc. } f_{by} = \frac{Pe_y}{S_y} = f_c\left(\frac{6e_y}{d_y}\right) = 546\left(\frac{6 \times 1.0}{9.5}\right) = 345 \text{ psi}$$

Determine the allowable bending stress for the y axis. Even with an unbraced length of 24 ft, there is little or no tendency for lateral buckling when the moment is about the y axis. The depth for bending about the y axis is 9.5 in.

$$d = 9.5 < 12$$

$$\therefore C_F = 1.0$$

$$F'_{by} = F_b(C_D)(C_M)(C_t)(C_F)(C_{fu})\dagger$$

$$= 1600(1.15)(1.0)(1.0)(1.0)(0.88)$$

$$= 1619 \text{ psi} > 345 \quad OK$$

COMBINED STRESSES:

Amplification factor for eccentric bending stress

The eccentric bending moment being considered is about the y axis, and the amplification factor is a function of the slenderness ratio for the y axis.

$$\left(\frac{l_e}{d}\right)_y = 20.2$$

$$F_{cEy} = \frac{K_{cE}E'}{[(l_e/d)_y]^2} = \frac{0.3(1,600,000)}{(20.2)^2} = 1175 \text{ psi}$$

$$\left(\frac{f_c}{F'_c}\right)^2 + \frac{f_{by} + f_c(6e_y/d_y)[1 + 0.234(f_c/F_{cEy})]}{F'_{by}[1 - f_c/F_{cEy} - (f_{bx}/F_{bEx})^2]}$$

$$= (0.690)^2 + \frac{0 + 546[6(1.0)/9.5][1 + 0.234(546/1175)]}{1619[1 - 546/1175 - (0/13,255)^2]}$$

$$= 0.917 < 1.0$$

---

†It is recommended that the designer contact the appropriate lumber rules-writing agency to obtain values of F_b about the y axis for Beams and Stringers.

Eccentric load is OK for bending about y axis.

> *Use* 10 × 14   Select Structural DF-L column.

7.18 Problems

Allowable stresses and section properties for the following problems are to be in accordance with the 1991 NDS. Dry service conditions, normal temperatures, and bending about the strong axis apply unless otherwise indicated.

The loads given in a problem are to be applied directly. In practice, the use of the *load combination factor* (Sec. 2.8) may be permitted. Check local code acceptance before using the load combination factor together with the load duration factor C_D. The load duration factor of 1.6 for problems involving wind or seismic is based on 1991 NDS recommendations. Check local code acceptance before using.

Some problems require the use of a microcomputer spreadsheet. Problems that are solved on a spreadsheet can be saved and used as a template for other similar problems. Templates can have many degrees of sophistication. Initially, a template may only be a hand (i.e., calculator) solution worked on a spreadsheet. In a simple template of this nature, the user will be required to provide many of the lookup functions for such items as

Tabulated stresses

Lumber dimensions

Duration factor

Wet service factor

Size factor

Volume factor

As the user gains experience with spreadsheets, the template can be expanded to perform lookup and decision-making functions that were previously done manually.

Advanced computer programming skills are not required to create effective spreadsheet templates. Valuable templates can be created by designers who normally do only hand solutions. However, some programming techniques are helpful in automating *lookup* and *decision-making* steps.

The first requirement for a spreadsheet template is that it operate correctly (i.e., calculate correct values). Another major requirement is that the input and output be structured in an orderly manner. A sufficient number of intermediate answers should be displayed and labeled so that the solution can be verified by hand.

7.1   A 3 × 8 member in a horizontal diaphragm resists a tension force of 20 k caused by the lateral wind pressure. Lumber is Select Structural DF-L. A single line of ⅞-in.-diameter bolts is used to make the connection of the member to the diaphragm. C_M = 1.0, and C_t = 1.0.

Find: The allowable axial tension load.

7.2   A 5⅛ × 15 DF axial combination 5 glulam is used as the tension member in a large roof truss. A single row of 1-in.-diameter bolts occurs at the net section of the member. Loads are a combination of (DL + SL). Joints are assumed to be pin-connected. MC = 10 percent. C_t = 1.0.

Find: a. The allowable axial tension load.
b. Repeat part *a* except that the MC = 15 percent.
c. Repeat part *a* except that the MC = 18 percent.
d. Repeat part *a* except that the member is a bending combination 24 F-V3 glulam.

7.3   The truss in Fig. 7.A has a 2 × 4 lower chord of Sel. Str. Spruce-Pine-Fir (South). The loads shown are the result of (DL + SL). There is no reduction of area for fasteners. C_M = 1.0, and C_t = 1.0. Joints are assumed to be pin-connected.*

Find: Check the tension stress in the member.

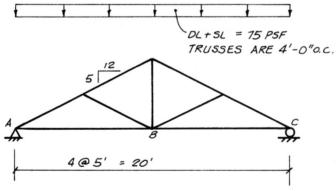

Figure 7.A

7.4   Use the hand solution to Prob. 7.1 as a guide to develop a microcomputer spreadsheet template to solve similar problems.
a. Consider only the specific criteria given in Prob. 7.1.
b. Expand the template to handle any sawn lumber size. The spreadsheet is to include a list (i.e., database) of tabulated stresses for all size categories (Dimension lumber, B&S, P&T) of Sel. Str. DF-L.
c. Expand the database in part *b* to include all stress grades of DF-L from No. 2 through Sel. Str.

---

*For trusses with joints which are not pinned (such as toothed metal gusset plates and others), the continuity of the joints must be taken into consideration. For the design of metal-plate-connected trusses, see Ref. 23.1.

7.5 The truss in Fig. 7.A has a 2 × 6 lower chord of No. 1 DF-L. In addition to the loads shown on the sketch, the lower chord supports a ceiling load of 5 psf (20 lb/ft). There is no reduction of member area for fasteners. Joints are assumed to be pin-connected. $C_M = 1.0$, and $C_t = 1.0$.

Find: Check combined stresses in the lower chord.

7.6 The truss in Fig. 7.B supports the roof DL of 16 psf shown in the sketch. Trusses are spaced 24 in o.c., and the RLL is to be in accordance with UBC Table 23.C, Method 1. Lumber is No. 2 DF-L. Fasteners do not reduce the area of the members. Truss joints are assumed to be pin-connected. $C_M = 1.0$, and $C_t = 1.0$.

Find: The required member size for the tension (bottom) chord.

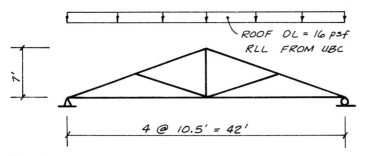

ROOF DL = 16 psf
RLL FROM UBC

7'

4 @ 10.5' = 42'

Figure 7.B

7.7 Repeat Prob. 7.6 except that in addition there is a ceiling load applied to the bottom chord of 8 psf (16 lb/ft). Neglect deflection.

7.8 The door header in Fig. 7.C supports the loads shown. Lumber is No. 2 Hem-Fir. $C_M = 1.0$, and $C_t = 1.0$. There are no bolt holes at the point of maximum moment. Lateral stability is not a problem.

Find: a. Check the given member size under the following loading conditions:
Vertical loads only
UBC-required combinations of vertical loads and lateral forces
b. Which loading condition is the more severe?

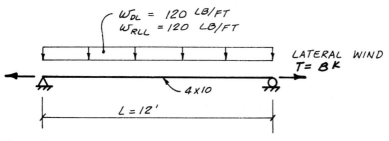

W_{DL} = 120 LB/FT
W_{RLL} = 120 LB/FT

LATERAL WIND
T = 8 K

4 × 10

L = 12'

Figure 7.C

7.9   Repeat Prob. 7.8 except the unbraced length is one-half of the span length (that is, $l_u = 0.5L$).

7.10 Use the hand solution to Prob. 7.9 as a guide to develop a microcomputer spreadsheet template to solve similar problems.
   a. Consider only the specific criteria given in Prob. 7.9.
   b. Expand the template to handle any span length and any unbraced length. The user should be able to choose any trial size of Dimension lumber and any grade of Hem-Fir from No. 2 through Sel. Str.

7.11 A 4 × 4 carries an axial compressive force caused by (DL + FLL + RLL). Lumber is No. 1 DF-L. $C_M = 1.0$, and $C_t = 1.0$.

   Find: The allowable column load if the unbraced length of the member is
   a. 3 ft
   b. 6 ft
   c. 9 ft
   d. 12 ft

7.12 Repeat Prob. 7.11 except that the member is a 4 × 6.

7.13 A 6 × 8 carries an axial compressive force caused by (DL + SL). Lumber is No. 1 DF-L. $C_M = 1.0$, and $C_t = 1.0$.

   Find: The allowable column load if the unbraced length of the member is
   a. 5 ft
   b. 9 ft
   c. 11 ft
   d. 15 ft
   e. 19 ft

7.14 Use the hand solution to Probs. 7.11 through 7.13 as a guide to develop a microcomputer spreadsheet template to solve similar problems.
   a. The user should be able to specify any sawn lumber member size, column length, and tabulated values of F_c and E. Initially limit the template to No. 1 DF-L, and assume that the user will look up and provide the appropriate size factor (if required) for compression.
   b. Expand the template to access a database of tabulated stresses for any size and grade of DF-L sawn lumber from No. 2 through Sel. Str. Include provision for the database to furnish the appropriate size factor.

7.15 *Given:*   The glulam column in Fig. 7.D with the following information:

$$P = 150 \text{ k} \qquad L_2 = 10 \text{ ft}$$

$$L_1 = 22 \text{ ft} \qquad L_3 = 12 \text{ ft}$$

   The load is an axial force caused by a combination of (DL + FLL + RLL). The member is axial combination 2 DF glulam without special tension laminations. The column effective length factor is $K_e = 1.0$. $C_M = 1.0$, and $C_t = 1.0$.

   Find: Is the column adequate to support the design load?

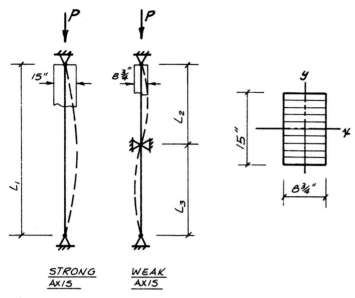

Figure 7.D

7.16   *Given:*   The glulam column in Fig. 7.D with the following information:

$$P = 150 \text{ k} \qquad L_2 = 10 \text{ ft}$$

$$L_1 = 24 \text{ ft} \qquad L_3 = 14 \text{ ft}$$

The load is an axial force caused by a combination of (DL + FLL + RLL). The member is axial combination 2 DF glulam without special tension laminations. The column effective length factor is $K_e = 1.0$. $C_M = 1.0$, and $C_t = 1.0$.

Find: Is the column adequate to support the design load?

7.17   Use the hand solution to Prob. 7.15 or 7.16 as a guide to develop a microcomputer spreadsheet template to solve similar problems.

    a. Initially the template may be limited to axial combination 2 DF-L, and assume that the user will look up and provide the tabulated properties for the material. The template should handle different loads and unbraced lengths for the x and y axes.

    b. Expand the template to access a database of tabulated stresses for any DF-L glulam combination. Consider either *axial* combinations or *bending* combinations as assigned.

7.18   A sawn lumber column is used to support an axial load (DL + SL) of 75 k. Use No. 1 DF-L. The unbraced length is the same for both the x and y axes of the member. The effective length factor is $K_e = 1.0$ for both axes. $C_M = 1.0$, and $C_t = 1.0$.

Find: The minimum column size if the unbraced length is
a. 8 ft
b. 10 ft
c. 14 ft
d. 18 ft
e. 22 ft
A spreadsheet template may be used provided sufficient output is
displayed to allow hand checking.

7.19   *Given:*   The glulam column in Fig. 7.D with the following information:

$$P = 75 \text{ k} \qquad L_2 = 10 \text{ ft}$$

$$L_1 = 26 \text{ ft} \qquad L_3 = 16 \text{ ft}$$

The load is a combination of (DL + FLL + RLL), and the minimum
eccentricity described in Sec. 7.16 is to be considered. The member
is a bending combination 24F-V3 DF glulam. The column effective
length factor is $K_e = 1.0$. $C_M = 1.0$, and $C_t = 1.0$.

Find: Is the column adequate to support the design load?

7.20   An 8×12 column of No. 1 S-P-F(S) has an unbraced length for buckling
about the strong (x) axis of 16 ft and an unbraced length for buckling about
the weak (y) axis of 8 ft. $C_M = 1.0$, and $C_t = 1.0$.

Find: The allowable axial (DL + FLL).

7.21   A stud wall is to be used as a bearing wall in a wood-frame building. The
wall carries an axial load of (DL + RLL). Studs are 2×4 Construction-
grade Hem-Fir and are located 16 in. o.c. Studs have sheathing attached.
$C_M = 1.0$, and $C_t = 1.0$.

Find: The allowable load per lineal foot of wall if the wall height is
a. 8 ft
b. 9 ft
c. 10 ft

7.22   A stud wall is to be used as a bearing wall in a wood-frame building. The
wall carries an axial load of (DL + SL). Studs are 2×6 No. 2 Southern
Pine and are 24 in. o.c. Studs have sheathing attached. $C_M = 1.0$, and $C_t = 1.0$.

Find: The allowable load per lineal foot of wall if the wall height is
a. 10 ft
b. 14 ft

7.23   *Given:*   The exterior column in Fig. 7.E is a 6×10 Sel. Str. DF-L. It supports
a vertical load due to a girder reaction and a lateral wind force from
the horizontal wall framing. The lateral force causes bending about
the strong axis of the member, and wall framing provides continuous

lateral support about the weak axis. The following values are to be used:

$$P_{DL} = 5 \text{ k} \qquad L = 16 \text{ ft}$$

$$P_{SL} = 15 \text{ k} \qquad C_M = 1.0$$

$$w_{wind} = 200 \text{ lb/ft} \qquad C_t = 1.0$$

Find: Check the column for combined stresses.

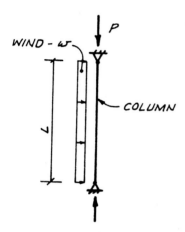

WIND - ఐ

P

COLUMN

Figure 7.E

7.24 Repeat Prob. 7.23 except that the following values are to be used:

$$P_{DL} = 5 \text{ k} \qquad L = 21 \text{ ft}$$

$$P_{SL} = 15 \text{ k} \qquad C_M = 1.0$$

$$w_{wind} = 100 \text{ lb/ft} \qquad C_t = 1.0$$

7.25 The truss in Fig. 7.A has a 2 × 10 top chord of No. 2 Hem-Fir. The top of the truss is fully supported along its length by roof sheathing. There is no reduction of area for fasteners. $C_M = 1.0$, and $C_t = 1.0$. Joints are assumed to be pin-connected.

Find: Check combined stresses in the top chord. A spreadsheet template may be used provided sufficient output is displayed to allow hand checking.

7.26 A truss is similar to the one shown in Fig. 7.A except the span is 36 ft and the load is 30 psf. The top chord is a 2 × 10 of No. 2 Hem-Fir, and it is laterally supported along its length by roof sheathing. There is no reduction of member area for fasteners. $C_M = 1.0$, and $C_t = 1.0$. Joints are assumed to be pin-connected.

Find: Check combined stresses in the top chord. A spreadsheet template may be used provided sufficient output is displayed to allow hand checking.

7.27   A 2 × 6 exterior stud wall is 14 ft tall. Studs are 16 in. o.c. The studs support the following vertical loads per foot of wall:

$$w_{DL} = 800 \text{ lb/ft}$$

$$w_{FLL} = 800 \text{ lb/ft}$$

$$w_{RLL} = 400 \text{ lb/ft}$$

In addition, the wall carries a uniform wind force of 15 psf (horizontal). Lumber is No. 1 DF-L. $C_M = 1.0$, and $C_t = 1.0$. Sheathing provides lateral support in the weak direction.

Find: Check the studs, using the UBC-required load combinations. Neglect uplift.

Plywood and Other Structural-Use Panels

8.1 Introduction

Plywood is a widely used building material with a variety of structural and nonstructural applications. Some of the major structural uses are

1. Roof, floor, and wall sheathing
2. Horizontal and vertical (shearwall) diaphragms
3. Structural components
   a. Lumber-and-plywood beams
   b. Stressed-skin panels
   c. Curved panels
   d. Folded plates
   e. Sandwich panels
4. Gusset plates
   a. Trusses
   b. Rigid frame connections
5. Wood foundation systems
6. Concrete formwork

Numerous other uses of plywood can be cited, including a large number of industrial, commercial, and architectural applications.

As far as the types of buildings covered in this text are concerned, the first two items in the above list are of primary interest. The relatively high allowable loads and the ease with which sheets of plywood can be installed have made plywood widely accepted for use in these applications. The other topics listed above are beyond the scope of this text. Information on these and other subjects is available from the American Plywood Association (APA).

This chapter will essentially serve as a turning point from the design of the vertical-load-carrying system (beams and columns) to the design of the lateral-force-resisting system (horizontal diaphragms and shearwalls). Plywood provides this transition because it is often used as a structural element in *both* systems.

In the vertical system, plywood functions as the *sheathing* material. As such, it directly supports the roof and floor loads and distributes these loads to the framing system. See Example 8.1. Wall sheathing, in a similar manner, distributes the normal wind force to the studs in the wall. In the lateral-force-resisting system (LFRS), plywood serves as the *shear*-resisting element.

EXAMPLE 8.1   Plywood Sheathing

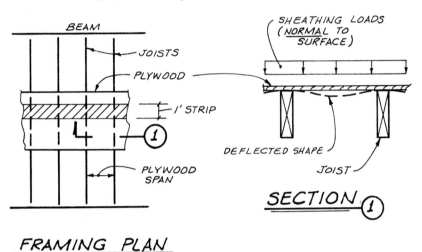

FRAMING PLAN

Figure 8.1   Plywood spanning between framing.

The term *sheathing load,* as used in this book, refers to loads that are normal to the surface of the sheathing. See Fig. 8.1. Sheathing loads for floors and roofs include DL and LL (or snow). For walls, the wind force is the sheathing load. Typical plywood sheathing applications use the plywood continuous over two or more spans. For common joist spacings and typical loads, *design aids* have been developed so that the required plywood sheathing can be chosen without having to perform beam design calculations. A number of these design aids are included in this chapter. When required, cross-sectional properties for a 1-ft-wide section of plywood can be obtained from Ref. 14.1

The required *thickness* of the plywood is often determined by *sheathing-type loads* (loads normal to the surface of the plywood). On the other hand, the *nailing* requirements for the plywood are determined by the *unit shears* in the horizontal or vertical diaphragm. When the shears are high, the required thickness of plywood may be governed by the diaphragm unit shears instead of by the sheathing loads.

It should be noted that the required thickness of plywood for roof, floor, and wall sheathing may usually be determined from *design aids* provided in Code tables or APA literature. It is important to realize that the bases for the design aids are beam calculations or concentrated load considerations, whichever are more critical. The need may arise for beam calculations if the design aids are found not to cover a particular situation. However, structural calculations for plywood are usually necessary only for the design of a structural-type component (e.g., a lumber-and-plywood beam or stressed-skin panel).

This chapter introduces plywood properties and grades and reviews the procedures used to determine the required thickness and grade of plywood for *sheathing applications.* Some of the design aids for determining sheathing requirements are included, but the calculation of stresses in plywood is beyond the scope of this text. However, the basic structural behavior of plywood is explained, and some of the unique design aspects of plywood are introduced. Understanding these basic principles is necessary for the proper use of plywood.

In addition to plywood, a number of other panel products have been developed for use in sheathing and diaphragm applications. These newer products include *composite panels, waferboard, oriented strand board,* and *structural particleboard.* Panel products other than plywood usually involve some form of reconstituted wood product. As research continues, other structural applications for these products will be developed.

Structural-use panels is the term that is commonly used to refer collectively to these new products as well as plywood. At this time traditional plywood constitutes the majority of total structural-use panel production, but the newer panel products continue to increase market share. However, plywood is still the standard by which the other panel products are judged.

Because of its wider use in structural applications, plywood and its use as a sheathing material are covered first (Secs. 8.3 to 8.7), and the new-generation panels are introduced in Sec. 8.8. Chapter 9 continues with an introduction to *diaphragm design,* and Chap. 10 covers *shearwalls.* There the calculations necessary for the design of the LFRS are treated in considerable detail.

8.2 Panel Dimensions and Installation Recommendations

The standard size of a structural-use panel is 4 ft × 8 ft. Certain manufacturers are capable of producing larger sizes, but the standard 4 ft × 8 ft dimensions should be assumed in design unless the availability of other sizes is known.

Plywood and the other products are dimensionally quite stable. However, some change in dimensions can be expected under varying moisture conditions, especially during the early stages of construction when the material is adjusting to local atmospheric conditions. For this reason, installation instructions for many roof, floor, and wall sheathing applications recommend a clearance between panel edges and panel ends. See Example 8.2.

EXAMPLE 8.2   Panel Installation Clearances

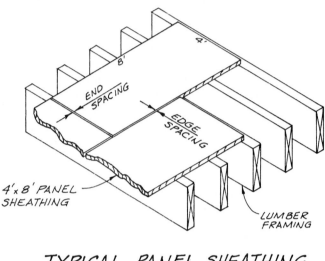

Figure 8.2   Clearance between panels.

Many panel sheathing applications for roofs, floors, and walls recommend an *edge* and *end spacing* of ⅛ in. to permit panel movement with changes in moisture content. Other spacing provisions may apply, depending on the type of panel, application, and moisture content conditions. Refer to the APA's publication *Design/Construction Guide—Residential and Commercial* (Ref. 14.4) for specific recommendations.

The tolerances for panel length and width depend on the panel type. Typical tolerances are $+0$, $-\frac{1}{16}$ in., and $+0$, $-\frac{1}{8}$ in. Some panel grade stamps include the term *sized for spacing,* and in this case the larger tolerance ($+0$, $-\frac{1}{8}$ in.) applies.

The installation clearance recommendations explain the negative tolerance on panel dimensions. By having the panel dimension slightly less than the stated size, the clearances between panels can be provided while maintaining the basic 4-ft module that the use of a structural-use panel naturally implies.

Another installation recommendation is aimed at avoiding *nail popping.* This is a problem that principally affects floors, and it occurs when the sheathing is nailed into green supporting beams. As the lumber supports dry, the members shrink and the nails appear to "pop" upward through the sheathing. This can cause problems with finish flooring (especially linoleum and similar products). Squeaks in floors may also develop.

Popping can be minimized by proper nailing procedures. Nails should be driven flush with the surface of the sheathing if the supporting beams are dry. If the supports are green, the nails should be "set" below the surface of the sheathing and the nail holes should not be filled. Squeaks can also be reduced by field-gluing the panels to the supporting beams. For additional information, contact the APA.

Structural-use panels are available in a number of standard thicknesses ranging from ¼ to 1⅛ in. The tolerances for thickness vary depending on the thickness and surface condition of the panel. Panels with veneer faces may have several different surface conditions including unsanded, touch-sanded, sanded, overlaid, and others. See the appropriate specification for thickness tolerances.

8.3 Plywood Makeup

A plywood panel is made up of a number of veneers (thin sheets or pieces of wood). Veneer is obtained by rotating *peeler logs* (approximately 8½ ft long) in a lathe. A continuous veneer is obtained as the log is forced into a long knife. The log is simply unwound or "peeled." See Example 8.3. The veneer is then clipped to the proper size, dried to a low moisture content (2 to 5 percent), and graded according to quality.

EXAMPLE 8.3 Fabrication of Veneer

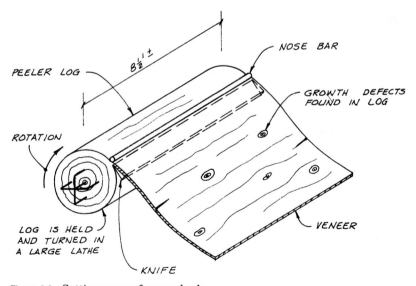

Figure 8.3 Cutting veneer from peeler log.

The log is rotary-cut or peeled into a continuous sheet of *veneer*. Thicknesses range between ⅟₁₆ and ⁵⁄₁₆ in. As with sawn lumber, the veneer is graded visually by observing the size and number of defects. Most veneers may be repaired or patched to improve their grade. Veneer grades are discussed in Sec. 8.5.

The veneer is spread with glue and cross-laminated (adjacent layers have the wood grain at right angles) into a plywood panel with an *odd* number of *layers*. See Example 8.4. The panel is then cured under pressure in a large hydraulic press. The glue bond obtained in this process is stronger than the wood in the plies. After curing, the panels are trimmed and finished (e.g., sanded) if necessary. Finally the appropriate grade-trademark is stamped on the panel.

It is the cross-laminating that provides plywood with its unique strength characteristics. It provides increased dimensional stability over wood that

---

EXAMPLE 8.4   Plywood Cross-Laminated Construction

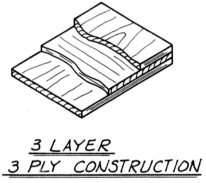

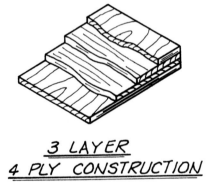

3 LAYER
3 PLY CONSTRUCTION

Figure 8.4a

3 LAYER
4 PLY CONSTRUCTION

Figure 8.4b

In its simplest form, plywood consists of 3 plies. Each ply has wood grain at right angles to the adjacent veneer (Fig. 8.4a).

An extension of the simple 3-ply construction is the 3-layer 4-ply construction (Fig. 8.4b). The two center plies have the grain running in the same direction. However, the basic concept of cross-laminating is still present because the two center plies are viewed as a single layer. It is the *layers* which are *cross-laminated*.

Three-layer construction is used in the thinner plywood panels. Depending on the thickness and grade of the plywood, 5- and 7-layer constructions are also fabricated. Detailed information on plywood panel makeup is contained in Ref. 14.8.

---

is not cross-laminated. Cracking and splitting are reduced, and fasteners, such as nails and staples, can be placed close to the edge without a reduction in load capacity.

In summary, *veneer* is the thin sheet of wood obtained from the peeler log. When *veneer* is used in the construction of plywood, it becomes a *ply*. The cross-laminated pieces of wood in a plywood panel are known as *layers*. A layer is often simply an individual ply, but it can consist of more than one ply.

The direction of the grain in a finished panel must be clearly understood. See Example 8.5. The names assigned to the various layers in the makeup of a plywood panel are

1. *Face*—outside ply. If the outside plies are of different veneer quality, the face is the better veneer grade.

2. *Back*—the other outside ply.

3. *Crossband*—inner layer(s) placed at right angles to the face and back plies.

4. *Center*—inner layer(s) parallel with outer plies.

EXAMPLE 8.5   Direction of Grain

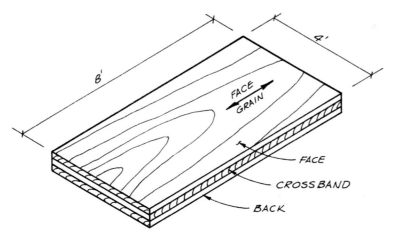

Figure 8.5 Standard plywood layup.

In standard plywood construction, the face and back plies have the grain running parallel to the 8-ft dimension of the panel. Crossbands are inner plies that have the grain at right angles to the face and back (i.e., parallel to the 4-ft dimension). If a panel has more than three layers, some inner plies (centers) will have grain that is parallel to the face and back.

When the stress in plywood is parallel to the 8-ft dimension, there are more "effective" plies (i.e., there are more plies with grain parallel to the stress *and* they are placed farther from the neutral axis of the panel). The designer should be aware that different section properties are involved, depending on how the panel is turned. This is important even if stress calculations are not performed.

If structural calculations are required, the cross-laminations in plywood make stress analysis somewhat more involved. Wood is stronger parallel to the grain than perpendicular to the grain. This is especially true in tension, where wood has little strength across the grain; it is also true in compression but to a lesser extent. In addition, wood is much stiffer parallel to the grain than perpendicular to the grain. The modulus of elasticity across the grain is approximately $\frac{1}{35}$ of the modulus of elasticity parallel to the grain.

Because of the differences in strength and stiffness, the *plies that have the grain parallel to the stress are much more effective* than those that have the grain perpendicular to the stress. In addition, the odd number of layers used in plywood construction causes further differences in strength properties for one direction (say, parallel to the 8-ft dimension) compared with the section properties for the other direction (parallel to the 4-ft dimension). Thus, two sets of cross-sectional properties apply to plywood. One set is used for stresses parallel to the 8-ft dimension, and the other is used for stresses parallel to the 4-ft dimension.

Even if the sheathing thickness and allowable load are read from a table (structural calculations not required), the orientation of the panel and its directional properties are important to the proper use of the plywood. To illustrate the effects of panel orientation, two different panel layouts are considered. See Fig. 8.6. With each panel layout, the corresponding 1-ft-wide beam cross section is shown. The bending stresses in these beams are parallel to the span. For simplicity, the plywood in this example is 3-layer construction.

In the first example, the 8-ft dimension of the plywood panel is parallel to the span (sheathing spans between joists). When the plywood is turned this way (face grain perpendicular to the supports), it is said to be used in the *strong direction*. In the second example, the 4-ft dimension is parallel to the span of the plywood (face grain parallel to the supports). Here the panel is used in the *weak direction*.

From these sketches it can be seen that the cross section for the strong direction has more plies with the grain running parallel to the span. In addition, these plies are located a larger distance from the neutral axis. These two facts explain why the effective cross-sectional properties are larger for plywood oriented with the long dimension of the panel perpendicular to the supports.

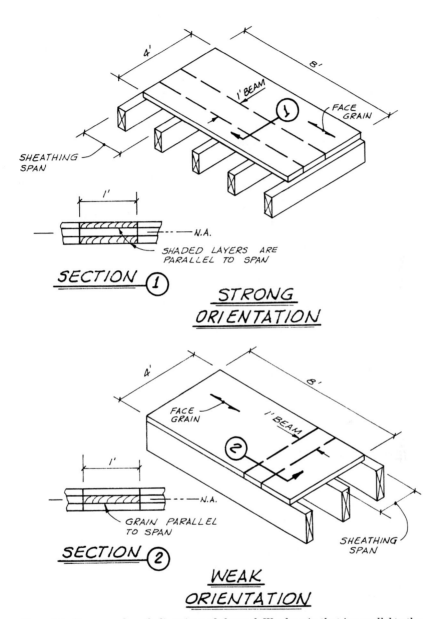

Figure 8.6 Strong and weak directions of plywood. Wood grain that is *parallel* to the span and stress is *more effective* than wood grain that is perpendicular.

8.4   Species Groups for Plywood

A large number of species of wood can be used to manufacture plywood. See Fig. 8.7. The various species are assigned, according to strength and stiffness, to one of five different groups. Group 1 species have the highest-strength characteristics, and Group 5 species have the lowest-strength properties. Allowable stresses have been determined for species groups 1 to 4, and plywood made up of these species can be used in structural applications. Group 5 has not been assigned allowable stresses.

Group 1	Group 2	Group 3	Group 4	Group 5
Apitong	Cedar, Port	Alder, Red	Aspen	Basswood
Beech,	Orford	Birch, Paper	Bigtooth	Poplar,
American	Cypress	Cedar, Alaska	Quaking	Balsam
Birch	Douglas	Fir,	Cativo	
Sweet	Fir 2 (a)	Subalpine	Cedar	
Yellow	Fir	Hemlock,	Incense	
Douglas	Balsam	Eastern	Western	
Fir 1 (a)	California	Maple,	Red	
Kapur	Red	Bigleaf	Cottonwood	
Keruing	Grand	Pine	Eastern	
Larch,	Noble	Jack	Black	
Western	Pacific	Lodgepole	(Western	
Maple, Sugar	Silver	Ponderosa	Poplar)	
Pine	White	Spruce	Pine	
Caribbean	Hemlock,	Redwood	Eastern	
Ocote	Western	Spruce	White	
Pine, South.	Lauan	Engelmann	Sugar	
Loblolly	Almon	White		
Longleaf	Bagtikan			
Shortleaf	Mayapis			
Slash	Red			
Tanoak	Tangile			
	White			
	Maple, Black			
	Mengkulang			
	Meranti,			
	Red (b)			
	Mersawa			
	Pine			
	Pond			
	Red			
	Virginia			
	Western			
	White			
	Spruce			
	Black			
	Red			
	Sitka			
	Sweetgum			
	Tamarack			
	Yellow-			
	Poplar			

(a) Douglas Fir from trees grown in the states of Washington, Oregon, California, Idaho, Montana, Wyoming, and the Canadian Provinces of Alberta and British Columbia shall be classed as Douglas Fir No. 1. Douglas Fir from trees grown in the states of Nevada, Utah, Colorado, Arizona and New Mexico shall be classed as Douglas Fir No. 2.
(b) Red Meranti shall be limited to species having a specific gravity of 0.41 or more based on green volume and oven dry weight.

Figure 8.7   Species of wood used in plywood. *(APA.)*

The specifications for the fabrication of plywood allow the mixing of various species of wood in a given plywood panel. This practice allows the more complete usage of raw materials. If it should become necessary to perform stress calculations, the allowable stresses for plywood calculations have been simplified for use in design. This is accomplished by providing allowable values based on the species group of the face and back plies. The species group of the outer plies is included in the grade stamp of certain grades of plywood (Sec. 8.7). Tabulated section properties are calculated for Group 4 inner plies (the weakest species group allowed in structural plywood). The assumption of Group 4 inner plies is made regardless of the actual makeup. Allowable stresses and cross-sectional properties are given in the APA publication *Plywood Design Specification* (PDS, Ref. 14.1).

Although plywood grades have not yet been covered, it should be noted that some grade modifications can be added to the *sheathing grades* which limit the species used in the plywood. For example, the term STRUCTURAL I can be added to certain plywood grades to provide increased strength properties. The addition of the STRUCTURAL I designation restricts all veneers in the plywood to Group 1 species. Thus the greatest section properties apply to plywood with this designation, because the inner plies of Group 1 species (rather than Group 4 species) are used in calculations. (It should also be noted that there is another term, known as STRUCTURAL II, which limits the species to those in Groups 1, 2, and 3. However, STRUCTURAL II is not generally available, and its use in design and building specifications is not recommended.)

Besides limiting the species of wood used in the manufacture of plywood, the STRUCTURAL I designation requires the use of exterior glue and provides further restrictions on layup, knot sizes, and repairs over the same grades without the designation. STRUCTURAL I should be added to the plywood grade specification when the increased strength is required, particularly in shear or cross-panel properties (parallel to the 4-ft dimension).

Before the methods for determining the required plywood grade and thickness for sheathing applications can be reviewed, some additional topics should be covered. These include veneer grades, exposure durability classifications, and plywood grades.

8.5   Veneer Grades

The method of producing the veneers which are used to construct a plywood panel was described in Sec. 8.3. Before a panel is manufactured, the individual veneers are graded according to quality. The *grade of the veneers* is one of the factors that determine the *grade of the panel.*

The six basic veneer grades are designated by a letter name:

N	Special-order "natural finish" veneer. Not used in ordinary structural applications.
A	Smooth, paintable surface. Solid-surface veneer without knots, but may contain a limited number (18 in a 4 ft × 8 ft veneer) of neatly made repairs.
B	Solid-surface veneer. May contain knots up to 1 in. in width across the grain if they are both sound and tight-fitting. May contain an unlimited number of repairs.
C-plugged	An improved grade of C veneer which meets more stringent limitations on defects than the normal C veneer. For example, open defects such as knotholes may not exceed $\frac{1}{4}$ in. by $\frac{1}{2}$ in. Further restrictions apply.
C	May contain open knotholes up to 1 in. width across the grain and occasional knotholes up to $1\frac{1}{2}$ in. across the grain. This is the minimum-grade veneer allowed in exterior-type plywood.
D	Allows open knotholes up to $2\frac{1}{2}$ in. in width across the grain and occasional knotholes up to 3 in. across the grain. This veneer grade is not allowed in exterior-type plywood.

The veneer grades in this list are given in order of decreasing quality. Detailed descriptions of the defects and patching provisions for each veneer grade can be found in Ref. 14.8. Although A and B veneer grades have better surface qualities than C and D veneers, on a structural basis A and C grades are more similar. Likewise, B and D grades are similar, structurally speaking. The reason for these structural similarities is that C veneers can be upgraded through patching and other repairs to qualify as A veneers. See Example 8.6. On the other hand, a B veneer grade can be obtained by upgrading a D veneer. The result is more unbroken wood fiber with A and C veneers.

Except for the special "Marine" exterior grade of plywood, A- and B-grade veneers are used only for face and back veneers. They may be used for the inner plies, but, in general, C and D veneers will be the grades used for the inner plies. It should be noted that D veneers represent a large percentage of the total veneer production, and their use, where appropriate, constitutes an efficient use of materials.

EXAMPLE 8.6   Veneer Grades and Repairs

A veneers are smooth and firm and free from knots, pitch pockets, open splits, and other open defects. A-grade veneers can be obtained by upgrading (repairing) C-grade veneers.

Another upgraded C veneer is C-plugged veneer. Although it has fewer open defects than C, it does not qualify as an A veneer.

B veneers are solid and free from open defects with some minor exceptions. B veneers can be obtained by upgrading (repairing) D-grade veneers. A and B veneers have similar surface qualities, but A and C are structurally similar. Likewise, B and D grades have similar strength properties.

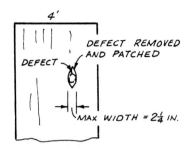

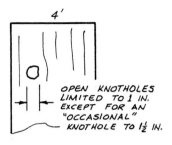

TYP. PATCH IN AN "A" VENEER

TYP. KNOTHOLE IN A "C" VENEER

Figure 8.8a A- and C-grade veneers are structurally similar.

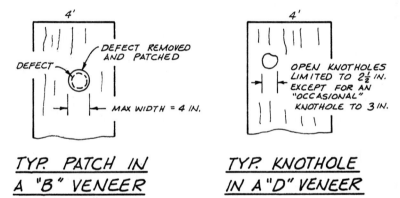

TYP. PATCH IN A "B" VENEER

TYP. KNOTHOLE IN A "D" VENEER

Figure 8.8b B- and D-grade veneers are structurally similar.

8.6 Exposure Durability Classifications

There are two similar exposure durability classification systems for structural wood panels. One applies to plywood fabricated under PS 1 (Ref. 14.8), and the other applies to panels (both all-veneer plywood and other panels) that are performance-rated. See Sec. 8.7 for additional information on PS 1 and performance-rated panels.

For plywood manufactured under PS 1 there are two exposure types: exterior and interior. *Exterior* plywood is glued with an insoluble "waterproof" glue *and* is constructed with a minimum of C-grade veneers. It will retain its glue bond when repeatedly wetted and dried. Exterior plywood is required when it will be permanently exposed to the weather or when the moisture content in use will exceed 18 percent, either continuously or in repeated cycles. In high-moisture-content conditions, the use of pressure-treated panels should be considered.

Interior-type plywood may be used if it is not exposed to the weather and if the MC in service does not continuously or repeatedly exceed 18 percent. Interior plywood can be manufactured with exterior, intermediate, or interior glue, but it is generally available with exterior glue. Thus, *plywood manufactured with exterior glue is not necessarily classified as exterior-type plywood*. If a plywood panel contains a D-grade veneer, it cannot qualify as an exterior panel even if it is manufactured with exterior glue. The reason for this veneer grade restriction is that the knotholes allowed in the D veneer grade are so large that the glue bond, even with exterior glue, may not stand up under continuous exposure to the weather. Such exposure may result in localized delamination in the area of the knothole.

Interior plywood with any glue type is intended for use in interior (protected) applications. Interior plywood bonded with exterior glue is known as Exposure 1 and is intended for use where exposure to moisture due to long construction delays may occur. In addition, the UBC *requires* that the plywood used for roof sheathing be bonded with exterior (or intermediate) glue. Although the roofing materials provide protection to the plywood, the Code specifies the added glue bond requirements to protect against leakage and possible higher moisture contents in roofing systems.

Under PS 1 the three exposure durability classifications for plywood are Exterior, Exposure 1 (interior type with exterior glue), and interior type with intermediate glue. Under APA's performance rating system, the three corresponding classifications for plywood and other panel products are Exterior, Exposure 1, and Exposure 2. For additional information on durability application recommendations, see Ref. 14.4.

8.7 Plywood Grades

For many years the specifications covering the manufacture of plywood have been prescriptive in nature. This means that a method of constructing a plywood panel was fully described by the specification. For a given grade of plywood the species group, veneer grades, and other important factors were specified.

U.S. Product Standard PS 1 for Construction and Industrial Plywood (Ref. 14.8) covers the manufacture of traditional *all-veneer* panels known as plywood. For many years PS 1 was a prescriptive-only specification. Although PS 1 still contains prescriptive requirements (a recipe for manufacturing plywood), it now also contains requirements for plywood that can be qualified on the basis of performance tests.

The concept of a *performance standard* was adapted to manufacturing of structural-use panels because a prescriptive type of specification did not lend itself to the development of some of the newer panel products (Sec. 8.8). These panels can be manufactured in a number of different ways using a variety of raw materials. Rather than prescribing how a panel product is to be constructed, a performance standard specifies what the product must do, e.g., load-carrying capability, dimensional stability, and ability to perform satisfactorily in the presence of moisture.

Although performance rating was developed for these newer panel products, it was noted that plywood can also be performance-rated. The performance rating of traditional all-veneer plywood has resulted in the development of newer, thinner thicknesses. For example, $^{15}/_{32}$ in. now replaces $^1/_2$ in., $^{19}/_{32}$ in. replaces $^5/_8$ in., and $^{23}/_{32}$ in. replaces $^3/_4$ in. For more information see APA's publication *Performance Rated Panels* (Ref. 14.9).

There are a large number of grades of plywood. Several examples are given here, but for a comprehensive summary of plywood grades and their appropriate uses, the reader is referred to APA's publication *Design/Construction Guide—Residential and Commercial* (Ref. 14.4) and Ref. 14.3.

Each plywood panel is stamped with a grade-trademark which allows it to be fully identified. A *sanded panel* will have an A- or B-veneer-grade face ply. The back ply may be an A, B, C, or D veneer. The grade-trademark on a sanded plywood panel will include the following:

1. Veneer grade of the face and back
2. Minimum species group (highest species group number from Fig. 8.7) of the outer plies
3. Exposure durability classification

These items essentially identify the plywood. See Example 8.7. Other information included in the stamp indicates the product standard, the manufacturer's mill number (000 shown), and the abbreviation of the "qualified inspection and testing agency." The American Plywood Association is the agency that provides this quality assurance for most of the plywood manufacturers in the United States.

EXAMPLE 8.7   Sanded Plywood Panel

Figure 8.9 Sanded plywood panel. *(APA.)*

A typical grade-trademark for a *sanded panel* is shown in Fig. 8.9. Outer plies of A- and B-grade veneers will be sanded. C-plugged will be touch-sanded. Others will be unsanded. For the given example only one side of the panel will be fully sanded.

The sanding operation improves the surface condition of the panel, but in doing so it reduces the thickness of the outer veneers by a measurable amount. In fact, the relative thickness of the layers is reduced by such an amount that different cross-sectional properties (Ref. 14.1) are used in strength calculations for sanded, touch-sanded, and unsanded panels.

Although a sanded plywood grade can be used in a structural application, it is normally not used because of cost. Plywood used in structural applications is often covered with a finish material, and a less expensive plywood grade may be used.

The plywood *sheathing grades* are normally used for roof, floor, and wall sheathing. These are

C-C

C-D

Note that C-C is generally Exterior-type plywood, and C-D is generally available with exterior glue which qualifies it as Exposure 1. Where added strength is required, these grades can be upgraded by adding STRUCTURAL I to the designation:

C-C STR I

C-D STR I

This grade modification affects both allowable stresses and effective section properties for the plywood. Although Ref. 14.8 allows the manufacture of an upgrade for C-C and C-D plywood known as STRUCTURAL II, it is not generally available.

A sheathing grade of plywood has several different items in the grade-trademark compared with a sanded panel, including the panel thickness and span rating. See Example 8.8.

The *span rating* on sheathing panels is a set of two numbers. The number on the left in the span rating is the maximum recommended span in inches when the plywood is used as roof sheathing. The second number is the maximum recommended span in inches when the plywood is used as subflooring. For example, a span rating of 48/24 indicates that the panel can be used to span 48 in. in a roof system and 24 in. as floor sheathing. In both roof and floor applications it is assumed the panel will be continuous over two or more spans. The purpose of the span rating is to allow the selection of a proper plywood panel for sheathing applications without the need for structural calculations. Allowable roof and floor sheathing loads are covered in later sections of this chapter.

The use of the span rating to *directly* determine the allowable span for a given panel requires that the plywood be oriented in the strong direction (i.e., the long dimension of the panel perpendicular to the supports). In addition, certain plywood *edge support* requirements must be satisfied in order to apply the span rating without a reduction in allowable span.

EXAMPLE 8.8   Plywood Sheathing Grade

Figure 8.10 A sheathing panel (such as C-C) is unsanded. *(APA.)*

A typical grade-trademark for a *sheathing grade* of plywood is shown in Fig. 8.10. The stamp indicates the panel is APA Rated Sheathing, *and* it conforms to the Product Standard PS 1. Because it conforms to PS 1, this is an all-veneer (i.e., plywood) panel. Some APA Rated Sheathing is not traditional all-veneer plywood. These other structural-use panels are usually manufactured with some form of reconstituted wood product (Sec. 8.8), and the Product Standard PS 1 will not be referenced in the grade-trademark of these other panels.

The example in Fig. 8.10 also indicates that the plywood is C-C Exterior with the STRUCTURAL I upgrade. The panel is ²³/₃₂ in. thick, and it has a *span rating* of 48/24. Other information includes the manufacturer's mill number (000 shown), and the panel conforms to the *performance standard* PRP-108 recognized by the three model codes in NER-108 (Ref. 15.1).

The basic Code reference for the span rating of plywood is UBC Table 25-S-1, and this table applies to both roof and floor applications. This and other selected tables from the UBC are included in Appendix C of this book. The fact to note at this time is that a given span rating may be found on panels of *different* thicknesses. The span rating theoretically accounts for the equivalent strength of panels fabricated from different species of wood. Thus, the same span rating may be found on a thin panel that is fabricated from a strong species of wood *and* a thicker panel that is manufactured from a weaker species. Practically speaking, however, plywood for a given span rating is usually constructed so that the thinner (or thinnest) of the panel thicknesses given in UBC Table 25-S-1 will be generally available.

This fact is significant because of the dual function of plywood in many buildings. The minimum *span rating* should be specified for sheathing loads, *and* the minimum *plywood thickness* as governed by lateral diaphragm design (or the minimum thickness compatible with the span rating) should be specified. Thus both span rating and panel thickness are required in specifying a sheathing grade of plywood.

To summarize, panels can be manufactured with different thicknesses for a given span rating. Generally speaking, the thickness that is *available* is the smaller of those listed for a given span rating in UBC Table 25-S-1. If the minimum span rating and minimum thickness are specified, then a panel with a larger span rating and/or thickness may properly be used in the field.

8.8   Other Structural-Use Panels

Reference to structural-use panels in addition to plywood has been made in previous sections of this chapter. These newer panel products include composite panels, waferboard, oriented strand board, and structural particleboard. APA Rated Sheathing and APA Rated Sturd-I-Floor panels include plywood and all the others mentioned. These are recognized under a *performance standard* by the three model building code bodies in NER-108 (Ref. 15.1). Alternatively certain structural wood panels may be produced under a more prescriptive type of specification such as ANSI A208.1 (UBC Standard 25-25 in Ref. 1.2). These panels can be used for structural roof, floor, and wall sheathing applications. In addition, they can be used to resist lateral forces in horizontal diaphragms and shearwalls.

The structural-use panels that are not all-veneer plywood usually involve some form of reconstituted wood product. A brief description of these panels is given here.

Composite panels have a veneer face and back and a reconstituted wood core. They sometimes also have a veneer crossband.

Waferboard is a nonveneer panel manufactured from reconstituted wood wafers. These wafer-like wood particles or flakes are compressed and bonded with phenolic resin. The wavers may vary in size and thickness, and the direction of the grain in the flakes is usually randomly oriented. The wafers may also be arranged in layers according to size and thickness.

Oriented strand board (OSB) is a nonveneer panel manufactured from reconstituted wood strands or wafers. The strand-like or wafer-like wood particles are compressed and bonded with phenolic resin. As the name implies, the wood strands or wafers are directionally oriented. The wood fibers are arranged in perpendicular layers (usually three to five) and are thus cross-laminated in much the same manner as plywood.

Structural particleboard is a nonveneer panel manufactured from small wood particles (as opposed to larger wafers or strands) bonded with resins under heat and pressure. See Fig. 8.11.

As noted, some structural-use panels that are not plywood may involve the use of veneers. For example, composite panels have outer layers that are veneers and an inner layer that is a reconstituted wood core. Other nonplywood panels are completely nonveneer products.

A typical grade-trademark for a nonveneer performance-rated panel includes a number of the same items found in a plywood sheathing stamp.

Composite
Panels of reconstituted wood cores bonded between veneer face and back piles.

Waferboard
Panels of compressed wafer-like particles or flakes randomly oriented.

Oriented-Strand Board
Panels of compressed strand-like or wafer-like to particles arranged in layers oriented at right angles to one another.

Structural Particleboard
Panels made of small particles usually arranged in layers by particle size, but not usually oriented.

Figure 8.11   APA Rated Sheathing. Of the four types of sheathing other than plywood, oriented strand board (OSB) is the most widely used. *(APA.)*

See Example 8.9. However, the grade-trademark found on panels that are not all-veneer plywood does not contain reference to PS 1, and nonveneer panels will not have veneer grades (e.g., C-D) shown in the stamp.

EXAMPLE 8.9   Nonveneer Sheathing Grade

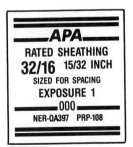

Figure 8.12 Nonveneer sheathing grade. *(APA.)*

A typical grade-trademark for a *nonveneer* panel is shown in Fig. 8.12. The stamp indicates that the panel is APA Rated Sheathing, and it has a span rating of 32/16 (Sec. 8.7). In addition, the thickness ($^{15}\!/_{32}$ in.) and durability classification (Exposure 1) are shown.

Other information includes the manufacturer's mill number (000 shown), and the panel is "sized for spacing" (Sec. 8.2). The panel conforms to APA's performance standard PRP-108, recognized by the three model building codes in NER-108 (Ref. 15.1).

8.9 Roof Sheathing

Plywood and the newer structural-use panels account for much of the wood roof sheathing used in the United States. These materials are assumed to be continuous over two or more spans. Plywood and panels with directional properties (e.g., oriented strand board) are normally used in the strong direction (long dimension of the panel perpendicular to the supports). However, in panelized roof systems (Sec. 3.2) the panels are often turned in the weak direction for sheathing loads. In this latter case, a thicker panel may be required, but this type of construction results in a savings in labor. In addition, higher diaphragm shears can be carried with the increased panel thickness.

The *span rating* described in Sec. 8.7 appears in the grade-trademark of both traditional plywood and APA's performance-rated sheathing. Recall that plywood in addition to other structural wood panels may be performance-rated.

The span rating can be used *directly* to determine the sheathing requirements for panels used in the strong direction under typical roof live loading conditions. When used directly, the actual span agrees with the roof span in the two-number span rating.

For larger roof loads, the span rating can be used *indirectly* to determine panel sheathing requirements. See Fig. 8.13. For example, if the span is 24 in. on a roof with a 75-psf snow load, the required span rating of 40/20 can be read from the table. In this case the roof span in the span rating (40 in.) does not agree with the actual span (24 in.).

The allowable roof loads given in Fig. 8.13 are recognized by the three model code groups in NER-108 (Ref. 15.1), which contains a similar table. These tables cover a number of different performance-rated panels, and the tabulated values are therefore *minimum* load capacities. Consequently many structural-use panels have load capacities that are greater than those listed. For example, UBC Table 25-S-1 applies to *plywood only,* and it contains values of allowable roof LL that exceed the loads in Fig. 8.13.

Both Fig. 8.13 and UBC Table 25-S-1 list the maximum allowable spans *with edge support* and *without edge support* (the UBC table refers to "edges blocked" and "edges unblocked"). Thus the panel edges parallel to the span may be *supported* or *unsupported*. See Example 8.10. Generally support to the edge perpendicular to the roof framing can be provided by *blocking, tongue-and-groove panel edges,* or *panel clips.*

Panel edge support is intended to limit differential movement between adjacent panel edges. Consequently if some form of edge support is not provided, a thicker panel or a reduced spacing of supports will be required.

ALLOWABLE UNIFORM ROOF LIVE LOADS FOR APA RATED SHEATHING AND APA RATED STURD-I-FLOOR WITH LONG DIMENSION PERPENDICULAR TO SUPPORTS[1, 6]

APA RATED SHEATHING APA RATED SHEATHING/CEILING DECK		ROOF											FLOOR
		MAXIMUM SPAN (inches)		ALLOWABLE LIVE LOADS (psf)									MAXIMUM SPAN (inches)
				Spacing of Supports Center-to-Center (inches)									
SPAN RATING	PANEL THICKNESS	With Edge Support[2]	Without Edge Support	12	16	20	24	32	40	48	54	60	
Roof/Floor Span	(inch)												
12/0	5/16	12	12	30									0
16/0	5/16, 3/8	16	16	70	30								0
20/0	5/16, 3/8	20	20	120	50	30							0
24/0	3/8, 7/16, 1/2	24	20[3]	190	100	60	30						0
24/16	7/16, 1/2	24	24	190	100	65	40						16
32/16	15/32, 1/2, 5/8	32	28	325	180	120	70	30					16[5]
40/20	9/16, 19/32, 5/8, 3/4, 7/8	40	32	—	305	205	130	60	30				20[4, 5]
48/24	23/32, 3/4, 7/8	48	36	—	—	280	175	95	45	35			24
54/32	7/8, 1	54	40	—	—	—	245	130	75	50	35		32
60/48	7/8, 1, 1-1/8	60	48	—	—	—	305	165	100	70	50	35	48

APA RATED STURD-I-FLOOR		ROOF											FLOOR
		MAXIMUM SPAN (inches)		ALLOWABLE LIVE LOADS (psf)									MAXIMUM SPAN (inches)
				Spacing of Supports Center-to-Center (inches)									
SPAN RATING	PANEL THICKNESS	With Edge Support[2]	Without Edge Support	12	16	20	24	32	40	48	54	60	
	(inch)												
16 o.c.	19/32, 5/8, 21/32	24	24	185	100	65	40						16[5]
20 o.c.	19/32, 5/8, 3/4	32	32	270	150	100	60	30					20[4, 5]
24 o.c.	11/16, 23/32, 3/4	48	36	—	240	160	100	50	30	25			24
32 o.c.	7/8, 1	48	40	—	—	295	185	100	60	40			32
48 o.c.	1-3/32, 1-1/8	60	48	—	—	—	290	160	100	65	50	40	48

[1] The allowable spans were determined using a dead load of 10 psf. If the dead load exceeds 10 psf then the live load should be reduced accordingly.

[2] Tongue-and-groove edges, panel edge clips (one midway between each support, except two equally spaced between supports 48 inches on center), lumber blocking, or other. Only lumber blocking will satisfy blocked diaphragm requirements of Table No. II, except as noted in Section III.B.3.

[3] Twenty-four inches for 1/2-inch panels.

[4] May be used over framing spaced 24 inches on center for floors where 1-1/2 inches of cellular or lightweight concrete is applied over the panels.

[5] May be used over framing of 24 inches on center where 3/4-inch wood strip flooring is installed at right angles to joist.

[6] Applies to panels 24 inches or wider.

Figure 8.13 Allowable roof live loads on APA Rated Sheathing. *(APA.)*

A point about the support of panel edges should be emphasized. The use of T&G edges or panel clips is accepted as an alternative to lumber blocking for sheathing loads only. If blocking is required for diaphragm action (Chap. 9), panel clips or T&G edges (except 1⅛-in.-thick 2-4-1 plywood with stapled T&G edges) cannot be substituted for lumber blocking.

EXAMPLE 8.10 Roof Sheathing Edge Support Requirements

Alternative forms of support for panel edge that is perpendicular to roof framing (Fig. 8.14).

   a. *Unsupported edge.* In most cases Fig. 8.13 and UBC Table 25-S-1 require closer roof joist spacing than given by the *span rating* when the 8-ft panel edges are not supported. Note that panel thickness may be increased as an alternative to providing support to all edges (or reducing the roof beam spacing).

   b. *Lumber blocking.* Cut and fitted between roof joists.

   c. *Tongue-and-groove (T&G) edges.*

   d. *Panel clips.* Metal H-shaped clips placed between plywood edges. For the number of panel clips refer to Fig. 8.13, footnote 2.

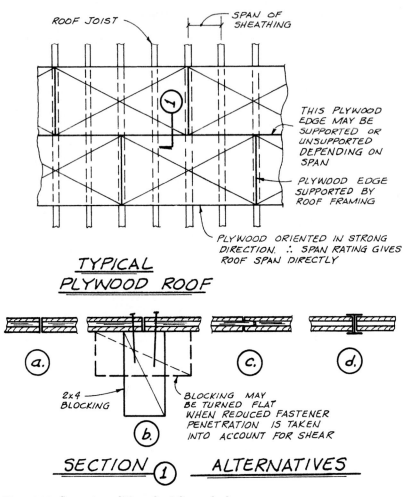

Figure 8.14 Support conditions for 8-ft panel edge.

Use of lumber blocking, T&G edges, and panel clips constitutes edge support for vertical loads. T&G edges and panel clips cannot be used in place of blocking if blocking is required for diaphragm action. Exception: 1⅛-in.-thick plywood with properly stapled T&G edges qualifies as a blocked diaphragm. Diaphragms are covered in Chap. 9.

It was noted at the beginning of this section that panels may be oriented in the weak direction in panelized roof systems. The span rating does not apply directly when panels are used in this manner. For the common roof support spacing of 24 in. o.c., UBC Table 25-S-2 gives the sheathing re-quirements for a *plywood* roof with the long dimension of the panel parallel to the supports (weak orientation for sheathing loads). An expanded version of this table and a table covering nonveneer APA-rated sheathing with the long dimension of the panel parallel to the supports are included in APA's publication *Design/Construction Guide—Residential and Commercial* (Ref. 14.4).

The use of certain structural wood panels that are not plywood and are not performance-rated is allowed by the Code. For example, panels constructed using wood wafers and wood flakes in accordance with a prescriptive-type standard such as ANSI A208.1 (UBC Standard 25-25 in Ref. 1.2) may be used for roof sheathing. UBC Table 25-S-3 refers to these panels as *particleboard* and relates sheathing span and design roof loads to the required panel thickness.

8.10 Design Problem: Roof Sheathing

A common roof sheathing problem involves supports that are spaced 24 in. o.c. See Example 8.11. This building is located in a non-snow load area. Consequently the sheathing is designed for a roof live load of 20 psf (because the sheathing spans only 24 in., there is no tributary area reduction for roof LL).

Part 1 of the example considers panels oriented in the strong direction, and several alternatives are suggested.

In part 2, plywood sheathing requirements for a panelized roof are considered. In this case the number of plies used in the construction of the plywood panels is significant. If 5-ply construction is used, the effective section properties in the weak direction are larger. In 4-ply (3-layer) construction, the section properties are smaller, and either stronger wood (STRUCTURAL I) or a thicker panel is required.

EXAMPLE 8.11   Roof Sheathing with a 24-in. Span

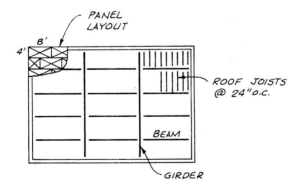

ROOF FRAMING PLAN

Figure 8.15 Panels turned in strong direction.

Loads

$$\text{Roof DL} = 8 \;\; \text{psf}$$

$$\underline{\text{Roof LL} = 20 \;\text{psf}} \quad\quad \text{(no snow load)}$$

$$\text{TL} = 28 \;\text{psf}$$

Part 1

For the roof layout shown, determine the panel sheathing requirements, using an appropriate sheathing grade of plywood and an APA Rated Sheathing nonveneer panel.

1. Plywood sheathing grades are

> C-C EXT
> C-C EXT STR I
> C-D INT
> C-D INT STR I

The UBC permits the use of interior-type plywood for roof sheathing protected from the weather by roofing materials. Exterior or intermediate glue is required. Interior plywood is generally available with exterior glue. This type of plywood is known as C-D Exposure 1 but is commonly abbreviated C-DX (X for exterior glue). STRUCTURAL I should be used when the added shear capacity is necessary for lateral forces.

In Fig. 8.15 the panels are oriented in the strong direction. From UBC Table 25-S-1 the required span rating is 24/0.

$$\text{Allow. roof LL} = 45 \;\text{psf} > 20$$

$$\text{Allow. roof TL} = 60 \;\text{psf} > 28 \quad\quad \textit{OK}$$

UBC Table 25-S-1 indicates that 24/0 plywood may be either $\frac{3}{8}$, $\frac{15}{32}$, or $\frac{1}{2}$ in. thick. Normally, however, plywood is constructed so that the thinner thickness qualifies for a given span rating.

UBC Table 25-S-1 also indicates that with unblocked edges the maximum allowable span for 24/0 plywood is 16 in. Therefore, plywood edges that are perpendicular to the roof joists must be supported. Edge support may be provided by

a. Blocking
b. T&G edges (available in plywood thicknesses $\frac{15}{32}$ in. and greater)
c. H-shaped metal clips (panel clips)

See Fig. 8.14.

Although $\frac{3}{8}$-in. plywood normally qualifies for a 24/0 span rating, $\frac{15}{32}$ in. (or $\frac{1}{2}$-in.) plywood is often used to span 24 in. for the roof in this type of building. Also from UBC Table 25-S-1, $\frac{15}{32}$-in. plywood normally qualifies for a span rating of 32/16. If plywood with a span rating of 32/16 is used, the maximum unsupported edge length is 28 in., which is greater than the actual span of 24 in. Therefore, edge support is not required for this alternative. When roofing is to be guaranteed by a performance bond, the roofing manufacturer should be consulted for minimum thickness and edge support requirements.

Summary: Plywood roof sheathing

The *minimum* plywood requirement for this building is ⅜-in. C-D EXP1 with a span rating of 24/0 and edges supported.

An alternative plywood sheathing is ¹⁵⁄₃₂-in. C-D EXP 1 with a span rating of 32/16 without edge support.

Blocking may be required for either choice for lateral forces (diaphragm action). See Chap. 9.

2. APA Rated Sheathing may be composite panels, waferboard, oriented strand board, structural particleboard, and plywood. From Fig. 8.13, a ⁷⁄₁₆-in. nonveneer panel with a span rating of 24/16 may be used to span 24 in. without edge support.

$$\text{Allow. roof LL} = 40 \text{ psf} > 20$$

$$\text{Allow. roof TL} = 40 + 10 = 50 \text{ psf} > 28 \quad OK$$

Other nonveneer panel choices exist; see UBC Table 25-S-3 for more. Blocking may be required for lateral forces.

Part 2

In the above building, assume that plywood is to be used in a panelized roof. Panels will be turned 90 degrees to that shown in Fig. 8.15, so that the long dimension of the panel is parallel to the supports (joists). Here the span rating cannot be used directly because panels are oriented in the weak direction. UBC Table 25-S-2 indicates that STRUCTURAL I plywood ¹⁵⁄₃₂ in. thick with 4-ply construction, when used in this manner, has

$$\text{Allow. roof LL} = 20 \text{ psf} \geqslant 20$$

$$\text{Allow. roof TL} = 30 \text{ psf} > 28 \quad OK$$

These same panels with 5-ply construction have larger allowable loads. A number of other panel choices exist.

8.11   Floor Sheathing

Structural wood panels are used in floor construction in two ways. One system involves *two layers* of panels, and the other system involves a *single layer*.

The terms used to refer to these different panel layers are:

1. *Subfloor*—the bottom layer in the two-layer system
2. *Underlayment*—the top layer in the two-layer system
3. *Combined subfloor-underlayment*—the single-layer system

A finish floor covering such as linoleum, tile, or carpeting is normally provided. See Ref. 14.4 for specific installation recommendations.

In the two-layer system, the subfloor is the basic structural sheathing material. See Example 8.12. It may be either a sheathing grade of plywood or a nonveneer panel. Recall the two-number span rating from Sec. 8.7. For panels with this span rating the second number is the recommended span in inches when the panel is used as a subfloor. Allowable floor live loads depend on the type of panel.

The basic Code reference for plywood subfloors is UBC Table 25-S-1. Footnote 4 to this table indicates that the allowable floor LL is 165 psf based on a deflection limit of 1/360. NER-108 (Ref. 15.1) indicates that the allowable floor LL for APA Rated Sheathing panels is 85 psf and the allowable dead load is 25 psf. These capacities apply at maximum span.

It should be noted that a number of floor panel applications are not controlled by *uniform* load criteria. Recommendations for plywood floors are based on deflection under concentrated loads, and how the floor *feels* to passing traffic. These and other subjective criteria relate to user acceptance of floor sheathing. For additional information see Ref. 14.10.

In subfloor construction, panels must be used in the strong direction and must be continuous over two or more spans. Differential movement between adjacent unsupported panel edges is to be limited by one of the following:

1. Tongue-and-groove edges

2. Blocking

3. ¼-in. underlayment with panel edges offset over the subfloor

4. 1½ in. of lightweight concrete over the subfloor

5. Finish floor of ¾-in. wood strips

The allowable floor live loads of 165 psf for PS 1 plywood and 85 psf for other APA Rated Sheathing are adequate for many floor applications. These allowable loads are obtained *directly* by matching the span rating with the actual span. If larger floor loads are encountered, the span rating can be used *indirectly* to determine panel requirements. See Fig. 8.16*b*.

In two-layer floor construction, the top layer is a grade of plywood known as UNDERLAYMENT. The underlayment layer lies under the finish floor covering and on top of the subfloor. It is typically either ¼ or ⅜ in. thick, and its purpose is to provide a solid surface for the direct application of nonstructural floor finishes. UNDERLAYMENT-grade plywood panels are touch-sanded to provide a reasonably smooth surface to support the nonstructural finish floor.

Single-layer floor construction is sometimes known as combination subfloor-underlayment because one layer serves both functions. Single-layer floor systems may use thicker grades of UNDERLAYMENT and C-C Plugged Exterior plywood or some form of nonveneer panel. APA's performance-rated

EXAMPLE 8.12   Two-Layer Floor Construction

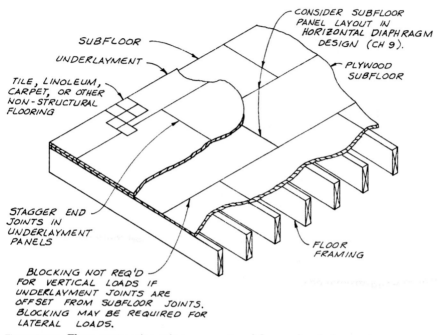

CONSIDER SUBFLOOR PANEL LAYOUT IN HORIZONTAL DIAPHRAGM DESIGN (CH 9).

SUBFLOOR

UNDERLAYMENT

TILE, LINOLEUM, CARPET, OR OTHER NON-STRUCTURAL FLOORING

PLYWOOD SUBFLOOR

STAGGER END JOINTS IN UNDERLAYMENT PANELS

FLOOR FRAMING

BLOCKING NOT REQ'D FOR VERTICAL LOADS IF UNDERLAYMENT JOINTS ARE OFFSET FROM SUBFLOOR JOINTS. BLOCKING MAY BE REQUIRED FOR LATERAL LOADS.

Figure 8.16a Floor construction using a separate subfloor and underlayment.

UNDERLAYMENT-grade plywood has C-plugged face veneer and special C-grade inner-ply construction to resist indentations. Typical underlayment thickness is ¼ in. for use over a panel subfloor and ⅜ in. for use over a lumber subfloor.

When flooring has some structural capacity, the underlayment layer is not required. Wood strip flooring and lightweight concrete are examples of flooring which do not require the use of underlayment over the subfloor.

panels known as Sturd-I-Floor include both plywood and nonveneer panels. The *span rating* for panels intended to be used in single-layer floor systems is composed of a single number. Here the span rating is the recommended maximum floor span in inches. See Example 8.13.

Single-layer floor systems can be installed with nails. However, the APA glued floor system increases floor stiffness and reduces squeaks due to nail popping (Sec. 8.2). This system uses a combination of field gluing and nailing of floor panels to framing members. For additional information see Ref. 14.4.

Recommended Uniform Floor Live Loads for APA RATED STURD-I-FLOOR and APA RATED SHEATHING with Long Dimension Perpendicular to Supports

Sturd-I-Floor Span Rating	Sheathing Span Rating	Maximum Span (in.)	Allowable Live Loads (psf)[a]						
			Joist Spacing (in.)						
			12	16	20	24	32	40	48
16 oc	24/16, 32/16	16	170	85					
20 oc	40/20	20	245	150	85				
24 oc	48/24	24	315	225	160	85			
32 oc		32		265	215	170	85		
48 oc		48			325	255	160	100	55

(a) 10 psf dead load assumed, except 25 psf dead load at maximum span for Span Ratings through 32 oc. Live load deflection limit is $\ell/360$.

Figure 8.16b Allowable floor live loads on APA Rated Sheathing. (*APA.*)

EXAMPLE 8.13   Single-Layer Floor Panels

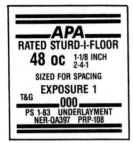

Figure 8.17a Typical grade-trademarks. *(APA.)*

Figure 8.17b Typical grade-trademarks. *(APA.)*

A typical grade-trademark for a plywood combination subfloor-underlayment is shown in Fig. 8.17a. In this example the panel can be identified as plywood because PS 1 is referenced. It is an UNDERLAYMENT grade of plywood that is an interior type with exterior glue (Exposure 1). The panel is APA Rated Sturd-I-Floor, which is also qualified under the performance standard PRP-108. The span rating is 48 o.c., and the panel thickness is 1⅛ in. Other information in the stamp includes the manufacturer's mill number (000 shown), the panel sized for spacing (+0, −⅛ in. tolerance on panel dimensions), and it has T&G edges.

A typical grade-trademark for a nonveneer single-layer floor panel is shown in Fig. 8.17b. Notice that the grade-trademark does not reference PS 1. Like the panel grade stamp in Fig. 8.17a, this panel is performance-rated under PRP-108. It has a span rating of 20 o.c., and the panel is ¹⁹⁄₃₂ in. thick. It has a durability rating of Exposure 1. The panel is sized for spacing and has T&G edges. By taking into account the T&G edges and the fact that it is sized for spacing, the panel has a net width of 47½ in.

The Code reference for plywood combination subfloor-underlayment is UBC Table 25-T-1. Allowable uniform floor loads are 125 psf (based on a deflection limit of 1/360) for all panels, except that the allowable total load on 1⅛-in.-thick plywood over a 48-in. span is 65 psf. NER-108 (Ref. 15.1) indicates that at maximum span the allowable floor live load for APA Sturd-I-Floor panels is 85 psf and the allowable floor DL is 25 psf, except that the Sturd-I-Floor panel with a span rating of 48 o.c. is limited to a total load of 65 psf. UBC Table 25-T-2 gives the allowable floor loads for combination subfloor-underlayment for nonveneer panels that are manufactured under ANSI A208.1 (UBC Standard 25-25 in Ref. 1.2), which is a prescriptive type of specification.

8.12 Design Problem: Floor Sheathing

In this example a typical floor sheathing problem for an office building is considered. See Example 8.14. The floor utilizes a two-layer floor system with a separate subfloor and underlayment. The subfloor is chosen from the sheathing grades using the two-number span rating described in Sec. 8.7. A ¼-in. plywood UNDERLAYMENT-grade panel is used over the subfloor. If the joints of the underlayment are staggered with respect to the joints in the subfloor, no special edge support is required for the subfloor panels.

A single-layer plywood floor could be used as an alternative. Plywood combination subfloor-underlayment (rather than a nonveneer panel) is recommended in Ref. 14.4 when the finish floor is a resilient nontextile flooring or adhered carpet without pad. The span rating for a combination subfloor-underlayment panel consists of a single number in the grade-trademark.

EXAMPLE 8.14   Floor Sheathing with 16-in. Span

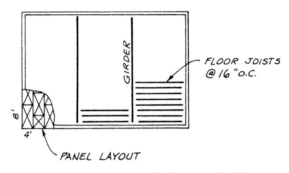

2ND FLOOR FRAMING PLAN

Figure 8.18 Floor construction requires panels in strong direction.

Loads:

$$\text{Floor DL} = 12 \text{ psf}$$

$$\text{Partition DL} = 20 \text{ psf}$$

$$\underline{\text{Floor LL} = 50 \text{ psf}}$$

$$\text{TL} = 82 \text{ psf}$$

For the floor layout, determine the sheathing requirements for vertical loads, assuming a separate plywood subfloor and underlayment construction. A thin resilient-tile finish floor will be used.

Sheathing grades of plywood are

C-C EXT
C-C EXT STR I
C-D INT
C-D INT STR I

Interior plywood is acceptable for the protected floor sheathing application above. Interior plywood is generally available with exterior glue. This type of plywood is known as C-D

Exposure 1 and is often abbreviated C-DX (X for exterior glue). Although interior-type plywood is generally available with exterior glue, exterior glue (Exposure 1) should be specified for plywood floors where moisture may be present (such as bathrooms and utility rooms). STRUCTURAL I should be used when the added shear capacity is necessary for lateral forces.

From the floor framing plan, the plywood is oriented in the strong direction over two or more spans. Therefore the span rating applies.

$$\text{Plywood span} = 16 \text{ in.}$$

$$\text{Req'd span rating} = \text{roof span/floor span}$$

$$= 32/16$$

From footnote 4 in UBC Table 25-S-1,

$$\text{Allow. floor TL} = 165 \text{ psf} > 82 \quad \textit{OK}$$

UBC Table 25-S-1 indicates that 32/16 plywood may be $^{15}/_{32}$, ½, $^{19}/_{32}$, or ⅝ in. thick. Normally plywood is constructed so that the thinner thickness is generally available. Therefore, the *minimum* plywood requirement for subflooring in this problem is

$^{15}/_{32}$-in. C-D EXP 1 with a span rating of 32/16

Because of the type of finish floor, a minimum thickness of ¼-in. UNDERLAYMENT-grade plywood should be installed over the subfloor. Underlayment panel edges should be offset with respect to subfloor edges to minimize differential movement between subfloor panels.

Other possible subfloor choices exist including nonveneer panels. As an alternative, a single-layer floor system can be used.

8.13 Wall Sheathing and Siding

Structural wood panels can be used in wall construction in *two basic* ways. In *one method,* the panels serve a structural purpose only. They are attached directly to the framing and serve as sheathing to distribute the normal wind force to the studs, and they may also function as the basic shear-resisting elements if the wall is a shearwall. See Example 8.15. Finished siding of wood or other material is then attached to the outside of the wall.

Typical sheathing grades of plywood (C-D interior and C-C exterior) and a variety of nonveneer panels are used when finished siding will cover the sheathing. In wall construction, the long dimension of the panel can be either parallel or perpendicular to the studs (supports). The Code reference for plywood wall sheathing is UBC Table 25-N-1, and the reference for APA Rated Sheathing (including both veneer and nonveneer panels) is NER-108. These references specify the minimum two-number span rating (Sec. 8.7) required for panel wall sheathing. UBC Table 25-N-2 gives wall sheathing requirements for nonveneer panels that are manufactured under ANSI A208.1 (UBC Standard 25-25 in Ref. 1.2). Different requirements apply when wall studs are spaced 16 and 24 in. o.c. For shearwall action all panel edges must be supported. This is provided by studs in one direction and wall plates or blocking between the studs in the other direction.

Finish siding material can be attached by nailing through the plywood sheathing into the wall framing, or it may be attached by nailing directly into the sheathing. See Ref. 14.4 for specific recommendations.

EXAMPLE 8.15   Panel Sheathing with Separate Siding

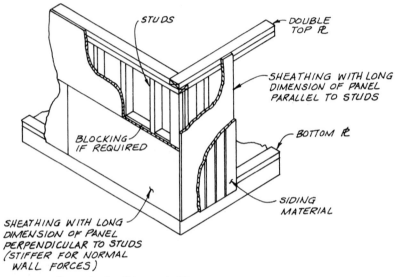

Figure 8.19 Separate sheathing and siding.

In this system the wood panels are basically a structural wall element. Wind forces normal to the wall are carried by the sheathing to the wall studs. In some cases the minimum panel requirements are increased if the face grain is not perpendicular to the studs. Finish siding is applied over the sheathing.

If the panel sheathing also functions as a shearwall (lateral forces parallel to wall), panel edges not supported by wall framing must be blocked and nailed (Chap. 10). *Minimum panel nailing* is 6d common or galvanized box nails at 6 in. o.c. at supported edges and 12 in. o.c. along intermediate supports (studs). Heavier nailing may be required for shearwall action.

In the *second method* of using wood panels in wall construction, a single panel layer is applied as combined sheathing-siding. If plywood is to serve as the siding as well as the structural sheathing, a siding grade of plywood will probably be used. See Example 8.16.

Common types of plywood used for this application are the APA proprietary products known as 303 sidings. These are exterior-type plywood panels available with a variety of textured surface finishes. A special 303 panel is known as Texture 1-11 and is manufactured in $^{19}/_{32}$- and $^5/_8$-in. thicknesses only. It has shiplap edges to aid in weather-tightness and to maintain surface pattern continuity. T 1-11 panels also have $^3/_8$-in.-wide grooves cut into the finished side for decorative purposes. A net panel thickness of $^3/_8$ in. is maintained at the groove. The required thickness of plywood for use as combined sheathing and siding is given in UBC Table 25-M-1. APA 303 siding includes a single-number span rating in the grade-trademark which indicates the maximum spacing of studs. Additional information on 303 siding is available in Ref. 14.4.

UBC Table 25-M-2 gives wall siding requirements for nonveneer panels that are manufactured under ANSI A208.1 (UBC Standard 25-25 in Ref. 1.2).

EXAMPLE 8.16   Plywood Combined Sheathing-Siding

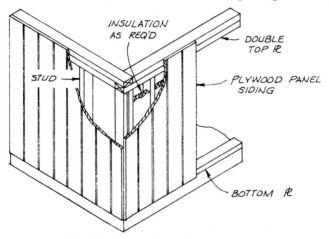

Figure 8.20a   Combined sheathing-siding.

In the combined sheathing-siding system, the plywood usually has a textured surface finish. These finishes include rough-sawn, brushed, and smooth finish for painting [medium density overlay (MDO)]. In addition to different surface textures, most siding panels are available with grooving for decorative effect.

Typical grade-trademarks for plywood combined sheathing-siding are shown in Fig. 8.20b. The examples are for APA 303 siding. A single-number span rating (e.g., 16 or 24 o.c.) indicates maximum recommended stud spacing. For additional information including an explanation of siding face grades, see Ref. 14.4.

Plywood panel siding is usually installed with the 8-ft panel dimension running vertically. However, these panels can also be installed horizontally. Various panel joint details can be used for protection against the weather (see Fig. 8.20c).

Nailing requirements for combined sheathing-siding are similar to the nailing for sheathing in the two-layer wall system (Example 8.15). However, hot-dipped galvanized nails are normally used to reduce staining. Casing nails may be used where the presence of a common or box nail head is objectionable. Additional information on plywood nailing for walls is included in Chap. 10. For panels grater than $^1/_2$ in. thick, the minimum nail size is increased to 8d nails.

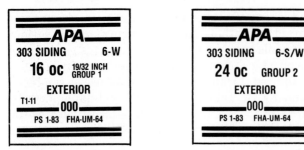

Figure 8.20b Typical grade-trademarks for combined sheathing-siding. *(APA.)*

Heavier nailing may be required for shearwall action. For shearwall design the thickness to be used is the *thickness where nailing occurs*. If grooves are nailed (see Fig. 8.20c), the net thickness at the groove is used.

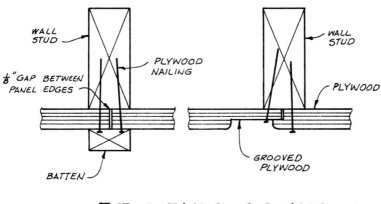

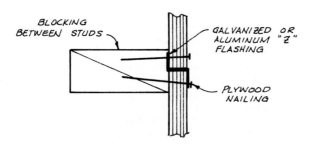

Figure 8.20c Panel edge details for sheathing-siding.

8.14   Stress Calculations for Plywood

The design aids which allow the required thickness of structural wood panel sheathing to be determined without detailed design calculations have been described in the previous sections. For most practical sheathing problems, these methods are adequate to determine the required grade and panel thickness of plywood or nonveneer panel.

In the design of *structural components* such as plywood and lumber beams and stress-skin panels, it will be necessary to have allowable stresses and cross-sectional properties available for use in design calculations.

If it becomes necessary to perform structural calculations for plywood, the designer must become familiar with a number of factors which interrelate to define plywood structurally. The document which gives effective cross-sectional properties and allowable stresses for PS 1 plywood is the *Plywood Design Specification* (PDS, Ref. 14.1). A number of supplements to the PDS are available (Ref. 14.2) that provide design information and examples for a variety of applications.

It will be helpful to review several factors which are unique to plywood structural calculations. These will provide a useful background to the designer even if structural calculations are not required. Although some of these points have been introduced previously, they are briefly summarized here.

Design properties for structural-use panels other than plywood are given in Ref. 14.20.

Cross-sectional properties.   The cross-sectional properties for plywood are tabulated in the PDS. The variables which affect the cross-sectional properties are

1. Direction of stress
2. Surface condition
3. Species makeup

The *direction of stress* relates to the two-directional behavior of plywood because of its cross-laminated construction. Because of this type of construction, two sets of cross-sectional properties are tabulated. One applies when plywood is stressed parallel to the face grain, and the other applies when it is stressed perpendicular to the face grain.

The *basic surface* conditions for plywood are

1. Sanded
2. Touch-sanded
3. Unsanded

It will be recalled that the relative thickness of the plies is different for these different surface conditions. Thus different section properties apply for the three surface conditions.

Finally, the *species makeup* of a panel affects is cross-sectional properties. A special table of section properties applies to STRUCTURAL I and Marine grades. Plywood panels made up of all other combinations of species are assigned a different set of cross-sectional properties.

The product standard (PS 1) allows some variation in the veneer and layer thicknesses used in the makeup of a plywood panel. Therefore, the tabulated cross-sectional properties are based on veneer thickness combinations which produce *minimum* properties. Thus for a given panel, the section properties for the strong and weak directions are not complementary.

Stress calculations.   Although plywood can be made up of a variety of wood species having different strengths and different values of modulus of elasticity, stress calculations are carried out on the assumption of uniform stress properties. This is made possible by use of the *effective* cross-sectional properties and the appropriate allowable stresses given in the PDS.

The use of effective cross-sectional properties differs somewhat from ordinary beam design calculations. For example, with sheathing-type loads, the bending stress in the plywood is to be calculated using the effective section modulus KS and not I/c (the normal definition of section modulus). See Example 8.17. The tabulated value for I is calculated by normalizing all ply areas relative to the face plies (transformed area technique), and I is to be used in stiffness (deflection) calculations only. Values for effective section modulus are then further adjusted based on the number and direction of plies using experimentally determined factors.

EXAMPLE 8.17   Plywood Beam Loading and Section Properties

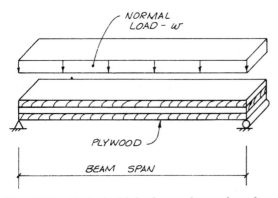

Figure 8.21a Plywood with load normal to surface of panel.

Plywood under Normal (Sheathing) Loads

For loads normal to the surface of the plywood (Fig. 8.21*a*), the effective section modulus *KS* is used for *bending* stress calculations, and the moment of inertia *I* is used for *deflection* calculations. For shear requirements see Example 8.18.

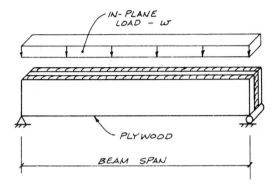

Figure 8.21*b*   Plywood with load in plane of panel.

Plywood under In-Plane Loads

Procedures for calculating cross-sectional properties for plywood loaded in its plane (Fig. 8.21*b*) are given in the *Plywood Design Specification,* Supplement 2 (Ref. 14.2). Plywood used in this manner is typically found in fabricated beams using lumber flanges and plywood webs (Fig. 8.21*c*).

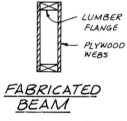

Figure 8.21*c*   Lumber and plywood beam.

Another factor that is unique to plywood structural calculations is that there are two different allowable shear stresses. The different allowable shear stresses are a result of the cross-laminations. The type and direction of the loading determine the type of shear involved, and the appropriate allowable shear must be used in checking the stress.

The PDS refers to these shear stresses as

1. Shear in a plane perpendicular to the plies, or *shear through the thickness* of the plywood
2. Shear in the plane of the plies, or *rolling shear*

The first type of shear occurs when the load is in the plane of the plywood, as in a diaphragm. See Fig. 8.22a in Example 8.18. This same type of stress occurs in fabricated beams using plywood webs. In the latter case, shear through the thickness of the plywood is the result of flexural (horizontal) shear. The design procedures for fabricated lumber and plywood beams are covered in PDS, Supplement 2 (Ref. 14.2).

Rolling shear can also be visualized as the horizontal shear in a beam, but in this case the loads are normal to the surface of plywood (as with sheathing loads). See Fig. 8.22b. The shear is seen to be "in the plane of the plies" rather than "through the thickness." With this type of loading, the wood fibers that are at right angles to the direction of the stress tend to slide or *roll* past one another. Hence the name *rolling shear*. If the stress is parallel to the face plies, the fibers in the inner crossband(s) are subjected to rolling shear.

The PDS provides different cross-sectional properties for the calculation of shear through the thickness and rolling shear. For shear through the thickness, the "effective thickness for shear" is used; and for rolling shear, the "rolling shear constant" Ib/Q is used. In addition to different cross-sectional properties, there are different allowable stresses for the two types of shear stress.

For a further study of structural calculations for plywood, the designer is referred to the PDS and its supplements.

EXAMPLE 8.18   Types of Shear in Plywood

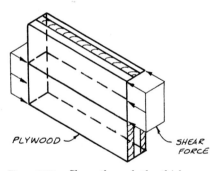

Figure 8.22a   Shear through the thickness.

Shear through the Thickness

Shear through the thickness can occur from the type of loading shown in Fig. 8.22a (as in diaphragm and shearwall action) or from flexural shear (horizontal shear) caused by the type of loading shown in Fig. 8.21b. The stress calculated for these types of loading conditions is based on the *effective thickness for shear*. See PDS.

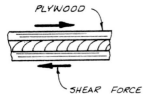

PLYWOOD

SHEAR FORCE

Figure 8.22b Rolling shear is shear in the plane of the plies.

Rolling Shear

Rolling shear occurs in the ply (or plies) that is (are) at right angles to the applied stress (Fig. 8.22b). This type of stress develops when plywood is loaded as shown in Fig. 8.21a. The stress is shear due to bending (horizontal shear) and is calculated from the rolling shear constant Ib/Q. The allowable stress for rolling shear is considerably less than the allowable shear through the thickness.

8.15 Problems

8.1 What two major types of loading are considered in designing a plywood roof or floor system that also functions as part of the LFRS?

8.2 Regarding the fabrication of plywood panels, distinguish between (1) veneer, (2) plies, and (3) layers.

8.3 In the cross section of plywood panel shown in Fig. 8A, label the names used to describe the 5 plies.

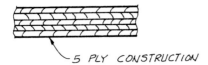

5 PLY CONSTRUCTION

Figure 8.A

8.4 Plywood panels (4 ft × 8 ft) of 5-ply construction (similar to that shown in Fig. 8A) are used to span between roof joists that are spaced 16 in. o.c.

Find: a. Sketch a plan view of the framing and the plywood, showing the plywood oriented in the strong direction.
    b. Sketch a 1-ft-wide cross section of the sheathing. Shade the plies that are effective in supporting the "sheathing" loads.

8.5 Repeat Prob. 8.4 except that the plywood is oriented in the weak direction.

8.6 How are the species of wood used in the fabrication of plywood classified?

8.7 The plywood in Fig. 8A has a grade stamp that indicates *Group 2*.

Find: a. What plies in the panel contain Group 2 species?
    b. If not all plies are of Group 2 species, what is assumed for the others?

8.8   What is the meaning of the term STRUCTURAL I? How is it used?

8.9   What are the veneer grades? Which veneers are the more similar in appearance and surface qualities? Which veneers are structurally more similar? State the reasons for similarities.

8.10   What is the most common type of glue used in the fabrication of plywood (interior, intermediate, or exterior)?

8.11   List and briefly describe the structural-use panels other than plywood.

8.12   What is the difference between a prescriptive specification and a performance standard for the production of structural-use panels?

8.13   Describe the exposure durability classifications for (*a*) plywood manufactured in accordance with the Product Standard PS 1 and (*b*) structural-use panels manufactured under APA's performance standard. (*c*) Which of the durability classifications in parts (*a*) and (*b*) are similar?

8.14   What is the difference between the construction of interior and exterior plywood?

8.15   Briefly describe the *span rating* found in the grade-trademark of the following panels:
  a. Sheathing grades
  b. APA Rated Sturd-I-Floor
  c. APA Rated 303 siding

8.16   Explain the significance of the following designations that may be found in the grade-trademarks of structural-use panels:
  a. PS 1
  b. PRP-108

8.17   What building code tables provide load/span information for the following?
  a. Plywood roof sheathing oriented in the strong direction
  b. Plywood floor sheathing
  c. Nonveneer APA structural-use panels for roof or floor sheathing
  d. Plywood roof sheathing oriented in the weak direction

8.18   What are the sheathing grades of plywood? Are these sanded, touch-sanded, or unsanded panels? What veneer grades are used for the face and back plies of a sanded plywood panel?

8.19   The spacing of rafters in a roof is 48 in. o.c. Roof DL = 5 psf. Snow load = 30 psf. Roof sheathing is to be a sheathing grade of plywood, and panels are oriented in the strong direction.

  Find: The minimum grade, span rating, thickness, and edge support requirements for the roof sheathing. Reference the UBC table used to select the sheathing.

8.20 The spacing of joists in a roof is 24 in. o.c. Roof DL = 8 psf. Snow load = 100 psf. Roof sheathing is to be APA Rated Sheathing (which can be either plywood or a nonveneer panel). Panels are oriented in the strong direction.

   Find: The minimum span rating, thickness, and edge support require-ments for the roof sheathing. Reference the table used to select the sheathing.

8.21 The spacing of joists in a floor system is 16 in. o.c., and the design floor (DL + LL) is 200 psf.

   Find: The required panel grade, span rating, thickness, edge support re-quirements, and panel orientation for the floor sheathing. Refer to the table used to select the sheathing.

8.22 Repeat Prob. 8.21 except that the joist spacing is 24 in o.c.

8.23 Describe the construction of UNDERLAYMENT-grade plywood. How is it used in floor construction?

8.24 A single-layer floor system is used to support a floor DL of 10 psf and a floor LL of 75 psf. Panels with a span rating of 16 in. will be used to span between floor joists that are 16 in. o.c.

   Find: *a.* Is an APA nonveneer panel able to support these loads, or is a plywood panel necessary?
   b. What are the advantages of field-gluing floor panels to the fram-ing members before they are nailed in place?
   c. What is meant by nail popping, and how is the problem mini-mized?

8.25 Describe the following types of plywood used on walls (include typical grades):
   a. Plywood sheathing
   b. Plywood siding
   c. Combined sheathing-siding

8.26 Grooved plywood (such as Texture 1-11) is used for combined sheathing-siding on a shearwall. Nailing to the studs is similar to that in Fig. 8.20c, the detail for a vertical plywood joint.

   Find: What thickness plywood is to be used in the shearwall design cal-culations?

8.27 Regarding the calculation of stresses in plywood,
   a. What is the effective section modulus KS, and when is it used?
   b. What is shear through the thickness?
   c. What is rolling shear?

Horizontal Diaphragms

9.1 Introduction

The lateral forces that act on conventional wood-frame buildings (bearing wall system) were described in Chap. 2, and the distribution of these forces was covered in Chap. 3. In the typical case, the lateral forces were seen to be carried by the wall framing to the horizontal diaphragms at the top and bottom of the wall sections. A horizontal diaphragm acts as a beam in the plane of a roof or floor that spans between shearwalls. See Fig. 9.1.

The examples in Chap. 3 were basically force calculation and force distribution problems. In addition, the calculation of the unit shear in a diaphragm was illustrated. Although the unit shear is a major factor in a diaphragm design, there are a number of additional items that must be addressed.

The basic design considerations for a horizontal diaphragm are

1. Sheathing thickness
2. Diaphragm nailing
3. Chord design
4. Strut design
5. Diaphragm deflection
6. Tie and anchorage requirements

The first item is often governed by loads normal to the surface of the sheathing (i.e., by sheathing loads). This subject is covered in Sec. 6.18 for lumber diaphragms and in Chap. 8 for plywood and other structural-use panel diaphragms. The nailing requirements, on the other hand, are a function of the unit shear. The sheathing thickness and nailing requirements

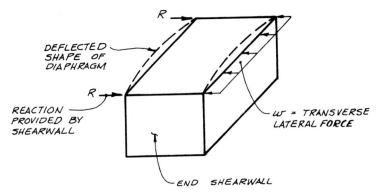

Figure 9.1 Typical horizontal roof diaphragm.

may, however, both be governed by the unit shears *when the shears are large*.

In this chapter the general behavior of a horizontal diaphragm is described, and the functions of the various items mentioned above are explained. This is followed by detailed design considerations for the individual elements. Tie and anchorage requirements are touched upon, but these are treated more systematically in Chap. 15. Shearwalls (vertical diaphragms) are covered in Chap. 10.

9.2 Basic Horizontal Diaphragm Action

A horizontal diaphragm can be defined as a large, thin structural element that is loaded in its plane. It is an assemblage of elements which typically includes

1. Roof or floor sheathing
2. Framing members supporting the sheathing
3. Boundary or perimeter members

When properly designed and connected together, this assemblage will function as a horizontal beam that spans between the vertical resisting elements in the lateral-force-resisting system (LFRS).

The diaphragm must be considered for lateral forces in both transverse and longitudinal directions. See Example 9.1. Like all beams, a horizontal diaphragm must be designed to resist both shear and bending.

In general, a horizontal diaphragm can be thought of as being made up of a shear-resisting element (the roof or floor sheathing) and boundary members. There are two types of boundary members in a horizontal diaphragm (chords and struts), and the direction of the applied force determines the function of the members (Fig. 9.2). The *chords* are designed to *carry the moment* in the diaphragm.

EXAMPLE 9.1   Horizontal Diaphragm Forces and Boundary Members

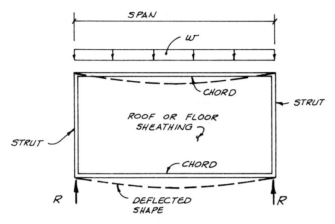

TRANSVERSE FORCE

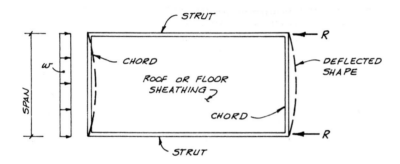

LONGITUDINAL FORCE

Figure 9.2   Diaphragm boundary members: Chords and Struts.

Diaphragm *boundary members* change functions depending on the direction of the lateral force.

   Chords are boundary members that are perpendicular to the applied force. *Struts* are boundary members that are parallel to the applied force.

An analogy is often drawn between a horizontal diaphragm and a steel wide-flange (W shape) beam. In a steel beam the flanges resist most of the moment, and the web essentially carries the shear. In a horizontal diaphragm, the sheathing corresponds to the web, and the chords are assumed to be the flanges. The chords are designed to carry axial forces created by the moment. These forces are obtained by resolving the internal moment into a couple (tension and compression forces). See Fig. 9.3. The shear is assumed to be carried entirely by the sheathing material. Proper nailing of the sheathing to the framing members is essential for this resistance to develop.

The *struts* are designed to trnasmit the horizontal diaphragm *reactions to the shearwalls*. This becomes a design consideration only when the supporting shearwalls are shorter in length than the horizontal diaphragm.

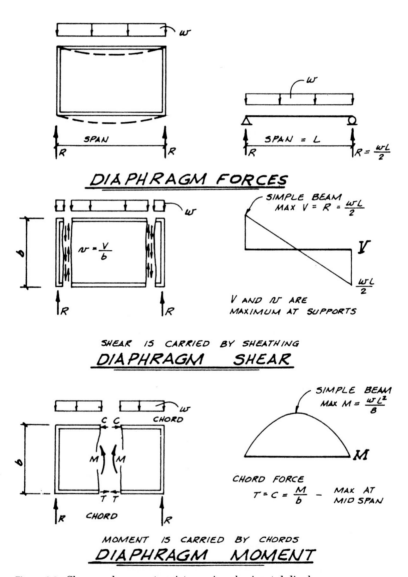

Figure 9.3 Shear and moment resistance in a horizontal diaphragm.

See Example 9.2. Essentially, the unsupported horizontal diaphragm unit shear over an opening in a wall must be transmitted to the shearwall elements by the strut. The strut load is also known as a *drag force* or *collector force* because the strut collects or drags the diaphragm shear into the shearwall. When the supporting shearwalls are of wood-frame construction, the unit shear in the shearwalls is usually assumed to be uniform throughout the length of the wall.

EXAMPLE 9.2   Function of Drag Strut

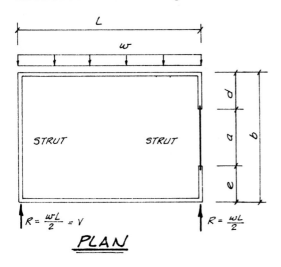

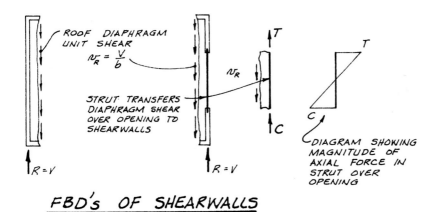

Figure 9.4 Drag strut over wall opening.

The left wall has no openings, and roof shear is transferred directly to the wall. The right wall has a large opening, and the strut transfers the roof diaphragm shear over the opening to the shearwalls. The strut here is assumed to function in both tension and compression. When shearwall lengths d and e are equal, the strut forces T and C are equal. Strut forces for other ratios of d and e are covered in Sec. 9.6.

9.3 Shear Resistance

The shear-resisting element in the horizontal diaphragm assemblage is the roof or floor sheathing. This can be either lumber sheathing or structural-use panels. The majority of wood horizontal diaphragms use plywood sheathing because of the economy of installation and the relatively high allowable unit shears it provides. However, today other panel products (Sec. 8.8) provide alternative choices for diaphragm sheathing. Because of its wide acceptance and for simplicity, this chapter deals primarily with plywood diaphragms, but the design procedures for other structural-use panels are the same as those for plywood diaphragms. Lumber-sheathed diaphragms are covered in Ref. 9.1.

For plywood diaphragms and diaphragms constructed from other panel products, the starting point is the determination of the required panel thickness for sheathing loads, i.e., loads perpendicular to the plane of the sheathing (Chap. 8). It has been previously noted that these loads often determine the final panel thickness. This is especially true for floors because the sheathing loads are larger and the deflection criteria are more stringent than those for roofs.

The shear capacity for plywood diaphragms is the shear "through the thickness" (Fig. 8.22a). However, in most cases the shear capacity of the plywood is not the determining factor. Unit diaphragm shears are usually limited by the *nail capacity* in the wood, rather than the strength of the plywood panel.

The nail spacing required for a horizontal diaphragm may be different at various points in the diaphragm. Because of the importance of the plywood nailing requirements, it is necessary for the designer to clearly understand the nailing patterns used in diaphragm construction.

The simplest nailing pattern is found in *unblocked diaphragms*. See Fig. 9.5a. An unblocked diaphragm is one that does *not* have two of the panel edges *supported* by lumber framing. These edges may be completely unsupported, or there may be some other type of edge support such as T&G edges or panel clips (Fig. 8.14). For an *unblocked diaphragm* the *standard nail spacing* requirements are

1. Supported plywood edges—6 in. o.c.

2. Along intermediate framing members (known also as *field* nailing)—12 in. o.c. (except 6 in. o.c. is required when supports are spaced 48 in. or greater—see UBC Table 25-Q, footnote 5)

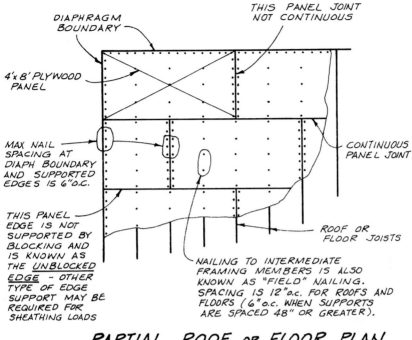

Figure 9.5a Unblocked diaphragm.

When a diaphragm has the plywood edges supported with *blocking,* the *minimum* nailing requirements are the same as for unblocked diaphragms. There are, however, more supported edges in a blocked diaphragm. See Fig. 9.5*b*.

Although the minimum nailing requirements (i.e., maximum nail spacing) are the same for both blocked and unblocked diaphragms, the allowable unit shears are much higher for blocked diaphragms. These higher unit shears are a result of the more positive, direct transfer of stress provided by nailing all four edges of the plywood panel. See Fig. 9.5*c*.

EXAMPLE 9.3   Plywood Diaphragm Nailing

Required nail size is a function of the plywood thickness and shear requirements. Plywood is shown spanning in the strong direction for normal (sheathing) loads. See Fig. 9.5*a* for an unblocked diaphragm and Fig. 9.5*b* for a blocked diaphragm.

The *direction of the continuous panel joint* and the *direction of the unblocked edge* are used to determine the *load case* for diaphragm design. Different panel layouts and framing arrangements are possible. The continuous panel joint and the unblocked edge are not necessarily along the same line. The diaphragm *load case* (described in Example 9.4) is considered in blocked diaphragms as well as unblocked diaphragms.

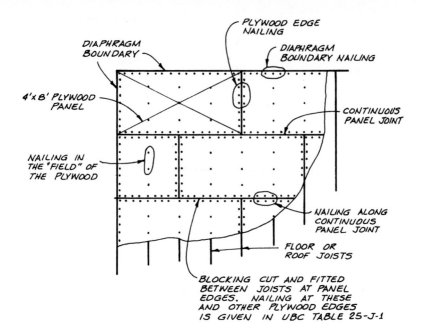

PLYWOOD EDGE NAILING

DIAPHRAGM BOUNDARY

DIAPHRAGM BOUNDARY NAILING

4'x 8' PLYWOOD PANEL

CONTINUOUS PANEL JOINT

NAILING IN THE "FIELD" OF THE PLYWOOD

NAILING ALONG CONTINUOUS PANEL JOINT

FLOOR OR ROOF JOISTS

BLOCKING CUT AND FITTED BETWEEN JOISTS AT PANEL EDGES. NAILING AT THESE AND OTHER PLYWOOD EDGES IS GIVEN IN UBC TABLE 25-J-1

PARTIAL ROOF or FLOOR PLAN

Figure 9.5b Blocked diaphragm.

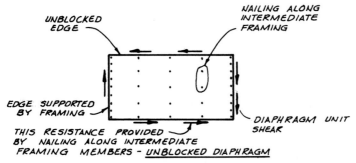

UNBLOCKED EDGE

NAILING ALONG INTERMEDIATE FRAMING

EDGE SUPPORTED BY FRAMING

DIAPHRAGM UNIT SHEAR

THIS RESISTANCE PROVIDED BY NAILING ALONG INTERMEDIATE FRAMING MEMBERS - UNBLOCKED DIAPHRAGM

ISOLATED PANEL FROM FIG 9.5.a

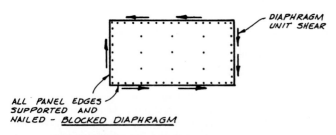

DIAPHRAGM UNIT SHEAR

ALL PANEL EDGES SUPPORTED AND NAILED - BLOCKED DIAPHRAGM

ISOLATED PANEL FROM FIG 9.5.b

Figure 9.5c Shear transfer in a plywood diaphragm.

From a comparison of the isolated panels in Fig. 9.5c it can be seen that the addition of nailing along the edge of a blocked panel will produce a much stronger diaphragm.

In diaphragms using relatively *thin* plywood, there is a tendency for the plywood to buckle. This is caused by the edge bearing of panels in adjacent courses as they rotate slightly under high diaphragm forces.

When loaded to failure, the nails in a plywood diaphragm deform, and the *head* of the nail may pull through the face of the plywood. Other possible modes of failure include pulling the nail through the *edge* of the plywood and *splitting* the framing members to which the plywood is attached. A minimum distance of ⅜ in. from the edge of a panel to the center of a nail is required to develop the design capacity of a nail in plywood. See Fig. 9.5d.

When loaded to ultimate, there are several possible modes of failure that can occur in a plywood diaphragm. Perhaps the most common type of failure is by the nail head pulling through the plywood. See Fig. 9.5d.

The nail spacing given above is used for all *unblocked* diaphragms. For *blocked* diaphragms, however, these spacing provisions are simply the maximum allowed spacing. Much higher allowable unit shears can be obtained by using a decreased nail spacing. Allowable unit shears for both unblocked

Figure 9.5d Nail deformation at ultimate load. *(APA.)*

and blocked diaphragms are given in UBC Table 25-J-1 for *plywood diaphragms,* NER-108 for *APA structural-use panels,* and UBC Table 25-J-2 for *panels qualified under UBC Standard 25-25* (Ref. 1.2). See Secs. 8.7 and 8.8 for a description of these panel products.

The design tables for the different types of panels are similar in organization and content. In order to simplify the discussion, the remaining portion of this chapter is limited to the consideration of plywood diaphragms, and design values are taken from UBC Table 25-J-1. The basic design procedure is similar for diaphragms using other structural-use panels.

Tabulated unit shears for horizontal diaphragms assume that the framing members are Douglas Fir-Larch or Southern Pine. If the diaphragm nailing penetrates into framing members of other species of wood, an adjustment is required that accounts for a reduced nail capacity. Reduction factors for other species of wood are given in a footnote to the allowable shear tables. In addition, it should be realized that the tabulated diaphragm values are for short-term (wind or seismic) forces. Because these represent the common loading conditions for horizontal diaphragms, the load duration factor C_D for wind and seismic is included in the tabulated allowable shears. Consequently, if a horizontal diaphragm is used to support loads of longer duration, allowable shears will have to be reduced in accordance with the appropriate load duration factors covered in Sec. 4.15.

When the design unit shears are large, the required *nail spacing* for *blocked diaphragms* must be carefully interpreted. The nail spacing along the following lines must be considered:

1. Diaphragm boundary
2. Continuous panel joints
3. Other plywood panel edges
4. Intermediate framing members (field nailing)

The field-nailing provisions are always the same: 12 in. o.c. for roofs and floors (except 6-in. o.c. spacing is required when framing is spaced at 48 in. or greater). The nail spacing along the other lines may all be the same (6 in. o.c. maximum), or some may be different. Allowable unit shears are tabulated for a nail spacing as small as 2 in. o.c.

A great deal of information is incorporated into UBC Table 25-J-1. Because of the importance of this table, the remainder of this section deals with a review of UBC Table 25-J-1 (this and certain other UBC tables are included in Appendix C).

The table is divided into several main parts. The top part gives allowable unit shears for diaphragms which have the STRUCTURAL I designation included in the plywood grade (Sec. 8.4). The values in the bottom half of the table apply to *all other plywood grades.*

The latter represents the large majority of plywood, and it includes both sanded and unsanded grades. STRUCTURAL I is stronger (and more expensive) and should be specified when the added strength is required. The allowable shear values for STRUCTURAL I are 10 percent larger than the values for other plywood grades. Although the table includes STRUCTURAL II, it should be remembered that this grade is not generally available.

In working across the table it will be noted that the left side is basically descriptive, and it requires little explanation. The two right-hand columns give the allowable unit shears for *unblocked* diaphragms. The next four columns give allowable shears for *blocked* diaphragms.

Throughout the allowable shear tables, reference is made to the *load cases*. Six load cases are defined, and some examples of these are given in UBC Table 25-J-1. Although somewhat different panel arrangements can be used, all layouts can be classified into one of the six load cases. Because the proper use of Table 25-J-1 depends on the load case, the designer must be able to determine the load case for any layout under consideration.

The *load case* essentially depends on two factors. The *direction of the lateral force* on the diaphragm is compared with the direction of the

1. Continuous panel joint

2. Unblocked edge (if blocking is not provided)

For example, in load case 1 the applied lateral force is perpendicular to the continuous panel joint, and it is also perpendicular to the unblocked edge. Load cases 1 through 4 consider the various combinations of these alternative arrangements. Load cases 5 and 6 have continuous panel joints running in both directions. Load cases 1 through 4 are more common than cases 5 and 6.

The panel layout must be shown on roof and floor framing plans along with the nailing and blocking requirements. It should be noted that the load case is defined by the criteria given above, and it does not depend on the direction of the plywood panel. See Example 9.4.

EXAMPLE 9.4   Plywood Diaphragm Load Cases

Determine the *load cases* for two horizontal diaphragms (Fig. 9.6a and b) in accordance with UBC Table 25-J-1. Consider both transverse and longitudinal directions.

Plywood in Fig. 9.6a is oriented in the strong direction for sheathing loads. In Fig. 9.6b the same building is considered except that the plywood layout has been revised. The plywood in Fig. 9.6b is oriented in the weak direction for sheathing loads.

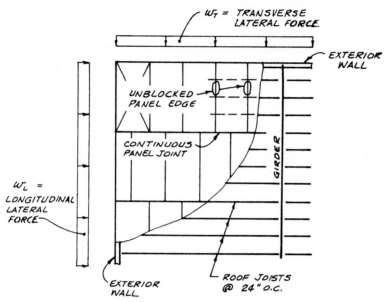

Figure 9.6a Partial roof framing plan.

Transverse Direction

Transverse force in Fig. 9.6a is perpendicular to continuous panel joint and parallel to unblocked edge.

∴ load case 2

Longitudinal Direction

Longitudinal force in Fig. 9.6a is parallel to continuous panel joint and perpendicular to the unblocked edge.

∴ load case 4

Practically speaking, for an unblocked diaphragm there is load case 1 and *all* others.

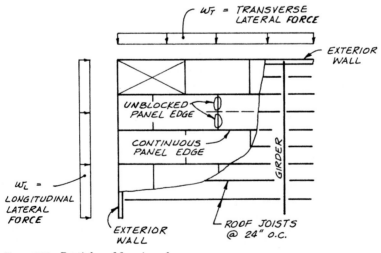

Figure 9.6b Partial roof framing plan.

When the criteria defining the load case are considered, it is seen that the load cases are the same in Fig. 9.6*b* as in Fig. 9.6*a*:

Traverse—case 2

Longitudinal—case 4

For a given horizontal diaphragm problem, two different load cases apply: one for the transverse load and the other for the longitudinal load. The lateral force in the transverse direction normally produces the larger unit shears in a horizontal diaphragm (this may not be the case for shearwalls), but the allowable unit shears may be different for the two load cases. Thus, the diaphragm shears should be checked in both directions.

Other factors regarding the makeup and use of UBC Table 25-J-1 should be noted. For example, the width of the framing members must be considered. Allowable shears for diaphragms using 2-in. nominal framing members are 11 percent less than for diaphragms using wider framing.

The *nail spacing* used for the *diaphragm boundary* on blocked diaphragms is also the nail spacing required along the *continuous panel joint* for load cases 3 and 4. This nail spacing is also to be used at all panel edges for load cases 5 and 6. If load case 1 or 2 is involved, the diaphragm boundary nail spacing is not required at the continuous panel joints, and the somewhat larger nail spacing for "other panel edges" may be used. The selection of the proper nailing specifications is illustrated in several examples later in the chapter.

When the spacing of nails is very close, UBC Table 25-J-1 requires special precautions to avoid the splitting of lumber framing. For example, under certain circumstances, 3-in. (or wider) nominal framing is required when the spacing of nails is 3 in. or less. Refer to UBC Table 25-J-1 footnotes for specific details.

A point should be made about the combination of nail sizes and plywood thicknesses in UBC Table 25-J-1. There are times when the nail size and plywood thickness for a given design will not agree with the combinations listed in the table. If the allowable shears in the tables are to be used without further justification, the following procedure should be followed: If a thicker plywood than that given in the table is used, the allowable shear from the table should be based on the nailing used. No increase in shear is permitted because of the increased thickness.

On the other hand, if a larger nail size is used for a plywood thickness given in the table, the allowable shear from the table should be based on the plywood thickness. No increase in shear is permitted because of the increased nail size. Thus, without further justification, the combination of plywood thickness and nail size given in UBC Table 25-J-1 is "compatible." Increasing one item only does not necessarily provide an increase in allowable unit shear. Reference 14.11 describes a method of calculating allowable diaphragm unit shears by principles of mechanics using the plywood shear values and nail strength values.

Another consideration about nail sizes has to do with the penetration of the nail into the framing members. UBC Table 25-J-1 indicates that 10d nails require a minimum penetration of 1⅝ in. into the framing members below the plywood panels. If 2 × 4 blocking is turned flat (dashed lines in Fig. 8.14, alternative b), the thickness available for nail penetration is simply the thickness of the 2 × 4 (that is, 1½ in.). This same thickness for nail penetration occurs when light-frame wood trusses use 2 × 4 top chords turned flat. The reduced penetration should be taken into account by reducing the tabulated allowable unit shears in UBC Table 25-J-1. The reduction is figured using a linear interpolation as the ratio of the furnished penetration to the required penetration. For the case of a 10d nail in a 2 × 4 flat, the reduction is 1.5/1.625 = 0.923 times the tabulated unit diaphragm shear (roughly an 8 percent reduction).

Finally, it should be noted that the other "approved" types of plywood edge support (such as T&G edges or panel clips—Fig. 8.14) are substitutes for lumber blocking for sheathing loads only. They do not qualify as substitutes for blocking for diaphragm design (except 1⅛-in.-thick 2-4-1 plywood with properly stapled T&G edges).

9.4 Diaphragm Chords

Once the diaphragm web has been designed (sheathing thickness and nailing), the flanges or chord members must be considered. The determination of the axial forces in the chords is described in Fig. 9.3. The axial force at any point in the chords can be determined by resolving the moment in the diaphragm at that point into a couple (equal and opposite forces separated by a lever arm—the lever arm is the distance between chords):

$$T = C = \frac{M}{b}$$

The tension chord is often the critical member. There are several reasons for this. One is that the allowable stress in compression is often larger than the allowable stress in tension. This assumes that the chord is laterally supported and that column buckling is not a factor. This is usually the case, but the possible effects of column instability in the compression chord must be evaluated.

Another reason that the tension chord may be critical is that the chords are usually not continuous single members for the full length of the building.

In order to develop the chord force, the members must be made effective by splicing separate members together. This is less of a problem in compression because the ends of chord members can transmit loads across a splice in end bearing. Tension splices, on the other hand, must be designed.

Because the magnitude of the chord force is calculated from the diaphragm moment, the *magnitude of the chord force follows the shape of the moment diagram*. The design force for any connection splice can be calculated by dividing the moment in the diaphragm at the location of the splice by the distance separating the chords. A simpler, more conservative approach would be to design all diaphragm chord splices for the maximum chord force.

It should also be noted that each chord member must be capable of functioning in either tension or compression. The applied lateral load can change direction and cause tension or compression in either chord.

Some consideration should be given at this point to what elements in a building can serve as the chords for a diaphragm. In a wood-frame building with stud walls, the doubled top plate is usually designed as the chord. See Example 9.5. This type of construction is accepted by contractors and carpenters as standard practice. Although it may be have developed through tradition, the concept behind its use is structurally sound.

The top plate members are not continuous in ordinary buildings unless the plan dimensions of the building are very small. Two plate members are used so that the splice in one plate member can be staggered with respect to the splice in the other member. This creates a continuous chord with at least one member being effective at any given point. When chord forces are large, more than two plate members may be required.

In order for the top plate members to act as a chord, they must be adequately connected together. If the chord forces are small, this connection can be made with nails, but if the forces are large, the connection will require the use of bolts. These are connection design problems, and the procedures given in Chaps. 12 and 13 can be used for the design of these splices. It should also be noted that the chord forces are usually the result of wind or seismic forces, and a C_D of 1.6* (Sec. 4.15) applies to the design of wood members and wood connections.

EXAMPLE 9.5   Horizontal Diaphragm Chord—Double Top Plate

The double top plate in a wood-frame wall is often used as the chord for the horizontal diaphragm. Splices are offset so that one member is effective in tension at a splice. Connections for anchoring the horizontal and vertical diaphragms together are covered in Chap. 15.

---

*Verify local code acceptance before using $C_D = 1.6$.

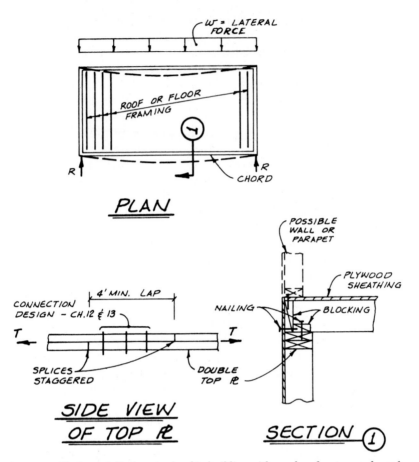

Figure 9.7 Horizontal diaphragm chord in building with wood roof system and wood-frame walls. Code minimum lap splice length is 4 ft to form a continuous chord member. Nail or bolt connection must be designed to transmit chord force T from one plate member to the other.

Plywood diaphragms are often used in buildings that have concrete tilt-up walls or masonry (concrete block or brick) walls. In these buildings the chord is made up of continuous horizontal reinforcing steel in the masonry or concrete wall. See Example 9.6. If the masonry or concrete is assumed to function in compression only (the usual assumption), the tension chord is critical. The stress in the steel is calculated by dividing the chord force by the cross-sectional area of the horizontal wall steel that is placed at the diaphragm level.

EXAMPLE 9.6   Horizontal Diaphragm Chord—Wall Steel

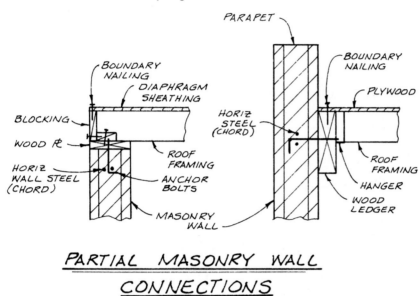

Figure 9.8   Typical connections of horizontal diaphragm to masonry walls.

The chord for the horizontal diaphragm usually consists of horizontal reinforcing steel in the wall at or near the level of the diaphragm. Attempts to design the wood top plate or ledger to function as the chord are usually considered inappropriate because of the larger stiffness of the masonry or concrete walls.

Development of the chord requires that the horizontal diaphragm be adequately attached (anchored) to the shearwalls. In this phase of the design, the spacing of anchor bolts, blocking, and nailing necessary to transfer the forces between these elements are considered. The *details in this sketch are not complete,* and these sketches (Fig. 9.8) are included here to illustrate the diaphragm chords. Anchorage connections are covered in detail in Chap. 15.

The double plate in wood walls and the horizontal steel in concrete and masonry walls are probably the two most common elements used as diaphragm chords. However, other building elements can be designed to serve as the chord. As an example of another type of chord member, consider a large window in the front longitudinal wall of a building. See Example 9.7.

The top plate in this longitudinal wall is not continuous. Here the window header supports the roof or floor framing directly, and the header may be designed to function as the chord. The header must be designed for both vertical loads and the appropriate combination of vertical loads and lateral forces. The connection of the header to the shearwall also must be designed. (*Note:* If a cripple stud wall occurs over the header and below the roof framing, a double top plate will be required over the header. In this case the plate can be designed as the chord throughout the length of the wall.)

EXAMPLE 9.7   Header Acting as a Chord

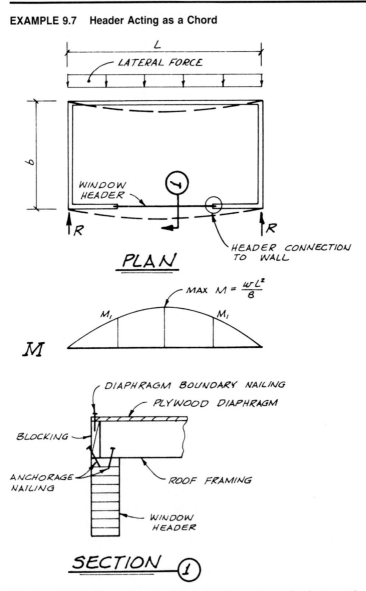

Figure 9.9   The header over an opening in a wall may be used as horizontal diaphragm chord.

Over the window the header serves as the chord. It must be capable of resisting the maximum chord force in addition to gravity loads. The maximum chord force is

$$T = C = \frac{\text{max. } M}{b}$$

The connection of the header to the wall must be designed for the chord force at that point:

$$T_1 = C_1 = \frac{M_1}{b}$$

NOTE: For simplicity, the examples in this book determine the chord forces using the dimension b as the width of the building. Theoretically b is the dimension between the centroids of the diaphragm chords, and the designer may choose to use this smaller, more conservative dimension.

The proper functioning of the chord requires that the horizontal diaphragm be effectively anchored to the chords and the supporting shearwalls. *Anchorage* can be provided by systematically designing for the transfer of gravity loads and lateral forces. This approach is introduced in Sec. 10.8, and the design for anchorage is covered in detail in Chap 15.

9.5 Design Problem: Horizontal Roof Diaphragm

In Example 9.8 a plywood roof diaphragm is designed for a one-story building. The design forces, diaphragm unit shears, and plywood thickness requirements for this building are all obtained from previous examples.

The maximum unit shear in the transverse direction is the basis for determining the blocking and *maximum* nailing requirements for the diaphragm. However, the shear in the diaphragm is not constant, and it is possible for the nail spacing to be increased in areas of reduced shear. Likewise, it is possible to omit the blocking where the actual shear in the diaphragm is less than the allowable shear for an *unblocked* diaphragm. The locations where these changes in diaphragm construction can take place are easily determined from the unit shear diaphragm.

The use of changes in nailing and blocking is fairly common, but these changes can introduce problems in construction and inspection. If changes in diaphragm construction are used, they should be clearly shown on the framing plan. In addition, if blocking is omitted in the center portion of the diaphragm, the requirements for some other type of edge support must be considered.

In this building the chord members are the horizontal reinforcing bars in the masonry walls, and a check of the chord stress in these bars is shown. The horizontal diaphragm is also checked for the lateral force in the longitudinal direction, and the effect of the change in the diaphragm load case on allowable unit shears is demonstrated.

EXAMPLE 9.8   Plywood Roof Diaphragm

This example considers a building that was analyzed for diaphragm unit shears in the examples in Sec. 3.5. Roof framing consists of light-frame wood trusses (top chords on edge) at 24 in. o.c. The plywood layout is given (Fig. 9.10a), and the shear and moment in the horizontal diaphragm are summarized below the framing plan. In this example, only the exterior walls are assumed to be shearwalls.

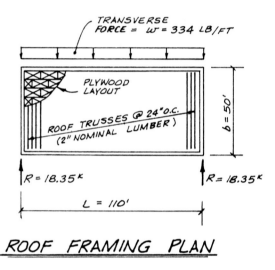

ROOF FRAMING PLAN

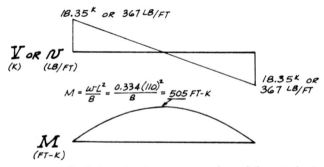

Figure 9.10a Roof plan showing transverse lateral force to horizontal diaphragm. Shear and moment diagrams for the diaphragm are also shown.

1. *Plywood for sheathing loads.*

$$\text{Roof LL} = 20 \text{ psf}$$

$$\text{Roof DL} = 8 \text{ psf}$$

Although the roof framing is different, the plywood sheathing spans the same distance (24 in.) as the sheathing in Fig. 8.15 (Sec. 8.10). In fact, since the roof is sloping in this example, the loads along the roof are even less.

The plywood choices given in Example 8.11, part 1, apply to the example at hand. These are

a. ⅜-in. C-D EXP 1 with a span rating of 24/0 with edge support

b. ¹⁵⁄₃₂-in. C-D EXP 1 with a span rating of 32/16 with edge support not required

For this problem the second alternative is selected.

> *Use* ¹⁵⁄₃₂-in. C-D EXP 1

2. *Diaphragm nailing.* Although ¹⁵⁄₃₂-in. C-D is available in STRUCTURAL I, the STRUCTURAL I upgrade will not be used in this problem. If a substantially higher unit shear were involved *or* if the nailing could be considerably reduced, then STRUCTURAL I should be considered.

Because the 2× top chord of the light-frame trusses is turned on edge, the 10d nails develop adequate penetration. If the 2× top chords were turned flat, the reduced nail penetration of 1½ in. would have to be taken into account (Sec. 9.3).

Plywood *load case* (transverse lateral force):

The lateral force is *perpendicular to the continuous panel joint* and *perpendicular to the unblocked edge.*

∴ load case 1

If blocking is not used, the maximum allowable unit shear is

$$\text{Allow. } v = 255 \text{ lb/ft}$$

This comes from UBC Table 25-J-1 for ¹⁵⁄₃₂-in. plywood (not STRUCTURAL I) in an unblocked diaphragm, load case 1, 2-in.-nominal framing, and 10d nails. The actual shear is greater than this allowable:

$$v = 367 \text{ lb/ft} > 255 \qquad NG$$

An increased allowable shear can be obtained by increasing the plywood thickness or using STRUCTURAL I plywood. Another method of increasing shear capacity used here is to provide blocking and increased nailing (i.e., reduced nail spacing). In order to develop adequate nail penetration, blocking will be turned on edge (not flat). As an alternative, the blocking can be used flat and the tabulated allowable diaphragm shears reduced. From the blocked diaphragm portion of UBC Table 25-J-1, the following design is chosen:

> *Use* ¹⁵⁄₃₂-in. C-D EXP 1 with 10d common nails
> at 4 in. o.c. boundary*
> 6 in. o.c. all other plywood edges
> 12 in. o.c. field
> Blocking required.
> Use 2 × 4 minimum (on edge).

$$\text{Allow. } v = 385 \text{ lb/ft} > 367 \qquad OK$$

---

*Because this diaphragm is load case 1, the 4-in. nail spacing is required at the diaphragm boundary only. The 6-in. nail spacing is used at continuous panel joints as well as other plywood edges.

The above nailing and blocking requirements can safely be used throughout the entire diaphragm because these were determined for the maximum unit shear. The variation of diaphragm shear can be shown on a sketch. The *unit shear diagram* is the total shear diagram divided by the diaphragm width (Fig. 9.10*b*).

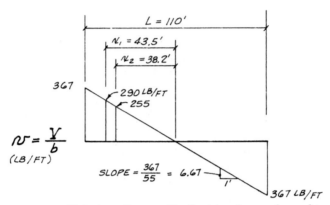

Figure 9.10*b* Unit shear diagram. Similar triangles may be used to determine locations of possible changes in diaphragm construction.

Some designers prefer to take into account the reduced unit shears toward the center of the diaphragm (away from the shearwall reactions). If this is done, the nail spacing can be increased to the Code maximum allowed spacing (that is, 6 in. o.c. at all edges including the diaphragm boundary) where the shear drops off to the corresponding allowable shear for this nailing. This location can be determined by similar triangles. For example,

$$\text{Allow. } v = 290 \text{ lb/ft}$$

when the nail spacing at the diaphragm boundary is 6 in. o.c. and blocking is provided. Then

$$x_1 = \frac{290}{6.67} = 43.5 \text{ ft}$$

This refinement can be carried one step further, and the location can be determined where blocking can be omitted:

$$\text{Allow. } v = 255 \text{ lb/ft} \quad \text{for unblocked diaphragm}$$

Then

$$x_2 = \frac{255}{6.67} = 38.2 \text{ ft}$$

If these changes in diaphragm construction are used, the locations calculated above should be rounded off to some convenient dimensions. These locations and the required types of construction in the various segments of the diaphragm must be clearly shown on the roof framing plan. In this regard, the designer must weigh the savings in labor and materials gained by the changes described above against the possibility that the diaphragm may be constructed improperly in the field. The more variations in nailing and blocking, the greater the chance for error in the field. Increased nail spacing and omission of blocking can represent substantial savings in labor and materials, but inspection becomes increasingly important.

3. *Chord.* Axial force in chord is obtained by resolving the diaphragm moment into a couple:

$$T = C = \frac{M}{b} = \frac{505}{50} = 10.1 \text{ k}$$

Depending on the type of wall system, various items can be designed to function as the *chord* member.

In this example, the walls are made from 8-in. grouted concrete block units, and the horizontal wall steel (two #5 bars) will be checked for chord stresses. (Examples of wood chords are covered elsewhere.)

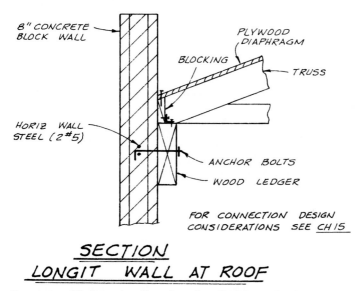

**SECTION
LONGIT WALL AT ROOF**

Figure 9.10c Horizontal wall steel used as diaphragm chord.

The tension chord is critical, and the stress in the horizontal wall steel can be calculated as the chord force divided by the area of steel. The minimum allowable stress in masonary wall reinforcing steel is 20 ksi under normal loads, and this can be increased by a factor of 1.33 for short-term forces (wind or seismic).

Stress in steel:

$$f_s = \frac{T}{A_s} = \frac{10.1}{2 \times 0.31} = 16.3 \text{ ksi}$$

Allow. $f_s = 20 \times 1.33 = 26.6$ ksi > 16.3 *OK*

The design of other wall-reinforcing steel is a problem in masonary design and is beyond the scope of this book. Steps must be taken to ensure that cross-grain bending (Example 6.1) in the ledger does not occur. The design of anchor bolts and other connections for attaching the horizontal diaphragm to the shearwall is covered in Chap. 15.

4. *Longitudinal lateral force.* Calculation of the lateral force in the longitudinal direction was not given in the examples in Sec. 3.5. However, the method used is similar to that illustrated for the transverse force. The longitudinal force and the corresponding shear and moment diagrams are shown in Fig. 9.10*d*.

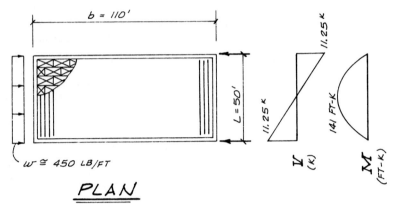

Figure 9.10*d* Roof plan showing longitudinal lateral force to horizontal diaphragm. Shear and moment diagrams are also shown.

The unit shear in a horizontal diaphragm is often critical in the transverse direction. However, the longitudinal shear should be checked, especially if changes in nailing occur. In any event, the longitudinal direction must be analyzed for anchorage forces for connecting the diaphragm and shearwall.

Unit shear:

$$v = \frac{V}{b} = \frac{11,250}{110} = 102 \text{ lb/ft}$$

The load in the longitudinal direction is *parallel* to the *continuous panel joint* and *parallel* to the *unblocked edge*.

∴ load case 3

If the blocking is omitted in the center portion of the diaphragm (up to 38.2 ft on either side of the centerline), the allowable unit shear for an unblocked diaphragm must be used. From UBC Table 25-J-1,

Allow. v = 190 lb/ft > 102   *OK*

If the unit shear in the longitudinal direction had exceeded 190 lb/ft, then blocking would have been required for the longitudinal lateral force. When blocking is required for load cases other than cases 1 and 2, the continuous panel joints must be nailed with the same spacing as the diaphragm boundary (UBC Table 25-J-1). The chord force in the transverse walls is less than the chord force in the longitudinal walls:

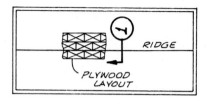

PLAN

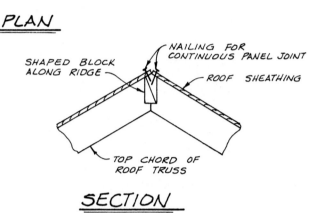

SECTION

Figure 9.10e Horizontal diaphragm detail at ridge.

$$T = C = \frac{M}{b} = \frac{141}{110} = 1.28 \text{ k} < 10.1 \text{ k}$$

∴ two #5 bars   *OK* for chord around entire building

5. *Nailing along ridge.* The plywood skin in this building is attached directly to the top chord of the light-frame wood roof trusses (see Fig. 9.10e). These trusses probably have sufficient strength and stiffness to maintain diaphragm continuity at the ridge. However, it is desirable to provide a positive attachment of the sheathing through doubled $2 \times$ blocking or a shaped $3 \times$ or $4 \times$ block.

See Ref. 8.2 for a discussion of diaphragm design considerations at ridges in steeply pitched roofs.

9.6 Distribution of Lateral Forces in a Shearwall

If a shearwall has door or window openings, the total lateral force in the wall is carried by the effective segments in the wall. In wood shearwalls these effective segments are known as *shear panels* (or shearwalls), and in concrete and masonry walls they are referred to as *wall piers*. The designer must understand how to distribute the total force to these resisting elements so that the unit wall shears can be calculated.

The procedures for designing wood shearwalls are given in Chap. 10, but the method for distributing the lateral force is covered at this time. The distribution needs to be understood at this point because it is used to determine the magnitude of the force for the horizontal diaphragm *strut*. A different procedure is used to distribute the horizontal diaphragm reaction to wood shearwalls and concrete or masonry shearwalls.

In a wood-frame shearwall, the most common approach is to assume that the unit shear is uniform throughout the total length of all shear panels. Thus the force in a given panel is in direct proportion to its length. See Example 9.9. The unit shear in one panel is the same as the unit shear in all other panels.

In order for this distribution to be reasonably correct, the wall must be constructed so that the panels function as separate shear-resisting elements. The height-to-width ratio h/b should be less than or equal to $3\frac{1}{2}$ for blocked plywood shear panels. In addition, the shear panels are assumed to all have the same height. This is obtained by using continuous full-height studs at each end of the shear panels. The panels must all deflect laterally the same amount. This is accomplished by tying the panels together with the strut.

EXAMPLE 9.9   Distribution of Shear in a Wood Shearwall

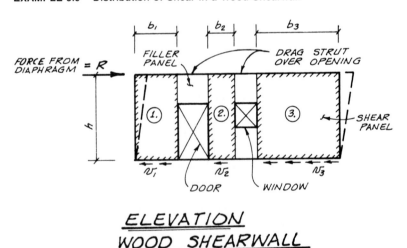

ELEVATION
WOOD SHEARWALL

Figure 9.11 Unit shears in a wood-frame shearwall are normally assumed to be uniform.

In a wood shearwall, the wall is usually assumed to be made up of *separate* shear panels. The shear panels are connected together so that they deflect laterally the same amount at the horizontal diaphragm level. Drag strut or tie members provide the connection between the shear panels.

The three shear panels in the wall shown in Fig. 9.11 all have the same height h. This behavior results from the use of double full-height studs at both ends of the shear panels and appropriate shearwall nailing (Chap. 10). Filler panels (wall elements above and below openings) may be nailed less heavily (i.e., with the Code minimum nailing) to further isolate the shear panels.

For the typical wood shearwall, the resistance to the applied lateral force is assumed to be uniform throughout the combined length of the shear panels. Thus

$$v_1 = v_2 = v_3 = \frac{R}{\Sigma b}$$

Several types of load resistance develop in a wall subjected to a lateral force. These include bending resistance and shear resistance. For wood-frame walls constructed as described above, the shear resistance is the significant form, and the unit shear in this case approaches a uniform distribution.

In buildings with reinforced-concrete or masonry shearwalls, the distribution of forces to the various elements in the wall differs from the uniform distribution assumed for wood shearwalls. Concrete and masonry walls may have significant combined bending and shear resistance. This combined resistance is measured by the *relative rigidity* of the various piers in the wall. Under a lateral force the piers are forced to undergo the same lateral deformation. The force required to deflect a long pier is larger than the force calculated on the basis of its length only.

Thus, in a concrete or masonry wall, the *unit shear* in a wider pier is greater than the unit shear in a narrower wall segment. The relative rigidity is a function of the height-to-width ratio h/b of the pier and not just its width. The relative rigidity and the question of force distribution are related to the *stiffness* of a structural element: The stiffer (more rigid) the element, the greater the force it "attracts." See Example 9.10. The calculation of relative rigidities for these wall elements is a concrete or masonry design problem and is beyond the scope of this text.

EXAMPLE 9.10   Distribution of Shear in a Concrete or Masonry Shearwall

In a concrete or masonry wall, the "piers" are analyzed to determine their *relative rigidities*. The smaller the height-to-width ratio h/b of a pier, the larger the relative rigidity. The larger the relative rigidity, the greater the percentage of total force R carried by the pier. Pier 2 in the wall shown in Fig. 9.12 has a greater rigidity and a greater unit shear (not just total shear) than pier 1; that is,

$$v_2 > v_1$$

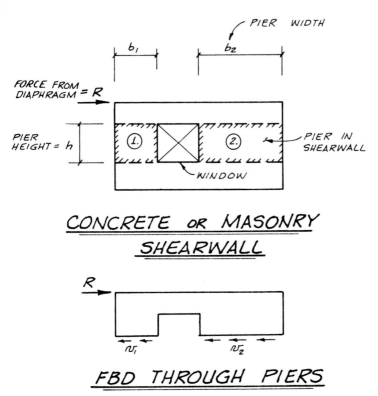

Figure 9.12 Unit shears in a concrete or masonry shearwall depend on relative rigidities of wall piers.

In buildings with concrete or masonry walls, the loads over openings in the walls can be supported in two different ways. In the first system, there is a concrete or masonry wall element over the openings in the wall. See Fig. 9.13a in Example 9.11. This element can be designed as a beam to carry the gravity loads across the opening. Concrete and masonry beams of this type are known as *lintels*. In the second case, a wood *header* may be used to span the opening (Fig. 9.13b).

EXAMPLE 9.11   Lintel and Header between Shearwalls

A concrete or masonry lintel, or a wood (or steel) header, can be used to span over an opening in a wall (see Fig. 9.13). The member over the opening must be designed for both vertical loads and lateral forces. Load combinations are

1. Vertical loads (DL + RLL) or (DL + SL).
2. Combined vertical and lateral (RLL can be omitted, but all or part of the snow load is required).
   a. For lateral forces parallel to the wall, the force in the header is the *strut* force.
   b. For lateral forces perpendicular to the wall, the force in the header is the diaphragm *chord* force.

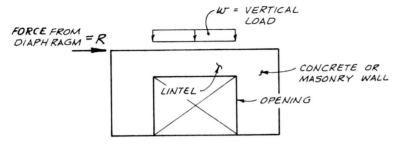

Figure 9.13a Wall with concrete or masonry lintel.

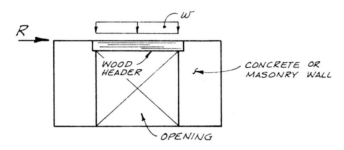

Figure 9.13b Wall with wood header.

A distinction is made between these systems because in the first case the load from the horizontal diaphragm is transmitted to the shearwalls through the lintel, and the diaphragm design is unaffected. In the case of the wood header, however, the unit shear from the horizontal diaphragm must be transmitted through the header/strut into the shearwalls. The load combinations required for the design of this member are given in Example 9.11.

In summary, the distribution of the *unit shear* in a wall subjected to a lateral force will be as follows:

1. Wood shearwalls—uniform distribution to all shear panels

2. Concrete and masonry shearwalls—distribution is a function of the relative rigidities of the wall piers

For problems in this book involving concrete or masonry walls, it is assumed that the distribution of wall forces and the unit shears are known by previous analysis.

9.7 Drag Strut Forces

The perimeter members of a horizontal diaphragm that are parallel to the applied lateral force are the struts. These members are also known as *collectors, drag members,* or *ties,* and their function is illustrated in Fig. 9.4 (Sec. 9.2). Essentially the strut pulls or drags the unit shear in an unsupported segment of a horizontal diaphragm (the portion over an opening in a shearwall, for example) into the supporting elements of the shearwall.

The members in a building that serve as the *struts* are typically the same members that are used as the *chords* for the lateral force in the perpendicular direction. Thus, the design of the chord and the strut for a given wall may simply involve the design of the same member for different forces. In fact, for a given perimeter member, the chord force is compared with the strut force, and the design is based on the critical force.

The wood design principles for struts and chords are covered in Chap. 7. These members are either tension or compression members, and they may or may not have bending. Bending may result from vertical loads, as in the header in Example 9.11. Connections are also an important part of the collector design. The member itself may be sufficiently strong, but little is gained unless the strut is adequately connected to the supporting shearwall elements. The design of connections is addressed in later chapters, but the calculation of the force in the drag strut is covered now.

The building in Fig. 9.4 has an end shearwall with an opening located in the *center* of the wall. This presents a simple problem for the determination of the drag strut forces because the total force is shared *equally* by both shear panels. This would be true for the equal-length piers in a concrete or masonry wall also. The force in the drag strut is maximum at each end of the wall opening. This maximum force is easily calculated as the unit shear in the horizontal diaphragm times one-half the length of the wall opening.

The force in the strut varies linearly throughout the length of the strut. At one end of the opening the strut is in tension, and at the other end it is in compression. Since the lateral force can come from either direction, the ends may be stressed in either tension or compression. The magnitude of the drag strut force in the two shear panels is not shown in Fig. 9.4. However, the force in a shearwall decreases from a maximum at the wall opening to zero at the outside end of the shearwall.

A somewhat more involved problem occurs when an opening is not symmetrically located in the length of the wall. See Example 9.12. Here a greater portion of the total wall load is carried by the longer shear panel. A correspondingly larger percentage of the unsupported diaphragm shear over the opening must be transmitted by the drag strut to the longer panel.

The magnitude of the force at some point in the strut can be determined in several ways. Two approaches are shown in Example 9.12. The *first method* simply involves summing forces on a free-body diagram (FBD) of the wall. The cut is taken at the point where the strut force is required. The other forces acting on the FBD are the unit shears in the roof diaphragm and the unit shears in the shearwall.

The *second method* provides a plot of the force in the drag strut along the length of the building. With this diagram the strut force at any point can be readily determined.

The procedure illustrated in Example 9.12 for plotting the drag strut force can be used for wood or concrete or masonry shearwalls. The only difference is that for masonry or concrete walls, the unit shear in the walls will probably be different.

The two methods presented in Example 9.12 graphically demonstrate the functioning of a drag strut. These methods are reasonable for the example shown. However, when there are multiple wall openings, some degree of engineering judgment must be exercised in determining the design force for the drag strut.

EXAMPLE 9.12   Calculation of Force in Drag Strut

Determine the magnitude of the drag strut force throughout the length of the front wall in the building shown in Fig. 9.14a. The walls are wood-frame construction.

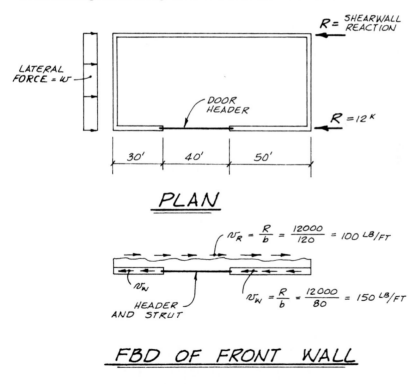

PLAN

FBD OF FRONT WALL

v_R = ROOF DIAPHRAGM UNIT SHEAR

v_W = SHEAR WALL UNIT SHEAR

Figure 9.14a Free body diagram of front longitudinal wall. The forces shown are (1) unit shear in roof diaphragm v_R, (2) unit shear in shearwalls v_W.

Method 1:   FBD Approach

The force in the strut at any point can be determined by cutting the member and summing forces. Two examples are shown (Fig. 9.14*b* and *c*). One cut is taken through the header, and the other is taken at a point in the wall.

   a. Strut force at point *A* (40 ft from left wall):

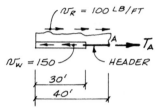

Figure 9.14*b*   Free body diagram of front longitudinal wall taken at point *A*.

$$\Sigma F_x = 0$$

$$T_A + 100(40) - 150(30) = 0$$

$$T_A = +500 \text{ lb} \qquad \text{(tension)}$$

NOTE: The lateral force can act toward the right or left. If the direction is reversed, the strut force at *A* will be in compression.

   b. Strut force at point *B* (100 ft from left wall):

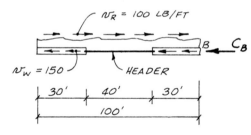

Figure 9.14*c*   Free body diagram of front longitudinal wall taken at point *B*.

$$\Sigma F_x = 0$$

$$C_B + 150(30 + 30) - 100(100) = 0$$

$$C_B = 1000 \text{ lb} \qquad \text{(compression)}$$

NOTE: This force would be tension if the direction of the lateral force were reversed.

Method 2:   Drag Strut Force Diagram

Construction of the strut force diagram (see Fig. 9.14*d*) involves
   a. Drawing the unit shear diagrams for the roof diaphragm and shearwalls.
   b. Drawing the *net* unit shear diagram by subtracting the diagrams in *a.*
   c. Constructing the strut force diagram by using the *areas* of the net unit shear diagram as *changes* in the magnitude of the strut force. The strut force is zero at the outside ends of the building.

The relationship between the net unit shear diagram and the strut force diagram is similar to the relationship between the shear and moment diagrams for a beam.

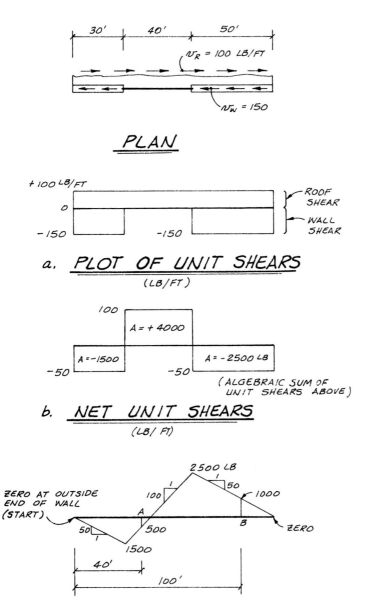

Figure 9.14d   Drag strut force diagram. The final plot (c. strut force) shows variation in the magnitude of the strut force over the entire length of the front longitudinal wall.

NOTE: Signs of forces are not important because forces can reverse direction.

The values obtained by taking FBDs at points A and B can be verified by similar triangles on the strut force diagram.

A third approach to strut force calculation is to determine the maximum force that might develop in a collector regardless of its location along the length of a wall. This force can be taken as the *unit shear in the horizontal diaphragm times the length of the wall opening.* If this is done for the building in Example 9.12, a strut force of $T = 100 \times 40 = 4000$ lb is obtained. Connections at both ends of the strut as well as the member itself would then conservatively be designed for this force.

Although a considerably higher design force is determined in this example (4000 lb versus 2500 and 1500 lb), the method has the advantage of being conservative and easy to apply. When there are multiple openings in a wall, the designer can extend this method to determine a very conservative value for the drag strut force by taking the unit shear in the horizontal diaphragm times the sum of the lengths of the wall openings. If the force obtained in this manner is overly conservative, a more detailed analysis can be made.

Once the strut forces have been determined, they can be compared with the chord forces at corresponding points along the wall to determine the critical design condition.

9.8   Diaphragm Deflections

The deflection of a horizontal diaphragm has been illustrated in a number of sketches in Chap. 9. This topic is the object of some concern because the walls that are attached to (actually supported by) the horizontal diaphragm are forced to deflect along with the diaphragm. See Example 9.13. If the walls are constructed so they can undergo or "accommodate" these deformations without failure, there is little need for concern. However, a potential problem exists when the deflection is large or when the walls are constructed so rigidly that they can tolerate little deflection. In this case, the diaphragm imposes a deflection on the wall that may cause the wall to be overstressed.

There are at this time two methods used to account for diaphragm deflections. The method that is the most widely used is basically a rule of thumb, in that no attempt is made to calculate the magnitude of the actual deflection. This method makes use of the span-to-width ratio of the diaphragm. In this simple approach, the span-to-width ratio L/b is checked to be less than some acceptable limit. For example, the Code sets an upper limit on the span-to-width ratio for horizontal plywood diaphragms of 4.

Thus, this approach says that if the *proportions* of the diaphragm are *reasonable*, deflection will not be excessive. Although no numerical value for the deflection of the diaphragm is calculated, this method has traditionally been applied. It is probably an acceptable approach for most wood-frame buildings, and many designers consider it to be sufficient for buildings with wood horizontal diaphragms and concrete or masonry walls.

EXAMPLE 9.13   Diaphragm Deflections and Span-to-Width Ratios

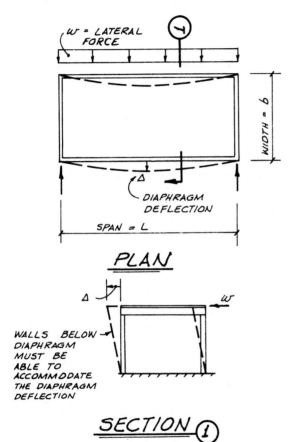

Figure 9.15 Plan and section views showing the deflections caused by lateral force on horizontal diaphragm.

Wood-frame walls are capable of accommodating larger deflections than are more rigid wall systems such as concrete or masonry.

Diaphragm Proportions

One method of controlling deflection is to limit the span-to-width ratio L/b for the diaphragm. For horizontal plywood diaphragms, $L/b \leq 4.0$. For other types of wood diaphragms, see UBC Table 25-I.

The second technique of accounting for diaphragm deflections is to calculate a numerical value for the deflection. The total deflection that occurs in an ordinary beam is made up of two deflection components: bending and shear. However, for most practical beams, the shear deflection is negligible, and only the bending deflection is calculated.

In a horizontal diaphragm, the total deflection is the sum of the deflections caused by a number of factors in addition to bending and shear. All these factors may contribute a significant amount to the total deflection. In the normally accepted formula, the deflection of a horizontal diaphragm is made up of four parts:

$$\text{Total } \Delta = \Delta_1 + \Delta_2 + \Delta_3 + \Delta_4$$

where Δ_1 = bending deflection

Δ_2 = shear deflection

Δ_3 = deflection due to nail slip (deformation)

Δ_4 = deflection due to slip in chord connection splices

The methods used to evaluate the various deflection components are described in Ref. 14.11 and are not included here. It should be noted that this formula applies only to *blocked* diaphragms. Attempts are being made to develop appropriate deflection calculation procedures for all types of diaphragms.

Reference 5.5 suggests that the basic elements in the existing formula should be generalized to handle a variety of diaphragm loading conditions. This reference also suggests an alternate method for calculating the deflection due to nail slip.

One problem with applying the deflection calculation is that there are no definite criteria against which the calculated deflection must be checked. The simple deflection limits used for ordinary beams (such as $L/180$ and $L/360$) are not applied to diaphragm deflections. These types of limits do not evaluate the effects that the deformations impose on the walls supported by the diaphragm.

Reference 10 suggests a possible deflection criterion for diaphragms that support concrete or masonry walls, but generally the evaluation of the calculated deflection is left to the judgment of the designer. It should be noted that the limits on the span-to-width ratio given in UBC Table 25-I are a requirement of the Code, and they must be satisfied.

In this introduction to diaphragm design, the limits on the span-to-width ratio will be relied upon for controlling deflections. As noted, this is fairly common practice in ordinary building design. For those interested in examining the problem of diaphragm deflections in greater detail, information is available from APA and in Refs. 8.2 and 8.3.

9.9 Diaphragms with Interior Shearwalls

All of the diaphragms considered up to this point have been supported by shearwalls that are the exterior walls of the building. Although it is convenient to introduce horizontal diaphragms by using this basic system, many buildings make use of interior shearwalls in addition to exterior shearwalls. In this case the roof or floor assemblage is assumed to act as a number of separate horizontal diaphragms. See Example 9.14.

Because the diaphragms are assumed to be separate elements, they are treated as simply supported beams that span between the respective shearwall supports. Thus the *shear in the diaphragm* can be determined using the methods previously covered for buildings with exterior shearwalls. The difference is that the span of the diaphragm is now measured between adjacent parallel walls and not simply between the exterior walls of the building. With these separate diaphragms there will be different unit shears in the diaphragms unless the spans and loads happen to be the same for the various diaphragms.

The *forces to the shearwalls* are calculated as the sum of the reactions from the horizontal diaphragms that are supported by the shearwall. Thus, for an exterior wall the shearwall force is the reaction of one horizontal diaphragm. For an interior shearwall, however, the force to the wall is the sum of the diaphragm reactions on either side of the wall.

The chord force for the diaphragms is determined in the same manner as for a building with exterior shearwalls. The moments in the respective diaphragms are calculated as simple beam moments. Once the chord forces are determined, the chords are designed in accordance with appropriate procedures for the type of member and materials used.

EXAMPLE 9.14   Horizontal Diaphragm with Interior Shearwall

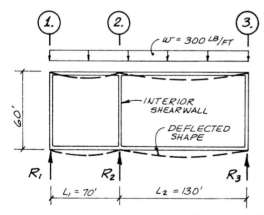

Figure 9.16a Plan view of building with interior and exterior shearwalls. Deflected shapes of assumed separate horizontal diaphragms are shown.

Determine the unit shear in the horizontal diaphragm and shearwalls in the building shown in Fig. 9.16*a* for the transverse lateral force of 300 lb/ft. Also calculate the diaphragm chord forces.

Horizontal Diaphragm

Flexible horizontal diaphragms are assumed to span between the exterior and interior shearwalls. The continuity at the interior wall is disregarded, and two simply supported diaphragms are analyzed for internal unit shears. See Fig. 9.16*b*.

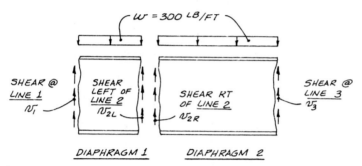

Figure 9.16b Free body diagrams of horizontal diaphragms.

$$V_1 = V_{2L} = \frac{wL_1}{2} = \frac{(0.300)70}{2} = 10.5 \text{ k}$$

$$v_1 = v_{2L} = \frac{V}{b} = \frac{10,500}{60} = 175 \text{ lb/ft}$$

$$V_{2R} = V_3 = \frac{wL_2}{2} = \frac{(0.300)130}{2} = 19.5 \text{ k}$$

$$v_{2R} = v_3 = \frac{V}{b} = \frac{19,500}{60} = 325 \text{ lb/ft}$$

The nailing requirements for each diaphragm can be determined separately on the basis of the respective unit shears. Note that both diaphragms 1 and 2 will have their own nailing requirements, including boundary nailing along line 2. These nailing provisions must be clearly shown on the design plans.

As an alternative to double boundary nailing, it is possible to design the nailing along line 2 for the combined shear from diaphragms 1 and 2:

$$v_2 = \frac{10,500 + 19,500}{60} = 500 \text{ lb/ft}$$

Shearwalls

The unit shears in the shearwalls can be determined by calculating the reactions carried by the shearwalls. Shearwall reactions must balance the loads (shears) from the horizontal diaphragm. See Fig. 9.16c.

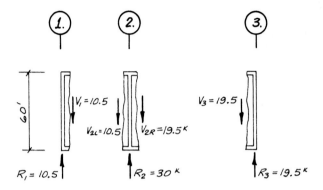

Figure 9.16c Plan view showing free body diagrams of the three transverse shearwalls.

Unit wall shears (no openings in walls):

$$v_1 = \frac{R}{b} = \frac{10,500}{60} = 175 \text{ lb/ft}$$

$$v_2 = \frac{30,000}{60} = 500 \text{ lb/ft}$$

$$v_3 = \frac{19,500}{60} = 325 \text{ lb/ft}$$

Alternate shearwall reaction calculation:

Because the diaphragms are assumed to be simply supported, the shearwall reactions can also be determined using the tributary widths to the shearwalls. See Fig. 9.16d.

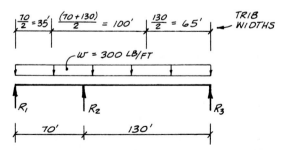

Figure 9.16d Lateral force diagram showing tributary widths to shearwalls (schematic similar to Fig. 9.16a).

$$R_1 = (0.300)35 = 10.5 \text{ k}$$

$$R_2 = (0.300)100 = 30 \text{ k}$$

$$R_3 = (0.300)65 = 19.5 \text{ k}$$

NOTE: The calculated unit shears for the shearwalls are from the horizontal diaphragm reactions. If the lateral force is a seismic force, there will be an additional wall shear generated by the dead load of the shearwall itself (Chap. 3).

Diaphragm Chord Forces

The distribution of force in the chord follows the shape of the simple beam moment diagram for the diaphragms. See Fig. 9.16*e*.

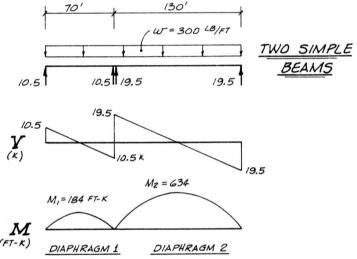

Figure 9.16e   Moment diagrams for determining the chord forces in the horizontal diaphragms.

$$T_1 = C_1 = \frac{M_1}{b} = \frac{184}{60} = 3.1 \text{ k}$$

$$T_2 = C_2 = \frac{M_2}{b} = \frac{634}{60} = 10.6 \text{ k}$$

The simple span procedure for handling horizontal diaphragms and interior shearwalls illustrated in Example 9.14 is probably the most common approach used to design the general class of buildings covered in this book. However, Ref. 8.2 suggests that the continuity of the horizontal diaphragm at an interior shearwall should not be disregarded. It also suggests that the relative rigidities of the diaphragm and the supporting shearwalls should be taken into account. See Refs. 8.2 and 8.3 for these proposed procedures and other advanced topics relating to the design of wood horizontal diaphragms. Additional diaphragm research is needed to better understand the interaction of the various components in a lateral-force-resisting system.

The 1991 UBC requires additional design considerations for seismic forces on buildings that are *structurally irregular*. An example of an irregularity is an interior shearwall on the second floor of a two-story building that is offset horizontally from the interior shearwall on the first floor. This and other types of seismic irregularities are covered in Chap. 16.

9.10   Interior Shearwalls with Drag Struts

If a horizontal diaphragm is supported by an interior shearwall that is not the full width of the building, or if there are openings in the wall, a drag tie will be required. As with the collectors in exterior walls (Sec. 9.7), the drag strut will transfer the unit shear from the unsupported portion of the horizontal diaphragm into the shearwall. In the case of an interior shearwall, the drag force will be the sum of the forces from the horizontal diaphragms on both sides of the shearwall. See Example 9.15.

The distribution of the force in the strut throughout its length can be plotted from the areas of the net unit shear diagram. From this plot it can be seen that the critical axial force in the drag strut is at the point where it connects to the shearwall. The member and the connection must be designed for this force. In addition, the effects of combined gravity loads and lateral forces must be considered.

EXAMPLE 9.15   Building with Interior Drag Strut

The building of Example 9.14 is modified in this example so that the interior shearwall is not the full width of the building. Determine the drag strut force for the interior shearwall. See Fig. 9.17.

$$\text{Unit shear in shearwall:} \quad v_2 = \frac{R}{b} = \frac{30{,}000}{40} = 750 \text{ lb/ft}$$

The interior shearwall carries the reactions of the horizontal diaphragms. Part of this force is transferred to the shearwall by the drag strut. The maximum drag strut force is 10 k and is obtained from the drag strut force diagram in Fig. 9.17.

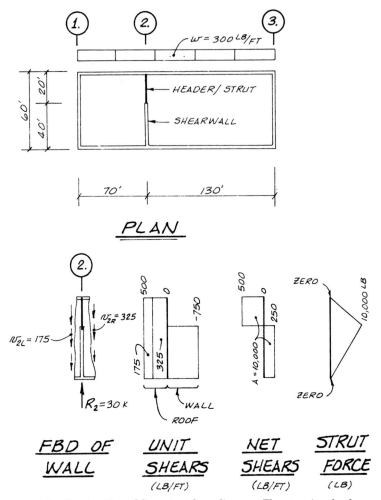

Figure 9.17 Construction of drag strut force diagram. The steps involved are similar to those introduced in Fig. 9.14d.

Not all interior walls are necessarily shearwalls. For an interior wood-frame wall to function as a shearwall, it must have sheathing of adequate strength, and it must be nailed to the framing so that the shear resistance is developed. In addition, the height-to-width ratio h/b of the shear panel must be less than the limits given in UBC Table 25-I. (Procedures for designing shearwalls are covered in Chap. 10.) The diaphragm must also be connected to the shearwall so that the shears are transferred.

In addition to these strength requirements, some consideration should be given to the relative widths and locations of the various walls. To illustrate this point, consider an interior wall with a width that is very small in comparison with the adjacent parallel wall. See Example 9.16.

Because of the large width b_e of the right exterior wall, it will be a more rigid support for the horizontal diaphragm than the small interior wall. The large rigidity of the exterior wall will "attract" and carry a large portion of the lateral force tributary to *both* walls.

Because of this, it would be better practice to ignore the small interior wall and design the nearby exterior wall for the entire tributary lateral force. The small interior wall should then be sheathed and nailed lightly to ensure that it does not interfere with the diaphragm span.

Attempts can be made to compare the relative rigidities of the various shearwalls. This is similar to the rigidity analysis of the various piers in a single concrete or masonry wall (Sec. 9.6). However, in wood-frame construction the question of whether to consider a wall as an "effective" shearwall is normally a matter of judgment. The relative widths of the shearwalls and their proximity to other effective walls are used in making this determination.

EXAMPLE 9.16   Effectiveness of Interior Shearwalls

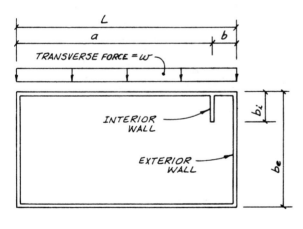

PLAN

Figure 9.18 Comparison of effective shearwalls.

Using tributary widths, the *calculated* load to the interior shearwall is

$$R_i = \left(\frac{a}{2} + \frac{b}{2}\right)w$$

The load to the right exterior wall would be much smaller:

$$R_e = \left(\frac{b}{2}\right)w$$

Under *actual* loading, however, the load carried by the right exterior wall will approach

$$R_e = \left(\frac{L}{2}\right)w$$

The reason for this is that the large exterior wall is more rigid than the interior wall. Thus, in order to distribute the force from the horizontal diaphragm to the walls using tributary widths, the shearwalls must be *effective*.

The effectiveness of a wall in providing true shearwall action depends on several factors, including

1. Relative lengths of the walls. If b_i and b_e were more nearly equal, the interior wall would be more effective.
2. Relative location of the walls. If b were larger in comparison to a, the interior shearwall would also begin to function as a separate support.

The evaluation of shearwall effectiveness is, to a large extent, a matter of judgment. Walls which are judged to be ineffective (i.e., ignored as shearwalls) should be constructed so that they do not interfere with the assumed action of the diaphragm.

9.11   Diaphragm Flexibility

Horizontal diaphragms can be classified according to their tendency to deflect under load. Concrete floor or roof slabs deflect very little under lateral forces and are defined as *rigid* diaphragms. Wood diaphragms, on the other hand, deflect considerably more and are classified as *flexible* diaphragms. There are other systems which classify diaphragms into additional categories such as semirigid, semiflexible, and very flexible (Ref. 10). For purposes of this text, only the basic classification of rigid and flexible diaphragms is considered.

The purpose of introducing these terms is to describe the differences between the distribution of lateral forces for the two types of diaphragms. In addition to describing the distribution of lateral forces to shearwalls, there is a second reason for introducing the classifications of *flexible* and *rigid* horizontal diaphragms. The 1991 UBC requires a significant increase in the anchorage force between walls and *flexible* horizontal diaphragms. Footnote 3 of UBC Table 23-P requires that the normal seismic force for anchoring walls and partitions (F_p) be increased 50 percent in the *center half* of the span of a flexible diaphragm. The reader can develop a feel for the reasoning behind this increase by reviewing the deflected shape of the flexible diaphragm in Fig. 9.15 (Sec. 9.8). The relatively large deflection near the center of a large flexible diaphragm causes a greater earthquake response that attempts to separate the walls from the diaphragm. This anchorage problem is addressed in detail in Chap. 15, and the remaining portion of this section deals with the distribution of lateral forces to shearwalls.

With a rigid diaphragm there is a torsional moment that must be considered. A *torsional moment* is developed if the centroid of the applied lateral force does not coincide with the center of resistance (center of rigidity) of the supporting shearwalls. See Example 9.17. The effect of the torsional moment is to cause wall shears in addition to those which would be developed if no eccentricity existed. This is essentially a combined stress problem in that shears are the result of direct loading and an eccentric moment.

EXAMPLE 9.17   Comparison of Flexible and Rigid Diaphragms

Basic classification of horizontal diaphragms:

1. Flexible, such as a wood roof or floor system
2. Rigid, such as a concrete roof or floor slab

Forces to supporting walls are simple beam (tributary) reactions for a *flexible* diaphragm (Fig. 9.19*a*).

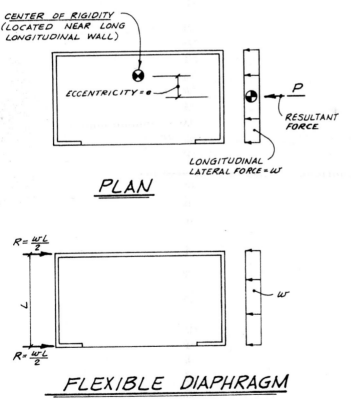

Figure 9.19a Distribution of lateral force in a flexible diaphragm. •

Forces to walls supporting a *rigid* diaphragm are the sum of the forces due to direct shear (as for the flexible diaphragm in Fig. 9.19*a*) and those due to the torsional moment *Pe* (Fig. 9.19*b*).

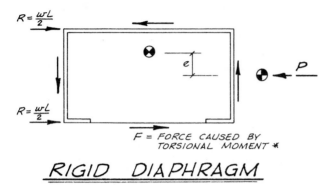

Figure 9.19*b*   Distribution of lateral force in a rigid diaphragm.

*Note that the force due to rotation adds to the direct shear force in the open front wall and subtracts from the force in the rear wall. Only the increases are considered in design. Calculation of torsional forces in buildings with rigid diaphragms is beyond the scope of this book.

It should be noted that the Code does not permit wood framing to support the dead load of concrete roof or floor slabs (except nonstructural coverings less than 4 in. thick). Thus, rigid diaphragms of reinforced concrete will not be supported by wood wall systems.

Wood diaphragms are, in most cases, assumed to be flexible, and rotation is usually not considered. Here the lateral force to the supporting shearwalls is simply determined using the respective tributary widths to the walls (Sec. 9.9). The force is then distributed to the various resisting elements in the wall by the methods covered in Sec. 9.6.

In certain wood buildings rotation may be used to resist lateral forces. This occurs in buildings with a side that is essentially open. In other words, there is no segment of a wall of sufficient length to provide an "effective" shear panel. See Example 9.18. The only way that a building of this nature can be designed is to take the torsional moment in rotation. The torsional moment is resolved into a couple with the forces acting in the transverse walls.

EXAMPLE 9.18   Rotation in a Flexible Diaphragm

In buildings with no effective shearwall on one side, rotation of a *flexible* diaphragm can be used to carry the torsional moment into the walls perpendicular to the applied lateral force (not allowed for buildings with concrete or masonry walls). Even in entirely wood-framed buildings, the Code limits the depth of the diaphragm normal to the open side to

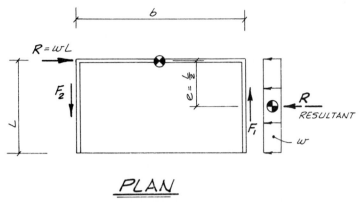

Figure 9.20 Plan of building with open side (i.e., no effective shearwall along one side).

25 ft or two-thirds the diaphragm width, whichever is smaller. (For one-story buildings, the width is limited to 25 ft or the full diaphragm width, whichever is smaller.)

Rear wall must carry the entire longitudinal load:

$$R = wL$$

Force to transverse walls due to rotation:

$$\text{Torsion} = T = Re = \frac{wL^2}{2}$$

Resolve torsion into a couple separated by the distance between transverse walls:

$$F_1 = F_2 = \frac{T}{b} = \frac{wL^2}{2b}$$

For more information see the APA publication *Diaphragms* (Ref. 14.14).

It should be noted that this is not necessarily a desirable design technique. In fact, the *Code does not allow the consideration of rotation of a wood diaphragm in a building with concrete or masonry walls.* The required approach in these types of buildings, and the desirable approach in all cases, is to provide a shearwall along the open side of the building.

The question of rotation brings up an important point. The designer, insofar as practical, should strive for structural *symmetry*. In Fig 9.20 it is quite unlikely that the design could be modified to have walls of exactly the same length at the front and back of the building. However, the design of a shearwall with an effective length sufficient to develop unit shears of a reasonable magnitude along the open side is recommended. The addition of this amount of symmetry will aid in reducing damage due to rotation.

Problems involving rotation were responsible for a number of the failures in residential buildings in the 1971 San Fernando earthquake. Reference 8.1 analyzes these failures and recommends construction details to avoid these problems. For additional recommendations on the design of horizontal wood diaphragms see Refs. 8.2, 9.4, and 14.14.

9.12 Problems

For simplicity the following horizontal diaphragm design problems all use PS 1 *plywood* sheathing. Plywood nailing and allowable unit shears are to be taken from UBC Table 25-J-1 (see Appendix C). The design of diaphragms using other types of structural-use panels is similar [e.g., diaphragm design values for APA Rated Sheathing are given in NER-108 (Ref. 15.1), and values for panels qualified under UBC Standard 25-25 (Ref. 1.2) are given in UBC Table 25-J-2].

Allowable stresses and section properties for wood members in the following problems are to be in accordance with the 1991 NDS. Dry-service conditions, normal temperatures, and bending about the strong axis apply unless otherwise noted. Based on recommendations in the 1991 NDS, a load duration factor of 1.6 is to be used for problems involving wind or seismic forces. Check acceptance by local code authority before using $C_D = 1.6$ in practice.

The loads given in a problem are to be applied directly. In practice, use of a load combination factor (Secs. 2.8 and 16.2) may be permitted. Check acceptance by local code authority before using the *load combination factor* together with the *load duration factor* C_D.

Some problems require the use of a *microcomputer spreadsheet*. Problems that are solved on a spreadsheet can be saved and used as a *template* for other similar problems. Templates can have many degrees of sophistication. Initially, a template may only be a hand (i.e., calculator) solution worked on a spreadsheet. In a simple template of this nature, the user will be required to provide many of the lookup functions for such items as

Allowable diaphragm unit shears (lb/ft)

Diaphragm nailing specifications

Tabulated stresses for wood members

As the user gains experience with spreadsheets, a template can be expanded to perform many of the lookup and decision-making functions that were previously done manually.

Advanced computer programming skills are not required to create effective spreadsheet templates. Valuable templates can be created by designers who normally do only hand solutions. However, some programming techniques are helpful in automating *lookup* and *decision-making* steps.

The first requirement is that a spreadsheet operate correctly (i.e., calculate correct values). Another major consideration is that the input and output should be structured in an orderly manner. A sufficient number of intermediate answers are to be displayed and labeled so that the solution can be verified by hand.

9.1 *Given:* The single-story commercial building in Fig. 9.A. Plywood is $^{15}/_{32}$-in. C-DX unblocked. Nails are 8d common. Critical lateral forces (wind or seismic) are

$$w_T = 140 \text{ lb/ft}$$

$$w_L = 320 \text{ lb/ft}$$

Vertical loads are

$$\text{Roof DL} = 10 \text{ psf}$$

$$\text{Snow} = 30 \text{ psf}$$

Find: *a.* For the transverse direction:
1. Roof diaphragm unit shear
2. Plywood load case (state criteria) and allowable unit shear
b. For the longitudinal direction:
1. Roof diaphragm unit shear
2. Plywood load case (state criteria) and allowable unit shear
c. What is the required nailing?
d. If blocking is not required, do the edges of the plywood need some other type of edge support?

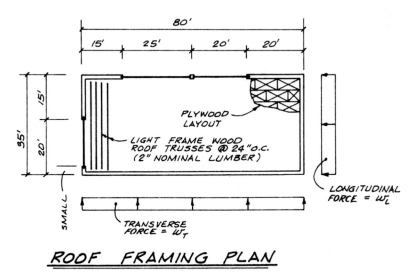

Figure 9.A

9.2   *Given:*   The single-story commercial building in Fig. 9.A. Plywood is $^{15}\!/_{32}$-in. C-DX STR I. Critical lateral forces (wind or seismic) are

$$w_T = 320 \text{ lb/ft}$$

$$w_L = 320 \text{ lb/ft}$$

   Find: a. Roof diaphragm unit shear.
   b. Is the UBC span-to-width ratio satisfied? Show criteria.
   c. Is blocking required for lateral forces? If it is required, calculate at what point it can be omitted. Show all criteria such as diaphragm load case, allowable unit shears, and nailing requirements.
   d. The maximum chord force.

9.3   Use the hand solution to Prob. 9.1 or 9.2 as a guide to develop a microcomputer spreadsheet *template* to solve similar problems.
   a. Consider only the specific criteria given in the problems.
   b. Expand the template to handle any diaphragm unit shear covered in UBC Table 25-J-1. In other words, input the values from the Code into a spreadsheet table or database, and have the template return the required nail specification and blocking requirements. Macros may be used as part of the spreadsheet.

9.4   *Given:*   The single-story wood-frame warehouse in Fig. 9.B. Roof sheathing of ⅜-in. C-DX STR I is adequate for vertical "sheathing" loads. Lateral forces to roof diaphragm are

$$w_T = 210 \text{ lb/ft}$$

$$w_L = 360 \text{ lb/ft}$$

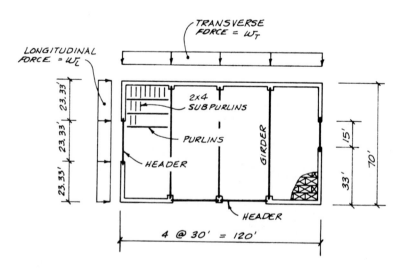

ROOF FRAMING PLAN

Figure 9.B

Find: *a.* Design the roof diaphragm, considering lateral forces in both directions. Show all criteria including design shears, load cases, allowable shears, and nailing requirements. If blocking is required, determine at what points it can be omitted.

          b. Calculate the maximum chord forces for both lateral forces. Also calculate the chord forces at the ends of all headers in the exterior walls.

          c. Plot the distribution of the strut force for each of the walls with openings. Compare the strut forces and chord forces to determine the critical loading.

9.5   Use the hand solution to Prob. 9.4 as a guide to expand the spreadsheet template from Prob. 9.3. The expanded template should evaluate the diaphragm *chord forces* and *drag strut* forces. In addition to maximum chord forces, the template should allow the user to select various arbitrary locations for the evaluation of chord and strut forces.

9.6   Repeat Prob. 9.4 except that the plywood in $^{15}\!/_{32}$-in. C-C STR I and the lateral forces are

$$w_T = 400 \text{ lb/ft}$$

$$w_L = 500 \text{ lb/ft}$$

9.7   *Given:*   The building in Fig. 9.A and the lateral forces

$$w_T = 300 \text{ lb/ft}$$

$$w_L = 500 \text{ lb/ft}$$

     Find: *a.* The maximum chord forces. Also determine the chord forces at each end of the wall openings.

          b. Plot the distribution of the strut forces for the two walls that have openings. Compare the magnitude of the strut forces with the chord forces.

NOTE: A spreadsheet template may be used to solve this problem. Verify results with hand solution.

9.8   *Given:*   Assume that the framing plan in Fig. 9.A is to be used for the second-floor framing of a two-story retail sales building. Lateral forces are

$$w_T = 450 \text{ lb/ft}$$

$$w_L = 450 \text{ lb/ft}$$

     Floor LL is to be in accordance with UBC. Plywood is C-C STR I.

Find: *a.* Required plywood thickness.
   b. Required plywood nailing. Check unit shears in both transverse and longitudinal directions. Show all criteria in design calculations.
   c. Calculate the maximum chord force and drag force in the building. Assume that three 2 × 6's of No. 1 DF-L are used as the top plate in the building. Check the maximum stress in this member if it serves as the chord and strut. At any point in the plate, two 2 × 6's are continuous (i.e., only one member is spliced at a given location). A single row of 1-in.-diameter bolts is used for the connections. $C_M = 1.0$, and $C_t = 1.0$.

NOTE: Design of the bolts is not part of this problem.

9.9   The one-story building in Fig. 9.C has the following loads:

Roof DL = 12 psf
Wall DL = 150 pcf (normal-weight concrete)
Wind = 20 psf
Seismic coefficient = 0.183W
Tributary wall height to roof diaphragm = 10 ft
Roof LL in accordance with UBC Table 23-C

Plywood is C-C (4-ply, 3-layer). Diaphragm chord consists of two #5 continuous horizontal bars in the wall at the diaphragm level.

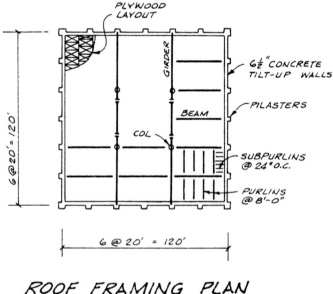

ROOF FRAMING PLAN

Figure 9.C

Find: a. Required plywood thickness.
b. Critical lateral forces.
c. Required plywood nailing based on the diaphragm unit shears. Show all design criteria. Consider forces in both directions.
d. Check the stress in the chord reinforcing steel. Allow. f_s = 20 ksi × 1.33.

9.10   *Given:*   The one-story building in Fig. 9.D. Roof sheathing is $^{15}\!/_{32}$-in. C-DX plywood spanning between roof joists spaced 24 in. o.c. Nails are 10d common. For the transverse lateral force, the plywood layout is load case 1.

         Find: a. Design the roof diaphragm, assuming that only the exterior walls are effective in resisting the lateral force. Show all design criteria including span-width ratio, nailing, and blocking requirements. Omit blocking where possible.
b. Redesign the roof diaphragm, assuming that the interior *and* exterior walls are effective shearwalls. Show all criteria.
c. Compare the maximum chord forces for a and b.
d. Plot the drag strut force diagram for the interior shearwall.

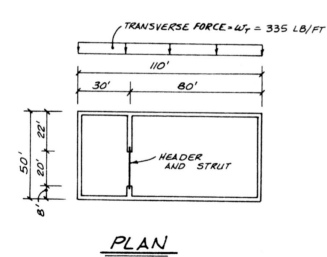

PLAN

Figure 9.D

9.11   *Given:*   The header/strut over the opening in the interior shearwall in Fig. 9.D is a 4 × 14 No. 1 DF-L. C_M = 1.0, and C_t = 1.0. The vertical load is

$$w_{DL} = 100 \text{ lb/ft}$$

$$w_{RLL} = 160 \text{ lb/ft}$$

The axial force is to be determined from a plot of the drag strut force.

Find: Analyze the member for combined stresses. Full lateral support is provided for the weak axis by the roof framing.

10

Shearwalls

10.1 Introduction

Shearwalls comprise the vertical elements in the lateral-force-resisting system (LFRS). They support the horizontal diaphragm and transfer the lateral forces down into the foundation. The procedures for calculating the forces to the shearwalls are covered in Chaps. 3 and 9.

Plywood horizontal diaphragms are often used in buildings with masonry or concrete shearwalls as well as buildings with wood-frame shearwalls. However, the design of masonry and concrete walls is beyond the scope of this book, and this chapter deals with the design of wood-frame shearwalls only.

A number of sheathing materials can be used to develop shearwall action in a wood-frame wall. These include

1. Plywood and other structural-use panels

2. Gypsum wallboard (drywall)

3. Interior and exterior plaster (stucco)

4. Fiberboard

5. Lumber sheathing

There may be other acceptable materials, but these are representative. When the design forces (wall shears) are relatively small, the normal wall covering material may be adequate to develop shearwall action. However, when the unit shears become large, it is necessary to design special sheathing and nailing to develop the required capacity.

10.2 Basic Shearwall Action

Essentially a shearwall cantilevers from the foundation as it is subjected to one or more lateral forces. See Example 10.1. As the name implies, the basic form of resistance is that of a shear element (Fig. 3.5c). The concept of "shear panels" in a wood-frame wall leads to the usual assumption that the lateral force is distributed uniformly throughout the total length of all panels (Sec. 9.6).

EXAMPLE 10.1   Cantilever Action of a Shearwall

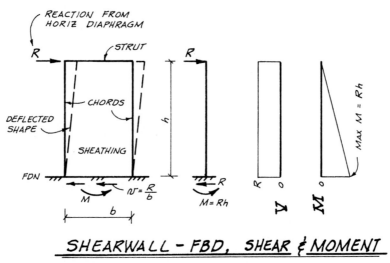

Figure 10.1 Deflected shape of one-story shearwall. Also shown are cantilever loading diagram (schematic), and shear and moment diagrams.

Figure 10.1 shows a typical shear panel for a one-story building. If there are additional stories, there will be additional forces applied to the shearwall at the diaphragm levels. If the lateral force is a seismic force, there will also be an inertial force generated by the mass of the shearwall (Chap. 3).

A variety of sheathing materials can be used to develop shearwall action for resisting lateral forces. The Code sets limits on the height-to-width ratios h/b for shear panels in order to develop effective shear (deep-beam) resistance. Limits on h/b vary with different sheathing materials.

A number of items should be considered in the design of a shearwall. These include

1. Sheathing thickness

2. Shearwall nailing

3. Chord design

4. Strut design

5. Shear panel proportions

6. Anchorage requirements

These factors are essentially the same as those required for a horizontal diaphragm, but there are some differences in procedures.

The *sheathing thickness* depends on the type of material used in the wall construction. Loads normal to the surface and the spacing of studs in the wall may determine the thickness of the sheathing, but the unit shear often controls the thickness. In other cases the sheathing thickness may be governed by the required fire rating of a wall. *Shearwall nailing* or stapling requirements are a function of the unit shear in the wall and the materials of construction.

As with a horizontal diaphragm, the *chords* are designed to carry the moment, and chords are required at both ends of a shearwall. The *strut* for a shearwall is the same member as the strut for the horizontal diaphragm. It is the connecting link between the shearwall and the horizontal diaphragm for loads parallel to the shearwall. Design forces for the strut are covered in detail in Chap. 9.

The *proportions* of a shear panel are measured by its height-to-width ratio h/b. In buildings with two or more stories, the height of the shearwall is the vertical distance between horizontal diaphragms. The Code sets upper limits on the height-to-width ratio for various wall sheathing materials used as shear panels. Specific values of these limits will be covered in the sections dealing with the various construction materials. Panels are considered as effective shearwall elements if these limits are not exceeded. Shear panels which satisfy the height-to-width ratio criteria are considered by many designers to also have proportions which will not allow the panel to deflect excessively under load (this is similar to the span-to-width ratios for horizontal diaphragms—Sec. 9.8).

10.3 Shearwalls Using Structural-Use Panels

Perhaps the most common wood-frame shearwall is the type that uses plywood sheathing or plywood siding. However, today other panel products provide additional choices for shearwall construction. The allowable unit shears for structural wood panel shearwalls are given in UBC Table 25-K-1 for plywood, NER-108 for APA structural-use panels, and UBC Table 25-K-2 for panels qualified under UBC Standard 25-25 (Ref. 1.2). See Secs. 8.7 and 8.8 for a description of these panel products.

The design tables for the different panel materials are similar in organization and content. In order to simplify the discussion, the remaining portion of this section deals specifically with plywood shearwalls, and allowable unit shears are taken from UBC Table 25-K-1. If some other type of structural-use panel is considered, the designer will simply have to refer to the appropriate table for shear values and nailing requirements. The basic design procedures will be similar.

Tabulated allowable unit shears for shearwalls assume that the framing members are Douglas Fir-Larch or Southern Pine. If the diaphragm nailing penetrates into framing members of other species of wood, an adjustment that accounts for a reduced nail capacity is required. Reduction factors for other species of wood are given in a footnote to the allowable shear tables. In addition it should be noted that the tabulated shearwall values are for short-term (wind or seismic) forces. Because these represent the common loading conditions for shearwalls, a load duration factor C_D for wind and seismic is included in the tabulated allowable shears. Consequently, if a shearwall is used to support forces of longer duration, allowable shears will have to be reduced in accordance with the load duration factors covered in Sec. 4.15.

Plywood sheathing is often provided on only one side of a wall, and then finish materials are applied to both sides of the wall. If the design unit shears are higher than can be carried with a single layer, another layer of plywood sheathing can be installed on the other side of the wall. See Fig. 10.2a. The addition of a second layer of plywood sheathing doubles the shear capacity of the wall (see footnotes to UBC Table 25-K-1 for nailing provisions). The capacity of the wall covering (drywall, plaster, stucco, etc.) is not additive to the shear capacity of the plywood.

Plywood siding can also be used to resist shearwall forces. This siding can be nailed directly to the studs, or it may be installed over a layer of ⅝-in. gypsum sheathing. See Fig. 10.2b. A wall construction that gives a 1-hour fire rating uses 2 × 4 studs at 16 in. o.c. with ⅝-in. type X gypsum sheathing and ⅜-in. plywood siding on the outside, and ⅝-in. type X gypsum wallboard on the interior. When grooved plywood panels are used, the thickness to be considered in the shearwall design is the net thickness where the plywood is nailed (i.e., the thickness at the groove).

In a few instances it is theoretically possible to nail certain grooved plywood siding panels through the full thickness of the panel (i.e., away from the grooves). For these relatively unusual circumstances, the shear capacity of the panel could govern, and the shear through the thickness (Sec. 8.14) should be checked using the net thickness at the groove. Sample calculations for unit shear values based upon the plywood strength and fastener capacity are given in Ref. 14.11.

EXAMPLE 10.2   Plywood Shearwalls

Allowable unit shears for plywood sheathing and siding are given in UBC Table 25-K-1. This table covers both siding attached directly to framing and siding applied over ½- or ⅝-in. gypsum sheathing.

Allowable shear values are given for plywood nailed with *common* or *galvanized box nails* and *galvanized casing nails*. Finishing nails are not allowed for plywood shearwalls.

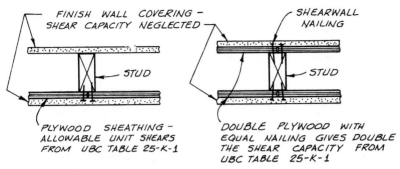

Figure 10.2a Plywood sheathing.

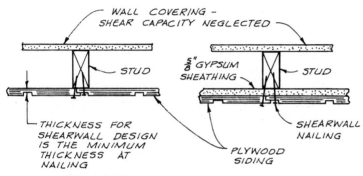

Figure 10.2b Plywood siding.

As noted, the allowable unit shears and nailing requirements for plywood shearwalls are given in UBC Table 25-K-1. It will be helpful at this point to review the organization of this table (included in Appendix C of this book). The shears given in the right side of the table are for plywood installed over ½- or ⅝-in. gypsum sheathing. The allowable shears to the left of these values apply to plywood that is nailed directly to the wall framing.

Ultimate load tests of plywood shear panels indicate that failure occurs by the nail head pulling through the plywood panel. Common nails and box nails have the same-diameter head, and for this reason, tests have shown that panels built with *common nails* and *galvanized box nails* develop approximately the same shear resistance. Allowable unit shears in the top portion of UBC Table 25-K-1 apply to both of these types of nails. The first section applies to plywood with the STRUCTURAL I addition to the plywood grade. The section below this applies to all other plywood grades, including plywood panel siding, when nailed with common or galvanized box nails.

Although common and galvanized box nails can be used to install finish plywood siding, the size of the nail head may be objectionable from an appearance standpoint. Therefore, allowable shears are tabulated at the bottom of Table 25-K-1 for plywood siding installed with *galvanized casing nails*.

Casing nails have a head diameter that is smaller than that of common or box nails but larger than that of finishing nails. Because of the tendency of the nail head to pull through the plywood, the allowable unit shears are considerably smaller when casing nails are used instead of common or galvanized box nails. The various types of nails are described more fully in Chap. 12.

UBC Table 25-K-1 applies to shear panels with the plywood installed either horizontally or vertically. In the table it is also assumed that all plywood edges are supported by either the wall studs, plates, or blocking. Footnotes give adjustments to the tabulated shears where appropriate. The table also gives special requirements designed to avoid the splitting of lumber framing when closely spaced nails are used. For example, when the nail spacing is 2 in. o.c., 3-in. nominal (or wider) framing is required at adjoining plywood panel edges.

UBC Table 25-I sets an upper limit on h/b of 3.5 for blocked plywood shearwalls. This is the largest height-to-width ratio permitted for wood-frame shear panels. For many other sheathing materials the maximum value for h/b is 1.5 or 2.0 (Sec. 10.4).

These limits can be important in the selection of the materials for a shear panel. See Example 10.3. The larger the allowable height-to-width ratio h/b, the shorter the permitted width of a shear panel for a given wall height. Thus if the width available for a shear panel is restricted, the use of a plywood shearwall may be required in order to satisfy the height-to-width limitations.

EXAMPLE 10.3   Height-to-Width Ratios for Wood-Frame Shearwalls

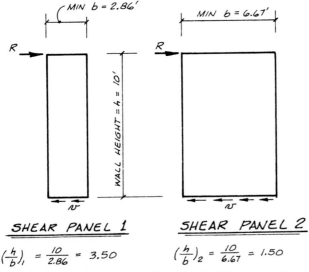

SHEAR PANEL 1

$$\left(\frac{h}{b}\right)_1 = \frac{10}{2.86} = 3.50$$

SHEAR PANEL 2

$$\left(\frac{h}{b}\right)_2 = \frac{10}{6.67} = 1.50$$

Figure 10.3 Minimum shearwall widths for different height-to-width ratios. Panels with smaller widths are ignored in design.

Blocked plywood shearwalls have an upper limit on h/b of 3.5. Thus, for a 10-ft-high shearwall the minimum width is 2.86 ft (shear panel 1).

Some common wall coverings can be used in shearwall design. Many of these materials have a limit on h/b of 1.5. Here a 10-ft-high wall must have a width of 6.67 ft (shear panel 2). A wall width less than this cannot be used as a shear panel. A number of these building materials can have the maximum h/b ratio increased to 2.0 if blocking is provided. See Sec. 10.4.

The discussion to this point has centered on one of the primary design tables for shearwalls, namely, UBC Table 25-K-1. This table has been in the Code for many years, and it serves as the basis for the design problems later in this chapter. However, there are a number of potential shearwall applications involving structural-use panels that are not covered in UBC Table 25-K-1. In addition, some points in the table needed confirmation and clarification. Some of these applications and needs include the use of

1. Unblocked shearwalls
2. Panels installed with staples
3. Panels attached to light-gage metal studs
4. Shearwalls with panels on both sides of wall
5. Panels installed over ⅝-in. gypsum sheathing
6. Increased stud spacing and the need for wider framing members to avoid splitting

A number of shearwall tests were recently conducted by the American Plywood Association (APA) to address these issues. The results, conclusions, and recommendations drawn from these and other tests are given in Ref. 14.6. In another research project, the APA studied the composite action of shearwalls that make use of glue, in addition to mechanical fasteners, for the attachment of sheathing materials. See. Ref. 14.15 for a summary of these results.

10.4   Other Sheathing Materials

It was mentioned at the beginning of this chapter that a number of wall materials other than plywood and structural-use panels can be used to develop shearwall action. If the design shears are high, plywood sheathing may be required. However, if the design forces are relatively low, other wall coverings may have sufficient strength to carry the shears directly.

Some of the more common materials are plaster, stucco (exterior plaster), and drywall. UBC Table 47-I gives allowable unit shears and construction requirements for several of these commonly used materials. The allowable unit shears for these materials range from 75 to 250 lb/ft, and the maximum height-to-width h/b is 1.5 (Example 10.3) for unblocked wall construction. The maximum height-to-width ratio for some materials may be increased from 1.5 to 2.0 if blocking is provided as described in UBC Sec. 4714 and UBC Table 47-I. This and other selected tables from the UBC are reproduced in Appendix C of this book.

The allowable shear values in UBC Table 47-I were obtained from tests in which the lateral force was applied to the wall from one direction. The results of recent tests indicate that *drywall* sheathing loses strength if the lateral force to the shearwall reverses direction. The reduced strength is attributed to a degradation of the gypsum material surrounding the nails under this type of *cyclic loading*. This has led to a 50 percent reduction in allowable shear capacity for gypsum products under strong *seismic forces* (i.e., in seismic zones 3 and 4). This reduction does not apply to lateral wind forces which are not subject to the force reversals that occur in an earthquake. See footnote 1 in UBC Table 47-I.

Other building materials that are not listed in the body of the Code may be tested and recognized as an alternative method of construction. For example, certain forms of stucco construction have been recognized for allowable unit shears up to 325 lb/ft. Values for the various recognized types of construction are available from Code evaluation reports and from the manufacturers of the specific construction products.

Fiberboard wall sheathing, often used for insulation, can also be designed for shearwall action when the design shears are relatively low. UBC Table 25-P gives the allowable unit shear for fiberboard as either 125 or 175 lb/ft, depending on panel thickness and nailing. The upper limit on h/b fiberboard shearwalls is also 1.5.

In the past, lumber sheathing was used extensively for wood-frame walls. Lumber sheathing can be applied horizontally (known as *transverse sheathing*), but it is relatively weak and flexible. Diagonally applied sheathing is considerably stronger and stiffer because of its triangulated (truss) action. See Fig. 10.4. Shearwalls using lumber sheathing have largely been replaced

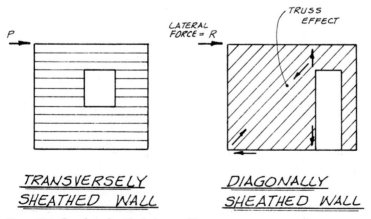

TRANSVERSELY SHEATHED WALL   DIAGONALLY SHEATHED WALL

Figure 10.4 Lumber-sheathed shearwalls.

with plywood and other structural-use panel shearwalls. Because of their relatively limited use, the design of lumber-sheathed walls is not covered in this text. A treatment of lumber shearwalls is given in Ref. 9.1.

10.5   Bracing in Wood-Frame Walls

The Code requires that most buildings and other structures be "designed" for both vertical loads and lateral forces. However, light-frame wood construction has a history of satisfactory performance, and the Code generally accepts this type of construction without further justification. Residential structures often fall into this category.

The requirements for this type of construction are given in the *Conventional Construction Provisions* of the Code (UBC Chap. 25). Lateral force resistance is ensured in these types of buildings by requiring some form of *wall bracing.*

Diagonal "let-in" (or light-gage-metal) braces have often been used in the past for this type of bracing. See Fig. 10.5. These braces are still allowed, but the Code also recognizes alternate forms of acceptable wall bracing for conventional construction. These alternate forms consist of a panel of solid sheathing (in effect, a nonengineered shearwall). Specific details are given in the Code (UBC Sec. 2517).

Experience in the San Fernando earthquake demonstrated the inadequacy of let-in braces. Many of these braces either failed in tension or pulled out of the bottom wall plate (Ref. 8.1). If these braces are used in buildings that require structural calculations, they are essentially ignored for design purposes.

A summary of the forms of wall bracing that qualify as conventional construction is given in UBC Table 25-V. It should be understood that the

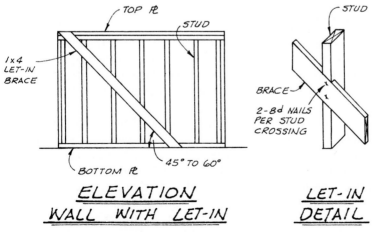

Figure 10.5   Let-in bracing.

alternative forms of wall bracing provided in this table are essentially *pre-scriptive requirements*. In other words, tradition and experience indicate that if a building follows these prescribed forms of bracing, reasonable perform-ance can be expected. Because of this, structural design for a building that qualifies as conventional construction is not required.

On the other hand, if a structure *clearly* does not satisfy the wall bracing criteria for conventional construction, a lateral force design should be pro-vided for the system. Futhermore, it is not acceptable practice to mix and match the *prescriptive requirements* for wall bracing *and* the requirements of a *lateral force design*.

A lateral force design requires more than a nailing schedule for a shear-wall. The shearwall is part of a system that also includes horizontal dia-phragms, drag struts, anchorage connections, and an overturning analysis. A lateral force design requires a *clearly identified path* for the transfer of lateral forces.

Reference 1.4*d* identifies an interesting development in the language of the construction industry that has taken place in recent years. Contractors and builders are generally aware of the need for shearwalls in wood-frame construction, and the phrases *shear the house* and *shear the building* have evolved. Here the word *shear* has become a verb that implies adding plywood sheathing to the walls of a building, perhaps throughout the entire structure.

For a building that does not meet the conventional wall bracing provisions, a proposal to "shear the entire building" may be made to a building official. This offer is usually made to obtain a building permit without the added time and expense required to obtain an appropriate lateral-force design. *Shearing* the structure by arbitrarily adding heavily nailed sheathing is not a substitute for proper design of the *lateral-force-resisting system* (LFRS). See Ref. 1.4*d* for additional discussion.

10.6 Shearwall Chord Members

The vertical members at both ends of a shear panel are the chords of the vertical diaphragm. See Example 10.4. As with a horizontal diaphragm, the chords are designed to carry the entire moment. The moment at the base of the shear panel is resolved into a couple which creates axial forces in the end posts.

Some designers analyze the chords in a shearwall for forces created by the *gross overturning moment* in the wall. This is a conservative approach in designing for *tension* because it neglects the reduction in moment caused by the dead load framing into the wall. For a definition of gross, net, and design net overturning moments, see Example 2.10 in Sec. 2.10.

Even if the dead-load-resisting moment is considered, the critical stress may be the tension at the net section. Reductions in the cross-sectional area often occur at the base of the tension chord for tie-down connections.

EXAMPLE 10.4   Shearwall Chord Members

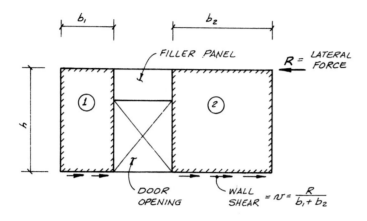

SHEARWALL WITH TWO PANELS

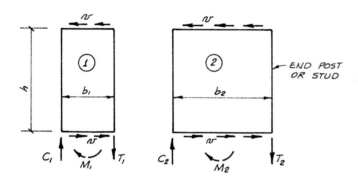

FBD's OF SHEAR PANELS

Figure 10.6 Elevation view of wall with two shearwall panels. Below are free body diagrams of shear panels. The moment at the base of a shear panel is resolved into a *couple*. The couple forms two concentrated chord forces: one in tension and the other in compression.

For a wood wall, the unit shear is generally assumed to be uniform throughout. For a lateral wind force, the unit shear is the same at the top and bottom of the two shear panels. The gross overturning moment (OM) is calculated at the base of each shear panel:

$$M_1 = v \times b_1 \times h$$

$$M_2 = v \times b_2 \times h$$

Chord forces are calculated by dividing gross OMs by the length of the shear panels:

$$T_1 = C_1 = \frac{M_1}{b_1} = vh$$

$$T_2 = C_2 = \frac{M_2}{b_2} = vh$$

Thus, considering the effects of the *gross OM*, the chord forces for the two panels are equal:

$$T_1 = C_1 = T_2 = C_2 = vh$$

A somewhat modified (but similar) procedure is used to calculate the gross chord forces when additional lateral forces are involved. These forces can be generated by additional stories (horizontal diaphragms) or, in the case of seismic forces, a lateral force due to the mass of the shearwall itself (Fig. 10.7d).

Chord forces for the two panels are *not equal* if the resisting dead load moments are considered. When the effects of the dead load are taken into account, larger chord forces will occur in the shorter-width shear panel.

Shearwall chord forces can be analyzed by using the expressions developed in this example or by using the basic statics approach described in Example 2.10 (Sec. 2.10). The chord forces should be in agreement regardless of the method used.

In the *compression* chord, the gross overturning force alone may not represent the critical design force. *Gravity loads* may be carried by the compression chord *in addition to the force due to overturning*. If the chord members are studs (rather than a post or column), compression perpendicular to the grain of the wall plates may be a consideration. With a column serving as a chord, a bearing plate may be used to reduce the bearing stress. Lateral forces to a shearwall may come from either direction, and chords must be designed for both tension and compression.

Recent tests conducted by APA demonstrated that compression perpendicular to grain on wall plates under a shearwall chord can, in fact, be a serious problem. The tests were conducted on heavily loaded shearwalls that had plywood sheathing on both sides of the wall. See Ref. 14.6 for details.

The usual assumption is that the shear is uniform throughout the width of a wood-frame shearwall. This common assumption is used throughout this book. However, one reference indicates that a nonuniform distribution of shear may develop, depending on how shearwall overturning is handled. See Ref. 9.4 for details about this alternative approach.

In order to ensure that the panels in a shearwall function as assumed (i.e., separate panels of equal height), double full-height studs should be used for the chords at the ends of the shear panels (Example 9.9 in Sec. 9.6). These tend to emphasize the vertical continuity of the panels. In addition, the lighter nailing of filler walls can be used to further isolate the shear panels.

10.7 Design Problem: Shearwall

In Example 10.5 the exterior transverse walls of a rectangular building are designed for a seismic force. There is a roof overhang on the left end of the building which develops a smaller, uniformly distributed, lateral seismic force than the main portion of the roof diaphragm. The difference in these two is the seismic force generated by the two longitudinal walls (i.e., the walls perpendicular to the direction of the earthquake force). The reaction of the left shearwall is made up of the cantilevered roof overhang plus the tributary force of the main roof diaphragm.

The total shear at the midheight of the transverse walls is made up of the tributary roof diaphragm reactions plus the seismic force due to the dead load of the top half of the shearwall.

The unit shear in the left wall can be carried by stucco of special construction. However, in this example a plywood shearwall is used. In the right wall, two shear panels are designed using the same type of plywood as the left wall, but the nailing is increased to meet the higher shear requirements.

The maximum chord force occurs in the walls with the higher unit shears. Calculations indicate that one 2 × 8 stud is sufficient to resist the tension chord force, but two 2 × 8 studs are required to carry the compression chord force. In order to function together, the two studs must be effectively connected together and attached to the sheathing.

EXAMPLE 10.5   Shearwall Design

Design the two transverse shearwalls in the building shown in Fig. 10.7a. Studs are 2 × 8's of No. 2 DF-L, and walls are of stucco construction. Seismic is critical, and the seismic coefficient is 0.183W. Wall DL = 20 psf. MC ≤ 19 percent, and C_M = 1.0. C_t = 1.0.

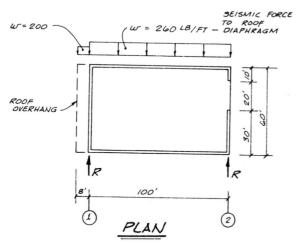

Figure 10.7a Plan view of building showing lateral seismic force to horizontal diaphragm.

Diaphragm Reactions

Forces to shearwalls from horizontal diaphragm are calculated on a tributary-width basis.

Wall 1: R = reaction from overhang + reaction from main roof

$$= (200 \times 8) + \left(260 \times \frac{100}{2}\right) = 14.6 \text{ k}$$

Wall 2: $R = 260 \times \dfrac{100}{2} = 13.0 \text{ k}$

Shearwall 1

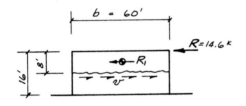

Figure 10.7b Elevation of left transverse wall (shearwall 1).

ELEV. WALL 1

Calculate wall seismic force, using the dead load of the *top half* of the wall (Chap. 3). Using the top half of the wall follows dynamic theory (Fig. 2.14*b*). Some designers use *entire* wall DL (conservative).

$$R_1 = 0.183W = 0.183(20 \text{ psf} \times 8 \times 60) = 1.76 \text{ k}$$

$$V = R + R_1 = 14.6 + 1.76 = 16.36 \text{ k}$$

$$v = \frac{V}{b} = \frac{16,360}{60} = 273 \text{ lb/ft}$$

From UBC Table 47-I,

$$\text{Shear capacity of cement plaster} = 180 \text{ lb/ft} < 273 \quad NG$$

Certain types of stucco construction have been recognized for unit shears in excess of 300 lb/ft. One of these recognized types of stucco can be used, or plywood sheathing may be provided.

Because the evaluation report for these higher-strength types of stucco construction is not included in this text, plywood sheathing will be shown. From UBC Table 25-N-1,

$\frac{5}{16}$-in. plywood can be used for normal sheathing loads, but $\frac{3}{8}$-in. C-D EXP 1 plywood is chosen. From UBC Table 25-K-1 with 6d common nails

$$\text{Allow. } v = 300 \text{ lb/ft} > 273 \quad OK$$

> *Use* $\frac{3}{8}$-in. C-D EXP 1 plywood
> with
> 6d common nails at
> 4-in. o.c. plywood edges
> 12-in. o.c. field
> Blocking required

Shearwall 2

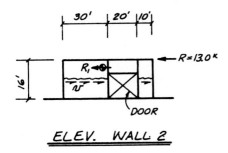

Figure 10.7c Elevation of right transverse wall (shearwall 2).

Use R_1 from wall 1 (conservative):

$$V = R + R_1 = 13.0 + 1.76 = 14.76 \text{ k}$$

$$v = \frac{V}{b} = \frac{14,760}{30 + 10} = 369 \text{ lb/ft}$$

> *Use* plywood similar to wall 1
> except
> 6d common nails at
> 3-in. o.c. plywood edges
> 12-in o.c. field
> Blocking required

$$\text{Allow. } v = 390 > 369 \text{ lb/ft} \quad OK$$

Tension Chord

The chord stresses are critical in wall 2 (Fig. 10.7*d*) because of the higher wall shears. The tension chord can be checked conservatively using the gross OM:

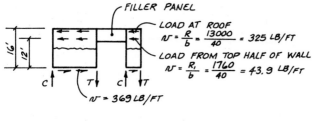

WALL 2 -   CHORD   FORCES

Figure 10.7d   Free body diagrams of panels in shearwall 2.

$$T = C = vh = 325(16) + (43.9)12 = 5.73 \text{ k} \qquad \text{(using gross OM)}$$

Check the tension stress in one 2 × 8 stud:

$$\text{Net area} = A_n = 1\tfrac{1}{2}(7\tfrac{1}{4} - 1) = 9.38 \text{ in.}^2$$

$$f_t = \frac{T}{A_n} = \frac{5730}{9.38} = 611 \text{ psi}$$

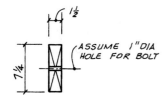

Figure 10.7e   Net area of one stud.

Lumber is No. 2 DF-L. A 2 × 8 is in the Dimension lumber size category, and tabulated stresses and size factors are from NDS Supplement Table 4A:

$F_t = 575$ psi $C_F = 1.2$ for F_t in a No. 2   2 × 8

$F_c = 1300$ psi $C_F = 1.05$ for F_c in a No. 2   2 × 8

$F_{c\perp} = 625$ psi

$E = 1{,}600{,}000$ psi

Allowable tension stress:

$$F'_t = F_t(C_D)(C_M)(C_t)(C_F)$$

$$= 575(1.6)(1.0)(1.0)(1.2)$$

$$= 1104 \text{ psi} > 611 \qquad OK$$

> One 2 × 8 is adequate for the
> tension chord of the shearwall.

The stress in the tension chord shown above is based on the gross chord force of 5.73 k. If the tension chord had been overstressed using the gross OM, the resisting DL moment could be considered.

Although not required in this problem, the reduced tension chord force* will be illustrated for comparison. Two approaches can be used to evaluate the effect of the resisting moment:

1. Basic statics using free-body diagrams (refer to Example 2.10 in Sec. 2.10).
2. Subtraction of the DL tributary to the tension chord from the gross chord force

The second method is illustrated in this example. However, both methods give the same results, and it is suggested that the reader apply both procedures and compare the results. The second method is quick and easy to apply to a one-story shearwall. In the case of a multistory shearwall, the second method requires careful attention to be applied properly, and the first method may be easier to use until experience is gained.

Recall from Chap. 2 that for overturning analysis the Code requires the DL to be reduced. This must be done regardless of which method is used. For overturning due to *wind* forces, the resisting DL is multiplied by 0.67, and for *seismic* forces the DL is multiplied by 0.85. Refer to Chap. 16 for a comprehensive treatment of overturning.

For a given unit shear v, the shorter-width panel in a given shearwall (10 ft in this example) will be critical. A wall DL of 20 psf was given in the problem statement. In addition, assume that the wall is a bearing wall that supports a portion of the roof. Say 12-ft-long roof joists (not shown) frame into the right end wall, and the roof DL = 15 psf. For the 10-ft-long shearwall, the tributary DL to the tension chord is one-half the shear panel length (5 ft).

$$\text{Roof DL} = 15 \text{ psf} \times (12/2) \text{ ft} = 90 \text{ lb/ft}$$

$$\underline{\text{Wall DL} = 20 \text{ psf} \times 16 \text{ ft} \quad = 320 \text{ lb/ft}}$$

$$\text{DL} = 410 \text{ lb/ft of wall}†$$

Subtract 0.85 times the DL tributary to the tension chord:

$$\text{Design uplift} = T_{\text{net}} = 5.73 \text{ k} - 0.85(0.410 \text{ k/ft})(5 \text{ ft})$$

$$= 3.99 \text{ k} \qquad \text{(considering 0.85 DL)}$$

---

*Reference 9.4 indicates that a nonuniform wall shear may occur if this is considered.
†Roof LL is omitted when overturning is checked.

The net uplift force is much less than the gross chord force of

$$T_{\text{gross}} = 5.73 \text{ k}$$

Compression Chord

Assume that the loads over the opening in wall 2 are supported by a separate column or trimmer.

Tributary DL to compression chord:

$$P_{\text{DL}} = 410 \text{ lb/ft} \times 5 \text{ ft} = 2050 \text{ lb}$$

(*Note*: The 0.85 multiplier for the tension chord is not applied to the compression chord.)
Add tributary DL to gross chord force:

$$C = 5.73 + 2.05 = 7.78 \text{ k}$$

Check the column capacity of one stud. Sheathing provides lateral support about the weak axis.

$$\left(\frac{l_e}{d}\right)_y = 0$$

$$\left(\frac{l_e}{d}\right)_x = \frac{16 \text{ ft} \times 12 \text{ in./ft}}{7.25} = 26.5$$

$$E' = E(C_M)(C_t) = 1{,}600{,}000(1.0)(1.0)$$

$$= 1{,}600{,}000 \text{ psi}$$

For visually graded sawn lumber used as a column, the values of K_{cE} and c are

$$K_{cE} = 0.3$$

$$c = 0.8$$

$$F_{cE} = \frac{K_{cE}E'}{(l_e/d)^2} = \frac{0.3(1{,}600{,}00)}{(26.5)^2} = 684 \text{ psi}$$

$$F_c^* = F_c(C_D)(C_M)(C_t)(C_F)$$

$$= 1300(1.6)(1.0)(1.0)(1.05) = 2184 \text{ psi}$$

$$\frac{F_{cE}}{F_c^*} = \frac{684}{2184} = 0.313$$

$$\frac{1 + F_{cE}/F_c^*}{2c} = \frac{1 + 0.313}{2(0.8)} = 0.821$$

$$C_P = \frac{1 + F_{cE}/F_c^*}{2c} - \sqrt{\left(\frac{1 + F_{cE}/F_c^*}{2c}\right)^2 - \frac{F_{cE}/F_c^*}{c}}$$

$$= 0.821 - \sqrt{(0.821)^2 - 0.313/0.8} = 0.290$$

$$F_c' = F_c(C_D)(C_M)(C_t)(C_F)(C_P)$$

$$= 1300(1.6)(1.0)(1.0)(1.05)(.0290)$$

$$= 633 \text{ psi}$$

Check bearing perpendicular to the grain on the wall plate: A stud serving as a shearwall chord occurs at the end of the wall plate. Therefore, $C_b = 1.0$.

$$F_{c\perp}' = F_{c\perp}(C_M)(C_t)(C_b)$$

$$= 625(1.0)(1.0)(1.0)$$

$$= 625 < 633$$

$$\therefore F_c' \text{ governs}$$

$$\text{Allow. } P = F_c'A = 0.625(1.5 \times 7.25) = 6.8 \text{ k} < 7.78 \quad NG$$

For two studs,

$$\text{Allow. } P = 2(6.8) = 13.6 \text{ k} > 7.78 \quad OK$$

NOTE: The column calculations given above for the compression chord are very conservative. The maximum compressive force at the base of the wall was used for the design load. However, the base of the chord is attached at the floor level, and column buckling is prevented at that point. Some reduced axial column force occurs at the critical location for buckling.

Check the compressive stress at the base of the chord, using the net area (Fig. 10.7e). Column buckling does not occur.

$$f_c = \frac{P}{A_n} = \frac{7780}{2(9.38)} = 415 \text{ psi}$$

$$F_c' = F_c(C_D)(C_M)(C_t)(C_F)(C_P)$$

$$= 1300(1.6)(1.0)(1.0)(1.05)(1.0)$$

$$= 2184 \text{ psi} \geqslant 415 \quad OK$$

> *Use*   two 2 × 8 studs of No. 2 DF-L
> for all shearwall chords

The load duration factor $C_D = 1.6$ used in Example 10.5 for checking the tension and compression chords is in accordance with the recommendations of the 1991 NDS for wind and seismic forces. The designer is advised to verify local code acceptance before using $C_D = 1.6$ in practice.

10.8   Anchorage Considerations

Six design considerations for shearwalls were listed in Sec. 10.2. The first five of these items have been covered (forces for designing the drag strut were covered in Chap. 9). The last item (anchorage) is considered now. Generally speaking, anchorage refers to the tying together of the main elements so that the building will function as a unit in resisting the design loads. Although gravity loads need to be considered, the term *anchorage* emphasizes the design for lateral forces.

Anchorage can be systematically provided by considering the transfer of the following loads:

1. Vertical (gravity) loads
2. Lateral forces parallel to a wall
3. Lateral forces perpendicular to a wall

If this systematic design approach is followed where the horizontal diaphragm connects to the various shearwalls, and where the shearwalls are attached to the foundation, the building will naturally be tied together. See Example 10.6.

The remainder of this chapter provides an introduction to anchorage considerations. The transfer of gravity loads is first summarized. For lateral forces, it is convenient to separate the discussion of anchorage into two parts. The transfer of lateral forces at the *base of the shearwall* is fairly direct, and this chapter concludes with a consideration of these anchorage problems. The anchorage of the *horizontal diaphragm to the shearwall* is somewhat more complicated, and this problem is covered in detail in Chap. 15.

The question of anchorage is basically a connection design problem. The scope of the discussion in this chapter is limited to the calculation of the forces involved in the connections. Once the magnitude of the forces is known, the techniques of Chaps. 12 through 14 can be used to complete the problem.

EXAMPLE 10.6   Basic Anchorage Criteria

The process of tying the building together can be approached systematically by considering loads and forces in the three principal directions of the building. The critical locations are where the horizontal diaphragms connect to the vertical diaphragms and shearwalls tie into the foundation. See Fig. 10.8.

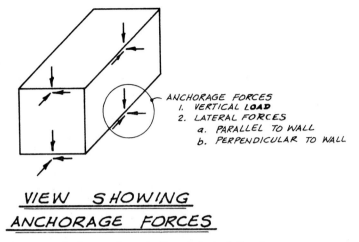

VIEW   SHOWING
ANCHORAGE   FORCES

Figure 10.8   Anchorage forces in three principal directions.

10.9   Vertical (Gravity) Loads

As noted, the term *anchorage* implies connection design for lateral forces. However, this can be viewed as part of an overall connection design process. In general connection design, the first loads that come to mind are the gravity loads. These start at the roof level and work their way down through the structure. The "flow" of these forces is fairly easy to visualize. See Example 10.7.

The magnitude of the loads required for the design of these connections can usually be obtained from the beam and column design calculations. The hardware used for these connections is reviewed in Chap. 14.

EXAMPLE 10.7   Connections for Gravity Loads

Design for gravity loads involves the progressive transfer of loads from their origin at the lightest framing member, through the structure, and eventually into the foundation. Consider the "path" for the transfer of gravity loads in the roof framing plan (Fig. 10.9). This requires the design of the following connections:

    a. Joist connections to roof beam and bearing wall
    b. Roof beam connections to girder and bearing wall
    c. Girder connections to column and header
    d. Header connection to column
    e. Column connection to footing, and stud connection to wall plate (these connections are not shown on the sketch)

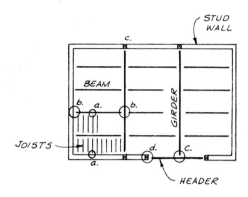

TYP ROOF FRAMING PLAN

Figure 10.9 Connections for the transfer of gravity loads.

10.10 Lateral Forces Parallel to a Wall

A shearwall resists lateral forces that are parallel to the wall. In doing so, it cantilevers from the foundation, and both a shear and a moment are developed at the base of the wall. Anchorage for the shear and moment is provided by separate connections.

The connections for resisting the *moment* will be considered first. It will be recalled that the moment is carried by the chords, and the chord forces are obtained by resolving the moment into a couple. See Fig. 10.10. The chord forces may be calculated from the gross overturning moment, or the resisting moment provided by the DL may be considered. Both procedures are illustrated in Example 10.5 (Sec. 10.7).

For connection design, the tension chord is generally of main concern. The tension chord force and the connection at the base of the tension chord will become important for

1. Tall shear panels (i.e., when h is large)

2. Narrow panels (i.e., when b is small)

3. Small resisting dead loads

When these conditions exist, a large tension uplift force develops at the base of the wall. If these conditions do not exist, there may be no uplift force at the base of the wall.

The tension tie for the shearwall anchorage is often made with a prefabricated metal bracket. These brackets are attached to the chord member with bolts, and to the foundation with an anchor bolt. The number and size

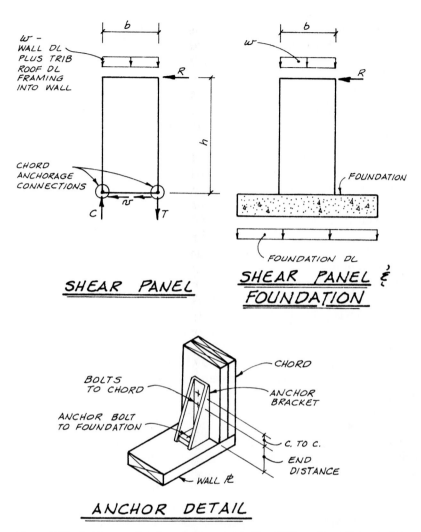

Figure 10.10   Anchorage for shearwall moment. The FBD on the left is used to design the anchorage connection of the shear panel to the foundation. The FBD on the right is used to check overall moment stability. The anchor bracket detail involves a connection between the bracket and the shearwall chord, and between the bracket and the foundation. Bolt spacing requirements (end distance and center-to-center) are important. See Chap. 13 for details.

of bolts, and the required embedment length for the anchor bolt, depend on the design force.

Connections of this type can be designed by using the wood design methods of Chap. 13 and the anchor bolt values in UBC Table 26-E. However, prefabricated brackets of this type usually have recognized load values which can be obtained from Code evaluation reports.

After the shearwall has been anchored to the foundation for the tension chord force, the overall stability of the wall system must be checked. In this case the dead load of the foundation is included in the resisting moment. In some cases the footing may also have to be designed for the compressive chord force. This becomes a concern with a large chord force, especially in areas with low soil-bearing values.

Recall that the factor of safety for overturning is handled differently by the Code for wind and seismic forces. These differences were discussed briefly in Example 2.10 and in Example 10.5. A more complete analysis of the requirements for overturning is given in Chap. 16.

The connection for transferring the *shear* to the foundation is considered now. This connection is normally made with a series of anchor bolts. See Example 10.8. These bolts are in addition to the anchor bolts used for the chord forces.

It will be recalled that the shear is essentially carried by the wall sheathing. The attachment of the sheathing to the bottom wall plate will transfer the shear to the base of the wall. The anchor bolts, then, are simply designed to transfer the shear from the bottom plate into the foundation.

Although the design of bolted connections is covered in a later chapter, the basic design procedure is briefly described here. The strength of the anchor bolt is determined as the bolt capacity parallel to the grain in the wood *or* by the strength of the anchor bolt in the concrete footing. The capacity of the bolt in the wood plate is covered in Chap. 13, and the capacity of the anchor bolt in the concrete footing is given in UBC Table 26-E. The smaller of these two values is used to determine the size and number of anchor bolts.

The anchor bolt values in UBC Table 26-E are based on a minimum required embedment length of bolt into the concrete footing. In addition, use of the full tabulated design values requires a minimum edge distance from the side of the footing to the center of the anchor bolt of 6 bolt diameters. However, the required edge distance can be reduced to 3 bolt diameters if the allowable loads are reduced 50 percent. Edge distance and other bolt spacings based on the requirements of the wood member are given in Chap. 13.

Because the bottom wall plate is supported directly on concrete, there is a potential problem with termites and decay. If a hazard exists, the Code requires that protection be provided. This is accomplished by using lumber for the sill plate which has been pressure-treated or wood that has a natural resistance to decay (e.g., foundation redwood). An introduction to pressure-treated lumber is given in Sec. 4.9.

EXAMPLE 10.8   Anchorage for Shearwall Shear

The anchor bolt requirement can be determined by first assuming a size of anchor bolt and determining the allowable load per bolt. If the allowable load per anchor bolt is Z'

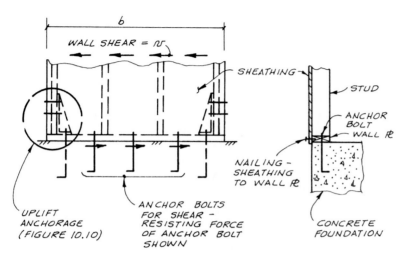

SHEAR PANEL   SHEAR ANCHORAGE

Figure 10.11 A separate set of anchor bolts is provided for shear transfer. These anchor bolts are in addition to those provided for the chord uplift connections.

(parallel-to-grain design value), and the total lateral force parallel to the shear panel is the unit shear times the panel width ($v \times b$), the required number of anchor bolts is

$$N = \frac{v \times b}{Z'}$$

The average spacing is approximately

$$\text{Spacing} = \frac{b}{N} = \frac{bZ'}{vb} = \frac{Z'}{v}$$

(This spacing is approximate because starting and ending anchor bolts must be set in from the panel ends a sufficient distance to clear the chords and tie-down brackets.)

The Code minimum anchor bolt requirement for wood-frame walls is

½-in. diameter anchor bolts at 6 ft-0 in. o.c. (UBC Chap. 29)

A minimum of two anchor bolts is required per wall plate, and one bolt is required within 12 in. of the end of each plate piece. Anchor bolts for shearwalls are usually larger and more closely spaced than the Code minimum.

10.11   Lateral Forces Perpendicular to a Wall

In addition to being designed for the shearwall forces covered in Sec. 10.10, walls must be designed for forces that are normal to the wall. The wall must be adequately anchored to the foundation and the roof diaphragm to resist design forces normal to the wall due to tributary wind and seismic forces.

The lateral seismic force normal to the wall is the force F_p. The seismic force F_p was compared with the wind force for a building with a wood roof and masonry walls in Example 2.17 (Sec. 2.15). In this earlier example, the seismic force was found to control because of the large dead load of the masonry wall. However, in buildings with wood-frame walls the seismic force is often less than the design wind pressure. See Example 10.9.

EXAMPLE 10.9   Force Perpendicular to a Wall

Compare the lateral design forces (wind and seismic) for the building in Example 2.17. Substitute wood-frame walls for the masonry walls, and calculate the anchorage force at the bottom of the wall. Wall DL = 20 psf. Wind pressures are from Example 2.17. Seismic coefficients from the previous example also apply.

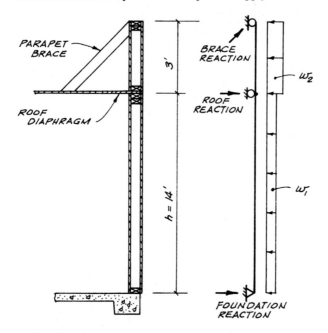

WALL SECTION

Figure 10.12 Section thru wall showing normal wall forces.

Seismic force to main wall:	*Seismic force to parapet wall:*
$w_1 = 0.3W_p$	$w_2 = 0.8W_p$
$= 0.3(20)$	$= 0.8(20)$
$= 6.0$ psf < 20.9 psf (wind)	$= 16$ psf < 22.6 psf (wind)

Wind pressures from Example 2.17 govern wall design and anchorage to footing. The given wind pressures are for elements *away* from discontinuities. Even higher wind pressures apply near building corners.

Anchorage force at bottom of wall (foundation reaction), calculated using tributary height:

$$R = w_1\left(\frac{h}{2}\right) = (20.9 \text{ psf})\left(\frac{14 \text{ ft}}{2}\right) = 146 \text{ lb/ft}$$

See Chap. 15 for anchorage considerations at the horizontal diaphragm level.

In the case of the lateral force *parallel* to the wall, the sheathing is assumed to transfer the force into the bottom plate of the wall. However, for the lateral force *normal* to the wall, the sheathing cannot generally be relied upon to transfer these forces. Connections should be designed to transfer the reaction from the stud to the bottom plate and then from the plate to the foundation. See Example 10.10.

EXAMPLE 10.10   Anchorage for Perpendicular to Wall Force

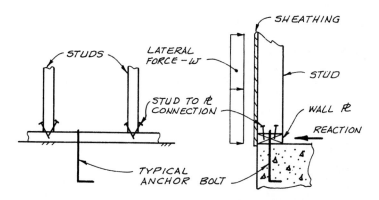

Figure 10.13 Two connections transfer normal wall forces to foundation: (1) nail connection between stud and bottom wall plate, (2) anchor bolt connection of wall plate to foundation. Anchor bolt design is governed by either the perpendicular to wall forces shown above or by the parallel to wall forces in Fig. 10.11.

The lateral force normal to the wall is usually transferred from the *stud to the bottom wall plate* by nails. The nailing schedule in UBC Table 25-Q gives the standard connection for the stud to the bottom (sole) plate as four 8d common or box toenails. An alternate connection is two 16d end nails.

The capacity of these connections can be evaluated by the techniques of Chap. 12. If the capacity of the standard stud-to-plate connections is less than the applied load, some other type of connection (such as a framing anchor—Chap. 14) will be required.

The connection of the *plate to the foundation* is accomplished with anchor bolts. The anchor bolt requirement can be determined by first assuming a size of anchor bolt and determining the allowable load per bolt.

If the allowable load per anchor bolt is Z' (perpendicular-to-grain design value), and the total foundation reaction (Example 10.9) is the reaction per foot R times the width of the wall b, then the required number of anchor bolts is

$$N = \frac{R \times b}{Z'}$$

This number must be compared with the required number of bolts determined for anchoring the parallel-to-wall forces (Example 10.8). The larger number of bolts controls.

The standard method of connecting wall studs to the bottom plate is with toenails or nails driven through the bottom plate into the end of the stud. The latter connection is often used when a wall panel is preframed and then lifted into place. Methods for evaluating the capacity of nailed connections are given in Chap. 12.

Experience during the 1971 San Fernando earthquake with conventional wood-frame houses proved the standard connection between wall studs and the bottom plate to be inadequate in many cases. Reference 8.1 was developed as a guide to home designers in an attempt to reduce these and other types of failures. This reference recommends the following anchorage for conventional wood-frame walls:

1. Framing anchors (Chap. 14) are to be used to fasten studs to the bottom wall plate at exterior corners. A ½-in.-diameter anchor bolt is to be installed within 2¾ in. of the corner studs (in addition to other anchor bolts). This is essentially an uplift connection.

2. In areas of high seismic risk (e.g., zone 4), the following additional anchorage is suggested. Framing anchors are to be used to connect the first two studs to the plate in each wall adjacent to the exterior corners.

3. Studs in the first story of two-story constructions are to be attached to the sole plate with framing anchors at 4-ft. intervals along the wall. This is required for all wall coverings except plywood.

For additional information see Ref. 8.1.

The force in the bottom plate is transferred to the foundation with anchor bolts. Because lateral forces parallel and perpendicular to the wall are not considered simultaneously, the same anchor bolts can be used for both of these forces.

The procedure for determining the required number of bolts is much the same as for parallel-to-wall loads. Here the strength of the anchor bolt is determined as the load capacity of the bolt perpendicular to the grain in the wood plate *or* by the strength of the anchor bolt in the concrete footing. The smaller of these two values is used as the allowable load per anchor bolt.

10.12 Problems

For simplicity the following shearwall problems that involve some type of structural-use panel are limited to PS 1 plywood. Plywood nailing and allowable unit shears are taken from UBC Table 25-K-1. The design of shearwalls using other types of structural-use panels is similar [e.g., shearwall design values for APA Rated Sheathing are given in NER-108 (Ref. 15.1), and values for panels qualified under UBC Standard 25-25 (Ref. 1.2) are given in UBC Table 25-K-2].

Allowable stresses and section properties for wood members in the following problems are to be in accordance with the 1991 NDS. Dry-service conditions, normal temperatures, and bending about the strong axis apply unless otherwise noted. Based on recommendations in the 1991 NDS, a load duration factor of 1.6 is to be used for problems involving wind or seismic forces. Check acceptance by local code authority before using $C_D = 1.6$ in practice.

The loads given in a problem are to be applied directly. In practice, use of a load combination factor (Secs. 2.8 and 16.2) may be permitted. Check acceptance by local code authority before using the *load combination factor* together with the *load duration factor* C_D.

Some problems require the use of a *microcomputer spreadsheet*. Problems that are solved on a spreadsheet can be saved and used as a *template* for other similar problems. Templates can have many degrees of sophistication. Initially, a template may only be a hand (i.e., calculator) solution worked on a spreadsheet. In a simple template of this nature, the user will be required to provide many of the lookup functions for such items as

Allowable shearwall unit shears (lb/ft)

Shearwall nailing specifications

Tabulated stresses for wood members

As the user gains experience with spreadsheets, a template can be expanded to perform many of the lookup and decision-making functions that were previously done manually.

Advanced computer programming skills are not required to create effective spreadsheet templates. Valuable templates can be created by designers who normally do only hand solutions. However, some programming techniques are helpful in automating *lookup* and *decision-making* steps.

The first requirement is that a spreadsheet operate correctly (i.e., calculate correct values). Another major consideration is that the input and output be structured in an orderly manner. A sufficient number of intermediate answers are to be displayed and labeled in a template so that the solution can be verified by hand.

10.1   *Given:*   The single-story wood-frame building in Fig. 10A. The critical lateral wind force in the longitudinal direction is given. Plywood sheathing is $^{15}/_{32}$-in. STR I with 8d common nails.

Find: a. The unit shear in the shear panel along line 1.
b. The required nailing for the shearwall along line 1.
c. The net maximum uplift force at the base of the wall along line 1. Consider the resisting moment provided by the weight of the wall (assume no roof load frames into longitudinal walls). Wall DL = 20 psf.
d. Are the proportions of the shear panel in the above wall within the limits given in the UBC?

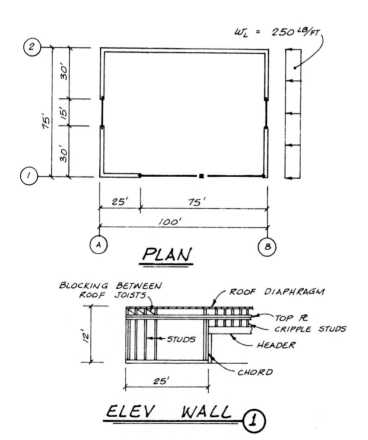

PLAN

ELEV   WALL ①

Figure 10.A

10.2 *Given:* The single-story wood-frame building in Fig. 10A. The critical lateral wind force in the longitudinal direction is given. Plywood wall sheathing (C-C exterior) will be designed to function as a shearwall. Studs are spaced 16 in. o.c.

     Find: *a.* The minimum required thickness of plywood sheathing, assuming that the face grain of the plywood may run either horizontally or vertically. (Plywood sheathing is used under a nonstructural wall covering.)

       b. The unit shear in the shear panel along line 1.

       c. Using the plywood thickness determined in *a*, select the required spacing of 6d common nails for the shearwall along line 1. Indicate blocking requirements (if any). Check the proportions of the shear panel.

       d. The maximum chord force in the shear panel along line 1, neglecting any resisting moment. Is a doubled 2×6 stud adequate to resist this chord force? Lumber is No. 2 DF-L. A single row of $\frac{3}{4}$-in.-diameter bolts is used for the anchorage connection at the base of the wall. $C_M = 1.0$, and $C_t = 1.0$.

       e. The uplift force for the design of the connection at the base of the tension chord. Consider the resisting moment provided by the wall and the roof dead load supported by the wall. The wall supports a 5-ft tributary width of roof DL. Roof DL = 10 psf. Wall DL = 15 psf.

10.3 *Given:* The single-story wood-frame building in Fig. 10A. The *transverse* lateral wind force (not shown in the sketch) is 375 lb/ft. The dead load of the roof and the wall is 250 lb/ft along the wall. Texture 1-11 (Sec. 8.13) plywood siding is applied directly to studs spaced 16 in o.c.

     Find: *a.* Unit shear in the roof diaphragm and in the shearwalls along lines *A* and *B*.

       b. The required nailing for the plywood siding to function as a shear panel. Use galvanized casing nails. Show all criteria. Check the proportions of the shear panel.

       c. The net design uplift force at the base of the shear panel chords.

10.4 *Given:* The wood-frame building in Fig. 10A. The critical lateral wind force in the longitudinal direction is given. The exterior wall finish is stucco ($\frac{7}{8}$-in. portland cement plaster over woven wire mesh).

     Find: Determine if the longitudinal wall along line 2 is capable of functioning as a shear wall for the given lateral force. Specify nailing. Check diaphragm proportions. Show all criteria.

10.5 Use the hand solution to Prob. 10.1, 10.2, or 10.3 as a guide to develop a microcomputer spreadsheet *template* to solve similar problems.

    a. Consider only the specific criteria given in the problems.

    b. Expand the template to handle any unit shear covered in UBC Table 25-K-1. In other words, input the values from the Code into a spreadsheet table *or* database and have the template return the required nail specification and blocking requirements. Macros may be used as part of the spreadsheet.

10.6   *Given:*   The one-story wood-frame building in Fig. 10B. The critical lateral force in the longitudinal direction is the given seismic force. The roof overhang has a higher lateral force because of the larger dead load of the plastered eave. Neglect the seismic force generated by the DL of the wall itself. Plywood wall sheathing is $^{15}/_{32}$-in. C-C STR I with 8d common or galvanized box nails. C_M = 1.0, and C_t = 1.0.

   Find: a. Design the plywood shear panels in the wall along line 1. Show all criteria including nailing, blocking, and shear panel proportions.

   b. Check shear panel chords using two 2 × 6s of No. 2 DF-L. Consider the resisting moment provided by a wall DL of 20 psf. Assume no roof DL frames into wall. A single row of $^3/_4$-in.-diameter bolts is used to anchor the chord to the foundation.

   c. Plot the distribution of the strut force along line 1. Check the stresses caused by the maximum strut force if a double 2 × 6 wall plate serves as the strut. A single row of $^7/_8$-in.-diameter bolts is used for the splices. Lumber is No. 2 DF-L.

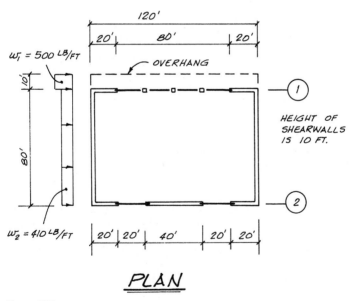

Figure 10.B

10.7   *Given:*   The one-story building in Fig. 10B. The longitudinal seismic force to the roof diaphragm is given. Texture 1-11 (Sec. 8.13) plywood siding is applied over $^5/_8$-in. gypsum sheathing for the wall along line 2. In addition to the load shown, consider the seismic force generated by the DL of the top half of the wall. Assume wall DL = 15 psf throughout and a seismic coefficient of 0.183.

Find: *a.* Design the shear panels in the wall along line 2, using galvanized casing nails. Show all criteria.
   b. Check the shear panels chords, using two 2 × 4s of No. 2 DF-L. Neglect any resisting moment. A single row of ⅝-in.-diameter bolts is used to anchor the chord to the foundation. C_M = 1.0 and C_t = 1.0.
   c. Plot the distribution of the strut force along line 2. Check the stresses caused by the maximum strut force if a double 2 × 4 wall plate serves as the strut. A single row of ⅝-in.-diameter bolts is used for the splices. Lumber is No. 2 DF-L.

10.8   *Given:*   The one-story wood-frame building in Fig. 10B. Roof DL = 10 psf. Wall DL = 18 psf (assume constant throughout). Wind = 20 psf. Seismic coefficient = 0.183.

Find: *a.* Calculate the critical lateral force in the transverse direction.
   b. The exterior wall covering for the transverse walls is stucco (⅞-in. portland cement plaster on expanded metal lath). Determine if these walls can function adequately as shearwalls. Consider the shear at the midheight of the wall. Show all criteria and give construction requirements.

10.9   *Given:*   The one-story wood-frame building in Chap. 9, Fig. 9D. The transverse lateral wind force is w_r = 355 lb/ft. The height of the building is 10 ft.

Find: *a.* The unit shears in the three transverse shearwalls.
   b. Design the three transverse shearwalls, using ⅜-in. C-DX plywood wall sheathing and 8d common or galvanized box nails. Studs are 16 in. o.c. Show all criteria including shearwall proportions.
   c. Calculate the chord forces for each of the three transverse shearwalls. Because the layout of the roof framing is not completely given, calculate the chord forces, using the gross overturning moments.

10.10   *Given:*   The elevation of the two-story wood-frame shearwall in Fig. 10C. The wind force reactions from the roof diaphragm and second-floor diaphragm are shown in the sketch. Vertical loads carried by the wall are also shown in the sketch (DL values include the weight of the wall). Plywood wall sheathing is ¹⁵⁄₃₂-in. C-C STR I with 8d common or galvanized box nails.

Find: *a.* The required nailing for the shear panel. Give full specifications.

        b. The required tie (drag strut) forces for the connections at *A*, *B*, *C*, and *D*.

        c. The net design uplift force for the tension chord at the first- and second-floor levels.

        d. The maximum force in the compression chord at the first- and second-floor levels. Consider the effects of both gravity loads and lateral forces. Assume that the header is supported by the shear panel chord.

        e. If the allowable load on one anchor bolt is 1500 lb, determine the number and approximate spacing of anchor bolts necessary to transfer the shear from the bottom wall plate to the foundation. These bolts are in addition to those required for uplift.

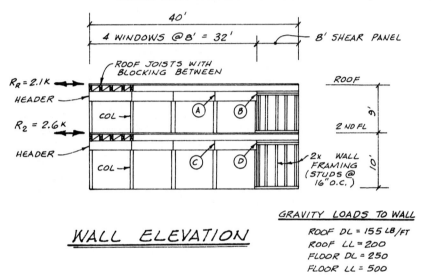

Figure 10.C

10.11 *Given:* The wood-frame shearwall in Fig. 10D. The lateral wind force from the roof diaphragm to the end shear panel is given. Gravity loads are also shown on the sketch. The DL includes both roof and wall DL. The shear panel has $^{15}\!/_{32}$-in. C-D plywood sheathing.

      Find: *a.* Determine the required nailing for the plywood.

         b. Calculate the net uplift force for the shear panel chord. Does this occur at column *A* or *B*?

         c. Determine the maximum compressive force in the shear panel chord. Consider the effects of gravity loads. Assume that the header is supported by the shear panel chord. What is the critical load combination? Specify which chord is critical.

         d. Assume that the allowable load per anchor bolt is 1000 lb. Determine the required number and approximate spacing of anchor bolts necessary to transfer the wall shear from the bottom plate to the foundation. These bolts are in addition to those required for uplift.

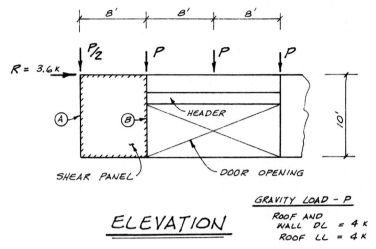

GRAVITY LOAD - P

ROOF AND
  WALL DL = 4 K
ROOF LL = 4 K

ELEVATION

Figure 10.D

10.12 *Given:* The elevation of the two-story wood-frame shearwall in Fig. 10E. Vertical loads and lateral wind forces are shown in the sketch. Wall framing is 2 in. nominal. Studs are 16 in. o.c. Wall sheathing is $^{15}/_{32}$-in. C-C STR I with 8d common or galvanized box nails.

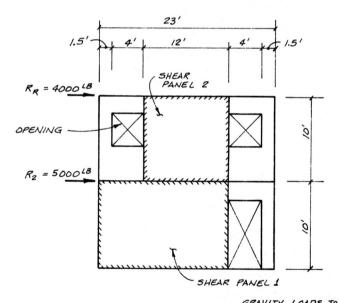

ELEVATION

GRAVITY LOADS TO WALL

ROOF DL = 140 LB/FT
ROOF LL = 200
FLOOR DL = 200
FLOOR LL = 500
WALL DL = 16 PSF

Figure 10.E

Find: a. The required nailing for the first- and second-story shear panels.
      b. The net uplift force at the base of shear panels 1 and 2.
      c. The maximum compressive force at the end of the first-floor shear panel. State the critical load combination.
      d. Assume that the capacity of an anchor bolt parallel to the wall is 1500 lb. Determine the required number and approximate spacing of anchor bolts necessary to transfer the shear from the wall into the foundation. These bolts are in addition to those required for uplift.

10.13   Repeat Prob. 10.12 except that shear panel 1 is 12 ft long and lies directly below shear panel 2.

Wood Connections—Background

11.1 Introduction

Design procedures for wood connections changed significantly in the 1991 NDS. The *equation format* of the 1991 NDS provides improved organization of the design requirements for fasteners. Coefficients and adjustment factors are now clearly identified by symbols, and it is much less likely that a design parameter will be overlooked. Use of a formal notation system will lead to more consistently designed connections.

In addition to the improved organization of design provisions, the 1991 NDS includes an entirely new method for evaluating the strength of laterally loaded connections. The new method is known as the *yield limit model for dowel-type fasteners,* and it represents a change to an engineering mechanics approach to the design of wood connections. It replaces the old empirical method of predicting the capacity of many common wood fasteners.

Although the equation format of the 1991 NDS provides a much better-organized design specification, the move to an engineering mechanics approach for fasteners has introduced some rather complicated equations for connection design. The designer, however, has the option of applying the formulas (which is best done on a microcomputer) or using a set of load tables that are based on the yield limit equations.

Chapter 11 starts by introducing the common types of fasteners used in typical wood connections, and the notation system for connection design is described. Greater detail about the connections and the required adjustment factors is included in the chapters that deal with specific fasteners. The chapter concludes with a review of the general concepts of the yield limit theory. Important strength considerations are included along with a summary of the various possible yield modes that are considered in this approach to connection design.

11.2 Types of Fasteners and Connections

There are a wide variety of fasteners and many different types of joint details that can be used in wood connections. When structural members are attached with fasteners or some other type of hardware, the joint is said to be a *mechanical connection.*

Mechanical connections are distinguished from connections made with *adhesives.* Adhesives are normally used in a controlled environment, such as a glulam, plywood, or wood I-joist manufacturing plant under the control of a formal quality assurance program. Other types of connections can be made with adhesives, but they are not common in conventional wood-frame buildings. The connections covered in this discussion are limited to mechanical connections.

The design of connections using the following types of fasteners is covered in this book:

1. Nails

2. Bolts

3. Lag bolts (lag screws)

4. Split ring and shear plate connectors

Some background material is introduced here, but much more detailed descriptions of the fasteners and design requirements for connections are given in Chaps. 12 and 13.

Connections are generally classified according to the direction of loading. *Shear connections* have the load applied *perpendicular* to the length of the fastener. See Example 11.1. These connections are further classified as to the number of shear planes. The most common applications are *single shear* and *double shear,* but additional shear planes are possible. According to the NDS, connections with more than two shear planes are to be analyzed by evaluating each shear plane as a single-shear connection. The design value for the weakest shear plane is then multiplied by the number of shear planes to obtain the total connection capacity.

EXAMPLE 11.1   Typical Wood Connections Subjected to Shear

The most common fasteners used in wood connections are nails, bolts, and lag bolts. In shear connections the load acts perpendicular to the length of the fasteners. One or more shear planes occur.

Split ring and shear plate connectors are also used in shear-type connections to provide additional bearing area on the wood members for added load capacity.

The symbol Z represents the nominal fastener load capacity for these types of connections. *Shear* connections are also known as *laterally loaded* connections. The other basic types of connections in wood design are withdrawal connections (Example 11.2).

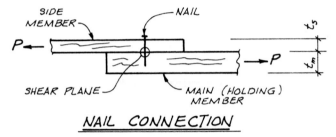

Figure 11.1a   Single-shear (two-member) wood-to-wood *nail connection*. A similar connection can be made with a steel side plate (wood-to-metal).

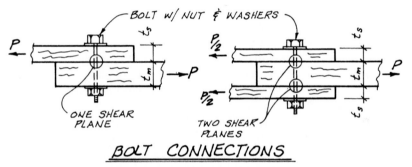

Figure 11.1b   Single-shear (two-member) and double-shear (three-member) *bolt connections*. Wood-to-wood connections are shown, but connections with steel side plates are common (wood-to-metal).

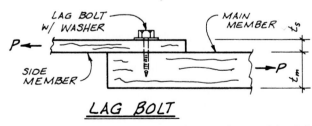

Figure 11.1c   Single-shear (two-member) wood-to-wood *lag bolt connection*. Another common application is with a steel side member (wood-to-metal).

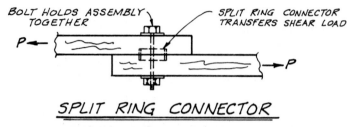

SPLIT RING CONNECTOR

Figure 11.1d *Split ring and shear plate connectors* fit into precut grooves. A split ring connector (shown in sketch) is used only for a wood-to-wood connection. Shear plate connectors can be used for either wood-to-wood *or* wood-to-metal connections. See Fig. 13.23 for photographs of split ring and shear plate connectors in partially assembled joints.

The second major type of loading in a wood connection has the applied load *parallel* to the length of the fastener, and the fastener is loaded in tension. When nails and lag bolts are subjected to this type of loading, the concern is that the fastener may pull out of the wood member. *Withdrawal loading* is the term applied to this situation (see Example 11.2). Nominal withdrawal values are tabulated in the NDS for nails and lag bolts.

Bolts may be loaded in tension, but such connections are not loaded in withdrawal. The strength of the fastener in tension is usually not critical, but technically it should be verified. Compression perpendicular to grain under the head of a bolt or lag bolt is a normal design consideration. A washer or plate of sufficient size must be provided between the wood member and the fastener head so that the allowable bearing stress $F'_{c\perp}$ is not exceeded. Refer to Sec. 6.8 for a review of allowable compressive stress perpendicular to grain. Finally, it should be noted that split rings and shear plate connectors are basically used in shear connections and are not subjected to tension.

EXAMPLE 11.2   Typical Wood Connections Loaded in Withdrawal and Tension

Withdrawal loading attempts to pull a nail or lag bolt (lag screw) out of the main (holding) wood member. The symbol W represents the nominal fastener load capacity for these types of connections. Note that the main member is the member that receives the pointed end of the fastener. In a withdrawal connection the load is parallel to the fastener, and the fastener is stressed in tension. Bolts can be loaded in tension, but they are not subject to withdrawal.

A washer of adequate size must be provided under the head of a bolt loaded in tension, and under the head of a lag bolt loaded in withdrawal, so that compression perpendicular to the grain is not exceeded.

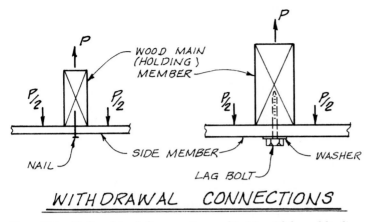

WITHDRAWAL   CONNECTIONS

Figure 11.2a   Nail and lag bolt connections subject to withdrawal loading.

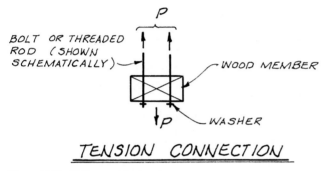

TENSION   CONNECTION

Figure 11.2b   Bolts used in tension.

The notation system for fastener design is based on the two types of loading just described. The following symbols are used:

Z = nominal design value for single fastener subjected to lateral *shear* load

W = nominal design value for single fastener subjected to *withdrawal* load

The term *nominal design value* refers to the basic load capacity for a fastener as defined by a table or equation in the NDS. As with all tabulated properties for wood design, the nominal fastener value applies to a specific set of conditions. These idealized conditions include such things as loads of *normal* (10-year) *duration,* lumber that is *initially dry* and *remains dry* in service, *temperature* range that is low to moderate (i.e., not high), and so on. The idealized conditions for connections are similar to the conditions that apply to the tabulated stresses for a wood member such as a beam. Thus, the nominal fastener value is simply the starting point for determining the allowable load capacity for a particular structural application.

Adjustment factors for load duration, moisture content conditions, temperature, and a number of other design considerations may be required to convert the nominal design value to an *allowable design value* for a single fastener. A prime is added to the symbol to indicate that the appropriate adjustments have been applied:

$Z' = Z \times$ (product of applicable adjustment factors for shear connection)

$W' = W \times$ (product of applicable adjustment factors for withdrawal connection)

It should be noted that the NDS provides design criteria for a number of fasteners in addition to those listed above. The appropriate adjustment factors for all fasteners covered in the NDS are summarized in NDS Table 7.3.1, *Applicability of Adjustment Factors for Connections*. A similar table for the fasteners covered in this book is included inside the back cover of this book for convenient reference. The specific adjustment factors for nails, bolts, lag bolts, and split ring and shear plate connectors are reviewed in detail in Chaps. 12 and 13.

The fasteners covered in this book are those that are most likely to be found in a typical wood-frame building. Other fasteners included in the NDS are

1. Wood screws

2. Metal plate connectors

3. Drift bolts and drift pins

4. Spike grids

Wood screws are similar to lag bolts, but wood screws are smaller in diameter and do not have a hex (or square) bolt head. Wood screws are inserted with a screwdriver or screw gun, but lag bolts are installed with a wrench. Wood screws have allowable structural design values, but the load capacities are relatively small. They have some application in manufactured housing, but because of their relatively low strength, wood screws are not often used in conventional wood-frame construction. For larger design loads, lag bolts are the more likely choice.

Metal plate connectors are frequently found in wood buildings that use prefabricated light-frame wood trusses. A photograph of metal plate connected trusses was given in Fig. 6.33*b*. Metal plate connectors are light-gage metal plates that connect the truss members together. Metal plate connectors are also known as *nail plates* or *truss plates* and are typically

Figure 11.3   Metal plate connectors. *(FPL.)*

produced by pressing or stamping sheet metal to form teeth or barbs which protrude from the side of the plate. See Fig. 11.3. The protrusions serve as the "nails" for the nail plate. Alternatively, conventional nails can be driven through holes punched (without protrusions) in metal nail plates. Metal plate connectors usually have teeth or barbs that become embedded in the wood members during the fabrication of a wood truss.

The load capacity of particular type of truss plate is determined by testing, and the load rating is usually given in pounds per square inch of contact area between the metal plate and the wood member. When a truss is analyzed, the forces to be transferred between the wood members are determined. The required size of metal plate connector is then obtained by dividing the force by the allowable load per square inch for the nail plate. The overall size and configuration of a metal plate connector must provide the necessary contact areas for each member in the joint. Truss plates can be found in many wood buildings, but they can be viewed as a specialty item. The design of metal plate connectors is usually handled by a truss manufacturer, and their use is typically restricted to a manufacturing plant operating under a formal quality control program. See Ref. 23.1 for information.

Drift bolts and *drift pins* are unthreaded steel rods that are driven into a hole bored through one wood member and into the adjacent member. *Spike grids* are intended for use in wood pile and pole construction. Drift pins and spike grids are also considered specialty fasteners. A number of fasteners are used in wood construction in addition to those included in the NDS.

Information on a variety of fasteners may be obtained from the *Wood Handbook* (Refs. 4.1 and 4.2), the *TCM* (Ref. 3.1), the International Staple, Nail and Tool Association (see Ref. 15.2), Ref. 34.3, and catalogs of other suppliers. The hardware used in conjunction with wood fasteners is covered in Chap. 14.

11.3   Yield Model for Laterally Loaded Fasteners

In the past the capacity of laterally loaded nails, bolts, and lag bolts was obtained from load tables given in earlier editions of the NDS. These tables were also included in building codes, typically in abbreviated form. The load values in these tables were obtained from empirical formulas which are summarized in various editions of the *Wood Handbook* (Refs. 4.1 and 4.2). Recall that the new symbol for the nominal design value of a laterally loaded fastener is Z.

The empirical formulas were based on the *proportional limit* strength of connections that were tested at the Forest Products Laboratory (FPL) during the 1930s. The empirical formulas from the *Wood Handbook* contain parameters that are important to connection performance such as fastener diameter and length. However, the empirical expressions simply reproduced load values that were obtained from laboratory testing programs. These formulas cannot be derived using principles of engineering mechanics and may not be appropriate for all connections.

In the 1940s an approach to connection analysis was developed in Europe that was based on the yielding of the various elements in the connection. In the 1980s a number of papers were published by FPL and other researchers that confirmed the yield model theory. Essentially these studies concluded that an engineering mechanics approach based on yield limit theory is appropriate for analyzing *dowel-type fasteners* in wood connections (Refs. 4.3 and 4.4).

Traditionally a dowel is thought to be a circular rod of wood or metal that is placed in a hole which has been drilled in a wood member or members. However, in the context of the 1991 NDS, the term *dowel-type fastener* simply refers to the yield theory of connection analysis for nails, bolts, and lag bolts.

The idea is that these fasteners act similar to a dowel as they bear against the grain in a wood member under a lateral load. The term *lateral load* here refers to a load that is perpendicular to the length of the fastener, i.e., a *shear connection*. The load may or may not include the effects of lateral wind or earthquake forces. The yield limit model applies only to shear connections and not to fasteners loaded in withdrawal. Withdrawal connections are still covered by empirical formulas from the *Wood Handbook*.

In utilizing the new system, the various yield modes that could occur in a given type of connection are analyzed. A load capacity is computed for each of the various modes. The yield limit is then taken as the smallest of these load capacities. This critical load defines the *yield mechanism* for the connection. It should be noted that the yield limit equations for Z in the NDS include an appropriate factor of safety.

An engineering mechanics approach to connection design, such as the yield limit model, has both advantages and disadvantages. The principal advantage is that the designer can mathematically analyze a connection of practically any configuration. Thus, the designer is not limited to joint configurations and details that are given in the NDS or Code tables. In the past, if a connection did not match the details in the table, the designer was forced either to revise the connection or to extrapolate values from a table that may not have been appropriate.

In addition, the yield limit model is able to take into account the strength of different fastener materials. In the older empirical method, a certain fastener strength was simply presumed. However, the yield theory directly incorporates the yield strength of a fastener into the analysis. A final advantage is that the yield limit model can be used to evaluate the strength of a connection involving wood members of different species, or a connection between a wood member and another material.

On the negative side, the application of the yield model to connection design can involve the use of some rather cumbersome equations. The number of equations varies with the fastener type (nails, bolts, and lag bolts) and whether the fastener is in single shear or double shear. However, regardless of the particular conditions, application of the yield limit model in equation form requires the consideration of a number of possible yield modes. The equations can be lengthy and awkward to solve by hand on a calculator. Fortunately the yield equations are easy to program and solve on a microcomputer using any of the popular spreadsheet programs.

In keeping with the *equation format,* the 1991 NDS contains a complete set of yield limit equations for the analysis of dowel-type fasteners. However, the NDS takes a balanced approach to this problem. It recognizes that some designers may not need or want the sophistication provided by the formal yield limit equations. Thus, for the designer who does only an occasional wood connection design, or for the designer who simply does not want to become involved with the yield equations, the 1991 NDS also provides a conservative set of load tables for the various types of fasteners.

The NDS load tables are based on the yield limit equations, but are simplified from the general theory by reducing the number of parameters used to obtain load capacity. For example, the tables apply to connections with all members from the same species of wood, and they cover only a limited number of species (specific gravities). Except for nails, the tables also handle only parallel- and perpendicular-to-grain loadings.

Therefore, the tables are simple, conservative, and relatively easy to use. They apply to a certain set of common but limited conditions. Although using the fastener tables may be easier than solving the yield equations on a calculator, the 1991 NDS tables are more involved than those found in previous editions.

The fastener load tables are limited in scope, and the real advantage of the yield limit model comes in the automated evaluation of the yield equations. In this way all of the details affecting a particular connection may be taken into account. In addition, there are some fastener problems that *require* use of the yield limit equations. For example, the NDS bolt tables cover only parallel- and perpendicular-to-grain loading, and the equations will be necessary to evaluate loading at some other angle to grain.

A programmed solution to the yield equations using a microcomputer spreadsheet can be easier than looking up a value in the NDS fastener tables. Solving the yield limit equations is, in fact, an elementary task on a spreadsheet. After the equations have been solved once, a spreadsheet *template* is created which can be used for other similar problems. The template can also be expanded to include some of the other design provisions such as the adjustment factors for wood connections.

The remaining portion of this chapter summarizes several of the important properties that affect the behavior of dowel-type connections. This is given in order to develop a general understanding of the rationale behind the theory, without attempting to derive the lengthy equations. The possible yield modes are also reviewed for typical two-member and three-member connections.

11.4   Factors Affecting Strength in Yield Model

It has been stated that the yield limit model is appropriate for the design of nails, bolts, lag bolts, and wood screws used in shear connections. For reasons given in Sec. 11.2, the design of wood screw connections is not covered in this book. Split rings and shear plate connectors may not behave as dowel-type fasteners, and because of their rather limited use, they are addressed only briefly (Chap. 13).

The yield limit model for dowel-type fasteners is based upon engineering mechanics, and it uses *connection geometry* and *material properties* to evaluate strength. The primary factors used to compute the nominal design value Z include

1. Fastener diameter D
2. Member thickness t
3. Fastener bending yield strength F_{yb}
4. Dowel bearing strength of wood member F_e
   a. Specific gravity (dry) of wood member SG
   b. Angle of load to grain of wood member θ
   c. Relative size of fastener (large or small diameter)
5. In the case of metal side plates, the dowel bearing strength F_e of the metal

The notation in the above list is usually expanded by adding subscripts m and s to the appropriate terms to indicate whether the symbols apply to the main member or the side member. For example, t_m, F_{em}, SG_m, and θ_m refer to the thickness, dowel bearing strength, specific gravity, and angle of load to grain for the *main member*. Likewise, t_s, F_{es}, SG_s, and θ_s represent the corresponding properties for the *side member*. *Member thicknesses* were labeled in Fig. 11.1. In a two-member bolted connection, the main member is the thicker member; and in a three-member connection, the main member is the center member. In a two-member nail or lag bolt connection, the member holding the pointed end of the fastener is the main member. The other members in the connections are the side members.

The bending *yield strength of the fastener* F_{yb} is a property which is used to predict the load capacity of a mechanism that involves the formation of a plastic hinge (Sec. 11.6) in the fastener. The NDS provides typical values of bending yield strength for various types of fasteners. These values may be used in the event that material properties for a specific fastener are not available. Values of F_{yb} for the fasteners given in the NDS are representative of those found in the field and are generally thought to be conservative. See NDS Appendix I for additional information.

The *dowel bearing strength* F_e is the strength property of the members in a connection that resists *embedding* of a dowel. Designers familiar with structural steel can best relate this property to the allowable bearing stress F_p on a steel plate in a bolted connection.

In wood design, the value of F_e depends on a number of different factors. The formulas for dowel bearing strength are given in Sec. 11.5. It is important to understand that the members in a connection can have different dowel bearing strengths. Because F_e depends on the specific gravity of the wood, one way to have different dowel bearing strengths in the same connection is to have main and side members from different species.

The angle of load to grain θ also may cause F_e to be different for the main and side members. Several typical uses of bolts and lag bolts in shear-type connections were illustrated in Example 11.1 (Sec. 11.2). The connections in this earlier example were made up of only wood members, and in each case the load was applied parallel to the length of the member. The load, therefore, was parallel to the grain, and the angle of load to grain was zero ($\theta = 0$ degrees).

The wood members in a connection may have different angles of load to grain. For example, the load from a fastener can cause bearing parallel to the grain in one member and bearing perpendicular to the grain in another member. Other connections may involve loading at an angle θ other than 0 or 90 degrees to the grain. See Fig. 11.4a in Example 11.3.

The dowel bearing strength for a wood member is greatest when the load is parallel to the grain and weakest for a load perpendicular to the grain. For intermediate angles, the bearing strength lies between the parallel- and perpendicular-to-grain values. (*Exception:* small-diameter fasteners have the same dowel bearing strength regardless of angle of load to grain—see Sec. 11.5.)

In other common connections, metal side members are used. These can be full-size structural-steel members, but often the side plates are some form of metal connection hardware. See Fig. 11.4*b*. The dowel bearing strength of a steel plate is much greater than it is for a wood member.

EXAMPLE 11.3   Examples of Different Dowel Bearing Strengths in the Same Connection

Different dowel bearing strengths can result from different angles of load to grain or the use of side members of different materials.

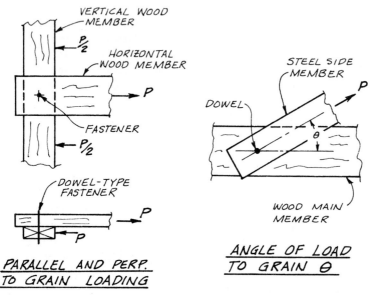

Figure 11.4*a*   Depending on fastener size, the angle of load to grain may have an effect on the dowel bearing strength of a wood member. In the sketch on the left, the load transmitted by the fastener is parallel to the grain in the horizontal wood member and perpendicular to the grain in the vertical member. On the right, the load is at an angle θ to the direction of the grain in the wood member.

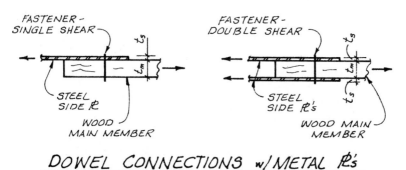

Figure 11.4*b*   Dowel-type fasteners are often used in wood connections with steel side plates. Single-shear and double-shear applications are common in wood-to-metal connections. The dowel bearing strength F_e for a steel plate is obviously much larger than F_e for a wood member.

If a metal side member is used in a connection, the plate is to be designed in accordance with recognized engineering practice. For example, a steel side plate should meet the requirements of the American Institute of Steel Construction (AISC) or the American Iron and Steel Institute (AISI). In addition, the *ultimate tensile strength* of the steel F_u is used to define the dowel bearing strength for the metal plate for use in the yield limit equations for the wood connection.

The major factors that affect the nominal design value Z of an individual dowel-type fastener according to the yield limit model have been briefly introduced. Some additional information regarding dowel bearing strength and the bending of fasteners in a connection is given in the following sections.

Recall that there are a number of other adjustments that may affect the allowable load Z'. These additional factors may apply to all types of connections (e.g., load duration factor C_D), or the factors may apply only to specific types of fasteners (e.g., penetration depth factor C_d for lag bolts). The strength adjustment factors that are not part of the yield limit model are covered in subsequent chapters which deal with specific fasteners.

11.5 Dowel Bearing Strength

The *property of wood* that affects the nominal design value Z of a nail, bolt, or lag bolt is known as *dowel bearing strength.* In much of the research literature, this property is termed *embedding strength,* hence the notation F_e. It is related to the crushing strength of the wood member under loading from a dowel subjected to a shear load. As noted in the previous section, the dowel bearing strength varies with the *specific gravity* of the wood and the relative size of the dowel. For large-diameter fasteners, the *angle of load to grain* also affects the dowel bearing strength.

Values of specific gravity for the various combinations of lumber species are given in a number of tables including NDS Table 8A for bolts, NDS Table 9A for lag bolts, and NDS Table 12A for nails. It is suggested that the reader briefly examine these tables, noting that values of SG are the same in all tables. Dowel bearing strengths, however, are not the same in all of these tables. In practice, the dowel bearing strength for use in a connection problem may be obtained from these tables. This will undoubtedly be the case for a hand solution of the yield limit equations. In contrast, if the equations for Z are programmed on the computer or solved on a spreadsheet, the *formulas for F_e* given in Example 11.4 may be useful.

Tests have shown that the dowel bearing strength of *large-diameter* fasteners depends on the angle of load to grain. Consequently, there is one formula for dowel bearing strength for parallel-to-grain loading ($F_{e\parallel}$) and another for perpendicular-to-grain loading ($F_{e\perp}$). For intermediate angles of load to grain, the Hankinson formula is used to obtain a dowel bearing strength ($F_{e\theta}$) that lies between $F_{e\parallel}$ and $F_{e\perp}$. The Hankinson formula was first introduced in Sec. 6.8 in a form for evaluating the allowable bearing stress in a wood member. The same expression, with a simple change in notation, is appropriate for determining the dowel bearing strength for fastener design.

Small-diameter dowels do not exhibit the directional strength characteristics of large fasteners, and a single expression defines dowel bearing strength regardless of the direction of loading. The shank diameter separating the categories of large dowels and small dowels is between ¼ and ⅜ in. Large-diameter fasteners (such as bolts and lag bolts) are installed in drilled holes. In contrast, small dowel-type fasteners (such as nails) are usually driven into the wood with a hammer or pneumatic gun.

EXAMPLE 11.4   Formulas for Dowel Bearing Strength

Numerical values of dowel bearing strength are listed in the 1991 NDS:

Bolts	NDS Table 8A
Lag bolts	NDS Table 9A
Nails and spikes	NDS Table 12A

The values in the NDS tables are based on the following expressions:

LARGE DOWELS:

Parallel-to-grain loading: $\qquad\qquad\qquad F_{e\parallel} = 11{,}200(\mathrm{SG})$

Perpendicular-to-grain loading: $\qquad\qquad F_{e\perp} = 6100(\mathrm{SG}^{1.45})D^{-0.5}$

The Hankinson formula gives F_e at an angle of load to grain θ

$$F_{e\theta} = \frac{F_{e\parallel}F_{e\perp}}{F_{e\parallel}\sin^2\theta + F_{e\perp}\cos^2\theta}$$

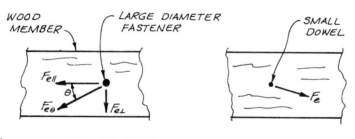

$F_{e\parallel}$ – PARALLEL TO GRAIN
$F_{e\perp}$ – PERPENDICULAR TO GRAIN
$F_{e\theta}$ – ANGLE TO GRAIN θ

F_e – ANY ANGLE TO GRAIN

LARGE DOWELS   SMALL DOWELS

Figure 11.5 Definition of dowel bearing strength depends on relative size of fastener. The dowel bearing strength F_e for *large*-diameter fasteners is a function of angle of load to grain. Specific gravity and diameter also are important. The F_e for *small*-diameter fasteners depends only on specific gravity.

SMALL DOWELS:

All angles of load to grain: $\qquad F_e = 16{,}600 \ \mathrm{SG}^{1.84}$

where F_e = dowel bearing strength; subscripts $\parallel$, $\perp$, and θ indicate strengths parallel
to grain, perpendicular to grain, and at an angle to grain θ
$\quad$ SG = specific gravity (dry) of wood member
$\qquad D$ = diameter of dowel-type fastener

The yield limit model is capable of handling a wide variety of wood connections including those in which the main and side members have different dowel bearing strengths. Several situations are described in Sec. 11.4 where F_{em} and F_{es} are not equal. On the other hand, in a number of design conditions the dowel bearing strength will be the same for the main and side members.

The formulas for dowel bearing strength in Example 11.4 are obtained from Ref. 4.5. Again, these formulas may be more convenient than the tables for F_e if the yield limit equations for Z are programmed on the computer. The dowel bearing strength formulas are evaluated for several fasteners in Example 11.5 to simply confirm the NDS tables.

EXAMPLE 11.5   NDS Dowel Bearing Values

Use the appropriate formulas from Example 11.4 to evaluate the dowel bearing strength values in the NDS tables for the following fasteners. Note that the values for F_e in the NSD tables are rounded to the nearest 50 psi.

LARGE DOWELS

Bolts:
 a. ⅝-in.-diameter bolt in DF-L with load applied parallel to grain ($\theta = 0$ degrees)
     Values of specific gravity are available in several NDS tables including Table 8A. For DF-L the specific gravity is 0.50.

$$F_{e\parallel} = 11{,}200(\mathrm{SG}) = 11{,}200 \times 0.50 = 5600 \ \mathrm{psi}$$

This value agrees with $F_{e\parallel}$ in NDS Table 8A.
 b. ¾-in.-diameter bolt in DF-L with load applied perpendicular to grain ($\theta = 90$ degrees)

$$F_{e\perp} = 6100(\mathrm{SG})^{1.45}D^{-0.5}$$

$$= 6100(0.50)^{1.45}(0.75)^{-0.5}$$

$$= 2578 \ \mathrm{psi} \approx 2600 \qquad \text{from NDS Table 8A}$$

Lag bolts:
 a. ½-in.-diameter lag bolt in DF-L with load applied parallel to grain ($\theta = 0$ degrees)

$$F_{e\parallel} = 11{,}200(\mathrm{SG}) = 11{,}200 \times 0.50 = 5600 \ \mathrm{psi}$$

This value agrees with $F_{e\parallel}$ in NDS Table 9A.

b. ¾-in.-diameter lag bolt in DF-L with load applied perpendicular to grain ($\theta = 90$ degrees)

$$F_{e\perp} = 6100(SG)^{1.45}D^{-0.5}$$

$$= 6100(0.50)^{1.45}(0.75)^{-0.5}$$

$$= 2578 \text{ psi} \approx 2600 \qquad \text{from NDS Table 9A}$$

NOTE: For a given D, θ, and SG, these examples show that F_e is the same for bolts and lag bolts.

SMALL DOWELS

Nails: 16d common nail at any angle of load to grain

$$F_e = 16{,}600(SG)^{1.84} = 16{,}600(0.50)^{1.84}$$

$$= 4637 \text{ psi} \approx 4650 \text{ psi} \qquad \text{from NDS Table 12A}$$

In the case of a connection between a wood member and a metal side plate, it is necessary to have the equivalent of an embedding strength value for the metal member. A conservative practice for a steel member is to use the ultimate tensile strength of steel F_u as the dowel bearing strength (that is, $F_e = F_u$). For the wood member in the same connection, F_e is defined as in Example 11.4. (*Note:* In steel design, Ref. 11.1 recommends $F_p = 1.2F_u$.)

This section concludes with a brief discussion of the dowel bearing capacity of a fastener in a *glulam* beam and in *plywood* sheathing. It will be recalled from Chap. 5 that higher-quality laminating stock is located at the outer tension and compression zones in a glulam bending member, and lower-quality material is placed in the inner core. In fact, the manufacturing specifications permit the mixing of different species of wood in the same member (i.e., the inner core may be from a weaker species than the outer laminations). Although mixing different species groups is permitted, most current practice is to manufacture a glulam member with material from a single species group.

If a glulam beam is produced from a single species group, a single specific gravity applies to the member. Values of SG can be obtained from the NDS tables that were previously described. Dowel bearing strength for the glulam may be computed using the expressions given in Example 11.4, or the value of F_e may be read from the appropriate table for bolts, lag bolts, or nails (NDS Tables 8A, 9A, or 12A).

In the event that a glulam is manufactured with material from more than one species group, there will be a different dowel bearing strength for each species group. See Example 11.6. A conservative approach to connection design is to use F_e based on the specific gravity for the inner core laminations. To take advantage of a larger F_e for the outer laminations, the designer will have to investigate the layup of a given member. In other words, to use the dowel bearing strength for the outer laminations, the designer must be assured that the fastener, or group of fasteners, is located entirely within the laminations with the higher F_e. Assistance can be obtained from the glulam manufacturer or AITC for special cases involving a larger F_e for a portion of the member.

EXAMPLE 11.6   Dowel Bearing Strength in Glulam Beams

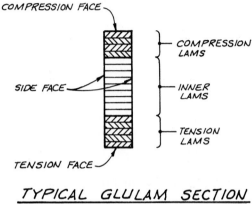

Figure 11.6 Distribution of laminations in a glulam follows bending stress distribution.

Most glulam beams produced today are manufactured with laminating stock from a single species group, and F_e is a function of a single specific gravity. In a member with outer laminations from one species group and inner laminations from another, two different specific gravities apply. To use the larger F_e, the fasteners must be located entirely inside the laminations from the denser species group.

Preliminary research (Ref. 4.4) indicates that the dowel bearing strength for a small-diameter fastener in *plywood* can be obtained by the formula given in Example 11.4. Several examples will be given in later chapters based on this assumption. However, the dowel bearing strength in plywood and other structural-use panels is still under investigation at APA, and the equation for F_e in plywood may be adjusted as additional information is obtained.

11.6   Plastic Hinge in Fastener

Dowel bearing strength is the primary factor that measures the strength of the wood members in a connection. In addition to this, the strength of the fastener can affect the yield limit mechanism of a connection. The mode of failure in a fastener is related to the formation of one or more *plastic hinges.* Designers who are familiar with the behavior of structural-steel members already understand the concept of a plastic hinge, but it is reviewed here briefly.

At normal temperatures, structural steel behaves in a ductile manner. In other words, the material can undergo large deformations before rupture occurs. This behavior is best seen on a stress-strain diagram for steel. See Fig. 11.7. The horizontal yield plateau is characteristic of the material. The ability of steel to undergo large deformations without rupture is essential to the formation of a plastic hinge.

In structural-steel design, a plastic hinge is usually introduced by examining the bending stress diagram in a beam as the member is loaded through several stages. See Example 11.7. In order for a plastic hinge to form, the beam must be braced so that buckling does not occur.

Consider what happens to the member as the load is increased to the point where the bending stress reaches yield F_y at the outside fibers. The beam does not collapse simply because the outer fibers in the member reach F_y. In fact, the member can carry additional load beyond this point as inner portions of the cross section reach yield. Because of the ductile nature of the material, this behavior continues until the entire section yields.

The deformation of the outside fibers of the beam takes place over a relatively small portion of the beam length. On either side of this localized yielding, the beam remains relatively straight. This behavior leads to the concept of a plastic hinge.

A plastic hinge corresponds to a rectangular bending stress block in which all of the fibers have reached the yield stress. By definition, a real hinge is a structural element that does not transmit moment. In contrast, a plastic hinge develops the plastic moment capacity M_p of the cross section. However, once M_p is reached at the point of local maximum moment, additional bend-

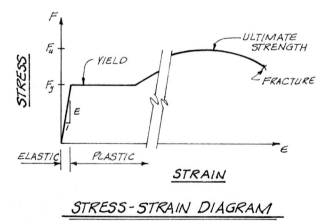

Figure 11.7 Typical stress-strain diagram for a ductile steel.

EXAMPLE 11.7   Formation of a Plastic Hinge in a Steel Beam

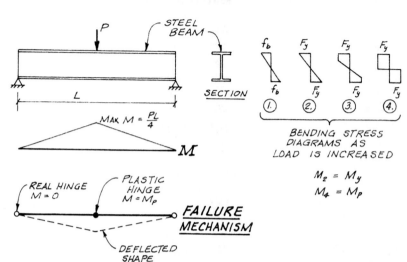

Figure 11.8 Formation of a plastic hinge (P.H.) in a structural steel beam. In a simply supported beam, the formation of a single plastic hinge causes a failure or collapse mechanism to develop.

The loading diagram for the W-shape beam has a concentrated load at the midspan. Several bending stress diagrams are given to show various stages as the load is increased. The steps in the formation of a plastic hinge are as follows:

1. Small load P causes a small bending stress f_b. The member is elastic, and the stress diagram is triangular with zero stress at the neutral axis and maximum stress at the outside fibers. The maximum bending stress is below the yield point.

2. Larger bending load causes the maximum bending stress to reach yield at the outside fibers ($f_b = F_y$). The moment in the beam that corresponds to this stress diagram is the yield moment M_y, and the load is known as the yield load P_y.

3. As the concentrated load is increased, the beam does not collapse (assuming that buckling is prevented). Because of the ductile nature of the material, the outer fibers simply continue to deform with no increase in stress. However, the inner fibers increase in stress until yielding occurs. This pattern of increasing the stress of the inner fibers continues until all of the fibers eventually yield.

4. When all fibers of the cross section have reached F_y, a *plastic hinge* has formed. The moment at the cross section is known as the plastic moment M_p, and the cross section at the point of maximum moment is incapable of carrying any additional moment. Thus, the plastic hinge functions as a real hinge as far as additional loading is concerned.

When a single plastic hinge forms in a simply supported beam, a failure mechanism develops. The plastic hinge at the midspan causes the formation of an unstable linkage (three hinges on a straight line) or failure mechanism. Note, in the sketch of the linkage, a real hinge is shown as an open circle, and the plastic hinge is shown as a solid circle. The load that causes a mechanism to form is known as the *ultimate* or *collapse load,* and it is given the symbol P_u.

ing moment cannot be developed by the member. Thus, a plastic hinge functions similar to a real hinge as far as *additional* loading is concerned.

The cross-sectional property that measures the plastic moment capacity of a member is known as the plastic section modulus Z. The plastic moment capacity is the product of the plastic section modulus and the yield stress ($M_p = ZF_y$). This relationship is analogous to the one for maximum elastic moment, which is the elastic section modulus times the yield stress ($M_y = SF_y$). Additional information on plastic section modulus can be found in books on steel structures.

Now that the concept of a plastic hinge has been introduced, the idea of a failure mechanism can be addressed in a little more detail. In a steel beam, a failure mechanism is a structural form that cannot support a load. It is characterized by large, unbounded displacements. In a beam or similar structure, the failure mechanism is associated with the collapse load.

The method of structural analysis that deals with the determination of collapse mechanisms is known as *plastic analysis*. Plastic analysis involves adding a sufficient number of plastic hinges to an initially stable structure to form a failure mechanism. The most elementary form of a collapse mechanism for a steel beam is a one with three hinges on a straight line. Once this form develops, the structure is unstable. One of the objectives in plastic analysis is to determine the collapse load P_u, which is the smallest load that will cause a failure mechanism to develop.

The linkage mechanism in Fig. 11.8 was created by the formation of a single plastic hinge in the beam. Whether or not a single plastic hinge causes the development of a collapse mechanism depends on the support conditions for the member. In a simply supported beam, only one plastic hinge is needed to produce a failure mechanism. However, for other support conditions, additional plastic hinges may be required. See Example 11.8. The beam in this example is fixed at one end and pinned at the other, and the development of a collapse mechanism occurs in several stages.

The first plastic hinge logically occurs at the point of maximum moment. However, the first plastic hinge does not produce a failure mechanism. For additional loading (beyond the loading required to cause the first plastic hinge), the beam appears to be a member that is pinned at both ends. There is a real hinge at one end of the member and a plastic hinge at the other end. A collapse mechanism with three hinges in line requires the formation of a second plastic hinge. The second plastic hinge develops under the concentrated load.

EXAMPLE 11.8   Formation of Two Plastic Hinges in a Steel Beam

A plastic hinge first develops at the fixed end, which is the point of maximum moment. However, a failure mechanism does not occur until an increased load causes a second plastic hinge under the concentrated load. The linkage created by the second plastic hinge has three hinges on a straight line: one real hinge and two plastic hinges.

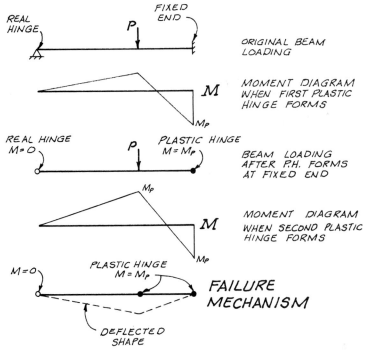

Figure 11.9 Steel beam fixed at one end and pinned at the other. Two plastic hinges are required to develop a mechanism.

The formation of a plastic hinge in a structural-steel member and the development of a failure mechanism have been discussed here for orientation and review. There are some major differences between the behavior of a dowel-type steel fastener used in a wood connection and the structural-steel beams just reviewed. One difference is that the cross section of a fastener is circular. However, the configuration of the cross section does not change the concept of a plastic hinge.

Another difference is that the mechanism in a wood connection is not that of a structural-steel beam. The behavior of a dowel-type fastener is more complex. In addition, there is a reserve capacity in a wood connection; hence the term *yield limit* is applied to wood connections rather than *collapse load*.

However, the elementary beam examples are useful to define the concept of a plastic hinge and a mechanism. At this point it should simply be understood that dowel-type fasteners (bolts, lag bolts, and nails) of a ductile metal can develop one or more plastic hinges as a *yield mechanism* is formed in a wood connection.

The 1991 NDS contains a complete set of yield limit equations to evaluate the nominal load capacity of the various yield mechanisms. Some of the mechanisms involve crushing of the wood fibers (exceeding the dowel bearing strength), and others are the result of a plastic hinge forming in the fastener combined with crushing of the wood fibers. The designer need not be fully conversant with the derivation of the yield limit equations, but an understanding of the various yield modes is important. A general summary of these modes is given in Sec. 11.7 for single-shear and double-shear wood connections.

11.7   Yield Limit Mechanisms

Several properties critical to the performance of dowel-type fasteners have been introduced in this chapter. These include connection geometry, dowel bearing strength of the members, and a plastic hinge in a fastener. These factors are used in the *yield limit equations* for laterally loaded nails, bolts, and lag bolts to evaluate the nominal design value Z for a single fastener.

To summarize the general procedure, there are several possible yield modes for dowel-type fasteners. An equation is provided in the NDS to evaluate the load capacity for each mode. The nominal design value Z for a particular fastener is then taken as the smallest value considering all of the appropriate modes.

The remaining portion of this chapter describes graphically the various yield limit modes that can occur in shear-type connections. The yield limit equations are lengthy and vary with the type of fastener. Therefore, only the yield limit modes are described here, and the specific equations for nails, bolts, and lag bolts are given in later chapters. The modes of failure are common to all dowel-type connections, and the yield limit mechanisms described here will be referenced in subsequent chapters.

Some modes that apply to single-shear (two-member) connections do not occur in double-shear (three-member) connections because of the symmetric loading that takes place in double-shear connections. See Example 11.9. The yield limit modes are as follows:

Mode I: Dowel bearing failure under uniform bearing.   The bearing stress in a Mode I failure is uniform because in this yield mechanism the fastener does not rotate or bend. The dowel bearing strength of a wood member is simply exceeded under uniform bearing. The possibility of a Mode I failure must be considered in each wood member in the connection. Consequently, a Mode I mechanism is further classified as a Mode I_m failure if the dowel bearing strength is exceeded in the main member. If the overstress occurs in the side member, the mechanism is a Mode I_s.

The need to check for a bearing failure in each member stems from the fact that the dowel bearing strength can be different for the main and side members (i.e., F_{em} and F_{es} may not be equal). Different strengths can be the result of mixing different species of wood in a connection or of having a different angle of load to grain for the main and side members.

It should be recalled that there is also a definition of dowel bearing strength for steel members as well as wood members. The F_e for a steel member is a necessary parameter for the general yield limit equations. However, there is not a load duration effect in steel. Consequently, the yield limit formula for a Mode I_s mechanism is not applied to steel side members (this is clearly called to the attention of the designer in the NDS). In other words, the designer should check the bearing stress in a steel side member in accordance with accepted (e.g., AISC or AISI) steel design practice.

Mode II: Dowel bearing failure under nonuniform bearing. The second principal failure mechanism also causes the dowel bearing strength to be exceeded. In this case, the fastener remains straight, but it undergoes rotation. Rotation causes a nonuniform bearing stress, and the wood fibers are crushed at the outside face of each member. Because of symmetry, a Mode II failure does not occur in a three-member connection.

Mode III: Plastic hinge located near each shear plane. In a Mode III mechanism, the dowel bends and a plastic hinge forms in the fastener. In a single-shear connection, the plastic hinge can occur within the side member or the main member, near the shear plane. There are two yield equations associated with a Mode III failure, and the mechanisms are further classified as Mode III_m and Mode III_s.

If the plastic hinge occurs inside one member, there is a corresponding crushing of the wood fibers in the other member. This is one reason why the failure mechanisms in a wood connection are more complex than those for the steel beams described in Sec. 11.6. The mechanism is classified as a Mode III_m failure when the dowel bearing strength is exceeded in the main member. Likewise, a Mode III_s indicates a crushing of the wood fibers in the side member. The notation emphasizes the member in which the dowel bearing strength is exceeded, rather than the member which contains the plastic hinge.

In a double-shear connection, two plastic hinges may form (one near each shear plane) with crushing of the wood fibers in the side members. This is known as a Mode III_s mechanism. A Mode III_m mechanism does not occur in three-member connections.

Mode IV: Two plastic hinges near each shear plane. The final mechanism covered by the yield model involves the formation of two plastic hinges at each shear plane. Mode IV failures can occur in both single-shear and double-shear connections.

The yield limit model for fasteners thus covers four general modes of failure. In a single-shear connection, Mode I and Mode III failures can occur in either the main member or side member, and these bring the total possible number of yield mechanisms to six. As noted, there is one yield equation for each yield mode. Because of symmetry there are only four yield mechanisms for a double-shear connection.

It should be noted that a commentary on the 1991 NDS is currently being developed by NFPA. The commentary will provide additional information on the historical development of the yield limit equations and a comprehensive summary of the supporting research.

EXAMPLE 11.9   Yield Modes

Dowel-type fasteners can yield in several modes. See Fig. 11.10. These modes are also sketched in *NDS Appendix I*.

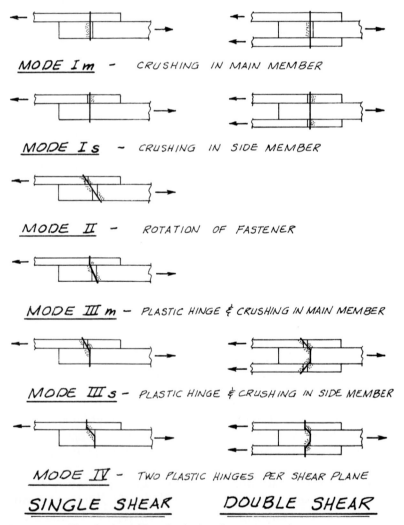

MODE I m – CRUSHING IN MAIN MEMBER

MODE I s – CRUSHING IN SIDE MEMBER

MODE II – ROTATION OF FASTENER

MODE III m – PLASTIC HINGE & CRUSHING IN MAIN MEMBER

MODE III s – PLASTIC HINGE & CRUSHING IN SIDE MEMBER

MODE IV – TWO PLASTIC HINGES PER SHEAR PLANE

SINGLE SHEAR   *DOUBLE SHEAR*

Figure 11.10 Four basic yield modes in dowel-type connections.

To fully cover the four basic yield modes, there are a total of six yield limit equations for single-shear connections. The two additional equations are required because Mode I and Mode III failures can occur in either the main or side members. In double-shear connections, Mode II and Mode III$_\mathrm{m}$ mechanisms do not occur, and three-member connections are fully covered by four yield model equations.

In practice, the designer will establish a trial configuration for a particular wood connection. This defines the geometry and strength parameters for use in determining the nominal design value Z for a single fastener. This nominal strength is the smallest load capacity obtained from all of the appropriate yield equations for the connection. The nominal strength is then subject to the other adjustments that account for the number of fasteners, duration of load, moisture content, and so on. The allowable fastener load with *all* adjustments taken into account is given the symbol Z'. Once the allowable load has been determined, a decision can be made about the trial joint configuration.

The basic concept of the yield model approach to wood connection design has been introduced in Chap. 11. With this background, the reader can explore the detailed design provisions for the common fasteners used in wood connections. To the designer who is familiar with the previous empirical design procedures, the yield limit model may seem overly complicated. This perception will undoubtedly be reinforced by the rather complex nature of the yield limit equations. However, much time and effort has gone into studying the behavior of wood connections, and the introduction of the yield limit equations into the NDS has brought wood engineering into the modern age.

In spite of the rather technical nature of the general yield theory, there are several factors that simplify the problem. First, all six of the general equations need be applied to only one type of connection problem: a bolted connection in single shear. Other connections do not require all six yield equations. It has already been noted that two modes of failure (Mode II and Mode III$_\mathrm{m}$) do not occur in double-shear connections. Two yield equations are thus eliminated for three-member joints. In connections involving fasteners other than bolts, the equations for still other yield modes need not be considered. This is justified through studies covering a wide range of fastener applications. These studies show that some yield modes simply do not control the design of certain connections. Therefore, a number of yield equations are eliminated in the NDS for some types of fasteners.

Finally, it should be recalled that the designer is not forced to obtain load capacities for all connections by evaluating the yield limit equations. The 1991 NDS contains a number of load tables that allow the designer to read directly a fastener value for many common applications. The tables are based on the appropriate yield limit equations and a simplified set of criteria. The intent of the 1991 NDS was to provide the occasional user with an alternative to programming the equations or to solving the equations by hand. Although the tables provide appropriate design values for many connections, the tables do not cover all loading conditions, and use of the yield limit equations cannot be avoided entirely. It has been noted previously that the yield limit equations are easy to solve on a modern spreadsheet program, and a spreadsheet template may involve less effort than reading the NDS tables.

11.8 Problems

11.1 Define the following terms and briefly describe how the terms relate to wood connections:
  a. Dowel-type fastener
  b. Plastic hinge
  c. Dowel bearing strength
  d. Yield mechanism
  e. Angle of load to grain

11.2 Sketch the yield mechanisms that may occur in a single-shear (two-member) connection that uses a dowel-type fastener. Along with the sketch, give a brief description of each mode.

11.3 Sketch the modes of failure that may occur in a double-shear (three-member) dowel-type connection. Give a brief description of each mode.

11.4 Describe the general concept behind the yield model theory of connection analysis.

11.5 Define the following symbols as used in the yield model for dowel-type fasteners: D, t_s, F_{em}, F_u, SG_s, θ_s, F_{yb}.

11.6 Use the appropriate expressions from Example 11.4 to compute the dowel bearing strengths for the following bolt connections. Compare the results with the values in NDS Table 8A.
  a. ½-in.-diameter bolt in Hem-Fir with load applied parallel to grain
  b. ½-in.-diameter bolt in Hem-Fir with load applied perpendicular to grain
  c. ½-in.-diameter bolt in Hem-Fir with angle of load to grain of 40 degrees
  d. 1-in.-diameter bolt in DF-L with load applied parallel to grain
  e. 1-in.-diameter bolt in DF-L with load applied perpendicular to grain
  f. 1-in.-diameter bolt in DF-L with angle of load to grain of 60 degrees

11.7 Use the appropriate expressions from Example 11.4 to compute the dowel bearing strengths for the following lag bolt (lag screw) connections. Compare the results with the values in NDS Table 9A.
  a. ⅝-in.-diameter lag bolt in Southern Pine with load applied parallel to grain
  b. ⅝-in.-diameter lag bolt in Southern Pine with load applied perpendicular to grain

c. ⅝-in.-diameter lag bolt in Southern Pine with angle of load to grain of 55 degrees

d. ⅝-in.-diameter lag bolt in DF-L with load applied parallel to grain

e. ⅝-in.-diameter lag bolt in DF-L with load applied perpendicular to grain

f. ⅝-in.-diameter lag bolt in DF-L with angle of load to grain of 45 degrees

11.8 Use the appropriate expressions from Example 11.4 to compute the dowel bearing strengths for the following nail connections. Compare the results with the values in NDS Table 12A.

a. 8d nail in Southern Pine with load applied parallel to grain

b. 8d nail in Southern Pine with load applied perpendicular to grain

c. 8d nail in Southern Pine with angle of load to grain of 30 degrees

d. 10d nail in DF-L with load applied parallel to grain

e. 10d nail in DF-L with load applied perpendicular to grain

f. 10d nail in DF-L with angle of load to grain of 45 degrees

12

Nailed and Stapled Connections

12.1 Introduction

The general use of nails in the construction of horizontal diaphragms and shearwalls was addressed in previous chapters. In addition, the two basic forms of nailed connections in structural applications (*shear* and *withdrawal*) were described in the introductory chapter on wood connections. It is recommended that the reader review the joint configurations, nomenclature, and yield modes for these connections in Chap. 11 before proceeding with the detailed design provisions given here.

The usual practice in the United States is to design nailed connections when the loads to be transmitted are relatively small, and to use other types of fasteners (e.g., bolts) for joints with larger loads. This is the general approach to connection design covered in this book. However, this contrasts with recent practice of some designers in Europe and New Zealand to also use nails in connections subjected to large forces. Obviously connections with heavy loads require the use of a large number of nails, and special fabrication practices are necessary. The preference for these types of connections is based on the expected ductile behavior of nailed joints and a corresponding concern about the possible lack of ductility in certain bolted connections, especially those involving large-diameter bolts.

The basic concept of a nail attaching one member to another member has undergone little change, but many developments have occurred in the configuration of nails and in the methods of installation. For example, Ref. 17 lists over 235 definitions and descriptions relating to the use of nails. The majority of these nails are fasteners for special applications, and the structural designer deals with a relatively limited number of nail types. Power-driving equipment has contributed substantially to the advances in this basic type of wood connection.

The different types of nails are distinguished by the following characteristics:

1. Nail head
2. Shank
3. Nail point
4. Material type
5. Surface condition

The first three items have to do with the configuration of the nail. See Fig.
12.1, in which four typical nail heads are shown along with the widely used
diamond-shaped nail point. Many other types of nails are described in Refs.
13.9, 17, and 18.

   This chapter introduces the main types of nails used in structural applications. The yield limit equations for laterally loaded nails are summarized,
and the modification factors for determining allowable fastener loads are
reviewed. Design procedures for the various types of nailed connections are
outlined.

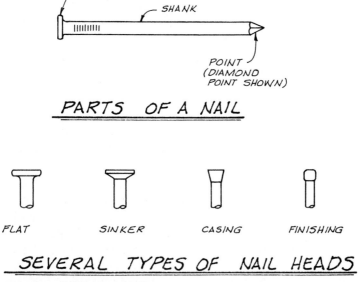

Figure 12.1 Definitions of nail terms.

12.2 Types of Nails

The NDS provides structural design values for the following basic types of
nails:

1. Common nails
2. Box nails

3. Common spikes

4. Threaded hardened steel nails

The size of nails is specified by the pennyweight of the nail, abbreviated d. The pennyweight for different types of nails specifies the length, shank diameter, and head size of the nail. The sizes of the nails listed above are given in NDS Tables 12.3A to 12.3H.

For a given pennyweight, all four basic types of nails have the same length. The first three types have the same basic form, but the diameters are different. They are fabricated from low-carbon-steel wire and have a flat head, plain shank, and diamond point (like the nail shown in Fig. 12.1). The fourth type of nail is made from high-carbon steel and has an annularly or helically threaded shank, a flat head, and a diamond point (some low-carbon threaded steel nails have sinker heads). See Fig. 12.2.

Common nails represent the basic structural nail. Design values for common wire nails are for a nail surface condition that is described as *bright*. This term is used to describe nails with a natural bare-metal finish, and load values for this surface condition can be considered conservative for other surface conditions. The diameter of common wire nails is larger than the diameter of box nails, and allowable loads are correspondingly higher. Because of their large diameter, common nails have less tendency to bend when driven manually.

Box nails are also widely used. They are available in several different surface conditions including bright, galvanized (zinc-coated), and cement-coated. Load values for nails in the bright condition may conservatively be used for other surface conditions. Coated nails are discussed below. The wire diameter of box nails is smaller than that for common nails, and the allowable loads are correspondingly smaller. Box nails also have a greater tendency to bend during driving.

Common spikes are similar in form to common wire nails except that they have a larger diameter. Because of their larger diameter, spikes have higher allowable loads, but the spacing requirements between fasteners are greater in order to avoid splitting of the wood. Predrilling of holes may also be necessary to avoid splitting.

Threaded hardened steel nails are made from high-carbon steel and are heat-treated and tempered to provide greater strength. These nails are especially useful when the lumber may have varying moisture contents. The threaded shank provides better withdrawal capacity in these circumstances. In addition, the higher yield strength values associated with high-carbon steel provide better lateral (shear) resistance.

Design values for threaded hardened steel nails are based on the wire diameter, except that for annularly threaded nails with threads on the shear plane, design values are to be based on the root diameter of the nail.

HELICAL THREAD
ALSO SPIRAL AND SCREW SHANK

Figure 12.2 Threaded hardened steel nails

ANNULAR THREAD
ALSO RING SHANK

The structural designer may encounter some types of *nails not covered in the NDS*. These may include

1. Finishing nails

2. Casing nails

3. Cooler nails

4. Zinc-coated nails

5. Cement-coated nails

Finishing nails are slender, bright, low-carbon-steel nails with a finishing head and a diamond point. These nails are used for finish or trim work, and they may be used for the installation of nonstructural paneling. However, because of the small nail head, finishing nails are not allowed for the attachment of structural sheathing or siding (Sec. 10.3).

Casing nails are slender, low-carbon nails with a casing head and a diamond point. These are available with a zinc coating to reduce staining of wood exposed to the weather. Galvanized casing nails can be used for the structural attachment of plywood siding when the appearance of a flat nail head is considered objectionable. Because of the smaller diameter of the nail head, allowable plywood shearwall values for casing nails are smaller than for common or galvanized box nails (Sec. 10.3).

Cooler nails are slender, low-carbon-steel nails with a flat head and diamond point, and are usually cement-coated. The head diameter is the same as or smaller than that of a common wire nail of the same length. When gypsum wallboard (drywall) of the required thickness is properly installed with the Code-required size and number of cooler nails, a wall may be designed as a shear panel using the allowable loads from UBC Table 47-I (Sec. 10.4).

It was noted earlier that nails can be obtained with a number of different surface conditions. The bright condition was previously described, and several others are introduced in the remainder of this section.

Zinc-coated (galvanized) nails are intended primarily for use where corrosion and staining resistance are important factors in performance and appearance. In addition, resistance to withdrawal may be increased if the zinc coating is evenly distributed. However, extreme irregularities of the coating may actually reduce withdrawal resistance. It should also be pointed out that the use of galvanized nails to avoid staining is not fully effective. Where staining should be completely avoided for architectural purposes, stainless steel nails can be used. The expense of stainless steel nails is much greater than that of galvanized nails.

Cement-coated nails are coated by tumbling or submerging in a resin or shellac (cement is not used). Resistance to withdrawal is increased because of the larger friction between the nail and the wood. However, there are substantial variations in the uniformity of cement coatings, and much of the coating may be removed in the driving of the nail. These variables cause large differences in the relative resistance to withdrawal for cement-coated nails. The increased resistance to withdrawal for these types of nails is, in most cases, only temporary.

12.3 Power-Driven Nails and Staples

Major advances in the installation of driven fasteners such as nails and staples have been brought about by the development of pneumatic, electric, and mechanical guns. The use of such power equipment greatly increases the speed with which fasteners can be installed. The installation of a nail or other fastener has been reduced to the pull of a trigger and can be accomplished in a fraction of a second. See Fig. 12.3.

Figure 12.3 Typical power fastening equipment. On the left, nailing through bottom wall plate with Senco SN325+ framing nailer. On the right, stapling plywood sheathing with Senco M series stapler. *(Senco Products, Inc.)*

Conventional round flathead nails can be installed with power equipment. To accomplish this, the nails are assembled in clips or coils that are fed automatically into the driving gun. The round head on these types of fasteners prevents the shanks of the nails from coming in close contact with adjacent nails, and therefore, a relatively large clip is required for a given number of nails.

The size of the clip can be reduced by modifying the shape of the conventional nail. A number of different configurations have been used to make more compact fastener clips. *Wire staples, T nails,* and *modified roundhead nails* are all in current use. See Fig. 12.4. Fasteners such as staples are often made from relatively thin wire. The tendency of this type of fastener to split the wood is reduced. In addition, standard power-driven nails are often thinner and shorter than corresponding pennyweight sizes of hand-driven nails.

Testing programs have resulted in Code recognition of a number of power-driven fasteners for use in structural design. For example, the International Staple, Nail and Tool Association has structural design values published in NER 272 (Ref. 15.2). National Evaluation Reports (NERs) are published jointly by the three model building codes under the name of the Council of American Building Officials (CABO). Recognition for other power-driven fasteners has also been obtained.

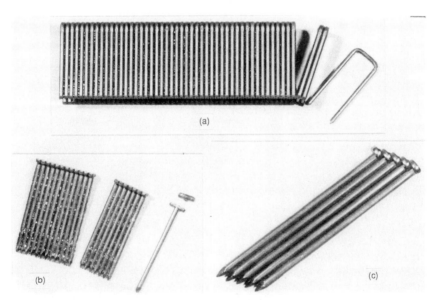

(a)

(b)

(c)

Figure 12.4 Typical power-driven fasteners. (*a*) Wire staples; (*b*) T nails; (*c*) modified roundhead nails. (*Photograph by Mike Hausmann.*)

The literature giving design information is extensive and is not reproduced in this text. The remainder of this chapter deals specifically with the four basic types of nails covered in the NDS. The designer, however, should be able to locate *equivalent* power-driven fasteners in the references.

It should be pointed out that the setting of power-driving guns is an important factor in the performance of a fastener. Care should be taken that the driving gun does not cause the head of a fastener to penetrate below the surface of the wood. Fasteners improperly installed will have a substantially lower load-carrying capacity. Precautions should also be taken in the manual driving of nails, and the head of a nail should not be "set" deeply below the surface of the wood. Because of the rapidity and consistency obtained with power-driving equipment, the installation setting is of particular importance with power-driven fasteners. The type of member will affect the setting of the gun. For example, when plywood roof sheathing is installed on a panelized roof, the gun should be adjusted for nailing into the different supporting members ($2 \times$'s, $4 \times$'s, and glulams).

12.4   Yield Limit Equations for Nails

A laterally loaded nail connection is usually a *single-shear* connection between a wood or steel *side member* and a wood *main member*. See Example 12.1. Recall from Chap. 11 that the dowel bearing strength F_e for a given species of wood is constant for a small-diameter fastener regardless of the angle of load to grain. Therefore, the angle of load to grain θ is not a concern in the design of nailed connections. Furthermore, if the wood members in a connection are *both from the same species,* the dowel bearing strengths are the same ($F_{em} = F_{es}$). The load tables for wood-to-wood connections in the NDS are limited to this simplified condition.

The dowel bearing strength for a nail connection is a function of the specific gravity of the wood (Example 11.4 in Sec. 11.5). Different values of F_e occur when the main member and side member are from different species. Connections involving mixed species are easily accommodated in the yield limit equations by using the corresponding dowel bearing strengths for the main and side members.

Mixing different species of wood in a nailed connection is a common occurrence. For example, plywood manufactured from Douglas Fir (specific gravity of 0.50) may be nailed to Hem-Fir sawn-lumber framing (specific gravity of 0.43). The respective dowel bearing strengths in this connection are $F_{es} = 4650$ psi for the plywood side member and $F_{em} = 3500$ psi for the framing or main member (see Example 12.5 later in this chapter).

If a nailed connection uses a metal side plate, the dowel bearing strengths for the main member and side member are also different. The bearing strength of a steel member may conservatively be taken as the ultimate tensile strength of the steel side plate $F_e = F_u$.

EXAMPLE 12.1   Single-Shear Nail Connections

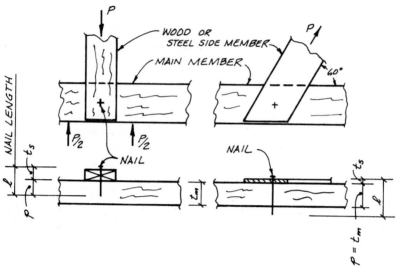

Figure 12.5a Wood-to-wood and wood-to-metal connections.

The most common nailed connections are single-shear (two-member) joints with a wood main member and either a wood or a steel side member. The nail passes through the *side member* and into the main member. The *main member* or *holding member* receives the pointed end of the fastener. The *penetration* is the length of the nail in the main member. The penetration is computed as the length of the nail minus the thickness of the side member. If the nail extends beyond the main member, the penetration is taken as the thickness of the main member:

$$\text{Penetration } p = l - t_s \le t_m$$

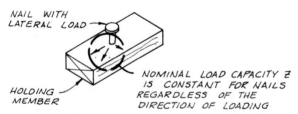

Figure 12.5b Angle of load to grain does not affect nominal strength of laterally loaded nail.

The *penetration* of a nail is defined as the distance that the nail extends into the main member. In order to use the full nominal design value Z of a nail according to the yield limit equations, the penetration should be a minimum of 12 times the shank diameter of the nail or spike. A reduced penetration may be used with a corresponding reduction in load capacity (see Sec. 12.6).

There are a number of possible nail connections in addition to those shown in Fig. 12.5a. For example, nails can be used in three-member connections, and the NDS provides the appropriate method for obtaining the nominal design value Z for joints in double shear. Another type of connection occurs between a plywood panel and light-gage metal studs. In this case the wood panel becomes the side member, and the sheet-metal stud is the main member because it receives the point of the fastener. Fasteners for this application may be nails, pins, or screws. These and other types of connections can be analyzed using yield limit theory. The reader should contact the American Plywood Association (APA) for information on this latter type of connection.

The purpose of this book is to provide a general introduction to nailed connections and the yield limit model, and it is not feasible to address all possible types of nailed connections. Only the basic *single-shear* connections in Fig. 12.5a are covered in this book. Four possible yield modes are to be considered, and the yield limit equations from the NDS for these modes are given in Example 12.2.

It is clear that the yield limit equations in the 1991 NDS are a radical departure from the old method of obtaining the load capacity of a nail from one rather simple table. The yield equations are cumbersome to solve by hand, and practically speaking, the equations need to be programmed.

As an alternative to using the yield limit equations, nominal design values for nails for a number of common applications are available in the NDS tables. These tables cover single-shear connections for the four basic types of nails: common, box, common wire spikes, and threaded hardened steel nails. The load tables are based on the yield limit equations and cover *wood-to-wood* connections for the case that both members are of the *same species* and *wood-to-metal* connections. The complex nature of the equations does not permit presentation of results in a single table. See NDS Tables 12.3A to 12.3H.

The load capacity for many nailed connection problems is covered by the NDS tables. However, once a program is developed or a spreadsheet template is created, it will often be more convenient to obtain nail design values from the computer. In addition, some problems will not be covered by the NDS tables, and application of the yield limit equations will be *required*. The examples in Sec. 12.5 illustrate the step-by-step solution of the yield equations.

Some mention should be made about the strength of the fasteners used in nailed connections. NDS Sec. 12.1.2 is titled *Quality of Nails and Spikes,* but it really says very little about the strength characteristics of the fasteners. In fact, the only specification in the NDS for common nails, box nails, and common wire spikes is that their dimensions shall agree with the sizes listed in Federal Specification FF-N-105B (Ref. 18). The same reference is

EXAMPLE 12.2   Yield Limit Equations for Nail in Single Shear

The basic strength of a single dowel-type fastener subjected to a lateral load is known as the *nominal design value* and is given the symbol Z. The nominal design value is taken as the smallest load capacity obtained by evaluating all of the yield limit equations for a given type of connection. The *allowable design value* Z' for a single fastener may then be obtained by multiplying the nominal design value by the appropriate adjustment factors described in Sec. 12.6.

Four yield modes apply to a single-shear nail connection. The yield modes are sketched in Fig. 11.10 (Sec. 11.7).

Mode I_s (NDS equation 12.3-1):

$$Z = \frac{Dt_sF_{es}}{K_D}$$

Mode III_m (NDS equation 12.3-2):

$$Z = \frac{k_1DpF_{em}}{K_D(1 + 2R_e)}$$

Mode III_s (NDS equation 12.3-3):

$$Z = \frac{k_2Dt_sF_{em}}{K_D(2 + R_e)}$$

Mode IV (NDS equation 12.3-4):

$$Z = \frac{D^2}{K_D}\sqrt{\frac{2F_{em}F_{yb}}{3(1 + R_e)}}$$

where Z = nominal design value for nail, spike, or similar fastener (Z is to be taken as smallest value from four yield model equations), lb

$$k_1 = -1 + \sqrt{2(1 + R_e) + \frac{2F_{yb}(1 + 2R_e)D^2}{3F_{em}p^2}}$$

$$k_2 = -1 + \sqrt{\frac{2(1 + R_e)}{R_e} + \frac{2F_{yb}(2 + R_e)D^2}{3F_{em}t_s^2}}$$

$R_e = \dfrac{F_{em}}{F_{es}}$

$p = l - t_s \le t_m$

    = penetration of nail

    = length of nail in main member (member holding point), in.

t_s = thickness of side member, in.

t_m = thickness of main member, in.

l = length of nail, in.

F_{es} = dowel bearing strength of side member, psi

F_{em} = dowel bearing strength of main (holding) member, psi

F_{yb} = bending yield strength of fastener, psi

D = diameter of nail or spike, in.

K_D = diameter coefficient for nail and spike connections

$$= \begin{cases} 2.2 & \text{for } D \le 0.17 \text{ in.} \\ 10D + 0.5 & \text{for } 0.17 < D < 0.25 \\ 3.0 & \text{for } D \ge 0.25 \text{ in.} \end{cases}$$

Values of F_e may be obtained from NDS Table 12A, *Dowel Bearing Strength for Nail or Spike Connections,* or they may be computed using the equation given in Sec. 11.5 of this book.

---

given for threaded hardened steel nails, but in addition, it is stated that threaded hardened nails are to be heat-treated and tempered to provide greater yield strength than that for common wire nails. However, F_{yb} is not specified for common wire nails.

It will be recalled that the bending yield strength F_{yb} of a dowel-type fastener is one of the major factors relating to the formation of a plastic hinge in a connection (Sec. 11.6). At this time a recognized national standard that establishes minimum strength properties for nails does not exist. Until such a standard is developed, the designer should specify the minimum F_{yb} for the nails being used.

The term *bending yield strength* indicates that the yield stress is obtained from a bending test of the nail rather than a tension test. See Fig. 12.6. The bending yield stress is obtained from an *offset* taken parallel to the initial slope of the load deflection curve. The nail is loaded as a simply supported beam with a concentrated load at the midspan (Ref. 4.4).

To provide guidance to the designer regarding the strength of nails generally available in the marketplace, a limited survey of box and common nails was conducted (NDS Appendix I). The survey found that bending yield strength is higher for smaller-diameter nails. The apparent reason for this increase in F_{by} is the additional work-hardening of the material that takes place in the manufacturing of small-diameter nails.

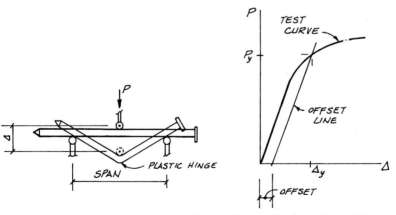

Figure 12.6 Test used to determine bending yield strength of a nail. An offset to the load deflection curve is used to obtain P_y and Δ_y from which the bending yield strength F_{yb} is computed.

Based on the results of the nail survey, the following formula for the bending yield strength of nails and spikes (Ref. 7.3) was developed:

$$F_{yb} = 130.4 - 213.9D$$

For threaded hardened steel nails, the bending yield strength is assumed to be 30 percent higher:

$$F_{yb} = 1.3(130.4 - 213.9D)$$

In these equations, D is the diameter of the fastener (in.), and F_{yb} is the bending yield strength (ksi). Note that F_{yb} in other equations is in psi. The 30 percent increase for threaded hardened nails is a soft conversion based on 1986 NDS load values. The diameters and lengths of nails and spikes are summarized for comparison in Fig. 12.7a. These dimensions are also available in NDS Tables 12.3A to 12.3H. The NDS load tables for nails are based on the above formulas, but values of F_{yb} in NDS Tables 12.3A to 12.3H were conservatively *truncated*. Formula values and truncated values of F_{yb} are compared in Fig. 12.7b. The truncated values of F_{yb} are listed in the footnotes to the NDS tables.

Sizes of Nails and Spikes

			Wire diameter, in.		
Pennyweight	Length, in.	Box nails	Common wire nails	Common wire spikes	Threaded hardened-steel nails
6d	2	0.099	0.113	—	0.120
8d	2½	0.113	0.131	—	0.120
10d	3	0.128	0.148	0.192	0.135
12d	3¼	0.128	0.148	0.192	0.135
16d	3½	0.135	0.162	0.207	0.148
20d	4	0.148	0.192	0.225	0.177
30d	4½	0.148	0.207	0.244	0.177
40d	5	0.162	0.225	0.263	0.177
50d	5½	—	0.244	0.283	0.177
60d	6	—	0.263	0.283	0.177
70d	7	—	—	—	0.207
80d	8	—	—	—	0.207
90d	9	—	—	—	0.207
⁵⁄₁₆	7	—	—	0.312	—
³⁄₈	8½	—	—	0.375	—

Figure 12.7a Table of nail sizes.

Box, Common, and Spikes

Nail diameter, in.	F_{yb} from formula, ksi	Truncated F_{by} used in NDS tables, ksi
0.099	109	100
0.113	106	100
0.128	103	100
0.131	102	100
0.135	102	100
0.148	99	90
0.162	96	90
0.192	89	80
0.207	86	80
0.225	82	80
0.244	78	70
0.263	74	70
0.283	70	60
$5/16$	64	60
$3/8$	50	45

Threaded Hardened-Steel Nails

Nail diameter, in.	F_{yb} used in NDS tables, ksi
0.120	130
0.135	130
0.148	115
0.177	115
0.207	100

Figure 12.7b Bending yield strengths for nails used to develop Z in NDS Tables 12.3A to 12.3H. Values of F_{yb} may be verified in the footnotes to NDS tables.

Several numerical examples of nail connections using the yield limit equations are given in the next section.

12.5 Applications of Yield Limit Equations

Example 12.3 evaluates the nominal load capacity of a 16d common nail in a connection between two sawn lumber members. The smallest value from the four yield equations is obtained from NDS equation 12.3-4, which indicates that a Mode IV failure governs. This type of yield mode has two plastic hinges in the fastener. See Fig. 11.10 (Sec. 11.7) for a sketch of the yield mode.

Because both members are the same species, the load capacity of the connection can be verified using NDS Table 12.3B.

EXAMPLE 12.3   Yield Limit Equations for Single-Shear Wood-to-Wood Nail Connection

Determine the nominal design value for the nail in Fig. 12.8. Both pieces of lumber are DF-L, and the nail is a 16d common nail. The angle of load to grain does not affect the problem and is not specified.

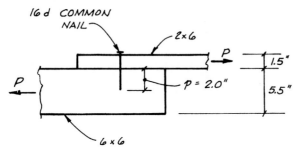

Figure 12.8   Single-shear wood-to-wood connection.

Dimensions of nail are obtained from the table in Fig. 12.7*a* or from NDS Table 12.3B:

$$D = 0.162 \text{ in.}$$

$$l = 3.5 \text{ in.}$$

Penetration

$$p = l - t_s \leq t_m$$

$$= 3.5 - 1.5 = 2.0 < 5.5$$

$$\therefore \ p = 2.0 \text{ in.}$$

Minimum penetration to obtain full nominal design value:

$$12D = 12(0.162) = 1.94 < 2.0 \text{ in.} \quad OK$$

The bending yield strength of a 16d common nail is assumed to be

$$F_{yb} = 90 \text{ ksi} = 90{,}000 \text{ psi}$$

This value can be obtained from the table in Fig. 12.7*b* or from NDS Table 12.3B. Specific gravity is the same for both main and side members and is obtained from NDS Table 12A:

$$SG_m = SG_s = 0.50$$

Dowel bearing strength can be computed or read from NDS Table 12A:

$$F_{em} = F_{es} = 4650 \text{ psi}$$

Coefficients for use in yield equations:

$$K_D = 2.2$$

$$R_e = \frac{F_{em}}{F_{es}} = \frac{4650}{4650} = 1.0$$

$$1 + R_e = 1 + 1.0 = 2.0$$

$$1 + 2R_e = 1 + 2(1.0) = 3.0$$

$$2 + R_e = 2 + 1.0 = 3.0$$

$$k_1 = -1 + \sqrt{2(1 + R_e) + \frac{2F_{yb}(1 + 2R_e)D^2}{3F_{em}p^2}}$$

$$= -1 + \sqrt{2(2.0) + \frac{2(90,000)(3.0)(0.162^2)}{3(4650)(2.0^2)}}$$

$$= 1.0625$$

$$k_2 = -1 + \sqrt{\frac{2(1 + R_e)}{R_e} + \frac{2F_{yb}(2 + R_e)D^2}{3F_{em}t_s^2}}$$

$$= -1 + \sqrt{\frac{2(2.0)}{1.0} + \frac{2(90,000)(3.0)(0.162^2)}{3(4650)(1.5^2)}}$$

$$= 1.1099$$

Yield limit equations:

Mode I_s (NDS equation 12.3-1):

$$Z = \frac{Dt_sF_{es}}{K_D} = \frac{0.162(1.5)(4650)}{2.2} = 514 \text{ lb}$$

Mode III_m (NDS equation 12.3-2):

$$Z = \frac{k_1DpF_{em}}{K_D(1 + 2R_e)} = \frac{1.0625(0.162)(2.0)(4650)}{2.2(3.0)} = 243 \text{ lb}$$

Mode III_s (NDS equation 12.3-3):

$$Z = \frac{k_2Dt_sF_{em}}{K_D(2 + R_e)} = \frac{1.1099(0.162)(1.5)(4650)}{2.2(3.0)} = 190 \text{ lb}$$

Mode IV (NDS equation 12.3-4):

$$Z = \frac{D^2}{K_D}\sqrt{\frac{2F_{em}F_{yb}}{3(1 + R_e)}}$$

$$= \frac{(0.162)^2}{2.2}\sqrt{\frac{2(4650)(90,000)}{3(2.0)}} = 141 \text{ lb}$$

Nominal design value is selected as the smallest value from the yield equations:

$$\boxed{Z = 141 \text{ lb}}$$

This agrees with the value listed in NDS Table 12.3B.

The second example of the yield limit equations uses an 8d box nail to connect a metal side plate to a sawn lumber main member of Southern Pine. See Example 12.4. The dowel bearing strength for a metal plate may conservatively be taken as the ultimate tensile strength of the steel. In this problem a Mode III$_s$ yield mechanism controls which indicates that a single plastic hinge forms in the nail.

EXAMPLE 12.4   Yield Limit Equations for Single-Shear Wood-to-Metal Nail Connection

Determine the nominal design value for the nail in Fig. 12.9. The side member is a 12-gage plate of ASTM A446 grade A steel, and the main member is a 4 × 4 of Southern Pine. The fastener is an 8d box nail. The angle of load to grain does not affect nailed connections and is not given.

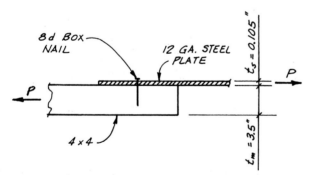

Figure 12.9 Single-shear wood-to-metal connection.

The dimensions of the nail are obtained from the table in Fig. 12.7a or NDS Table 12.3E:

$$D = 0.113 \text{ in.}$$

$$l = 2.5 \text{ in.}$$

Penetration:

t_s = 0.105 in. (12-gage plate thickness from Ref. 11.1 or NDS Table 12.3E)

$p = l - t_s \leq t_m$

 = 2.5 − 0.105 = 2.40 < 3.5

∴ p = 2.40 in.

Minimum penetration to obtain full nominal design value:

$$12D = 12(0.113) = 1.36 < 2.40 \text{ in.} \quad OK$$

Bending yield strength of an 8d box nail is assumed to be

$$F_{yb} = 100,000 \text{ psi}$$

Specific gravity for Southern Pine is obtained from NDS Table 12A:

$$SG_m = 0.55$$

Dowel bearing strength for Southern Pine can be computed or read from NDS Table 12A:

$$F_{em} = 5550 \text{ psi}$$

Dowel bearing strength of steel side member:

$$F_{es} = F_u = 45,000 \text{ psi}$$

Coefficients for yield equations:

$$K_D = 2.2$$

$$R_e = \frac{F_{em}}{F_{es}} = \frac{5550}{45,000} = 0.1233$$

$$1 + R_e = 1 + 0.1233 = 1.1233$$

$$1 + 2R_e = 1 + 2(0.1233) = 1.2467$$

$$2 + R_e = 2 + 0.1233 = 2.1233$$

$$k_1 = -1 + \sqrt{2(1 + R_e) + \frac{2F_{yb}(1 + 2R_e)D^2}{3F_{em}p^2}}$$

$$= -1 + \sqrt{2(1.1233) + \frac{2(100,000)(1.2467)(0.113^2)}{3(5550)(2.40^2)}}$$

$$= 0.5100$$

$$k_2 = -1 + \sqrt{\frac{2(1 + R_e)}{R_e} + \frac{2F_{yb}(2 + R_e)D^2}{3F_{em}t_s^2}}$$

$$= -1 + \sqrt{\frac{2(1.1233)}{0.1233} + \frac{2(100,000)(2.1233)(0.113^2)}{3(5550)(0.105^2)}}$$

$$= 5.9106$$

Yield limit equations:

Mode I$_s$ (NDS equation 12.3-1):

$$Z = \frac{Dt_s F_{es}}{K_D} = \frac{0.113(0.105)(45,000)}{2.2} = 243 \text{ lb}$$

Mode III$_m$ (NDS equation 12.3-2):

$$Z = \frac{k_1 Dp F_{em}}{K_D(1 + 2R_e)} = \frac{0.5100(0.113)(2.40)(5550)}{2.2(1.2467)} = 279 \text{ lb}$$

Mode III$_s$ (NDS equation 12.3-3):

$$Z = \frac{k_2 Dt_s F_{em}}{K_D(2 + R_e)} = \frac{5.9106(0.113)(0.105)(5550)}{2.2(2.1233)} = 83 \text{ lb}$$

Mode IV (NDS equation 12.3-4):

$$Z = \frac{D^2}{K_D}\sqrt{\frac{2F_{em}F_{yb}}{3(1 + R_e)}}$$

$$= \frac{(0.113)^2}{2.2}\sqrt{\frac{2(5550)(100,000)}{3(1.1233)}} = 105 \text{ lb}$$

Nominal design value is selected as the smallest value from the yield equations:

$$\boxed{Z = 83 \text{ lb}}$$

This agrees with value listed in NDS Table 12.3E.

The first two nail examples were given to clarify the use of the yield formulas and to verify the NDS tables. The concept behind the tables is to cover many of the common nail applications. However, in going to the equation format, the 1991 NDS has placed the emphasis on the yield limit equations as the basis for the design of wood structures. This allows the designer to evaluate a much wider variety of connections. The final nail problem in this section requires use of the yield equations because the specific conditions are not addressed by the tables.

The 10d common nail in Example 12.5 is driven through a thickness of Douglas Fir plywood into a sawn lumber framing member of Hem-Fir. Because different species are involved, there are different dowel bearing strengths for the main and the side members. This application is not covered by the NDS tables. The yield mechanism is Mode III$_s$ because NDS equation 12.3-3 produces the smallest nominal design value.

EXAMPLE 12.5   Yield Limit Equations for Single-Shear Plywood-to-Lumber Nail Connection

Determine the nominal design value for the nail in Fig. 12.10. The side member is ½-in. STR I DF plywood panel, and the main member is a 2 × 6 piece of Hem-Fir. The fastener is a 10d common nail. The angle of load to grain does not affect nailed connections and is not given.

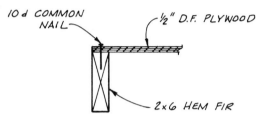

Figure 12.10 Single-shear plywood-to-lumber connection.

The dimensions of the nail are obtained from the table in Fig. 12.7a or NDS Table 12.3B:

$$D = 0.148 \text{ in.}$$

$$l = 3.0 \text{ in.}$$

Penetration: The nail is driven into the edge of the 2 × 6, and $t_m = 5.5$.

$$t_s = 0.5 \text{ in.}$$

$$p = l - t_s \le t_m$$

$$= 3.0 - 0.5 = 2.5 < 5.5$$

$$\therefore \ p = 2.5 \text{ in.}$$

Minimum penetration to obtain full nominal design value:

$$12D = 12(0.148) = 1.78 < 2.5 \text{ in.}   OK$$

Bending yield strength of 10d common nail is assumed to be

$$F_{yb} = 90,000 \text{ psi}$$

Specific gravity for Hem-Fir is obtained from NDS Table 12A:

$$SG_m = 0.43$$

Dowel bearing strength for Hem-Fir can be computed or read from NDS Table 12A:

$$F_{em} = 3500 \text{ psi}$$

Because plywood is STR I, the panel contains veneer from all Group I species, and the specific gravity for DF can be used to determine dowel bearing strength. Values are obtained from NDS Table 12A:

$$SG_s = 0.50$$

$$F_{es} = 4650 \text{ psi}$$

Coefficients for yield equations:

$$K_D = 2.2$$

$$R_e = \frac{F_{em}}{F_{es}} = \frac{3500}{4650} = 0.7527$$

$$1 + R_e = 1 + 0.7527 = 1.7527$$

$$1 + 2R_e = 1 + 2(0.7527) = 2.5054$$

$$2 + R_e = 2 + 0.7527 = 2.7527$$

$$k_1 = -1 + \sqrt{2(1 + R_e) + \frac{2F_{yb}(1 + 2R_e)D^2}{3F_{em}p^2}}$$

$$= -1 + \sqrt{2(1.7527) + \frac{2(90,000)(2.5054)(0.148^2)}{3(3500)(2.5^2)}}$$

$$= 0.9120$$

$$k_2 = -1 + \sqrt{\frac{2(1 + R_e)}{R_e} + \frac{2F_{yb}(2 + R_e)D^2}{3F_{em}t_s^2}}$$

$$= -1 + \sqrt{\frac{2(1.7527)}{0.7527} + \frac{2(90,000)(2.7527)(0.148^2)}{3(3500)(0.5^2)}}$$

$$= 1.9651$$

Yield limit equations:

Mode I$_s$ (NDS equation 12.3-1):

$$Z = \frac{Dt_sF_{es}}{K_D} = \frac{0.148(0.5)(4650)}{2.2} = 156 \text{ lb}$$

Mode III$_m$ (NDS equation 12.3-2):

$$Z = \frac{k_1DpF_{em}}{K_D(1 + 2R_e)} = \frac{0.9120(0.148)(2.5)(3500)}{2.2(2.5054)} = 214 \text{ lb}$$

Mode III_s (NDS equation 12.3-3):

$$Z = \frac{k_2 D t_s F_{em}}{K_D(2 + R_e)} = \frac{1.9651(0.148)(0.5)(3500)}{2.2(2.7527)} = 84 \text{ lb}$$

Mode IV (NDS equation 12.3-4):

$$Z = \frac{D^2}{K_D} \sqrt{\frac{2 F_{em} F_{yb}}{3(1 + R_e)}}$$

$$= \frac{(0.148)^2}{2.2} \sqrt{\frac{2(3500)(90,000)}{3(1.7527)}} = 109 \text{ lb}$$

Nominal design value is selected as the smallest value from the yield equations:

$$\boxed{Z = 87 \text{ lb*}}$$

Whether the NDS tables or the yield limit equations are used, the determination of the nominal design value Z is the first step in developing the allowable load Z' for a single nail. Other important strength properties and the required adjustment factors that may be necessary to obtain the allowable load for a single fastener are covered in the next section.

12.6   Adjustment Factors for Laterally Loaded Nails

The yield limit equations for laterally loaded nailed connections were reviewed in Sec. 12.5. As a reminder, *nominal design value Z* is the notation assigned to the load capacity of a single fastener as obtained from the *yield equations*. In order to be used in the design of a particular connection, the nominal design value must be converted to an *allowable design value Z'*.

This is done by multiplying the nominal value by a series of adjustment factors. Depending on the circumstances, the adjustment factors could have a major or minor effect on the allowable load capacity. The adjustment factors required in the design of connections are summarized in NDS Table 7.3.1. See the inside back cover of this book for a similar table. If the particular design conditions agree with the conditions for the nominal design value, the adjustment factors simply default to unity.

---

*Reference 4.4 indicates that the yield limit equations may conservatively be applied to the evaluation of nail capacity in plywood. Additional research is currently being conducted. Contact APA for the latest information.

The base conditions associated with the nominal design value of a nail connection are as follows:

1. Load is normal (10-year) duration.

2. Wood is initially dry at the time of fabrication of a connection and remains dry in service.

3. Temperature range is normal.

4. Penetration of nail is at least 12 fastener diameters.

5. Nail is driven into the side grain of the main (holding) member.

6. Nail is not part of diaphragm or shearwall nailing (Chaps. 9 and 10).

7. Nail is not driven as a toenail.

If a nailed connection is used under exactly these conditions, the adjustment factors are all unity and $Z' = Z$.

For a laterally loaded nailed connection that does not satisfy the base conditions described above, the following adjustment factors may be required:

$$Z' = Z(C_D C_M C_t C_d C_{eg} C_{di} C_{tn})$$

where C_D = load duration factor (Sec. 4.15)

C_M = wet service factor (Sec. 4.14)

C_t = temperature factor (Sec. 4.20)

C_d = penetration depth factor

C_{eg} = end grain factor

C_{di} = diaphragm factor

C_{tn} = toenail factor

The total allowable load for a connection using two or more nails is the sum of the individual allowable load values Z'. This summation is appropriate if the nails are all of the same type and size because each fastener will have the same yield mode. The load capacity for the connection is, then, the number of nails N times the allowable load for one fastener:

$$\text{Allow. } P = N(Z')$$

A number of adjustment factors have been described in previous sections, and these are reviewed only briefly. Other adjustments apply only to nailed connections and require greater explanation.

Load duration factor C_D. The load duration factor for nailed connections is the same as that applied to allowable stresses in the design of structural members such as beams, tension members, and columns. Refer to Sec. 4.15 for a review of load duration and the numerical values for C_D.

Wet service factor C_M. The concept of an allowable stress adjustment based
moisture content was introduced in Sec. 4.14. It will be recalled that the
wet service factors for member design vary with the type of stresses. Different adjustments also apply in connection design depending on the type
of fastener and the moisture content of the wood at several stages. The
moisture content is considered (1) at the time of fabrication of the joint and
(2) in service. The nominal design value applies to nailed connections in
which the wood is initially dry and remains dry in service. For connection
design the term *dry* refers to wood that has a moisture content of 19 percent
or less.

If the moisture content exceeds the dry limits, either at the time of fabrication *or* in service, a reduction in load capacity is required for common
nails, box nails, and common wire spikes. For laterally loaded connections
$C_M = 0.75$ for these conditions. A reduction in load capacity for high moisture
content is not required for threaded hardened steel nails. Values of C_M are
listed in NDS Table 7.3.3, *Wet Service Factors, C_M, for Connections.*

Temperature factor C_t. If wood is used in an application with higher-than-
normal temperature conditions, the allowable stresses for member design
and the allowable design loads for connections are to be reduced by an
appropriate temperature factor C_t. Refer to Sec. 4.20 for a brief review of
the temperature factor. Numerical values of C_t for connections are obtained
from NDS Table 7.3.4. The temperature range for most wood-frame buildings
does not require adjustment of design values, and C_t can usually be set equal
to one.

Penetration depth factor C_d. The penetration of a nail was defined in Fig.
12.5a as the distance that the nail extends into the main or holding member.
To use the full nominal design load for a nail, the penetration must be at
least 12 times the diameter of the nail ($p \geq 12D$). A reduced penetration
is permitted, but a corresponding reduction in allowable load is required.
The multiplying factor used to reduce the allowable load is known as the
penetration depth factor C_d.

To obtain any load capacity Z for a nail, the absolute minimum penetration
is $6D$. When the penetration is in the range $6D \leq p < 12D$, a linear interpolation is used to obtain a reduced nail capacity. Therefore, the penetration
depth factor is defined as follows:

$$C_d = \begin{cases} 0 & \text{when } p < 6D \\ \dfrac{p}{12D} & \text{when } 6D \leq p < 12D \\ 1.0 & \text{when } p \geq 12D \end{cases}$$

End grain factor C_{eg}. The nominal design value applies to a laterally loaded
connection with the nail driven into the *side grain* of the main member.
Recall that the main member receives the pointed end of the fastener. In

this basic shear connection, the load is perpendicular to the length of the fastener, and the axis of the nail is perpendicular to the wood fibers in the holding member. This is the strongest and most desirable type of nailed connection. See Fig. 12.11a in Example 12.6. When a nail is driven into the side grain, the end grain factor does not apply or may be set equal to one.

In another type of single-shear connection, the nail penetrates into the *end grain* of the holding member (Fig. 12.11b). The load is still perpendicular to the length of the nail, but the fastener axis is now parallel to the grain. This is a much weaker type of connection. To determine the reduced allowable load, the nominal design value is multiplied by the end grain factor $C_{eg} = 0.67$.

EXAMPLE 12.6   Comparison of Side Grain and End Grain Nailing

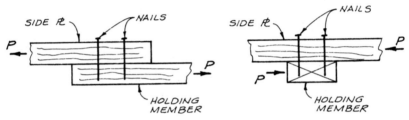

Figure 12.11a Nails in side grain.

Lateral Resistance in Side Grain

Two examples of nails used in the *basic* shear connection are shown in Fig. 12.11a. The basic connection has the nail driven into the *side grain* (i.e., perpendicular to the grain) of the holding member, and the load is applied perpendicular to the length of the nail. For nails driven into the side grian, $C_{eg} = 1.0$.

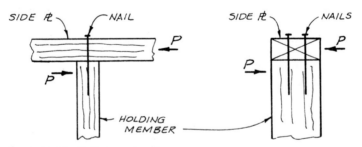

Figure 12.11b Nails in end grain.

Lateral Resistance in End Grain

The second main type of lateral load connection has the nail driven into the end grain (i.e., parallel to the grain) of the holding member, and the load is applied perpendicular to the length of the nail. The front and side views of an end grain connection are shown in Fig. 12.11*b* with two different sets of lateral loads. For nails driven into the end grain, $C_{eg} = 0.67$.

Diaphragm factor C_{di}. Design of nailing for horizontal diaphragms and shear-walls using standard Code tables was covered in detail in Chaps. 9 and 10. The allowable unit shears in UBC Tables 25-J-1 and 25-K-1 are the result of diaphragm tests conducted by APA. As an alternative to designing diaphragms and shearwalls with Code tables, the designer may compute the allowable unit shear. The allowable shear will be controlled by the shear capacity of the plywood panel *or* by the lateral load capacity of the fasteners.

Tests on diaphragms and shearwalls have demonstrated that the load capacity of nails used in diaphragms is greater than the load capacity of nails used in other structural connections. The diaphragm factor C_{di} is used to adjust the nominal design value Z to an allowable load for use in diaphragm and shearwall design. Note that the diaphragm factor is only to be used for nails that attach plywood sheathing to framing members; C_{di} does not apply to other connections that may simply be a part of the diaphragm. For example, C_{di} is not used in the design of diaphragm chord splices or drag strut connections made with nails. See Ref. 14.11 for an example of how to compute the allowable unit shear for a diaphragm using C_{di} and other appropriate factors. See also the note in Example 15.4 (Sec. 15.3).

Toenail factor C_{tn}. In many cases it is not possible to nail directly through the side member into the holding member. In these circumstances toenails may be used. See Example 12.7. Toenails are nails that are driven at an angle of 30 degrees to the side member and are started approximately one-third of the nail length from the intersection of the two members.

Anyone who has ever driven a toenail realizes that the installation details shown in Fig. 12.12*a* are only approximated in the field. However, the geometry given allows the designer to evaluate the thickness of the side member t_s and the penetration p_L of the toenail into the holding member for use in the yield limit equations.

Penetration requirements for a laterally loaded toenail are the same as those for a conventional shear connection. If a reduced penetration exists, the allowable load Z' for the toenail is to be reduced using the penetration depth factor C_d described above. Common applications of toenails are for stud to wall plate, beam to wall plate, and blocking to plate connections.

The capacity of a toenail is obtained by multiplying the nominal design value Z by the toenail factor C_{tn}. The toenail factor is $C_{tn} = 0.83$ for a laterally loaded toenail, and a different toenail factor applies to withdrawal connections (Sec. 12.12). The toenail factor does not apply to conventional laterally loaded connections. In other words, C_{tn} defaults to unity ($C_{tn} = 1.0$) for the ordinary single-shear connections in Fig. 12.11*a*.

Finally, it will be noted that some authors draw a distinction between the types of connections shown in Fig. 12.12*a* and *b*. The difference has to

EXAMPLE 12.7   Toenail Connection

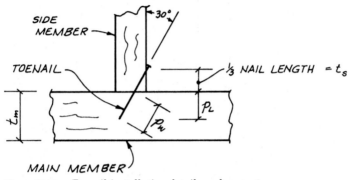

Figure 12.12a   Toenail installation details and geometry.

Dimensions for toenails for use in yield limit equations:

l = length of nail

t_s = thickness of side member for toenail design

= projected length of toenail in side member

= one-third nail length

= $l/3$

p_L = penetration of toenail for *laterally loaded* connection

= projected length of toenail in main (holding) member

= $l \cos 30 - t_s \leq t_m$

There are two different definitions of penetration for toenails. The penetration p_L of a toenail in a laterally loaded connection is the *projected* length of the toenail in the main member. The definition of penetration p_W for a toenail in a *withdrawal* connection changes to the actual length of the nail in the main member. Although the yield limit equations do not apply to withdrawal connections, the two definitions of nail penetration are shown in Fig. 12.12a for comparison.

p_W = penetration of toenail for a connection *loaded in withdrawal*

= total length of nail in main member

= $l - \dfrac{l/3}{\cos 30} \leq \dfrac{t_m}{\cos 30}$

The capacity of a toenail in a withdrawal connection is related to the surface area of the nail in the holding member. Nail connections loaded in withdrawal are addressed in Sec. 12.12.

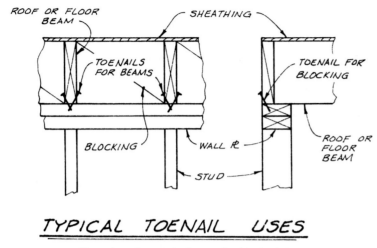

TYPICAL   TOENAIL   USES

Figure 12.12b   Typical applications of toenails. On the left, toenails connect beams to top plate of stud wall. On the right, toenails attach blocking to wall plate.

do with the direction of the grain in the side member. For example, assume that the vertical member in Fig. 12.12a is a wall stud. The toenail, therefore, goes through the *end grain* of the side member. In contrast, the toenails in Fig. 12.12b run through the *side grain* of the beams and the blocking.

When this difference is recognized, the connection in Fig. 12.12a is referred to as a *toenail,* and the connections in Fig. 12.12b are termed *slant nails.* According to Ref. 9.3, toenails require a reduction in design value ($C_{tn} = 0.83$), and slant nails do not ($C_{tn} = 1.0$).

There is a problem with semantics here, because field personnel refer to both types of installations as toenails. Perhaps to avoid confusion, the 1991 NDS does not recognize the difference between the two applications, and $C_{tn} = 0.83$ is currently used for both.

Several numerical examples will now be given to demonstrate the practical design of nails in single-shear connections. In many cases the nominal design values for the nails can be determined from either the yield limit equations or the NDS nail tables.

12.7   Design Problem: Nail Connection for Knee Brace

The type of brace used in this example is typical for a number of unenclosed structures including carports, sheds, and patios. See Example 12.8. The design load is the lateral seismic force. It is assumed to be carried equally by all of the columns, and the reaction at the base of the column is determined first.

The horizontal component of force in the brace is then calculated using the free-body diagram of a column. After the horizontal component is known, the axial force in the brace can be evaluated. The force in the brace is used to determine the required number of nails to attach the brace. The same connection will be used at the top and bottom of the brace.

The nominal design value Z for the nail is obtained from a previous example, and the problem essentially deals with the determination of the allowable load capacity Z'.

EXAMPLE 12.8   Knee Brace Connection

The carport shown in Fig. 12.13a uses 2×6 knee braces to resist the longitudinal seismic force. Determine the number of 16d common nails required for the connection of the brace to the 4×4 post. Material is DF-L lumber that is dry at the time of construction. Normal temperatures apply.

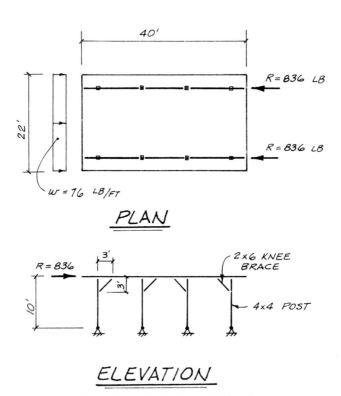

Figure 12.13a Lateral force in longitudinal direction.

Force to one row of braces:

$$R = \frac{wL}{2} = 76\left(\frac{22}{2}\right) = 836 \text{ lb}$$

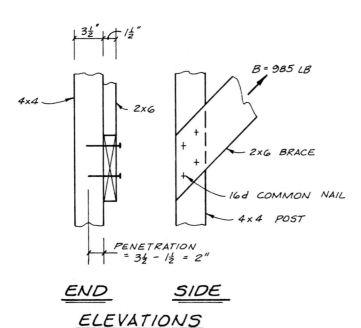

FBD OF COLUMN

Figure 12.13b   FBD to determine axial force B in brace.

Assume the force is shared equally by all braces.

$$\Sigma M_O = 0$$

$$3H - 209(10) = 0$$

$$H = 697 \text{ lb}$$

$$B = \sqrt{2}H = \sqrt{2}(697)$$

$$= 985 \text{ lb axial force in knee brace}$$

$$= \text{force on nailed connection}$$

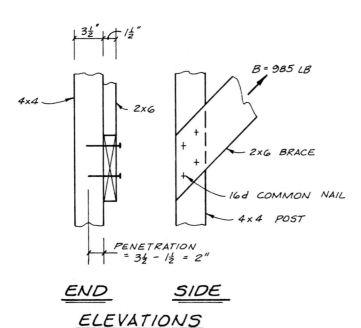

END   SIDE

ELEVATIONS

Figure 12.13c   Nail connection of brace to column.

The nominal design value for a 16d common nail in DF-L can be evaluated using the yield equations (Sec. 12.4), or it can be obtained from NDS Table 12.3B. Although the sizes of the wood members are different, the dimensions and other properties that affect nail strength are the same as those in Example 12.3.
Nominal design value from Example 12.3:

$$Z = 141 \text{ lb/nail}$$

Adjustment Factors

Penetration
Required penetration to use the full value of Z

$$12D = 12(0.162) = 1.94 \text{ in.} < 2.0$$

$$\therefore \quad \text{Penetration depth factor is}$$

$$C_d = 1.0$$

Moisture content

Because the building is "unenclosed," the brace connection may be exposed to the weather, and the severity of this exposure must be judged by the designer. Assume that a reduction for high moisture content is deemed appropriate, and the wet service factor C_M is obtained from NDS Table 7.3.3.

$$C_M = 0.75$$

Load duration

The load duration factor recommended in the 1991 NDS for seismic forces is $C_D = 1.6$. The designer is cautioned to verify local code acceptance before using this value in practice.

Other adjustment factors

All other adjustment factors for allowable nail capacity do not apply to the given problem, and each can be set equal to unity:

$C_t = 1.0$ because normal temperature range is assumed

$C_{eg} = 1.0$ because nails are driven into side grain of holding member

$C_{di} = 1.0$ because connection is not part of nailing for diaphragm or shearwall

$C_{tn} = 1.0$ because nails are not toenailed

Allowable load for 16d common nail in DF-L:

$$Z' = Z(C_D C_M C_t C_d C_{eg} C_{di} C_{tn})$$

$$= 141(1.6)(0.75)(1.0)(1.0)(1.0)(1.0)(1.0)$$

$$= 169 \text{ lb/nail}$$

Required number of nails:

$$N = \frac{B}{Z'} = \frac{985}{169} = 5.82$$

> *Use*   six 16d common nails each end of knee
> brace for high-moisture conditions.*

If the reduction for wet service is not required, $C_M = 1.0$. The revised connection is

$$Z' = 141(1.6)(1.0) = 226 \text{ lb/nail}$$

$$N = \frac{985}{226} = 4.37$$

> *Use*   five 16d common nails each end of knee
> brace if moisture is not a concern.

For an unenclosed building of this nature, the designer must evaluate the exposure of the connections and the moisture content of the members. This example illustrates the effects of different assumed moisture conditions. The load duration factor for seismic forces has been increased from 1.33 to $C_D = 1.6$ in the 1991 NDS. Acceptance of this larger value should be confirmed before using.

In this problem the furnished nail penetration is greater than the required, and the full load capacity of the nail may be used ($C_d = 1.0$). Other adjustment factors for converting Z to Z' also default to 1.0 in this example. The reasons for the defaults to unity are listed in this first nail example, but in subsequent problems the adjustments are set equal to 1.0 without detailed explanation.

The number of nails that can be accommodated in a connection may be limited by the spacing requirements (joint details). The layout of this connection is considered in Sec. 12.13.

12.8   Design Problem: Top Plate Splice

In Example 12.9, a splice in the double top plate of a wood-frame wall is designed. The forces in the plate are caused by the horizontal diaphragm action of the roof. The longitudinal wall plate is designed for the *chord force*

---

*The use of preservative pressure-treated wood should be considered (Sec. 4.9).

(produced by the transverse lateral force) or the *drag strut force* (produced by the longitudinal lateral force). The larger of the two forces is used for the connection design. In this building the chord force controls, but the drag force could have been the critical force if the opening in the wall had been somewhat longer than 14 ft.

In buildings with larger lateral forces, the magnitude of the chord or drag force may be too great for a nailed connection. In this case, bolts or some form of connection hardware could be used for the plate splice.

At any splice, either the top or bottom member of the chord will be continuous. If a check of the stress in the chord were shown, the tension force would be divided by the cross-sectional area of *one* of the plate members. This example concentrates on the design of the connection only, and the stress in the chord/drag-strut member is not included.

An interesting point about the yield limit equations is highlighted in this example. The results of three of the four required equations are the same as those in a previous nail problem (Example 12.3). However, the value given by the Mode III_m equation is considerably less in the current example (190 lb compared with 243 lb). The lower value of Z in the Mode III_m equation is the result of a reduced nail penetration caused by a main member that is only 1.5 in. thick. In Example 12.9, the values of Mode III_m and Mode III_s are the same because the thicknesses of the main and side members are equal.

The designer needs to be aware of the subtle way this problem changed from the earlier example. The outcome was the same (that is, $Z = 141$ lb in both examples), but the results could have been different.

It should be noted that the tables in the NDS *do not* take into account the thickness of the main member. In other words, the tables assume that the nail does not protrude out of the holding member. This does not affect the result of Example 12.9 because the Mode III_m yield mechanism does not control. Consequently the nominal design value agrees with the value listed in NDS Table 12.3B. However, this may not always be the case.

Another consideration is related to the penetration of the nail. The 1.5-in. thickness of the main member is less than the minimum penetration necessary to obtain the full design capacity. This requires use of a penetration depth factor C_d that is less than 1.0.

EXAMPLE 12.9   Top Plate Splice

The building shown in Fig. 12.14a has stud walls with a double 2× top plate around the entire building. Lateral seismic forces to the horizontal diaphragm are given. Splices in the double top plate for the *longitudinal wall* are to be designed for the horizontal diaphragm chord force or drag force (whichever is larger). Lumber is dry DF-L that will remain dry in service. Normal temperatures apply. Connection is to be made with 16d common nails.

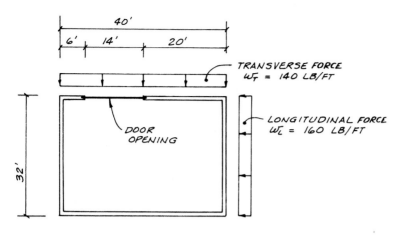

PLAN

Figure 12.14a Lateral forces to roof diaphragm. Consider force in each direction separately.

Transverse Lateral Force

Top plate of wall serves as diaphragm chord.
 Moment in diaphragm:

$$M = \frac{wL^2}{8} = \frac{140(40)^2}{8} = 28{,}000 \text{ ft-lb}$$

Chord force:

$$T = C = \frac{M}{b} = \frac{28{,}000}{32} = 875 \text{ lb}$$

For a discussion of horizontal diaphragm chords and drag struts, see Chap. 9.

Longitudinal Lateral Force

Wall plate serves as drag strut (Fig. 12.14b).
 Shearwall reaction:

$$R = \frac{wL}{2} = \frac{160(32)}{2} = 2560 \text{ lb}$$

Wall with opening has the critical drag strut force.
Roof diaphragm unit shear:

$$v_r = \frac{R}{b} = \frac{2560}{40} = 64 \text{ lb/ft}$$

Unit shear in shearwall:

$$v_r = \frac{R}{b} = \frac{2560}{6 + 20} = 98.5 \text{ lb/ft}$$

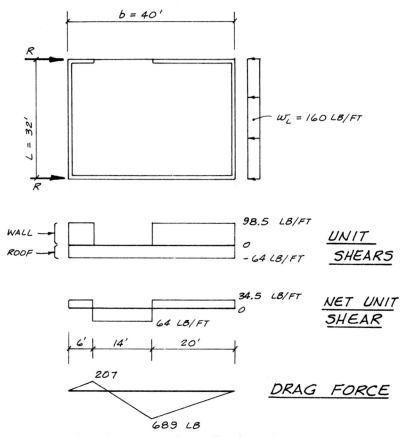

Figure 12.14b Force in drag strut along wall with opening.

Splice Connection

Max. chord force = 875 lb   governs

Max. drag force = 689 lb

If the code minimum lap of 4 ft is used for the top plate splice, the connection within the lap must transmit the full chord force.

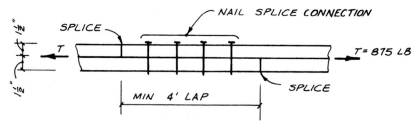

Figure 12.14c Splice in top wall plate.

The yield limit equations for a 16d common nail in Fig. 12.14c are the same as the yield limit equations in Example 12.3 with one exception: The Mode III$_m$ yield mechanism depends on the penetration of the nail. In this problem the nail protrudes beyond the thickness of the main member, and the furnished penetration is less. NDS equation 12.3-2 is reevaluated here, and the results of the other three yield equations are obtained from the previous example.

Information from Example 12.3 that applies to the problem at hand:

$$D = 0.162 \text{ in.}$$

$$l = 3.5 \text{ in.}$$

$$F_{yb} = 90,000 \text{ psi}$$

$$SG_m = SG_s = 0.50$$

$$F_{em} = F_{es} = 4650 \text{ psi}$$

$$K_D = 2.2$$

$$R_e = \frac{F_{em}}{F_{es}} = \frac{4650}{4650} = 1.0$$

$$1 + R_e = 2.0$$

$$1 + 2R_e = 3.0$$

$$2 + R_e = 3.0$$

Reduced nail penetration:

$$p = l - t_s \leq t_m$$

$$= 3.5 - 1.5 = 2.0 > 1.5$$

$$\therefore \ p = 1.5 \text{ in.}$$

Revised value of k_1 with penetration of 1.5 in.:

$$k_1 = -1 + \sqrt{2(1 + R_e) + \frac{2F_{yb}(1 + 2R_e)D^2}{3F_{em}p^2}}$$

$$= -1 + \sqrt{2(2.0) + \frac{2(90,000)(3.0)(0.162^2)}{3(4650)(1.5^2)}}$$

$$= 1.1099$$

Mode III$_m$ (NDS equation 12.3-2):

$$Z = \frac{k_1 Dp F_{em}}{K_D(1 + 2R_e)} = \frac{1.1099(0.162)(1.5)(4650)}{2.2(3.0)} = 190 \text{ lb}$$

This is less than the value of 243 lb for Mode III$_m$ for the connection in Example 12.3.

Results of other yield equations from Example 12.3:

Mode I_s (NDS equation 12.3-1)

$$Z = 514 \text{ lb}$$

Mode III_s (NDS equation 12.3-3)

$$Z = 190 \text{ lb}$$

Mode IV (NDS equation 12.3-4)

$$Z = 141 \text{ lb}$$

Refer to Fig. 11.10 in Sec. 11.7 for sketches of the yield modes. Notice that the same value of Z is obtained for Mode III_m and Mode III_s for the top plate splice. This is to be expected because of the equal thicknesses of the main and side members. The length of the nail is the same in both members.

The nominal design value is taken as the smallest value from the yield formulas:

$$Z = 141 \text{ lb}$$

Adjustment factors for this problem are all unity except the load duration factor and penetration depth factor.

For seismic forces the 1991 NDS recommends

$$C_D = 1.6 \qquad \text{(Verify local code acceptance before using.)}$$

Required penetration to use full value of Z:

$$12D = 12(0.162) = 1.94 \text{ in.} > 1.5 \text{ in.}$$

$$\therefore \quad \text{Reduce load capacity with } C_d$$

Absolute minimum allowed penetration:

$$6D = 6(0.162) = 0.97 < 1.5 \text{ in.} \qquad OK$$

Penetration depth factor is a linear reduction:

$$C_d = \frac{1.5}{1.94} = 0.772$$

Allowable load for a 16d common nail in DF-L:

$$Z' = Z(C_D C_M C_t C_d C_{eg} C_{di} C_{tn})$$

$$= 141(1.6)(1.0)(1.0)(0.772)(1.0)(1.0)(1.0)$$

$$= 174 \text{ lb/nail}$$

Required number of nails:

$$N = \frac{T}{Z'} = \frac{875}{174} = 5.03$$

Use   six 16d common nails between splice points.

Although it was not done in this example, the designer can specify the location of the splices in the top plate. If these locations are clearly shown on the plans, the design forces (chord and strut loads) that occur at these points may be used for connection design. In this example the *maximum* forces were used, and consequently the top plate splices may occur at any point along the length of the wall.

12.9 Design Problem: Shearwall Chord Tie

The requirements for anchoring a shearwall panel to the foundation were discussed in Chap. 10. A similar problem occurs in the attachment of a second-story shearwall to the supporting first-story shearwall. The same basic forces must be considered.

In Example 12.10 the tension chord of the second-story wall is spliced to the chord of the first-story wall. This splice is required because in typical *platform* construction the studs are not continuous from the roof level to the foundation. The first-story studs stop at the double wall plate that supports the second-floor framing. Separate second-story studs are then constructed on top of the second-floor platform.

The purpose of the splice, then, is to develop a continuous shearwall chord from the roof level to the foundation. Splices of this type are referred to as *continuity ties* or splices. Various types of connections can be used for these ties. In this example the connection consists of a steel strap connected to the first- and second-story chords with 8d box nails. For larger forces, bolts or lag screws can be used in place of nails. Calculations to verify the tension capacity of the strap are not shown in this example, but they would normally be required in design. In addition, the layout and spacing requirements of the nails in the connection should be considered.

Chord forces can be calculated using either the gross overturning moment or the net overturning moment. Both are illustrated, and the choice of which method to use in a particular situation is left to the judgment of the designer.

EXAMPLE 12.10   Shearwall Chord Tie

Design the connection tie between the first- and second-story shearwall chords for the right end wall (Fig. 12.15a). A 12-gage ASTM A446 grade A steel strap with 8d box nails is to be used. Lumber is dry Southern Pine that will remain dry in service. Normal temperatures apply. Wind force reactions from the horizontal roof and second-floor diaphragms are given.

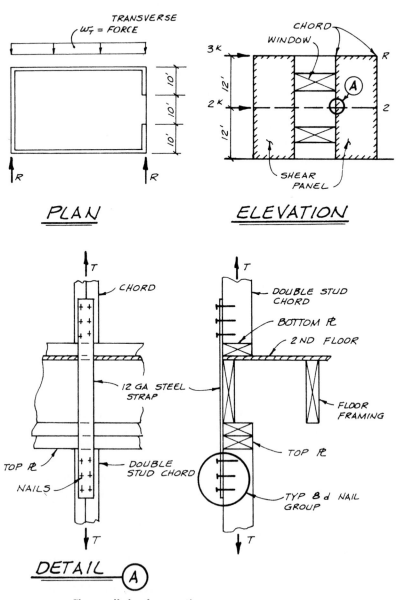

Figure 12.15a Shearwall chord connection.

Chord Force

The chord forces at the second-story level are caused by the lateral forces at the roof level. See Fig. 12.15*b*.

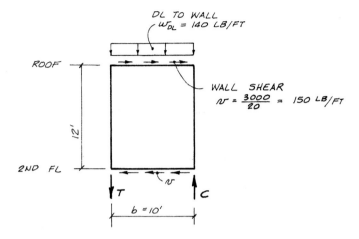

FBD OF SHEAR PANEL

Figure 12.15*b*   Shearwall overturning.

From the gross overturning moment OM (refer to Example 10.4),

$$\text{Gross } T = C = vh = (150)(12) = 1800 \text{ lb} \qquad \text{(conservative)}$$

From the design net OM (refer to Example 2.10),

$$\text{Design net OM} = \text{gross OM} - \tfrac{2}{3}(\text{dead load RM})$$

$$= (150 \times 10)(12) - \tfrac{2}{3}(140 \times 10)(5)$$

$$= 13.3 \text{ ft-k}$$

$$\text{Net } T = \frac{M}{b} = \frac{13{,}300}{10} = 1330 \text{ lb}$$

Alternate calculation (refer to Example 10.5):

$$\text{Net } T = \text{gross } T - \tfrac{2}{3}(\text{trib. DL})$$

$$= 1800 - \tfrac{2}{3}(140 \times 5) = 1330 \text{ lb}$$

Nail Connection

The nominal design value for an 8d box nail installed through a metal side plate into a Southern Pine main member was computed using the yield model formulas in Example 12.4. The same value applies to the problem at hand.

$$Z = 83 \text{ lb}$$

Nail penetration was shown in the previous example to be greater than the minimum required to use the full design value.

$$\therefore \quad C_d = 1.0$$

Load duration factor for wind is

$$C_D = 1.6 \quad \text{(Verify local code acceptance before using.)}$$

All other adjustment factors are unity for this problem, and the allowable design value is

$$Z' = Z(C_D) = 83(1.6) = 133 \text{ lb/nail}$$

For the gross overturning moment:

$$N = \frac{1800}{133} = 13.6$$

> *Use*   fourteen 8d box nails each end of steel strap into multiple studs.

For the net overturning moment:

$$N = \frac{1330}{133} = 10.0$$

> *Use*   ten 8d box nails each end of steel strap to multiple studs.

12.10   Design Problem: Laterally Loaded Toenail

The example to illustrate the load capacity of a toenail connection is the Code attachment of a stud to the bottom plate of a wall. See Example 12.11. The nailing schedule in UBC Table 25-Q lists four 8d common or box toenails as one of the acceptable methods of attaching a stud to the sole plate. Design forces and special considerations for this attachment in areas of high seismic risk were discussed in Sec. 10.11.

The force on the given connection is wind perpendicular to the wall. The penetration of the nail and the thickness of the side member for use in the yield limit equations are determined using the geometry from Fig. 12.12a (Sec. 12.6). Recall that t_s and p_L are to be taken as the *projected* lengths of the nail in the side and main members.

The geometry thus established is not directly covered by the NDS fastener load tables, and the yield limit expressions are evaluated in the example. This would normally be done on the computer, and the full numerical example is given for illustration.

EXAMPLE 12.11   Capacity of Toenail Connection

Determine the allowable wind force reaction at the base of a wood-frame shearwall which uses the standard Code toenailing of four 8d common or box nails (Fig. 12.16). Lumber is dry DF-L that will remain dry in service. Normal temperatures apply.

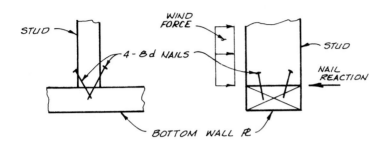

TYPICAL   STUD   TO   ℝ   CONNECTION

Figure 12.16   Toenail connection at bottom of stud subject to lateral wind force.

Box nails have a smaller diameter than common nails. Therefore, calculations are shown for *box nails,* and a larger load capacity will be obtained if common nails are used.

Geometry:

Dimensions of an 8d box nail are obtained from the table in Fig. 12.7a or NDS Table 12.3A:

$$D = 0.113 \text{ in.}$$

$$l = 2.5 \text{ in.}$$

For a toenail, the thickness of the side member and penetration are determined using the geometry given in Fig. 12.12a. The bottom wall plate is a nominal 2×, and $t_m = 1.5$ in.

$$t_s = \frac{l}{3} = \frac{2.5}{3} = 0.83 \text{ in.}$$

$$p_L = l \cos 30 - t_s \leq t_m$$

$$= 2.5 \cos 30 - 0.83 \leq 1.5$$

$$\therefore \quad p_L = 1.33 \text{ in.}$$

Coefficients for yield equations:

Bending yield strength of an 8d box nail is obtained from the table in Fig. 12.7b or NDS Table 12.3A:

$$F_{yb} = 100,000 \text{ psi}$$

Specific gravity and dowel bearing strength are the same for both the main member and side member and are obtained from NDS Table 12A:

$$SG_m = SG_s = 0.50$$

$$F_{em} = F_{es} = 4650 \text{ psi}$$

Coefficients for use in yield equations:

$$K_D = 2.2$$

$$R_e = \frac{F_{em}}{F_{es}} = \frac{4650}{4650} = 1.0$$

$$1 + R_e = 2.0$$

$$1 + 2R_e = 3.0$$

$$2 + R_e = 3.0$$

$$k_1 = -1 + \sqrt{2(1 + R_e) + \frac{2F_{yb}(1 + 2R_e)D^2}{3F_{em}p^2}}$$

$$= -1 + \sqrt{2(2.0) + \frac{2(100{,}000)(3.0)(0.113^2)}{3(4650)(1.33)^2}}$$

$$= 1.076$$

$$k_2 = -1 + \sqrt{\frac{2(1 + R_e)}{R_e} + \frac{2F_{yb}(2 + R_e)D^2}{3F_{em}t_s^2}}$$

$$= -1 + \sqrt{\frac{2(2.0)}{1.0} + \frac{2(100{,}000)(3.0)(0.113^2)}{3(4650)(0.83)^2}}$$

$$= 1.189$$

Yield equations:

Mode I_s (NDS equation 12.3-1):

$$Z = \frac{Dt_sF_{es}}{K_D} = \frac{0.113(0.83)(4650)}{2.2} = 199 \text{ lb}$$

Mode III_m (NDS equation 12.3-2):

$$Z = \frac{k_1DpF_{em}}{K_D(1 + 2R_e)} = \frac{1.076(0.113)(1.33)(4650)}{2.2(3.0)} = 114 \text{ lb}$$

Mode III_s (NDS equation 12.3-3):

$$Z = \frac{k_2Dt_sF_{em}}{K_D(2 + R_e)} = \frac{1.189(0.113)(0.83)(4650)}{2.2(3.0)} = 79 \text{ lb}$$

Mode IV (NDS equation 12.3-4):

$$Z = \frac{D^2}{K_D} \sqrt{\frac{2F_{em}F_{yb}}{3(1 + R_e)}}$$

$$= \frac{(0.113)^2}{2.2} \sqrt{\frac{2(4650)(100,000)}{3(2.0)}} = 72 \text{ lb}$$

Nominal design value:

Nominal design value is taken as the smallest value from the yield formulas:

$$Z = 72 \text{ lb}$$

Adjustment factors:

Load duration factor for wind is

$$C_D = 1.6 \qquad \text{(Verify local code acceptance before using.)}$$

Limits for penetration depth factor:

$$12D = 12(0.113) = 1.36 \text{ in.}$$

$$6D = 6(0.113) = 0.68 \text{ in.}$$

$$0.68 < 1.33 < 1.36$$

∴   Penetration depth factor:

$$C_d = \frac{p_L}{12D} = \frac{1.33}{1.36} = 0.982$$

Toenail factor for laterally loaded toenails:

$$C_{tn} = 0.83$$

All other adjustments do not apply to this problem and are set equal to unity.

Allowable design value:

$$Z' = Z(C_D C_d C_{tn})$$

$$= 72(1.6)(0.982)(0.83) = 94 \text{ lb/nail}$$

Allowable reaction:

Allowable wind reaction at base of stud:

$$R = N \times Z' = 4(94) = \boxed{377 \text{ lb/stud}}$$

12.11   Design Problem: Laterally Loaded Connection in End Grain

The final example of a shear connection involves nailing a member into the end grain of a roof beam. See Example 12.12. This is not a very desirable type of connection, but it is frequently seen in the field and serves as an illustration of when the end grain factor C_{eg} is required. There are a number of alternative connections, with nails driven into the side grain, that can be used in place of the given connection. These alternative connections are generally preferred and become necessary for larger loads. The alternative connections may involve some type of metal hardware (Chap. 14).

EXAMPLE 12.12   Nail into End Grain of Roof Beam

Determine the allowable load that can be transmitted by the nail connection in Fig. 12.17. Lumber is DF-L that is initially dry and remains dry in service. Normal temperatures apply. The connection is made with two 16d common nails into the end grain of the main member. Loads are (DL + snow).

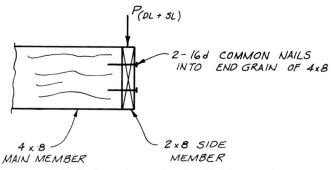

Figure 12.17   Nails driven into end grain of holding member.

Nominal design value:

The nominal design value in this example is the same as the nail in Example 12.3. The member sizes are different, but the dimensions and other factors affecting the nominal design value are the same in the two problems. Thus, from Example 12.3

$$Z = 141 \text{ lb}$$

Allowable design value:

Load duration factor for (DL + snow):

$$C_D = 1.15$$

End grain factor:

$$C_{eg} = 0.67$$

Other adjustment factors have default values of unity.

$$Z' = Z(C_D C_{eg}) = 141(1.15)(0.67)$$

$$= 109 \text{ lb/nail}$$

Allowable load on connection:

$$P_{(DL+SL)} = N \times Z' = 2 \times 109$$

$$= \boxed{218 \text{ lb} \quad \text{(dry service)}}$$

NOTE: If the connection is exposed to the weather or if high-humidity conditions exist, the wet service factor will apply, and the allowable load becomes

$$Z' = Z(C_D C_M C_{eg}) = 141(1.15)(0.75)(0.67)$$

$$= 82 \text{ lb/nail}$$

$$P_{(DL+SL)} = 2 \times 82 = \boxed{164 \text{ lb} \quad \text{(wet service)}}$$

12.12   Nail Withdrawal Connections

The concept of a fastener loaded in withdrawal was introduced in Chap. 11 (Fig. 11.2). In the *basic withdrawal connection,* the nail passes through the side member and into the *side grain* of the main member. In this connection the load is parallel to the length of the nail, and the load attempts to pull the nail out of the holding member. Generally speaking, connections loaded in withdrawal are weaker and less desirable than the same connections subjected to shear loading. The NDS provides tabulated design loads for fasteners subjected to "pullout," but the usual recommendation is that withdrawal connections should be avoided (in favor of other more positive types of connections) where practical.

The yield limit model for dowel-type fasteners applies only to shear connections, and the load capacities for nails in withdrawal are based on empirical test results. The *nominal design value* for the basic withdrawal connection is given the symbol W. In addition to nail size and type, the withdrawal capacity depends on the specific gravity of the wood and the penetration p of the nail into the holding member.

NDS Table 12.2A gives the nominal withdrawal design value *per inch of penetration* for common nails, box nails, common wire spikes, and threaded hardened steel nails. If the value from the table is given the symbol w, the nominal design value for a single nail is

$$W = w \times p$$

As explained previously, the nominal design value W represents the load capacity for a nail used under a set of base conditions, similar to the base conditions for laterally loaded connections:

1. Load is normal (10-year) duration.

2. Wood is initially dry at the time of fabrication of a connection, and it remains dry in service.

3. Temperature range is normal.

4. Nail is driven into the side grain of the main (holding) member.

5. Nail is not driven as a toenail.

To obtain the *allowable design value* W' for another set of conditions, the nominal design value is multiplied by the appropriate adjustment factors:

$$W' = W(C_D C_M C_t C_{tn})$$

where C_D = load duration factor (Sec. 4.15)
  C_M = wet service factor (Sec. 4.14)
  C_t = temperature factor (Sec. 4.20)
  C_{tn} = toenail factor

If more than one nail of the same size and type is used, the allowable withdrawal load for the connection is the allowable withdrawal load for one fastener W' times the number of nails N:

$$P = N(W')$$

Perhaps the most basic point to understand about nails loaded in withdrawal has to do with the direction of the grain of the holding member. See Example 12.13. The nominal design values apply only to connections with the nail penetrating into the *side grain* of the holding member (Fig. 12.18a). This has been referred to as the *basic* withdrawal connection. The other possible arrangement is to have the nail penetrate into the *end grain* of the holding member (Fig. 12.18b).

Nails that are driven into the end grain have very low capacities and exhibit considerable variation in withdrawal values. Consequently, the NDS does not provide withdrawal load values for nails driven into the end grain. This point could be emphasized by introducing an end grain factor of $C_{eg} = 0$ into the allowable load formula for withdrawal loading.

EXAMPLE 12.13   Comparison of Withdrawal Connections

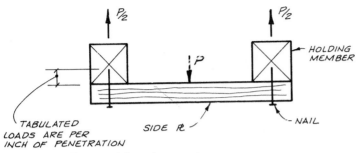

Figure 12.18a Basic withdrawal connection.

Withdrawal from Side Grain

The *basic* withdrawal connection has the nail driven into the *side grain* (i.e., perpendicular to the grain) of the holding member, and the load is parallel to the length of the nail (Fig. 12.18a).

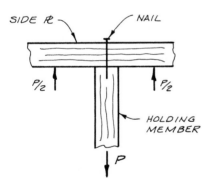

Figure 12.18b Withdrawal from end grain—not allowed.

Withdrawal from End Grain—Not Permitted

The second example is a withdrawal connection with the nail driven into the *end grain* (i.e., parallel to the grain) of the holding member. The load is again parallel to the length of the nail (Fig. 12.18b). This is an inherently weak connection, and it is not permitted in design (i.e., it has no allowable load).

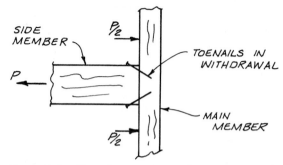

Figure 12.18c Toenail connection withdrawal from side grain.

Toenail Loaded in Withdrawal

A *toenail* connection may be loaded in withdrawal as long as the nails penetrate the *side grain* of the holding member. For withdrawal loading, the toenail factor is $C_{tn} = 0.67$ (compared with 0.83 for toenails subjected to shear loading). For a toenail in withdrawal, the NDS indicates that the wet service factor need not be applied. In other words, C_M may be set equal to 1.0 for toenails loaded in withdrawal.

   A brief summary of the adjustment factors for withdrawal connections is given. This is followed by two numerical examples.

Load duration factor C_D.   The load duration factor C_D for nail connections subject to withdrawal is the same as that applied in the design of structural members such as beams, tension members, and columns. Refer to Sec. 4.15 for a review of load duration and the numerical values for C_D.

Wet service factor C_M.   The concept of an adjustment factor based on moisture content was introduced in Sec. 4.14. In most cases, nails loaded in withdrawal are more negatively affected by variations in moisture content than are other connections. As with shear connections, the moisture content of the wood is considered (1) at the time of fabrication of the joint and (2) in service. The nominal design value applies to withdrawal connections in which the wood is initially dry and remains dry in service. For other moisture content conditions, values of C_M are obtained from NDS Table 7.3.3.
   The performance of threaded hardened steel nails is better than other types of nails, and $C_M = 1.0$ for all moisture content conditions. The NDS also specifies $C_M = 1.0$ for all toenail connections loaded in withdrawal, regardless of nail type.

Temperature factor C_t.   If wood is used at higher-than-normal temperatures, the nominal design values for connections are to be reduced by the temperature factor C_t. Numerical values of C_t are obtained from NDS Table

7.3.4. It should be noted that the temperature range in most wood-frame buildings does not require a reduction in fastener load capacity, and C_t is usually taken as 1.0.

Toenail factor C_{tn}.   The installation of toenails was covered earlier in this chapter. The geometry in Fig. 12.12a is used to evaluate penetration in determining the nominal withdrawal value W. The nominal design value is then reduced by the toenail factor for withdrawal $C_{tn} = 0.67$. Note again that the wet service factor does not apply to toenails loaded in withdrawal $(C_M = 1.0)$.

Because withdrawal connections are not the preferred connection, only two brief examples are given. The first is a withdrawal connection with the nail driven perpendicular to the member and into the side grain. See Example 12.14. The second problem demonstrates the procedure for a toenail connection loaded in withdrawal. See Example 12.15.

EXAMPLE 12.14   Basic Withdrawal Connection

Assume that the hanger in Fig. 12.18a is used to suspend a dead load P. The side member is a 2 × 8, and the holding members are 6 × 6s. Lumber is Western Hemlock that is initially green, and seasoning occurs in service. Normal temperatures apply. Six 16d box nails are used at both ends of the side member. Determine the allowable load P.

Nail diameter and length are obtained from the table in Fig. 12.7a or from NDS Table 12.3A:

$$D = 0.135 \text{ in.}$$

$$l = 3.5 \text{ in.}$$

Specific gravity is obtained from NDS Table 12A:

$$SG = 0.47$$

Tabulated withdrawal value from NDS Table 12.2A:

$$w = 28 \text{ lb/in.}$$

Penetration:

$$p = l - t_s \leq t_m$$

$$= 3.5 - 1.5 \leq 5.5$$

$$\therefore \ p = 2.0 \text{ in.}$$

Nominal design value:

$$W = p \times w = 2.0(28) = 56 \text{ lb/nail}$$

Allowable design value:

$$W' = W(C_D C_M C_t C_{tn})$$

$$= 56(0.9)(0.25)(1.0)(1.0) = 12.6 \text{ lb/nail}$$

The load is applied symmetrically, and the total load capacity is

$$\text{Allow. } P = N(W') = 12(12.6) = \boxed{151 \text{ lb}}$$

EXAMPLE 12.15   Toenail Withdrawal Connection

Assume that the connection in Fig. 12.18c has three 8d common nails. Both members are 2-in. nominal DF-L that is initially dry and remains dry in service. Normal temperatures apply. Determine the allowable wind force P.

Nail diameter and length are obtained from the table in Fig. 12.7a or NDS Table 12.3B:

$$D = 0.131 \text{ in.}$$

$$l = 2.5 \text{ in.}$$

Penetration for a toenail in a withdrawal connection (Fig. 12.12a):

$$p_W = l - \frac{l/3}{\cos 30} \le \frac{t_m}{\cos 30}$$

$$= 2.5 - \frac{2.5}{3 \cos 30} \le \frac{1.5}{\cos 30}$$

$$= 1.54 < 1.73$$

$$\therefore \ p_W = 1.54 \text{ in.}$$

Specific gravity from NDS Table 12A:

$$SG = 0.50$$

Tabulated withdrawal value from NDS Table 12.2A:

$$w = 32 \text{ lb/in.}$$

Nominal design value:

$$W = p_W \times w = 1.54(32) = 49.3 \text{ lb/nail}$$

Allowable design value:

$$W' = W(C_D C_t C_{tn})$$

$$= 49.3(1.6)(1.0)(0.67) = 53 \text{ lb/nail}$$

Total load capacity:

$$\text{Allow. } P = N(W') = 3(53) = \boxed{159 \text{ lb}}$$

12.13   Spacing Requirements

The spacing requirements for nail connections given in the NDS are rather general. Nail spacing "shall be sufficient to prevent splitting of the wood."

In the past, the layout of nails in a connection has typically been left to the discretion of the field personnel fabricating the connection. However, because an increasingly large number of nails are used in some structural connections, the designer may need to address the layout of fasteners in certain cases. Judgment must be used in the detailing of nail connections because there is not a recognized standard for the placement of nails. The UBC provides partial guidance.

In order to discuss the spacing of mechanical fasteners, it is necessary to define some terms that are used in detailing wood connections. See Fig. 12.19. These definitions apply to nails as well as other types of fasteners, but there are additional clarifications required for bolts and other connectors.

End distance is the distance, measured parallel to the grain, from the center of the nearest fastener to the end grain of a square-cut piece of lumber. *Edge distance* is the distance, measured perpendicular to the grain, from the center of the nearest fastener to the edge of the member. *Center-to-center distance* (also known as *nail spacing*) is the distance from the center of one fastener to the center of an adjacent fastener in a row. A *row* of fasteners is defined as two or more fasteners in a line parallel to the direction of load, and *row spacing* is the perpendicular distance between rows of fasteners.

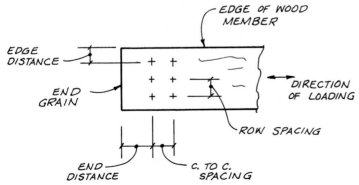

Figure 12.19   Definition of terms for nail spacing. Drawing shows *three rows* of nails.

The UBC gives the following spacing requirements for *wood-to-wood* nailed connections. The center-to-center spacing in the direction of stress should not be less than the required penetration of the nail. The minimum end and edge distances *in the direction of stress* are taken as one-half the required penetration. Spacing requirements perpendicular to the loading are not addressed, except that splitting of wood is to be avoided.

In most cases, nails are simply driven into wood members without drilling. However, preboring nail holes may be used to avoid splitting the wood. The NDS limits the diameter of a pilot hole to a maximum of 90 percent of the nail diameter for wood with a specific gravity greater than 0.6, and 75 percent of the nail diameter for less dense wood (SG $\leq$ 0.6). The full lateral design value Z' and withdrawal design value W' apply to connections with or without prebored holes. Preboring is an effective method of avoiding the splitting of wood members.

There are many connection detailing questions that are left unanswered under the Code criteria. As noted, the Code criteria are limited to spacings parallel to the direction of the stress. Another problem occurs in members that do not have square-cut ends. See Example 12.16. As the angle θ in Fig. 12.20 becomes small, the perpendicular distance from the end cut on the diagonal member to the center of the nail becomes small if the end distance (parallel to the grain) is kept constant. A similar problem occurs with the edge distance for the vertical member.

For an end cut that is not square, the TCM (Ref. 3.1) recommends that the *perpendicular distance from the end cut* should not be less than the *edge distance*. Similar logic may reasonably be applied to the perpendicular distance from the nail to the edge of the vertical member. It should be noted that the recommendation just cited from the TCM is a general recommendation for fasteners, and the TCM does not provide specific spacing criteria for nail connections. For nails, the TCM indicates that "unusual" splitting is to be avoided.

EXAMPLE 12.16   Nail Spacing

Determine the nail spacing for the knee brace connection designed in Example 12.8 (Sec. 12.7). See Fig. 12.20 for a scale drawing. Apply the UBC criteria to the extent possible. Can six 16d common nails be accommodated?

Required penetration according to 1991 NDS is

$$p = 12D = 12(0.162) = 1.94 \quad say \quad 2 \text{ in.}$$

UBC spacings are *parallel to load:*

$$\text{Min. end distance} = \tfrac{1}{2}p = \tfrac{1}{2} \times 2 = 1 \text{ in.}$$

$$\text{Min. edge distance} = \tfrac{1}{2}p = 1 \text{ in.}$$

$$\text{Min. spacing (c. to c. distance)} = p = 2 \text{ in.}$$

NOTE: As the angle θ becomes small, the perpendicular distance from the nail to the end cut may become too small. Therefore, use the general recommendation from AITC that the perpendicular distance from the end cut be not less than the edge distance. The Code edge distance will also be applied to the edge distance for the vertical member, even though the load is not parallel to the axis of the vertical member.

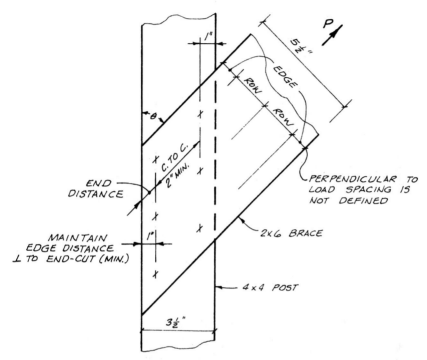

Figure 12.20 Detailing of nail connection for brace.

For this connection, the layout of six nails meets the parallel-to-load spacing criteria from the UBC. In addition, the connection can accommodate the perpendicular distance from the end cut of the diagonal, and the edge distance for the vertical member, equal to one-half of the required penetration. Row spacings is not addressed.

A scale drawing is helpful in determining the spacing requirements for a connection. Because the spacing provisions perpendicular to the load are not specified, the total number of nails that can be used in a limited area is not fully defined.

The spacings given in Example 12.16 represent a mix of very limited criteria for nail connections from several sources:

1. A nail penetration value of $12D$ is the 1991 NDS requirement to obtain the full design value of a nail. (Note that the NDS permits nail pene-

tration to be reduced to 6D with a corresponding reduction in allowable load.)

2. Center-to-center spacing equal to the required penetration, and end and edge distances equal to one-half the required penetration come from the UBC. According to the Code, these apply in the direction of the stress.

3. Distance perpendicular to the end cut equal to the edge distance comes from the general spacing recommendations in the TCM.

Clearly there are a number of other possible interpretations of nail spacing criteria. Furthermore, other sources offer much different spacing recommendations. For example, without prebored holes, Ref. 9.3 recommends an end distance of 20D and other spacings from this reference are generally larger than those cited.

It should be noted that a *Commentary* to the *1991 NDS* is currently being developed by NFPA. The plan is to include a set of proposed nail spacings in the *Commentary* which will be offered for trial use by the design community. After appropriate input, a set of spacing requirements will be incorporated into a later edition of the NDS. It is likely that the spacing criteria to be included in the *NDS Commentary* will be more restrictive than the criteria used in Example 12.16.

At this point the reader should understand that certain connections will require careful consideration of nail spacing, and that considerable judgment is required in detailing connections. Nail patterns should be chosen by the designer with a basic understanding of the material and the tendency of wood to split if adequate spacing is not provided.

Definitive criteria for spacing in a nail connection does not exist at this time. The proposed criteria to be included in the NDS Commentary represents committee consensus, but additional research is necessary to confirm spacing criteria.

12.14   Nailing Schedule

UBC Table 25-Q is a *nailing schedule* which gives the minimum nailing that is to be used for a number of common connections in wood-frame construction. The table covers such items as the nailing of beams (joists and rafters) to the top plate of a wall. For this connection three 8d toenails are specified (Fig. 12.12*b*). The required nailing for numerous other connections is covered by this schedule. Copies of a number of UBC tables are included in Appendix C of this book.

The requirements given by the Code should be regarded as a *minimum*. They apply to conventional wood-frame construction as well as construction that has been structurally designed. A larger number of nails (or some other type of connection hardware) may be required when structural calculations are performed. Special consideration should be given to the attachment of the various elements in the lateral-force-resisting system.

12.15 Problems

Many of the nail problems in this section require the *nominal design value*
Z and the *allowable design value Z'* as either final or intermediate answers.
These values are to be identified as part of the general solution along with
the information specifically requested.

The nominal design values for a given nail may be obtained by solving
the yield limit equations or by using the NDS nail tables. Tables are to be
used only if they apply directly to the design conditions stated in the problem
and are to be referenced in the solution. Yield limit equations may be evaluated by either calculator or computer. If the computer is used, output must
be sufficient so that all steps in the solution can be verified.

In all problems normal temperatures are assumed, and $C_t = 1.0$. Except
for the load duration factor C_D, all adjustment factors are to be referenced
to the appropriate NDS table or section so that the source of the value may
be verified.

Based on recommendations in the 1991 NDS, a load duration factor of 1.6
is used for problems involving wind or seismic forces. Check acceptance by
local code authority before using $C_D = 1.6$ in practice. The loads given in
a problem are to be applied directly. In practice, use of a load combination
factor (Secs. 2.8 and 16.2) may be permitted. Check acceptance by local code
authority before using the *load combination factor* together with the *load
duration factor C_D*.

Some problems require the use of a microcomputer spreadsheet. Problems
that are solved on a spreadsheet can be saved and used as a *template* for
other similar problems. Templates can have many degrees of sophistication.
Initially, a template may only be a hand (i.e., calculator) solution worked
on a spreadsheet. In a simple template of this nature, the user will be
required to provide many of the lookup functions for such items as

1. Nail diameter and length

2. Bending yield strength of nail

3. Specific gravity and dowel bearing strength of wood member

4. Dowel bearing strength of metal side member

As the user gains experience with spreadsheets, a template can be expanded
to perform many of the lookup and decision-making functions that were
previously done manually.

Advanced programming skills are not required to create effective spreadsheets templates. Valuable templates can be created by designers who normally do only hand solutions. However, some programming techniques are
helpful in automating *lookup* and *decision-making* functions.

The first requirement is that a spreadsheet operate correctly (i.e., calculate
correct values). Another major consideration is that the input and output
must be structured in an orderly manner. A sufficient number of interme-

diate answers are to be displayed and labeled in a template so that the solution can be verified by hand.

12.1   Use a microcomputer spreadsheet to set up the solution of the yield limit equations for a laterally loaded nail. Consider a single-shear wood-to-wood connection, using the following variables for input:

> Nail diameter D
>
> Nail length l
>
> Thickness of side member t_s
>
> Specific gravity of the side member SG_s
>
> Thickness of main member t_m
>
> Specific gravity of main member SG_m

The spreadsheet is to do the following:
a. Compute the dowel bearing strength for the main and side members F_{es} and F_{em}.
b. Determine the penetration of the nail p.
c. Evaluate the coefficients for use in the yield limit equations.
d. Solve the four yield limit equations and select the smallest value as the *nominal design value Z*.

12.2   Expand or modify the spreadsheet template from Prob. 12.1 to handle a single-shear connection with a steel side plate. Input remains the same except the ultimate tensile strength of the metal side plate F_u replaces the specific gravity of the side member SG_s.

12.3   Expand the spreadsheet template from Prob. 12.1 to handle laterally loaded *toenail* connections *in addition to* conventional shear connections. Input is to essentially remain the same as Prob. 12.1, but some method of distinguishing between a toenail and a nail not driven as a toenail is required.

   One approach is to leave the thickness of the side member blank (i.e., $t_s = 0$) to indicate a toenail connection. The spreadsheet would then evaluate t_s for the toenail using the geometry in Fig. 12.12a.

12.4   Expand the spreadsheet template in Prob. 12.1, 12.2, or 12.3 (as assigned) to convert the *nominal design value Z* to an *allowable design value Z'*. The input must be expanded to include the appropriate adjustment factors. Include, as a minimum, the adjustments for:
a. Load duration factor C_D
b. Moisture content factor C_M
c. Penetration depth factor C_d
d. End grain factor C_{eg}
e. Toenail factor C_{tn} (applies only if expanding Prob. 12.3)

12.5 The shed in Fig. 12.A has double 2 × 6 knee braces on each column to resist the lateral force. Lumber is Southern Pine. The braces are to be connected to the columns with 16d common nails. Lateral force to roof diaphragm w_L is 67 lb/ft. Heights: h_1 = 9 ft, h_2 = 2 ft.

Find: a. The required number of nails for the brace connection, assuming that C_M = 1.0.
            b. The required number of nails for the brace connection, assuming that the connection is exposed to the weather
            c. How would *a* and *b* change if threaded hardened nails were used?

12.6 The shed in Fig. 12.A has double 2 × 6 knee braces on each column to resist the lateral force. Lumber is California Redwood. The braces are to be connected to the columns with 16d common nails. Lateral force to roof diaphragm w_L = 46 lb/ft. Heights: h_1 = 12 ft, h_2 = 4 ft.

Find: a. The required number of nails for the brace connection, assuming that C_M = 1.0.
            b. The required number of nails for the brace connection, assuming that the connection is exposed to the weather.
            c. How would *a* and *b* change if threaded hardened nails were used?

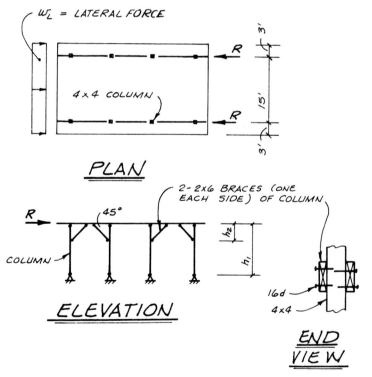

Figure 12.A

12.7   Repeat Prob. 12.6 except that 16d box nails are to be used.

12.8   The single-story wood-frame building in Fig. 12.B has a double 2×4 top wall plate of Southern Pine. This top plate serves as the chord and drag strut along line 1. Loads are $w_T = 134$ lb/ft and $w_L = 223$ lb/ft. $C_M = 1.0$.

   Find: *a.* The maximum chord force along line 1.
      b. The maximum drag force along line 1.
      c. Determine the number of 16d common nails necessary to splice the top plate for the maximum force determined in *a* and *b*.

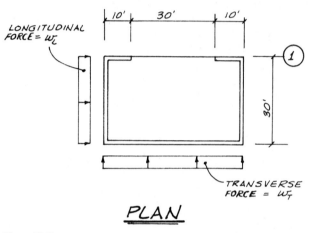

LONGITUDINAL FORCE = w_L

TRANSVERSE FORCE = w_T

10'   30'   10'

30'

1

PLAN

Figure 12.B

12.9   Repeat Prob. 12.8 except that 16d box nails are to be used.

12.10   The single-story wood-frame building in Fig. 12.B has a double 2×4 top wall plate of Douglas Fir-Larch. The top plate serves as the chord and drag strut along line 1. The loads are $w_T = 100$ lb/ft and $w_L = 250$ lb/ft. $C_M = 1.0$.

   Find: *a.* The maximum chord force along line 1.
      b. The maximum drag force along line 1.
      c. Determine the number of 16d common nails necessary to splice the top plate for the maximum force determined in *a* and *b*.

12.11   Repeat Prob. 12.10 except that 16d box nails are to be used.

12.12   *Given:*   The elevation of the shearwall in Fig. 12.C. The lateral force and the resisting dead load of the shearwall are shown on the sketch. The uplift force at the bottom of the wall is anchored to the foundation by a metal strap embedded in the concrete foundation. The 10-gage ASTM A446 grade A steel strap is attached to the shearwall chord (two 2×4s) with 10d common nails. Lumber is Hem-Fir. $C_M = 1.0$. Assume that the steel strap is adequate.

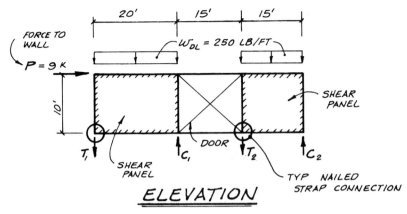

Figure 12.C

Find: Determine the number of nails required to attach the metal anchor strap to the chord. Consider the resisting DL when calculating the anchorage force.

12.13 Repeat Prob. 12.12 except that nails are 16d common nails.

12.14 The two-story wood-frame building in Fig. 12.D has plywood shear panels along line 1. The lateral forces are shown in the sketch. Diaphragm span length $L = 30$ ft. Resisting dead loads to line 1 are roof DL = 100 lb/ft, floor DL = 120 lb/ft, and wall DL = 10 psf. Tie-down anchorage is to be with 12-gage ASTM A446 grade A steel straps and 16d common nails. Studs are 2 × 6 of Spruce-Pine-Fir (South). Assume that the metal strap is adequate. $C_M = 1.0$.

Find: The number of nails required for the anchorage connections at A and B.

12.15 Repeat Prob. 12.14 except that the diaphragm span length is $L = 40$ ft.

12.16 The attachment of a roof diaphragm to the supporting shearwall is shown in Fig. 12.E. The shear transferred to the wall is $v = 230$ lb/ft. Toenails in the blocking are used to transfer the shear from the roof diaphragm into the double top plate. Lumber is DF-L. $C_M = 1.0$.

Find: The required number of 8d common toenails per block if roof beams are 16 in o.c.

12.17 Repeat Prob. 12.16 except $v = 180$ lb/ft and nails are 8d box toenails.

12.18 The studs in the wood-frame wall in Fig. 12.F span between the foundation and the horizontal diaphragm. Roof beams are anchored to the wall top plate with 8d box toenails. Lumber is Hem-Fir. Roof beams are spaced 24 in o.c. Wind = 20 psf. Wall height = 10 ft. $C_M = 1.0$.

Find: The required number of toenails per roof beam.

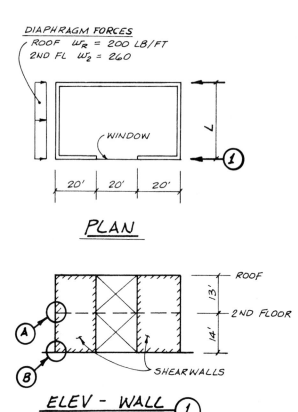

DIAPHRAGM FORCES
ROOF w_R = 200 LB/FT
2ND FL w_2 = 260

WINDOW

20'   20'   20'

L

1

PLAN

ROOF

13'

2ND FLOOR

14'

A

B

SHEARWALLS

ELEV - WALL   1

Figure 12.D

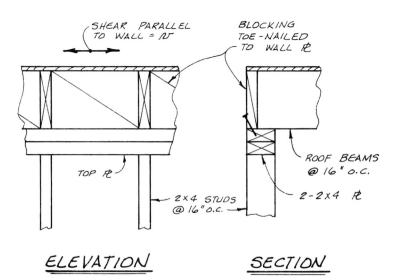

SHEAR PARALLEL
TO WALL = $\wp$

BLOCKING
TOE-NAILED
TO WALL $\wp$

TOP $\wp$

2×4 STUDS
@ 16" O.C.

ROOF BEAMS
@ 16" O.C.

2-2×4 $\wp$

ELEVATION   ## SECTION

Figure 12.E

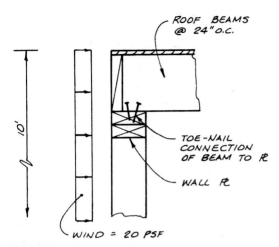

Figure 12.F

12.19 The support shown in Fig. 12.G carries a DL of 500 lb. Lumber is DF-L. Nails are 20d common nails driven into the side grain of the holding member.

Find: The required number of nails, assuming that
a. $C_M = 1.0$
b. The connection is exposed to the weather.
c. The connection is exposed to the weather and threaded hardened nails are used in place of common nails.

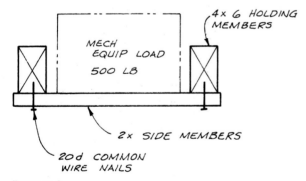

Figure 12.G

12.20 Determine the UBC minimum required nailing for the following connections. Give nail size, type, and required number.
a. Joist to sill or girder, toenail
b. Bridging to joist, toenail each end
c. Sole plate to joist or blocking, face nail
d. Top plate to stud, end nail
e. Stud to sole plate, toenail
Problem continues on next page.

f. Doubled studs, face nail
g. Doubled top plates, face nail
h. Top plates, laps, and intersections; face nail
i. Ceiling joists to plate, toenail
j. Continuous header to stud, toenail
k. Ceiling joists to parallel rafters, face nail
l. Rafter to plate, toenail

Bolts, Lag Bolts, and Other Connectors

13.1 Introduction

Once the vertical-load-supporting system and lateral-force-resisting system of a building have been designed, attention is turned to the design of the connections. The importance of connection design has been emphasized in previous chapters, and the methods used to calculate the forces on several types of connections have been illustrated.

When the design forces are relatively small, the connections may often be made with nails (Chap. 12). However, bolts, lag bolts, and other connectors are normally used for larger loads. There are several additional reasons why nailed connections were covered in a separate chapter. Recall from Chap. 11 that the load capacity for a small-diameter fastener, such as a nail, is independent of the angle of load to grain. The angle of load to grain, however, is a major consideration in the design of large-diameter fasteners. The other principal reason is that there are a number of adjustment factors that apply to bolts, lag bolts, and other connectors which do *not* apply to nails.

Connections made with larger-diameter fasteners often involve the use of some form of structural steel hardware. For many common connections this hardware may be available prefabricated from manufacturers or suppliers. Other connections, however, will require the fabrication of special hardware. Prefabricated hardware, when available, is often more economical than made-to-order hardware. Chapter 14 continues the subject of connection design by giving examples of common types of hardware. These examples are accompanied by comments about both good and poor connection layout practices.

The types of fasteners covered in this chapter include

1. Bolts
2. Lag bolts (lag screws)

3. Other connectors
   a. Split rings
   b. Shear plates

Examples of several connections using these fasteners were given in the introductory chapter on connections. It is recommended that the reader review the joint configurations, nomenclature, and yield modes that are summarized in Chap. 11 before proceeding with the detailed design provisions given here. Because of their greater use, the majority of the coverage in Chap. 13 is devoted to bolted connections. This is followed by lag bolts. Split ring and shear plate connectors are often viewed as specialty connections, and for this reason their use is covered only briefly.

13.2 Bolt Connections

Most bolts are used in laterally loaded dowel-type connections. These are further described by giving the number of shear planes and the types of structural members connected. For example, the most common connections are either *single-shear* (two-member) or *double-shear* (three-member) joints. See Example 12.1. Connections can be *wood-to-wood* or *wood-to-metal*. A single-shear connection also occurs when a wood member is attached by anchor bolts to a concrete foundation or a concrete or masonry wall. These can be referred to as *wood-to-concrete* or *wood-to-masonry* connections, but they are often simply termed *anchor bolt* connections.

EXAMPLE 13.1   Bolts in Shear Connections

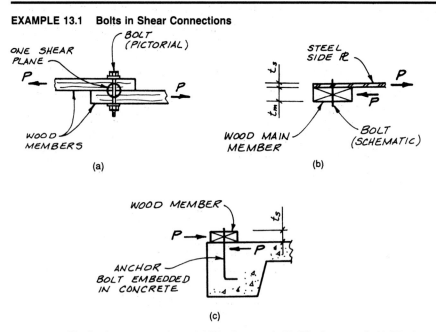

Figure 13.1 Single-shear connections. (*a*) Wood-to-wood. (*b*) Wood-to-metal. (*c*) Wood-to-concrete anchor bolt.

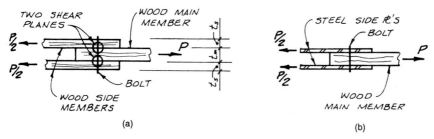

Figure 13.2 Double-shear connections. (*a*) Wood-to-wood. (*b*) Wood-to-metal.

In shear connections the load is perpendicular to the axis of the bolt. The angle of load to grain in the wood can be zero (load parallel to grain), 90 degrees (load perpendicular to grain), or at some intermedite angle θ. The angle of load to grain affects the load capacity of bolted connections.

Bolted connections can have more than two shear planes (i.e., more than three members). For multiple shear planes, the NDS states that the load capacity is to be evaluated by first determining the single-shear capacity for each shear plane. The nominal design value for the connection is determined by multiplying the value for the weakest shear plane by the number of shear planes. In this book, only the common cases of single- and double-shear bolt connections are covered.

Washers of adequate size are to be provided between a wood member and the bolt head, and between the wood member and the nut. Washers can be circular or square. The use of washers applies to bolts in shear as well as to those loaded in tension. For bolts in tension (Fig. 11.2*b* in Sec. 11.2), the size of washer needs to be such that the bearing stress in the wood member does not exceed the allowable compressive stress perpendicular to grain $F'_{c\perp}$.

The size of the washer is not particularly critical for bolts loaded in shear, and the washer simply protects the wood as the nut is tightened. The nut should be snugged tight, but care should be taken so that the nut is not installed too tight. In other words, the washer should not be embedded in the wood member by overtightening the nut. On the other hand, if a wood member seasons in service, the width of the wood member may shrink so that the nut may need to be retightened after a period of time.

The quality of bolts used in wood connections has not been a major concern in the past. However, with the move to a design procedure based on the yield model for dowel-type fasteners, there is a need to have recognized mechanical properties for bolts. Recall that some yield modes are based on the formation of one or more plastic hinges in the fastener, and this requires bolts with predictable bending yield strengths F_{yb} and ductility characteristics.

Designers familar with steel know that the trend in steel structures is away from the use of low-strength A307 bolts and toward the use of high-strength

A325 bolts. However, this is not the case in wood structures, and A307 bolts are often used in wood connections. The current problem with specifying A307 bolts is that the ASTM standard for these bolts provides only an ultimate tensile strength F_u, and there is no minimum F_y covered by the specification.

Without a published value for yield strength, there is a conceptual problem in using the yield limit model with ASTM A307 bolts. As a practical matter, A307 bolts have performed satisfactorily in the past, and these fasteners must have a reasonable F_y. The tables in the 1991 NDS are based on $F_{yb} = 45$ ksi, which is generally thought to be a conservative value of bending yield strength for A307 bolts.

As an alternative to specifying A307 bolts, the designer may choose to use another bolt specification such as SAE J429, *Mechanical and Material Requirements for Externally Threaded Fasteners*. This specification provides a more complete set of strength criteria for bolts including F_y. Note that F_y is the yield strength determined from a tension test. See NDS Appendix I for an approximate relationship for bending yield strength F_{yb} as a function of tension yield F_y and tension ultimate F_u.

Bolts should be installed in properly drilled holes, and members in a connection should be aligned so that only light tapping is required to insert the bolts. If the bolt holes are too small, an excessive amount of driving will be required to install the bolts, and splitting of the wood may be induced. Obviously, splitting will greatly reduce the shear capacity of a bolted connection. On the other hand, if bolt holes are too large, nonuniform bearing stresses may occur. The NDS specifies that bolt holes are to be a minimum of $\frac{1}{32}$ in. to a maximum of $\frac{1}{16}$ in. larger than the bolt diameter.

The manner in which the holes are bored in the wood also has an effect on load capacity. A bolt hole with a smooth surface develops a higher load with less deformation than one that has a rough surface. See Fig. 13.3. Smooth surfaces are obtained with sharp drill bits, a proper drill speed, and a slow rate of feed. See the *Wood Handbook* (Ref. 4.1) for more information.

Bolt sizes used in wood connections typically range from $\frac{1}{2}$ through 1 in. in diameter, in increments of $\frac{1}{8}$ in. In the past, large bolts ($1\frac{1}{4}$- and $1\frac{1}{2}$-in. diameter) were also used. However, for a number of years AITC expressed concern about the use of large-diameter bolts in wood members (see Ref. 3.7). The reasons cited for this concern are the difficulty in accurately cutting larger holes and the difficulty in aligning large-diameter bolts in a multiple-bolt connection. There is some opinion that the greater stiffness of large-diameter bolts may not allow uniform bearing on all fasteners in a connection.

If there is nonuniform bearing in a connection as the result of inaccuracies in fabrication (Sec. 7.2), small-diameter bolts may be flexible enough to allow a redistribution of stresses in the connection so that the bolts become more uniformly loaded. With large-diameter bolts there is concern that splitting of the wood member may occur before a redistribution of stress to less highly loaded bolts can occur. For these reasons, the 1991 NDS limits bolts in wood connections to 1 in. and less in diameter. Additional research should clarify

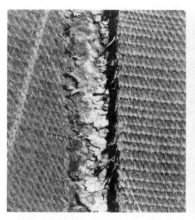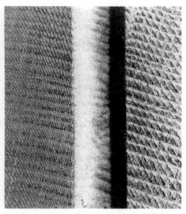

Figure 13.3 Fabrication technique affects performance of bolt connection. Bolt hole on left has a rough surface as the result of torn wood fibers due to improper drilling. Hole on right is smooth and will make a better connection. Both holes were made with the same twist drill bit. The smooth hole was produced by using a higher drill speed (rpm) and a lower rate of feed (in./min) through the piece. *(FPL.)*

the effect of fabrication tolerances on the strength of large- and small-diameter bolts.

13.3 Bolt Yield Limit Equations for Single Shear

The yield limit equations for bolts in single shear are covered in this section. The value obtained from the yield limit equations is the *nominal design value Z* for a single bolt. The adjustment factors necessary to convert the nominal value to an *allowable design value Z'* are covered in the next section.

Many of the coefficients needed to evaluate the yield limit equations have been previously defined. Recall that for a large-diameter fastener, such as a bolt, the dowel bearing strength may be different for the main and side members even if the members are from the same species. This occurs when the angle of load to grain is different for the main and side members $(\theta_m \neq \theta_s)$.

Recall also from Sec. 11.5 that the dowel strength parallel to grain $F_{e\parallel}$ depends only on the specific gravity of the wood. However, dowel bearing strength perpendicular to grain $F_{e\perp}$ is a function of both specific gravity and bolt diameter. $F_{e\parallel}$ and $F_{e\perp}$ can be computed given the specific gravity of the wood and the fastener diameter, or values can be obtained from NDS Table 8A, *Dowel Bearing for Bolted Connections*. If needed, the dowel bearing strength at an angle of load to grain $F_{e\theta}$ can be determined using the Hankinson formula. Finally, the dowel bearing strength of a metal member may be taken equal to the ultimate tensile strength of the steel plate (that is, $F_e = F_u$).

Yield limit equations from the 1991 NDS for a *bolt* in *single shear* are given in Example 13.2. This type of connection requires the largest number of yield equations because any of the six possible yield modes (Fig. 11.10 in Sec. 11.7) may control. All six equations are required for wood-to-wood and wood-to-concrete connections, but only five are needed for a wood-to-steel connection.

The equations require the use of several coefficients that are, in turn, defined by some rather lengthy expressions. Again, the use of a microcomputer spreadsheet greatly aids in the solution of the yield model equations.

EXAMPLE 13.2   Bolt Yield Limit Equations for Single Shear

The following yield limit equations apply to the three types of single-shear bolt connections that were illustrated in Fig. 13.1. Yield modes are sketched in Fig. 11.10 (Sec. 11.7).

Wood-to-Wood Connection

The nominal design value for one bolt in a single-shear connection between two wood members is the smallest load capacity obtained from the following six equations.

Mode I_m (NDS equation 8.2-1):

$$Z = \frac{Dt_m F_{em}}{4K_\theta}$$

Mode I_s (NDS equation 8.2-2):

$$Z = \frac{Dt_s F_{es}}{4K_\theta}$$

Mode II (NDS equation 8.2-3):

$$Z = \frac{k_1 Dt_s F_{es}}{3.6K_\theta}$$

Mode III_m (NDS equation 8.2-4):

$$Z = \frac{k_2 Dt_m F_{em}}{3.2(1 + 2R_e)K_\theta}$$

Mode III_s (NDS equation 8.2-5):

$$Z = \frac{k_3 Dt_s F_{em}}{3.2(2 + R_e)K_\theta}$$

Mode IV (NDS equation 8.2-6):

$$Z = \frac{D^2}{3.2K_\theta} \sqrt{\frac{2F_{em}F_{yb}}{3(1 + R_e)}}$$

where Z = nominal design value for bolt in single shear (Z is to be taken as smallest value from six yield limit equations), lb

$$k_1 = \frac{\sqrt{R_e + 2R_e^2(1 + R_t + R_t^2) + R_t^2 R_e^3} - R_e(1 + R_t)}{(1 + R_e)}$$

$$k_2 = -1 + \sqrt{2(1 + R_e) + \frac{2F_{yb}(1 + 2R_e)D^2}{3F_{em}t_m^2}}$$

$$k_3 = -1 + \sqrt{\frac{2(1 + R_e)}{R_e} + \frac{2F_{yb}(2 + R_e)D^2}{3F_{em}t_s^2}}$$

$$R_e = \frac{F_{em}}{F_{es}}$$

$$R_t = \frac{t_m}{t_s}$$

$$K_\theta = 1 + \frac{\theta}{360}$$

D = bolt diameter, in.
t_m = thickness of main (thicker) member, in.
t_s = thickness of side (thinner) member, in.
F_{em} = dowel bearing strength of main member, psi:

$$= \begin{cases} F_{e\parallel} & \text{for load parallel to grain} \\ F_{e\perp} & \text{for load perpendicular to grain} \\ F_{e\theta} & \text{for load at angle to grain } \theta \text{ (see Hankinson formula below)} \end{cases}$$

F_{es} = dowel bearing strength of side member, psi:

$$= \begin{cases} F_{e\parallel} & \text{for load parallel to grain} \\ F_{e\perp} & \text{for load perpendicular to grain} \\ F_{e\theta} & \text{for load at angle to grain } \theta \text{ (see Hankinson formula below)} \end{cases}$$

(For a steel side member, $F_{es} = F_u$.)
F_{yb} = bending yield strength of bolt, psi
θ = maximum angle of load to grain ($0 \leq \theta \leq 90$ degrees) for any member in connection

Dowel bearing strength at an angle of load to grain θ is given by the Hankinson formula:

$$F_{e\theta} = \frac{F_{e\parallel} F_{e\perp}}{F_{e\parallel} \sin^2 \theta + F_{e\perp} \cos^2 \theta}$$

Wood-to-Metal Connection

The nominal design value for one bolt in a single-shear connection between a wood main member and a steel side plate is the smallest load capacity obtained from five of the six equations given above.

A Mode I_s mechanism represents a bearing failure in the side member. Because the yield limit equation for Mode I_s contains an adjustment for load duration in a *wood* member, it is not appropriate to apply NDS equation 8.2-2 to a bearing failure in a *steel* plate. Therefore, NDS equation 8.2-2 is not used to evaluate wood-to-metal connections. However, the designer must ensure that the bearing capacity of the steel side member is not exceeded in accordance with recognized steel design practice.

Wood-to-Concrete Connection

The nominal design value for one anchor bolt embedded in concrete or masonry and used in a single-shear connection with a wood member is the smallest load capacity obtained from the six equations given above. The following relationships are to be used in evaluating the six wood-to-wood equations for anchor bolt applications:

$$t_m = 2t_s = \text{twice thickness of wood member}$$

$$F_{em} = F_{es} = \text{dowel bearing strength of wood member}$$

These equations essentially determine the capacity of the connection between the wood member and the anchor bolt. In addition, the strength of the anchor bolt embedded in the concrete or masonry should be verified. This can be done for concrete in UBC Table 26-E and for masonry in UBC Table 24-E. See Example 15.6 (Sec. 15.4) for two sample anchor bolt problems.

As an alternative to solving the yield limit equations, the nominal design values for a number of common *single-shear* connections are available in NDS Tables 8.2A to 8.2D.

For *wood-to-wood* connections, three nominal design values are given in the NDS tables. Three values are listed because the equations used to generate the tables produce a different bolt capacity depending on the *angle of load to grain* for the members in the connection. Values of Z are given for the following conditions:

1. Load *parallel* to grain in *both* main member and side member. The notation in the NDS tables for this condition is $Z_\parallel$.

2. Load *perpendicular* to grain in *side* member and parallel to grain in main member, $Z_{s\perp}$.

3. Load *perpendicular* to grain in *main* member and parallel to grain in side member, $Z_{m\perp}$.

For *wood-to-steel* connections, the NDS tables provide two values of Z based on the angle of load to grain for the wood member:

1. Load parallel to grain in wood main member, $Z_\parallel$.

2. Load perpendicular to grain in wood main member, $Z_\perp$.

Metal side plates are assumed to be ¼-in.-thick ASTM A36 steel.

The NDS tables may be helpful in providing nominal bolt design values for a number of loading conditions without the need to evaluate the yield limit formulas. However, the NDS tables are restricted to parallel- and perpendicular-to-grain loadings, and the yield limit equations must be evaluated for connections with an intermediate angle of load to grain ($0 < \theta < 90$ degrees).

Two examples are given to illustrate the application of the yield limit equations. The first problem verifies a bolt value in one of the NDS tables. See Example 13.3. The load is perpendicular to the grain in the main member and parallel to the grain in the side member. Both wood pieces are of the same species, but there are different dowel bearing strengths for the two members because of the angle of load to grain. The problem is not a complete design because the conditions necessary to convert the nominal design value to an allowable design load are not given. The example is simply intended to illustrate the yield limit equations and the NDS tables.

EXAMPLE 13.3   Nominal Design Value: Single-Shear Bolt in Wood-to-Wood Connection

The horizontal load in the connection shown in Fig. 13.4 is parallel to the grain in the horizontal member and perpendicular to the grain in the vertical member. Lumber is DF-L. Determine the nominal design value of the single ¾-in.-diameter A307 bolt.

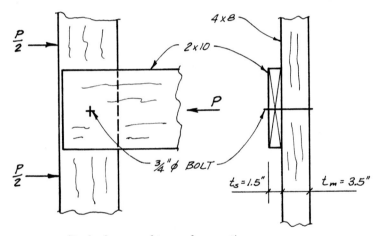

Figure 13.4 Single-shear wood-to-wood connection.

Summary of Known Values

Summarize the information necessary to evaluate the yield model equations. Bolt diameter, member thicknesses, and angles of load to grain are obtained from the sketch. Dowel bearing strengths can be computed using the formulas from Example 11.4 (Sec. 11.5), or they can be read from NDS Table 8A. Specific gravity is also given in NDS Table 8A.

$$D = 0.75 \text{ in.}$$

$$F_{yb} = 45 \text{ ksi} \quad \text{(assumed for A307 bolt)}$$

$$t_m = 3.5 \text{ in.}$$

$$\theta_m = 90 \text{ degrees}$$

$$F_{em} = 2600 \text{ psi} \quad (F_{e\perp} \text{ for ¾-in. bolt in DF-L})$$

$$t_s = 1.5 \text{ in.}$$

$$\theta_s = 0 \text{ degrees}$$

$$F_{es} = 5600 \text{ psi} \qquad (F_{e\parallel} \text{ for bolt in DF-L})$$

$$SG_m = SG_s = 0.50$$

Coefficients for Yield Limit Equations

$$R_e = \frac{F_{em}}{F_{es}} = \frac{2600}{5600} = 0.464$$

$$1 + R_e = 1 + 0.464 = 1.464$$

$$1 + 2R_e = 1 + 2(0.464) = 1.929$$

$$2 + R_e = 2 + 0.464 = 2.464$$

$$R_t = \frac{t_m}{t_s} = \frac{3.5}{1.5} = 2.333$$

$$1 + R_t = 1 + 2.333 = 3.333$$

$$1 + R_t + R_t^2 = 3.333 + (2.333)^2 = 8.778$$

$$\theta = 90 \text{ degrees} \qquad (\textit{Note: } \theta \text{ is the larger of } \theta_m \text{ and } \theta_s.)$$

$$K_\theta = 1 + \frac{\theta}{360} = 1 + \frac{90}{360} = 1.25$$

$$k_1 = \frac{\sqrt{R_e + 2R_e^2(1 + R_t + R_t^2) + R_t^2 R_e^3} - R_e(1 + R_t)}{(1 + R_e)}$$

$$= \frac{\sqrt{0.464 + 2(0.464^2)(8.778) + (2.333)^2(0.464^3)} - 0.464(3.333)}{1.464}$$

$$= 0.4383$$

$$k_2 = -1 + \sqrt{2(1 + R_e) + \frac{2F_{yb}(1 + 2R_e)D^2}{3F_{em}t_m^2}}$$

$$= -1 + \sqrt{2(1.464) + \frac{2(45{,}000)(1.929)(0.75^2)}{3(2600)(3.5^2)}}$$

$$= 0.9876$$

$$k_3 = -1 + \sqrt{\frac{2(1 + R_e)}{R_e} + \frac{2F_{yb}(2 + R_e)D^2}{3F_{em}t_s^2}}$$

$$= -1 + \sqrt{\frac{2(1.464)}{0.464} + \frac{2(45{,}000)(2.464)(0.75^2)}{3(2600)(1.5^2)}}$$

$$= 2.663$$

Yield Limit Equations

Mode I_m (NDS equation 8.2-1):

$$Z = \frac{Dt_m F_{em}}{4K_\theta} = \frac{0.75(3.5)(2600)}{4(1.25)} = 1365 \text{ lb}$$

Mode I_s (NDS equation 8.2-2):

$$Z = \frac{Dt_s F_{es}}{4K_\theta} = \frac{0.75(1.5)(5600)}{4(1.25)} = 1260 \text{ lb}$$

Mode II (NDS equation 8.2-3):

$$Z = \frac{k_1 Dt_s F_{es}}{3.6K_\theta} = \frac{0.4383(0.75)(1.5)(5600)}{3.6(1.25)} = 614 \text{ lb}$$

Mode III_m (NDS equation 8.2-4):

$$Z = \frac{k_2 Dt_m F_{em}}{3.2(1 + 2R_e)K_\theta} = \frac{0.9876(0.75)(3.5)(2600)}{3.2(1.929)(1.25)} = 874 \text{ lb}$$

Mode III_s (NDS equation 8.2-5):

$$Z = \frac{k_3 Dt_s F_{em}}{3.2(2 + R_e)K_\theta} = \frac{2.663(0.75)(1.5)(2600)}{3.2(2.464)(1.25)} = 790 \text{ lb}$$

Mode IV (NDS equation 8.2-6):

$$Z = \frac{D^2}{3.2K_\theta} \sqrt{\frac{2F_{em}F_{yb}}{3(1 + R_e)}}$$

$$= \frac{0.75^2}{3.2(1.25)} \sqrt{\frac{2(2600)(45,000)}{3(1.464)}} = 1026 \text{ lb}$$

Nominal design value is selected as the smallest value from the yield limit equations:

$$\boxed{Z = 614 \text{ lb}}$$

Compare with value from NDS Table 8.2A, *Bolt Values (Z) for Single Shear (two member) Connections.* Enter table with $t_m = 3.5$, $t_s = 1.5$, $D = 0.75$, and SG $= 0.50$:

$$Z_{m\perp} = 610 \approx 614 \text{ lb} \qquad OK$$

The second example is a bolt in single shear that is not covered by the NDS tables, and the yield limit equations must be used. The connection is between a $4\times$ wood member and a $\frac{1}{2}$-in.-thick hot-rolled angle. The angle is A36 steel, and the minimum tensile strength is $F_u = 58$ ksi. Example

13.4 has an angle of load to grain of 45 degrees, and $F_{e\theta}$ is computed with the Hankinson formula.

EXAMPLE 13.4   Nominal Design Value: Single-Shear Bolt in Wood-to-Metal Connection

The bolt through steel angle in Fig. 13.5 provides a load to the horizontal wood member at an angle of 45 degrees to the grain. The angle is A36 steel, and the wood member is Hem-Fir. Determine the nominal design value of a single ⅝-in.-diameter A307 bolt.

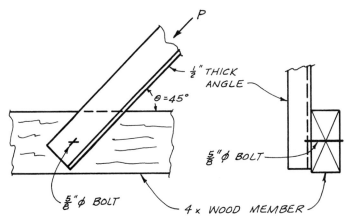

Figure 13.5 Single-shear wood-to-steel connection.

Summary of Known Values

Dowel bearing strength parallel and perpendicular to grain in Hem-Fir can be computed using the formulas in Example 11.4 (Sec. 11.5), or they can be obtained from NDS Table 8A.

$$D = 0.625 \text{ in.}$$

$$F_{yb} = 45 \text{ ksi} \quad \text{(assumed for A307 bolt)}$$

$$t_m = 3.5 \text{ in.}$$

$$\theta_m = 45 \text{ degrees}$$

$$F_{em\parallel} = 4800 \text{ psi}$$

$$F_{em\perp} = 2250 \text{ psi} \quad (F_{e\perp} \text{ for ⅝-in. bolt in Hem-Fir})$$

$$t_s = 0.5 \text{ in.}$$

$$F_{es} = F_u = 58{,}000 \text{ psi} \quad \text{(for A36 steel)}$$

Coefficients for Yield Limit Equations

$$F_{e\theta} = \frac{F_{e\parallel}F_{e\perp}}{F_{e\parallel}\sin^2\theta + F_{e\perp}\cos^2\theta}$$

$$= \frac{4800(2250)}{4800\sin^2 45 + 2250\cos^2 45} = 3064 \text{ psi}$$

$$R_e = \frac{F_{em}}{F_{es}} = \frac{3064}{58,000} = 0.05282$$

$$1 + R_e = 1 + 0.05282 = 1.053$$

$$1 + 2R_e = 1 + 2(0.05282) = 1.106$$

$$2 + R_e = 2 + 0.05282 = 2.053$$

$$R_t = \frac{t_m}{t_s} = \frac{3.5}{0.5} = 7.0$$

$$1 + R_t = 1 + 7.0 = 8.0$$

$$1 + R_t + R_t^2 = 8.0 + 7.0^2 = 57.0$$

$$\theta = 45 \text{ degrees}$$

$$K_\theta = 1 + \frac{\theta}{360} = 1 \cdot \frac{45}{360} = 1.125$$

$$k_1 = \frac{\sqrt{R_e + 2R_e^2(1 + R_t + R_t^2) + R_t^2 R_e^3} - R_e(1 + R_t)}{(1 + R_e)}$$

$$= \frac{\sqrt{0.05282 + 2(0.05282^2)(57.0) + 7.0^2(0.05282^3)} - 0.05282(8.0)}{1.053}$$

$$= 0.1827$$

$$k_2 = -1 + \sqrt{2(1 + R_e) + \frac{2F_{yb}(1 + 2R_e)D^2}{3F_{em}t_m^2}}$$

$$= -1 + \sqrt{2(1.053) + \frac{2(45,000)(1.106)(0.625^2)}{3(3064)(3.5^2)}}$$

$$= 0.5655$$

$$k_3 = -1 + \sqrt{\frac{2(1 + R_e)}{R_e} + \frac{2F_{yb}(2 + R_e)D^2}{3F_{em}t_s^2}}$$

$$= -1 + \sqrt{\frac{2(1.053)}{0.05282} + \frac{2(45,000)(2.053)(0.625^2)}{3(3064)(0.5^2)}}$$

$$= 7.442$$

Yield Limit Equations

Mode I_m ((NDS equation 8.2-1):

$$Z = \frac{Dt_mF_{em}}{4K_\theta} = \frac{0.625\,(3.5)(3064)}{4(1.125)} = 1489\text{ lb}$$

Mode II (NDS equation 8.2-3):

$$Z = \frac{k_1Dt_sF_{es}}{3.6K_\theta} = \frac{0.1827\,(0.625)(0.5)(58,000)}{3.6(1.125)} = 818\text{ lb}$$

Mode III_m (NDS equation 8.2-4):

$$Z = \frac{k_2Dt_mF_{em}}{3.2(1 + 2R_e)K_\theta} = \frac{0.5655\,(0.625)(3.5)(3064)}{3.2(1.106)(1.125)} = 952\text{ lb}$$

Mode III_s (NDS equation 8.2-5):

$$Z = \frac{k_3Dt_sF_{em}}{3.2(2 + R_e)K_\theta} = \frac{7.442\,(0.625)(0.5)(3064)}{3.2(2.053)(1.125)} = 964\text{ lb}$$

Mode IV (NDS equation 8.2-6):

$$Z = \frac{D^2}{3.2K_\theta} \sqrt{\frac{2F_{em}F_{yb}}{3(1 + R_e)}}$$

$$= \frac{0.625^2}{3.2(1.125)} \sqrt{\frac{2(3064)(45,000)}{3(1.053)}} = 1014\text{ lb}$$

Nominal design value is selected as the smallest value from the yield limit equations:

$$\boxed{Z = 818\text{ lb}}$$

13.4   Bolt Yield Limit Equations for Double Shear

The yield limit equations and several numerical examples for bolts in single-shear connections were given in the previous section. In addition to this application, bolts are frequently used in double shear. From a review of the various yield modes in Fig. 11.10 (Sec. 11.7), it should be clear that there are a different set of yield limit equations for double- and single-shear connections.

The yield limit equations for bolt connections in double shear are given in Example 13.5. Because of symmetric behavior, only four yield equations are required for a double-shear wood-to-wood connection. In the case of a wood-to-metal connection, one of these yield limit equations is eliminated, but the steel side members must be designed in accordance with recognized practice (Ref. 11.1).

EXAMPLE 13.5   Yield Limit Equations for Bolts in Double Shear

The following yield limit equations from the 1991 NDS apply to the two common types of double-shear connections illustrated in Fig. 13.2. The yield modes are sketched in Fig. 11.10.

Wood-to-Wood Connection

The nominal design value for one bolt in a double-shear connection between three wood members is the smallest load capacity obtained from the following four equations. The thicknesses of the *side* members are assumed to be equal. See the NDS for the case of unequal thickness.

Mode I_m (NDS equation 8.3-1):

$$Z = \frac{Dt_m F_{em}}{4K_\theta}$$

Mode I_s (NDS equation 8.3-2):

$$Z = \frac{Dt_s F_{es}}{2K_\theta}$$

Mode III_s (NDS equation 8.3-3):

$$Z = \frac{k_3 Dt_s F_{em}}{1.6(2 + R_e)K_\theta}$$

Mode IV (NDS equation 8.3-4):

$$Z = \frac{D^2}{1.6K_\theta} \sqrt{\frac{2F_{em}F_{yb}}{3(1 + R_e)}}$$

where Z = nominal design for bolt in double shear (Z is to be taken as smallest value from four yield limit equations), lb

$$k_3 = -1 + \sqrt{\frac{2(1 + R_e)}{R_e} + \frac{2F_{yb}(2 + R_e)D^2}{3F_{em}t_s^2}}$$

$$R_e = \frac{F_{em}}{F_{es}}$$

$$K_\theta = 1 + \frac{\theta}{360}$$

D = bolt diameter, in.

t_m = thickness of main (center) member, in.

t_s = thickness of one of the side members, in.

F_{em} = dowel bearing strength of main (center) member, psi:

$$= \begin{cases} F_{e\parallel} & \text{for load parallel to grain} \\ F_{e\perp} & \text{for load perpendicular to grain} \\ F_{e\theta} & \text{for load at angle to grain } \theta \text{ (see Hankinson formula below)} \end{cases}$$

F_{es} = dowel bearing strength of side member, psi:

$$= \begin{cases} F_{e\parallel} & \text{for load parallel to grain} \\ F_{e\perp} & \text{for load perpendicular to grain} \\ F_{e\theta} & \text{for load at angle to grain } \theta \text{ (see Hankinson formula below)} \end{cases}$$

(For a steel side members, $F_{es} = F_u$.)

F_{yb} = bending yield strength of bolt, psi

θ = maximum angle of load to grain ($0 \leq \theta \leq 90$ degrees) for any member in connection

Dowel bearing strength at an angle of load to grain θ is given by the Hankinson formula:

$$F_{e\theta} = \frac{F_{e\parallel} F_{e\perp}}{F_{e\parallel} \sin^2 \theta + F_{e\perp} \cos^2 \theta}$$

Wood-to-Metal Connections

For one bolt in a double-shear connection between a *wood main member* and *two steel side plates*, the nominal design value is taken as the smallest load capacity obtained from three of the four equations given above for a wood-to-wood connection. A Mode I_s mechanism represents a bearing failure in the steel side member. Because the yield limit equation for Mode I_s contains an adjustment for load duration in a *wood* member, it is not appropriate to apply NDS equation 8.3-2 to a bearing failure in a *steel* plate. Therefore, NDS equation 8.3-2 is eliminated for this type of wood-to-metal connection. However, the designer must ensure that the bearing capacity of the steel side members is not exceeded in accordance with accepted steel design practice.

A less frequently encountered double-shear connection involves a *steel main (center) member* and *two wood side members*. In this situation a Mode I_m mechanism represents a bearing failure in the main steel member, and NDS equation 8.3-1 is the one that is eliminated. The remaining three yield limit equations are evaluated to determine the nominal design value for the bolt. In this case also, the designer must ensure that the bearing capacity of the steel member is adequate in accordance with recognized practice.

As with single shear, the NDS bolt tables may be helpful in providing nominal design values for a number of loading conditions without the need to evaluate the yield limit formulas. Values of Z for double-shear connections are given in NDS Tables 8.3A to 8.3D. Again, the NDS tables are limited to parallel- and perpendicular-to-grain loading only, and the yield limit equations are required for connections with an intermediate angle of load to grain ($0 < \theta < 90$ degrees).

One example is given to illustrate the yield limit equations for double shear and to gain familiarity with the NDS bolt tables. See Example 13.6. Although the example deals with a connection that can be read from an NDS table, a computer solution on a spreadsheet or other program will normally be used for the cases not covered by a table. The example illustrates the yield limit formulas, and the adjustment factors necessary to convert the nominal design value to an allowable bolt capacity are covered in the next section.

EXAMPLE 13.6   Nominal Design Value: Double-Shear Bolt in Wood-to-Metal Connection

Determine the nominal design value of the single ⅞-in.-diameter A307 bolt in Fig. 13.6. The load in the connection is parallel to the grain in the 6× wood member, and ¼-in.-thick steel side plates are used. The wood member is DF-L, and the side plates are A36 steel with F_u = 58 ksi.

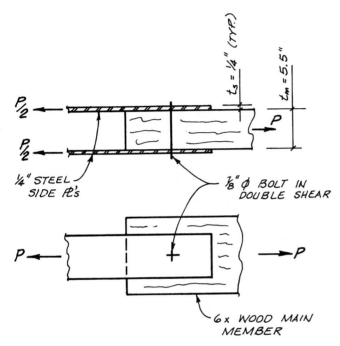

Figure 13.6   Double-shear wood-to-steel connection.

Summary of Known Values

Dowel bearing strength of the wood member can be computed using the formulas in Example 11.4 (Sec. 11.5), or it can be read from NDS Table 8A. Specific gravity is also available in NDS Table 8A.

$$D = 0.875 \text{ in.}$$

$$F_{yb} = 45 \text{ ksi} \quad \text{(assumed for A307 bolt)}$$

$$t_m = 5.5 \text{ in.}$$

$$\theta_m = 0 \text{ degrees}$$

$$F_{em} = 5600 \text{ psi} \quad (F_{e\parallel} \text{ for DF-L})$$

$$SG_m = 0.50$$

$$t_s = 0.25 \text{ in.}$$

$$F_{es} = F_u = 58,000 \text{ psi} \quad \text{(for A36 steel)}$$

Coefficients for Yield Limit Equations

$$R_e = \frac{F_{em}}{F_{es}} = \frac{5600}{58,000} = 0.09655$$

$$1 + R_e = 1 + 0.09655 = 1.097$$

$$2 + R_e = 2 + 0.09655 = 2.097$$

$$\theta = 0 \text{ degrees}$$

$$K_\theta = 1 + \frac{\theta}{360} = 1 + \frac{0}{360} = 1.0$$

$$k_3 = -1 + \sqrt{\frac{2(1 + R_e)}{R_e} + \frac{2F_{yb}(2 + R_e)D^2}{3F_{em}t_s^2}}$$

$$= -1 + \sqrt{\frac{2(1.097)}{0.09655} + \frac{2(45,000)(2.097)(0.875^2)}{3(5600)(0.25^2)}}$$

$$= 11.66$$

Yield Limit Equations

Mode I_m (NDS equation 8.3-1):

$$Z = \frac{Dt_mF_{em}}{4K_\theta} = \frac{0.875(5.5)(5600)}{4(1.0)} = 6783 \text{ lb}$$

Mode III_s (NDS equation 8.3-3):

$$Z = \frac{k_3Dt_sF_{em}}{1.6(2 + R_e)K_\theta} = \frac{11.66(0.875)(0.25)(5600)}{1.6(2.097)(1.0)}$$

$$= 4258 \text{ lb}$$

Mode IV (NDS equation 8.3-4):

$$Z = \frac{D^2}{1.6K_\theta} \sqrt{\frac{2F_{em}F_{yb}}{3(1 + R_e)}}$$

$$= \frac{(0.875)^2}{1.6(1.0)} \sqrt{\frac{2(5600)(45,000)}{3(1.097)}} = 5922 \text{ lb}$$

Nominal design value is selected as the smallest value from the yield limit equations:

$$\boxed{Z = 4258 \text{ lb}}$$

Compare with the value from NDS Table 8.3B.

$$Z_\| = 4260 \approx 4258 \text{ lb} \quad OK$$

13.5 Adjustment Factors for Bolts

The yield limit equations for single- and double-shear bolt connections were reviewed in previous sections. The term *nominal design value* is assigned to the load capacity of a single bolt as obtained from the yield limit equations. For use in the design of a particular connection, the nominal design value Z must be converted to an *allowable design value Z'*. As with nails, this is done by multiplying the nominal value by a series of adjustment factors.

The adjustments convert the base conditions for a bolt to the design conditions for a given problem. Depending on the circumstances, the adjustment factors could have a major or minor effect on the allowable load capacity. The adjustment factors required in the design of connections are summarized in NDS Table 7.3.1. See the inside back cover of this book for a similar table. If the particular design conditions agree with the conditions for the nominal design value, the adjustment factors simply default to unity.

The base conditions associated with the nominal design value are as follows:

1. Load is normal (10-year) duration.
2. Wood is initially dry at the time of fabrication of a connection and remains dry in service.
3. Temperature range is normal.
4. There is one bolt in a line parallel to the applied load (i.e., only one bolt per row).
5. Spacing provisions for bolts (geometry requirements for the connection) are satisfied.

If a bolt connection is used under exactly these conditions, the adjustment factors are all unity, and $Z' = Z$.

For a laterally loaded bolt connection that does not satisfy the base conditions described above, the following adjustment factors may be required:

$$Z' = Z(C_D C_M C_t C_g C_\Delta)$$

where C_D = load duration factor (Sec. 4.15)
$\quad C_M$ = wet service factor (Sec. 4.14)
$\quad C_t$ = temperature factor (Sec. 4.20)
$\quad C_g$ = group action factor
$\quad C_\Delta$ = geometry factor

The total allowable load for a connection using two or more bolts is the sum of the individual allowable load values Z'. This summation is appropriate if the bolts are all the same type and size, because each fastener will have the same yield mode. The load capacity for the connection is the number of bolts N times the allowable load for one fastener:

$$\text{Allow. } P = N(Z')$$

A number of adjustment factors were described previously and are mentioned only in summary. Other adjustments require greater explanation. Some of these new factors will also be required for other connectors such as lag bolts, split rings, and shear plates.

Load duration factor C_D. The load duration factor C_D for bolted connections is the same as that applied to allowable stresses in the design of structural members such as beams, tension members, and columns. Refer to Sec. 4.15 for a review of load duration and the numerical values for C_D.

Wet service factor C_M. The concept of an allowable stress adjustment based on moisture content was introduced in Sec. 4.14. However, the wet service factors for member design vary with the type of stress. Different adjustments also apply in connection design depending on the type of fastener and the moisture content of the wood at several stages. The moisture content is considered (1) at the time of fabrication of the joint and (2) in service. The nominal design value applies to a bolt connection in which the wood is initially dry and remains dry in service. For connection design, the term *dry* refers to wood that has a moisture content of 19 percent or less. For these conditions, there is no reduction in the load capacity of a bolt for moisture content, and $C_M = 1.0$. Other moisture content conditions may require significant reductions of the nominal design value (that is, $C_M < 1.0$).

The proper design of bolted connections requires that the effects of changes in moisture content be considered in the design of a wood structure. In the past, problems were created in certain bolted connections by designers who were not familiar with the unique characteristics of wood.

It is necessary for the designer to understand the material if it is to be used properly. Wood undergoes dimensional changes as the moisture content changes. Shrinkage (or swelling) is caused by changes in moisture content below the fiber saturation point (Sec. 4.7). The large majority of the dimensional change takes place across the grain, and very little occurs parallel to the grain. These volumetric changes require that the *arrangement of bolts* in a connection be taken into account *in addition to the moisture content conditions* mentioned above.

Problems involving volume changes develop when bolts are held rigidly in position. Perhaps the best illustration is in a connection that uses a metal side plate and parallel rows of bolts. See Example 13.7. The bolts are essentially fixed in position by the metal side plates (the only movement permitted is that allowed by the clearance between the bolts and the holes). If the lumber is at an initially high moisture content and is allowed to season in place after fabrication of the connection, a serious cracking situation can develop.

The shrinkage that occurs is essentially across the grain. Wood is very weak in tension perpendicular to grain, and the result will be the development of cracking parallel to the grain. Obviously this type of cracking greatly reduces the strength of a connection.

The problem of cross-grain shrinkage can often be eliminated by proper detailing of a connection. This can be accomplished by providing for the unrestricted movement of the bolts across the grain. For example, in the case of the steel side plate, separate side members for the two rows of bolts can be used. These separate plates will simply move with the bolts as the moisture content changes, and cross-grain tension and the associated cracking will be avoided. Another approach is to use slotted holes in the steel side plates so that movement is not restricted. Other examples of proper connection detailing to avoid splitting are given in Chap. 14.

EXAMPLE 13.7   Cross-Grain Cracking

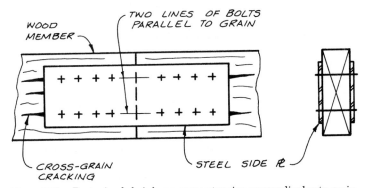

Figure 13.7a   Restrained shrinkage causes tension perpendicular to grain.

Figure 13.7a shows a critical connection for cross-grain cracking. As the wood loses moisture, cross-grain shrinkage occurs, and the bolts are rigidly held in position by the steel plates. The lumber becomes stressed in tension across the grain (a weak state of stress for wood).

Wet Service Factors (C_M):

In the 1991 NDS the following definitions apply to connections:

"Wet" condition—MC at or above FSP (approximately 30 percent)

"Dry" condition—MC ≤ 19 percent

For the type of connection in Fig. 13.7a, the following values of C_M are specified in NDS Table 7.3.3:

1. When the lumber is initially dry and remains dry in service, $C_M = 1.0$.
2. When the lumber used to fabricate a connection is initially wet and seasons in place to a dry condition, the allowable load is reduced by 60 percent (i.e., $C_M = 0.40$).
3. For lumber that is between the wet and dry condition (partially seasoned) at fabrication and later seasons in place, an intermediate C_M can be used.

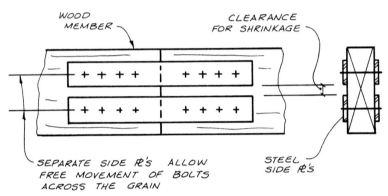

Figure 13.7b   Proper connection detailing eliminates restraint across the grain.

The cross-grain cracking problem can be eliminated by proper joint detailing. The use of separate side plates for each line of bolts allows the free movement of the bolts across the grain. Slotted holes can also be used. With proper detailing C_M can be taken as 1.0. See Fig. 13.7b.

NDS spacing criteria (see below) limit the spacing between outer rows of bolts to a maximum of 5 in. unless separate side plates are used. If separate plates are not used, the 5-in. limit on the spacing across the grain provides a limited width across the grain in which shrinkage can occur.

It was noted that very little volume change occurs parallel to the grain. This fact can cause a cross-grain cracking problem when wood members frame together at right angles. See Fig. 13.8. The problem develops when there are multiple rows of bolts passing through the two members and significant changes in moisture content occur. Here the problem is caused by cross-grain shrinkage in the mutually perpendicular members with little or no shrinkage parallel to the grain. The use of a single fastener for this connection is desirable. The problem is not critical in connections which are initially dry and remain dry in service.

The importance of proper connection detailing can be seen by the magnitude of the wet service factor required when severe cross-grain cracking can develop. Example 13.7 indicates that a C_M of 0.40 is required when these connections are fabricated with wood members that are initially wet and season to a dry condition in service. A summary of the C_M values for wood

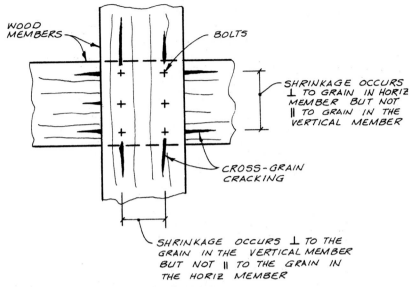

Figure 13.8 Cracking in wood-to-wood connection.

connections is given in NDS Table 7.3.3, *Wet Service Factors, C_M, for Connections.*

It should be noted that a C_M of 0.40 does not apply to connections where cross-grain cracking is prevented (e.g., connections that are initially dry and remain dry). The NDS also indicates that the following connections have $C_M = 1.0$:

1. One fastener only
2. Two or more fasteners in a single line parallel to the grain (no shrinkage parallel to grain)
3. Fasteners in two or more lines parallel to the grain with separate side plates for each line (movement not restricted)

Note there can be a fairly large difference between the initial and final moisture contents in the *dry* range, and shrinkage can occur (Sec. 4.7). This is especially true in dry climate zones. In view of the concern about the effects of cross-grain shrinkage in critical connections, the designer may want to make reductions of allowable stress when large differences in moisture content are expected even in the dry range.

As noted earlier, however, the most desirable solution is to detail the connection so that shrinkage cannot induce cross-grain cracking in the first place. Providing for unrestricted movement is a key factor. Recommended connection detailing practices with this intention are given in Chap. 14.

Temperature factor C_t. If wood is used in an application with higher-than-normal temperature conditions, the allowable design loads for connections are to be reduced by an appropriate temperature factor C_t. Refer to Sec. 4.20 for a brief review of the temperature factor. Numerical values of C_t for connections are given in NDS Table 7.3.4. The temperature range for most wood-frame buildings does not require adjustment of bolt values, and C_t is often unity.

Group action factor C_g. Research has shown that the end bolts in a row carry a greater portion of the total load on a connection than the intermediate bolts. This is also true for other large-diameter fasteners such as lag bolts, split rings, and shear plate connectors. To account for this behavior, the nominal design value is reduced based on the number of fasteners in a row. A *row* is considered to be a *group of fasteners in a line parallel* to the direction of *loading*. The term *group action factor* C_g is the reduction factor that accounts for the nonuniform loading of fasteners. The value of C_g decreases as the number of fasteners in a row increases. The group action factor does not apply to small-diameter fasteners such as nails.

In previous editions of the NDS, the group action factor was given in a set of tables. However, the tables covered a rather limited set of conditions, and the 1991 NDS defines the group action factor with an equation (Ref. 5.10). This is consistent with the move to an equation format in the 1991 NDS. It is also true that the formula for the group action factor is rather cumbersome to solve by hand on a calculator, and it is preferable to solve the expression on the computer. The definition of group action factor in equation form will allow the designer to handle a much wider variety of loading conditions and joint details. See Example 13.8.

The primary consideration in determining C_g is the number of bolts in a row n. The number of bolts in a row n should not be confused with the number of bolts in the connection N. If there is only one row of bolts, then n and N are equal.

In addition to the number of bolts in a row, the group action factor depends on

Ratio of the stiffnesses of members being connected

Diameter of fastener

Spacing of fasteners in a row

Load/slip modulus for the fastener

Although net area is used to evaluate member stresses at a connection, the distribution of forces to the fasteners is a function of relative stiffness. For an axial force member, the stiffness of a member is the product of *gross* cross-sectional and modulus of elasticity.

EXAMPLE 13.8 Formula for Group Action Factor C_g

The nominal design value for a bolt Z is reduced by the group action factor C_g. The value of C_g decreases as the number of fasteners in a row increases.

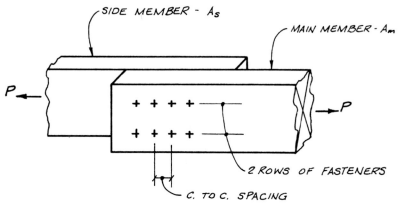

Figure 13.9 Definition of terms for C_g. Group action factor primarily depends on the number of fasteners in a row. For sample connection: Number of fasteners in row = n = 4; number of fasteners in connection = N = 8.

The number of fasteners in a row n is used to determine the group action factor C_g. The total number of fasteners N is used to determine the total allowable load for the connection

$$\text{Allow. } P = N(Z')$$

The formula for C_g is the same for bolts, lag bolts, split rings, and shear plates. The differences in these fasteners are reflected in the load/slip modulus γ for the connection. The group action factor is given by the following formula:

$$C_g = \left[\frac{m(1 - m^{2n})}{n[(1 + R_{EA}m^n)(1 + m) - 1 + m^{2n}]} \right] \left[\frac{1 + R_{EA}}{1 - m} \right]$$

where n = number of fasteners in a row
R_{EA} = smaller ratio of member stiffnesses
  = lesser of $\dfrac{E_s A_s}{E_m A_m}$ or $\dfrac{E_m A_m}{E_s A_s}$
E_m = modulus of elasticity of main member, psi
A_m = gross cross-sectional area of main member, in.²
E_s = modulus of elasticity of side member, psi
A_s = gross cross-sectional area of side member, in.² (*Note:* If there is more than one side member, A_s is the sum of the gross cross-sectional areas of the side members.)
$m = u - \sqrt{u^2 - 1}$
$u = 1 + \gamma \left(\dfrac{s}{2}\right) \left[\dfrac{1}{E_m A_m} + \dfrac{1}{E_s A_s} \right]$
s = center-to-center spacing between adjacent fasteners in a row, in.

γ = load/slip modulus for a connection, lb/in.
 = 180,000($D^{1.5}$) for bolts or lag bolts in a wood-to-wood connection
 = 270,000($D^{1.5}$) for bolts or lag bolts in a wood-to-metal connection
 = 500,000 for 4-in.-diameter split ring or shear plate connectors
 = 400,000 for 2½-in.-diameter split ring or 2⅝-in.-diameter shear plate connectors
D = diameter of bolt or lag bolt, in.

As an alternative to the equation for group action factor, the 1991 NDS provides expanded tables for C_g that may be used for certain applications. Again, the concept in the 1991 NDS is to define terms, to the extent possible, with general formulas that can be readily programmed, *and* to provide tables for use by the designer who does only an occasional wood design problem. Numerical values of C_g are given in NDS Tables 7.3.6A to 7.3.6D.

Geometry factor C_Δ.   The NDS provides spacing requirements for bolts. These are typically given as a number of bolt diameters D (e.g., $4D$ is the required end distance for a wood member in compression). In many cases the NDS provides two sets of spacings. The larger ones can be viewed as *base dimensions* that are required in order to use the full *nominal design value* for the fastener. The *geometry factor* C_Δ is the multiplier that is used to reduce the nominal design value Z if the spacings furnished in a given connection are less than the base dimensions. Thus, if the base spacing requirements for a connection are all satisfied, the geometry factor defaults to unity (C_Δ = 1.0). Note that C_Δ does not exceed 1.0 if additional space is provided.

The second set of spacings given in the NDS is the *minimum permitted spacings*. For example, the minimum permitted end distance for a member in compression is $2D$. An end distance less than this minimum is unacceptable. The geometry factor could be viewed as zero (C_Δ = 0) if the furnished spacings are less than the minimums.

A practical application of the geometry factor occurs when the furnished spacing lies between the base dimension and the minimum spacing. The geometry factor is a simple straight-line reduction. See Example 13.9. If there is more than one spacing that does not satisfy the basic spacing requirements, C_Δ is governed by the worst case. In other words, the smallest C_Δ for a given connection is to be used for all fasteners in a connection. However, the reductions are not cumulative, and several geometry factors need not be multiplied together.

EXAMPLE 13.9   Geometry Factor C_Δ

The geometry factor C_Δ is used to reduce the nominal design value for a bolt if the base dimensions are not satisfied. As an illustration, determine the geometry factor for the connection shown in Fig. 13.10 considering end distance only. Assume that all other base dimensions are provided.

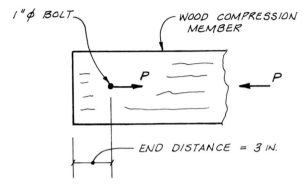

Figure 13.10 End distance for compression member.

From NDS Table 8.5.4, the end distances for a member loaded in axial compression are as follows:

Base end distance = $4D$ = 4(1) = 4 in.   (end distance required to obtain *full* design value)

Minimum end distance = $2D$ = 2(1) = 2 in.   (end distance required to obtain *any* design value)

The end distance provided in Fig. 13.10 is between the base dimension of 4 in. and the minimum of 2 in. The geometry factor is the ratio of the furnished end distance to the end distance required to obtain the full design value

$$C_\Delta = \frac{\text{furnished end distance}}{\text{base end distance}} \le 1.0$$

$$= \frac{3 \text{ in.}}{4 \text{ in.}} = 0.75$$

A geometry factor is to be calculated for each spacing that does not satisfy the base dimensions. However, geometry factors are not cumulative, and if more than one geometry factor is calculated, the *smallest* C_Δ is used for *all* fasteners in a connection. The other geometry factors are disregarded.

Although the NDS allows the bolt spacings to be reduced below the base dimensions (provided the allowable load is reduced using the appropriate C_Δ), it is considered good detailing practice to provide the full base spacings whenever possible.

Now that the concept of the geometry factor has been introduced, the spacing requirements for bolted connections can be considered in detail. The dimensions for locating bolts in a connection are given to the centerline of the bolts. The detailing of a bolted connection requires consideration of

1. End distance
2. Edge distance
3. Center-to-center (c. to c.) spacing of bolts in a row
4. Row spacing

Bolted connections are somewhat more complicated than nailed connections because the direction of loading in relation to the direction of the grain must be considered. Other factors such as bolt slenderness l/D and the sense of force in the member (tension or compression) may also affect the spacing requirements. The *bolt slenderness ratio* is defined as the *smaller* value of

$$\frac{l}{D} = \frac{\text{length of bolt in main member}}{\text{bolt diameter}}$$

$$\frac{l}{D} = \frac{\text{length of bolt in side member(s)}}{\text{bolt diameter}}$$

If there is more than one side member, l is taken as the combined thickness of the side members.

Because of the complexity, the spacing requirements are best summarized on a sketch. The NDS spacing criteria for *parallel-to-grain loading* are given in Example 13.10. The spacing requirements to obtain the full design value ($C_\Delta = 1.0$) are shown first, followed by the minimum permitted spacings in parentheses.

Note that there are different end distances for members stressed in tension and compression. For tension members it further depends on whether the member is a softwood or hardwood species. The 5-in. limit on the distance between outer rows of bolts was addressed previously (see Wet Service Factor above).

EXAMPLE 13.10   Bolt Spacing Requirements: Parallel-to-Grain Loading

Parallel-to-grain loading spacing requirements (Fig. 13.11) are as follows:
1. *End distance*
   a. Members in tension
      Softwood species = 7*D*   (3.5*D* minimum)
      Hardwood species = 5*D*   (2.5*D* minimum)
   b. Members in compression = 4*D*   (2*D* minimum)
2. *Edge distance* − bolt slenderness = *l*/*D*
   a. For *l*/*D* ≤ 6.0: edge distance = 1.5*D*
   b. For *l*/*D* > 6.0: edge distance = 1.5*D* or 0.5 × row spacing, whichever is larger

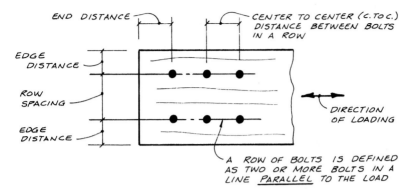

Figure 13.11 Bolt spacing requirements: parallel to grain loading.

  3. *Center-to-center* spacing = s = $4D$ ($3D$ minimum)
  4. *Row spacing* = $1.5D$. Row spacing between outer rows of bolts shall not exceed 5 in. unless separate side plates are used for each row.

The NDS spacing criteria for *perpendicular-to-grain loading* are given in Example 13.11. Again, the spacing requirements to obtain the full design value (C_Δ = 1.0) are shown first, followed by the minimum permitted spacings in parentheses. Note that there are different edge distances for the *loaded edge* and the *unloaded edge*. The bolt can be viewed as delivering a load to the wood member. The loaded edge is the edge of the piece toward which the load is acting. The unloaded edge is the other side of the member.

EXAMPLE 13.11   Bolt Spacing Requirements: Perpendicular-to-Grain Loading

Perpendicular-to-grain loading spacing requirements (Fig. 13.12) are as follows:

  1. *End distance* = $4D$ ($2D$ minimum)
  2. *Edge distance*
      a. Loaded edge = $4D$
      b. Unloaded edge = $1.5D$
  3. *Center-to-center* spacing to obtain full design value is governed by the spacing requirements of the member(s) to which the bolts are attached (e.g., steel side plates* or wood member loaded parallel to grain).   ($3D$ minimum)
  4. *Row spacing*
      a. For $l/D \leq 2.0$: row spacing = $2.5D$.
      b. For $l/D \geq 6.0$: row spacing = $5D$.
      c. For $2.0 < l/D < 6.0$: interpolate between $2.5D$ and $5D$.

---

*The center-to-center and edge spacing requirements for steel plates are given in Ref. 11.

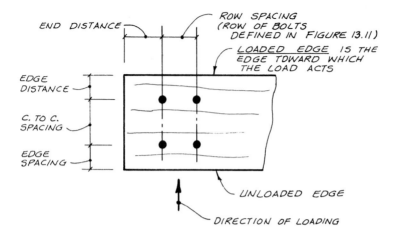

Figure 13.12 Bolt spacing requirements: perpendicular to grain loading.

NOTE: Shear in the member must be checked in accordance with NDS Sec. 3.4.5.

Specific requirements for the spacing of bolts in a connection where the load is at some angle other than 0 or 90 degrees to the direction of the grain are not given in the NDS. It is stated, however, that "the gravity axis of each member shall pass through the center of resistance of the group of bolts to insure uniform stress in the main member and a uniform distribution of load to all bolts." In addition to providing this symmetry, the spacing provisions for both parallel and perpendicular loading can be used as a guide in detailing the connection.

This concludes the basic summary of adjustment factors for bolted connections. Several numerical examples are provided in the following sections to illustrate the design procedures for bolts.

13.6   Design Problem: Bolted Chord Splice for Diaphragm

For the building in Example 13.12, the top plate of a 2 × 6 stud wall serves as the chord for the roof diaphragm. The connections for the splice in the top plate are to be designed. The magnitude of the chord force is large, and the splice will be made with bolts instead of nails.

The location of the splices in the chord should be considered. In this building the chord is made up of farily long members (say 20 ft), and the splices are offset by half the length of the members (10 ft in this example). At some point between the splices, the chord force is shared equally by the two members. Therefore, the connections at each end of a chord member may be designed for one-half of the total chord force.

This is in contrast to the nailed chord splice designed in Example 12.9 (Sec. 12.8). If the lap of the members in the chord is kept to a minimum, the entire chord force must be transmitted by the single connection within the lap. Either method of splicing the chord may be used in practice.

The connection is designed by first assuming a bolt size and determining the nominal design value for the fastener. In this problem Z can be found using the yield limit equations or the NDS bolt tables. Except for t_m and θ_m, the current example is very similar to Example 13.3. Therefore, the determination of the nominal value Z is not shown and is left to the reader as an exercise.

With Z known, the approximate number of bolts is estimated, and the allowable load for the connection is determined and compared with the design load. As with many practical problems, a number of the possible adjustment factors default to unity. However, the load duration factor and the group action factor are required to obtain Z'.

Part 1 of the example follows the recommended practice of providing the full base dimensions for the end distance and center-to-center spacing. Part 2 is given for illustrative purposes only, to show how the geometry factor is applied should the base dimensions not be provided.

EXAMPLE 13.12   Bolt Splice for Tension Chord

A large wood-frame warehouse uses 2×6 stud walls. A double 2×6 top plate functions as the chord of the horizontal roof diaphragm. See Fig. 13.13a. Determine the number and spacing of ¾-in.-diameter bolts for the splice connection in the top plate. The bolts are in a single row. Lumber is Select Structural DF-L. The chord force at the connection has been determined, and the splice is to be designed for one-half of this load. The stress in the member is also to be evaluated. $C_M = 1.0$, and $C_t = 1.0$.

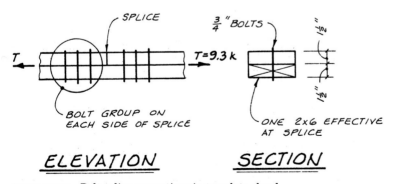

Figure 13.13a Bolt splice connections in top plate chord.

Bolt Design—Part 1

In part 1, spacings are to be determined in accordance with the base dimensions to obtain the full design load for the bolt. The following parameters are known about the connection. The nominal design value for the bolt can be determined from the yield limit equations for a single-shear wood-to-wood connections. As an alternative to the equations, Z can be obtained from NDS Table 8.2A. Evaluation of Z is left as an exercise for the reader.

$$D = 0.75 \text{ in.}$$

$$F_{yb} = 45 \text{ ksi} \qquad \text{(assumed for A307 bolts)}$$

$$t_m = 1.5 \text{ in.}$$

$$\theta_m = 0 \text{ degrees}$$

$$F_{em} = 5600 \text{ psi} \qquad (F_{e\parallel} \text{ for bolt in DF-L})$$

$$t_s = 1.5 \text{ in.}$$

$$\theta_s = 0 \text{ degrees}$$

$$F_{es} = 5600 \text{ psi} \qquad (F_{e\parallel} \text{ for bolt in DF-L})$$

$$SG_m = SG_s = 0.50$$

Nominal design value:

$Z = 725$ lb   (Mode II yield mechanism given by NDS equation 8.2-3. This compares with $Z = 720$ lb in NDS Table 8.2A.)

Adjustment factors:

$C_D = 1.6$ for lateral loading due to wind or seismic (verify local code acceptance before using)

$C_M = 1.0$ given

$C_t = 1.0$ given

$C_g \approx 0.95$ (assumed) before the group action factor can be determined, it is necessary to know the number of bolts. C_g will be verified later.

$C_\Delta = 1.0$ for bolt spacings given by base dimensions.

Base dimensions:

$$\text{End distance} = 7D = 7(0.75) = 5.25 \text{ in.} \qquad \text{(tension member)}$$

$$\text{c.-to-c. spacing} = s = 4D = 4(0.75) = 3.0 \text{ in.}$$

$$\text{Bolts will be located in the center of the 2} \times \text{6s.}$$

$$\text{Edge distance} = 0.5(5.5) = 2.75 \text{ in.}$$

$$l/D = 1.5/0.75 = 2.0 < 6.0$$

$$\text{Min. edge distance} = 1.5D = 1.5(0.75)$$

$$= 1.125 \text{ in.} < 2.75 \quad OK$$

Estimate number of bolts:

$$\text{Load on one bolt group} = \frac{T}{2} = \frac{9300}{2} = 4650 \text{ lb}$$

$$\text{Approx. } Z' = Z(C_D C_M C_t C_g C_\Delta)$$

$$= 725(1.6 \times 1.0 \times 1.0 \times 0.95 \times 1.0)$$

$$= 1102 \text{ lb/bolt}$$

$$N \approx \frac{4650}{1102} = 4.22 \quad say \quad 5 \text{ bolts}$$

Allowable load capacity:
Verify group action factor by evaluating the equation for C_g for five bolts in a row.

$$\gamma = \text{load/slip modulus for wood-to-wood bolt connection}$$

$$= 180{,}000(D^{1.5}) = 180{,}000(0.75^{1.5}) = 116{,}900$$

$$E_m = E_s = 1{,}900{,}000 \text{ psi}$$

$$A_m = A_s = 8.25$$

$$R_{EA} = 1.0$$

Note R_{EA} is the minimum ratio of member stiffnesses [i.e., the smaller of $E_m A_m/(E_s A_s)$ and $E_s A_s/(E_m A_m)$]. In this example, the member stiffnesses are equal, hence $R_{EA} = 1.0$.

$$u = 1 + \gamma\left(\frac{s}{2}\right)\left[\frac{1}{E_m A_m} + \frac{1}{E_s A_s}\right]$$

$$= 1 + 116{,}900 \left(\frac{3.0}{2}\right)\left[\frac{1}{1{,}900{,}000(8.25)} + \frac{1}{1{,}900{,}000(8.25)}\right]$$

$$= 1.022$$

$$m = u - \sqrt{u^2 - 1}$$

$$= 1.022 - \sqrt{1.022^2 - 1} = 0.8097$$

$$1 + m = 1 + 0.8097 = 1.810$$

$$1 - m = 1 - 0.8097 = 0.1903$$

$$m^{2n} = 0.8097^{2(5)} = 0.1211$$

$$1 + R_{EA} = 1 + 1.0 = 2.0$$

$$1 + R_{EA}m^n = 1 + 1.0(0.8097^5) = 1.348$$

$$C_g = \left[\frac{m(1 - m^{2n})}{n[(1 + R_{EA}m^n)(1 + m) - 1 + m^{2n}]} \right] \left[\frac{1 + R_{EA}}{1 - m} \right]$$

$$= \left[\frac{0.8097(1 - 0.1211)}{5[(1.348)(1.810) - 1 + 0.1211]} \right] \left[\frac{2.0}{0.190} \right]$$

$$= 0.958$$

Allowable load on one splice connection:

$$\text{Allow. } P = N(Z') = 5(725)(1.6 \times 0.958)$$

$$= 5(1111)$$

$$= 5556 \text{ lb} > 4650 \quad \textit{OK}$$

> *Use*   five ¾-in.-diameter bolts each side of splice.

NOTE: The spacing of bolts must be shown on the design plans.

Bolt Design—Part 2

The bolt spacings given in part 1 are the preferred spacings even though the allowable load is greater than the design load. For illustration, determine the effect on the load capacity of the connection if reduced spacings are used.

Reduced spacings and geometry factor:

$$\text{Reduced end distance} = 5.0 \text{ in.} < 7D = 5.25 \text{ in.} \quad \text{(base)}$$

$$> 3.5D = 2.625 \quad \text{(minimum)}$$

$$\therefore \text{End } C_\Delta = \frac{5.0}{5.25} = 0.952$$

$$\text{Reduced c.-to-c. spacing} = s = 2.5 \text{ in.} < 4D = 3.0 \text{ (base)}$$

$$> 2D = 1.5 \text{ (minimum)}$$

$$\therefore \text{Center-to-center } C_\Delta = \frac{2.5}{3.00} = 0.833$$

A single geometry factor is used for the entire connection, and the smaller value applies:

$$C_\Delta = 0.833$$

Revised group action factor:

$$u = 1 + \gamma\left(\frac{s}{2}\right)\left[\frac{1}{E_m A_m} + \frac{1}{E_s A_s}\right]$$

$$= 1 + 116{,}900\left(\frac{2.5}{2}\right)\left[\frac{1}{1{,}900{,}000(8.25)} + \frac{1}{1{,}900{,}000(8.25)}\right]$$

$$= 1.019$$

$$m = u - \sqrt{u^2 - 1}$$

$$= 1.019 - \sqrt{1.019^2 - 1} = 0.8246$$

$$1 + m = 1 + 0.8246 = 1.825$$

$$1 - m = 1 - 0.8246 = 0.1754$$

$$m^{2n} = 0.8246^{2(5)} = 0.1454$$

$$1 + R_{EA} = 1 + 1.0 = 2.0$$

$$1 + R_{EA}m^n = 1 + 1.0(0.8246^5) = 1.381$$

$$C_g = \left[\frac{m(1 - m^{2n})}{n[(1 + R_{EA}m^n)(1 + m) - 1 + m^{2n}]}\right]\left[\frac{1 + R_{EA}}{1 - m}\right]$$

$$= \left[\frac{0.8246(1 - 0.1454)}{5[(1.381)(1.825) - 1 + 0.1454]}\right]\left[\frac{2.0}{0.1754}\right]$$

$$= 0.965$$

Allowable load on one splice connection:

$$\text{Allow. } P = N(Z') = 5(725)(1.6 \times 0.965 \times 0.833)$$

$$= 5(932)$$

$$= 4662 \text{ lb} > 4650 \quad OK$$

Although the allowable load is greater than the design load, the connection capacity has been substantially reduced (4662 versus 5556 lb) as a result of bolt spacing.

Member

One 2×6 is effective at a splice in the chord. Check the stress at the net section.

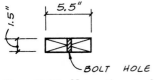

Figure 13.13b   Net section at splice.

$$A_n = 1.5[5.5 - (\tfrac{3}{4} + \tfrac{1}{8})] = 6.94 \text{ in.}^2$$

The $\tfrac{1}{8}$ in. was arbitrarily added to the bolt diameter for clearance and possible damage to wood fibers resulting from the drilling process. Actual clearance is $\tfrac{1}{16}$ in.

$$f_t = \frac{T}{A_n} = \frac{9300}{6.94} = 1340 \text{ psi}$$

$$F_t' = F_t(C_D)(C_M)(C_t)(C_F)$$

$$= 1000(1.6)(1.0)(1.0)(1.3)$$

$$= 2080 \text{ psi} > 1340 \qquad OK$$

Use   double 2 × 6 Sel. Str. DF-L for top plate.

13.7   Shear Stresses in a Beam at a Connection

The evaluation of shear stresses in a beam is covered in Chap. 6. When a beam is supported by a connection with bolts, lag bolts, split rings, or shear plates, there are additional considerations for horizontal shear (NDS Sec. 3.4.5). The computed shear stress is determined using the *effective depth* d_e, which is taken as the depth of the member minus the distance from the unloaded edge of the member to the *center* of the nearest bolt or lag bolt. For timber connectors d_e is taken as the depth of the beam minus the distance from the unloaded edge to the *edge* of the nearest connector. See Example 13.13.

It should be clear that the tendency of a beam to develop a crack parallel to the grain will be affected by the magnitude of the shear stress in the member. In addition, the tendency of the member to split will be affected by the proximity of the connection to the end of the beam. Consequently, when the connection is less than 5 times the depth of the beam d from the end of the member, the computed shear stress is increased by the ratio of the depth to the effective depth d/d_e. The allowable shear stress is as defined in Chap. 6.

When the connection is greater than $5d$ from the end of the member, the splitting tendency is reduced, and the shear stress is computed without the d/d_e increase and the allowable shear stress may be increased (multiplied) by 1.5. However, when this more liberal stress check on the effective depth is used, the shear stress on the gross cross section must be checked in the conventional manner.

EXAMPLE 13.13 Shear Stresses at a Connection

The shear in a beam supported by fasteners is checked using the effective depth d_e (Fig. 13.14). For bolts and lag bolts, d_e is the depth of the member minus the distance from the unloaded edge to the center of the nearest fastener. For split ring and shear plate connectors, d_e is the depth of the member minus the distance from the unloaded edge to the nearest edge of a connector. The loaded and unloaded edges are determined by examining the *force on the beam* at the fastener. The loaded edge is the edge toward which the force acts. The unloaded edge is the opposite edge.

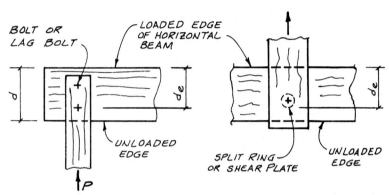

Figure 13.14 Definition of effective depth d_e for evaluation of shear in a beam supported by fasteners.

The total shear V in the beam at a connection is computed in the usual manner (Chap. 6). Depending on the location of the connection, the actual shear stress is then compared with the allowable shear stress as follows:

When the connection is less than $5d$ from the end of the member,

$$f_v = \frac{3V}{2bd_e}\left(\frac{d}{d_e}\right) \leq F'_v$$

When the connection is more than $5d$ from the end of the member,

$$f_v = \frac{3V}{2bd_e} \leq 1.5F'_v$$

Also

$$f_v = \frac{3V}{2bd} \leq F'_v$$

For a discussion of the allowable shear stress F'_v, see Chap. 6.

13.8 Design Problem: Bolt Connection for Diagonal Brace

This final bolt example involves a connection that must be evaluated with the yield limit equations because the NDS bolt tables cover only parallel- and perpendicular-to-grain loading, and they handle only wood members with the same specific gravity.

The load in the side member in Example 13.14 is parallel to the grain ($\theta = 0$ degrees), and the angle of load to grain for the main member is 45 degrees. In addition, the beam and brace are from different species. Many of the adjustment factors default to unity in this connection problem.

The center of resistance of the fastener coincides with the centroid of the members, and there is no eccentricity in the connection. However, the horizontal shear in the beam should be evaluated using the effective depth to the bolt (Sec. 13.7). Because the connection is more than 5 times the beam depth from the end of the member, the computed shear stress need not be multiplied by the ratio d/d_e. In addition, the allowable shear stress may be increased 50 percent. Shear on the gross section is also checked.

EXAMPLE 13.14   Bolt Connection for Diagonal Brace

The beam in Fig. 13.15a supports a DL of 575 lb at its free end and is connected to the diagonal brace with a single ¾-in.-diameter bolt. The horizontal beam is a 24F-V3 DF glulam, and the diagonal brace is No. 1 Hem-Fir sawn lumber. Wood is initially dry and remains dry in service. Normal temperature conditions apply.

Determine if the bolt is adequate, and check the shear stress in the beam at the connection. Assume that other stresses in the members are OK.

Solve for force in brace.

$$\Sigma M_c = 0$$

$$6T_v = 575(10)$$

$$T_v = 958 \text{ lb}$$

$$T = \sqrt{2}T_v = \sqrt{2}(958) = 1355 \text{ lb}$$

NOTE: Segment BC of the beam is subjected to combined axial and bending stresses (Chap. 7).

Bolt Capacity

Summary of values for yield limit equations:

$$D = 0.75 \text{ in.}$$

$$F_{yb} = 45 \text{ ksi} \quad \text{(assumed for A307 bolts)}$$

$$t_m = 3.125 \text{ in.}$$

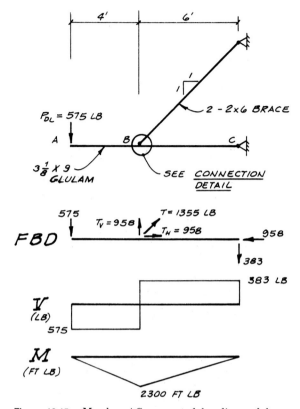

Figure 13.15a Member AC supported by diagonal brace at B.

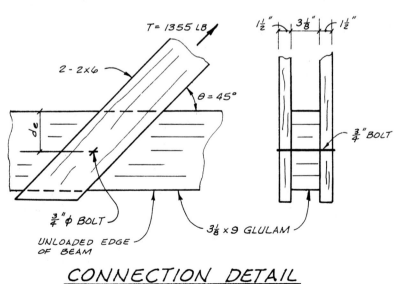

CONNECTION DETAIL

Figure 13.15b Bolt connection at B: double shear wood-to-wood.

$$\theta_m = 45 \text{ degrees}$$

$$SG_m = 0.50 \qquad \text{(dowel bearing strength may be computed using SG or read from NDS Table 8A.)}$$

$$F_{e\parallel} = 5600 \text{ psi} \qquad \text{for bolt in DF-L}$$

$$F_{e\perp} = 2600 \text{ psi} \qquad \text{for } \tfrac{3}{4}\text{-in. bolt in DF-L}$$

$$t_s = 1.5 \text{ in.}$$

$$\theta_s = 0 \text{ degrees}$$

$$SG_s = 0.43$$

$$F_{es} = F_{e\parallel} = 4800 \text{ psi} \qquad \text{for bolt in Hem-Fir}$$

Coefficients for yield equations:

$$F_{em} = F_{e\theta} = \frac{F_{e\parallel}F_{e\perp}}{F_{e\parallel} \sin^2 \theta + F_{e\perp} \cos^2 \theta}$$

$$= \frac{5600(2600)}{5600 \sin^2 45 + 2600 \cos^2 45} = 3551 \text{ psi}$$

$$R_e = \frac{F_{em}}{F_{es}} = \frac{3551}{4800} = 0.7398$$

$$1 + R_e = 1 + 0.7398 = 1.740$$

$$2 + R_e = 2 + 0.7398 = 2.740$$

$$\theta = \text{larger value of } \theta_m \text{ and } \theta_s$$

$$= 45 \text{ degrees}$$

$$K_\theta = 1 + \frac{\theta}{360} = 1 + \frac{45}{360} = 1.125$$

$$k_3 = -1 + \sqrt{\frac{2(1 + R_e)}{R_e} + \frac{2F_{yb}(2 + R_e)D^2}{3F_{em}t_s^2}}$$

$$= -1 + \sqrt{\frac{2(1.740)}{0.7398} + \frac{2(45,000)(2.740)(0.75^2)}{3(3551)(1.5^2)}}$$

$$= 2.239$$

Yield limit equations:
Mode I_m (NDS equation 8.3-1):

$$Z = \frac{Dt_m F_{em}}{4K_\theta} = \frac{0.75(3.125)(3551)}{4(1.125)} = 1850 \text{ lb}$$

Mode I_s (NDS equation 8.3-2):

$$Z = \frac{Dt_s F_{es}}{2K_\theta} = \frac{0.75(1.5)(4800)}{2(1.125)} = 2400 \text{ lb}$$

Mode III_s (NDS equation 8.3-3):

$$Z = \frac{k_3 Dt_s F_{em}}{1.6(2 + R_e)K_\theta}$$

$$= \frac{2.239(0.75)(1.5)(3551)}{1.6(2.740)(1.125)} = 1814 \text{ lb}$$

Mode IV (NDS equation 8.3-4):

$$Z = \frac{D^2}{1.6K_\theta} \sqrt{\frac{2F_{em} F_{yb}}{3(1 + R_e)}}$$

$$= \frac{0.75^2}{1.6(1.125)} \sqrt{\frac{2(3551)(45,000)}{3(1.740)}} = 2445 \text{ lb}$$

Nominal design value:

$$Z = 1814 \text{ lb}$$

Allowable design value:
   The bolt is located on the center lines of the two members.
   The required edge distance to the loaded edge of the horizontal member is $4D$.

$$4D = 4(0.75) = 3.0$$

$$\text{Edge distance} = \frac{9}{2} = 4.5 > 3.0 \quad OK$$

   Assume that all other dimensions in the connection (including end distance for the tension member) will be chosen to satisfy the base dimension spacings for the connection in accordance with Sec. 13.5. Thus $C_\Delta = 1.0$.

$$Z' = Z(C_D C_M C_t C_g C_\Delta)$$

$$= 1814(0.9)(1.0)(1.0)(1.0)(1.0)$$

$$= 1633 \text{ lb} > 1355 \quad OK$$

> ¾-in.-diameter bolt   *OK*

Shear Stress

The shear stress in the 3⅛ × 9 glulam beam is not critical, but calculations will be shown to demonstrate the criteria given in Sec. 13.7. Compare *5 times the beam depth* with the distance of the connection from the end of the beam.

$$5d = 5 \times 9 = 45 \text{ in.} < 48 \text{ in.}$$

The joint is more than 5 times the depth from the end. The computed stress need not be multiplied by d/d_e, and the allowable stress may be increased:

$$f_v = \frac{3V}{2bd_e} = \frac{3(575)}{2(3.125)(9.0/2)} = 61.3 \text{ psi}$$

For 24F-V3 DF glulam:

$$F_v = 165 \text{ psi} \quad \text{(from NDS Supplement Table 5A)}$$

$$F'_v = 1.5F_v(C_D C_M C_t)$$

$$= 1.5(165)(0.9)(1.0)(1.0)$$

$$= 223 \text{ psi} > 61.3 \text{ psi} \quad OK$$

Shear stress on the gross section:

$$f_v = \frac{3V}{2bd} = \frac{3(575)}{2(3.125)(9.0)} = 30.7 \text{ psi}$$

$$F'_v = F_v(C_D C_M C_t)$$

$$= 165(0.9)(1.0)(1.0)$$

$$= 149 \text{ psi} > 30.7 \quad OK$$

> Shear in beam is OK.

13.9   Lag Bolt Connections

Lag bolts are relatively large-diameter fasteners that have a *wood* screw thread and a square or hexagonal bolt head. See Fig. 13.16*a*. The NDS refers to these fasteners as lag screws, but the TCM (Ref 3.1) uses the term *lag bolt*. The term *lag bolt* implies a large-diameter fastener with a bolt head, and the term *lag screw* indicates a fastener with a wood screw thread. Both refer to the same type of fastener, and the term *lag bolt* is generally used in this book.

A distinction should be made between large-diameter lag bolts (lag screws) and similar small-diameter fasteners known as *wood screws*. Recall from Chap. 11 that the dowel bearing strength is different for large- and small-diameter fasteners. For lag bolts F_e is a function of diameter. The methods of installation for lag bolts and wood screws are also different. Because of their large size, lag bolts are installed with a wrench, and wood screws are usually installed with a screwdriver or screw gun. The NDS covers the design of both lag bolts and wood screws, but only lag bolts are addressed in this text.

Lag bolts are used when an excessively long bolt would be required to make a connection or when access to one side of a through-bolted connection may be prevented. Lag bolts can be used in shear connections (Fig. 13.16*b*) or withdrawal connections (Fig. 13.16*c*). As with nails, the laterally loaded (shear) connection is more positive and is preferred over the withdrawal type. However, both applications are used in practice, and the designer should be familiar with the design procedures for both types of problems.

EXAMPLE 13.15   Lag Bolt Connections

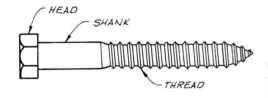

Figure 13.16a   Lag bolt. Large-diameter fastener with wood screw thread and bolt head. Also known as lag screw.

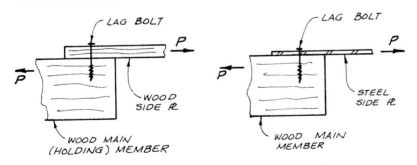

Figure 13.16b   Lag bolts in single-shear connections. Wood-to-wood and wood-to-metal connections are the common applications.

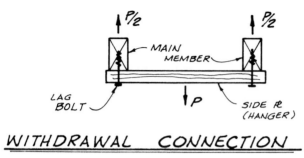

WITHDRAWAL   CONNECTION

Figure 13.16c   Lag bolts in withdrawal connection.

Lag bolts are installed in special prebored holes that accommodate the shank diameter and provide holding material for the thread. Washers are required under the fastener head (similar to bolts).

As with the majority of other fasteners used in wood connections, there is not a currently recognized national standard that defines mechanical properties for lag bolts. However, lag bolts are typically manufactured from the same wire stock as bolts, and $F_{yb} = 45$ ksi appears to be conservative for commonly available lag bolts ⅜ in. or greater in diameter. For smaller diameters, the bending yield strength is assumed to increase because of work-hardening (similar to nails): $F_{yb} = 70$ ksi for ¼-in. diameter, and $F_{yb} = 60$ ksi for 5⁄16-in. diameter. It is felt that these values can reasonably be used in the yield limit equations until a standard is developed. In the meantime, the designer should list the bending yield strength as part of the design specifications.

The configuration of lag bolts is given in NDS Appendix L *Typical Dimensions of Standard Lag Screws*. This table provides a number of important dimensions that are used in the installation and design calculations for a lag bolt. These dimensions include the nominal length, shank diameter and length, root diameter and thread length, and length of tapered tip.

Lag bolts are installed in prebored holes that accommodate the shank and the threaded portion. See Example 13.16. The hole involves drilling with two different-diameter bits. The larger-diameter hole has the same diameter and length as the unthreaded shank of the lag bolt. The diameter of the lead hole for the threaded portion is given as a percentage of the shank diameter that depends on the specific gravity of the wood.

It is important that lag bolts be installed properly with a wrench. Driving with a hammer is an unacceptable method of installation. Soap or another type of lubricant should be used on the lag bolt or in the pilot hole to facilitate installation and to prevent damage to the fastener.

EXAMPLE 13.16   Installation of Lag Bolt

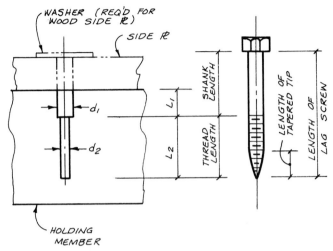

Figure 13.17a   Hole sizes.

A lag bolt is installed in a pilot hole. The dimensions of the pilot hole in the main or holding member are as follows:

For the shank:

$$L_1 = \text{shank length} - \text{side plate thickness} - \text{washer thickness}$$

$$d_1 = \text{shank diameter}$$

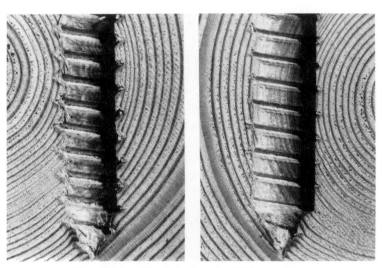

Figure 13.17b   Photographs of lag bolt threads. *(FPL.)*

For the threaded portion:

$$L_2 \geq \text{thread length}$$

$$d_2 = \begin{cases} (0.65 \text{ to } 0.85) \times d_1 & \text{for wood with SG} > 0.6 \\ (0.60 \text{ to } 0.75) \times d_1 & \text{for wood with } 0.5 < \text{SG} \leq 0.6 \\ (0.40 \text{ to } 0.70) \times d_1 & \text{for wood with SG} \leq 0.5 \end{cases}$$

For a given specific-gravity range, the larger percentages of d_1 should be used for larger-diameter lag bolts. It is important that lag bolts be installed by turning with a wrench into lead holes of proper size.

The photograph on the left in Fig. 13.17b shows deep, clean-cut threads of a lag bolt that was properly installed in the correct size lead hole. On the right, the threads have shallow penetration into the wood because of an oversize pilot hole.

The shear capacity of a lag bolt is covered by a set of yield limit equations (Sec. 13.10). The withdrawal load capacity is empirically based on test results (Sec. 13.13).

13.10   Yield Limit Equations for Lag Bolts

Many of the parameters that are used in the yield limit equations for lag bolts are similar to those for bolt connections (Sec. 13.3). There are, however, fewer yield modes that need to be checked for lag bolts compared with conventional through-bolted connections. For example, a single-shear lag bolt connection requires only three yield equations for a wood-to-wood connection, compared with six equations for a similar connection made with bolts. Likewise, for a lag bolt wood-to-steel connection, there are only two yield equations compared with five for bolts.

The yield limit equations for lag bolts in single-shear (two-member) connections are summarized in Example 13.17. Lag bolts are not generally used in double-shear applications. The dowel bearing strength F_e can be computed given the specific gravity of the wood, or values can be obtained from NDS Table 9A, *Dowel Bearing Strength for Lag Screw Connections.*

EXAMPLE 13.17   Lag Bolt Yield Limit Equations for Single Shear

Wood-to-Wood Connection

For one lag bolt in a single-shear connection between two wood members, the nominal design value is taken as the smallest load capacity obtained from the following three equations. The yield modes are sketched in Fig. 11.10 (Sec. 11.7).

Mode I_s (NDS equation 9.3-1):

$$Z = \frac{Dt_s F_{es}}{4K_\theta}$$

Mode III$_s$ (NDS equation 9.3-2):

$$Z = \frac{kDt_sF_{em}}{2.8(2 + R_e)K_\theta}$$

Mode IV (NDS equation 9.3-3):

$$Z = \frac{D^2}{3K_\theta}\sqrt{\frac{1.75F_{em}F_{yb}}{3(1 + R_e)}}$$

where $k = -1 + \sqrt{\dfrac{2(1 + R_e)}{R_e} + \dfrac{F_{yb}(2 + R_e)D^2}{2F_{em}t_s^2}}$

$R_e = \dfrac{F_{em}}{F_{es}}$

$K_\theta = 1 + \dfrac{\theta}{360}$

D = diameter of unthreaded shank of lag bolt, in.

t_m = thickness of main member, in.

t_s = thickness of side member, in.

F_{em} = dowel bearing strength of main member, psi:

$= \begin{cases} F_{e\parallel} & \text{for parallel-to-grain loading} \\ F_{e\perp} & \text{for perpendicular-to-grain loading} \\ F_{e\theta} & \text{for load at angle to grain } \theta \text{ (see Hankinson formula below)} \end{cases}$

F_{es} = dowel bearing strength of side member, psi:

$= \begin{cases} F_{e\parallel} & \text{for parallel-to-grain loading} \\ F_{e\perp} & \text{for perpendicular-to-grain loading} \\ F_{e\theta} & \text{for load at angle to grain } \theta \text{ (see Hankinson formula below)} \end{cases}$

(For a steel side member, $F_{es} = F_u$.)

F_{yb} = bending yield strength of lag bolt:

$= \begin{cases} 70{,}000 \text{ psi} & \text{for } D = \frac{1}{4} \text{ in.} \\ 60{,}000 \text{ psi} & \text{for } D = \frac{5}{16} \text{ in.} \\ 45{,}000 \text{ psi} & \text{for } D \geq \frac{3}{8} \text{ in.} \end{cases}$

θ = maximum angle of load to grain ($0 \leq \theta \leq 90$ degrees) for any member in connection

$F_{e\theta} = \dfrac{F_{e\parallel}F_{e\perp}}{F_{e\parallel}\sin^2\theta + F_{e\perp}\cos^2\theta}$

Wood-to-Metal Connection

For one lag bolt in a single-shear connection between a wood main member and a steel side plate, the nominal design value is taken as the smallest load capacity obtained from two of the three equations given above. Equation 9.3-1 is eliminated for wood-to-metal connections. In applying the yield limit equations, F_{es} may conservatively be taken equal to the ultimate tensile strength F_y of the steel side plate.

A Mode I$_s$ yield mechanism represents a bearing failure in the side plate. Because the yield limit equation for Mode I$_s$ contains an adjustment for load duration in a *wood* member, it is not appropriate to apply NDS equation 9.3-1 to a bearing failure in a *steel* plate. However, the designer must ensure that the bearing capacity of the steel side member is not exceeded in accordance with recognized steel design practice (Ref. 11.1).

As an alternative to solving the yield limit equations, the nominal design value for a lag bolt used in certain common applications may be read from NDS Tables 9.3A and 9.3B. Values are given for parallel- and perpendicular-to-grain loading. The notation is similar to that used in the bolt tables:

1. Load *parallel* to grain in *both* main member and side member, $Z_\parallel$.
2. Load *perpendicular* to grain in *side* member and parallel to grain in main member, $Z_{s\perp}$.
3. Load perpendicular to grain in main member and parallel to grain in side member, $Z_{m\perp}$.

When the load is at an intermediate angle of load to grain, the yield limit equations must be evaluated.

One example is given to illustrate the application of the yield limit equations for lag bolts. See Example 13.18. The connection is between a steel side plate and a glulam beam.

EXAMPLE 13.18   Lag Bolt Nominal Design Value: Single-Shear Wood-to-Metal Connection

Determine the nominal design value of a ⅝-in.-diameter lag bolt used to connect a ¼-in.-thick metal side plate of A36 steel and a DF-L glulam beam. Load is parallel to grain in the glulam.

Summary of Known Values

Dowel bearing strength can be computed (Sec. 11.5) given the specific gravity of the glulam beam, or it can be read as $F_{e\parallel}$ from NDS Table 9A.

$$D = 0.625 \text{ in.}$$

$$F_{yb} = 45 \text{ ksi} \quad (\text{assumed for } \tfrac{5}{8}\text{-in.-diameter lag bolt})$$

$$\theta_m = 0 \text{ degrees}$$

$$SG_m = 0.50$$

$$F_{em} = 5600 \text{ psi} \quad (F_{e\parallel} \text{ for lag bolt in DF-L})$$

$$t_s = 0.375 \text{ in.}$$

$$F_{es} = F_u = 58{,}000 \text{ psi} \quad (\text{for A36 steel plate})$$

Coefficients for Yield Limit Equations

$$R_e = \frac{F_{em}}{F_{es}} = \frac{5600}{58{,}000} = 0.09655$$

$$1 + R_e = 1 + 0.09655 = 1.097$$

$$2 + R_e = 2 + 0.09655 = 2.097$$

$$\theta = 0 \text{ degrees}$$

$$K_\theta = 1 + \frac{\theta}{360} = 1 + \frac{0}{360} = 1.0$$

$$k = -1 + \sqrt{\frac{2(1 + R_e)}{R_e} + \frac{F_{yb}(2 + R_e)D^2}{2F_{em}t_s^2}}$$

$$= -1 + \sqrt{\frac{2(1.097)}{0.09655} + \frac{45,000(2.097)(0.625^2)}{2(5600)(0.25^2)}}$$

$$= 7.681$$

Yield Limit Equations

Mode III_s (NDS equation 9.3-2):

$$Z = \frac{kDt_sF_{em}}{2.8(2 + R_e)K_\theta}$$

$$= \frac{7.681(0.625)(0.25)(5600)}{2.8(2.097)(1.0)} = 1145 \text{ lb}$$

Mode IV (NDS equation 9.3-3):

$$Z = \frac{D^2}{3K_\theta} \sqrt{\frac{1.75F_{em}F_{yb}}{3(1 + R_e)}}$$

$$= \frac{0.625^2}{3(1.0)} \sqrt{\frac{1.75(5600)(45,000)}{3(1.097)}} = 1508 \text{ lb}$$

Nominal design value is selected as the smaller value from the two yield formulas:

$$\boxed{Z = 1145 \text{ lb}}$$

Compare with values from NDS Table 9.3B:

$$Z = 1140 \approx 1145 \text{ lb}$$

13.11   Adjustment Factors for Lag Bolts in Shear Connections

The yield limit equations for lag bolts in single shear were reviewed in Sec. 13.10. The *nominal design value Z* represents the load capacity of a single lag bolt or lag screw as obtained from the yield equations. In the design of a given connection, the nominal design value is converted to an *allowable design value Z'* by a series of adjustment factors.

The adjustment factors convert the base conditions to the conditions for a specific design situation. The adjustment factors required in the design of connections are summarized in NDS Table 7.3.1. See the inside back cover of this book for a similar table.

The base conditions associated with the nominal design value are as follows:

1. Load is normal (10-year) duration.

2. Wood is initially dry at the time of fabrication of a connection and remains dry in service.

3. Temperature range is normal.

4. There is one lag bolt in a line parallel to the applied load (i.e., only one bolt per row).

5. Spacing provisions for lag bolts (geometry requirements for the connection) are satisfied.

6. Penetration of lag bolt in the holding member (not including the tapered tip) is a minimum of 8 times the shank diameter (that is, $p \geq 8D$).

7. Lag bolt penetrates the side grain (not the end grain) of the main (holding) member.

If a lag bolt is used in a connection under exactly these conditions, the adjustment factors all default to unity, and $Z' = Z$.

For a shear connection that does not satisfy the base conditions described above, the following adjustment factors may be required:

$$Z' = Z(C_D C_M C_t C_g C_\Delta C_d C_{eg})$$

where C_D = load duration factor (Sec. 4.15)
C_M = wet service factor (Sec. 4.14)
C_t = temperature factor (Sec. 4.20)
C_g = group action factor
C_Δ = geometry factor
C_d = penetration depth factor
C_{eg} = end grain factor

The total allowable load for a connection using two or more lag bolts is the sum of the individual allowable load values Z'. This summation is appropriate if the lag bolts are all the same type and size because each fastener will have the same yield mode. The load capacity for the connection is the number of lag bolts N times the allowable load for one fastener:

$$\text{Allow. } P = N(Z')$$

A number of adjustment factors are described elsewhere in this book and are mentioned only in summary. Some of these were covered in Chap. 4, and others, which apply to both lag bolts and bolts, were summarized in Sec. 13.5. Only the adjustment factors that are unique to lag bolts are covered in detail.

Load duration factor C_D. The load duration factor for a lag bolt connection is the same as that applied to the design of a structural member or other fastener. Refer to Sec. 4.15 for a review of load duration and the numerical values for C_D.

Wet service factor C_M. The concept of an adjustment factor based on moisture content was introduced in Sec. 4.14. The discussion regarding possible damage in a wood connection due to cross-grain volume changes applies to both lag bolts and bolts. See Sec. 13.5 for a discussion of this potentially serious problem. The numerical values of C_M are also the same for lag bolts and bolts and are given in NDS Table 7.3.3, *Wet Service Factors, C_M, for Connections*.

The first objective in good design practice is to keep the connection dry where possible. Second, the connection should be detailed so that cross-grain cracking does not occur. Wood is very weak in tension perpendicular to grain, and the conditions that cause tension across the grain can be eliminated, or minimized, by proper detailing. For example, separate steel side plates for rows of bolts parallel to the grain will allow volume changes to occur without locking in stresses.

Temperature factor C_t. If wood is used in an application with high temperatures, the allowable load for a lag bolt is to be reduced by the temperature factor C_t. Refer to Sec. 4.20 for a brief review of the temperature factor. Numerical values of C_t for connections are given in NDS Table 7.3.4. The temperature range for most wood-frame buildings does not require a reduction of design values, and the temperature factor is often taken as unity.

Group action factor C_g. In a connection that has more than one lag bolt in a row, it is necessary to reduce the nominal design value by a multiplier known as the group action factor C_g. The group action factor primarily depends on the number of fasteners in a row. The group action factor for a lag bolt connection is the same as a bolt connection. Refer to Sec. 13.5 for a discussion and definition of C_g. Note that C_g does not exceed unity ($C_g \le$ 1.0).

Geometry factor C_Δ. End distance, edge distance, center-to-center spacing, and row spacing requirements for lag bolts are the same as for bolts. Refer to Sec. 13.5 for a discussion of spacing requirements. Specific criteria are given in Example 13.10 for parallel-to-grain loading and in Example 13.11 for perpendicular-to-grain loading.

Examples 13.10 and 13.11 summarize the base dimensions for fastener spacing. It is recommended that the base dimensions be used in designing and detailing a connection whenever practical. However, if conditions do not permit the use of the full base dimensions, it is possible to reduce certain spacings with a corresponding reduction in allowable load. The minimum spacing limits are also given in these examples.

The geometry factor C_Δ is the multiplier that is used to reduce the nominal design value Z if the furnished spacings are less than the base dimensions. If the base requirements for a connection are all satisfied, the geometry factor defaults to unity $(C_\Delta = 1.0)$. For other conditions, the geometry factor for lag bolts is the same as for bolts. Refer to Sec. 13.5 for the definition of C_Δ for reduced spacings. Note that C_Δ does not exceed unity $(C_\Delta \leq 1.0)$.

Penetration depth factor C_d.   The penetration of a lag bolt is defined as the distance that the fastener extends into the main (holding) member minus the length of the tapered tip. Dimensions of typical lag bolts are given in NDS Appendix L, and the length of tapered tip E is included in this table. Thus, the penetration of a lag bolt can be computed as the length of the lag bolt minus the thickness of the side member minus the washer thickness minus the length of the tapered end:

$$p = L - t_s - t_{\text{washer}} - E$$

Equations for the nominal design value Z are based on a minimum lag bolt penetration of 8 times the fastener shank diameter D. If the furnished penetration is less than $8D$, the nominal design value is reduced by multiplying by the penetration depth factor C_d. A similar factor is used in the design of nailed connections.

The absolute minimum penetration for a lag bolt is $4D$. In other words, if $p < 4D$, the penetration depth factor is zero $(C_d = 1.0)$. On the other hand, if the penetration exceeds $8D$, there is no increase in load capacity $(C_d \leq 1.0)$. In the event that the penetration is between the two limits, the penetration depth factor is taken as the ratio of the furnished penetration to the required penetration:

$$C_d = \begin{cases} 0 & \text{when } p < 4D \\ \dfrac{p}{8D} & \text{when } 4D \leq p < 8D \\ 1.0 & \text{when } p \geq 8D \end{cases}$$

End grain factor C_{eg}.   The nominal design value Z applies to a laterally loaded shear connection with the lag bolt installed into the *side grain* of the main member. Again, the main member is the member that receives the pointed end of the fastener. See Fig. 13.18a. This is the strongest and most desirable type of lag bolt connection. When a lag bolt is installed in the side grain, the end-grain factor does not apply, or it can be viewed as having a default value of unity ($C_{eg} = 1.0$).

EXAMPLE 13.19   Comparison of Lag Bolts in Side Grain and End Grain

Lateral Resistance in Side Grain

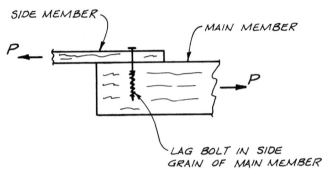

Figure 13.18a   Lag bolt in side grain.

The basic shear connection has the lag bolt installed in the side grain of the main member (Fig. 13.18a). The full nominal design value applies to this type of loading, and the end grain factor is $C_{eg} = 1.0$.

Lateral Resistance in End Grain

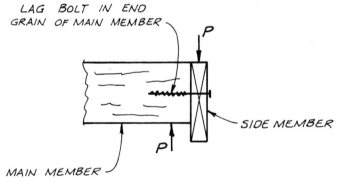

Figure 13.18b   Lag bolt in end grain.

A second type of shear connection has the lag bolt installed in the end grain of the holding member (Fig. 13.18b). In other words, the lag bolt is installed parallel to the grain of the main member. The connection still qualifies as a laterally loaded connection because the load is perpendicular to the axis of the fastener. For lag bolts installed in the end grain, $C_{eg} = 0.67$. For a lag bolt in the end grain, $F_{em} = F_{e\perp}$.

In another type of shear connection, the lag bolt is installed in the end grain of the holding member (Fig. 13.18*b*). This is a much weaker and less desirable connection. However, laterally loaded connections of this type are permitted, but the nominal design value is reduced by an end grain factor of $C_{eg} = 0.67$. A similar factor is used in connections with nails driven into the end grain (Sec. 12.6).

This concludes the review of adjustment factors for lag bolts in shear connections. One design example is provided in the next section. Many of the possible adjustment factors in this example are shown to default to unity. Although this occurs frequently in practice, the designer needs to be aware of the base conditions associated with the nominal design value. When other circumstances occur, adjustment factors are required.

13.12   Design Problem: Drag Strut Splice with Lag Bolts

This example makes use of lag bolts to attach a glulam beam to a concrete shearwall. The load is the result of a wind or seismic force on the horizontal diaphragm. See Example 13.20. The force on the connection is obtained from the drag strut force diagram which is given in the problem. For a review of drag strut force diagrams, refer to Sec. 9.10.

The force is transferred from the glulam beam by lag bolts in a shear connection to a steel plate. A second connection transfers the load from the steel plate to the shear wall with anchor bolts. The example is limited to the lag bolt connection, and calculations for the anchor bolts used in the second connection are not illustrated. The nominal design value for the lag bolt is obtained from a previous example, and the yield limit equations are not repeated.

The glulam beam in this example is manufactured with laminations that are all from one species. The designer is reminded of special considerations for connections in glulam members that are fabricated from more than one species. These were discussed in Example 11.6 (Sec. 11.5), but do not affect the problem at hand.

EXAMPLE 13.20   Splice with Lag Bolts

The roof beam in the building in Fig. 13.19 serves as the drag strut for two horizontal diaphragms. The maximum collector force occurs at the connection of the roof beam and the concrete shearwall, and the magnitude of the load is obtained from the drag strut force diagram.

Determine the number of ⅝-in.-diameter, × 6-in. lag bolts necessary to connect the steel splice plate to the Douglas Fir (24F-V3) glulam beam. The nominal design value for the lag bolt is obtained from Example 13.18. Assume that the splice plate and the connection to the wall are adequate. A single row of lag bolts is to be used, and the base dimensions for lag bolt spacings are to be summarized. $C_M = 1.0$, and $C_t = 1.0$.

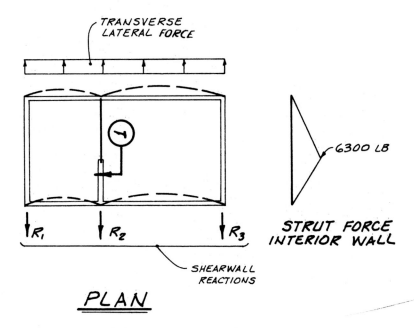

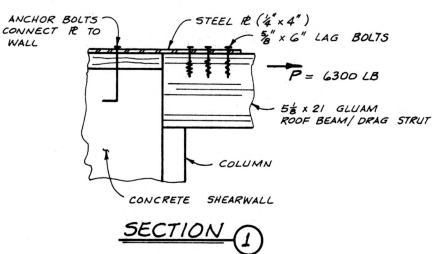

Figure 13.19 Drag strut connection made with lag bolts.

Trial Design

The nominal design value for a ⅝-in.-diameter 6-in. lag bolt from Example 13.18 is

$$Z = 1145 \text{ lb}$$

For an initial trial, assume all adjustment factors default to unity except load duration factor:

$$Z' \approx Z(C_D) = 1145(1.6) = 1832 \text{ lb/lag bolt}$$

Approximate number of bolts

$$N = \frac{P}{Z'} = \frac{6300}{1832} = 3.44 \qquad say \quad 4 \text{ lag bolts}$$

Final Design

The possible adjustment factors that can affect the capacity of a lag bolt connection include C_D, C_M, C_t, C_g, C_Δ, C_d, and C_{eg}. At this point the following factors are known or assumed:

$C_D = 1.6$ for wind or seismic (verify local code acceptance before using)

$C_M = 1.0$ given (assumes connection is initially dry and remains dry in service)

$C_t = 1.0$ assumes normal temperature range

$C_{eg} = 1.0$ lag bolts installed in side grain (top face) of glulam

The remaining adjustments will now be considered.

Penetration depth factor:
    Thickness of the metal side plate $t_s = \frac{1}{4}$ in.

    Assume washer thickness $t_{\text{washer}} = \frac{1}{8}$ in.

    From NDS Appendix L, the length
    of the tapered tip is $E = \frac{13}{32}$ in.

$$p = L - t_s - t_{\text{washer}} - E$$

$$= 6 - 0.25 - 0.125 - 0.406$$

$$= 5.22 \text{ in.}$$

Minimum penetration (base value) to develop the full design capacity is

$$p = 8D = 8(0.625) = 5.0 \text{ in.} < 5.22$$

$$\therefore C_d = 1.0$$

Geometry factor:
    Connection is a single row of lag bolts with load parallel to grain. Spacing requirements for lag bolts are the same as for bolts. For parallel-to-grain loading, spacing requirements are summarized in Example 13.10. If there is adequate room, it is recommended that base dimensions be used in detailing a connection.
    Base dimensions for a single row of bolts in a tension member (softwood species):

End distance $= 7D = 7(0.625) = 4.375$ use   5 in.
c.-to-c. spacing $= s = 4D = 4(0.625) = 2.5$ use   3 in.
Edge distance $= 1.5D = 1.5(0.625) = 0.94$ in.
The row of lag bolts will be installed along the centerline of the beam.

$$\text{Edge distance} = \frac{5.125}{2} = 2.56 \text{ in.} > 0.94 \qquad OK$$

The furnished spacings all exceed the base dimensions.

$$\therefore C_{\Delta} = 1.0$$

Group action factor:

The formula and coefficients for the group action factor are summarized in Example 13.8 (Sec. 13.5).

Load/slip modulus $\gamma = 270{,}000(D^{1.5})$ for lag bolts in wood-to-metal connection

$$= 270{,}000(0.625^{1.5}) = 133{,}400 \text{ lb/in.}$$

Member stiffnesses:

$$E_m = E_{\text{axial}} = 1{,}600{,}000 \text{ psi}   \text{(NDS Supplement Table 5A)}$$

$$A_m = 5.125 \times 21 = 107.6 \text{ in.}^2$$

$$E_m A_m = 1{,}600{,}000(107.6) = 172{,}200{,}000$$

$$E_s = E_{\text{steel}} = 29{,}000{,}000 \text{ psi}$$

$$A_m = 0.25 \times 4 = 1.0 \text{ in.}^2$$

$$E_m A_m = 29{,}000{,}000(1.0) = 29{,}000{,}000$$

Spacing of fasteners in a row

$$s = \text{c.-to-c. spacing} = 3 \text{ in.}$$

Coefficients for C_g:

$$n = \text{number of lag bolts in row} = 4$$

$$u = 1 + \gamma\left(\frac{s}{2}\right)\left[\frac{1}{E_m A_m} + \frac{1}{E_s A_s}\right]$$

$$= 1 + 133{,}400\left(\frac{3.0}{2}\right)\left[\frac{1}{172{,}200{,}000} + \frac{1}{29{,}000{,}000}\right]$$

$$= 1.008$$

$$m = u - \sqrt{u^2 - 1}$$

$$= 1.008 - \sqrt{1.008^2 - 1} = 0.8808$$

$$1 + m = 1 + 0.8808 = 1.881$$

$$1 - m = 1 - 0.8808 = 0.1192$$

$$m^{2n} = 0.8808^{2(4)} = 0.3623$$

$$\frac{E_m A_m}{E_s A_s} = \frac{172{,}200{,}000}{29{,}000{,}000} = 5.937$$

$$\frac{E_s A_s}{E_m A_m} = \frac{1}{5.937} = 0.1684$$

$$R_{EA} = \text{smaller of ratios of member stiffnesses}$$

$$= 0.1684$$

$$1 + R_{EA} = 1 + 0.1684 = 1.168$$

$$1 + R_{EA}m^n = 1 + 0.1684(0.8808)^4 = 1.101$$

$$C_g = \left[\frac{m(1 - m^{2n})}{n[(1 + R_{EA}m^n)(1 + m) - 1 + m^{2n}]}\right]\left[\frac{1 + R_{EA}}{1 - m}\right]$$

$$= \left[\frac{0.8808(1 - 0.3623)}{4[(1.101)(1.881) - 1 + 0.3623]}\right]\left[\frac{1.168}{0.1192}\right]$$

$$= 0.960$$

Allowable load:

$$Z' = Z(C_D C_M C_t C_g C_\Delta C_d C_{eg})$$

$$= 1145(1.6 \times 1.0 \times 1.0 \times 0.960 \times 1.0 \times 1.0 \times 1.0)$$

$$= 1759 \text{ lb}$$

$$\text{Allow. } P = N(Z') = 4(1759) = 7035 \text{ lb} > 6300 \qquad OK$$

> *Use* 4 lag bolts in a single row
> $\frac{5}{8}$-in. diameter $\times$ 6 in. long.
> End distance = 5 in.
> c.-to-c. spacing = 3 in.

13.13 Lag Bolts in Withdrawal

The concept of a lag bolt being subject to a withdrawal load was introduced in Chap. 11 (Fig. 11.2a). Withdrawal loading attempts to pull the fastener out of the holding member. Withdrawal connections are generally less desirable than shear-type connections.

The yield limit equations for dowel-type fasteners apply only to shear-type connections, and the yield limit theory does not apply to lag bolts in withdrawal. The withdrawal values for lag bolts are based on an empirical formula that simply reproduces laboratory test results. The formula is summarized in the *Wood Handbook* (Ref. 4.1).

Although the 1991 NDS has essentially gone to an equation format, design values for connections loaded in withdrawal (both nails and lag bolts) are still covered by tables. The *nominal design value* for the basic withdrawal connection is given the symbol W. The basic withdrawal connection is with the lag bolt installed in the side grain of the holding member. NDS Table 9.2A gives the nominal withdrawal design value *per inch of thread penetration* into the main member.

If the value from the table is given the symbol w and the *thread* penetration for withdrawal is given the symbol p_w, the nominal design value for a single lag bolt is

$$W = w \times p_w$$

The penetration p for a shear connection was explained in Sec. 13.11 under the discussion of the penetration depth factor C_d. For shear, the penetration is taken as the length of the lag bolt in the main (holding) member minus the length of the tapered end. In other words, in a shear connection, a portion of the unthreaded shank may be included in the penetration length. However, the effective penetration for withdrawal loading p_w depends on the effective thread length in the holding member. See Fig. 13.20. NDS Appendix L gives the length of the threaded portion of the lag bolt T, the length of the tapered tip E, and the length of the full-diameter threads $T - E$. Assuming that the threads are all within the main member, the effective penetration for withdrawal is

$$p_w = T - E$$

The nominal design value W represents the load capacity for a lag bolt used under a set of base conditions. The base conditions associated with the nominal design value are as follows:

1. Load is normal (10-year) duration.

2. Wood is initially dry at the time of fabrication of connection and remains dry in service.

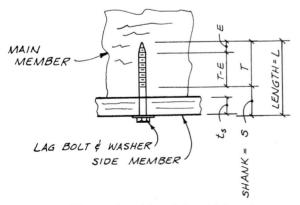

Figure 13.20 Effective thread length for withdrawal.

3. Temperature range is normal.

4. Lag bolt is installed in the side grain of the holding member.

To obtain the allowable design value W' for a different set of conditions, the nominal design value is multiplied by adjustment factors:

$$W' = W(C_D C_M C_t C_{eg})$$

where C_D = load duration factor (Sec. 4.15)

C_M = wet service factor (Sec. 4.16)

C_t = temperature factor (Sec. 4.20)

C_{eg} = end grain factor

A discussion of adjustment factors for lag bolts in *shear* connections was given in Sec. 13.11. The majority of this material also applies to lag bolts in *withdrawal* connections.

However, the end grain factor is different for a withdrawal connection. The default condition for $C_{eg} = 1.0$ still applies to the base condition of a lag bolt installed into the *side grain* of the main member. But for a withdrawal connection into the *end grain* of the holding member, the end grain factor is $C_{eg} = 0.75$ instead of the 0.67 value used for shear connections. Connections into the end grain should be avoided where possible. Although the loading shown is not withdrawal, Fig. 13.18*a* and *b* illustrates lag bolts installed in the side grain and end grain.

The total allowable withdrawal load for a connection is the number of lag bolts N times the allowable load for one fastener:

$$\text{Allow. } P = N(W')$$

An example of a simple lag bolt withdrawal connection is given in Example 13.21.

EXAMPLE 13.21   Lag Bolt Withdrawal Connection

The load P is an equipment DL which is suspended from two Southern Pine supporting beams (Fig. 13.21). The load is centered between the two beams. Determine the allowable load based on the strength of the ½ in.-diameter × 6 in. lag bolts. Lumber is initially dry and is exposed to the weather in service. $C_t = 1.0$.

Nominal design value:

Length of lag bolt in main member $= L - t_s - t^*_{\text{washer}} = 6 - 1.5 - 0.125 = 4.375$ in.

---

*Washer must be sufficiently large to keep the bearing stress perpendicular to grain below the allowable ($f_{c\perp} \leq F'_{c\perp}$).

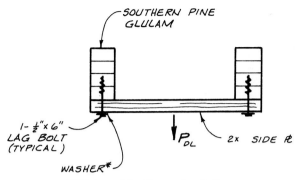

Figure 13.21   Withdrawal loading on lag bolts.

Thread length $= T = 3\frac{1}{2}$ in.   (NDS Appendix L)
All of the threads are inside the main member.
Effective penetration for withdrawal $p_w = T - E = 3\frac{3}{16}$ in.
Specific gravity for Southern Pine:

$$SG = 0.55$$

From NDS Table 9.2A

$$w = 437 \text{ lb/in.}$$

$$W = w(p_w) = 437(3\tfrac{3}{16}) = 1393 \text{ lb/lag bolt}$$

Allowable design load:

$$W' = W(C_D C_M C_t C_{eg})$$

$$= 1393(0.9 \times 0.75 \times 1.0 \times 1.0)$$

$$= 940 \text{ lb}$$

$$\text{Allow. } P = 2(940) = 1880 \text{ lb}$$

In addition to the direct withdrawal problem, there are occasions when lag bolts are subjected to combined lateral and withdrawal loading. See Fig. 13.22. The resultant load acts at an angle α to the surface of the main member. The practice for this type of loading is to determine an allowable resultant load capacity Z'_α which must equal or exceed the design load.

The first step in computing the allowable resultant load is to evaluate the nominal design value Z of the lag bolt for *shear* loading using the appropriate yield limit equations. For the next step, the nominal *withdrawal* design value W is computed using the tabulated value from NDS Table 9.2A and the effective thread length for withdrawal ($W = w \times p_w$). The necessary adjustment factors are then applied to the nominal values to obtain allow-

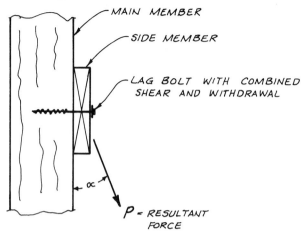

Figure 13.22 Lag bolt subjected to combined lateral and with-drawal loading.

able values Z' and W'. The interaction between these values is finally taken into account by the Hankinson formula, to give the allowable resultant:

$$Z'_\alpha = \frac{Z'W'}{Z' \sin^2 \alpha + W' \cos^2 \alpha}$$

13.14   Split Ring and Shear Plate Connectors

Split rings and shear plates are connectors that are installed into precut grooves in wood members. Connectors provide a large bearing surface to resist shearing-type forces in a wood connection. A bolt or lag bolt is required through the center of the split ring or shear plate to hold the assembly together. A sketch of the load transfer was shown in the introductory chapter on connections in Fig. 11.1d.

Split rings are only for wood-to-wood connections because the steel ring fits into a groove cut into the mating surfaces of the members being connected. See Fig. 13.23a. The steel ring is "split" to provide simultaneous bearing on the inner core and the outer surface of the groove.

Shear plates can be used for wood-to-metal connections because the shear plate is flush with the surface of the wood. Shear plates may also be used for wood-to-wood connections, but a shear plate is required in each wood member. Both wood-to-wood and wood-to-steel connections are shown in Fig. 13.23b. Shear plate wood-to-wood connections are easier to assemble or disassemble than split-ring connections and may be desirable where ease of erection is important.

EXAMPLE 13.22   Split Ring and Shear Plate Connectors

Split rings are for wood-to-wood connections only. Figure 13.23*a* is an unassembled joint showing the split ring installed in the center member and the precut groove in one of the side members ready for installation. Also shown are the bolt, washer, and nut required to hold the assembly together. In a three-member joint, a second split ring is required at the mating surface between the center member and the other side member.

Figure 13.23a Split ring connection. *(FPL.)*

Joint *A* at the top of Fig. 13.23*b* shows a wood-to-wood connection ready for assembly. A shear plate is required in each mating face of the wood members. Therefore, in the three-member joint illustrated, a total of four shear plates are required. Shear plates have the advantage of creating a surface that is flush with the surface of the wood member. Although more connectors are required, joints made with shear plates are easier to assemble than a similar split ring connection. Joint *B* is a three-member wood-to-steel connection. One shear plate is required at each interface between the wood and steel members.

Figure 13.23b Shear plate connections. *(FPL.)*

The allowable loads for split rings and shear plates are higher than those for bolts or lag bolts. However, split-ring and shear plate connectors require special fabrication equipment, and their use is limited by fabrication costs. These types of connectors may be used where relatively large loads must be transferred in a fairly limited amount of space, but they are much less common than simple bolted connections. Split ring and shear plate connectors are more widely used in glulam arches and heavy timber trusses than in shearwall-type buildings. See Example 13.23.

EXAMPLE 13.23   Typical Arch Connection Using Timber Connectors

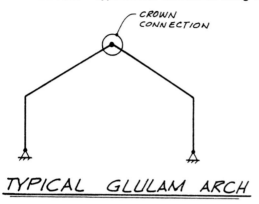

Figure 13.24a

Arch connections are shown in Fig. 13.24a and b to illustrate how shear plates can be used in the end grain of a member. Allowable loads for timber connectors are given in NDS Tables 10.2A and 10.2B. Similar tables are available in the TCM. Information on the design of arches can also be found in the TCM.

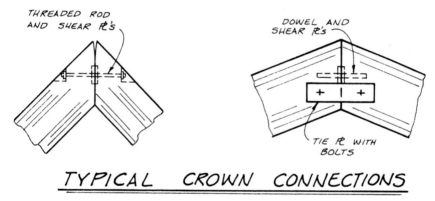

Figure 13.24b

For arches with steep slopes, two shear plates can be used with a threaded rod. Washers are counterbored into the arch.

For flat arches, two shear plates can be used on a dowel for vertical reactions. The tie plate keeps the arch from separating.

Split rings are available in 2½- and 4-in. diameters, and shear plates are available in 2⅝- and 4-in. diameters. Other pertinent dimensions are given in NDS Appendix K. For the design of split rings and shear plates, commercial lumber species are divided into four groups (A to D) in NDS Table

10A. Information on the species groupings for timber connectors in glulam members is available in the TCM (Ref. 3.1) and Ref. 3.2.

Design values for split rings and shear plates are not covered by the yield limit theory that is applied to nails, bolts, and lag bolts. Nominal design values for split rings are listed NDS Table 10.2A, and values for shear plates are found in NDS Table 10.2B. The basic connection for both split rings and shear plates is with the connector installed in the side grain of the wood member. Tabulated load values include *parallel-to-grain design value P* and *perpendicular-to-grain design value Q*. Adjustment factors are provided to convert tabulated values to allowable loads P' and Q'.

The Hankinson formula is used to obtain the load capacity N' at an angle of load to grain other than 0 or 90 degrees. Further adjustment are used for obtaining design values for connectors installed in the end grain of a member (as in the arch crown connection in Fig. 13.24b). Spacing requirements are important for split rings and shear plates, and design criteria are given in the NDS. A detailed review of this material is beyond the scope of this book. Additional information for obtaining allowable loads and connector spacings is available in Refs. 3.1 and 34.3.

A brief example will illustrate the use of the NDS tables for timber connectors. See Example 13.24. The connection involves the design of shear plates for the splice of a chord in a horizontal diaphragm.

EXAMPLE 13.24   Shear Plate Connection

Determine the number of 4-in.-diameter shear plates necessary to develop the chord splice in Fig. 13.25. The member is a 24F-V3 DF glulam that is dry and remains dry in service. Temperature range is normal. Assume that the metal splice plates and the glulams* are adequate.

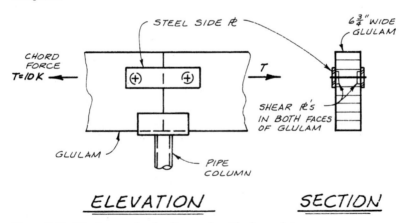

Figure 13.25 Diaphragm chord splice made with shear plates.

---

*For tension calculations, the net area of a wood member with shear plates must allow for the projected area of the connectors in addition to the projected area of the bolt hole. See NDS Appendix K.

Reference 3.2 indicates that the compression and inner core laminations of a 24F-V3 DF glulam are in timber connector group B (this agrees with NDS Table 10A for DF-L). From NDS Table 10.2B, the nominal design value for parallel-to-grain loading is

$$P = 4320 \text{ lb}$$

The following adjustment factors apply to this problem:

$C_D = 1.6$ wind or seismic force (verify local code acceptance before using)

$C_M = 1.0$ moisture content factor

$C_t = 1.0$ normal temperature range

$C_g = 1.0$ one shear plate in a row

$C_\Delta = 1.0$ spacings will exceed base dimensions

$C_{st} = 1.11$ steel side plate factor for parallel-to-grain loading in species group B (NDS Table 10.2.4)

Allowable design value for one shear plate:

$$P' = P(C_D C_M C_t C_g C_\Delta C_{st})$$

$$= 4320(1.6 \times 1.0 \times 1.0 \times 1.0 \times 1.0 \times 1.11)$$

$$= 7672 \text{ lb}$$

There is a shear plate in each face of the glulam (two connectors each side of splice).

$$\text{Allow. } T = 2(7670) = 15,300 \text{ lb} > 10,000 \text{ lb} \quad OK$$

> *Use* total of four 4-in.-diameter shear plates (two each side of splice).

13.15 Problems

Problems 13.1 through 13.9 involve work with a microcomputer spreadsheet. The first requirement is for a spreadsheet to operate correctly, (i.e., to compute correct values). Another major consideration is the format of input and output. A sufficient number of intermediate results should be displayed so that the computer solution can be conveniently verified by hand.

It will be necessary to test a number of different connection configurations to verify that the equation for each yield limit mode is programmed correctly. Save each spreadsheet as a template for use on other connection problems.

Many of the problems require the nominal design value Z and the allowable design value Z' as either final or intermediate answers. These values are to be identified as part of the general solution along with the information specifically requested.

Nominal design values may be obtained by solving the yield limit equations or by using the NDS tables. Tables are to be used only if they apply directly to the design conditions stated in the problem and are to be referenced in the solution. Yield limit equations may be evaluated by either calculator or computer.

All solutions are to be in accordance with the 1991 NDS. The designer should verify acceptance by local code authority before using $C_D = 1.6$ in practice. The loads given in a problem are to be applied directly. In practice, use of a load combination factor (Secs. 2.8 and 16.2) may be permitted. Check acceptance by local code authority before using the *load combination factor* together with the *load duration factor C_D*.

In all problems, normal temperatures are assumed, and $C_t = 1.0$. Except for the load duration factor C_D, all adjustment factors are to be referenced to the appropriate NDS table or section so that the source of the values may be verified.

13.1   Use a microcomputer spreadsheet to solve the yield limit equations for a bolt in a single-shear wood-to-wood connection. Input the following:

Diameter of bolt D (in.)

Bending yield strength of bolt F_{yb} (ksi)

Thickness of main member t_m (in.)

Specific gravity of main member SG_m

Angle of load to grain for main member θ_m (degrees)

Thickness of side member t_s (in.)

Specific gravity of side member SG_s

Angle of load to grain for side member θ_s (degrees)

The spreadsheet is to do the following:

a. Compute the dowel bearing strengths parallel ($F_{e\parallel}$), perpendicular ($F_{e\perp}$), and at angle θ ($F_{e\theta}$) to the grain for both the main and side members.

b. Evaluate the coefficients for use in the yield limit equations: R_e, R_t, θ, K_θ, k_1, k_2, and k_3. Other intermediate answers may be provided to aid in checking.

c. Solve the six yield limit equations, and select the smallest value as the *nominal design value Z*.

13.2   Expand or modify the template from Prob. 13.1 to handle a bolt in a single-shear connection with a steel side plate (wood-to-metal connection). Input remains the same, except SG_s and θ_s are not required, and the ultimate tensile strength of the metal side plate F_u is an input.

13.3   Expand or modify the template from Prob. 13.1 to handle a single-shear connection with an anchor bolt (wood-to-concrete connection). Input remains the same, except there is no input for the side member.

NOTE: If desired, this spreadsheet may be expanded to include a database or table of nominal design values for the capacity of the anchor bolt in the concrete (UBC Chap. 26) and/or masonry (UBC Chap. 24).

13.4 Expand the spreadsheet template in Prob. 13.1, 13.2, or 13.3 (as assigned) to convert the *nominal design value Z* to an *allowable design value Z'*. Input must be expanded to include the appropriate adjustment factors. Include, as a minimum, adjustments for

a. Load duration factor C_D
b. Wet service factor C_M
c. Group action factor C_g
d. Geometry factor C_Δ

NOTE: C_D and C_M may be input by the user, but C_g and C_Δ should be generated by the spreadsheet with a minimum of input. Necessary input is to be determined as part of the problem. Macros may be used if desired but are not required.

13.5 Use a microcomputer spreadsheet to solve the yield limit equations for a double-shear wood-to-wood connection, using the following variables for input:

Bolt diameter D (in.)
Bending yield strength of bolt F_{yb} (ksi)
Thickness of main member t_m (in.)
Specific gravity of main member SG_m
Angle of load to grain for main member θ_m (degrees)
Thickness of side member t_s (in.)
Specific gravity of side member SG_s
Angle of load to grain for side member θ_s (degrees)

The spreadsheet is to do the following:

a. Compute the dowel bearing strengths parallel $(F_{e\parallel})$, perpendicular $(F_{e\perp})$, and at angle θ $(F_{e\theta})$ to the grain for both the main and side members.
b. Evaluate the coefficients for use in the yield limit equations: R_e, R_t, θ, K_θ, and k_3. Other intermediate answers may be provided to aid in checking.
c. Solve the four yield limit equations, and select the smallest value as the *nominal design value Z*.

13.6 Expand or modify the template from Prob. 13.5 to handle a bolt in a double-shear connection with steel side plates (wood-to-metal connection). Input remains the same, except SG_s and θ_s are not required, and the ultimate tensile strength of the metal side plate F_u is an input.

13.7 Expand the spreadsheet template in Prob. 13.5 or 13.6 (as assigned) to convert the *nominal design value Z* to an *allowable design value Z'*. Input is to be expanded to include the appropriate adjustment factors. Include as a minimum:

Load duration factor C_D
Wet service factor C_M
Group action factor C_g
Geometry factor C_Δ

NOTE: C_D and C_M may be input by the user, but C_g and C_Δ should be generated by the spreadsheet with a minimum of input. Necessary input is to be determined as part of the problem. Macros may be used if desired but are not required.

13.8   Use a microcomputer spreadsheet to set up the solution of the yield equations for a single-shear lag bolt connection. Consider both *wood-to-wood* and *wood-to-steel* connections, using the following variables for input:

> Diameter of lag bolt D (in.)
> Length of lag bolt L (in.)
> Bending yield strength of lag bolt F_{yb} (ksi)
> Specific gravity of main member SG_m
> Angle of load to grain for main member θ_m (degrees)
> Thickness of side member t_s (in.)
> Specific gravity of side member SG_s
> Angle of load to grain for side member θ_s (degrees)

The spreadsheet is to do the following:
a. Compute the dowel bearing strengths parallel $(F_{e\parallel})$, perpendicular $(F_{e\perp})$, and at angle θ $(F_{e\theta})$ to the grain for both the main and side members.
b. Evaluate the coefficients for use in the yield limit equations: R_e, θ, K_θ, and k. Other intermediate answers may be provided to aid in checking.
c. Solve the three yield limit equations for a *wood-to-wood* connection or the two yield limit equations for a *wood-to-steel* connection. Select the smallest value as the *nominal design value Z*.

13.9   Expand the spreadsheet template in Prob. 13.8 to convert the *nominal design value Z* to an *allowable design value Z'*. Input must be expanded to include the appropriate adjustment factors. Include as a minimum:

> Load duration factor C_D
> Wet service factor C_M
> Group action factor C_g
> Geometry factor C_Δ
> Penetration depth factor C_d
> End grain factor C_{eg}

NOTE: C_D, C_M, and C_{eg} may be input by the user, but C_g, C_Δ, and C_d should be generated by the spreadsheet with a minimum of input. Necessary input is to be determined as part of the problem. Macros may be used if desired but are not required.

13.10   The connection in Fig. 13.A uses a single row of five ¾-in.-diameter bolts. Lumber is No. 1 Hem-Fir. The load is the result of (DL + wind). $C_M = 1.0$.

> *Find:*   *a.* Allowable load on the bolt connection.
> *b.* Allowable tension in the wood members.
> *c.* Indicate the base spacing requirements for the bolts.

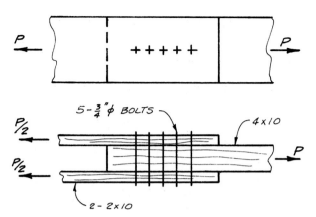

Figure 13.A

13.11 A connection similar to the connection in Fig. 13.A has a single row of *six* (instead of five) ¾-in.-diameter bolts. Lumber is No. 1 DF-L. Load is the result of (DL + snow). $C_M = 1.0$.

> *Find:* *a.* Allowable load on the bolt connection.
> *b.* Allowable tension in the wood members.
> *c.* Indicate the base spacing requirements for the bolts.

13.12 Repeat Prob. 13.10 except that the lumber is green at the time of fabrication and it later seasons in service.

13.13 Repeat Prob. 13.11 except that the lumber is green at the time of fabrication and it later seasons in service.

13.14 Repeat Prob. 13.10 except that the connection is exposed to the weather.

13.15 Repeat Prob. 13.11 except that the connection is exposed to the weather.

13.16 The connection in Fig. 13.B uses side plates of A36 steel and four 1-in. bolts on each side of the splice. Lumber is No. 1 DF-L. The force is seismic.

> *Find:* Allowable load on the bolts if:
> *a.* $C_M = 1.0$.
> *b.* Green lumber is used that later seasons in service.
> *c.* Connection is exposed to the weather.
> *d.* Lumber is above the FSP in service.

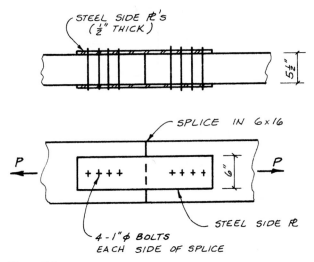

STEEL SIDE ℞'S
(½" THICK)

5½"

SPLICE   IN   6 × 16

P →

← P

6"

+ + + +   + + + +

STEEL SIDE ℞

4 - 1"φ BOLTS
EACH SIDE OF SPLICE

Figure 13.B

13.17 The beam in Fig. 13.C is suspended from a pair of angles (2 L 4 × 3 × ⁵⁄₁₆ of A36 steel). The load is (DL + FLL). Lumber is Select Structural Spruce-Pine-Fir (S) that is initially dry and remains dry in service. Assume that the angles are adequate.

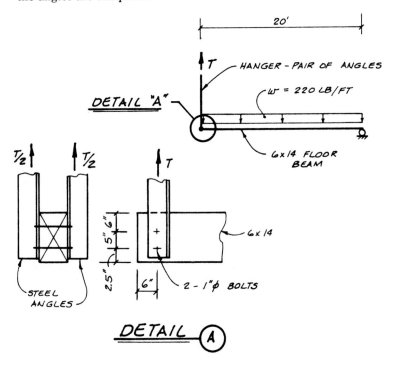

20'

T

HANGER - PAIR OF ANGLES

w = 220 LB/FT

DETAIL "A"

6 × 14 FLOOR
BEAM

T/₂   T/₂

T

6 × 14

5" 6"

2.5"

6"

2 - 1"φ BOLTS

STEEL
ANGLES

DETAIL Ⓐ

Figure 13.C

Find: a. Determine if the bolts are adequate.
b. Check the shear stress in the beam at the connection.
c. Are the base spacing requirements satisfied?

13.18 Repeat Prob. 13.17 except the hanger is not vertical. It forms an angle of 60 degrees to the horizontal upward to the right.

13.19 Repeat Prob. 13.17 except that the lumber is initially at the FSP and it seasons in service.

13.20 The connection in Fig. 13.D uses two rows of $7/8$-in.-diameter bolts with three fasteners in each row. The load carried by the connection is (DL + FLL). The wood member is a $63/4 \times 16.5$ DF glulam with SG = 0.50. It is initially dry (at or near the EMC) and remains dry in service.

Find: a. Allowable connection load based on the capacity of the bolts. Show the base dimension spacing requirements on a sketch of the connection.
b. Check the stresses in the main member and side plates for the load in (a). Assume A36 steel plate (Ref. 11.1) which has an allowable tensile stress on the gross area of 22 ksi ($0.6F_y$) and an allowable tensile stress on the net area of 29 ksi ($0.5F_u$).

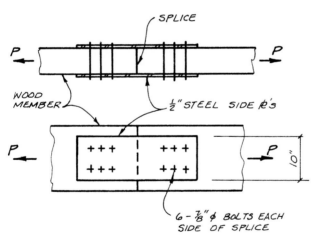

Figure 13.D

13.21 The connection in Fig. 13.D uses two rows of $7/8$-in.-diameter bolts with *five* (instead of three) fasteners in each row. Load carried by the connection is (DL + snow). The wood member is a 6×14 Select Structural DF-L that is initially wet, and it later seasons in place.

Find: a. Allowable load on the connection, based on the strength of the bolts.
b. Allowable load on the connection if separate side plates are used for the two rows of bolts. Show the base dimension spacing requirements for the bolts in the connection.

c. Check the stresses in the main member and side plates for the load in (*b*). Assume A36 steel plate (Ref. 11.1) which has an allowable tensile stress on the gross area of 22 ksi ($0.6F_y$) and an allowable tensile stress on the net area of 29 ksi ($0.5F_u$).

13.22   The connection in Fig. 13.E uses ¾-in.-diameter bolts in single shear. Lumber is DF-L that is initially dry (near the EMC) and it remains dry in service. The load is caused by (DL + FLL). Assume that the members are adequate.

Find: *a.* The allowable load on the connection, based on the strength of the bolts.

b. Show the spacing requirements for the bolts on a sketch of the connection.

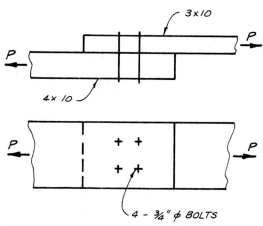

Figure 13.E

13.23   The connection in Fig. 13.F uses 1-in.-diameter bolts and serves as a tie for lateral wind forces. Lumber is DF-L that is initially dry (near the EMC) and it remains dry in service. Assume that the members are adequate.

Find: *a.* Allowable load on the connection is based on the strength of the bolts.

b. Show the base dimension spacing requirements for the bolts on a sketch of the connection.

c. If initially green lumber is used, what will be the effect on the allowable load?

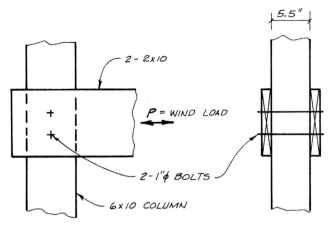

Figure 13.F

13.24 The connection in Fig. 13.G uses one 1-in.-diameter bolt that carries a lateral wind force. Lumber is Southern Pine that is dry ($C_M = 1.0$). Assume that the members are adequate.

Find: Allowable load on the connection.

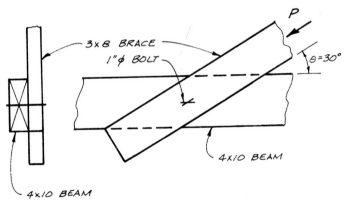

Figure 13.G

13.25 The building in Fig. 13.H uses 2×6 wall framing of No. 1 Hem-Fir. The double top wall plate serves as the horizontal diaphragm chord and drag strut. The top plate is fabricated from 20-ft-long lumber, and splices occur at 10-ft intervals. Design lateral forces are given. $C_M = 1.0$.

Find: Design and detail the connection splice in the top plate of wall 1, using ¾-in.-diameter bolts.

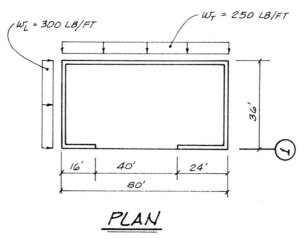

Figure 13.H

13.26   Repeat Prob. 13.25 except that the lumber is No. 1 DF-L and the bolts are ⅞ in. in diameter.

13.27   *Given:*   The shearwall and anchorage detail in Fig. 13.I. The gravity loads and the lateral wind force are shown in the sketch. The chords in the shearwall are 4 × 4 members of No. 2 DF-South. Assume the bracket is adequate. $C_M = 1.0$.

   Find: a. Number of ¾-in.-diameter bolts necessary to anchor the chord to the hold-down bracket. Assume an area of 2.5 in.² for the bracket. Sketch the base dimension spacing requirements for the bolts.
   b. Check the tension capacity of the chord at the critical section (bolts are in a single row).
   c. Determine the required size of anchor bolt to tie the bracket to the foundation. Use UBC Table 26-E.

13.28   *Given:*   The wood shearwall in Fig. 13.I. Lumber is DF-L, and $C_M = 1.0$.

   Find: a. The required number of ¾-in.-diameter anchor bolts necessary to transfer the 4-k lateral force from the 2× bottom plate to the 2000-psi concrete foundation. These bolts are in addition to the anchor bolt shown in the sketch for the uplift anchor bracket. See Sec. 10.10 for design considerations for the anchor bolts for this problem.
   b. For the anchor bolts found in part a, determine the total allowable foundation reaction (Fig. 10.12) perpendicular to the wall for short-term (wind or seismic) forces.

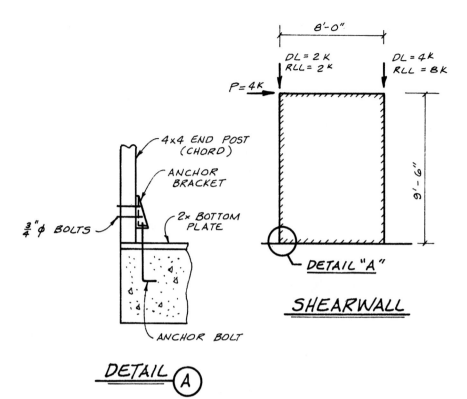

4x4 END POST
(CHORD)

ANCHOR
BRACKET

2× BOTTOM
PLATE

$\frac{3}{4}"\ \phi$ BOLTS

ANCHOR BOLT

DETAIL (A)

8'-0"

DL = 2 K
RLL = 2 K

DL = 4 K
RLL = 8 K

P = 4K

9'-6"

DETAIL "A"

SHEARWALL

Figure 13.I

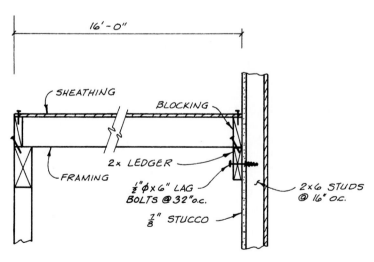

16'-0"

SHEATHING

BLOCKING

2× LEDGER

$\frac{1}{2}"\ \phi \times 6"$ LAG
BOLTS @ 32" o.c.

FRAMING

$\frac{7}{8}"$ STUCCO

2×6 STUDS
@ 16" o.c.

SECTION - PATIO ROOF

Figure 13.J

13.29 The connection of the ledger to the stud wall in Fig. 13.J uses ½-in.-diameter × 6-in. lag bolts. Patio DL = 6 psf, and roof LL = 10 psf (UBC Appendix Chap. 49). Lumber is DF-L.

> *Find:* *a.* Determine if the connection is adequate to carry the design loads if the lumber is initially dry and remains dry in service.
>
>   *b.* Is the connection adequate if the lumber is exposed to the weather?

13.30 Repeat Prob. 13.29 except that the roof LL is 20 psf.

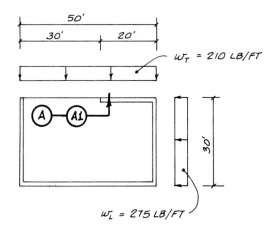

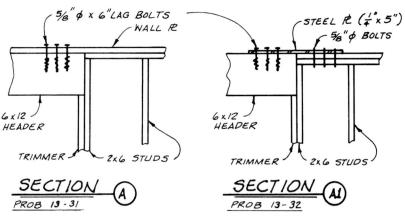

Figure 13.K

13.31 The building in Fig. 13.K uses the connection shown in section *A* to transfer the lateral force (chord force and strut force) from the wall plate to the header. Lumber is No. 1 DF-L, and $C_M = 1.0$.

Find: Determine the required number of ⅝-in.-diameter × 6-in. lag bolts for the connection.

13.32   Repeat Prob. 13.31 except that the lateral force transfer is made with the connection shown in section *A*1. In addition to the number of lag bolts, determine the required number of ⅝-in.-diameter machine bolts (A307) necessary to connect the steel splice plate to the double 2× top plate.

14

Connection
Hardware

14.1 Introduction

Chapters 12 and 13 covered the basic fasteners that are used in the construction of wood buildings. In addition to these fasteners, most wood connections involve some type of metal connection hardware. This hardware may be a simple tension strap, but considerably more complicated devices are often used.

This chapter introduces some typical connection hardware details. A critique of the connection accompanies a number of the details, and particular attention is given to the effects of cross-grain shrinkage. These principles should be given special attention if it is necessary to design, detail, and fabricate special connection hardware. An example of several connection hardware calculations is given after the general review.

In a number of cases, prefabricated connection hardware may be available for common connections. In any event, the basic principles of connection design should be understood by the designer. The chapter concludes with a review of some typical prefabricated connection hardware.

14.2 Connection Details

The hardware used in a connection must itself be capable of supporting the design loads, and the structural steel design principles of Ref. 11.1 should be used to determine the required plate thickness and weld sizes. Some of these principles are demonstrated in examples, but a comprehensive review of steel design is beyond the scope of this book.

Some suggested details for common wood connections are included in Refs. 3.1 and 3.4, with an emphasis on avoiding cross-grain cracking caused by changes in moisture content. These details are aimed at minimizing restraint in connections that will cause splitting. Where restraint does occur, the distance across the grain between the restraining elements should be kept small so that the total shrinkage between these points is minimized. Where possible, the connections should be designed to accommodate the shrinkage (and swelling) of the wood without initiating built-in stresses.

The majority of the details in this section are taken or adapted from Ref. 3.4 by permission of AITC. The sketches serve as an introduction to the types of connections that are commonly used in wood construction. See Example 14.1. Both good and poor connection design practices are illustrated. The details were developed specifically for glulam construction, where members and loads are often large. The principles are valid for both glulam and sawn lumber of any size, but the importance of these factors increases with increasing member size.

The connection details in Example 14.1 are not to scale and are to be used as a guide only. Actual designs will require complete drawings with dimensions of the connection and hardware. The designs must take into consideration the spacing requirements for bolts (Examples 13.10 and 13.11 in Sec. 13.5) or the other types of fasteners. Examples of the following connections are included in Example 14.1:

1. Typical beam-to-column connections
2. Beam-to-girder saddle connection
3. Beam face hanger connection
4. Beam face clip connection
5. Cantilever beam hinge connection
6. Beam connection for uplift
7. Beam connection to continuous column
8. Beam with notch in tension side
9. Beam with end notch
10. Inclined beam—lower support detail
11. Inclined beam—upper support detail
12. Suspending multiple loads from beam
13. Suspending isolated loads from beam
14. Truss heel connection
15. Additional truss joint considerations
16. Moisture protection at column base

References 3.1 and 3.4 cover a number of connections in addition to these. However, the details given here illustrate the basic principles involved in proper connection design. A numerical example is provided in the following section for the design of a beam-to-column connection. This is followed by some additional considerations for beam hinge connections.

EXAMPLE 14.1   Connection Details*

Beam-to-Column Connections

If compression perpendicular to grain $F_{c\perp}$ at the beam reaction is satisfactory, the beam may be supported directly on a column. A T bracket can be used to tie the various members together (Fig. 14.1a).

The bottom face of the beam bears on the column. If cross-grain shrinkage occurs in length a, cracking or damage to the bracket will result. The problem can be minimized by keeping a small.

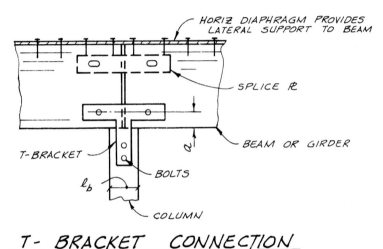

Figure 14.1a   Beam-to-column connection with T bracket.

For larger loads the T bracket will be replaced with a U bracket (Fig. 14.1b). The U bracket can provide a bearing length l_b which is greater than the width of the column. The spacing requirements for the fasteners must also be considered in determining the length of the bracket.

If a separate splice plate is used near the top of the beam (Fig. 14.1a), the effects of the end rotation and beam separation should be considered. Bolts in tightly fitting holes can restrict the movement of the end of the beam, and splitting may be induced. Slotted holes can reduce this problem. If the beam carries an axial drag or chord force, the T bracket or U bracket can be designed to transmit the lateral force.

U brackets (Fig. 14.1b) may be fabricated from bent plates when the bracket does not cantilever a long distance beyond the width of the column. For longer U brackets, the vertical plates will probably be welded to a thicker base plate. Calculations for a U-bracket connection are given in Sec. 14.3.

---

*Adapted from Ref. 3.4, courtesy of AITC.

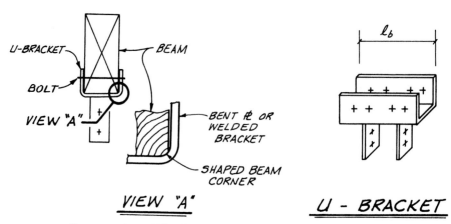

Figure 14.1b Beam-to-column U bracket hardware.

In U brackets and similar connection hardware, it is important that the wood member be fully seated on the bearing surface *before* the bolts are installed. This may require that the bottom edges of the beam be shaped to conform to the inside of the bracket. Without such precautions the squared corners of the beam could initially rest on the inside radius of a bent plate (or on a weld), and the member may not fully seat until it is loaded heavily in service. In this case the bolt capacity perpendicular to the grain may become overstressed as the member moves downward, and a split in the beam may develop.

Beam Saddle Connection

Beam saddle connections are the preferred means of transferring beam reactions to girders (Fig. 14.2a). The beam reaction is transferred by bearing perpendicular to the grain on the *bottom* of the hanger. The load on the hanger is then transferred by bearing perpendicular to the grain through the *top* of the saddle to the girder. This type of connection is recommended for larger loads.

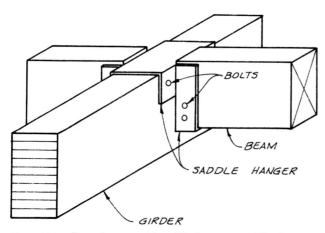

Figure 14.2a Beam hanger with saddle feature providing bearing on the *bottom* of beam and on the *top* of girder.

The tops of beams are shown higher than the girder to allow for shrinkage in beams without affecting roof sheathing or flooring. The idea is to have the tops of beams and girders at the same level after shrinkage occurs. For shrinkage calculations see Example 4.3 (Sec. 4.7).

Note in Fig. 14.2a that the bolts are located *near* the bearing points to minimize cross-grain effects. Figure 14.2b illustrates the possible effects of cross-grain shrinkage if the bolts are located *improperly*. The bolt in the beam is located some distance away from the initial point of bearing (section 1). After the beam is in service for some time, it loses moisture and shrinks across the grain. The bolt is held rigidly in position by the hanger bracket. Under a relatively small applied load, the bolt capacity may be large enough to support the beam reaction, and the bottom face of the member may shrink *up* from its intended bearing point (section 2).

However, when the member finally becomes heavily loaded, the bearing capacity of the bolt perpendicular to the grain may be exceeded, and a split at the end of the member will develop as the beam seats again on the hanger (section 3). The end split not only reduces the capacity of the member, but it also renders the bolt ineffective in resisting lateral (wind or seismic) forces that may create an axial force in the beam. Improperly located bolts as shown in Fig. 14.2b should be *avoided*.

Although the bolts should be located near the bearing face of the member, care should be taken to avoid boring holes in the high-quality outer lamination in bending glulams. This is especially important when bolts occur in the tension zone of the member.

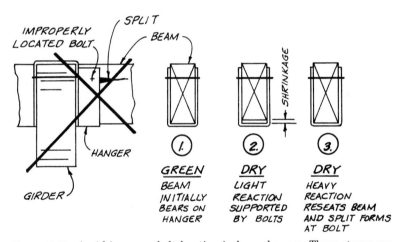

Figure 14.2b *Avoid* improper bolt location in beam hanger. Three stages are identified that lead to the formation of a split. Proper detailing will avoid split by placing bolt in beam closer to its bearing surface.

Beam Face Hanger Connection

When the reaction of the beam or purlin is relatively small, the hanger can be bolted to the face of the girder (Fig. 14.3). The bolts in the main supporting beam or girder should be placed in the upper half of the member, but not too close to the top of the beam where extreme fiber-bending stresses are maximized. This is especially important in the tension zone which occurs on the top side of cantilever girders.

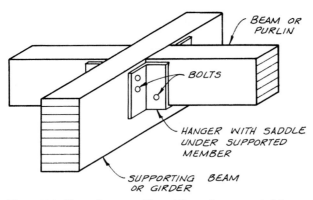

Figure 14.3 Beam hanger with saddle under supported beam.
Beam reaction is transferred to girder through fasteners instead
of bearing as in Fig. 14.2a.

Beam Face Clip Connection

Face connections without the saddle feature shown in Fig. 14.3 may be used for light
loads (Fig. 14.4a). However, construction is more difficult than with the saddle because
the beams must be held in place while the bolts are installed. The connection at the end
of the supported beam must be checked for shear in accordance with the procedures
outlined in Sec. 13.7.

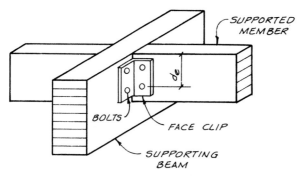

Figure 14.4a Face clip connection is limited to light loads.
Beam reaction is transferred through fasteners in both members.

Face clips should be limited to connections with light loads. Larger loads will require
a long row of bolts perpendicular to the grain through steel side plates. Glulam timbers,
although relatively dry at the time of manufacture, may shrink as the EMC is reached
in service. The problems associated with cross-grain tension should be avoided by not
using the type of connection in Fig. 14.4b.

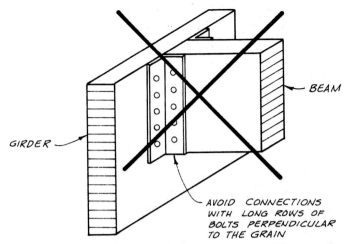

Figure 14.4b *Avoid* long rows of bolts perpendicular to grain through steel side plates. Changes in moisture content will result in cross grain volume changes, and cross grain tension and splitting may occur. The saddle connection in Fig. 14.2a is the preferred method of transferring heavy loads.

Cantilever Beam Hinge Connection

PROBLEM

For vertical loads the *suspended* beam in Fig. 14.5a bears on the *bottom* of the hinge connector, and the hinge connector in turn bears on the *top* of the *supporting* (cantilever) member. Cantilever systems may be subjected to lateral forces as well as gravity bending loads. Some designers have used a tension connector with bolts lined up in both members near the bottom of the beam. The problem with this arrangement is that as the wood shrinks, the supporting member will permit the saddle to move downward. The bolts in the cantilever, however, will restrain this movement, and a split may occur. The revised detail (Fig. 14.5b) avoids this problem.

SUGGESTED REVISION

The connection in Fig. 14.5b does not interfere with possible shrinkage in the members and cracking is avoided. It also allows a slight rotation in the joint. A positive tension tie for lateral forces can be provided with a separate tension strap at the middepth of the joint. This tension strap may also be an integral part of the hanger if the holes in the tension tie are slotted vertically in deep members. Also see Sec. 14.4.

Beam Connection for Uplift

In this example, gravity loads are transferred by bearing perpendicular to grain. Adequate fastenings must also be provided to carry horizontal and uplift forces. See Fig. 14.6. These loads are usually of a transient nature and are of short duration. The fastener is usually placed toward the lower edge of the member. The distance d_e must be no less than the required perpendicular-to-grain edge distance for the type of fastener used. It must also

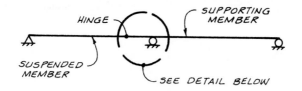

TYP CANTILEVER BEAM SYSTEM

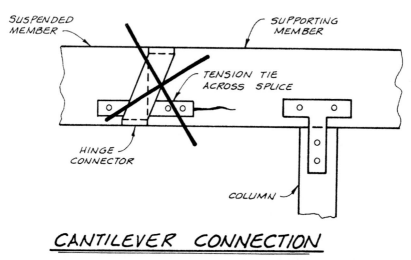

CANTILEVER CONNECTION

Figure 14.5a *Avoid* cantilever beam hinge connections with improperly located tension tie which causes cracking as cross-grain shrinkage occurs.

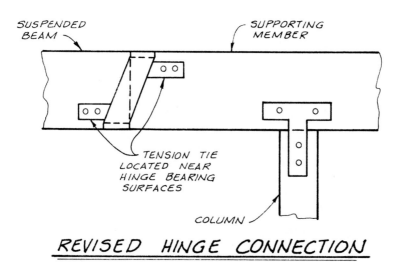

REVISED HINGE CONNECTION

Figure 14.5b *Revised* cantilever beam hinge connection with tension ties properly located near top and bottom bearing surfaces.

be large enough so that the shear stresses caused by uplift (calculated in accordance with the methods of Sec. 13.7) are not excessive. The end distance *e* must also be adequate for the type of fastener used.

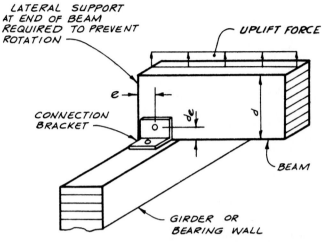

Figure 14.6 Gravity loads are transferred by bearing. Connection hardware may be necessary for uplift and lateral forces. Proper detailing considers fastener spacing requirements.

Beam Connection to Continuous Column

PROBLEM

Connections of the type shown in Fig. 14.7*a* should not be used on large beams or girders because tension perpendicular to the grain and horizontal shear at the lower fastener tend to cause splitting of the member.

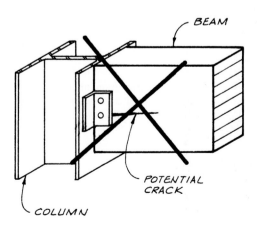

Figure 14.7a *Avoid* transferring large reactions at the end of a beam with fasteners.

SUGGESTED REVISION

When the design is such that the bending member does not rest on the top of a column, wall, or pilaster, but frames into another member, several methods can be used to support the ends. The preferred method is to transfer the end reaction by bearing perpendicular to grain. See Fig. 14.7*b*.

1. Vertical beam reaction is transferred by bearing perpendicular to grain on the beam seat angle.
2. Positive connection is made between the beam and the column with fasteners in the tie clip.
3. Clip angle at top provides lateral stability to beam, but it is not attached to the top of the beam with fasteners. In other words, the clip angle prevents rotation perpendicular to the plane of the beam, and it thereby braces the member against lateral torsional buckling. However, because there is no fastener in the beam at the top, rotation in the plane of the beam is accommodated as the member is loaded in bending. This provides a stable member that will not split the end.

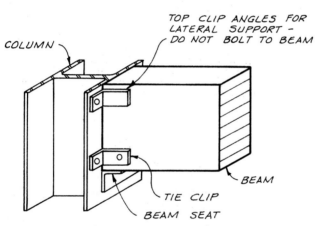

Figure 14.7b *Revised* connection transfers beam reaction by bearing on the bottom of the member.

Beam with Notch in Tension Side

PROBLEM

The detail in Fig. 14.8 is critical in cantilever framing (negative moment at support). The top *tension* fibers have been cut to provide space for recessed connection hardware or for the passage of conduit or other elements over the top of the beam. This is particularly serious in glulam construction because the tension laminations are critical in the performance of the structure.

SUGGESTED REVISION

Notches in the tension zone are serious stress raisers and should be avoided. Revise the detail in Fig. 14.8 so that the cut in the beam is eliminated. Also see Sec. 6.2.

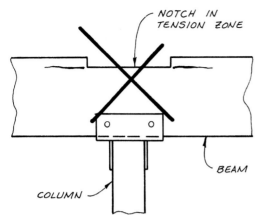

Figure 14.8 *Avoid* notching the tension side of a wood member.

Beam with End Notch

PROBLEM

An abrupt notch in the end of a wood member creates two problems (Fig. 14.9a). One is that the effective shear strength of the member is reduced because of the smaller depth d_n and stress concentration. In addition, the exposure of end grain in the notch will permit a more rapid migration of moisture in the lower portion of the member, and a split may develop.

For horizontal shear calculations at notched end of a beam, see Sec. 6.5.

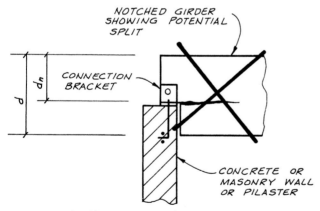

Figure 14.9a *Avoid* square cut notches.

SUGGESTED REVISION

Where the height of the top of a beam is limited, the beam seat should be lowered to a pilaster or specially designed seat in the wall (Fig. 14.9b).

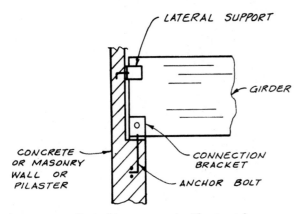

Figure 14.9b *Revised* beam support without notch.

Lateral support connection at top of girder is required for stability. There is no fastener between wood member and lateral support hardware. Therefore, the lateral support connection prevents rotation perpendicular to the plane of the girder, but it allows rotation of the end of the member for in-plane loading.

Inclined Beam—Lower Support Details

PROBLEM

The condition in Fig. 14.10*a* is similar to the problem in Fig. 14.9*a*, but it may not be as evident. The shear strength of the end of the member is reduced, and the exposed end grain may result in splitting.

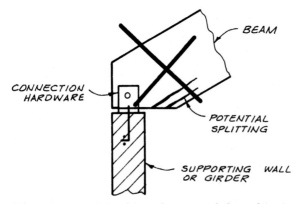

Figure 14.10a *Avoid* end cuts that exposed the end grain on the *tension* side of a beam.

SUGGESTED REVISION

Where the end of the beam must be flush with outer wall, the beam seat should be lowered so that the tapered cut is loaded in bearing (Fig. 14.10*b*).

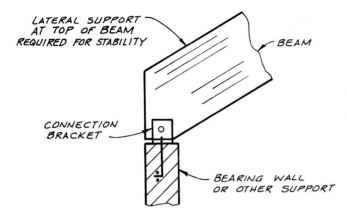

Figure 14.10b *Revised* taper cut is detailed so that the end grain is stressed in compression.

Inclined Beam—Upper Support Details

PROBLEM

The bird's mouth cut in Fig. 14.11a is commonly used in rafters to obtain a horizontal bearing surface. In major, heavily loaded beams, large cuts of this nature substantially reduce the effective depth of the member at the notch and should be avoided. Stress concentrations also cause high shear stress at the notch and may cause splitting.

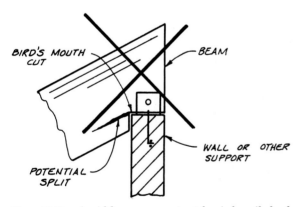

Figure 14.11a *Avoid* deep square cut notches in heavily load members.

SUGGESTED REVISION

A welded bracket with a sloping seat can be used to avoid notching the member (Fig. 14.11b). The bracket must be properly designed to support the beam reaction. Eccentricity in the connection should be avoided.

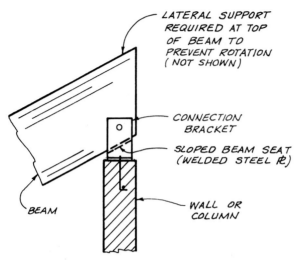

Figure 14.11b *Revised* beam support without end notch.

Suspending Multiple Loads from Beam

PROBLEM

Suspending multiple loads below the neutral axis (NA) of a wood member is not recommended (Fig. 14.12a). Tension stresses perpendicular to the grain tend to concentrate at the fastenings. Wood is weak in cross-grain tension, and tension perpendicular to grain can interact with horizontal shear to cause splitting. Hanger loads may be mechanical or electric equipment suspended below the beam, or they may be reactions from joists, purlins, or other members framing into the side of the beam.

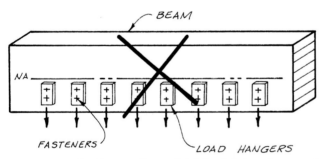

Figure 14.12a *Avoid* suspending multiple loads below the neutral axis.

SUGGESTED REVISION 1

It is better design practice to locate the fasteners above the neutral axis, as shown in Fig. 14.12b. Where possible, the loads should be transferred by bearing (Fig. 14.12c).

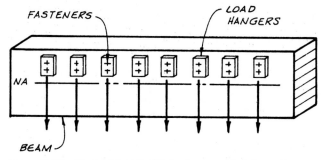

Figure 14.12b *Revised* detail with loads suspended above the neutral axis.

SUGGESTED REVISION 2

The preferred method is to suspend loads from the top of a beam or girder, as in Fig. 14.12c. This approach transfers the loads by bearing on the top of the beam. It avoids tension perpendicular to grain and stress concentrations from large loads being transferred by fasteners. Transferring loads by compression perpendicular to grain is generally the preferred method of load transfer in all cases, but it becomes increasingly important as the magnitude of the load increases.

Note that this method was recommended previously for the transfer of beam reactions to a girder in Fig. 14.2a. The saddle transfers the load by bearing rather than by fasteners.

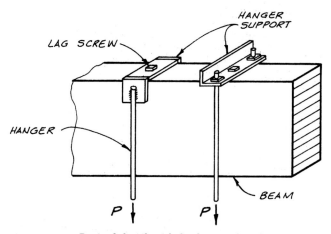

Figure 14.12c *Revised* detail with loads transferred by bearing (compression perpendicular to grain).

Suspending Isolated Loads from Beam

The connections shown in Fig. 14.13 are for isolated loads. Recommendations for suspending isolated loads are similar to those for multiple loads.

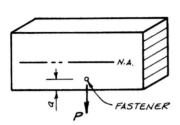 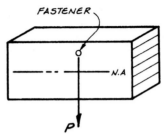

Figure 14.13 Isolated loads suspended from a beam.

An isolated light load may be suspended below the neutral axis of a beam. However, the load should be limited to one that can be transferred with small fasteners (e.g., small conduit loads). The distance a must equal or exceed the required edge distance, and Ref. 3.4 recommends a minimum of 6 in. Shear stresses in the member must be checked according to Sec. 13.7.

It is good practice to locate fasteners above the neutral axis. Even better practice is to detail the connection as shown in Fig. 14.12c.

Truss Heel Connection

PROBLEM

The truss heel connection in Fig. 14.14a has structural steel gusset plates with bolts or shear plates for fasteners. There are two problems with this detail. First, the connection involves an eccentricity because the forces at the joint do not intersect at a common point. Second, the steel gusset plates hold the fasteners rigidly in position, and this can cause the wood truss members to split as the joint attempts to rotate when the truss is loaded.

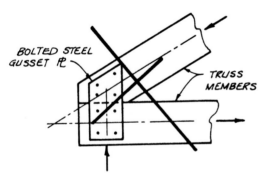

Figure 14.14a *Avoid* eccentric forces and rigid truss connections.

SUGGESTED REVISION

A truss connection is shown in Fig. 14.14b in which the force in the top chord is taken by bearing. This connection has the advantage of concentric forces. The single fastener in the top chord member and the clearance provided between the chord members allow free joint rotation as the truss is loaded. Cross-grain shrinkage in the bottom chord of the truss can be eliminated by the proper placement of bolts in vertically slotted holes.

See the TCM (Ref. 3.1) for a numerical example of a truss design.

NOTE: For the design of light-frame wood trusses using light-gage metal plates, see Ref. 23.1.

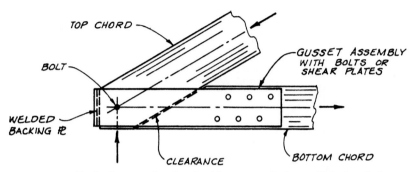

Figure 14.14b *Revised* connection detail with concentric forces. This detail also accommodates rotation between truss members.

Additional Truss Joint Considerations

PROBLEM

When the centerlines of members (and correspondingly the axial forces in the truss) do not intersect at a common point, considerable shear and moment may result in the bottom chord (Fig. 14.15a). When these stresses are combined with a high tension stress in the member, failure may occur.

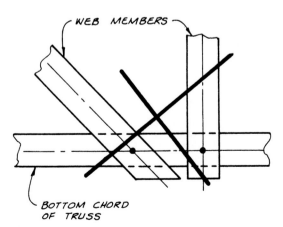

Figure 14.15a *Avoid* truss connections with eccentric forces.

PROBLEM

The welded steel gusset plate in Fig. 14.15*b* has a rigidity problem similar to the solid gusset plate in Fig. 14.14*a*. The welded plates are rigidly held in position, and splitting of the wood members may occur as the truss attempts to deform under load.

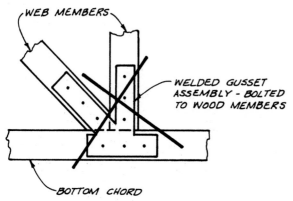

Figure 14.15b *Avoid* rigid truss connections which do not allow rotation between truss members. Prying and splitting may occur.

SUGGESTED REVISION

For trusses with single-piece members, the chords and web members should be in the same plane, and separate straps or gusset plates should be used for the connection. See Fig. 14.15c. The separate gusset plates should accommodate truss deflection and joint rotation without splitting of the wood members.

Steel gusset plates must be properly designed for the applied tension or compression forces. Shims should be provided between the steel plates and the wood members where necessary to maintain gusset plate alignment. For example, shims should be used between the vertical gusset plate and the vertical wood member to account for the thickness of

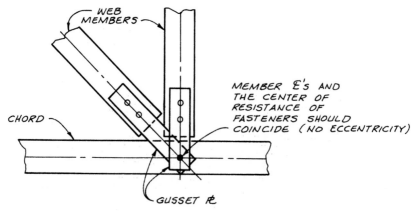

Figure 14.15c *Revised* connection detail with separate gusset plates. Fastener arrangement allows joint rotation without prying or splitting.

the diagonal gusset plate. Without these shims the vertical gusset plate may become damaged as the bolts are tightened.

See the TCM (Ref. 3.1) for a numerical example of a truss design.

Moisture Protection at Column Base

PROBLEM

Some designers try to conceal the base of a column or an arch by placing concrete around the connection (Fig. 14.16a). Moisture may migrate into the lower portion of the wood and cause decay.

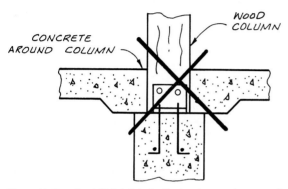

Figure 14.16a *Avoid* joint details that entrap moisture and promote decay.

SUGGESTED REVISION

Detail the column base at the top of the floor level (Fig. 14.16b). Note that the base of the column is separated from concrete by a bottom bearing plate. Where subjected to splashing water, untreated columns should be supported by piers projecting up at least 1 in. (UBC Chap. 25) above the finished floor.

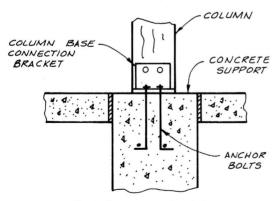

Figure 14.16b *Revised* connection detail does not entrap moisture.

14.3   Design Problem: Beam-to-Column Connection

Example 14.2 illustrates a typical beam-to-column connection. The beam is a 5⅛ × 27 glulam, and the column is a 4-in. steel tube. Steel tubes and steel pipe columns are commonly used to support wood beams.

The design of this connection starts with a consideration of the required bearing length for the wood beam. Calculations of this nature were introduced in Chap. 6. The required overall length of the U bracket for bearing stresses is 8 in. In later calculations this length is shown to be less than the length required to satisfy the bolt spacing criteria.

The example concludes with a check of the bending stresses in the U bracket. Because of the small cantilever length, a bent plate is used for the bracket. For longer cantilever lengths, a welded U bracket will be required. For special connection hardware, complete details of the bracket should be included on the structural plans. However, U brackets of the type covered in this example are generally available prefabricated from commercial sources.

EXAMPLE 14.2   U-Bracket Column Cap

Design a U bracket to connect two glulam beams to the 4-in. steel tube column. Gravity loads are given in Fig. 14.17a. There is no uplift force on the beam-to-column connection.

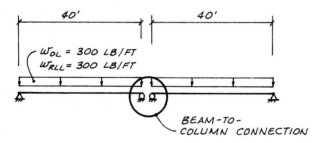

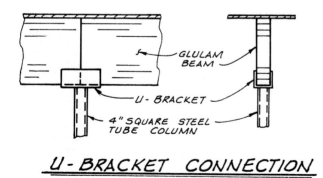

Figure 14.17a Beam to column connection.

The lateral seismic force causes an axial force of 6 k in the glulam beams. Glulam is 24F-V3 Douglas Fir which is initially dry and remains dry in service. Temperature range is normal.

Vertical Load

Reaction from one beam:

$$R = \frac{wL}{2} = \frac{600(40)}{2} = 12{,}000 \text{ lb}$$

Allowable bearing stress:

$$F'_{c\perp} = F_{c\perp}(C_M C_t C_b) = 650(1.0)(1.0)(1.0)$$

$$= 650 \text{ psi}$$

$$\text{Req'd bearing length} = \frac{R}{b \times F'_{c\perp}} = \frac{12{,}000}{5.125 \times 650}$$

$$= 3.6 \text{ in./beam}$$

Minimum length of bracket = 2(3.6) = 7.2 in.   *say*   8 in. minimum

Lateral Force

Assume that the lateral force will be transferred from one glulam to the other through the U bracket made from $\frac{1}{4}$-in.-thick A36 steel. Use $\frac{3}{4}$-in.-diameter bolts in double shear with steel side plates.

$$D = 0.75 \text{ in.}$$

$$F_{yb} = 45 \text{ ksi}\quad\text{(assumed for A307 bolt)}$$

$$t_m = 5.125 \text{ in.}$$

$$\theta_m = 0 \text{ degrees}$$

$$F_{em} = 5600 \text{ psi}\quad(F_{e\parallel} \text{ for DF-L})$$

$$t_s = 0.25 \text{ in.}$$

$$F_{es} = 58{,}000 \text{ psi} = F_u\quad\text{for A36 steel}$$

The nominal design value for the bolt may be computed as the smallest value from the three yield limit equations for a double-shear wood-to-metal connection (Example 13.5 in Sec. 13.4). However, the given conditions are covered directly by an NDS table, and Z is obtained from NDS Table 8.3D as

$$Z = 3170 \text{ lb}$$

The reader may wish to verify this value by applying the yield limit equations.

Allowable design value:
    Load duration factor C_D from the 1991 NDS is 1.6 for seismic forces (verify acceptance of $C_D = 1.6$ by local code authority before using in practice). Both C_m and C_t are 1.0. The

is defined as a line of fasteners *parallel* to the direction of loading. Assume $C_g = 1.0$. The geometry factor C_Δ will also be unity because the base dimensions for bolt spacing will be provided as a minimum. Therefore,

$$Z' = Z(C_D C_M C_t C_g C_\Delta)$$

$$= 3170(1.6 \times 1.0 \times 1.0 \times 1.0 \times 1.0)$$

$$= 5070 \text{ lb/bolt}$$

$$\text{Req'd number of bolts} = \frac{6000}{5070} \approx 2$$

> *Use* two ¾-in.-diameter bolts each side of splice.

Although there are two bolts on each side of the splice, two rows will be provided with one bolt in each row.

$$\therefore C_g = 1.0 \quad OK$$

Connection Details

A number of possible connection details can be used. One possible design is included in Fig. 14.17*b*.

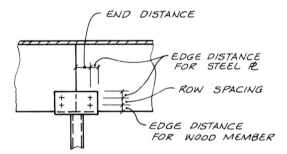

BOLT SPACINGS

Figure 14.17b Connection details.

Lateral force is carried by U bracket in tension, and vertical load is carried by bearing. Spacing requirements are governed by the lateral force (parallel-to-grain loading criteria—Example 13.10 in Sec. 13.5).

HORIZONTAL SPACING

$$\text{End distance} = 7D = 7(¾) = 5¼ \text{ in.}$$

$$\text{Steel plate edge distance} = 1½ \text{ in.} \quad \text{(minimum from Ref. 11.1)}$$

Total bracket length = (5¼ + 1½)2 = 13½ in.

13½ > 8 in.

Base dimension spacing provisions govern over bearing ($f_{c\perp}$).

VERTICAL SPACING

Steel plate edge distance = 1½ in.

Row spacing = 1½D = 1½(¾) = 1⅛ in.   say 1½ in.

$$\text{Bolt slenderness} = \frac{l}{D} = \frac{5.125}{0.75} = 6.83 > 6.0$$

∴ Edge distance* = 1½D = 1⅛ in.

or   ½ row spacing = ¾ in.   (the larger governs)

Say 1½ in.

Minimum bracket height = 3(1½) = 4½ in.

PROPORTIONS OF U BRACKET

As a rule of thumb, a bracket height of one-third the length is reasonable:

⅓ × 13.5 = 4.5 in.   (agrees with vertical bolt spacing requirements)

U-Bracket Stresses

The plan and elevation of the connection detail are shown in Fig. 14.17c. The bracket essentially cantilevers from the face of the column. [If a round column (e.g., a pipe column) is used, the cantilever length is figured from the face of an equivalent square column of equal area.]

The width of the U bracket is determined by adding a clearance to the width of the beam to allow installation of the member. Reference 3.4 recommends a maximum clearance of ¼ in. In this example a clearance of ⅛ in. is used (inside bracket width = 5⅛ + ⅛ = 5¼ in.). See uniform bearing considerations in Fig. 14.1b.

At this point it can be determined whether a bent plate bracket or welded plate bracket should be used (Fig. 14.17d). If the cantilever length of the bracket is small in comparison to the distance between the vertical legs, a bracket of uniform thickness throughout can be used. This can be obtained by folding a plate into the desired shape. The bending stresses in the bracket caused by the cantilever action must be evaluated.

On the other hand, if the cantilever length is long in comparison to the distance between the vertical legs, the bottom plate may have to be thicker than the vertical legs. In this case the bottom plate of the bracket should first be designed for the bending stresses developed as it spans horizontally between the vertical plates. After the thickness of the bottom plate is determined, the composite section of the U bracket can be checked for cantilever stresses (as in the analysis of the stresses in the bent plate bracket). The weld

---

*Uplift force was given as zero. If uplift occurs, the edge distance is 4D as governed by perpendicular-to-grain criteria (Example 13.11 in Sec. 13.5) or horizontal shear criteria (Sec. 13.7).

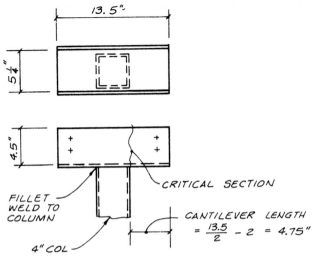

Figure 14.17c U bracket plan and elevation views.

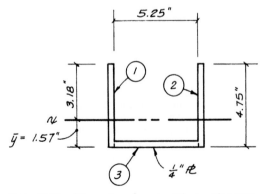

BENT PLATE

WELDED
BRACKET

Figure 14.17d Alternative ways of forming U bracket. For lighter loads a folded (bent) plate may be used. Larger loads may require a welded bracket with a thicker bottom plate capable of spanning between the vertical legs.

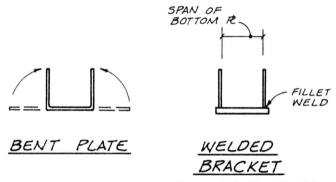

Figure 14.17e Dimensions for computing section properties of U bracket.

between the vertical and horizontal plates must also be designed. The minimum weld size based on the plate thickness (Ref. 11.1) often governs the weld size.

In the problem at hand, a bent plate bracket will be used because the cantilever length of 4.75 in. (Fig. 14.17c) is less than the distance between vertical plates (5¼ in.). Check cantilever bending stresses using ¼-in. plate (Fig. 14.17e).

Section properties are conveniently calculated in a table from the formula

$$I_x = \Sigma I_g + \Sigma A d^2$$

Element	A	y	Ay	$I_g = \dfrac{bh^3}{12}$	d	Ad^2
1	4.75 × ¼ = 1.19	2.38	2.82	2.23	0.80	0.76
2	1.19	2.38	2.82	2.23	0.80	0.76
3	5.25 × ⅛ = 1.31	0.125	0.16	—	1.45	2.76
	3.69		5.80	4.47		4.28

$$\bar{y} = \frac{A_y}{A} = \frac{5.80}{3.69} = 1.57 \text{ in.}$$

$$I_x = \Sigma I_g + \Sigma A d^2 = 4.47 + 4.28 = 8.75 \text{ in.}^4$$

Uniform load on bracket:

$$w = \frac{R}{A} = \frac{12,000 \times 2}{5.125 \times 13.5} = 347 \text{ psi}$$

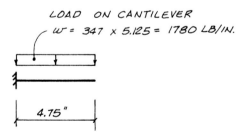

LOAD ON CANTILEVER
w = 347 × 5.125 = 1780 LB/IN.

4.75"

Figure 14.17f

$$M = \frac{wL^2}{2} = \frac{1780(4.75)^2}{2} = 20 \text{ in.-k}$$

$$f_b = \frac{Mc}{I} = \frac{20(3.18)}{8.75} = 7.28 \text{ ksi}$$

For A36 steel plate,

$$F_b = 22 \text{ ksi*} > 7.28 \quad OK$$

> *Use* ¼-in.-thick plate U bracket.

The U bracket must be welded to the top of the column. Without design loads, the weld size is governed by plate thickness requirements (Ref. 11.1).

14.4   Cantilever Beam Hinge Connection

The type of connection used for an internal hinge in a wood cantilever beam system was introduced in Fig. 14.5. There the detailing of the connection was considered to minimize the effects of shrinkage. In the design of this type of connection, the equilibrium of the hinge must also be considered. See Fig. 14.18. The saddle hinge with tension ties located near the bearing surfaces is recommended for gravity loads. The tension ties are required to balance the eccentric moment generated by the vertical reactions.

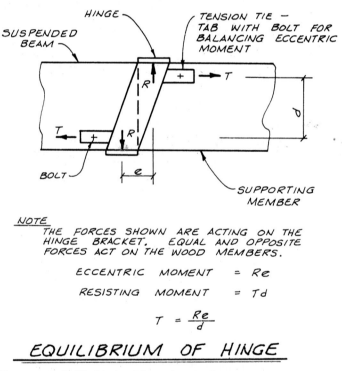

Figure 14.18 Saddle hinge with tension ties for gravity loads.

---

*The width-to-thickness ratios of plate elements in the compression zone are less than the limits given in Sec. B5. of Ref. 11.1.

Once the dimensions of the hinge connection have been established, the force on the tension ties can be calculated. This force is used to determine the number and size of bolts in the tension ties as well as the size and length of the weld between the tension tie and the main portion of the hinge connector.

Other considerations include spacing requirements for the bolts in the connection. The top and bottom bearing plates for the hinge must be capable of spanning horizontally between the vertical plates, and the welds between the vertical and horizontal plates must be designed.

In many cases there will be a tension force at the hinge due to an axial force in the beam. This is in addition to the tension load caused by gravity loads. This typically occurs in buildings with concrete and masonry walls under seismic forces. Here the beams are designed as continuous cross ties between horizontal diaphragm chords (Chap. 15). A tension force can also result from diaphragm chord or drag strut action.

The addition of a lateral force to the hinge connection problem can be handled in several ways. One solution is to provie a *welded* splice across the connection. See Fig. 14.19.

In the example shown, the seismic ties are located at the midheight of the hinge connector. Vertically slotted holes are required in the welded seismic ties to allow for cross-grain shrinkage. Note that the bolts must be located properly in the vertical slots to accommodate the movement between the bolts and the points of bearing in the connection. In addition, the nuts on these bolts should be hand-tightened only to permit movement.

In a different approach, *separate* tension ties for the seismic force are provided across the hinge in a typical double-shear bolt connection. This connection is similar to Fig. 14.19 except the tie plates are continuous across the hinge and are not welded to the hinge connector. In this case the use

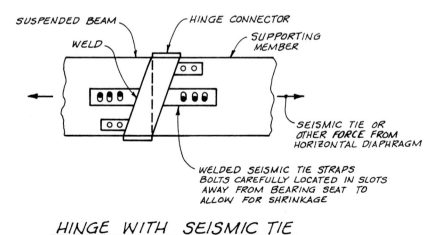

Figure 14.19 Saddle hinge with seismic tie.

of vertically slotted holes is not required because the separate splice plates will not restrain movement across the grain. Shims may be used to isolate the seismic tension tie from the hinge connector.

Other solutions to the seismic force problem are possible, but the two described are representative.

14.5 Prefabricated Connection Hardware

A number of manufacturers produce prefabricated connection hardware for use in wood construction. Catalogs (e.g., Refs. 32 to 35) are available from manufacturers or suppliers which show the configurations and dimensions of the hardware. In addition, the catalogs generally indicate allowable design loads for connections using the hardware. However, the designer should verify that the hardware and the allowable loads are recognized by the local building code authority.

In many cases prefabricated hardware will be the most economical solution to a connection problem. This is especially true if the hardware is a "shelf item." For example, light-gage steel joist or purlin hangers (similar in configuration to the beam face hanger in Fig. 14.3) are usually available as a stock item. Allowable loads for some hardware have been established through testing, and design values may be higher than can be justified by stress calculations. Obviously this type of hardware represents an efficient use of materials.

For connections involving larger loads, the appropriate hardware may be available from a manufacturer. However, the designer should have the ability to apply the fastener design principles of the previous chapters *and* basic structural steel design principles (Ref. 11.1) to develop appropriate connection details for a particular job. In some cases it may be more economical to fabricate special hardware, *or* there may not be suitable prefabricated hardware for a certain application.

Many manufacturers offer a number of variations of the hardware illustrated in Example 14.1. The fittings may range from light-gage steel to ¼-in. and thicker steel plate. Allowable loads vary correspondingly. Several other types of connection hardware are generally available from manufacturers. See Example 14.3. These include

1. Framing anchors

2. Diaphragm-to-wall anchors

3. Tie straps

Some hardware that has been illustrated in previous chapters is also available commercially. For example, shearwall tie-down brackets (Fig. 10.10) are produced by a number of manufacturers. Metal knee braces (Fig. 6.26*b*) and metal bridging (mentioned in Example 6.7) are also available.

With some knowledge of structural steel design and the background provided in Chaps. 11 to 14, the designer should be prepared to develop appropriate connections for the transfer of both vertical loads and lateral forces. Chapters 15 and 16 conclude the discussion of the lateral force design problem with final anchorage considerations and an introduction to some advanced problems in diaphragm design, structural irregularity, and overturning.

EXAMPLE 14.3   Connection Hardware

Framing Anchors

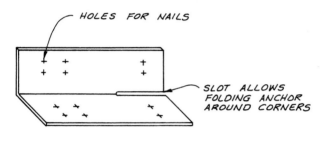

Figure 14.20a

Framing anchors (Fig. 14.20a) are light-gage steel connection brackets that are usually installed with nails. They have a variety of uses, especially where conventional nail connections alone are inadequate. Framing anchors generally can be bent and nailed in a number of different ways (Fig. 14.20b). Allowable loads depend on the final configuration of the anchor and the direction of loading (different allowable loads apply to loadings *A* through *E*).

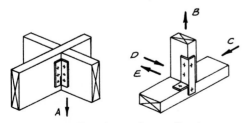

Figure 14.20b Framing anchor applications.

Diaphragm-to-Wall Anchors

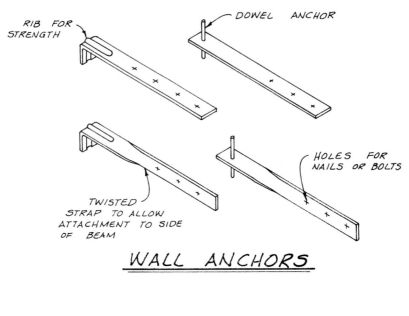

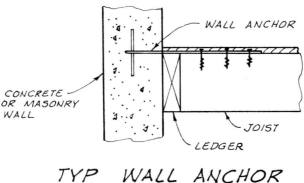

Figure 14.21 Wall anchors are used to tie a concrete or masonry wall to a horizontal diaphragm.

Diaphragm-to-wall anchors (Fig. 14.21) are known commercially by various names (purlin anchors, joist anchors, strap anchors, etc.). These anchors are used to tie concrete or masonry walls to horizontal diaphragms (Chap. 15). Their purpose is to prevent the ledger from being stressed in cross-grain bending (Example 6.1).

Note that the connection in Fig. 14.21 is only part of the total wall-to-diaphragm connection. It carries the lateral force that acts perpendicular to the wall. The anchor-bolt-to-ledger connection in Fig. 6.1*b* is used for vertical loads and lateral forces parallel to the wall. See Example 15.6 (Sec. 15.4) for additional information.

Tie Straps

HOLES FOR
NAILS OR BOLTS

TIE   STRAP

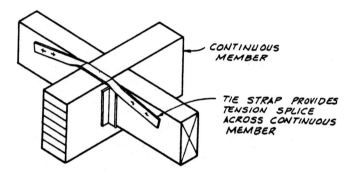

CONTINUOUS
MEMBER

TIE STRAP PROVIDES
TENSION SPLICE
ACROSS CONTINUOUS
MEMBER

TYP   TIE   STRAP   APPLICATION

Figure 14.22

Tie straps (Fig. 14.22) are typically used to provide a connection across an intervening member. Ties of this type may be required if the beams are part of a horizontal diaphragm (Chap. 15).

14.6   Problems

The design of connection hardware usually involves the use of structural steel design principles as well as wood design calculations. For the following problems, structural steel is A36, and design methods and allowable stresses should conform to the specifications contained in Ref. 11.1. Design of wood members and fasteners shall be in accordance with the 1991 NDS. $C_t = 1.0$.

14.1   *Given:*   The beam-to-column connection in Fig. 14.A. The two beams are 6 × 16, and the column is a 6 × 6. Lumber is No. 1 DF-L. $C_M = 1.0$. Bolts in the connection are ⅞-in.-diameter A307.

Find: Design and detail a U-bracket connection for the following loads:
a. An axial load in the column of DL = 5 k and snow = 15 k.
b. The vertical load from part *a* plus a tension force in the beam of 8 k. The tension force is a result of a seismic force.

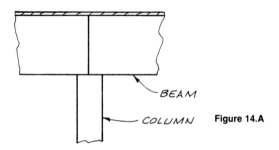

Figure 14.A

14.2   Repeat Prob. 14.1 except that the lumber is Select Structural Hem-Fir.

14.3   *Given:*   The beam-to-column connection in Fig. 14.A. The two beams are 6¾ × 31.5 24F-V3 DF glulam. C_M = 1.0. Bolts in the connection are ¾-in. diameter. The column is an 8-in. standard steel pipe column.

Find: Design and detail a U-bracket connection for the following loads:
a. A total axial load in the column of (DL + snow) = 70 k.
b. The vertical load from *a* plus a tension force in the beam of 6 k. The tension force is a result of a seismic force.

NOTE: The cantilever length of the U bracket is to be determined using the dimensions of an effective square column. The effective square column has an area equal to the area of a circle with a diameter of 8.625 in. (the outside diameter of an 8-in. standard pipe). Design the bottom plate of the U bracket for bending between the vertical side plate supports.

14.4   *Given:*   The beam-to-girder connection in Fig. 14.B. The members are 20F-V3 DF glulam. The girder is a 6¾ × 30, and the beams are 3⅛ × 15. C_M = 1.0.

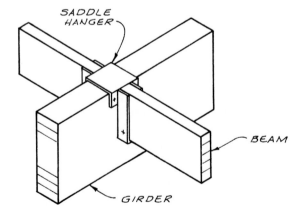

Find: Design and detail the connection hardware if each beam transmits a reaction of 4.5 k to the girder. Load is (DL + RLL).

14.5 *Given:* The beam-to-girder connection in Fig. 14.C. The girder is a 5¾ × 25.5 16F-V3 DF glulam, and the beam is a 4 × 14 sawn member No. 1 DF-L. Bolts are ¾-in. diameter. $C_M = 1.0$.

Find: Design and detail the connection hardware if the beam reaction on the girder is 2000 lb. Load is (DL + RLL).

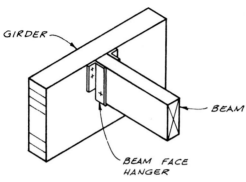

GIRDER

BEAM

BEAM FACE HANGER

Figure 14.C

14.6 *Given:* The hinge connector in Fig. 14.D. The girders are 6¾ × 31.5 20F-V3 DF glulam. $C_M = 1.0$. Bolts are ⅞-in. diameter.

Find: Design and detail the hinge connector for the following loads:
a. A vertical load of 16 k. Load is (DL + snow).
b. The vertical load from part *a* plus a tension force in the girder of 8 k.

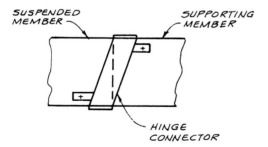

SUSPENDED MEMBER

SUPPORTING MEMBER

HINGE CONNECTOR

Figure 14.D

14.7 *Given:* The hinge connector in Fig. 14.E. The members are 24F-V1 SP glulams. The supporting member is 5 × 24.75, and the suspended member is a 5 × 28.875. $C_M = 1.0$. Bolts are ¾-in. diameter.

Find: Design and detail the hinge connector for the following loads:
a. A vertical load of 12 k. Load is (DL + RLL).
b. The vertical load from part *a* plus a tension force in the girder of 4 k.

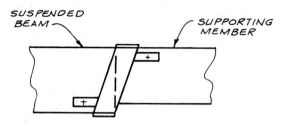

Figure 14.E

14.8   Design and detail a shearwall anchor bracket similar to the one shown in Fig. 10.10. The lateral wind force causes a tension force in the chord of 4 k. The chord is composed of two 2 × 6 studs of No. 1 DF-L. Use ¾-in. bolts for the connection to the chord, and choose the proper anchor bolt for the connection to the foundation from UBC Table 26-E.

15

Diaphragm-to-Shearwall Anchorage

15.1 Introduction

Anchorage was defined previously as the tying together of the major elements of a building with an emphasis on the transfer of lateral (wind and earthquake) forces. A systematic approach to anchorage involves a consideration of load transfer in the three principal directions of the building.

Chapter 10 illustrated the anchorage requirements at the base of a wood-frame shearwall. This chapter continues the anchorage problem with a detailed analysis of the connection between the horizontal diaphragm and the shearwalls. Additional considerations for shearwall anchorage and overturning are addressed in Chap. 16. Several typical anchorage details are analyzed including connections to wood-frame shearwalls and concrete or masonry shearwalls.

Following the subject of diaphragm-to-wall anchorage, the subdiaphragm concept is introduced. This design technique was developed to ensure the integrity of a horizontal plywood diaphragm that supports seismic forces generated by *concrete* or *masonry walls*. Its purpose is to satisfy the Code requirement that "continuous ties" be provided to distribute these larger seismic forces into the diaphragm (UBC 2337, *Earthquake Design*). This is also an anchorage problem, but it is unique to buildings with concrete or masonry walls.

15.2 Anchorage Summary

Horizontal diaphragm anchorage refers to the design of connections between the horizontal diaphragm and the vertical elements of the building. These elements may support the horizontal diaphragm, or they may transfer a force to the diaphragm.

A systematic approach to anchorage is described in Example 10.6 (Sec. 10.8). This simply involves designing the connections between the various resisting elements for the following loads and forces:

1. Vertical loads
2. Lateral forces parallel to a wall
3. Lateral forces perpendicular to a wall

In designing for these gravity loads and lateral forces, it is important that a *continuous path* be developed. The path must take the load or force from its source, through the connections, and into the supporting element.

The "path" in the progressive transfer of *vertical loads* is described in Example 10.7 (Sec. 10.9) and is not repeated here. Many of the connections for vertical loads can be made with the hardware described in Chap. 14.

There are several types of *lateral forces parallel* to a wall. See Example 15.1. These include

1. Basic unit shear transfer
2. Drag strut force
3. Horizontal diaphragm chord force

The methods used to calculate drag strut forces and horizontal diaphragm chord forces were given in Chap. 9, and several connection designs were demonstrated in Chaps. 12 and 13. These forces are listed here simply to complete the anchorage design summary. However, the connection for the transfer of the unit shear has not been discussed previously, and it requires some additional consideration. The connections used to transfer this shear are different for different types of walls. Typical details of these connections and the calculations involved are illustrated in the following sections.

EXAMPLE 15.1   Anchorage Forces Parallel to Wall

Consider the anchorage forces *parallel* to the right end wall in the building shown in Fig. 15.1a. Three different forces are involved.

Unit Shear Transfer

The unit shear in the roof diaphragm v_R (Fig. 15.1a) must be transferred to the supporting elements (drag strut and shearwall).

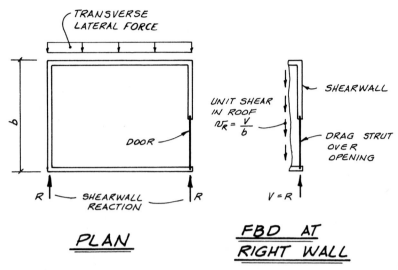

Figure 15.1a   Plan view showing lateral force to horizontal diaphragm, and free body diagram cut a small distance away from right shearwall and drag strut.

Drag Strut Connection to Shearwall

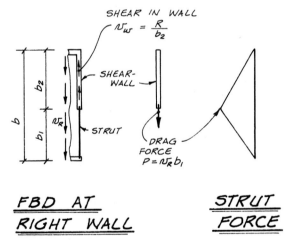

Figure 15.1b   *Drag strut force* caused by lateral force to diaphragm in the transverse direction.

The force in the drag strut must be transferred to the shearwall (Fig. 15.1b). The magnitude of the connection force may be read from the drag strut force diagram (Sec. 9.7).

Diaphragm Chord Connection

The diaphragm chord force in Fig. 15.1c is an alternative design criterion to the drag strut force in Fig. 15.1b. The connection between the member over the door and the wall should be designed for the *chord force* or the *drag strut force*, whichever is larger.

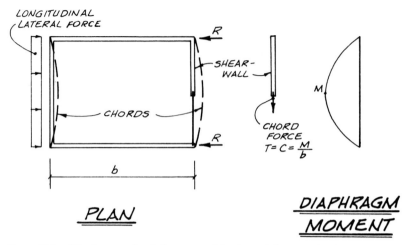

Figure 15.1c *Diaphragm chord force* caused by lateral force to diaphragm in the longitudinal direction.

There are also several types of *lateral forces perpendicular* to a wall that must be considered in designing the anchorage of the horizontal diaphragm. These include

1. Wind force on elements and components
2. Seismic force normal to the wall F_p
3. In cases of masonry and concrete walls, an arbitrary Code minimum force of 200 lb/ft

These are alternate design forces, and anchorage must be designed for the maximum value. These forces act normal to the wall (either inward or outward) and attempt to separate the wall from the horizontal diaphragm. See Example 15.2.

These types of forces were introduced in Examples 2.17 (Sec. 2.15) and 10.9 (Sec. 10.11). In the sketches in these examples, the force labeled *roof reaction* corresponds to the anchorage force being discussed.

In wood-frame buildings, wind usually controls the design of anchorage for perpendicular-to-wall forces. For masonry and concrete walls, however, the seismic force F_p often governs because of the large dead load of these walls. The Code minimum force of 200 lb/ft for these types of walls ensures a minimum connection regardless of the calculated seismic forces. (Some designers also apply the 200-lb/ft minimum load parallel to the wall as a lower limit on the unit shear anchorage force—Example 15.1.)

EXAMPLE 15.2   Anchorage Forces Perpendicular to Wall

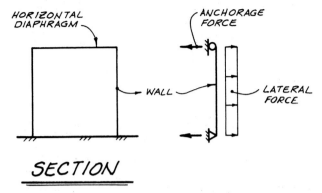

Figure 15.2 Schematic of one-story building. In most buildings, wall framing is assumed to span vertically between the foundation and the roof diaphragm.

Anchorage for normal-to-wall forces must be designed for the largest of the following:

1. Wind force tributary to horizontal diaphragm.
2. Seismic force F_p tributary to horizontal diaphragm. Recall that the 1991 UBC (UBC Table 23-P, footnote 3) requires a 50 percent increase in the F_p anchorage force in the center one-half of flexible diaphragms.
3. For concrete and masonry walls, a separation force of 200 lb/ft at the diaphragm level.

Anchorage must be provided for normal forces acting inward and outward.

A large number of connection details can be used to anchor the horizontal diaphragm to the walls for both parallel and perpendicular forces. The type of wall framing (wood frame, concrete, or masonry) and the size and direction of the framing members for the horizontal diaphragm affect the choice of the anchorage connection. Examples of two typical anchorage details are given in Secs. 15.3 and 15.4.

15.3   Connection Details—Horizontal Diaphragm to Wood-Frame Wall

A typical anchorage connection of a horizontal plywood diaphragm to a wood-frame wall is considered here. Two anchorage details are shown in Example 15.3: one for the transverse wall and one for the longitudinal wall.

In practice, additional details will be required. For example, the connection where the girder ties into the transverse wall must be detailed in the structural plans. The vertical reaction of the girder, and the horizontal diaphragm chord force caused by lateral forces in the longitudinal direction, need to be considered. However, the two connection details given in the sketches are intended to define the problem and be representative of the methods used for anchorage.

As noted previously, the key to the anchorage problem is to provide a continuous *path* for the "flow" of forces in the connection. Each step in this flow is labeled on the sketch, and a corresponding explanation is given. Sample calculations are provided for the transverse wall anchorage detail. See Example 15.4.

EXAMPLE 15.3   Anchorage to Wood-Frame Walls

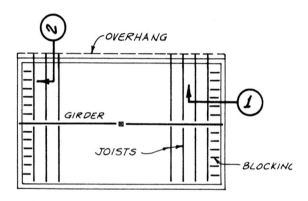

FRAMING   PLAN

Figure 15.3a One story building with wood roof system and wood-frame stud walls.

Different anchorage details are required for the diaphragm attachment to the transverse and longitudinal walls. More complicated roof or floor framing will require additional anchorage details.

The following details shown are representative only, and other properly designed connections are possible. The path for the transfer of anchorage forces is described for each connection.

Transverse Wall Anchorage

Parallel-to-wall force (diaphragm shear)

a. Diaphragm boundary nailing transfers shear into end joist (Fig. 15.3b).
b. The shear must be transferred from the end joist into the wall plate. The top plate here serves as the diaphragm chord and strut. Various types of connections can be used for this transfer. Framing anchor is shown. Alternate connections not shown are toenails (not allowed for concrete or masonry walls) or additional blocking, as in Example 9.5.
c. Shearwall edge nailing transfers shear into wall sheathing.

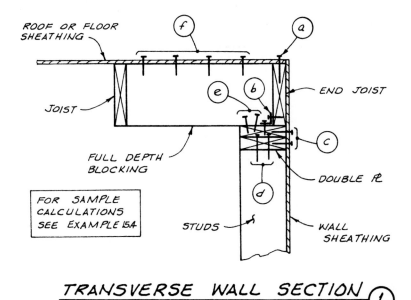

Figure 15.3b Anchorage connections between roof and transverse shearwall.

*Perpendicular-to-wall force (wind critical for
most wood-frame walls)*

d. Connect stud to double plate for reaction at top of stud. Standard connection from
 UBC Table 25-Q is two 16d nails into end grain of study. Alternate connection for
 larger forces is framing anchor.
e. Full-depth blocking normal to wall is required to prevent the rotation of the joists
 under this type of force. This blocking is necessary whether or not the horizontal
 diaphragm is a "blocked" diaphragm. Spacing of blocks depends on lateral force (2 to
 4 ft is typical). Connect top plate to block for tributary lateral force. Toenails are shown
 (not allowed for concrete or masonry walls). Alternate connection not shown is framing
 anchor.
f. Connect block to horizontal diaphragm sheathing for same force considered in *e*. For
 consistency, use the same size of nail as for diaphragm nailing.

Longitudinal Wall Anchorage

Parallel-to-wall force (diaphragm shear)

a. Diaphragm boundary nailing transfers shear into blocking (Fig. 15.3c).
b. Connection of blocking to double plate transfers shear into top plate. Framing anchor
 is shown. Alternate connections not shown are toenails (not allowed for concrete or
 masonry walls) or additional blocking, as in Example 9.5.
c. Shearwall edge nailing transfers shear from top plate to wall sheathing.

*Perpendicular-to-wall force (wind critical for
most wood-frame walls)*

d. Same as transverse wall connection d (Fig. 15.3b).
e. Connect top plate to joist for the tributary lateral force. Framing anchor is shown.

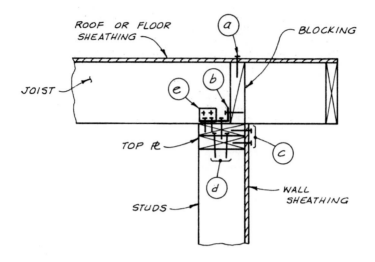

Figure 15.3c Anchorage connections between roof and longitudinal shear-wall.

Alternate connection not shown is with toenails (not allowed for concrete or masonry walls). The connection of the joist to the horizontal diaphragm sheathing is provided directly by the diaphragm nailing. Specific nail design similar to the transverse wall connection f is usually not required.

EXAMPLE 15.4   Anchorage of Transverse Wood-Frame Wall

Design the connection for the anchorage of the transverse wall for the building in Example 15.3 (section 1), using the following loads. The letter designations in this example correspond to the designations of the connection details in Fig. 15.3b. Lumber is DF-L, and plywood is ½-in. STR I DF with 10 d common nails. $C_M = 1.0$, and $C_t = 1.0$.

Known Information

$$\text{Roof unit shear} = v = 205 \text{ lb/ft} \quad \text{(parallel to wall)}$$

$$\text{Wind} = 26 \text{ psf} \quad \text{(wall height} = 10 \text{ ft)}$$

$$\text{Separation force} = w = (26)\left(\frac{10}{2}\right)$$

$$= 130 \text{ lb/ft} \quad \text{(perpendicular to wall)}$$

Assume allowable load on framing anchor.

$$\text{Allow. } P = 410 \text{ lb*} \qquad \text{(normal duration)}$$

$$= 410 \times 1.6\dagger = 656 \text{ lb} \quad \text{(wind)}$$

Parallel-to-Wall Forces

a. The nailing for item a in Fig. 15.3b is obtained from UBC Table 25-J-1.
Minimum allowable roof shear = 215 lb/ft > 205   *OK*
Minimum edge nailing (10d common nails at 6 in. o.c.) will transfer roof shear into end joist.

b. Item b in Fig. 15.3b connects end joist to plate with framing anchors (assume diaphragm width = b = 40 ft):

$$V = vb = 205 \times 40 = 8200 \text{ lb}$$

$$\text{Number of anchors} = \frac{8200}{656} \approx 13$$

$$\text{Spacing of anchors} \approx \frac{40}{13} = 3.08 \text{ ft}$$

Connection b:	*Use* 13 framing anchors total. Space anchors at approximately 3 ft-0 in. o.c.

Alternate toenail connection:
Assume 10d common toenails. The yield limit equations from Chap. 12 for the strength of the toenails will be shown for review. In practice, the yield limit equations will be solved on a spreadsheet template or other computer program. For the remaining nail problems in this example, the nominal fastener capacity will be obtained from NDS tables.

Dimensions and bending yield strength of 10d common nail can be obtained from the tables in Fig. 12.7a and b (Sec. 12.4) or from NDS Table 12.3B.

$$D = 0.148 \text{ in.}$$

$$l = 3.0 \text{ in.}$$

$$F_{yb} = 90 \text{ ksi}$$

For a toenail the thickness of the side member (for use in the yield limit equations) and penetration is determined using the geometry given in Fig. 12.12a (Sec. 12.6). The thick-

---

*In practice, the capacity of the framing anchor is obtained from the evaluation report giving code-recognized design values of proprietary product.

†Verify acceptance of C_D = 1.6 by local code authority before using in practice.

ness of the main member t_m is assumed to be the combined thicknesses of the double $2\times$ members forming the top wall plate.

$$t_m = 2(1.5) = 3.0 \text{ in.}$$

$$t_s = \frac{l}{3} = \frac{3.0}{3} = 1.0 \text{ in.}$$

$$p_L = l \cos 30 - t_s \le t_m$$

$$= 3.0 \cos 30 - 1.0 \le 3.0$$

$$\therefore p_L = 1.60 \text{ in.}$$

Coefficients for yield limit equations:

The specific gravity and dowel bearing strength are the same for both the main member and the side member and are obtained from NDS Table 12A:

$$SG_m = SG_s = 0.50$$

$$F_{em} = F_{es} = 4650 \text{ psi}$$

$$K_D = 2.2 \qquad \text{for } D \le 0.17 \text{ in.}$$

$$R_e = \frac{F_{em}}{F_{es}} = \frac{4650}{4650} = 1.0$$

$$1 + R_e = 1 + 1.0 = 2.0$$

$$1 + 2R_e = 1 + 2(1.0) = 3.0$$

$$2 + R_e = 2 + 1.0 = 3.0$$

$$k_1 = -1 + \sqrt{2(1 + R_e) + \frac{2F_{yb}(1 + 2R_e)D^2}{3F_{em}p^2}}$$

$$= -1 + \sqrt{2(2.0) + \frac{2(90,000)(3.0)(0.148)^2}{3(4650)(1.60)^2}}$$

$$= 1.081$$

$$k_2 = -1 + \sqrt{\frac{2(1 + R_e)}{R_e} + \frac{2F_{yb}(2 + R_e)D^2}{3F_{em}t_s^2}}$$

$$= -1 + \sqrt{\frac{2(2.0)}{1.0} + \frac{2(90,000)(3.0)(0.148)^2}{3(4650)(1.0)^2}}$$

$$= 1.202$$

Yield limit equations:

Mode I_s (NDS equation 12.3-1):

$$Z = \frac{Dt_sF_{es}}{K_D} = \frac{0.148(1.0)(4650)}{2.2} = 313 \text{ lb}$$

Mode III$_m$ (NDS equation 12.3-2):

$$Z = \frac{k_1 D p F_{em}}{K_D(1 + 2R_e)} = \frac{1.081(0.148)(1.60)(4650)}{2.2(3.0)} = 180 \text{ lb}$$

Mode III$_s$ (NDS equation 12.3-3):

$$Z = \frac{k_2 D t_s F_{em}}{K_D(2 + R_e)} = \frac{1.202(0.148)(1.0)(4650)}{2.2(3.0)} = 125 \text{ lb}$$

Mode IV (NDS equation 12.3-4):

$$Z = \frac{D^2}{K_D} \sqrt{\frac{2F_{em}F_{yb}}{3(1 + R_e)}}$$

$$= \frac{(0.148)^2}{2.2} \sqrt{\frac{2(4650)(90,000)}{3(2.0)}} = 118 \text{ lb}$$

Nominal design value:

The nominal design value is taken as the smallest value from the yield formulas:

$$Z = 118 \text{ lb}$$

Adjustment factors:

Load duration factor from 1991 NDS for wind:

$$C_D = 1.6 \quad \text{(Verify acceptance by local code authority before using in practice.)}$$

Limits for penetration depth factor:

$$12D = 12(0.148) = 1.78 \text{ in.} \quad \text{(base penetration)}$$

$$6D = 6(0.148) = 0.89 \text{ in.} \quad \text{(minimum penetration)}$$

$$0.89 < 1.60 < 1.78$$

∴ Penetration depth factor:

$$C_d = \frac{p_L}{12D} = \frac{1.60}{1.78} = 0.90$$

Toenail factor for laterally loaded toenails:

$$C_{tn} = 0.83$$

All other adjustment factors default to unity in this problem.

Allowable design value:

$$Z' = Z(C_D C_M C_t C_d C_{eg} C_{di} C_{tn})$$

$$= 118(1.6)(1.0)(1.0)(0.90)(1.0)(1.0)(0.83)$$

$$= 141 \text{ lb/nail}$$

$$\text{Req'd spacing} = \frac{141 \text{ lb/nail}}{205 \text{ lb/ft}} = 0.688 \text{ ft} = 8.3 \text{ in.} \qquad say \quad 8 \text{ in. o.c.}$$

> Alternate connection *b*:   *Use*   10d common toenails
> at 8 in. o.c.

c. Plywood shearwall edge nailing transfers shear from wall plate into shearwall (UBC Table 25-K-1).

Perpendicular-to-Wall Forces

d. Check connection of stud to wall plate for separation force. Assume two 16d common nails through wall plate into end grain of stud (UBC Table 25-Q).

Lumber is DF-L, and the thickness of the side member is the thickness of one of the wall plates ($t_s = 1\frac{1}{2}$ in.). The nominal design value for a 16d nail could be obtained from the yield limit equations. However, the plate-to-stud connection is covered directly in NDS Table 12.3B. The reader may wish to verify the results of the yield limit equations as an exercise.

$$Z = 141 \text{ lb}$$

The following adjustments apply:

$$C_D = 1.6 \qquad \text{for wind (verify acceptance by local code authority before using in practice.)}$$

$$C_{eg} = 0.67 \qquad \text{Nail is driven into end grain of stud.}$$

Check nail penetration:

$$p = l - t_s = 3.5 - 1.5 = 2.0 \text{ in.}$$

$$12D = 12(0.162) = 1.94 \text{ in.} < 2.0$$

$$\therefore C_d = 1.0$$

All other adjustment factors are unity.

$$Z' = Z(C_D C_M C_t C_d C_{eg} C_{di} C_{tn})$$

$$= 141(1.6)(1.0)(1.0)(1.0)(0.67)(1.0)(1.0)$$

$$= 151 \text{ lb/nail}$$

Allowable load for stud connection:

$$\text{Allow. } P = N(Z') = 2(151) = 302 \text{ lb/stud}$$

Load on one stud connection is the force per foot of wall times the spacing of the studs.

$$P = 130 \text{ lb/ft} \times 1.33 \text{ ft}$$

$$= 173 \text{ lb/stud} < 302 \qquad OK$$

e. Assume that blocking is spaced 24 in. o.c.

$$\text{Load per block} = 130 \text{ lb/ft} \times 2 \text{ ft} = 260 \text{ lb}$$

Capacity of 10d common toenails:

$$Z' = 141 \text{ lb/nail} \qquad (\text{from } b)$$

$$\text{Number of toenails} = \frac{260 \text{ lb/block}}{141 \text{ lb/nail}} \approx 2$$

> *Use* two 10d common toenails per block.
> Blocks at 24 in. o.c.

f. Attach blocking to roof sheathing.

$$\text{Load per block} = 260 \text{ lb} \qquad (\text{from } e)$$

For the general diaphragm nailing 10d common nails in ½-in. STR I DF plywood are used. Determine the number of 10d nails required to transmit the load from the block into the roof diaphragm.

The yield limit equations could be evaluated for a 10d common nail through ½-in. DF plywood into DF-L blocking. However, the nominal design value will be obtained from NDS Table 12.3B:

$$Z = 90 \text{ lb/nail}$$

The following adjustments apply:

$C_D = 1.6$ for wind (verify acceptance by local code authority before using.)

$C_{di} = 1.1$ Nail is into plywood diaphragm.

Check nail penetration:

$$p = l - t_s = 3.0 - 0.5 = 2.5 \text{ in.}$$

$$12D = 12(0.148) = 1.78 \text{ in.} < 2.5$$

$$\therefore C_d = 1.0$$

Other adjustment factors default to unity.

$$Z' = Z(C_D C_M C_t C_d C_{eg} C_{di} C_{tn})$$

$$= 90(1.6)(1.0)(1.0)(1.0)(1.0)(1.1)(1.0)$$

$$= 158 \text{ lb/nail}$$

NOTE: Reference 14.11 recommends a 10 percent reduction in nail value when diaphragm nailing is driven into narrow (2-in. nominal) framing. The 0.9 multiplying factor in the next step is to account for this reduction. Depending on materials, other adjustments may apply. Contact APA for the latest information regarding allowable nail design values for diaphragms using the yield limit equations.

$$\text{Modified } Z' = 158(0.9) = 142 \text{ lb/nail}$$

$$\text{Number of nails} = \frac{260 \text{ lb/block}}{142 \text{ lb/nail}} \approx 2$$

Length of block will depend on spacing of roof joists (assume joists are 24 in. o.c.). If nails are spaced 6 in. o.c.,

$$N = \frac{24}{6} \approx 4 \text{ nails/block} > 2 \qquad OK$$

> *Use* 10d common nails at 6 in. o.c.
> through plywood into blocking.

15.4 Connection Details—Horizontal Diaphragm to Concrete or Masonry Walls

The anchorage of concrete tilt-up and masonry (concrete block and brick) walls to horizontal plywood diaphragms has been the subject of considerable discussion in the design profession. The use of plywood diaphragms in buildings with concrete or masonry walls is very common, especially in one-story commercial and industrial buildings. Some failures of these connections occurred in the San Fernando earthquake, and revised design criteria have been included in the Code to strengthen these attachments.

The Code seismic forces introduced in Chaps. 2 and 3 are larger than the forces that were previously used for the design of these types of buildings. In addition, the Code has the following requirements for the anchorage of concrete and masonry walls for seismic forces:

1. Anchorage connections may not stress lumber in cross-grain bending or cross-grain tension (Example 6.1 in Sec. 6.2).

2. Toenails and nails loaded in withdrawal are not allowed for anchorage in seismic zones 2, 3, and 4.

3. When the spacing of anchors exceeds 4 ft, the wall must be designed to resist bending between the anchors.

4. Continuous ties are to be provided between diaphragm chords in order to distribute the anchorage forces well into the diaphragm. Subdiaphragms (Sec. 15.5) may be used to transmit the anchorage forces to main cross ties.

Two different anchorage problems are considered in this section, and the path used to transfer the forces is described. The first anchorage detail involves a *ledger connection* to a wall with a parapet. See Example 15.5. The vertical load must be transferred in addition to the lateral forces. The anchor bolts are designed to carry both the vertical load and the lateral force parallel to the wall. This requires that two different load combinations be checked, and the capacity of the bolts in the wall and in the ledger must be determined.

A special anchorage device is provided to transmit the lateral force normal to the wall into the framing members. This is required to prevent crossgrain bending in the ledger. A numerical example is provided for the anchorage of a masonry wall with a ledger. See Example 15.6.

EXAMPLE 15.5 Typical Ledger Anchorage to Masonry Wall

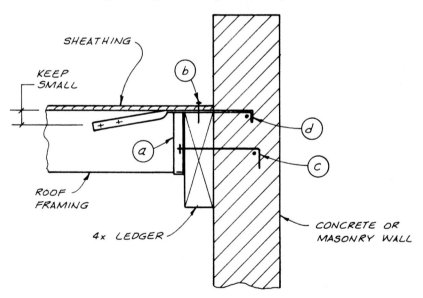

TYPICAL LEDGER CONNECTION

Figure 15.4a Anchorage connections to masonry wall with ledger.

a. Vertical loads (DL + RLL) are transferred from roof framing members to ledger with prefabricated metal hangers.
b. Horizontal diaphragm unit shear parallel to the wall is transferred to ledger by diaphragm boundary nailing.
c. The vertical load and unit shear from a and b are transferred from the ledger to the wall by the anchor bolts. The strength of the anchor bolts is governed by the capacity of the bolts in the
   1. *Wall*
      Concrete walls—UBC Table 26-E
      Masonry walls—UBC Table 24-E
   2. *Wood ledger* with bolt in single shear (Chap. 13)
      The following load cases must be considered to determine the bolt capacity in the wood ledger:
      (a) *Vertical load* (DL + RLL)
          Single-shear capacity perpendicular to grain Z'.
      (b) *Vertical load plus lateral force parallel to wall* (DL + roof shear). RLL is not considered simultaneously with lateral force. Snow load (or floor LL), if applicable, must be included.

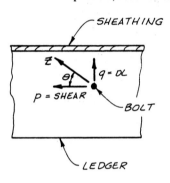

Figure 15.4b Anchor bolt connection between ledger and masonry wall. Vectors shown are resisting forces provided by anchor bolt under gravity load and lateral force parallel to wall.

      i. Assume bolt size and spacing.
      ii. Calculate tributary DL and tributary shear.
      iii. Determine resultant force Z at angle θ.
      iv. Compare resultant to allowable load Z' using the yield limit equations with the Hankinson formula.
d. Lateral forces perpendicular to the wall are carried by diaphragm-to-wall anchors (Fig. 14.21 in Sec. 14.5) or similar-type hardware. If the strap is bent down to allow bolting through the framing member, the fold-down distance should be kept small to minimize eccentricity. However, the required edge distance for the fasteners should be provided. The anchors are embedded in the wall (preferably hooked around horizontal wall steel) and nailed, bolted, or lag bolted to the roof framing. The purpose of this separate anchorage connection for normal wall forces is to avoid cross-grain bending in the wood ledger (Example 6.1 in Sec. 6.2).

Subdiaphragm Problem

Once the perpendicular-to-wall force has been transferred into the framing members, it is carried into the sheathing. Because these normal wall forces may be large for concrete and masonry walls, it is important that the framing members extend back into the diaphragm (i.e., away from the wall) in order to make this transfer. The concept of subdiaphragms (Sec. 15.5) was developed to ensure that the framing is sufficiently anchored into the diaphragm.

EXAMPLE 15.6 Anchorage of Masonry Wall with Ledger

Design the connections for the ledger anchorage in Example 15.5. The letter designations in this example correspond to the designations of the connection details in Fig. 15.4a. The following information is known.

Loads

Roof DL = 60 lb/ft   (along wall)

Roof LL = 100 lb/ft

Roof diaphragm shear = 300 lb/ft   (parallel to wall)

Seismic separation force F_p = 130 lb/ft.

Increased separation force for center one-half of diaphragm = 1.5(130) = 195 lb/ft < 200   (UBC Table 23-P footnote 3).

∴ Use Code minimum of 200 lb/ft normal to wall.

Construction

½-in. STR I plywood roof sheathing is used.

Roof framing members are 2 × 6 at 24 in. o.c.

Ledger is 4 × 12 DF-L that is dry and remains dry in service. Normal temperature conditions apply.

Walls are grouted concrete block.

Anchorage

a. Roof beams are 2 ft o.c. Reaction of roof beam on ledger (DL + RLL):

$$R = (60 + 100)2 = 320 \text{ lb}$$

Choose prefabricated metal hanger from manufacturer with Code-recognized capacity greater than 320 lb.

b. From UBC Table 25-J-1, for ½ (or ¹⁵⁄₃₂)-in. STR I plywood, allow. v = 320 lb/ft (>300) for a *blocked* diaphragm with 2-in. nominal framing and 10d common nails at:

6-in. o.c. edges

12-in. o.c. field

c. Assume ¾-in. anchor bolts at 32 in. o.c. For this anchor bolt spacing, compare the *actual* load and *allowable* load for two cases:

1. Vertical load (DL + RLL).
2. Vertical load and lateral force parallel to wall (DL + roof shear).

(1) *Vertical loads:*

$$DL + LL = (60 + 100)\left(\frac{32}{12}\right) = 427 \text{ lb/bolt}$$

Check bolt capacity in grouted masonry wall with f'_m = 1500 psi (UBC Table 24-E).

$$B_v = 1780 \text{ lb/bolt} > 427 \quad OK$$

Check bolt capacity in ledger.

The capacity of an anchor bolt in a wood member is defined in NDS Sec. 8.2.3. The nominal design value for a wood-to-masonry connection is taken as the single-shear capacity for a wood-to-wood connection with the following definitions:

t_s = thickness of wood side member

$t_m = 2t_s$ thickness of main member for use in yield limit equations is taken as twice the thickness of wood side member.

$F_{em} = F_{es}$ dowel bearing strength of main member for use in yield limit equations is taken equal to dowel bearing strength of wood side member.

Application of the yield limit equations from Chap. 13 will be shown to demonstrate the procedure for anchor bolt capacity in a wood member. Evaluation of the yield limit equations is, in fact, required in many cases because of the way F_{em} is defined for anchor bolt problems.

In other words, the capacity of an anchor bolt in a wood member is based on the yield limit equations for a single-shear wood-to-wood connection. The dowel bearing strength F_{em} of the imaginary second wood main member is taken equal to F_{es}. The NDS bolt tables do not cover the two load cases required in this problem. As a result of the way F_{em} is defined for anchor bolt problems, NDS Table 8.2A may be used to evaluate Z *only* when the load is parallel to the grain ($Z_{\parallel}$).

In practice, the yield limit equations will be solved on a spreadsheet template or other computer program, and the cumbersome details of the hand solution are avoided.

For vertical (gravity) loads, the load is perpendicular to grain:

$D = 0.75$ in.

$F_{yb} = 45$ ksi   (assumed for A307 bolt)

$t_s = 3.5$ in.

$\theta_s = 90$ degrees

$F_{es} = 2600$ psi   ($F_{e\perp}$ for ¾-in. bolt in DF-L from NDS Table 8A)

For an anchor bolt problem:

$$t_m = 2(3.5) = 7.0 \text{ in.}$$

$$F_{em} = F_{es} = 2600 \text{ psi}$$

Coefficients for yield limit equations:

$$R_e = \frac{F_{em}}{F_{es}} = \frac{2600}{2600} = 1.0$$

$$1 + R_e = 1 + 1.0 = 2.0$$

$$1 + 2R_e = 1 + 2(1.0) = 3.0$$

$$2 + R_e = 2 + 1.0 = 3.0$$

$$R_t = \frac{t_m}{t_s} = \frac{7.0}{3.5} = 2.0$$

$$1 + R_t = 1 + 2.0 = 3.0$$

$$1 + R_t + R_t^2 = 3.0 + 2.0^2 = 7.0$$

$$\theta_{max} = 90 \text{ degrees}$$

$$K_\theta = 1 + \frac{\theta_{max}}{360} = 1 + \frac{90}{360} = 1.25$$

$$k_1 = \frac{\sqrt{R_e + 2R_e^2(1 + R_t + R_t^2) + R_t^2 R_e^3} - R_e(1 + R_t)}{(1 + R_e)}$$

$$= \frac{\sqrt{1.0 + 2(1.0^2)(7.0) + (2.0^2)(1.0^3)} - 1.0(3.0)}{2.0}$$

$$= 0.6794$$

$$k_2 = -1 + \sqrt{2(1 + R_e) + \frac{2F_{yb}(1 + 2R_e)D^2}{3F_{em}t_m^2}}$$

$$= -1 + \sqrt{2(2.0) + \frac{2(45,000)(3.0)(0.75^2)}{3(2600)(7.0^2)}}$$

$$= 1.097$$

$$k_3 = -1 + \sqrt{\frac{2(1 + R_e)}{R_e} + \frac{2F_{yb}(2 + R_e)D^2}{3F_{em}t_s^2}}$$

$$= -1 + \sqrt{\frac{2(2.0)}{1.0} + \frac{2(45,000)(3.0)(0.75^2)}{3(2600)(3.5^2)}}$$

$$= 1.364$$

Yield limit equations:

Mode I_m (NDS equation 8.2-1):

$$Z = \frac{Dt_m F_{em}}{4K_\theta} = \frac{0.75(7.0)(2600)}{4(1.25)} = 2730 \text{ lb}$$

Mode I_s (NDS equation 8.2-2):

$$Z = \frac{Dt_s F_{es}}{4K_\theta} = \frac{0.75(3.5)(2600)}{4(1.25)} = 1365 \text{ lb}$$

Mode II (NDS equation 8.2-3):

$$Z = \frac{k_1 Dt_s F_{es}}{3.6 K_\theta} = \frac{0.6794\,(0.75)(3.5)(2600)}{3.6\,(1.25)} = 1030 \text{ lb}$$

Mode III$_m$ (NDS equation 8.2-4):

$$Z = \frac{k_2 Dt_m F_{em}}{3.2(1 + 2R_e)K_\theta} = \frac{1.097\,(0.75)(7.0)(2600)}{3.2\,(3.0)(1.25)} = 1248 \text{ lb}$$

Mode III$_s$ (NDS equation 8.2-5):

$$Z = \frac{k_3 Dt_s F_{em}}{3.2(2 + R_e)K_\theta} = \frac{1.365\,(0.75)(3.5)(2600)}{3.2\,(3.0)(1.25)} = 776 \text{ lb}$$

Mode IV (NDS equation 8.2-6):

$$Z = \frac{D^2}{3.2 K_\theta} \sqrt{\frac{2 F_{em} F_{yb}}{3(1 + R_e)}}$$

$$= \frac{0.75^2}{3.2\,(1.25)} \sqrt{\frac{2\,(2600)(45{,}000)}{3\,(2.0)}} = 878 \text{ lb}$$

Nominal design value is selected as the smallest value from the yield limit formulas:

$$Z = 776 \text{ lb}$$

Load duration factor for the combination (DL + RLL) is $C_D = 1.25$. With a minimum edge distance for the loaded edge of $4D = 4(0.75) = 3.0$ in., the full bolt capacity can be used (i.e., $C_\Delta = 1.0$). Other adjustment factors are unity for this problem.

$$Z' = Z(C_D C_M C_t C_g C_\Delta)$$

$$= 776(1.25)(1.0)(1.0)(1.0)(1.0)$$

$$= 970 \text{ lb/bolt} > 427 \quad OK$$

(2) *DL + Lateral Force:*
   RLL may be omitted when lateral forces are considered (Fig. 15.5).
   Perpendicular-to-grain component q:

$$q = DL = 60\left(\frac{32}{12}\right) = 160 \text{ lb/bolt}$$

Parallel-to-grain component p:

$$p = \text{lateral force} = 300\left(\frac{32}{12}\right) = 800 \text{ lb/bolt}$$

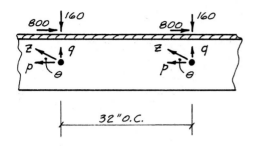

Figure 15.5 Anchor bolt in ledger carrying gravity load and lateral force parallel to wall.

Resultant load on one bolt:

$$z = \sqrt{800^2 + 160^2} = 816 \text{ lb/bolt}$$

Bolt capacity in grouted masonry wall with $f'_m = 1500$ psi is obtained from UBC Table 23-E. UBC Chap. 23 permits an allowable load increase of 1.33 for load combinations involving wind or seismic forces. See the discussion of load combination factor in Secs. 2.8 and 16.2.

$$B_v = 1780(1.33) = 2367 \text{ lb} > 816 \qquad OK$$

Bolt capacity in ledger:

Evaluation of the anchor bolt capacity in the ledger is similar to the previous yield limit equations except there is a different angle of load to grain. Computer solutions handle this problem by simply changing θ.

Angle of load to grain of θ:

$$\theta = \tan^{-1} \frac{160}{800} = 11.3 \text{ degrees}$$

$$D = 0.75 \text{ in.}$$

$$F_{yb} = 45 \text{ ksi} \qquad \text{(assumed for A307 bolt)}$$

$$t_s = 3.5 \text{ in.}$$

$$\theta_s = 11.3 \text{ degrees}$$

$$F_{e\parallel} = 5600 \text{ psi} \qquad (F_{e\parallel} \text{ for bolt in DF-L from NDS Table 8A})$$

$$F_{e\perp} = 2600 \text{ psi} \qquad (F_{e\perp} \text{ for } \tfrac{3}{4}\text{-in. bolt in DF-L from NDS Table 8A})$$

$$F_{es} = F_{e\theta} = \frac{F_{e\parallel} F_{e\perp}}{F_{e\parallel} \sin^2 \theta + F_{e\perp} \cos^2 \theta}$$

$$= \frac{5600(2600)}{5600 \sin^2 11.3 + 2600 \cos^2 11.3} = 5362 \text{ psi}$$

For an anchor bolt problem:

$$t_m = 2(3.5) = 7.0 \text{ in.}$$

$$F_{em} = F_{es} = 5362 \text{ psi}$$

Coefficients for yield limit equations:

$$R_e = \frac{F_{em}}{F_{es}} = \frac{5362}{5362} = 1.0$$

$$1 + R_e = 1 + 1.0 = 2.0$$

$$1 + 2R_e = 1 + 2(1.0) = 3.0$$

$$2 + R_e = 2 + 1.0 = 3.0$$

$$R_t = \frac{t_m}{t_s} = \frac{7.0}{3.5} = 2.0$$

$$1 + R_t = 1 + 2.0 = 3.0$$

$$1 + R_t + R_t^2 = 3.0 + 2.0^2 = 7.0$$

$$\theta_{max} = 11.3 \text{ degrees}$$

$$K_\theta = 1 + \frac{\theta_{max}}{360} = 1 + \frac{11.3}{360} = 1.031$$

$$k_1 = \frac{\sqrt{R_e + 2R_e^2(1 + R_t + R_t^2) + R_t^2 R_e^3} - R_e(1 + R_t)}{(1 + R_e)}$$

$$= \frac{\sqrt{1.0 + 2(1.0^2)(7.0) + (2.0^2)(1.0^3)} - 1.0(3.0)}{2.0}$$

$$= 0.6794 \qquad \text{(This value is unchanged from the gravity load case.)}$$

$$k_2 = -1 + \sqrt{2(1 + R_e) + \frac{2F_{yb}(1 + 2R_e)D^2}{3F_{em}t_m^2}}$$

$$= -1 + \sqrt{2(2.0) + \frac{2(45,000)(3.0)(0.75^2)}{3(5362)(7.0^2)}}$$

$$= 1.048$$

$$k_3 = -1 + \sqrt{\frac{2(1 + R_e)}{R_e} + \frac{2F_{yb}(2 + R_e)D^2}{3F_{em}t_s^2}}$$

$$= -1 + \sqrt{\frac{2(2.0)}{1.0} + \frac{2(45,000)(3.0)(0.75^2)}{3(5362)(3.5^2)}}$$

$$= 1.184$$

Yield limit equations:

Mode I_m (NDS equation 8.2-1):

$$Z = \frac{Dt_m F_{em}}{4K_\theta} = \frac{0.75(7.0)(5362)}{4(1.031)} = 6824 \text{ lb}$$

Mode I_s (NDS equation 8.2-2):

$$Z = \frac{Dt_s F_{es}}{4K_\theta} = \frac{0.75(3.5)(5362)}{4(1.031)} = 3412 \text{ lb}$$

Mode II (NDS equation 8.2-3):

$$Z = \frac{k_1 Dt_s F_{es}}{3.6K_\theta} = \frac{0.6794(0.75)(3.5)(5362)}{3.6(1.031)} = 2576 \text{ lb}$$

Mode III_m (NDS equation 8.2-4):

$$Z = \frac{k_2 Dt_m F_{em}}{3.2(1 + 2R_e)K_\theta} = \frac{1.047(0.75)(7.0)(5362)}{3.2(3.0)(1.031)} = 2979 \text{ lb}$$

Mode III_s (NDS equation 8.2-5):

$$Z = \frac{k_3 Dt_s F_{em}}{3.2(2 + R_e)K_\theta} = \frac{1.184(0.75)(3.5)(5362)}{3.2(3.0)(1.031)} = 1684 \text{ lb}$$

Mode IV (NDS equation 8.2-6):

$$Z = \frac{D^2}{3.2K_\theta} \sqrt{\frac{2F_{em}F_{yb}}{3(1 + R_e)}}$$

$$= \frac{0.75^2}{3.2(1.031)} \sqrt{\frac{2(5362)(45,000)}{3(2.0)}} = 1529 \text{ lb}$$

Nominal design value is selected as the smallest value from the yield limit formulas:

$$Z = 1529 \text{ lb}$$

Load duration factor from NDS for a combination of (DL + seismic) is $C_D = 1.6$.* Other adjustment factors are unity for this problem.

$$Z' = Z(C_D C_M C_t C_g C_\Delta)$$

$$= 1529(1.6 \times 1.0 \times 1.0 \times 1.0 \times 1.0)$$

$$= 2446 \text{ lb/bolt} > 816 \quad OK$$

Use ¾-in.-diameter anchor bolts at 32 in. o.c.

---

*Verify acceptance of $C_D = 1.6$ by local code authority before using in practice.

d. Provide wall anchors at every other roof framing member (i.e., 4 ft-0 in. o.c.). Perpendicular-to-wall force:

$$P = 200 \text{ lb/ft} \times 4 \text{ ft} = 800 \text{ lb}$$

Choose a wall anchor from manufacturer with Code-recognized load capacity that is greater than 800 lb.

The second anchorage detail example is for a diaphragm that connects to the *top* of a concrete or masonry wall. See Example 15.7. The anchor bolts in the wall are used to transfer the lateral forces both parallel and perpendicular to the wall. These forces are not checked concurrently, and the bolt values parallel and perpendicular to grain in the wood plate are used independently. The strength of the bolt in the wall must also be checked.

The problem in this connection centers on the need to avoid cross-grain tension in the wood plate when forces normal to the wall are considered. Two possible connections for preventing cross-grain tension are presented.

Calculations for the anchorage of this type of connection are similar in many respects to those for the ledger connection (Example 15.6), and a numerical example is not provided.

EXAMPLE 15.7   Anchorage at Top of Masonry Wall

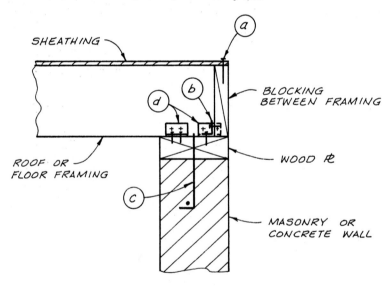

Figure 15.6a Anchorage connections to top of masonry wall.

Parallel-to-Wall Force (Diaphragm Shear)

a. Boundary nailing transfers diaphragm shear from sheathing into blocking.

b. Connection for transferring shear from blocking to plate. Framing anchor is shown. Alternate connection is additional blocking as in Example 9.5 (Sec. 9.4). Toenails are not allowed for anchorage of concrete or masonry walls.

c1. Shear is transferred from plate to wall by anchor bolts. Bolt strength is governed by wall capacity (UBC Table 24-E or 26-E) or by the allowable load parallel to grain of the bolt in the wood plate.

Perpendicular-to-Wall Force (Wind, Seismic, or Code Minimum)

c2. Lateral force normal to wall is transferred from wall to plate by anchor bolts. Bolt strength is governed by wall capacity (UBC Table 24-E or 26-E) or by the allowable load perpendicular to the grain of the bolt in the wood plate.

d. The attachment of the wall plate to the framing presents a problem. The Code requires that anchorage of concrete and masonry walls be accomplished without cross-grain bending or *cross-grain tension*.

The connection in Fig. 15.6*b* is shown with framing anchors on both the right and left sides of the wall plate. In this way cross-grain tension in the plate is not being relied upon for load transfer. The framing anchors shown with solid lines are those that stress the plate in compression perpendicular to grain.

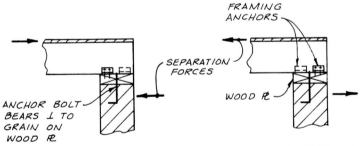

Figure 15.6*b* For each case, the framing anchor shown with solid lines is capable of transferring the lateral force to the anchor bolt by compression perpendicular to grain.

For a given direction of lateral force, the effective framing anchors cause the wood plate to bear on the anchor bolt in compression. Without fasteners on both sides of the anchor bolt, cross-grain tension would be developed in the plate for one of the directions of loading. The shear in the wood plate should be checked in accordance with the procedures given in Sec. 13.7.

Other connection details can be used to avoid cross-grain tension. One alternative, shown in Fig. 15.6*c*, avoids the problem by tying the framing member directly to the anchor bolt. Use of this type of anchorage requires close field coordination. The anchor bolts must be set accurately when the wall is constructed to match the future location of the roof or floor framing.

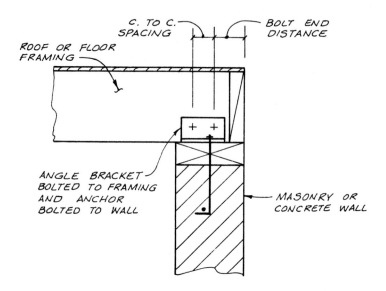

C. TO C.
SPACING

BOLT END
DISTANCE

ROOF OR FLOOR
FRAMING

ANGLE BRACKET
BOLTED TO FRAMING
AND ANCHOR
BOLTED TO WALL

MASONRY OR
CONCRETE WALL

PARTIAL CONNECTION DETAIL
SHOWING ALT. ANCHORAGE FOR
NORMAL TO WALL FORCES

Figure 15.6c Angle bracket is connected directly to framing and anchor bolt. Therefore, normal wall force is transferred directly to the framing without placing the wood plate on top of wall in cross-grain tension.

Subdiaphragm Anchorage

For a discussion of the subdiaphragm anchorage of concrete and masonry walls, see Example 15.5 and Sec. 15.5.

15.5 Subdiaphragm Anchorage of Concrete and Masonry Walls

The anchorage requirements for concrete and masonry walls were outlined in Sec. 15.4. There it was noted that the Code requires *continuous ties* between the diaphragm chords in order to distribute the anchorage forces perpendicular to a wall into the diaphragm. The concept of subdiaphragms (also known as minidiaphragms) was developed to satisfy this Code requirement. The concept was first presented in Ref. 1.4*a*, and it was subsequently restated and clarified in Refs. 1.4*b* and 1.4*c*. Reprints of these latter two references are available in Ref. 14.13 from the American Plywood Association.

If the framing members in a horizontal diaphragm are continuous members from one side of the building to the other, the diaphragm would naturally have continuous ties between the chords. See Example 15.8. This is possible, however, only in very small buildings or in buildings with closely spaced trusses. Even if continuous framing is present in one direction, it would normally not be present in the other direction.

EXAMPLE 15.8   Diaphragm with Continuous Framing

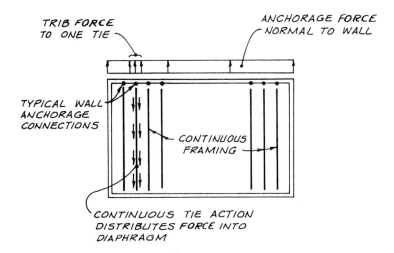

Figure 15.7 Building with continuous cross ties between diaphragm chords in one direction provided by continuous framing.

Continuous framing in the transverse direction would provide continuous ties between diaphragm chords for the transverse lateral force. For this force the chords are parallel to the longitudinal walls. Continuous ties distribute the anchorage force back into the diaphragm. The action of a continuous tie is similar in concept to a drag strut. The tie drags the wall force into the diaphragm.

If the spacing of wall anchors exceeds 4 ft, the wall must be designed to resist bending between the anchors. For the lateral force in the longitudinal direction, no intermediate ties are shown perpendicular to the continuous framing (Fig. 15.7). Ties must be designed and spliced across the transverse framing, or the transverse wall must be designed for bending (at the diaphragm level) between the longitudinal shearwalls (not practical in most buildings).

The majority of buildings do not have continuous framing. In a typical panelized roof system, for example, the subpurlins span between purlins,

purlins span between girders, and girders span between columns. See Example 15.9. In addition, the tops of the beams are usually kept at the same elevation, and the diaphragm sheathing is nailed directly to these members. In order for this type of construction to be used, the lighter beams are not continuous across supporting members. Lighter beams are typically suspended from heavier beams with metal hangers (Chap. 14).

If continuous cross ties are to be provided between diaphragm chords in both directions of the building, a larger number of additional connections will be required. In order to meet the continuous-tie requirement literally, each beam would have to be spliced for an axial drag-type force across the members to which it frames.

EXAMPLE 15.9   Diaphragm without Continuous Framing

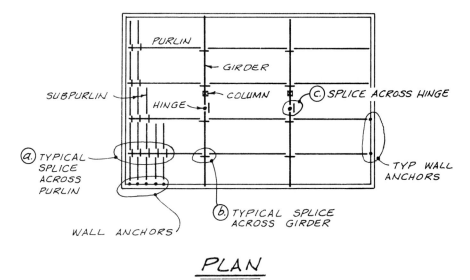

PLAN

Figure 15.8 Continuous cross ties between diaphragm chords by splicing each framing member would require an excessive number of connections.

In a building without continuous framing between the diaphragm chords, a large number of cross-tie splices would be required (Fig. 15.8).

a. Subpurlins spliced across purlins
b. Purlins spliced across girders
c. Girders spliced across hinges

Splices must be capable of transmitting the wall anchorage force tributary to a given member (Fig. 15.7). With the use of subdiaphragms, the continuous-tie requirement may be satisfied *without* connection splices at every beam crossing.

The idea of a *subdiaphragm* was developed to ensure the proper anchorage of the wall seismic forces without requiring a cross-tie splice at every beam crossing. With this method the designer selects a portion of the total diaphragm (known as a subdiaphragm) which is designed as a separate diaphragm. See Example 15.10. The unit *shear* capacity (plywood thickness and nailing) must be sufficient to carry the tributary wall lateral forces, and the subdiaphragm must have its own *chords* and *continuous cross ties* between the chords. Subdiaphragm chords and cross ties are also referred to as *subchords* and *subcross ties* (or simply *subties*).

The subdiaphragm reactions are in turn carried by the main cross ties which must be continuous across the full horizontal diaphragm. Use of the subdiaphragm avoids the requirement for continuous ties across the full width of the diaphragm except at the subdiaphragm boundaries.

EXAMPLE 15.10   Subdiaphragm Analysis

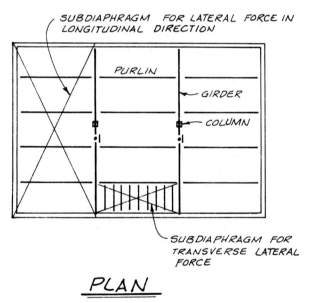

PLAN

Figure 15.9a Subdiaphragms may be used to provide wall anchorage without requiring the large number of connections described in Fig. 15.8.

The building from the previous example is redrawn in Fig. 15.9a showing the subdiaphragms which will be used for the wall anchorage. The assumed action of the subdiaphragms for resisting the lateral forces is shown in Figs. 15.9b and 15.9c. The subdiaphragm concept is only a computational device that is used to develop adequate anchorage of concrete and masonry walls. It is recognized that the subdiaphragms are actually part of the total horizontal diaphragm, and they do not deflect independently as shown.

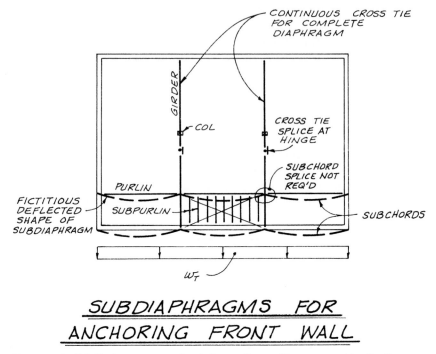

SUBDIAPHRAGMS FOR ANCHORING FRONT WALL

Figure 15.9b Subdiaphragms spanning between the continuous cross ties for the complete diaphragm.

For construction using plywood and other structural-use panels, subdiaphragm proportions (span-to-width ratios) are limited to a maximum of 4:1 (the same as for the total horizontal diaphragm).

Three subdiaphragms for the anchorage of the front longitudinal wall are shown in Fig. 15.9b. Three similar subdiaphragms will also be used for the anchorage of the rear wall. Note that the transverse anchorage force can act in either direction.

The purlin and wall serve as the chords (subchords) for the subdiaphragms. The purlin must be designed for combined bending and axial forces. Because the subdiaphragms are treated as separate diaphragms, the subchord forces are zero at the girder. The purlins, therefore, need not be spliced across the girders.

The subpurlins serve as continuous cross ties (subties) between the subdiaphragm chords and do not have to be spliced across the purlin. The girders act as continuous cross ties for the complete diaphragm, and a cross-tie splice at the hinge is required. The splice must carry the reactions from two subdiaphragms.

The subdiaphragm for anchorage of the left wall is shown in Fig. 15.9c. A similar subdiaphragm is required for anchoring the right wall. The girder and wall serve as chords for the subdiaphragm. The girder must be designed for combined bending from gravity loads plus axial tension or compression caused by lateral forces.

The splice at the girder hinge must be designed for the subdiaphragm chord force. This is an alternate force to the continuous cross-tie force caused by the transverse lateral

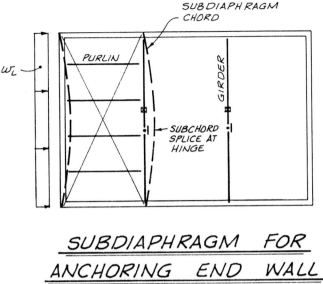

SUBDIAPHRAGM FOR
ANCHORING END WALL

Figure 15.9c A subdiaphragm can have the same span as the complete diaphragm. However, the subdiaphragm is designed for the wall anchorage force, and the complete diaphragm is designed for the total lateral force to the horizontal diaphragm.

force in Fig. 15.9b. The purlins serve as continuous ties between subdiaphragm chords and do not have to be spliced across the girder.

The designer has some flexibility in the choice of what portions of the complete diaphragm are used as subdiaphragms. See Example 15.11. Figure 15.10a in this example shows that a number of small subdiaphragms are used to anchor the transverse wall. In Fig. 15.10b, one large subdiaphragm is used to anchor the same wall force between the longitudinal walls only. For additional examples illustrating subdiaphragm choices, see Refs. 1.4b, 1.4c, and 1.4i.

The flexibility permitted in the choice of subdiaphragm arrangements results from the fact that the subdiaphragm concept is a computational device only. The independent deflection of the subdiaphragms is not possible, and the analysis is used arbitrarily to ensure adequate anchorage connections.

Various types of connections can be used to provide the splices in the cross ties and chords of the diaphragm and subdiaphragms. Because most beams frame into the sides of the supporting members, compression forces are normally assumed to be taken by bearing. Thus the connections are usually designed for tension. This tension tie can be incorporated as part of the basic connection hardware (e.g., the seismic tie splice on the hinge connection in

Fig. 14.19), or a separate tension strap may be provided (Fig. 14.22). The connections may be specially designed using the principles of Chaps. 12, 13, and 14, or some form of prefabricated connection hardware may be used.

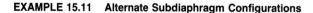

EXAMPLE 15.11   Alternate Subdiaphragm Configurations

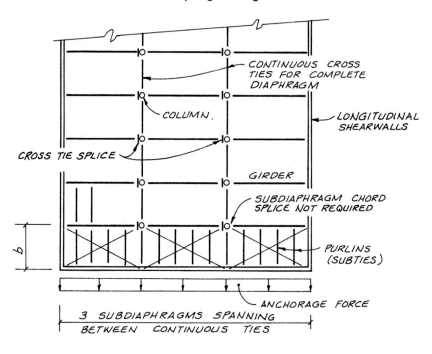

Figure 15.10a Three small subdiaphragms used to anchor transverse end wall.

The subdiaphragm arrangement in Fig. 15.10a uses three small subdiaphragms. The two outside subdiaphragms span between the longitudinal shearwalls and the continuous cross ties for the complete diaphragm. The center subdiaphragm spans between the two continuous cross ties. The line of purlins forming the two main cross ties must be spliced at each girder crossing (in this example a column happens to occur at each of these locations) for the tributary wall anchorage force.

The other purlins in the subdiaphragms serve as continuous ties (subties) between the subdiaphragm chords, and they need not be spliced for lateral forces across the girder line.

The transverse wall and first row of girders serve as the subchords. The subdiaphragm chord force is zero at the ends of the girders, and subchord splices are not required at the columns.

In the second subdiaphragm layout (Fig. 15.10b), one large subdiaphragm spans between the exterior walls. Continuous subtie splices are required for the purlins across

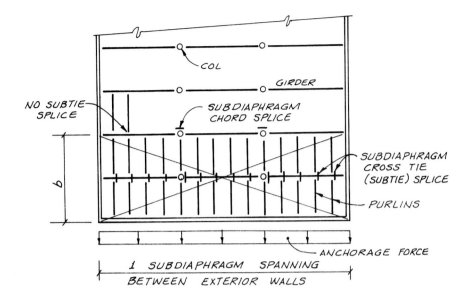

PLAN

Figure 15.10*b* One large subdiaphragm used to anchor transverse end wall.

the first girder only. The subdiaphragm chord formed by the second line of girders must be tied across the columns for the appropriate subchord force.

The choice of the subdiaphragm configuration in practice will depend on the required number of connections when both the transverse and longitudinal forces are considered.

The reader is reminded that the lateral forces shown in the examples in this section are *wall anchorage forces*. In other words, the forces represent one of the three perpendicular-to-wall forces described in Example 15.2, and they are not the lateral forces for designing the main horizontal diaphragm.

Subdiaphragms are really a design concern in structures with concrete and masonry walls, and the typical anchorage force is the seismic force $F_p = (ZIC_p)W_p \geq 200$ lb/ft. This force was first introduced in Example 2.17 (Sec. 2.15). The primary purpose of Examples 15.8 to 15.11 was to define the concept of a subdiaphragm and to illustrate where additional seismic connections may be required. It should be noted that the forces in these examples are simply shown as uniformly distributed lateral forces, and they do not reflect the 50 percent increase in F_p required for the center one-half of the diaphragm. The increase in the F_p anchorage force for the center part of a flexible diaphragm is illustrated in Example 15.12.

15.6   Design Problem: Subdiaphragm

In Example 15.12 the wall anchorage requirements for a large one-story building are analyzed. Exterior walls are of reinforced brick masonry construction.

In order to check the unit shear in the subdiaphragms, the construction of the entire roof diaphragm must be known. For this reason the unit shear diagrams for the complete diaphragm are shown along with the nailing and the allowable unit shears. Two different nailing patterns are used for the roof diaphragm. The heavier nailing occurs near the ends of the building in areas of high diaphragm shear. This different nailing is important when the unit shears in the subdiaphragms are checked.

Along the longitudinal wall a series of small subdiaphragms is used to anchor the wall. Subdiaphragm 1 spans between girders which serve as continuous cross ties for the entire roof diaphragm in the transverse direction. Because subdiaphragm 1 occurs in both areas of diaphragm nailing, the unit shear in the subdiaphragm is first checked against the lower allowable shear for the complete diaphragm.

When the lower shear capacity is found to be inadequate for subdiaphragm 1, an 8-ft-wide strip of heavier nailing is added next to the longitudinal wall. An alternative solution would be to increase the size of subdiaphragm 1.

The transverse wall is anchored by a large subdiaphragm that spans between the longitudinal walls. Continuous cross ties are required only between the subdiaphragm chords. Because subdiaphragm 2 coincides with the area of heavy nailing for the complete diaphragm, the unit shear can be checked against the larger shear capacity of the diaphragm.

The use of the larger-diaphragm shear capacity (425 lb/ft) in a number of locations requires that the heavier boundary nailing be provided at the perimeter of each subdiaphragm. Care must be taken to avoid potential splitting of lumber that might result from the use of closely spaced nails at adjacent subdiaphragm boundaries. See UBC Table 25-J-1, footnote 2, for possible considerations.

EXAMPLE 15.12   Subdiaphragm Anchorage for Masonry Walls

The complete roof diaphragm for the building in Example 15.11 has been designed for seismic forces in both the transverse and longitudinal directions. The unit shears and plywood nailing are summarized below. A subdiaphragm analysis is to be performed using subdiaphragm 1 (Fig. 15.11b) for the longitudinal walls and subdiaphragm 2 (Fig. 15.11c) for the transverse walls. The calculation of subdiaphragm unit shears and tie forces is demonstrated.

Given Information

Total wall height is 16 ft. Tributary wall height to roof diaphragm:

$$h = \frac{16}{2} = 8 \text{ ft}$$

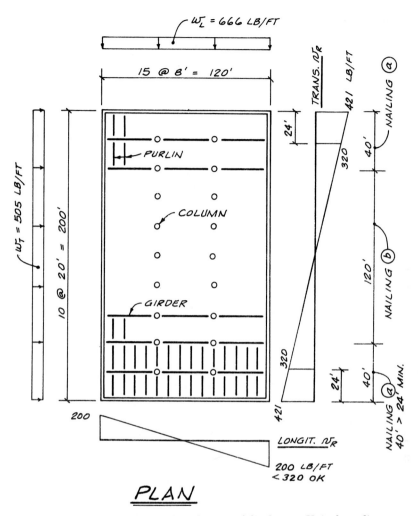

Figure 15.11a Lateral forces on entire horizontal diaphragm. Unit shear diagrams caused by transverse and longitudinal lateral forces are also shown.

Dead loads:

$$Roof\ DL\ =\ 11\ psf$$

$$Wall\ DL\ =\ 90\ psf$$

Seismic coefficient:

$$w\ =\ 0.183\ W_1$$

Entire Roof Diaphragm

Seismic force to roof diaphragm:

$$\text{Transverse } w = 0.183[11 \text{ psf}(120 \text{ ft}) + 90 \text{ psf}(8 \text{ ft})(2 \text{ walls})]$$

$$= 505 \text{ lb/ft}$$

$$\text{Longitudinal } w = 0.183[11 \text{ psf}(200 \text{ ft}) + 90 \text{ psf}(8 \text{ ft})(2 \text{ walls})]$$

$$= 666 \text{ lb/ft}$$

Roof unit shears: See unit shear diagrams (Fig. 15.11a).

$$\text{Transverse } V = \frac{wL}{2} = \frac{505(200)}{2} = 50,500 \text{ lb}$$

$$v = \frac{V}{b} = \frac{50,500}{120} = 421 \text{ lb/ft}$$

$$\text{Longitudinal } V = \frac{wL}{2} = \frac{666(120)}{2} = 39,960 \text{ lb}$$

$$v = \frac{V}{b} = \frac{39,960}{200} = 200 \text{ lb/ft}$$

Plywood sheathing and nailing:

½-in. STR I plywood.

All edges supported and nailed into 2-in. minimum nominal framing.

Assume plywood load cases 2 and 4 (UBC Table 25-J-1). Note that plywood layout is not shown, but will eventually be included on the plans.

> *Diaphragm nailing a.*   10d common nails at:
>   4-in. o.c. boundary and continuous panel edges
>   6-in. o.c. other panel edges
>   12-in. o.c. field

$$\text{Allow. } v = 425 \text{ lb/ft} > 421 \quad \textit{OK}$$

> *Diaphragm nailing b.*   10d common nails at:
>   6-in. o.c. all edges
>   12-in. o.c. field

$$\text{Allow. } v = 320 \text{ lb/ft}$$

From similar triangles on the unit shear diagram, a unit shear of 320 lb/ft occurs 24 ft from the transverse shearwalls.

∴ Use diaphragm *nailing a* for distance of 40 ft from transverse shearwalls (24 ft is minimum), and use diaphragm *nailing b* in central 120 ft of horizontal diaphragm.

NOTE: In the longitudinal direction two allowable shears apply: 425 lb/ft for *nailing a* and 320 lb/ft for *nailing b*. Both of these allowable shears exceed the actual shear of 200 lb/ft. Therefore, unit shear in longitudinal direction is not critical.

Subdiaphragm Anchorage of Longitudinal Masonry Wall

Subdiaphragm 1(8 ft × 20 ft):

The seismic force for wall anchorage was introduced in Chap. 2 (see note in Example 2.17). The seismic coefficient from Example 2.17 (Sec. 2.15) applies to the current problem:

$$F_p = ZIC_pW_p = 0.4(1.0)(0.75)W_p = 0.3W_p$$

This seismic coefficient is used to obtain the force normal to the wall.

$$w = 0.3W_p = 0.3(90 \text{ psf})$$

$$= 27 \text{ psf} > \text{design wind pressure} \quad \text{(wind analysis not shown)}$$

Anchorage force is the "roof reaction" which is obtained as the uniform seismic force times the tributary height to the roof level.

$$w_T = 27 \text{ psf} \times 8 \text{ ft} = 216 \text{ lb/ft} > \text{Code minimum of 200}$$

The 1991 UBC requires that the coefficient C_p be increased 50 percent for the center one-half of flexible diaphragms (UBC Table 23-P, footnote 3). This causes the wall-to-diaphragm anchorage force to increase 50 percent in this area. See Fig. 15.11*b*.

$$w_T = 216(1.5) = 324 \text{ lb/ft} \quad \text{for central 100 ft of diaphragm span}$$

Technically the anchorage connections could be different in the area of the smaller anchorage force of 216 lb/ft (i.e., over a distance of 50 ft from the transverse shearwalls). However, any potential savings in cost, resulting from the lower design force, must be weighed against the increased field control and inspection necessary to ensure that the different anchorage details are located and installed properly in the field. For this reason, the designer may wish to consider using the larger design force of 324 lb/ft over the entire length of the wall.

Although the designer may choose to use the larger value throughout, the remainder of this example, in most cases, illustrates the evaluation of connection design forces for both sets of lateral forces.

Subdiaphragm span-to-width ratio:

$$\frac{L}{b} = \frac{20}{8} = 2.5 < 4 \quad OK$$

Subdiaphragm unit shear:

A typical 8 ft × 20 ft subdiaphragm (subdiaphragm 1) in the central 100 ft of the building will have the critical unit shear.

$$\text{Max. } V = \frac{wL}{2} = \frac{324(20)}{2} = 3240 \text{ lb}$$

$$v = \frac{V}{b} = \frac{3240}{8} = 405 \text{ lb/ft} > 320 \text{ lb/ft} \quad NG$$

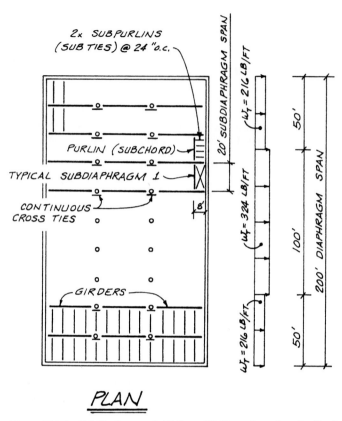

PLAN

Figure 15.11b Subdiaphragm 1 (8 ft × 20 ft) anchors longitudinal masonry wall for seismic force w_T in transverse direction. The 1991 UBC requires an increased seismic anchorage force for the center one-half of a flexible diaphragm.

The nailing for the entire roof diaphragm in the center portion of the building (i.e., diaphragm nailing *b*) is not adequate for subdiaphragm 1. There are several possible solutions to this problem. For example, the 8-ft width of subdiaphragm 1 could be increased to 16 ft to reduce the unit shear. In other words, subdiaphragm 1 could be changed from an 8 × 20 ft subdiaphragm to a 16 × 20 ft subdiaphragm. Although this would reduce the unit shear in the subdiaphragm, it would require the addition of subtie splice connections across the first line of purlins next to the longitudinal wall.

The alternative solution chosen in this example is to provide increased nailing for the original 8 × 20 ft subdiaphragm 1. This will be done by extending nailing *a* for the entire roof diaphragm, to include an 8-ft-wide strip along the longitudinal walls. See Fig. 15.11c.

$$\text{Allow. } v = 425 \text{ lb/ft} > 405 \text{ lb/ft} \quad OK$$

NOTE: Nailing *a* includes boundary nailing that must be provided at the perimeter of each subdiaphragm 1. Technically this requirement could be limited to subdiaphragms in the central 100-ft portion of the building.

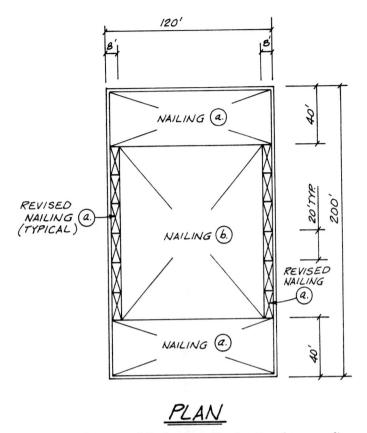

PLAN

Figure 15.11c Summary of diaphragm nailing locations for proper diaphragm and subdiaphragm action. See calculations below for *revised nailing a.*

For the following anchorage force calculations, refer to Fig. 15.11*b*.
Girder—continuous cross-tie force at columns:

Central 100-ft portion (area of increased anchorage force)

$$T = (324 \text{ lb/ft})(20 \text{ ft}) = 6480 \text{ lb}$$

Outer 50-ft segments (without the 50 percent increase)

$$T = (216 \text{ lb/ft})(20 \text{ ft}) = 4320 \text{ lb}$$

Depending on the location, the continuous-cross-tie connections along the girders at the columns could be designed for these different forces. As a practical matter, all of the girder splices at the columns may conservatively be designed for a force of 6480 lb.

NOTE: The purpose of this example is to define the subdiaphragm problem and to determine the associated design forces. Detailed connection designs for these forces are beyond the scope of the example. See Chaps. 12 to 14 for design principles.

Subpurlin—anchor wall to subpurlin at 4 ft-0 in. o.c.

Every other subpurlin will serve as a continuous cross tie (subtie) for subdiaphragm 1. The masonry wall need not be designed for bending between wall anchors that are spaced 4 ft-0 in. o.c. or less. As with the girder splices above, subpurlin anchors may be different for the central 100-ft portion of the building and the outer 50-ft segments. Alternatively, the anchors for the more heavily loaded portion may be used throughout.
Central 100-ft portion:

$$T = (324 \text{ lb/ft})(4 \text{ ft}) = 1296 \text{ lb}$$

Outer 50-ft segments:

$$T = (216 \text{ lb/ft})(4 \text{ ft}) = 864 \text{ lb}$$

An anchor bracket with a Code-recognized load capacity in excess of these values should be provided between the masonry wall and the $2 \times$ subpurlins (subties).

These anchorage brackets may be attached to subpurlins that occur at the edge of a plywood panel. However, unless the designer is assured of this, it should be assumed that the anchors occur at subpurlins located at the center of a plywood panel. In this case, the capacity of the diaphragm *field nailing* should be checked against the wall anchorage force. The capacity of a 10d common nail in a plywood diaphragm nailed to DF-L framing is determined to be

$Z = 90 \text{ lb/nail}$ (Obtained from NDS Table 12.3B. As an alternative
to the NDS table yield limit equations may be evaluated.)

The following adjustments apply:

$C_D = 1.6$ for seismic force (verify local code acceptance
before using in practice)

$C_{di} = 1.1$ plywood diaphragm nailing (Sec. 12.6)

Nail penetration is adequate by inspection,

$$\therefore C_d = 1.0$$

All other adjustment factors are unity.

$$Z' = Z(C_D C_M C_t C_d C_{eg} C_{di} C_{tn})$$

$$= 90(1.6)(1.0)(1.0)(1.0)(1.0)(1.1)(1.0)$$

$$= 158 \text{ lb/nail}$$

NOTE: Reference 14.11 recommends a 10 percent reduction in nail value when diaphragm nailing is driven into narrow (2-in. nominal) framing. The 0.9 multiplying factor in the next step is to account for this reduction. Depending on materials, other adjustments may apply. Contact APA for the latest information regarding allowable nail design values for diaphragms based on yield limit theory.

$$\text{Modified } Z' = 0.9(158) = 142 \text{ lb/nail}$$

The usual spacing of nails in the field (i.e., along intermediate framing) of a plywood panel is 12 in. o.c. Subpurlins are 8 ft long, and a minimum of 8 (probably 9) nails is available to develop the anchorage force.

$$P = 8(142) = 1136 \text{ lb}$$

This load capacity exceeds the 864 lb for the anchorage force for the outer 50-ft segments, but it is less than the 1296-lb force for the central 100-ft portion. Determine the nailing required for the increased force in the center one-half of the building.

$$N = \frac{1296}{142} = 9+ \text{ nails per subpurlin}$$

Use a minimum of ten 10d common nails per subpurlin for the 8-ft-wide strip of nailing a immediately adjacent to the longitudinal walls. This may be expressed as an average nail spacing of

$$S = \frac{L}{N-1} = \frac{96 \text{ in.}}{10-1} \approx 10 \text{ in. o.c.}$$

> *Revised nailing a* (Fig. 15.11c). 10d common nails at:
> 4-in. o.c. boundary and continuous panel edges
> 6-in. o.c. other panel edges
> 10-in. o.c. field

The diaphragm nailing in Fig. 15.11c is not extremely complex, and it is provided here because it adds to the understanding of subdiaphragms. However, as a practical matter, the various nailings in this example do not differ substantially from one another, and use of a single nailing specification should be considered. With a single nailing specification, layout and inspection in the field could be simplified at the expense of a relatively small amount of additional nailing.

Subdiaphragm chord force purlins (refer again to Fig. 15.11b):

The first line of purlins parallel to the masonry wall serves as the subchord for subdiaphragm 1. Although a subchord force could be computed for the outer 50-ft segments, the subchord force for the central 100-ft section is critical.

$$T_{\max} = C_{\max} = \frac{M}{b} = \frac{wL^2}{8b} = \frac{324(20)^2}{8(8)} = 2025 \text{ lb}$$

A subchord splice across the girders is not required. However, the subchord must be checked for combined axial stress (from the subchord force) plus bending stress (from gravity loads).

Subdiaphragm Anchorage of Transverse
Masonry Wall

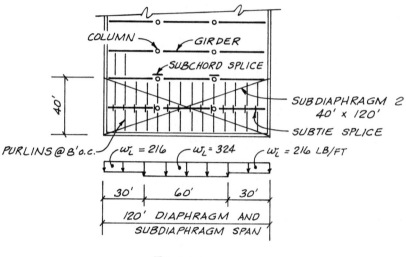

Figure 15.11d Subdiaphragm 2 (40 ft × 120 ft) anchors transverse masonry wall for seismic force w_L in longitudinal direction.

Subdiaphragm 2 (40 ft × 120 ft):

Wall anchorage forces (from subdiaphragm 1):

w_L = 216 lb/ft   for two 30-ft outer segments of diaphragm span

w_L = 324 lb/ft   for central 60-ft portion of diaphragm span

Span-to-width ratio:

$$\frac{L}{b} = \frac{120}{40} = 3 < 4 \quad OK$$

Subdiaphragm shear:

$$V = \frac{216(30 + 30) + 324(60)}{2} = 16{,}200 \text{ lb}$$

$$v = \frac{V}{b} = \frac{16{,}200 \text{ lb}}{40 \text{ ft}} = 405 \text{ lb/ft} < 425 \text{ lb/ft} \quad OK$$

Diaphragm nailing a is adequate for subdiaphragm 2. However, in order for subdiaphragm 2 to qualify for an allowable shear of 425 lb/ft, the boundary nailing of 10d common nails at 4 in. o.c. must be provided along the second girder line in addition to the usual boundary nailing locations for nailing a.

Purlin—subtie splice force across the first girder line:
Two different subtie splice forces may be determined:
Central 60-ft portion (for the increased anchorage force):

$$T = (324 \text{ lb/ft})(8 \text{ ft}) = 2592 \text{ lb}$$

Outer 30-ft segments (without the 50 percent force increase):

$$T = (216 \text{ lb/ft})(8 \text{ ft}) = 1728 \text{ lb}$$

All the subtie splices across the first girder line may conservatively be designed for the larger of these anchorage forces. Again, the designer must weigh the pros and cons of the two approaches.
Purlin—anchor wall to purlins at 8 ft-0 in. o.c.:
The connection hardware between the masonry wall and the purlins has the same design forces as the subtie splices just determined:

$$T = \begin{cases} 2592 \text{ lb/purlin} & \text{central 60-ft portion} \\ 1728 \text{ lb/purlin} & \text{outer 30-ft segments} \end{cases}$$

The nailing between the plywood sheathing and the cross tie for subdiaphragm 2 is not as critical as subdiaphragm 1. The maximum subtie force has doubled ($2 \times 1296 = 2592$ lb), but the cross-tie length has more than doubled (the length is 40 ft instead of 8 ft). In addition, plywood edge nailing (not just the field nailing) will occur along the subties (purlins) due to the plywood layout. Therefore, a less critical subtie nailing situation exists for subdiaphragm 2.
Note that the masonry wall must be designed for bending because the 8-ft spacing of anchors exceeds the 4-ft Code limit. This is a masonry design problem and is not included here.
Subdiaphragm chord force in second girder line:
The maximum moment in subdiaphragm 2 (Fig. 15.11d) is 534.6 ft-k.

$$T = C = \frac{M}{b} = \frac{534,600 \text{ ft-lb}}{40 \text{ ft}} = 13,365 \text{ lb}$$

The subdiaphragm chord along the second girder should be spliced at the columns for the subchord force of 13,365 lb, instead of the continuous-cross-tie force of 4320 lb for this location (see calculations for subdiaphragm 1).
An alternate for subdiaphragm 2 is to use several smaller subdiaphragms similar to the first arrangement in Example 15.11.

The design of anchorage for concrete and masonry walls to wood roof systems using the concept of subdiaphragms has been utilized since the early 1970s.
It was noted in Chap. 2 that a major change to the seismic design requirements of the UBC was introduced in 1988. A number of significant changes are concerned with seismicly irregular structures. A different approach to handling the design for overturning of shearwalls has evolved for wind and seismic forces. These subjects are introduced in Chap. 16.

15.7 Problems

15.1 *Given:* The roof framing of Fig. 9.A (Chap. 9) and the typical section of the same building in Fig. 15.A. The lateral wind pressure is 20 psf. Roof DL = 15 psf and RLL = 20 psf.

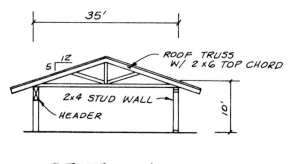

Figure 15.A

> *Find:* Design and sketch the roof-to-wall anchorage details for:
> a. The rear longitudinal wall at the 25- and 20-ft headers.
> b. The longitudinal bearing walls.
> c. The right transverse wall. Consider one case with full-height wall studs and a second case with 10-ft studs to a double plate and a filler truss over.

15.2 *Given:* The roof framing plan of Fig. 9.A (Chap. 9) and the typical section of the same building in Fig. 15.B. Roof DL = 20 psf; roof LL = 20 psf; wall DL = 75 psf. Seismic base shear coefficient = 0.183.

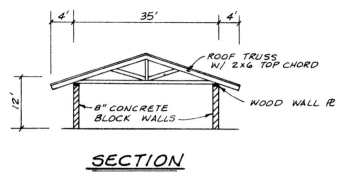

Figure 15.B

> *Find:* Design and sketch the roof-to-wall anchorage details for:
> a. The longitudinal bearing walls.
> b. The transverse walls, assuming continuous full-height masonry from foundation to roof level. Include cross ties at 4 ft-0 in. o.c.

16

Advanced Topics in
Lateral Force Design

16.1 Introduction

The seismic base shear and the distribution of this force over the height of
the structure were covered in Chap. 2. It was noted that the format of the
base shear equation has been improved in the new seismic code (1988 and
1991 UBC). The terms in the base shear coefficient are more rational, but
for a typical wood-frame building with standard occupancy, the numerical
results obtained using the new formula for base shear

$$V = \left(\frac{ZIC}{R_w}\right)W$$

are not substantially different from those given by the old formula

$$V = (ZIKCS)W$$

However, a number of important changes were incorporated into the new
seismic code. One significant change is the need to consider whether or not
a structure is *regular* or *irregular*.

In addition, specific overturning requirements for earthquake forces were
introduced. The Code has also modified the overturning requirements for
the moment stability analysis of certain low-profile buildings under wind
forces. It is important for the designer to understand the similarities and
differences in the overturning requirements for wind and seismic forces.

This chapter provides an introduction to seismic irregularity considerations and gives a more detailed review of the overturning requirements for
both wind and seismic forces.

The reader is reminded of the general convention in this book to use the term *load* to refer to a *gravity* effect such as dead load, live load, snow load, and so on. On the other hand, *force* generally refers to a *lateral* effect such as wind force and seismic force. Therefore, the phrase *combination of loads and forces* implies that both gravity and lateral effects are involved. Although there are not hard-and-fast rules regarding the use of these terms, the pattern of addressing vertical (gravity) loads *and* lateral (wind and seismic) forces seems to be emerging.

16.2   Seismic Forces—Regular Structures

Experience has proven that regular structures perform much better in earthquakes than irregular structures. The subject of irregularity has added to the length and complexity of the seismic code. Recall how the SEAOC *Blue Book* and its commentary (Ref. 6.1) have grown in size, and to a large extent this increase is the result of the need to consider structural irregularity.

To demonstrate how involved this subject has become, the new seismic code identifies 10 types of structural irregularity. In order to organize these into a workable system, the UBC summarizes these irregularities in tables, and the tables then reference appropriate sections of the Code which give the detailed requirements for each type of irregularity. The commentary to the Blue Book expands on each item. Obviously a comprehensive treatment of structural irregularity is beyond the scope of this introductory text. However, it is essential that the designer of a wood-frame building have some knowledge of this subject.

Several examples of *regular* and *irregular* structures are given in this chapter to illustrate the general concepts. The wood-frame buildings that were considered in previous chapters meet the basic definition of a seismicly regular structure. Dealing with these basic types of structures allowed a number of important subjects to be covered without becoming overly complicated. These subjects included horizontal diaphragms, shearwalls, chords, drag struts, and anchorage forces.

However, regular structures are rather limited in plan and elevation, and many buildings do not qualify as regular structures. It is important for the designer to be able to recognize what constitutes a structural irregularity and to know what, if any, additional requirements are imposed because of the irregularity. A number of the features that can cause a structure to be classified as irregular are addressed in Sec. 16.3.

Regular structures are those which have no significant physical or structural irregularities in either plan view or elevation. For example, a simple rectangular wood-frame building with a uniform distribution of mass can fit this description. However, in order to be classified as structurally regular, an additional requirement for multistory buildings is that the shearwalls in an upper story must be located directly over the shearwalls in a lower story. See Example 16.1.

EXAMPLE 16.1   Regular Structure

Regular structures have a history of good performance in resisting earthquake forces. These structures have no *plan irregularities* or *vertical irregularities.*

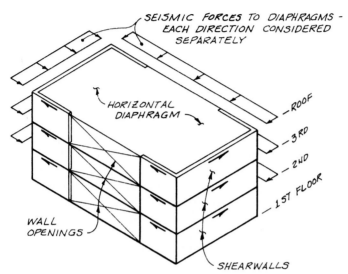

Figure 16.1   Regular structure. Recall from Chaps. 2 and 3 that two different distributions of seismic forces are provided by the Code: F_x for shearwall design, and F_{px} for diaphragm design. Although the sketch shows lateral forces in both directions, each principal direction of the structure is considered separately.

A building will be classified as structurally regular if

1. The plan is essentially *rectangular.*
2. The *mass* is reasonably uniform over the height.
3. The *shearwalls* in a lower story are directly below the shearwalls in an upper story.

Both transverse and longitudinal lateral seismic forces are shown in the sketch. Normal practice is to consider the force in each direction separately.

For regular structures the seismic forces are computed and distributed as illustrated in Chaps. 2 and 3. The design of the lateral-force-resisting systems (LFRSs) for these buildings follows the procedures given in Chaps. 9 and 10, and the anchorage details are handled as described in Chap. 15.

Traditional allowable stress design for lateral forces has involved an allowable-stress increase of one-third (allowable stress multiplier of 1.33) when the actual stresses are the result of wind or seismic forces acting alone or in combination with other loads. This allowable-stress increase is permitted for *all materials* (UBC Chap. 23).

ASCE 7 (Ref. 5.1) has a similar provision except that the adjustment is stated as a 25 percent reduction in the combination of design loads and forces (0.75 multiplier for the combination) when wind or seismic forces are included in the combination being considered. In the ASCE Standard the 0.75 multiplier is known as a *load combination factor*.

A significant difference between the two approaches just described is that ASCE 7 requires at least two transient loads or forces in order to apply the 0.75 multiplier. In contrast, UBC Chap. 23 permits an allowable-stress increase in all cases that include wind or seismic forces. Thus, the UBC permits allowable stresses to be increased one-third for the combinations

DL + wind

DL + seismic

Dead load is obviously a permanent load, and these two cases each involve a *single* transient force (i.e., the lateral force). However, the concept of a 0.75 load combination factor in ASCE 7 requires *at least two* transient loads or forces in addition to the dead load. Other transient loads include roof live load, snow load, floor live load, and so on. Further discrepancies exist between the UBC and ASCE 7 loading criteria.

The point of mentioning the two conflicting loading criteria is not to point out the differences in design loads and forces between the UBC and ASCE 7. The purpose is to note the long-term national practice of either increasing allowable stresses *or* reducing the loads and forces when the combination includes either wind or seismic. The 1991 NDS (NDS Sec. 1.4 and NDS Appendix B.4) notes that the 0.75 reduction in loads and forces (or the 1.33 increase in allowable stress) is essentially related to the *reduced probability* that the *maximum* loads and forces will act *simultaneously,* and it is independent of the type of material being used.

The NDS distinguishes between this universal adjustment and the material property in wood design known as the load duration factor C_D. Because the strength of wood is dependent on the duration of loading, the NDS states that both the *load combination factor* and the *load duration factor* should be permitted. It should be noted that some Code authorities have taken the position that the two factors are one and the same. This question should be settled automatically when the wood industry moves to an LRFD format. Design loads will be modified with a load combination factor on one side of the equation, and material properties including the "time-effect factor" for wood will be handled on the resistance side of the equation.

In summary, opinion is currently divided on whether or not the general adjustment for wind and seismic permitted for all materials should be taken concurrently with the load duration factor for wood. The position taken throughout this book has been that the designer should verify local code acceptance before applying the 1.33 allowable-stress increase (0.75 load multiplier) simultaneously with C_D. If the two adjustments are acceptable, the recommendation of the National Forest Products Association (NFPA) is that the load combination factor not be applied unless there are at least two transient effects in the combination of loads and forces being considered.

It is important also to recognize that only those elements of a structure which resist the *combination* of loads and forces can use the combination reduction factor. For example, a shear panel acting only to resist lateral forces cannot use the reduction factor.

These subjects have been discussed previously in this book, and the reader may find it helpful to review this material (Secs. 2.8 and 4.15) before continuing with this chapter. The reason for developing a thorough understanding of these problems is that the Code assigns additional design requirements to buildings classified as irregular structures. One of the common penalties assessed is that the traditional 1.33 multiplier for allowable stress (UBC Chap. 23) is not permitted in the design of an irregular structure in seismic zones 3 and 4. However, regular structures located in seismic zones 3 and 4 may be designed using the 1.33 multiplying factor.

Again, the designer should verify local code acceptance before combining the general allowable stress increase of 1.33 with C_D. Furthermore, the designer should verify local code acceptance of $C_D = 1.6$ before using this increased value of C_D in practice.

16.3 Seismic Forces—Irregular Structures

An *irregular structure* has one or more significant discontinuities in its configuration or in its lateral-force-resisting system. Several examples of irregular structures are given in this section to illustrate the general concept of structural irregularities.

The 10 general types of irregularity identified in the Code are classified as either *vertical irregularities* (UBC Table 23-M) or *plan irregularities* (UBC Table 23-N). Detailed descriptions of the irregular features are given in these tables and UBC Chap. 23. As mentioned previously, the commentary in the SEAOC *Blue Book* expands these descriptions and helps to clarify the intent of the Code.

The first form of irregularity considered in this introduction has an effect on the dynamic properties of a building that is easy to visualize. It is a type of vertical irregularity known as *weight (mass) irregularity* (UBC Table 23-M, Type B). This is best described by considering the lumped-mass model of the three-story building in Fig. 2.14b (Sec. 2.12). In this figure the F_x story forces are shown to follow a triangular distribution with zero force at the bottom and maximum force at the roof level. This linear distribution is obtained if the masses at the story levels are all equal. Obviously some other distribution will result (using the Code formula for F_x) if the masses are not all the same magnitude.

Now, if one of the masses is significantly larger or smaller than the mass at an adjacent level, the dynamic behavior of the system will be altered.

Thus, *mass irregularity* is said to exist if the mass of any story is more than 150 percent of the mass of an adjacent story. However, a roof which is lighter than the floor below need not be considered as being mass-irregular. The fundamental mode (first mode) of vibration may not be the critical mode for a structure that has mass irregularity.

Recall that the Code permits two forms of seismic analysis. The *static lateral force procedure* is generally applied to smaller structures, and a *dynamic analysis* is used for larger structures. The Code now requires that a dynamic analysis be performed for a greater number of structures than it did in the past. A dynamic analysis is to be used in the design of an *irregular* structure that is *more* than five stories or 65 ft in height. It should be clear that very few wood structures exceed these height limitations, and consequently a dynamic analysis is not required in the design of a wood-frame structure even if the building is classified as irregular.

The example of mass irregularity is given here as a simple illustration of a vertical irregularity. One can easily visualize how the mode shape in Fig. 2.14*b* could be significantly altered by having one of the lumped masses in the system much larger or smaller than the others.

Because the Code permits the use of the static lateral force procedure for low-rise irregular structures, no specific additional requirements are imposed on a typical wood-frame building that is mass-irregular. However, the designer of any structure should generally be aware of mass irregularity and should pay particular attention to tying the structure together for lateral force transfer and continuity.

A number of other types of irregularity can affect the design of a wood-frame structure even when the static lateral force procedure is used. For these buildings the Code imposes additional design requirements or penalties for the irregularity. The *penalty* generally takes the form of

1. A *reduced allowable* stress for use in designing certain members and connections in the lateral-force-resisting system

2. An *increased seismic design force*

Typically the Code imposes these penalties only in areas of high seismic risk such as seismic zones 3 and 4. In some cases they may be required in seismic zone 2 in addition to zones 3 and 4.

Perhaps the most common penalty for an irregularity is a reduced allowable stress. It was noted in the previous section and in Sec. 2.8 that the Code usually permits an allowable-stress increase of one-third (allowable-stresses multiplier = 1.33) when the effects of wind or seismic forces are considered. This applies to all structural materials including steel, concrete, masonry, wood, and soil bearing values. However, this universal increase of allowable stress is no longer permitted for certain types of irregularity.

Thus, the penalty imposed by the Code for these irregular features in seismic zones 3 and 4 is the use of a much smaller allowable stress. The reduced stress applies to the design of drag struts (diaphragm collectors) and the anchorage connections between horizontal diaphragms and shear-walls. On the other hand, buildings that are structurally regular may still use the traditional one-third increase for the design of these elements (i.e., *no penalty for regular structures*). The design penalty does not apply to diaphragm unit shear values. In other words, the diaphragm nailing given by UBC Table 25-J-1 is not affected by the penalty assigned to irregular structures.

The penalty just described applies to buildings with the following forms of plan irregularity (UBC Table 23-N):

Type A: Torsional irregularity

Type B: Reentrant corners

Type C: Diaphragm discontinuity

Type D: Out-of-plane offset

The question of diaphragm flexibility was discussed briefly in Chap. 9, and it was noted that wood diaphragms have usually been classified as *flexible* diaphragms. If a building uses a flexible diaphragm in its lateral-force-resisting system, the Code does not require that *torsional irregularity* (Type A) be considered. Further consideration of torsional irregularity is not given here, but the other types are addressed. In the future, more attention will be paid to whether a wood diaphragm behaves as a flexible or rigid diaphragm.

Reentrant corners (Type B) occur frequently in wood-frame structures. Typical L-, T-, and U-plan shaped buildings are common examples of structures with reentrant corners. When *both projections* beyond a reentrant corner are greater than 15 percent of the plan dimension of the structure in a given direction, the building is classified as plan-irregular. See Fig. 16.2. A method of calculating the design forces for drag struts and related connections for a typical L-shaped building is demonstrated in Sec. 16.9.

Another type of plan irregularity is described as a *diaphragm discontinuity* (Type C). An example of a diaphragm discontinuity is a large opening in a floor or roof diaphragm. See Fig. 16.3.

Diaphragms with openings have additional diaphragm chords. These chords are framing members at the boundary of the diaphragm opening. If a free-body diagram is cut through the diaphragm at the opening, the chords at the opening plus the chords at the boundary of the diaphragm carry the moment in the diaphragm. A method of analyzing the diaphragm chord and drag strut forces in a horizontal diaphragm with an opening is given in Ref. 14.11, and additional information is available in Refs. 8.2 and 9.4. The evaluation of forces described in these references applies whether or not the opening in the diaphragm is large enough to be classified as a Type C plan irregularity.

Tests of diaphragms with openings are also reported in Ref. 14.11. These indicate that large forces can develop at the corners of the openings in the

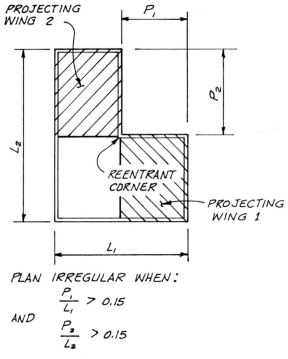

PLAN IRREGULAR WHEN:

$$\frac{P_1}{L_1} > 0.15$$

AND

$$\frac{P_2}{L_2} > 0.15$$

PLAN OF L-SHAPED BUILDING

Figure 16.2 A building with a *reentrant corner* is classified as plan irregularity Type B when both projections exceed 15 percent of the corresponding side lengths.

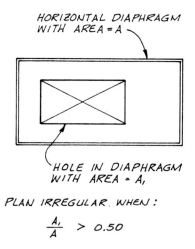

PLAN IRREGULAR WHEN:

$$\frac{A_1}{A} > 0.50$$

PLAN - DIAPHRAGM WITH OPENING

Figure 16.3 A horizontal diaphragm with a large opening is a *diaphragm discontinuity* and is known as plan irregularity Type C. The discontinuity is classified as plan-irregular if the size of the opening A_1 is greater than 50 percent of the gross area A.

diaphragm and that the magnitude of the forces increases with increased opening size. If the opening in the diaphragm is large enough to be classified as a diaphragm discontinuity, the collector members and connections are to be designed without the one-third increase of allowable stress normally permitted for seismic design.

On the other hand, if an opening is small, Ref. 14.11 offers the following general guide to designers: "... When openings are relatively small, chord forces do not increase significantly and it is usually sufficient to simply reinforce perimeter framing and assure that it is continuous. Continuous framing should extend from each corner of the opening both directions into the diaphragm a distance equal to the largest dimension of the opening."

The fourth type of plan irregularity which is assigned the penalty of a reduced allowable stress in zones 3 and 4 is known as an *out-of-plane offset* (Type D). This is a particularly serious type of discontinuity because it interrupts the flow in the normal path of lateral forces down through the structure and into the foundation. Because of this, a second design penalty is assigned to an out-of-plane offset. As noted previously, the second penalty usually takes the form of an increased design force.

To describe this type of plan irregularity, consider a two-story building with a horizontal diaphragm at the second floor and roof levels. See Example 16.2. The supporting walls include an interior shearwall as well as the usual exterior shearwalls. This example focuses on the interior shearwall, and the exterior walls are not shown in detail.

Initially the building is considered *without* a plan irregularity (i.e., an out-of-plane offset does not exist) so that the *normal flow* of forces down through the structure can first be understood. See Fig. 16.4a. Note that the interior shearwall on the second story is vertically in line with the shearwall on the first-story level.

Because one shearwall is immediately above the other, the lateral force from the upper wall can be transferred *directly* to the lower wall. Note that the shearwall on the first story carries a lateral force from the second-floor diaphragm in addition to the force from the second-story shearwall. The drag struts transfer the shears in the horizontal diaphragms to the interior shearwall. See Sec. 9.10 for a review of drag struts.

In Fig. 16.4b the interior shearwalls have been revised so that there is a horizontal offset between the shearwall on the first- and second-story levels. Two problems are created by the *out-of-plane offset*:

1. The force from the second-story wall must travel horizontally through the diaphragm at the second-floor level before it can be transferred into the shearwalls on the first story.

2. The resistance to the overturning moment at the base of the second-story interior shearwall requires special consideration.

These are described in greater detail in Fig. 16.4c and d.

EXAMPLE 16.2   Out-of-Plane Offset Added to a Regular Structure

The interior shearwalls in the two-story building in Fig. 16.4a do not involve an out-of-plane offset. The shearwalls on the first and second floors are aligned vertically, one over the other.

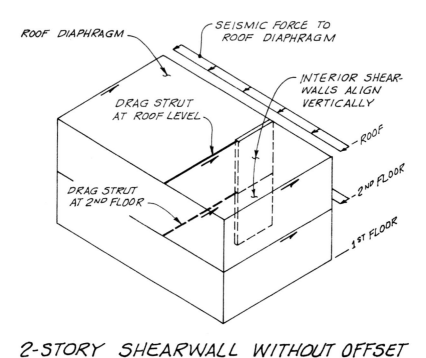

2-STORY SHEARWALL WITHOUT OFFSET

Figure 16.4a Structurally *regular* two-story building. The alignment of the shearwalls provides a *direct path* for the continuous flow of the lateral force from the roof level down to the foundation. Drag struts function as described in Sec. 9.10.

The revised layout of this building in Fig. 16.4b has the interior shearwall at the first-story level relocated to the left of its original position. A much more critical situation has been created because the shear from the second-story shearwall must now be transferred *horizontally* through the second-floor diaphragm before it can be picked up by the shearwalls on the first floor. The second problem involves the overturning moment at the base of the second-story shearwall. Neither of these problems occurs in the original configuration (Fig. 16.4a) which was structurally regular.

The horizontal seismic force from the roof is carried by the second-story shearwall. At the second-floor diaphragm this force must be distributed horizontally to the shearwalls at the first-story level. See Fig. 16.4c. Although it is possible to develop a continuous path for the transfer of lateral forces down through the structure, the forces do not follow a direct route. The discontinuity introduced by the out-of-plane offset causes the shear to travel horizontally in its path to the foundation. This places a concentrated force on the second-floor diaphragm that is in addition to the usual distributed force.

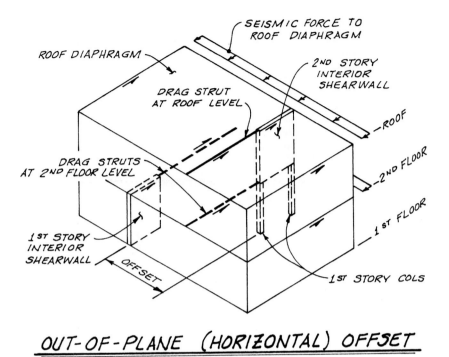

OUT-OF-PLANE (HORIZONTAL) OFFSET

Figure 16.4b Interior shearwall with *out-of-plane offset.* This is classified in UBC Table 23-N as plan irregularity Type D.

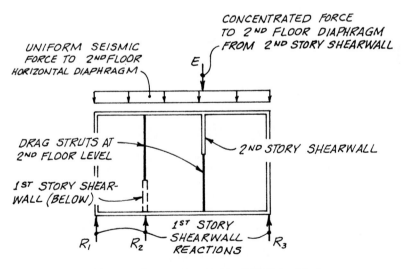

PLAN - 2ND FLOOR DIAPHRAGM

Figure 16.4c *Shear* transfer as a result of out-of-plane offset. The shear from the second-story shearwall is transferred as a concentrated force E to the second-floor diaphragm.

The concentrated force in Fig. 16.4c accounts for the transfer of the *shear* at the base of the second-story shearwall. The force to the second-floor horizontal diaphragm includes the usual uniformly distributed force plus a concentrated earthquake force E from the second-story shearwall. The second-floor horizontal diaphragm is supported by the first-story shearwall reactions R_1, R_2, and R_3.

The *moment* at the base of the second-story shearwall must also be transferred. This overturning moment is resolved into a couple, and the moment is replaced by a pair of equal and opposite forces (one tension and one compression) separated by a lever arm at the ends of the second-story interior shearwall.

One approach to handling this moment is to provide columns in the story directly below these forces for the purpose of carrying the overturning moment to the foundation. See Fig. 16.4d. These columns may carry gravity loads in addition to the forces due to overturning. Note that these are isolated *columns* in the first story, and there is *no shearwall* between them. Other solutions to the overturning moment problem are possible.

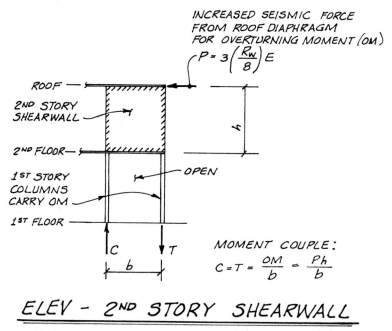

ELEV - 2ND STORY SHEARWALL

Figure 16.4d *Overturning moment* at base of second-story shearwall. Note that the OM is at the *base* of the shearwall and is computed using height h. The overturning at the first-floor level is taken into account by an overturning analysis of the first-story shearwalls.

Because of its critical nature, the Code assigns a *double penalty* to the discontinuity caused by an out-of-plane offset for buildings in seismic zones 3 and 4.

The first penalty required for a building with a Type D irregularity (out-of-plane offset) is the same one assessed for plan irregularity Types B and C. In other words, drag struts and related connections and diaphragm-to-shearwall anchorages are to be designed without the one-third increase in allowable stress usually permitted for seismic forces.

The overturning moment below the second-story interior shearwall may be carried by columns in the first story. The forces T and C are determined by dividing the overturning moment OM by the lever arm b. In seismic zones 3 and 4, an out-of-plane offset requires that the columns carrying the overturning moment be designed for an increased seismic force. The increased seismic force to be considered for overturning is significantly larger than the usual earthquake force E.

The nominal increase in seismic force for overturning is *3 times* the usual seismic force. The large order of magnitude of this force indicates the severe nature of this type of discontinuity in the lateral-force path. The Code specifies the increased seismic force for overturning as

$$3\left(\frac{R_w}{8}\right)$$

times the usual seismic force E.

The reason for this added force requirement is to guard against the collapse of the lateral-force-resisting system that would be triggered by a failure of the columns carrying the overturning moment. This force level was selected because the columns at such a discontinuity must be capable of supporting the lateral-force-resisting system (LFRS) as it is forced well into the inelastic range. Thus, the performance of these columns is essentially a *strength* design requirement.

Obviously these force levels represent an extreme loading condition. Thus, when a working stress design method (ASD) is used, the allowable stresses for this loading condition may be factored up to an ultimate strength level. This is accomplished by multiplying the allowable stresses for use in the design for overturning by 1.7. Thus, the *net increase* in seismic force for overturning is the load multiplier divided by the allowable-stress increase:

$$\frac{3(R_w/8)}{1.7}$$

The structural system quality factor R_w (Sec. 2.13) reflects the ability of the lateral-force-resisting system to sustain cyclic deformations in the inelastic range without collapse. Recall that for the types of buildings covered in this book the value of R_w ranges between 6 and 9. A common value of R_w is 8, and for this case the term in the parentheses becomes unity. Therefore, the net increase for this common situation is

$$\frac{3}{1.7} = 1.76$$

times the usual seismic force.

The value of 1.76 is given here to understand the relative order of magnitude of the increase for overturning brought about by the out-of-plane offset. However, for consistency it is recommended that, in practice, the individual *force* and *allowable-stress* multipliers be used in design calculations. The subject of overturning is addressed in greater detail later in this chapter.

In summary, the discontinuity resulting from an out-of-plane offset causes the lateral *shear force* and the *overturning moment* from the second-story shearwall to follow two different paths. The shear is transferred horizontally through the second-floor diaphragm to the first-story shearwalls, and the overturning moment is transferred vertically to the columns directly below the second-story shearwall. The design penalties assigned by the Code indicate the level of concern about Type D discontinuities.

The final type of irregularity to be covered in this section is a form of *vertical irregularity* (Type D in UBC Table 23-M). Although this type of irregularity is classified as a vertical irregularity, it is very similar in concept to the out-of-plane offset (plan irregularity) that was just reviewed. An in-plane-offset of a lateral-force-resisting element also interrupts the normal lateral-force path of the system.

To illustrate an in-plane discontinuity, again consider the regular structure in Fig. 16.4a. The building has shearwalls on the second story that are located directly over the shearwalls on the first story. In Fig. 16.5 this building is reconfigured to have a Type D vertical irregularity. The interior shearwalls on the first and second stories are offset by a distance greater than the length of the shearwall elements.

Essentially the same overturning problem occurs with the in-plane offset in Fig. 16.5 and the out-of-plane offset in Fig. 16.4d. For this reason the Code requires that the columns supporting the second-story shearwall also be designed for the overturning effects caused by an increased seismic force of

$$3\left(\frac{R_w}{8}\right)E$$

Again, the symbol E represents the usual earthquake force to the second-story shearwall that would be required in the design of a structure that is classified as structurally regular. Because the increased force represents a collapse limit state, the usual allowable stresses for this severe loading condition may be multiplied by 1.7.

A full understanding of the design requirements for irregular structures requires the reader to first understand the simple regular buildings that are covered in Chaps. 1 to 15. The intent of Sec. 16.3 is to summarize some of the common discontinuities that may be encountered in a typical wood-frame building. The next section continues the discussion of overturning under lateral forces and provides a comparison of the practices for wind and seismic forces.

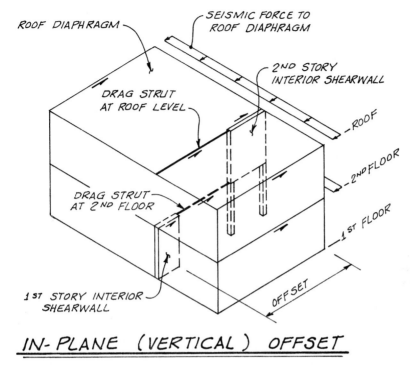

ROOF DIAPHRAGM

SEISMIC FORCE TO
ROOF DIAPHRAGM

DRAG STRUT
AT ROOF LEVEL

2ND STORY
INTERIOR SHEARWALL

ROOF

2ND FLOOR

DRAG STRUT
AT 2ND FLOOR

1ST FLOOR

1ST STORY INTERIOR
SHEARWALL

OFFSET

IN-PLANE (VERTICAL) OFFSET

Figure 16.5 An *in-plane-discontinuity in vertical lateral-force-resisting element* is classified as vertical irregularity Type D in UBC Table 23-M.

16.4 Overturning—Background

The general combinations of loads and forces that are required by the Code were summarized briefly in Sec. 2.16. These combinations essentially define which loads and forces must be applied simultaneously in the design of a building. To a certain extent, a combination reflects the probability that the various loads and forces will occur concurrently. Some of these probabilities were discussed previously and are not repeated here. The combinations described in Chap. 2 have been integrated into design practice over many years, and the numerical examples throughout this book made use of these combinations where appropriate.

As the Code requirements for wind and seismic forces have become increasingly complex, the considerations for moment stability have also become more involved. The overturning analysis for a shearwall under wind forces was introduced in Example 2.10 (Sec. 2.10), and additional overturning moment problems were covered in Chap. 10. The reader may find it useful to review these sections in preparation for the detailed summary given here.

The Code provides several additional load and force combinations for use in the moment stability analysis of a structure. These combinations for overturning are not directly reflected in the five general combinations covered in Sec. 2.16. The Code incorporates the additional combinations for overturning into the wind force and seismic force portions of the UBC.

The Code may specifically call out an additional combination for overturning, or it may state the combination in a less obvious manner. For example, the Code-required factor of safety for overturning under wind can be viewed as a combination of wind force plus a portion of the dead load. Furthermore, overturning requirements for wind are handled differently from those for seismic.

Not only does the Code provide different factors of safety for overturning under wind and seismic forces, but different factors of safety may apply within a given type of lateral loading. Although this approach may seem inconsistent, the different factors of safety are intentional and are based on the relative magnitudes of the design-level lateral forces, expected return periods for the design-level forces, and the observed performance of structures in service.

A comprehensive study of overturning is introduced by first reviewing a simple statics problem. The principles of statics are then expanded to cover moment stability at the following locations:

1. Base of a wood-frame shearwall
2. Base of the foundation for a shearwall (known as the foundation-soil interface)

It is important that the designer understand how to evaluate the overturning effects at both locations. Initially these problems are treated purely from a statics approach, without concern for the Code-required factors of safety (or load and force combinations). This essentially defines the moment stability problem, and it introduces the analysis necessary to evaluate soil bearing pressures under combined gravity loads and lateral forces.

After the statics of these two problems is understood, the Code-required factors of safety (or required load and force combinations) are finally introduced. Although this book is not a text on foundation design, some lateral-force criteria make it desirable to cover the evaluation of soil bearing pressure under overturning. The need for the detailed review given here is the result of the new seismic code as well as modifications to some of the wind force requirements.

16.5   Overturning—Review

Most designers are first exposed to the subject of *moment stability* in a course in statics or engineering mechanics. See Example 16.3. In this type of problem, the dimensions and weight of an object are given. In addition, the coefficient of static friction μ of the surface upon which the block rests is known.

A typical requirement in such a problem is to determine whether the block *moves* or *remains in static equilibrium* when subjected to a lateral force. If the block moves, the problem is to indicate whether it *slides* along the supporting surface or whether it *tips* (overturns). If the block remains at rest, the *factors of safety* against *sliding* and *overturning* are to be calculated.

EXAMPLE 16.3   Typical Moment Stability Problem from a Course in Statics

GIVEN:

The dimensions and weight of a block are known. See Fig. 16.6. The coefficient of static friction μ of the surface upon which the block rests is given.

FIND:

If a lateral force P is applied at height h above the base, determine whether or not the block remains in static equilibrium. If the block moves, indicate whether it slides or tips. If the block remains static, determine the factors of safety against sliding and overturning.

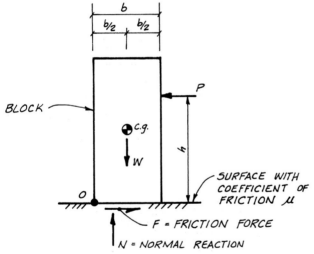

Figure 16.6   Typical statics problem involving moment stability of a block.

SOLUTION:

Sliding:

By summing forces in the y direction, the normal reaction at the base equals the weight of the block:

$$\Sigma F_y = 0$$

$$N = W$$

By summing forces in the x direction, the friction force at the base equals the applied lateral force P:

$$\Sigma F_x = 0$$

$$F = P$$

The maximum available friction force for resisting the lateral force is the normal reaction times the coefficient of static friction:

$$\text{Max. } F = \mu N$$

If the lateral force exceeds the maximum available resisting force

$$P > \text{max. } F$$

sliding will occur.
   On the other hand, if

$$P < \text{max. } F$$

the object does not slide, and the *factor of safety against sliding* can be computed as

$$\boxed{\text{FS}_{\text{sliding}} = \frac{\text{max. } F}{P} = \frac{\mu N}{P} = \frac{\mu W}{P}}$$

Moment stability:

If the block tips, the normal force N shifts to the pivot point at O. By summing moments about point O, N drops out, and the maximum overturning moment OM is the lateral force times the height above the base:

$$\Sigma M_O$$

$$\text{OM} = Ph$$

Also by summing moments about point O, the resisting moment RM is the weight of the block times the lever arm to the line of action of this force:

$$\text{RM} = W\left(\frac{b}{2}\right)$$

If the maximum overturning moment exceeds the available resisting moment

$$\text{OM} > \text{RM}$$

tipping will occur.
   On the other hand, if

$$\text{OM} < \text{RM}$$

the object remains in static equilibrium, and the *factor of safety against overturning* can be computed as

$$\boxed{\text{FS}_{\text{overturning}} = \frac{\text{RM}}{\text{OM}}}$$

Although the example of a block sliding or tipping is an elementary problem, it is helpful to begin a review of overturning for a wood-frame shearwall with these basic principles in mind.

Most wood-frame buildings use a combination of horizontal diaphragms and shearwalls to resist lateral forces. In checking overturning for these types of structures, the usual practice is to examine the moment stability of the vertical elements (i.e., the shearwalls) in the primary LFRS of the strucutre. If the individual shearwalls are stable, the overall moment stability of the structure is ensured. With other structural systems (such as steel rigid frames) it may be common practice to check overturning of the entire building, but this is usually not done in a conventional shearwall building.

It has been noted throughout this book that the key to successful lateral force design is to adequately tie the elements together so that a continuous path is provided for the transfer of forces from the roof level down into the foundation. The simple statics problem is expanded to a shearwall overturning analysis by considering the forces acting on a shearwall from a one-story building. See Example 16.4.

In this example the stability of a free-body diagram (FBD) taken at the base of a shearwall is analyzed. Similar problems were considered in Chap. 10. The approach taken here is purely from a statics point of view, and consideration is not given to whether the lateral force is wind or seismic, and the FS required by the Code is not defined. The expressions necessary to determine the forces in the *shearwall chords* and *anchorage connections* for overturning are again reviewed.

EXAMPLE 16.4   Overturning at Base of Shearwall

If the lateral forces to a shearwall are relatively small, the dead load of the wall plus any roof or floor dead load supported by the wall may be sufficient to resist overturning (see Fig. 16.7). On the other hand, if the lateral forces are large or if the dead loads above the foundation are small, it may be necessary to attach the shearwall to the foundation with anchorage hardware so that the weight of the foundation can be included in the moment stability analysis.

The gross overturning moment at the *base of the shearwall* is the lateral force (the reaction from the roof diaphragm) times the height from the top of the foundation to the roof level:

$$\text{Gross OM} = Rh$$

The resisting moment is the sum of any dead loads supported by the wall (including the weight of the wall and any other dead loads framing into the wall) times the lever arm from the pivot point O to the line of action of the dead loads. For a uniformly distributed dead load, the lever arm is simply one-half of the shearwall length:

$$\text{RM} = W_{\text{DL}}\left(\frac{b}{2}\right)$$

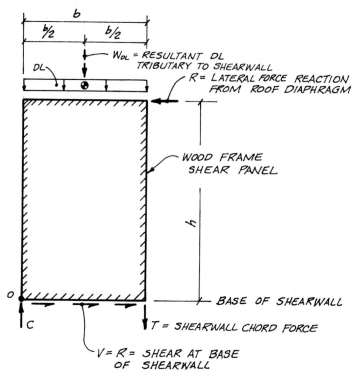

Figure 16.7 Moment stability of a one-story shearwall. FBD cut at base of wall (top of foundation).

In order for the shearwall to be stable, the maximum available resisting moment must be greater than or equal to the gross overturning moment:

$$RM \geq OM$$

Alternatively, this could be expressed by requiring the factor of safety against overturning to be 1.0 or larger:

$$FS = \frac{RM}{OM} \geq +1.0$$

For specific lateral force combinations the Code may require the FS to be greater than 1.0.

Because of the relatively small dead loads involved in wood-frame buildings, it is not uncommon for the OM at the base of a shearwall to exceed the RM. The typical solution in such a case is to attach the shearwall to the supporting foundation with hardware of adequate strength so that the *net overturning moment* is transferred to the foundation. According to statics, the net OM is the difference between the gross OM and the dead load RM:

$$Net\ OM = gross\ OM - RM$$

$$= Rh - RM$$

Obviously if the sign of the net OM is negative, the shearwall is stable without special hold-down attachments to the foundation. In this case the only force to be transferred to the foundation with hardware is the shear force $V = R$. Generally the friction force between the wall and the foundation is ignored, and *anchor bolts* are designed to transfer the shear from the shearwall into the foundation (see Example 10.8 in Sec. 10.10 for additional information).

If the sign of the net OM is positive, additional anchorage hardware is required to transfer the net OM to the foundation. The net OM is resolved into a couple by dividing the moment by the width of the shearwall (distance between shearwall chords). One force from the resulting couple is a tension force T, and the other is a compression force C. Since the force can originate from either direction, anchorage at either end of the shearwall must be designed for both tension and compression forces. See Sec. 10.6 and Fig. 10.10 (Sec. 10.10) for additional information.

When the magnitude of the dead-load-resisting moment is relatively small, the designer may choose to ignore the resisting dead load. In this case the net OM equals the gross OM, and the tension and compression chord forces obtained by resolving the OM into a couple are known as *gross chord forces:*

$$\text{Gross } T = \text{gross } C = \frac{\text{gross OM}}{b}$$

On the other hand, when the resisting dead load is considered, the tension chord force is based on the net OM. The *net tension chord force* is

$$\text{Net } T = \frac{\text{net OM}}{b} = \frac{\text{gross OM} - \text{RM}}{b}$$

It is important to realize that only the dead load of the structure is used to resist overturning. This again reflects the conservative approach used in structural design. There may or may not be gravity *live* loads acting on the shearwall system when lateral forces are applied. There is a greater chance of having floor live loads present during a major windstorm or earthquake than roof live loads. However, the presence of neither type of live load can be ensured, and consequently only gravity dead loads are considered in checking uplift due to overturning.

16.6 Overturning—Foundation-Soil Interface

Once the shearwall and the anchorage connections to the foundation have been addressed (Example 16.4), the entire system including the shearwall and the foundation must satisfy the moment stability requirements at the foundation-soil interface. See Example 16.5.

The FBDs in this example are taken at the *bottom* of the foundation to determine the footing requirements for the shearwall. The term used to refer to this location is the *foundation-soil interface*. Depending on the details of a given problem, one of two alternative soil pressure diagrams (trapezoidal or triangular) can apply at the foundation-soil interface. The formulas necessary to determine the magnitude of the vertical soil-bearing pressure are derived in this example.

EXAMPLE 16.5   Overturning at Foundation-Soil Interface

At the base of the footing for a shearwall, resistance to sliding under lateral force R is provided by the friction force V_1 acting on the bottom of the footing and by horizontal bearing V_2 on the end of the footing (Fig. 16.8a):

$$R = V_1 + V_2$$

The horizontal bearing resistance V_2 can be developed by the passive soil bearing pressure acting on the end of the footing or by the bearing resistance provided by a concrete slab.

In analyzing the overturning at the base of the foundation (i.e., at the interface), it will be noted that the vertical lever arm has increased from h in Example 16.4 to h_1 in Fig. 16.8a. The overturning moment is now

$$OM = Rh_1$$

Assuming that the anchorage connections between the shearwall and the foundation have been adequately designed, the resisting moment RM at the foundation-soil interface includes the dead load of the foundation in addition to the dead load used in the first part of the stability analysis.

$$RM = (W_{DL} + W_{foot})\frac{b}{2}$$

Note that the lever arm h_2 is usually small, and the resisting moment provided by the force V_2 is often neglected. To be in static equilibrium, the resisting moment must exceed the overturning moment:

$$RM \geq OM$$

In other words, the factor of safety against overturning must be greater than 1.0.

$$FS = \frac{RM}{OM} \geq +1.0$$

As noted previously, a factor of safety of 1.0 may not always be appropriate, and different factors of safety for wind and seismic forces are required.

Depending on the magnitude of the lateral forces and the geometry of the shearwall-footing combination, two different soil pressure diagrams at the foundation soil interface are possible.

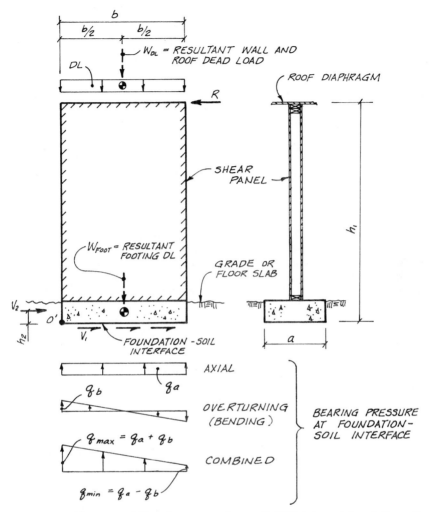

Figure 16.8a Moment stability of one-story shearwall. FBD taken at foundation-soil interface. *Trapezodal* soil pressure diagram occurs when $q_b < q_a$.

Several points about the foundation in Fig. 16.8a need to be discussed. The footing width *a* for a *bearing wall* that is *not a shearwall* is usually determined by dividing the resultant gravity loads (dead and live) by the allowable vertical soil bearing pressure. However, in the case of a *shearwall*, the size of the footing can be governed by two other factors:

1. Dead load necessary to resist overturning
2. Vertical soil bearing pressure (caused by overturning plus gravity loads)

The first consideration is the *dead load* required to resist overturning. The volume of concrete in the footing may be determined by the need to develop a sufficiently large resisting moment. In other words, the provision of anchorage hardware at the base of the shearwall (Fig. 16.7) is meaningless unless the footing to which it is attached is large enough to hold the shearwall down.

A *continuous wall footing* is shown for this purpose in Fig. 16.8a; however, a number of other configurations are possible. For example, a concrete mass (known as a *deadman*) could be located directly under the end of the shear panel to counter the tension chord force.

Another possibility is to continue the footing past the ends of the shear panel to form a *grade beam*. Grade beams are designed as reinforced-concrete beams that are simply cast as part of the foundation system of the structure. In fact, any foundation (including those that do not run past the end of the shearwall) must be designed in accordance with the principles of reinforced concrete. The foundation must have an adequate amount of reinforcing steel so that the system functions as intended by the designer.

The size of the footing can also be controlled by the *vertical soil bearing pressure* at the foundation-soil interface. An *axial soil bearing pressure* is determined by dividing the uniformly distributed dead load by the contact area between the footing and the soil:

$$q_a = \frac{W_{DL} + W_{foot}}{a \times b}$$

The uniform soil pressure diagram for q_a is shown in Fig. 16.8a.

The soil bearing pressure caused by the overturning moment is determined using the flexure formula from strength of materials ($q_b = Mc/I$). In an overturning problem of this type, I is the moment of inertia of the footprint of the foundation as it resists bending about an axis perpendicular to the length of the shearwall. The footprint is a rectangular area with a moment of inertia of

$$I = \frac{ab^3}{12}$$

The distance from the neutral axis to the point of maximum bending stress is

$$c = \frac{b}{2}$$

The *soil bearing stress* due to the *overturning moment* then becomes

$$q_b = \frac{(OM)c}{I} = \frac{(Rh_1)(b/2)}{ab^3/12} = \frac{Rh_1}{ab^2/6}$$

One side of the overturning soil pressure diagram is in compression, and the other is in tension, and by symmetry $q_{bc} = q_{bt}$. As long as q_b is less than q_a, the combined vertical soil bearing pressure diagram can be determined by adding the axial and bending soil pressure diagrams together algebraically. Thus

$$q_{max} = q_a + q_{bc}$$

and

$$q_{min} = q_a - q_{bt}$$

In this case, the combined vertical soil bearing pressure diagram forms a *trapezoid*.

The dimensions of the foundation system are adequate if the maximum soil bearing pressure is less than the allowable vertical soil bearing capacity. In other words, the dimensions a and b are acceptable if

$$q_{max} \leq q_{allowable}$$

In some cases the soil pressure diagram will not be trapezoidal, and a different analysis will be required to determine q_{max}. If the axial soil pressure is less than the bending soil pressure ($q_a < q_b$), a *triangular* soil pressure diagram will result instead of a trapezoidal one. Unlike many structural materials, soil is not capable of resisting tension, and the resulting vertical soil pressure distribution cannot be obtained by the algebraic summation of q_a and q_b. See Fig. 16.8b.

In the case that the soil pressure due to overturning q_b exceeds the axial soil pressure q_a, the calculation for maximum soil bearing pressure is best performed by resolving the resisting moment at the foundation-soil interface into a resultant vertical reaction N that acts at an eccentricity e from the center of the foundation. By statics, N is equal and opposite to the sum of the gravity loads.

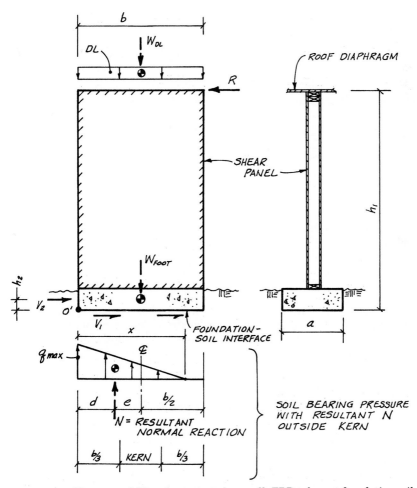

Figure 16.8b Moment stability of one-story shearwall. FBD taken at foundation-soil interface. *Triangular* soil pressure diagram occurs when $q_b > q_a$.

The eccentricity of the resultant force e can be obtained by summing moments about the centerline of the foundation. However, it is generally more convenient to sum moments about one end of the foundation (e.g., point O'), and the location of the resultant is determined as the distance d.

$$\Sigma M_{O'} = 0$$

$$W_{DL}\left(\frac{b}{2}\right) + W_{foot}\left(\frac{b}{2}\right) - R(h_1) - N(d) = 0$$

from which

$$d = \frac{W_{DL}(b/2) + W_{foot}(b/2) - R(h_1)}{N}$$

If it recognized that the resisting moment is

$$RM = W_{DL}\left(\frac{b}{2}\right) + W_{foot}\left(\frac{b}{2}\right)$$

and the gross overturning moment is

$$OM = Rh_1$$

then the expression used to solve for d can be written succinctly as

$$d = \frac{OM - RM}{N}$$

Note that the normal reaction N in this expression is simply equal to the sum of the gravity dead loads

$$N = \Sigma DL = W_{DL} + W_{foot}$$

With the location of the resultant normal reaction known, it is a simple statics problem to determine the magnitude of the maximum soil pressure on the triangular stress block. Again refer to Fig. 16.8b. The width of the triangular stress block is given the symbol x, and it is noted that the centroid of the triangle is located at one-third of the base. Thus the width of the stress block is

$$x = 3d$$

From statics the resultant force N is equal to the volume of the stress block

$$N = \tfrac{1}{2}(q_{max} \times x)a$$

Thus, for a triangular stress block the maximum soil pressure is

$$q_{max} = \frac{2N}{xa}$$

At the foundation-soil interface there are two basic problems. The entire shearwall-foundation system must be stable against overturning, and the maximum vertical soil bearing pressure must not exceed the allowable vertical soil capacity.

Example 16.5 shows the two possible soil pressure distributions (trapezoidal or triangular) on the bottom of a footing when a shearwall is subject to overturning. The example outlines the method for calculating the maximum soil bearing pressure for each case.

To review the design process, trial dimensions of the foundation system are first assumed. The axial soil bearing pressure q_a and the bending soil pressure due to overturning q_b are then computed in accordance with the analysis accompanying Fig. 16.8a. If the axial pressure exceeds the bending

$$q_a > q_b$$

the soil pressure diagram is trapezoidal, and the maximum soil bearing pressure is computed as

$$q_{max} = q_a + q_b$$

On the other hand, if the axial pressure is less than the bending

$$q_a < q_b$$

the soil pressure diagram is triangular instead of trapezoidal. In this case the initial values of q_a and q_b must be set aside, and the maximum soil bearing pressure is obtained using the analysis accompanying Fig. 16.8b, where

$$q_{max} = \frac{2N}{xa}$$

Whether the soil pressure diagram is *trapezoidal* (Fig. 16.8a) or *triangular* (Fig. 16.8b), a final decision about the trial dimensions of the foundation system depends on a comparison of the maximum soil bearing pressure and the allowable soil bearing value. Therefore, if

$$q_{max} \leq q_{allowable}$$

the trial dimensions of the shearwall footing are acceptable. If not, the foundation system should be redesigned.

The question about which configuration of soil pressure diagram (trapezoidal or triangular) develops under a given loading condition can be answered by the procedures outlined in Example 16.5. The methods described for obtaining q_{max} are direct and easy to apply.

However, another method is sometimes used to determine whether the soil pressure diagram is trapezoidal or triangular. The alternate system may be familiar to designers of earth retaining walls, and consequently it is described briefly. The principal difference between the two problems is that in a shearwall the lateral force is *parallel* to the wall, and in a retaining wall the lateral force from the retained earth is *perpendicular* to the wall. However, the basic foundation design principles for overturning are essentially the same for both problems.

The starting place in the alternate method is to determine the location of the resultant soil pressure force (Fig. 16.8*b*). The resultant force is given the symbol N, and the location of N is given by the distance d. With a triangular soil pressure diagram, the limiting condition occurs when the distance d is equal to one-third of the length of the foundation. In this case the triangular soil pressure diagram completely covers the length of the footing. In other words, when the resultant is located at

$$d = \frac{b}{3}$$

the width of the triangular stress block is equal to the length of the footing:

$$x = b$$

This limiting condition can be used to determine the configuration of the soil pressure diagram as follows.

If the location of the resultant force N (i.e., the dimension d) is less than one-third of the footing length

$$d < \frac{b}{3}$$

the soil pressure diagram will obviously be triangular, and the length of the stress block x will be less than the length of the wall b.

On the other hand, if d is greater than one-third of the footing length

$$d > \frac{b}{3}$$

the soil bearing diagram will not be triangular, and a trapezoidal stress block will occur.

Some books on foundation engineering define the center one-third of the footing length as the *kern*. Then if the resultant force N lies inside the kern, the pressure diagram is known to be trapezoidal. On the other hand, if the resultant lies outside the kern, the soil pressure will be triangular.

Either of the two methods (i.e., comparing q_a with q_b or determining whether the resultant N falls inside or outside the kern) is a convenient tool for determining the configuration of the stress block for the soil bearing pressure. Once the type of soil pressure diagram has been determined, the analysis of q_{max} proceeds as described in Example 16.5.

Relatively small overturning moments produce the trapezoidal stress block, while large overturning moments produce the triangular distribution. The allowable soil bearing pressure is obtained from a soil report for the building site, or a conservative allowable soil bearing value can be determined in accordance with the provisions of UBC Chap. 29. For further information on footing design, the reader is referred to books on foundation engineering.

The shearwall overturning problem considered to this point has made use of the principles of statics only, and additional Code provisions have not been discussed. The only requirement thus far has been that the structure be in static equilibrium (i.e., FS $\geq$ 1.0), and from a conceptual standpoint the problem is relatively simple. This introduction should provide the designer with a good understanding of the basics of the moment stability of a structure.

However, in practice more is required. Some of the difficulties in applying the basic principles of moment stability to the Code-required wind and seismic overturning problems were mentioned in Sec. 16.4. Various factors of safety (or different combinations of loads and forces) are required or implied by the Code. The specific provisions for overturning under wind and seismic forces will be given in the next sections.

To do this, four general classes of practical moment stability problems are identified, and a summary of the important design criteria for each type is given. The intent is to provide the information in a form in which the similarities and differences are clear for each situation. The four classes of overturning problems include two wind and two earthquake problems:

1. Wind overturning
   a. General wind requirements (Example 16.6)
   b. Reduced requirements for low-profile buildings (Example 16.7)
2. Seismic overturning
   a. Regular structures (Example 16.8)
   b. Irregular structures (Example 16.9)

Each of these cases produces an overturning situation which, according to the Code, is unique in some way. For each overturning problem there are certain basic requirements, including the following:

1. Check the moment stability using the appropriate FS (or combination of loads and forces) at the
   a. Base of the shearwall (excluding the weight of the foundation)
   b. Foundation-soil interface (including the weight of the foundation)

2. Determine shearwall chord forces.
   a. Net tension chord force (known also as the *uplift* or *anchorage* force)
   b. Maximum compression chord force (including tributary gravity load)
3. Analyze the vertical soil bearing pressure.
4. Determine what allowable stress increase may (or may not) be used for the chords, connections, and soil bearing values.

16.7 Overturning—Wind

The general wind force requirements from the UBC were introduced in Secs. 2.9 to 2.11. The specific requirements for checking overturning under wind forces are summarized in this portion of Chap. 16.

It was previously noted that only the DL of the structure is used to resist overturning. When the dead load of a structure is estimated, designers often take an approach that is conservative for vertical load analysis. This may be done by rounding the summation of gravity loads upward and by slightly overestimating the weight of the members so that it will not be necessary to revise design calculations once member sizes have been determined. The practice of overestimating loads is generally considered to be on the side of greater safety.

However, in the moment stability analysis of a structure, an overestimation of dead loads is *unconservative* because the larger loads will produce a calculated resisting moment that is larger than is actually available. For this and other reasons, a factor of safety of 1.5 is implied by the Code for checking overturning at the base of a structure. The specific wording from UBC Chap. 23 indicates that the base OM on all or part of the primary wind-resisting system "shall not exceed two-thirds of the dead-load-resisting moment." This can be stated mathematically in several different forms. The factor of safety for moment stability can be written as

$$FS = \frac{RM}{OM} \geq 1.5$$

Alternatively the moment stability requirement could be stated as a load case, similar to the five combinations listed in Sec. 2.16. For moment stability under wind, this combination would be

$$\tfrac{2}{3}DL + wind$$

The consideration of this combination for the moment stability of the complete shearwall-foundation system *and* the corresponding shearwall tension chord force leads to an interesting problem. It is one that has been debated by designers for many years.

The *allowable stresses* for use in the design of shearwall chords and their anchorage connections have a factor of safety already incorporated into the design values. Some designers logically reason that it is not necessary, then, to incorporate the 1.5 factor of safety required for overall moment stability into the design forces for the shearwall chords. It is argued that the full dead-load-resisting moment above the foundation should be used to compute the tension chord force (instead of two-thirds of the DL-resisting moment). Again, the reasoning is that the wood tension member and the tie-down connection hardware already have appropriate factors of safety included their allowable design values.

The anomaly with this logic occurs when the DL-resisting moment just equals the overturning moment (i.e., when RM = OM). In this situation, the calculated tension chord force is zero. Accordingly, it would, theoretically, be unnecessary to anchor the shear panel to the concrete footing, because the resisting dead load moment exactly counters the overturning effect. However, *without a tie-down connection to the foundation,* it is clearly not possible to develop the required factor of safety of 1.5 at the base of the foundation. In other words, the DL of the foundation will not be effective unless there is an adequate connection between the shearwall tension chord and the foundation.

Consequently, in this book it is recommended that the FS used for base overturning also be used to determine the tension chord force at the connection between the shearwall and the foundation. This can be done by computing the anchorage requirements for the shearwall using two-thirds of the DL-resisting moment. A similar analysis may be used to calculate the forces for connecting a shear panel in the second story of a structure to a shear panel in the first story. Thus, the combination of (⅔DL + wind) is recommended for all tension chord problems involving general wind force design. See Example 16.6.

The anomaly just described applies to the *tension chord* of a shearwall and its connection to the foundation. However, this problem does not occur with the *compression chord*. The combination of (⅔DL + wind) applies to base overturning and to the tension chord and *not* to the compression chord. The critical combination of gravity loads and wind forces for the compression chord will be combination 3 or 4 from the list of five combinations given in Sec. 2.16. Therefore, the design force for the compression chord is the gross chord force caused by the wind overturning moment plus the tributary gravity loads.

It was noted in Chap. 2 that the UBC wind design provisions require wind uplift, if any, to be considered *simultaneously* with horizontal wind forces. Whether or not wind uplift acts on a given shearwall depends on the roof framing system and whether the shearwall is a bearing or nonbearing wall for vertical loads. If the wall supports gravity loads in addition to its own weight, it is classified as a bearing wall. The same framing members that cause additional gravity loads to be supported by the wall may also cause wind uplift to be transferred to the shearwall.

EXAMPLE 16.6   Overturning Requirements for Wind—General

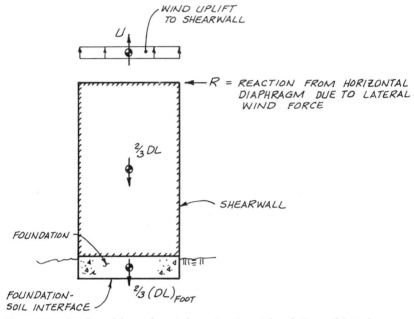

Figure 16.9a   Loads and forces for wind overturning at foundation-soil interface.

General UBC requirements are that horizontal wind forces and uplift wind are to be considered simultaneously. See Fig. 16.9a. Base overturning requirements are

Implied FS for base overturning: $\text{FS} = \dfrac{1}{\frac{2}{3}} = 1.5$

Combination of loads and forces incorporating FS = 1.5:   ⅔DL + horizontal wind + uplift wind

Allowable stress increase: 1.33

The allowable stress increase is from UBC Chap. 23 and applies to all structural materials including wood, steel, concrete, and soil bearing values. Any structural element (such as a reinforced-concrete foundation) that is designed on a strength basis should use the appropriate load factors instead of the allowable stress increase.

To develop an FS of 1.5 for base overturning, it is recommended that the shearwall tension chord force T be determined by using two-thirds of the resisting moment. Dead load only is considered in computing the resisting moment for the tension chord. See Fig. 16.9b. The critical shearwall compression chord force C will be governed by a combination of loads and forces that uses the full DL (not ⅔DL).

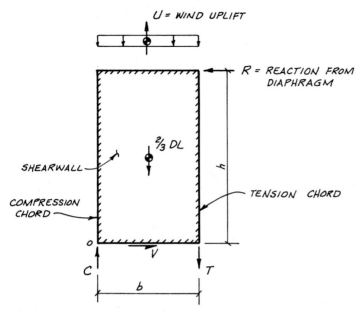

Figure 16.9b Loads and forces for wind overturning at shearwall connection to foundation for *tension chord*.

The gross overturning moment is

$$\text{Gross OM} = Rh + U\left(\frac{b}{2}\right)$$

The expressions developed in the statics analysis of the overturning problem in Example 16.4 are revised as follows to reflect the appropriate factors of safety:

Tension chord

Load combination: ⅔DL + horizontal wind + uplift wind
Net overturning moment (ΣM_O): net OM = gross OM − ⅔RM
Net tension chord force:

$$\text{net } T = \frac{\text{net OM}}{b}$$

$$= \frac{\text{gross OM} - \text{⅔RM}}{b}$$

Allowable stress increase: 1.33

Compression chord:

Load combinations: DL + FLL + wind + ½(snow)

DL + FLL + snow + ½(wind)

Compression chord force:

$$C = \frac{\text{gross OM} + \text{RM}}{b}$$

Allowable stress increase: 1.33

Note that the free body diagram (FBD) in Fig. 16.9*b* shows the load and force combination for the tension chord analysis. The DL in the sketch represents all of the dead load to the shearwall above the foundation.

For designing the compression chord, the FBD would have to be revised to reflect the two required load cases. Recall that roof live load is an alternative to snow load. However, the Code does not require that roof live load be considered in wind design, because it is not likely that the RLL will be present during a major windstorm.

The calculation of the shearwall chord forces may be carried out using the expressions given above. A similar approach with a slightly different format was described in Chap. 10.

Example 16.6 deals with the *general* wind overturning requirements, which involve the addition of overturning due to horizontal wind and overturning due to uplift wind. If the uplift force U is large, the requirement to consider overturning due to the two wind effects simultaneously can be a significant force increase over previous codes. For low-rise buildings this burden has recently been mitigated as the result of wind tunnel tests and statistical wind load studies. The UBC wind force requirements were revised in 1988 to permit a *one-third reduction* of the *combined* effects of horizontal wind and uplift wind on certain *low-profile* buildings. See Example 16.7.

EXAMPLE 16.7   Reduced Wind Overturning Effects on Low-Profile Buildings

The effect of overturning caused by horizontal wind *plus* uplift wind may be reduced by *one-third* for buildings with a height-to-width ratio of 0.5 or less in the direction of the wind force. See Fig. 16.10. In addition to a maximum h/b ratio of 0.5, the Code limits the one-third reduction to buildings 60 ft or less in height.

The design requirements from Example 16.4 are revised in the following summary to reflect the reduced effects caused by combined horizontal wind and uplift wind.

Base overturning

Reduced FS for base overturning: FS $= (1 - \frac{1}{3})(1.5) = 1.0$
Load combination incorporating FS $= 1.0$:   DL $+$ horizontal wind $+$ uplift wind
Allowable stress increase: 1.33

Overturning at shearwall connection to foundation

$$\text{Gross OM} = Rh + U\left(\frac{b}{2}\right)$$

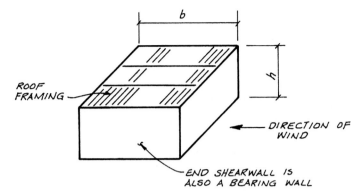

PICTORIAL OF LOW PROFILE BUILDING

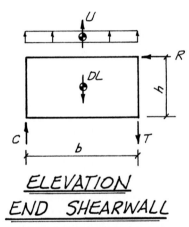

ELEVATION
END SHEARWALL

Figure 16.10 Low-profile buildings have $h/b \leq 0.5$ and $h \leq 60$ ft. These structures are subject to less critical overturning effects due to wind. The overturning due to *combined* horizontal wind *plus* uplift wind may be reduced by one-third. Therefore, the full DL (instead of ⅔DL) may be used to determine the net OM.

Tension chord

  Load combination: DL + horizontal wind + uplift wind
  Net overturning moment (ΣM_O):   Net OM = gross OM − RM
  Net tension chord force:

$$\text{Net } T = \frac{\text{net OM}}{b}$$

$$= \frac{\text{gross OM} - \text{RM}}{b}$$

  Allowable stress increase: 1.33

Compression chord

Design recommendations for the compression chord are the same as those given in Example 16.6.

The reduced overturning effects in Example 16.7 are for the *combined* effects from horizontal wind and uplift wind on low-profile buildings. Therefore, it may also be reasonable to consider the effects of overturning caused by the horizontal wind force and the overturning due to uplift wind force *separately*, without the one-third reduction permitted for the combined effects.

In Example 16.6 and 16.7, the maximum soil bearing pressure q_{max} should be investigated under the combination of loads and forces that produces the critical situation for the foundation design.

16.8   Overturning—Seismic

The seismic force requirements from the UBC were introduced in Secs. 2.12 to 2.15. The specific requirements for checking overturning under seismic forces are summarized in this section.

The current seismic code was first introduced in the 1988 UBC, and it contains detailed design provisions for *regular* and *irregular* structures. Because irregular structures are inherently more susceptible to earthquake damage, the Code assigns additional design requirements for these structures. As previously noted, these penalties may take the form of higher design force levels, or other requirements may be imposed. For comparison, the overturning requirements for regular structures will be reviewed first, followed by a summary of the design provisions for irregular structures.

Even in a regular structure the forces generated during an earthquake are erratic, and the magnitude of the force level changes rapidly with time. This is due in part to the changing ground accelerations and in part to the dynamic characteristics of the structure. The transient and reversing nature of seismic forces as compared to wind forces, and observed behavior of buildings in past earthquakes, indicates that the accumulated effects at the base (foundation-soil interface) of a structure are less critical than would be obtained by a direct addition of the seismic overturning forces acting on the structure above. Consequently, a lower factor of safety is implied for checking the moment stability of a structure under seismic forces compared with wind.

For moment stability and uplift considerations, a multiplier of 0.85 is used to reduce the dead load for seismic overturning (in place of the two-thirds factor used for wind overturning). See Example 16.8. For regular structures the Code permits the one-third increase in allowable stress traditionally used for wind and seismic forces.

It is interesting to note that very early seismic codes included a coefficient that was used to *reduce* the seismic overturning moment. Although this reduction factor has been deleted for some time, the current seismic code specifically states that the seismic force F_t (Sec. 2.12) may be ignored when overturning *at the foundation-soil interface* is checked.

EXAMPLE 16.8   Seismic Overturning Requirements—Regular Structures

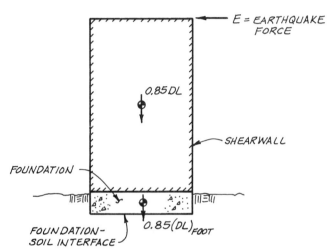

Figure 16.11a Loads and forces for seismic overturning at foundation-soil interface.

Seismic overturning effects are less critical at the foundation-soil interface (Fig. 16.11a) because of the transient and reversing nature of the seismic forces on the structure above. As an indication of this less critical situation, UBC Chap. 29 allows F_t to be omitted when overturning at the foundation-soil interface is checked.

This provision illustrates the point that *lateral* seismic forces are transient and reversing. However, it has little practical effect on the design of typical low-rise wood structures because F_t is zero for buildings with a period of vibration of 0.7 sec or less.

On the other hand, significant *vertical* ground accelerations have been recorded in earthquakes. These are recognized in the Code by requiring that the effects of overturning and uplift be considered by reducing the DL-resisting moment by 15 percent (0.85 multiplier for DL).

The 15 percent reduction in DL may, in some instances, be *unconservative* because ground motion records indicate vertical ground motion measurements of 30 to over 100 percent of the horizontal ground motion. However, the 15 percent reduction in resisting DL is intended to account for *vertical ground motion*. With this reduction, the implied FS for overturning under lateral seismic forces is 1.0.

Base overturning requirements are as follows:

Implied FS for base overturning: FS = 1.0

Load and force combination incorporating FS = 1.0:   0.85DL + E

Allowable stress increase: 1.33

The allowable stress increase may be applied to the vertical soil bearing value. A reinforced-concrete foundation that is designed on a strength basis should use the appropriate load factor instead of the allowable-stress increase.

Uplift connections to the foundation should be designed for overturning by considering 0.85 times the dead-load-resisting moment. See Fig. 16.11b.

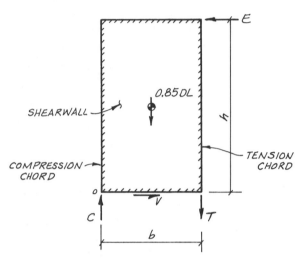

Figure 16.11b Loads and forces for seismic overturning at shearwall tension chord connection to foundation—regular structure.

The gross overturning moment is

$$\text{Gross OM} = Eh$$

The expressions developed in the statics analysis of the overturning problem in Example 16.4 are revised as follows:

Tension chord:

Load and force combination: $0.85DL + E$

Net overturning moment:

$$\text{Net OM} = \text{gross OM} - 0.85RM$$

Net tension chord force:

$$\text{Net } T = \frac{\text{net OM}}{b}$$

$$= \frac{\text{gross OM} - 0.85RM}{b}$$

Allowable stress increase: 1.33

Compression chord:

Load and force combination: DL + FLL + snow + *E*
Compression chord force:

$$C = \frac{\text{gross OM} + \text{RM}}{b}$$

Allowable stress increase: 1.33

Note that the free-body diagram in Fig. 16.11*b* shows the load and force combination for the tension chord analysis. For designing the compression chord, the FBD would have to be revised to reflect the appropriate combination of loads and forces. Snow load may be reduced (Sec. 2.16) when combined with seismic. Recall that roof live load is an alternative to snow load. However, the Code does not require that roof live load be considered in seismic design because it is not likely that RLL will be present during a major earthquake.

The calculation of the shearwall chord forces may be carried out by using the expressions given above. A similar but slightly different approach was described in Chap. 10.

The overturning requirements for a *regular structure* in any *seismic zone* are summarized in Example 16.8. The reader is cautioned that the sketches in Examples 16.6 and 16.8 show the DL of the structure multiplied by a factor (e.g., ⅔ and 0.85). These FBDs are given to illustrate the concept of the load and force combinations covered in the discussion.

However, it is advisable to work, as consistently as possible, in terms of the true dead load of the structure (i.e., the DL without the multipliers). Then, only when needed to make the final check, should the multiplier be introduced. This practice will avoid mistakenly using a *reduced DL* in a load combination that requires the *full dead load*. Again, the drawings show the reduced DL to illustrate the concept of load and force combinations, rather than to recommend an approach to be followed in practice.

The design penalties that are assigned to *irregular* structures in areas of high seismic risk were outlined in Sec. 16.3. It will be recalled that two particularly critical types of discontinuities are the out-of-plane offset (Fig. 16.4*b*) and the in-plane-discontinuity (Fig. 16.5). These are *plan irregularity Type D* and *vertical irregularity Type D,* respectively. For buildings in seismic zones 3 and 4 with either Type D irregularity, the Code requires that shearwall chords, connections, and columns supporting the shearwall system be designed for greatly increased earthquake force levels. The required load and force combinations for the design of these elements are given in Example 16.9.

EXAMPLE 16.9   Seismic Overturning Requirements—Irregular Structures

The overturning of a second-story shear panel with a Type D structural irregularity was introduced in Example 16.2. In areas of high seismic risk (seismic zones 3 and 4), a force that produces an approximate collapse limit state is to be considered. See Fig. 16.12.

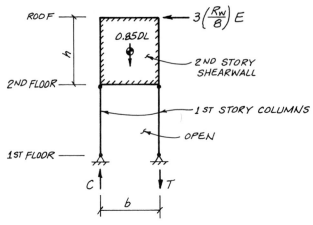

Figure 16.12   Overturning of second-story shearwall with Type D vertical or plan irregularity. Loads and forces shown are for seismic overturning for tension chord. Note that the shear from wall is transferred to second-floor horizontal diaphragm, as shown in Fig. 16.4c.

The gross overturning moment at the base of the shearwall is

$$\text{Gross OM} = 3\left(\frac{R_w}{8}\right)Eh$$

The design requirements for the first-story columns are as follows:

Tension chord:

   Load and force combination:

$$0.85\text{DL} + 3\left(\frac{R_w}{8}\right)E$$

   Net overturning moment:

$$\text{Net OM} = \text{gross OM} - 0.85\text{RM}$$

   Net tension chord force:

$$\text{Net } T = \frac{\text{net OM}}{b}$$

$$= \frac{\text{gross OM} - 0.85\text{RM}}{b}$$

   Allowable stress increase: 1.7

Compression chord:

Load combination:

$$\text{DL} + 0.8\text{LL} + 3\left(\frac{R_w}{8}\right)E$$

Compression chord force:

$$C = \frac{\text{gross OM} + \text{RM}}{b}$$

Allowable stress increase: 1.7

Note that the free-body diagram in Fig. 16.12 shows the load and force combination for the tension chord analysis. For the compression chord, the FBD would have to be revised to reflect the combination for the compression chord.

The large allowable stress increase of 1.7 permitted in this example reflects the severe (collapse) nature of the factored earthquake force.

In Example 16.8 and 16.9, the maximum vertical soil bearing pressure q_{max} should be investigated under the combination of loads and forces that produces the critical situation for the foundation design.

For a discussion of the one-third increase in allowable stress the reader is referred to Secs. 2.8 and 16.2. See Sec. 16.3 for background on the 1.7 allowable stress multiplier.

It is hoped that the fairly extensive treatment of the moment stability problem will give the reader a better appreciation of the problem and provide a convenient summary of the design criteria.

16.9   Lateral Analysis of Nonrectangular Buildings

Many of the buildings that have been considered thus far have been rectangular in plan view with exterior and possibly interior shearwalls. These types of buildings have been used to illustrate basic concepts about horizontal diaphragm design.

In practice, however, buildings are often not rectangular. Obviously, an unlimited number of plan configurations are possible. However, a simple L-shaped building can be used to illustrate how the lateral forces on a nonrectangular building can be resisted. See Example 16.10.

For seismic design, buildings of this nature are said to have a plan irregularity known as a *reentrant corner* (UBC Table 23-N, Type B). This type of discontinuity and the associated design penalty were described earlier (Fig. 16.2). In seismic zones 3 and 4, the presence of a reentrant corner requires that the traditional one-third increase in allowable stresses normally permitted for seismic design not be used. This restriction applies to the design of anchorage between the horizontal diaphragm and the vertical elements and to the design of drag struts and their connections. It does not affect plywood diaphragm nailing.

EXAMPLE 16.10   Lateral Analysis of Nonrectangular Buildings

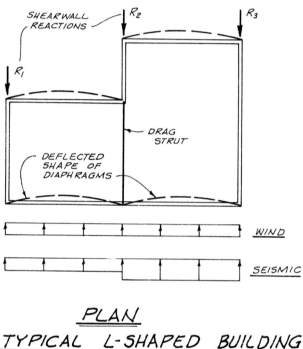

Figure 16.13 Wind and seismic forces to diaphragms in nonrectangular building.

A building with a nonrectangular plan may use rectangular horizontal diaphragms. Reactions to the shearwalls are calculated on a tributary width basis. The nonuniform seismic force results from the distribution of the dead load (Example 2.16 in Sec. 2.14). A similar analysis is used for lateral forces in the other direction.

In the approach illustrated, the building is divided into rectangles which are treated as separate horizontal diaphragms. The shearwall that is common to both diaphragms receives a portion of its force from the drag strut. The drag strut collects the roof diaphragm unit shear from the unsupported segments of the two horizontal diaphragms. A numerical example using this same building illustrates the method of calculating the design forces in both directions. See Example 16.11.

The simple span diaphragm approach illustrated in Example 16.11 has been used successfully by a number of designers to analyze buildings of nonrectangular configuration. However, Ref. 8.2 recommends that the continuity of the diaphragm at the interior shearwall be taken into account. In this case the chord in narrower diaphragms will have to be extended (see dashed line along line B in Fig. 16.14b and line 2 in Fig. 16.14c). See Ref. 8.2 for additional information.

EXAMPLE 16.11   L-Shaped Building

Determine the design unit roof shears, chord forces, and maximum drag strut connection forces for the one-story building in Fig. 16.14a. Consider lateral forces acting in both the N-S and E-W directions, and assume simple span diaphragms.

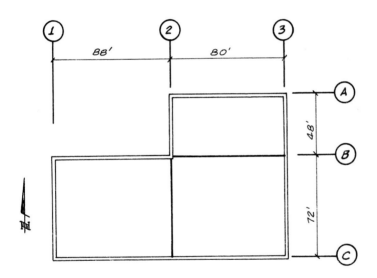

PLAN

Figure 16.14a L-shaped building.

Known Information

Roof DL = 20 psf
Wall DL = 75
Wind ≈ 20 psf
Seismic = 0.183W
Trib. wall height to roof level = 12 ft

Lateral Forces in N-S Direction

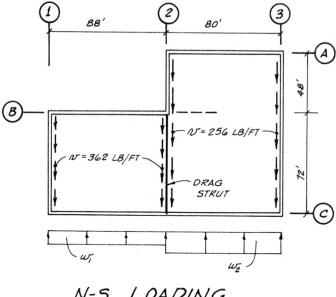

N-S LOADING

Figure 16.14*b* Diaphragm forces in N-S direction.

Diaphragm forces (Fig. 16.14*b*):

Wind

$$w = 20 \times 12 = 240 \text{ lb/ft}$$

Seismic

$$w_1 = 0.183[(20 \times 72) + 2(75 \times 12)]$$

$$= 593 \text{ lb/ft}$$

$$w_2 = 0.183[(20 \times 120) + 2(75 \times 12)]$$

$$= 769 \text{ lb/ft} \quad \text{seismic governs}$$

Roof shears:
Line 1 and west of line 2:

$$v = \frac{V}{b} = \frac{wL}{2b} = \frac{(593)(88)}{2(72)} = 362 \text{ lb/ft}$$

Line 3 and east of line 2:

$$v = \frac{wL}{2b} = \frac{(769)(80)}{2(120)} = 256 \text{ lb/ft}$$

Chord forces:
  Lines B and C between lines 1 and 2:

$$T = C = \frac{M}{b} = \frac{wL^2}{8b} = \frac{0.593(88)^2}{8(72)} = 7.97 \text{ k}$$

  Lines A and C between lines 2 and 3:

$$T = C = \frac{wL^2}{8b} = \frac{0.769(80)^2}{8(120)} = 5.12 \text{ k}$$

Drag tie force:
  Connection on line 2 at line B. Drag strut collects unsupported roof shear from both diaphragms.

$$T = (0.362 + 0.256)72 = 44.5 \text{ k}$$

Lateral Forces in E-W Direction

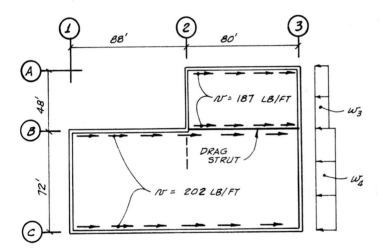

$$\underline{\underline{E\text{-}W \ \ LOADING}}$$

Figure 16.14c Diaphragm forces in E-W direction.

Diaphragm forces (Fig. 16.14c):
  Wind does not govern.
  Seismic

$$w_3 = 0.183[(20 \times 80) + 2(75 \times 12)]$$

$$= 622 \text{ lb/ft}$$

$$w_4 = 0.183[(20 \times 168) + 2(75 \times 12)]$$

$$= 944 \text{ lb/ft}$$

Roof shears:
Line A and north of line B:

$$v = \frac{V}{b} = \frac{wL}{2b} = \frac{622(48)}{2(80)} = 187 \text{ lb/ft}$$

Line C and south of line B:

$$v = \frac{wL}{2b} = \frac{944(72)}{2(168)} = 202 \text{ lb/ft}$$

Chord forces:
Lines 2 and 3 between lines A and B:

$$T = C = \frac{M}{b} = \frac{wL^2}{8b} = \frac{0.622(48)^2}{8(80)} = 2.24 \text{ k}$$

Lines 1 and 3 between lines B and C:

$$T = C = \frac{wL^2}{8b} = \frac{0.944(72)^2}{8(168)} = 3.64 \text{ k}$$

Drag tie force:
Connection on line B at line 2:

$$T = (0.187 + 0.202)(80) = 31.1 \text{ k}$$

16.10   Additional Topics in Horizontal Diaphragm Design

The lateral design forces required by the Code in areas of high seismic risk have increased substantially in recent years. In order to provide design values for more heavily loaded diaphragms, the American Plywood Association conducted a series of tests on diaphragms that were designed to develop high allowable unit shears. These diaphragms are referred to as *high-load* diaphragms, and test results are published in Ref. 14.11. High-load diaphragms are recognized in ICBO Evaluation Service, Inc., Report Number 1952.

One type of high-load diaphragm uses two layers of plywood sheathing. In the test the first layer was attached to the framing members with conventional nailing. The top layer was attached to the first layer with 14-gauge × 1¾-in. staples. The panel edges for the second layer were offset from the edges of the first layer, and the staples were purposely *not* driven into the framing members (i.e., staples penetrated the first layer of plywood only).

Another method of obtaining high-load diaphragms was with the use of relatively thick plywood (⅝ and ¾ in.) and closely spaced fasteners. Tests indicated that closely spaced 10d and 16d nails often caused the framing lumber to split. However, very closely spaced (1-in. o.c.) pneumatically driven wire staples were found to not cause splitting. High unit shears were obtained with these diaphragms.

Among other objectives, these diaphragm tests were designed to measure the effects of openings in horizontal diaphrams. See Refs. 8.2 and 14.11 for information on openings in diaphragms and other advanced topics in diaphragm design.

16.11 Problems

16.1 Discuss the differences between a structure that is seismicly regular and one that is irregular.

16.2 Give a brief description and sketch of the following seismic irregularities:
   a. Vertical mass irregularity
   b. Diaphragm discontinuity
   c. Reentrant corner
   d. Out-of-plane offset
   e. In-plane discontinuity

16.3 Classify each of the irregularities in Prob. 16.2 as either a vertical irregularity or a plan irregularity. List the section number in 1991 UBC that gives the design requirements for each type of irregularity.

16.4 Briefly describe the seismic design requirements for the irregularities in Prob. 16.2. Only the requirements that are *in addition* to those for a regular structure need to be discussed.

16.5 Regarding the overturning of a shearwall, describe the possible vertical soil bearing pressure diagrams. Give the formulas that are used to obtain the maximum soil pressure for the two distributions.

16.6 Refer to Fig. 16.8a and b. Determine the type of soil pressure distribution and the maximum soil bearing pressure for the following conditions:
   a. $R = 5000$ lb
   $h_1 = 12$ ft
   $b = 8$ ft
   $a = 24$ in.
   DL $= 200$ lb/ft   including weight of wall but not footing
   Footing thickness $= 16$ in.
   Unit weight of concrete $= 150$ pcf
   b. $R = 5000$ lb
   $h_1 = 12$ ft
   $b = 6$ ft
   $a = 24$ in.
   DL $= 200$ lb/ft   including weight of wall but not footing
   Footing thickness $= 16$ in.
   Unit weight of concrete $= 150$ pcf

16.7 Give the critical combinations of loads and forces required for designing the shearwall tension and compression chords for a typical single-story building. The structure is located in seismic zone 4, and the local snow loads govern over roof live loads. Give the corresponding allowable-stress increase (if any) for the following cases:

a. Seismic force for an irregular structure with an out-of-plane offset
b. Wind force on a low-profile building
c. Wind force on a building that does not qualify as a low-profile structure
d. Seismic force for a regular structure. In addition to the shearwall chords, give the loading condition for use in analyzing the overturning effects at the foundation-soil interface.

16.8 *Given:* The plan of the U-shaped building in Fig. 16.A. Exterior walls serve as shearwalls. Roof DL = 20 psf, and wall DL = 60 psf. Tributary wall height to roof diaphragm is 8 ft. Seismic coefficient = 0.183.

  Find: a. Unit shear in the horizontal diaphragms and shearwalls
b. The magnitude of the drag strut force at the point where these members connect to the shearwalls

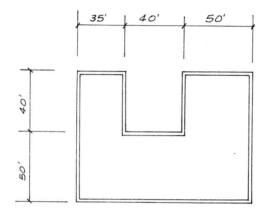

PLAN

Figure 16.A

A

Equivalent Uniform Weights of Wood Framing

Weights are for Douglas Fir-Larch lumber (S4S) used at an equilibrium moisture content of 15 percent (the maximum found in most covered structures). The unit weight of Douglas Fir-Larch equals or exceeds the unit weight of most softwood species, and the dead loads given below are conservative for most designs.

| | Spacing | | | | | |
| | 12 in. o.c. | | 16 in. o.c. | | 24 in. o.c. | |
Nominal size	Weight, psf	Board feet* per ft²	Weight, psf	Board feet* per ft²	Weight, psf	Board feet* per ft²
2 × 3	0.9	0.50	0.7	0.38	0.5	0.25
2 × 4	1.3	0.67	1.0	0.50	0.7	0.34
2 × 6	2.1	1.00	1.6	0.75	1.0	0.5
2 × 8	2.7	1.33	2.1	1.00	1.4	0.67
2 × 10	3.5	1.67	2.6	1.25	1.7	0.84
2 × 12	4.3	2.00	3.2	1.50	2.1	1.00
3 × 6	3.5	1.50	2.6	1.13	1.7	0.75
3 × 8	4.6	2.00	3.4	1.50	2.3	1.00
3 × 10	5.8	2.50	4.4	1.88	2.9	1.25
3 × 12	7.1	3.00	5.3	2.25	3.5	1.50
3 × 14	8.3	3.50	6.3	2.63	4.2	1.75
4 × 8	6.4	2.67	4.8	2.00	3.2	1.34
4 × 10	8.2	3.33	6.1	2.50	4.1	1.67
4 × 12	9.9	4.00	7.4	3.00	5.0	2.00
4 × 14	11.7	4.67	8.8	3.50	5.8	2.34
4 × 16	13.5	5.33	10.1	4.00	6.7	2.67

*Lumber is ordered and priced by the board foot. A board foot is a volume of lumber corresponding to 1 in. thick by 12 in. wide by 1 ft long. Nominal dimensions are used to calculate board measure.
SOURCE: Table from Ref. 9.1. Courtesy of Western Wood Products Association.

Weights of
Building
Materials

Loads given in Appendix B are typical values. Specific products may have weights which differ considerably from those shown, and manufacturer's catalogs should be consulted for actual loads.

		Roof dead loads	
Material		Weight, psf	
Lumber sheathing, 1 in. nominal		2.5	
Plywood, per inch of thickness		3.0	
Timber decking (MC = 15%):	2 in. nom.	3 in. nom.	4 in. nom.
DF-Larch	4.5	7.6	10.6
DF (South)	4.1	6.8	9.5
Hem-Fir	4.0	6.6	9.3
Mtn. Hemlock—Hem-Fir	4.0	6.6	9.3
Western Hemlock	4.0	6.6	9.3
Engelmann Spruce—Alpine Fir	3.1	5.2	7.3
Lodgepole Pine	3.7	6.2	8.6
Ponderosa Pine—Sugar Pine	3.7	6.2	8.6
Idaho White Pine	3.3	5.5	7.7
Western Cedars	3.3	5.5	7.7

Roof dead loads		
Material	**Weight, psf**	
Aluminum (including laps):	Flat	Corrugated (1½ and 2½ in.)
12 American or B&S gage	1.2	. . .
14	0.9	1.1
16	0.7	0.9
18	0.6	0.7
20	0.5	0.6
22	. . .	0.4
Galvanized steel (including laps):	Flat	Corrugated (2½ and 3 in.)
12 U.S. std. gage	4.5	4.9
14	3.3	3.6
16	2.7	2.9
18	2.2	2.4
20	1.7	1.8
22	1.4	1.5
24	1.2	1.3
26	0.9	1.0
Other types of decking (per inch of thickness):		
Concrete plank	6.5	
Insulrock	2.7	
Petrical	2.7	
Porex	2.7	
Poured gypsum	6.5	
Tectum	2.0	
Vermiculite concrete	2.6	
Corrugated asbestos (¼ in.)	3.0	
Felt:		
3-ply	1.5	
3-ply with gravel	5.5	
5-ply	2.5	
5-ply with gravel	6.5	
Insulation (per inch of thickness):		
Expanded polystyrene	0.2	
Fiber glass, rigid	1.5	
Loose	0.5	
Roll roofing	1.0	

Roof dead loads

Material	Weight, psf
Shingles:	
Asphalt (¼ in. approx.)	2.0
Book tile (2 in.)	12.0
Book tile (3 in.)	20.0
Cement asbestos (⅜ in. approx.)	4.0
Clay tile (for mortar add 10 psf)	9.0 to 14.0
Ludowici	10.0
Roman	12.0
Slate (¼ in.)	10.0
Spanish	19.0
Wood (1 in.)	3.0

Ceiling dead loads

Material	Weight, psf
Acoustical fiber tile	1.0
Channel-suspended system	1.0
For gypsum wallboard and plaster, see *Wall and partition dead loads*	

Floor dead loads

Material	Weight, psf
Hardwood (1 in. nominal)	4.0
Plywood (per inch of thickness)	3.0
Asphalt mastic (per inch of thickness)	12.0
Cement finish (per inch of thickness)	12.0
Ceramic and quarry tile (¾ in.)	10.0
Concrete (per inch of thickness)	
Lightweight	6.0 to 10.0
Reinforced (normal weight)	12.5
Stone	12.0
Cork tile (¹⁄₁₆ in.)	0.5
Flexicore (6-in. slab)	46.0
Linoleum (¼ in.)	1.0
Terrazo finish (1½ in.)	19.0
Vinyl tile (⅛ in.)	1.4

Wall and partition dead loads

Material	Weight, psf
Wood paneling (1 in.)	2.5
Wood studs (2 × 4 DF-Larch):	
12 in. o.c.	1.3
16 in. o.c.	1.0
24 in. o.c.	0.7
Glass block (4 in.)	18.0
Glass (¼-in. plate)	3.3
Glazed tile	18.0
Marble or marble wainscoting	15.0

Wall and partition dead loads

Material	Weight, psf
Masonry (per 4 in. of thickness):	
Brick	38.0
Concrete block	30.0
Cinder concrete block	20.0
Hollow clay tile, load bearing	23.0
Hollow clay tile, non-load-bearing	18.0
Hollow gypsum block	13.0
Limestone	55.0
Terra-cotta tile	25.0
Stone	55.0
(The average weights of completed reinforced and grouted concrete block and brick walls can be found in Ref. 12.)	
Plaster (1 in.)	8.0
Plaster (1 in.) on wood lath	10.0
Plaster (1 in.) on metal lath	8.5
Gypsum wallboard (1 in.)	5.0
Porcelain-enameled steel	3.0
Stucco (⅞ in.)	10.0
Windows (glass, frame, and sash)	8.0

SOURCE: Weights from Ref. 9.1. Courtesy Western Wood Products Association.

Appendix

C

Selected Tables from the *Uniform Building Code,* 1991 Edition*

	UBC Table No.
Tables for use in determining design loads	
1. Uniform and concentrated loads	23-A
2. Special loads	23-B
3. Minimum roof live loads	23-C
4. Maximum allowable deflection for structural members	23-D
5. Value of K	23-E
6. Wind stagnation pressure (q_s) at standard height of 33 ft	23-F
7. Combined height, exposure and gust factor coefficient (C_e)	23-G
8. Pressure coefficients (C_q)	23-H
9. Seismic zone factor Z	23-I
10. Site coefficients	23-J
11. Occupancy categories	23-K
12. Occupancy requirements	23-L
13. Vertical structural irregularities	23-M
14. Plan structural irregularities	23-N
15. Structural systems	23-O
16. Horizontal force factor, C_p	23-P
17. Minimum basic wind speeds in miles per hour	Figure 23-1
18. Seismic zone map of the United States	Figure 23-2
19. Normalized response spectra shapes	Figure 23-3

*Reproduced from the 1991 edition of the *Uniform Building Code,* copyright © 1991, with permission of the publisher, the International Conference of Building Officials.

TABLE NO. 23-A—UNIFORM AND CONCENTRATED LOADS

USE OR OCCUPANCY		UNIFORM LOAD[1]	CONCEN-TRATED LOAD
Category	**Description**		
1. Access floor systems	Office use	50	2,000[2]
	Computer use	100	2,000[2]
2. Armories		150	0
3. Assembly areas[3] and auditoriums and balconies therewith	Fixed seating areas	50	0
	Movable seating and other areas	100	0
	Stage areas and enclosed platforms	125	0
4. Cornices, marquees and residential balconies		60	0
5. Exit facilities[4]		100	0[5]
6. Garages	General storage and/or repair	100	6
	Private or pleasure-type motor vehicle storage	50	6
7. Hospitals	Wards and rooms	40	1,000[2]
8. Libraries	Reading rooms	60	1,000[2]
	Stack rooms	125	1,500[2]
9. Manufacturing	Light	75	2,000[2]
	Heavy	125	3,000[2]
10. Offices		50	2,000[2]
11. Printing plants	Press rooms	150	2,500[2]
	Composing and linotype rooms	100	2,000[2]
12. Residential[7]		40	0[5]
13. Restrooms[8]			
14. Reviewing stands, grandstands, bleachers, and folding and telescoping seating		100	0
15. Roof decks	Same as area served or for the type of occupancy accommodated		
16. Schools	Classrooms	40	1,000[2]
17. Sidewalks and driveways	Public access	250	6
18. Storage	Light	125	
	Heavy	250	
19. Stores	Retail	75	2,000[2]
	Wholesale	100	3,000[2]

[1]See Section 2306 for live load reductions.
[2]See Section 2304 (c), first paragraph, for area of load application.
[3]Assembly areas include such occupancies as dance halls, drill rooms, gymnasiums, playgrounds, plazas, terraces and similar occupancies which are generally accessible to the public.
[4]Exit facilities shall include such uses as corridors serving an occupant load of 10 or more persons, exterior exit balconies, stairways, fire escapes and similar uses.

(Continued)

[5]Individual stair treads shall be designed to support a 300-pound concentrated load placed in a position which would cause maximum stress. Stair stringers may be designed for the uniform load set forth in the table.

[6]See Section 2304 (c), second paragraph, for concentrated loads.

[7]Residential occupancies include private dwellings, apartments and hotel guest rooms.

[8]Restroom loads shall not be less than the load for the occupancy with which they are associated, but need not exceed 50 pounds per square foot.

TABLE NO. 23-B—SPECIAL LOADS[1]

USE		VERTICAL LOAD	LATERAL LOAD
Category	Description	(Pounds per Square Foot unless Otherwise Noted)	
1. Construction, public access at site (live load)	Walkway, see Sec. 4406	150	
	Canopy, see Sec. 4407	150	
2. Grandstands, reviewing stands, bleachers, and folding and telescoping seating (live load)	Seats and footboards	120[2]	See Footnote No. 3
3. Stage accessories (live load)	Gridirons and fly galleries	75	
	Loft block wells[4]	250	250
	Head block wells and sheave beams[4]	250	250
4. Ceiling framing (live load)	Over stages	20	
	All uses except over stages	10[5]	
5. Partitions and interior walls, see Sec. 2309 (live load)			5
6. Elevators and dumbwaiters (dead and live load)		2 x Total loads[6]	
7. Mechanical and electrical equipment (dead load)		Total loads	
8. Cranes (dead and live load)	Total load including impact increase	1.25 x Total load[7]	0.10 x Total load[8]
9. Balcony railings and guardrails	Exit facilities serving an occupant load greater than 50		50[9]
	Other		20[9]
10. Handrails		See Footnote No. 10	See Footnote No. 10
11. Storage racks	Over 8 feet high	Total loads[11]	See Table No. 23-P
12. Fire sprinkler structural support		250 pounds plus weight of water-filled pipe[12]	See Table No. 23-P
13. Explosion exposure	Hazardous occupancies, see Sec. 910		

(Continued)

[1]The tabulated loads are minimum loads. Where other vertical loads required by this code or required by the design would cause greater stresses, they shall be used.

[2]Pounds per lineal foot.

[3]Lateral sway bracing loads of 24 pounds per foot parallel and 10 pounds per foot perpendicular to seat and footboards.

[4]All loads are in pounds per lineal foot. Head block wells and sheave beams shall be designed for all loft block well loads tributary thereto. Sheave blocks shall be designed with a factor of safety of five.

[5]Does not apply to ceilings which have sufficient total access from below, such that access is not required within the space above the ceiling. Does not apply to ceilings if the attic areas above the ceiling are not provided with access. This live load need not be considered as acting simultaneously with other live loads imposed upon the ceiling framing or its supporting structure.

[6]Where Appendix Chapter 51 has been adopted, see reference standard cited therein for additional design requirements.

[7]The impact factors included are for cranes with steel wheels riding on steel rails. They may be modified if substantiating technical data acceptable to the building official is submitted. Live loads on crane support girders and their connections shall be taken as the maximum crane wheel loads. For pendant-operated traveling crane support girders and their connections, the impact factors shall be 1.10.

[8]This applies in the direction parallel to the runway rails (longitudinal). The factor for forces perpendicular to the rail is 0.20 x the transverse traveling loads (trolley, cab, hooks and lifted loads). Forces shall be applied at top of rail and may be distributed among rails of multiple rail cranes and shall be distributed with due regard for lateral stiffness of the structures supporting these rails.

[9]A load per lineal foot to be applied horizontally at right angles to the top rail.

[10]The mounting of handrails shall be such that the completed handrail and supporting structure are capable of withstanding a load of at least 200 pounds applied in any direction at any point on the rail. These loads shall not be assumed to act cumulatively with Item 9.

[11]Vertical members of storage racks shall be protected from impact forces of operating equipment, or racks shall be designed so that failure of one vertical member will not cause collapse of more than the bay or bays directly supported by that member.

[12]The 250-pound load is to be applied to any single fire sprinkler support point but not simultaneously to all support joints.

TABLE NO. 23-C—MINIMUM ROOF LIVE LOADS[1]

| ROOF SLOPE | METHOD 1 | | | METHOD 2 | | |
| | TRIBUTARY LOADED AREA IN SQUARE FEET FOR ANY STRUCTURAL MEMBER | | | UNIFORM LOAD[2] | RATE OF REDUC- TION r (Percent) | MAXIMUM REDUC- TION R (Percent) |
	0 to 200	201 to 600	Over 600			
1. Flat or rise less than 4 inches per foot. Arch or dome with rise less than one eighth of span	20	16	12	20	.08	40
2. Rise 4 inches per foot to less than 12 inches per foot. Arch or dome with rise one eighth of span to less than three eighths of span	16	14	12	16	.06	25
3. Rise 12 inches per foot and greater. Arch or dome with rise three eighths of span or greater	12	12	12	12		
4. Awnings except cloth covered[3]	5	5	5	5	No Reductions Permitted	
5. Greenhouses, lath houses and agricultural buildings[4]	10	10	10	10		

[1]Where snow loads occur, the roof structure shall be designed for such loads as determined by the building official. See Section 2305 (d). For special-purpose roofs, see Section 2305 (e).

[2]See Section 2306 for live load reductions. The rate of reduction r in Section 2306 Formula (6-1) shall be as indicated in the table. The maximum reduction R shall not exceed the value indicated in the table.

[3]As defined in Section 4506.

[4]See Section 2305 (e) for concentrated load requirements for greenhouse roof members.

TABLE 23-D—MAXIMUM ALLOWABLE DEFLECTION FOR STRUCTURAL MEMBERS[1]

TYPE OF MEMBER	MEMBER LOADED WITH LIVE LOAD ONLY *(L.L.)*	MEMBER LOADED WITH LIVE LOAD PLUS DEAD LOAD *(L.L. + K.D.L.)*
Roof member supporting plaster or floor member	$L/360$	$L/240$

[1]Sufficient slope or camber shall be provided for flat roofs in accordance with Section 2305 (f).

L.L. = live load.
D.L. = dead load.
K = factor as determined by Table No. 23-E.
L = length of member in same units as deflection.

TABLE 23-E—VALUE OF "K"

WOOD		REINFORCED CONCRETE[2]	STEEL
Unseasoned	Seasoned[1]		
1.0	0.5	$[2 - 1.2\,(A'_s/A_s)] \geq 0.6$	0

[1]Seasoned lumber is lumber having a moisture content of less than 16 percent at time of installation and used under dry conditions of use such as in covered structures.
[2]See also Section 2609.
A'_s = area of compression reinforcement.
A_s = area of nonprestressed tension reinforcement.

TABLE NO. 23-F—WIND STAGNATION PRESSURE (q_s) AT STANDARD HEIGHT OF 33 FEET

Basic wind speed (mph)[1]	70	80	90	100	110	120	130
Pressure q_s (psf)	12.6	16.4	20.8	25.6	31.0	36.9	43.3

[1]Wind speed from Section 2314.

TABLE NO. 23-G—COMBINED HEIGHT, EXPOSURE AND GUST FACTOR COEFFICIENT (C_e)[1]

HEIGHT ABOVE AVERAGE LEVEL OF ADJOINING GROUND (feet)	EXPOSURE D	EXPOSURE C	EXPOSURE B
0-15	1.39	1.06	0.62
20	1.45	1.13	0.67
25	1.50	1.19	0.72
30	1.54	1.23	0.76
40	1.62	1.31	0.84
60	1.73	1.43	0.95
80	1.81	1.53	1.04
100	1.88	1.61	1.13
120	1.93	1.67	1.20
160	2.02	1.79	1.31
200	2.10	1.87	1.42
300	2.23	2.05	1.63
400	2.34	2.19	1.80

[1]Values for intermediate heights above 15 feet may be interpolated.

TABLE NO. 23-H—PRESSURE COEFFICIENTS (C_q)

STRUCTURE OR PART THEREOF	DESCRIPTION	C_q FACTOR

1. Primary frames and systems	**Method 1** (Normal force method)
	Walls:
	  Windward wall
	  Leeward wall
	Roofs[1]:
	  Wind perpendicular to ridge
	  Leeward roof or flat roof
	  Windward roof
	    less than 2:12
	    Slope 2:12 to less than 9:12
	
	    Slope 9:12 to 12:12
	    Slope > 12:12
	  Wind parallel to ridge and flat roofs
		
		0.8 inward
		0.5 outward
		
		0.7 outward
		
		0.7 outward
		0.9 outward or
		  0.3 inward
		0.4 inward
		0.7 inward
		0.7 outward

	Method 2 (Projected area method)
	On vertical projected area
	  Structures 40 feet or less in height
	  Structures over 40 feet in height
	On horizontal projected area[1]
		
		1.3 horizontal any direction
		1.4 horizontal any direction
		0.7 upward

2. Elements and components not in areas of discontinuity[2]	Wall elements
	  All structures
	  Enclosed and unenclosed structures
	  Open structures
	  Parapets walls
		
		1.2 inward
		1.2 outward
		1.6 outward
		1.3 inward or outward

	Roof elements[3]
	Enclosed and unenclosed structures
	  Slope < 7:12
	  Slope 7:12 to 12:12
	
	Open structures
	  Slope < 2:12
	  Slope 2:12 to 7:12
	
	  Slope > 7:12 to 12:12
		
		1.3 outward
		1.3 outward or inward
		
		1.7 outward
		1.6 outward or 0.8 inward
		1.7 outward or inward

3. Elements and components in areas of discontinuities[2,4,6]	Wall corners[7]
	
	Roof eaves, rakes or ridges without overhangs[7]
	  Slope < 2:12
	  Slope 2:12 to 7:12
	  Slope > 7:12 to 12:12
	For slopes less than 2:12
	  Overhangs at roof eaves, rakes or ridges, and canopies
		1.5 outward or 1.2 inward
		
		2.3 upward
		2.6 outward
		1.6 outward
		
		0.5 added to values above

STRUCTURE OR PART THEREOF	DESCRIPTION	C_q FACTOR
4. Chimneys, tanks and solid towers	Square or rectangular Hexagonal or octagonal Round or elliptical	1.4 any direction 1.1 any direction 0.8 any direction

5. Open-frame towers[5,8]	Square and rectangular
	    Diagonal
	    Normal
	Triangular
		
		4.0
		3.6
		3.2

6. Tower accessories (such as ladders, conduit, lights and elevators)	Cylindrical members
	    2 inches or less in diameter
	    Over 2 inches in diameter
	Flat or angular members
		
		1.0
		0.8
		1.3

7. Signs, flagpoles, lightpoles, minor structures[8]		1.4 any direction

[1]For one story or the top story of multistory open structures, an additional value of 0.5 shall be added to the outward C_q. The most critical combination shall be used for design. For definition of open structures, see Section 2312.

[2]C_q values listed are for 10-square-foot tributary areas. For tributary areas of 100 square feet, the value of 0.3 may be subtracted from C_q, except for areas at discontinuities with slopes less than 7:12 where the value of 0.8 may be subtracted from C_q. Interpolation may be used for tributary areas between 10 and 100 square feet. For tributary areas greater than 1,000 square feet, use primary frame values.

[3]For slopes greater than 12:12, use wall element values.

[4]Local pressures shall apply over a distance from the discontinuity of 10 feet or 0.1 times the least width of the structure, whichever is smaller.

[5]Wind pressures shall be applied to the total normal projected area of all elements on one face. The forces shall be assumed to act parallel to the wind direction.

[6]Discontinuities at wall corners or roof ridges are defined as discontinuous breaks in the surface where the included interior angle measures 170 degrees or less.

[7]Load is to be applied on either side of discontinuity but not simultaneously on both sides.

[8]Factors for cylindrical elements are two thirds of those for flat or angular elements.

TABLE NO. 23-I
SEISMIC ZONE FACTOR *Z*

ZONE	1	2A	2B	3	4
Z	0.075	0.15	0.20	0.30	0.40

The zone shall be determined from the seismic zone map in Figure No. 23-2.

TABLE NO. 23-J
SITE COEFFICIENTS[1]

TYPE	DESCRIPTION	S FACTOR
S_1	A soil profile with either: (a) A rock-like material characterized by a shear-wave velocity greater than 2,500 feet per second or by other suitable means of classification, or (b) Stiff or dense soil condition where the soil depth is less than 200 feet.	1.0
S_2	A soil profile with dense or stiff soil conditions, where the soil depth exceeds 200 feet.	1.2
S_3	A soil profile 70 feet or more in depth and containing more than 20 feet of soft to medium stiff clay but not more than 40 feet of soft clay.	1.5
S_4	A soil profile containing more than 40 feet of soft clay characterized by a shear wave velocity less than 500 feet per second.	2.0

[1]The site factor shall be established from properly substantiated geotechnical data. In locations where the soil properties are not known in sufficient detail to determine the soil profile type, soil profile S_3 shall be used. Soil profile S_4 need not be assumed unless the building official determines that soil profile S_4 may be present at the site, or in the event that soil profile S_4 is established by geotechnical data.

TABLE NO. 23-K
OCCUPANCY CATEGORIES

OCCUPANCY CATEGORIES	OCCUPANCY TYPE OR FUNCTIONS OF STRUCTURE
I. Essential Facilities[1]	Hospitals and other medical facilities having surgery and emergency treatment areas.
	Fire and police stations.
	Tanks or other structures containing, housing or supporting water or other fire-suppression materials or equipment required for the protection of essential or hazardous facilities, or special occupancy structures.
	Emergency vehicle shelters and garages.
	Structures and equipment in emergency-preparedness centers.
	Standby power-generating equipment for essential facilities.
	Structures and equipment in government communication centers and other facilities required for emergency response.
II. Hazardous Facilities	Structures housing, supporting or containing sufficient quantities of toxic or explosive substances to be dangerous to the safety of the general public if released.
III. Special Occupancy Structure	Covered structures whose primary occupancy is public assembly–capacity > 300 persons.
	Buildings for schools through secondary or day-care centers–capacity > 250 students.
	Buildings for colleges or adult education schools–capacity > 500 students.
	Medical facilities with 50 or more resident incapacitated patients, but not included above.
	Jails and detention facilities.
	All structures with occupancy > 5,000 persons.
	Structures and equipment in power-generating stations and other public utility facilities not included above, and required for continued operation.
IV. Standard Occupancy Structure	All structures having occupancies or functions not listed above.

[1]Essential facilities are those structures which are necessary for emergency operations subsequent to a natural disaster.

TABLE NO. 23-L—OCCUPANCY REQUIREMENTS

OCCUPANCY CATEGORY[1]	IMPORTANCE FACTOR I	
	Earthquake[2]	Wind
I. Essential facilities	1.25	1.15
II. Hazardous facilities	1.25	1.15
III. Special occupancy structures	1.00	1.00
IV. Standard occupancy structures	1.00	1.00

[1]Occupancy types or functions of structures within each category are listed in Table No. 23-K and structural observation requirements are given in Sections 305, 306 and 307.
[2]For life-safety-related equipment, see Section 2336 (a).

TABLE NO. 23-M
VERTICAL STRUCTURAL IRREGULARITIES

IRREGULARITY TYPE AND DEFINITION	REFERENCE SECTION
A. **Stiffness Irregularity—Soft Story** A soft story is one in which the lateral stiffness is less than 70 percent of that in the story above or less than 80 percent of the average stiffness of the three stories above.	2333 (h) 3 B
B. **Weight (mass) Irregularity** Mass irregularity shall be considered to exist where the effective mass of any story is more than 150 percent of the effective mass of an adjacent story. A roof which is lighter than the floor below need not be considered.	2333 (h) 3 B
C. **Vertical Geometric Irregularity** Vertical geometric irregularity shall be considered to exist where the horizontal dimension of the lateral force-resisting system in any story is more than 130 percent of that in an adjacent story. One-story penthouses need not be considered.	2333 (h) 3 B
D. **In-plane Discontinuity in Vertical Lateral Force-resisting Element** An in-plane offset of the lateral load-resisting elements greater than the length of those elements.	2334 (g)
E. **Discontinuity in Capacity–Weak Story** A weak story is one in which the story strength is less than 80 percent of that in the story above. The story strength is the total strength of all seismic-resisting elements sharing the story shear for the direction under consideration.	2334 (i) 1

TABLE NO. 23-N
PLAN STRUCTURAL IRREGULARITIES

IRREGULARITY TYPE AND DEFINITION	REFERENCE SECTION
A. **Torsional Irregularity—to be considered when diaphragms are not flexible.** Torsional irregularity shall be considered to exist when the maximum story drift, computed including accidental torsion, at one end of the structure transverse to an axis is more than 1.2 times the average of the story drifts of the two ends of the structure.	2337 (b) 9 E
B. **Reentrant Corners** Plan configurations of a structure and its lateral force-resisting system contain reentrant corners, where both projections of the structure beyond a reentrant corner are greater than 15 percent of the plan dimension of the structure in the given direction.	2337 (b) 9 E 2337 (b) 9 F
C. **Diaphragm Discontinuity** Diaphragms with abrupt discontinuities or variations in stiffness, including those having cutout or open areas greater than 50 percent of the gross enclosed area of the diaphragm, or changes in effective diaphragm stiffness of more than 50 percent from one story to the next.	2337 (b) 9 E
D. **Out-of-plane Offsets** Discontinuities in a lateral force path, such as out-of-plane offsets of the vertical elements.	2334 (g), 2337 (b) 9 E
E. **Nonparallel Systems** The vertical lateral load-resisting elements are not parallel to or symmetric about the major orthogonal axes of the lateral force-resisting system.	2337 (a)

TABLE NO. 23-O—STRUCTURAL SYSTEMS

BASIC STRUCTURAL SYSTEM[1]	LATERAL LOAD-RESISTING SYSTEM—DESCRIPTION	R_w[2]	H[3]
A. Bearing Wall System	1. Light-framed walls with shear panels		
	a. Plywood walls for structures three stories or less	8	65
	b. All other light-framed walls	6	65
	2. Shear walls		
	a. Concrete	6	160
	b. Masonry	6	160
	3. Light steel-framed bearing walls with tension-only bracing	4	65
	4. Braced frames where bracing carries gravity loads		
	a. Steel	6	160
	b. Concrete[4]	4	—
	c. Heavy timber	4	65
B. Building Frame System	1. Steel eccentrically braced frame (EBF)	10	240
	2. Light-framed walls with shear panels		
	a. Plywood walls for structures three stories or less	9	65
	b. All other light-framed walls	7	65
	3. Shear walls		
	a. Concrete	8	240
	b. Masonry	8	160
	4. Concentrically braced frames		
	a. Steel	8	160
	b. Concrete[4]	8	—
	c. Heavy timber	8	65
C. Moment-resisting Frame System	1. Special moment-resisting frames (SMRF)		
	a. Steel	12	N.L.
	b. Concrete	12	N.L.
	2. Concrete intermediate moment-resisting frames (IMRF)[6]	8	—
	3. Ordinary moment-resisting frames (OMRF)		
	a. Steel	6	160
	b. Concrete[7]	5	—

D. Dual Systems	1. Shear walls		
	a. Concrete with SMRF	12	N.L.
	b. Concrete with steel OMRF	6	160
	c. Concrete with concrete IMRF[6]	9	160
	d. Masonry with SMRF	8	160
	e. Masonry with steel OMRF	6	160
	f. Masonry with concrete IMRF[4]	7	—
	2. Steel EBF		
	a. With steel SMRF	12	N.L.
	b. With steel OMRF	6	160
	3. Concentrically braced frames		
	a. Steel with steel SMRF	10	N.L.
	b. Steel with steel OMRF	6	160
	c. Concrete with concrete SMRF[4]	9	—
	d. Concrete with concrete IMRF[4]	6	—
E. Undefined Systems	See Sections 2333 (h) 3 and 2333 (i) 2	—	—

[1]Basic structural systems are defined in Section 2333 (f).
[2]See Section 2334 (c) for combination of structural system.
[3]*H*—Height limit applicable to Seismic Zones Nos. 3 and 4. See Section 2333 (g).
[4]Prohibited in Seismic Zones Nos. 3 and 4.
[5]N.L.—No limit.
[6]Prohibited in Seismic Zones Nos. 3 and 4, except as permitted in Section 2338 (b).
[7]Prohibited in Seismic Zones Nos. 2, 3 and 4.

TABLE NO. 23-P—HORIZONTAL FORCE FACTOR, C_P

ELEMENTS OF STRUCTURES AND NONSTRUCTURAL COMPONENTS AND EQUIPMENT[1]	VALUE OF C_P	FOOTNOTE
I. **Part or Portion of Structure**		
1. Walls including the following:		
a. Unbraced (cantilevered) parapets	2.00	
b. Other exterior walls above the ground floor	0.75	2,3
c. All interior bearing and nonbearing walls and partitions	0.75	3
d. Masonry or concrete fences over 6 feet high	0.75	
2. Penthouse (except when framed by an extension of the structural frame)	0.75	
3. Connections for prefabricated structural elements other than walls, with force applied at center of gravity	0.75	4
4. Diaphragms	—	5
II. **Nonstructural Components**		
1. Exterior and interior ornamentations and appendages	2.00	
2. Chimneys, stacks, trussed towers and tanks on legs:		
a. Supported on or projecting as an unbraced cantilever above the roof more than one half their total height	2.00	
b. All others, including those supported below the roof with unbraced projection above the roof less than one half its height, or braced or guyed to the structural frame at or above their centers of mass	0.75	
3. Signs and billboards	2.00	
4. Storage racks (include contents)	0.75	10
5. Anchorage for permanent floor-supported cabinets and book stacks more than 5 feet in height (include contents)	0.75	
6. Anchorage for suspended ceilings and light fixtures	0.75	4,6,7
7. Access floor systems	0.75	4,9
III. **Equipment**		
1. Tanks and vessels (include contents), including support systems and anchorage	0.75	
2. Electrical, mechanical and plumbing equipment and associated conduit, ductwork and piping, and machinery	0.75	8

[1]See Section 2336 (b) for items supported at or below grade.
[2]See Section 2337 (b) 4 C and Section 2336 (b).

[3]Where flexible diaphragms, as defined in Section 2334 (f), provide lateral support for walls and partitions, the value of C_p for anchorage shall be increased 50 percent for the center one half of the diaphragm span.

[4]Applies to Seismic Zones Nos. 2, 3 and 4 only.

[5]See Section 2337 (b) 9.

[6]Ceiling weight shall include all light fixtures and other equipment or partitions which are laterally supported by the ceiling. For purposes of determining the seismic force, a ceiling weight of not less than four pounds per square foot shall be used.

[7]Ceilings constructed of lath and plaster or gypsum board screw or nail attached to suspended members that support a ceiling at one level extending from wall to wall need not be analyzed provided the walls are not over 50 feet apart.

[8]Machinery and equipment include, but are not limited to, boilers, chillers, heat exchangers, pumps, air-handling units, cooling towers, control panels, motors, switch gear, transformers and life-safety equipment. It shall include major conduit, ducting and piping serving such machinery and equipment and fire sprinkler systems. See Section 2336 (b) for additional requirements for determining C_p for nonrigid or flexibly mounted equipment.

[9]W_p for access floor systems shall be the dead load of the access floor system plus 25 percent of the floor live load plus a 10 psf partition load allowance.

[10]In lieu of the tabulated values, steel storage racks may be designed in accordance with U.B.C. Standard No. 27-11.

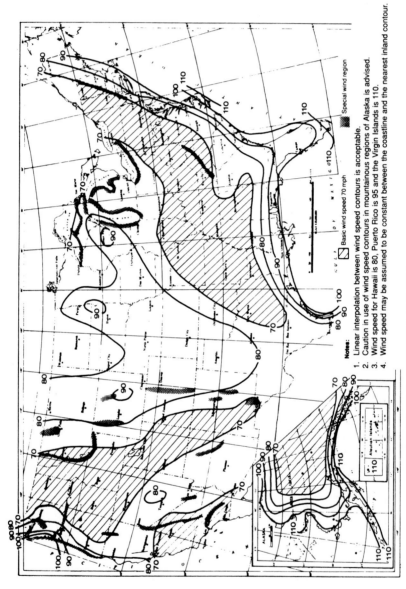

FIGURE NO. 23-1—MINIMUM BASIC WIND SPEEDS IN MILES PER HOUR

Notes:

1. Linear interpolation between wind speed contours is acceptable.
2. Caution in use of wind speed contours in mountainous regions of Alaska is advised.
3. Wind speed for Hawaii is 80, Puerto Rico is 95 and the Virgin Islands is 110.
4. Wind speed may be assumed to be constant between the coastline and the nearest inland contour.

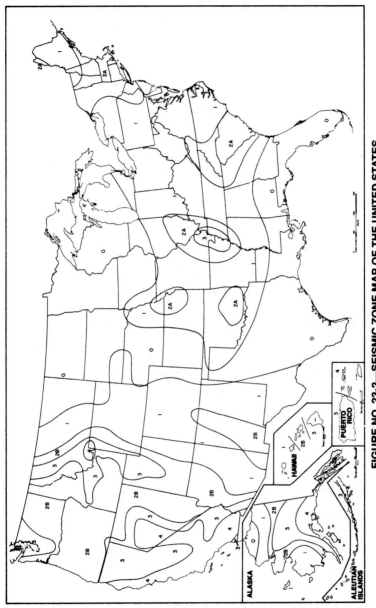

FIGURE NO. 23-2—SEISMIC ZONE MAP OF THE UNITED STATES

For areas outside of the United States, see Appendix Chapter 23.

853

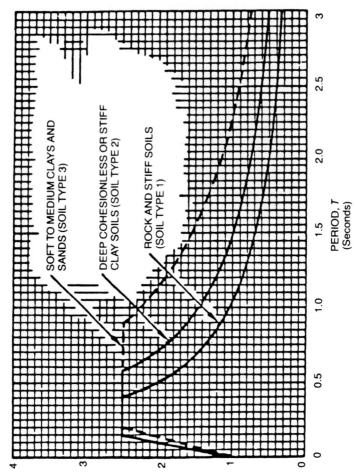

FIGURE NO. 23-3—NORMALIZED RESPONSE SPECTRA SHAPES

TABLE NO. 25-I—MAXIMUM DIAPHRAGM DIMENSION RATIOS

MATERIAL	HORIZONTAL DIAPHRAGMS	VERTICAL DIAPHRAGMS
	Maximum Span-Width Ratios	Maximum Height-Width Ratios
1. Diagonal sheathing, conventional	3:1	2:1
2. Diagonal sheathing, special	4:1	$3^{1}/_{2}$:1
3. Plywood and particleboard, nailed all edges	4:1	$3^{1}/_{2}$:1
4. Plywood and particleboard, blocking omitted at intermediate joints	4:1	2:1

TABLE NO. 25-J-1—ALLOWABLE SHEAR IN POUNDS PER FOOT FOR HORIZONTAL PLYWOOD DIAPHRAGMS WITH FRAMING OF DOUGLAS FIR-LARCH OR SOUTHERN PINE[1]

| PLYWOOD GRADE | Common Nail Size | Minimum Nominal Penetration in Framing (In Inches) | Minimum Nominal Plywood Thickness (In Inches) | Minimum Nominal Width of Framing Member (In Inches) | BLOCKED DIAPHRAGMS — Nail spacing at diaphragm boundaries (all cases), at continuous panel edges parallel to load (Cases 3 and 4) and at all panel edges (Cases 5 and 6) / Nail spacing at other plywood panel edges (Cases 5 and 6) | | | | UNBLOCKED DIAPHRAGM — Nails spaced 6" max. at supported end | |
					6 / 6	4 / 6	2½ / 4	2 / 3	Load perpendicular to unblocked edges and continuous panel joints (Case 1)	Other configurations (Cases 2, 3, 4, 5 and 6)
STRUCTURAL I	6d	1¼	5/16	2 / 3	185 / 210	250 / 280	375 / 420	420 / 475	165 / 185	125 / 140
	8d	1½	3/8	2 / 3	270 / 300	360 / 400	530 / 600	600 / 675	240 / 265	180 / 200
	10d[3]	1⅝	15/32	2 / 3	320 / 360	425 / 480	640 / 720	730 / 820	285 / 320	215 / 240
C-D, C-C, STRUCTURAL II and other grades covered in U.B.C. Standard No. 25-9	6d	1¼	5/16	2 / 3	170 / 190	225 / 250	335 / 380	380 / 430	150 / 170	110 / 125
			3/8	2 / 3	185 / 210	250 / 280	375 / 420	420 / 475	165 / 185	125 / 140
	8d	1½	3/8	2 / 3	240 / 270	320 / 360	480 / 540	545 / 610	215 / 240	160 / 180
			15/32	2 / 3	270 / 300	360 / 400	530 / 600	600 / 675	240 / 265	180 / 200
	10d[3]	1⅝	15/32	2 / 3	290 / 325	385 / 430	575 / 650	655 / 735	255 / 290	190 / 215
			19/32	2 / 3	320 / 360	425 / 480	640 / 720	730 / 820	285 / 320	215 / 240

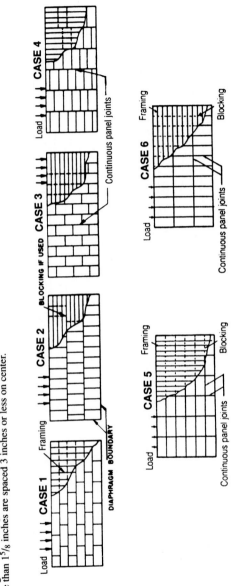

¹These values are for short-time loads due to wind or earthquake and must be reduced 25 percent for normal loading. Space nails 12 inches on center along intermediate framing members.

Allowable shear values for nails in framing members of other species set forth in Table No. 25-17-J of the U.B.C. Standards shall be calculated for all grades by multiplying the values for nails in Structural 1 by the following factors: Group III, 0.82 and Group IV, 0.65.

²Framing at adjoining panel edges shall be 3-inch nominal or wider and nails shall be staggered where nails are spaced 2 inches or 2¹/₂ inches on center.

³Framing at adjoining panel edges shall be 3-inch nominal or wider and nails shall be staggered where 10d nails having penetration into framing of more than 1⁵/₈ inches are spaced 3 inches or less on center.

Note: Framing may be oriented in either direction for diaphragms, provided sheathing is properly designed for vertical loading.

TABLE NO. 25-K-1—ALLOWABLE SHEAR FOR WIND OR SEISMIC FORCES IN POUNDS PER FOOT FOR PLYWOOD SHEAR WALLS WITH FRAMING OF DOUGLAS FIR-LARCH OR SOUTHERN PINE[1][4]

PLYWOOD GRADE	MINIMUM NOMINAL PLYWOOD THICKNESS (Inches)	MINIMUM NAIL PENETRATION IN FRAMING (Inches)	NAIL SIZE (Common or Galvanized Box)	PLYWOOD APPLIED DIRECT TO FRAMING — Nail Spacing at Plywood Panel Edges				NAIL SIZE (Common or Galvanized Box)	PLYWOOD APPLIED OVER 1/2-INCH OR 5/8-INCH GYPSUM SHEATHING — Nail Spacing at Plywood Panel Edges			
				6	4	3	22		6	4	3	22
STRUCTURAL I	5/16	1 1/4	6d	200	300	390	510	8d	200	300	390	510
	3/8	1 1/2	8d	230[3]	360[3]	460[3]	610[3]	10d[5]	280	430	550	730[2]
	15/32	1 1/2	8d	280	430	550	730	10d[5]	280	430	550	730
	15/32	1 5/8	10d[5]	340	510	665	870	—	—	—	—	—
C-D, C-C STRUCTURAL II, plywood panel siding and other grades covered in U.B.C. Standard No. 25-9.	5/16	1 1/4	6d	180	270	350	450	8d	180	270	350	450
	3/8	1 1/4	6d	200	300	390	510	8d	200	300	390	510
	3/8	1 1/2	8d	220[3]	320[3]	410[3]	530[3]	10d[5]	260	380	490	640
	15/32	1 1/2	8d	260	380	490	640	10d[5]	260	380	490	640
	15/32	1 5/8	10d[5]	310	460	600	770	—	—	—	—	—
	19/32	1 5/8	10d[5]	340	510	665	870	—	—	—	—	—
			NAIL SIZE (Galvanized Casing)					NAIL SIZE (Galvanized Casing)				
Plywood panel siding in grades covered in U.B.C. Standard No. 25-9	5/16	1 1/4	6d	140	210	275	360	8d	140	210	275	360
	3/8	1 1/2	8d	130[3]	200[3]	260[3]	340[3]	10d[5]	160	240	310	410

[1] All panel edges backed with 2-inch nominal or wider framing. Plywood installed either horizontally or vertically. Space nails at 6 inches on center along intermediate framing members for 3/8-inch plywood installed with face grain parallel to studs spaced 24 inches on center and 12 inches on center for other conditions and plywood thicknesses. These values are for short-time loads due to wind or earthquake and must be reduced 25 percent for normal loading.

Allowable shear values for nails in framing members of other species set forth in Table No. 25-17-J of U.B.C. Standards shall be calculated for all grades by multiplying the values for common and galvanized box nails in STRUCTURAL I and galvanized casing nails in other grades by the following factors: Group III, 0.82 and Group IV, 0.65.

[2] Framing at adjoining panel edges shall be 3-inch nominal or wider and nails shall be staggered where nails are spaced 2 inches on center.

[3] The values for 3/8-inch-thick plywood applied direct to framing may be increased 20 percent, provided studs are spaced a maximum of 16 inches on center or plywood is applied with face grain across studs.

[4] Where plywood is applied on both faces of a wall and nail spacing is less than 6 inches on center on either side, panel joints shall be offset to fall on different framing members or framing shall be 3-inch nominal or thicker and nails on each side shall be staggered.

[5] Framing at adjoining panel edges shall be 3-inch nominal or wider and nails shall be staggered where 10d nails having penetration into framing of more than 1 5/8 inches are spaced 3 inches or less on center.

TABLE NO. 25-M-1—EXPOSED PLYWOOD PANEL SIDING

MINIMUM THICKNESS[1]	MINIMUM NO. OF PLIES	STUD SPACING (INCHES) PLYWOOD SIDING APPLIED DIRECT TO STUDS OR OVER SHEATHING
1. ⅜"	3	16[2]
2. ½"	4	24

[1]Thickness of grooved panels is measured at bottom of grooves.
[2]May be 24 inches if plywood siding applied with face grain perpendicular to studs or over one of the following: (a) 1-inch board sheathing, (b) $^{15}/_{32}$-inch plywood sheathing or (c) $^{3}/_{8}$-inch plywood sheathing with face grain of sheathing perpendicular to studs.

TABLE NO. 25-M-2—ALLOWABLE SPANS FOR EXPOSED PARTICLEBOARD PANEL SIDING

GRADE	STUD SPACING (Inches)	MINIMUM THICKNESS (Inches)		Exterior Ceilings and Soffits
		Siding		Direct to Supports
		Direct to Studs	Continuous Support	
2-M-W	16	⅜	$^{5}/_{16}$	$^{5}/_{16}$
	24	½	$^{5}/_{16}$	⅜
2-M-1 2-M-2 2-M-3	16	⅝	⅜	—
	24	¾	⅜	—

TABLE NO. 25-N-1—PLYWOOD WALL SHEATHING[1]
(Not Exposed to the Weather, Face Grain Parallel or Perpendicular to Studs)

MINIMUM THICKNESS AND CONSTRUCTION	PANEL SPAN RATING	STUD SPACING (Inches)		
		Siding Nailed to Studs	Sheathing Under Coverings Specified in Section 2516 (g) 4	
			Sheathing Parallel to Studs	Sheathing Perpendicular to Studs
1. $^{5}/_{16}$"	12/0, 16/0, 20/0	16	—	16
2. ⅜", $^{15}/_{32}$", ½"—3 ply	16/0, 20/0, 24/0, 32/16	24	16	24
3. $^{15}/_{32}$", ½"—4 and 5 ply	24/0, 32/16	24	24	24

[1]In reference to Section 2517 (g) 3, blocking of horizontal joints is not required.

TABLE NO. 25-N-2—ALLOWABLE SPANS FOR PARTICLEBOARD WALL SHEATHING[1]
(Not exposed to the weather, long dimension of the panel parallel or perpendicular to studs)

GRADE	THICKNESS (Inches)	STUD SPACING (Inches)	
		Siding Nailed to Studs	Sheathing Under Coverings Specified in Section 2516 (g) 4 Parallel or Perpendicular to Studs
2-M-W	5/16	16	—
	3/8	24	16
	7/16	24	24
2-M-1 2-M-2	3/8	16	—
2-M-3	1/2	16	16

[1]In reference to Section 2517 (g) 3, blocking of horizontal joints is not required.

TABLE NO. 25-P—ALLOWABLE SHEARS FOR WIND OR SEISMIC LOADING ON VERTICAL DIAPHRAGMS OF FIBERBOARD SHEATHING BOARD CONSTRUCTION FOR TYPE V CONSTRUCTION ONLY[1]

SIZE AND APPLICATION	NAIL SIZE	SHEAR VALUE 3-INCH NAIL SPACING AROUND PERIMETER AND 6-INCH AT INTERMEDIATE POINTS
1. 1/2" x 4' x 8'	No. 11 gauge galvanized roofing nail 1½" long, 7/16" head	125[2]
2. 25/32" x 4' x 8'.	No. 11 gauge galvanized roofing nail 1¾" long, 7/16" head	175

[1]Fiberboard sheathing diaphragms shall not be used to brace concrete or masonry walls.
[2]The shear value may be 175 for ½-inch x 4-foot x 8-foot fiberboard nail-base sheathing.

TABLE NO. 25-Q—NAILING SCHEDULE

CONNECTION	NAILING[1]
1. Joist to sill or girder, toenail	3-8d
2. Bridging to joist, toenail each end	2-8d
3. 1″ x 6″ subfloor or less to each joist, face nail	2-8d
4. Wider than 1″ x 6″ subfloor to each joist, face nail	3-8d
5. 2″ subfloor to joist or girder, blind and face nail	2-16d
6. Sole plate to joist or blocking, face nail	16d at 16″ o.c.
7. Top plate to stud, end nail	2-16d
8. Stud to sole plate	4-8d, toenail or 2-16d, end nail
9. Double studs, face nail	16d at 24″ o.c.
10. Doubled top plates, face nail	16d at 16″ o.c.
11. Top plates, laps and intersections, face nail	2-16d
12. Continuous header, two pieces	16d at 16″ o.c. along each edge
13. Ceiling joists to plate, toenail	3-8d
14. Continuous header to stud, toenail	4-8d
15. Ceiling joists, laps over partitions, face nail	3-16d
16. Ceiling joists to parallel rafters, face nail	3-16d
17. Rafter to plate, toenail	3-8d
18. 1″ brace to each stud and plate, face nail	2-8d
19. 1″ x 8″ sheathing or less to each bearing, face nail	2-8d
20. Wider than 1″ x 8″ sheathing to each bearing, face nail	3-8d
21. Built-up corner studs	16d at 24″ o.c.
22. Built-up girder and beams	20d at 32″ o.c. at top and bottom and staggered 2-20d at ends and at each splice

(Continued)

CONNECTION	NAILING[1]
23. 2″ planks	2-16d at each bearing
24. Plywood and particleboard:[5] **Subfloor, roof and wall sheathing (to framing):** 1/2″ and less	6d[2]
19/32″-3/4″	8d[3] or 6d[4]
7/8″-1″	8d[2]
1 1/8″-1 1/4″	10d[3] or 8d[4]
Combination Subfloor-underlayment (to framing): 3/4″ and less	6d[4]
7/8″-1″	8d[4]
1 1/8″-1 1/4″	10d[3] or 8d[4]
25. Panel Siding (to framing): 1/2″ or less	6d[6]
5/8″	8d[6]
26. Fiberboard Sheathing:[7] 1/2″	No. 11 ga.[8] 6d[3] No. 16 ga.[9]
25/32″	No. 11 ga.[8] 8d[3] No. 16 ga.[9]

[1]Common or box nails may be used except where otherwise stated.
[2]Common or deformed shank.
[3]Common.
[4]Deformed shank.
[5]Nails spaced at 6 inches on center at edges, 12 inches at intermediate supports except 6 inches at all supports where spans are 48 inches or more. For nailing of plywood and particleboard diaphragms and shear walls, refer to Section 2513 (c). Nails for wall sheathing may be common, box or casing.
[6]Corrosion-resistant siding or casing nails conforming to the requirements of Section 2516 (j) 1.
[7]Fasteners spaced 3 inches on center at exterior edges and 6 inches on center at intermediate supports.
[8]Corrosion-resistant roofing nails with $7/16$-inch-diameter head and $1 1/2$-inch length for $1/2$-inch sheathing and $1 3/4$-inch length for $25/32$-inch sheathing conforming to the requirements of Section 2516 (j) 1.
[9]Corrosion-resistant staples with nominal $7/16$-inch crown and $1 1/8$-inch length for $1/2$-inch sheathing and $1 1/2$-inch length for $25/32$-inch sheathing conforming to the requirements of Section 2516 (j) 1.

TABLE NO. 25-R-3—SIZE, HEIGHT AND SPACING OF WOOD STUDS[1]

STUD SIZE (Inches)	BEARING WALLS				NONBEARING WALLS	
	LATERALLY UNSUPPORTED STUD HEIGHT[3] (Feet)	SUPPORTING ROOF AND CEILING ONLY	SUPPORTING ONE FLOOR, ROOF AND CEILING	SUPPORTING TWO FLOORS, ROOF AND CEILING	LATERALLY UNSUPPORTED STUD HEIGHT[3] (Feet)	SPACING (Inches)
		SPACING (Inches)				
1. 2 x 3[2]	—	—	—	—	10	16
2. 2 x 4	10	24	16	—	14	24
3. 3 x 4	10	24	24	16	14	24
4. 2 x 5	10	24	24	—	16	24
5. 2 x 6	10	24	24	16	20	24

[1]Utility grade studs shall not be spaced more than 16 inches on center, or support more than a roof and ceiling, or exceed 8 feet in height for exterior walls and load bearing or 10 feet for interior nonload-bearing walls.

[2]Shall not be used in exterior walls.

[3]Listed heights are distances between points of lateral support placed perpendicular to the plane of the wall. Increases in unsupported height are permitted where justified by an analysis.

TABLE NO. 25-S-1—ALLOWABLE SPANS FOR PLYWOOD SUBFLOOR AND ROOF SHEATHING CONTINUOUS OVER TWO OR MORE SPANS AND FACE GRAIN PERPENDICULAR TO SUPPORTS[1] [8]

PANEL SPAN RATING[3]	PLYWOOD THICKNESS (Inch)	ROOF[2]				FLOOR MAXIMUM SPAN[4] (In Inches)
		Maximum Span (In Inches)		Load (In Pounds per Square Foot)		
		Edges Blocked	Edges Unblocked	Total Load	Live Load	
1. 12/0	5/16	12		135	130	0
2. 16/0	5/16, 3/8	16		80	65	0
3. 20/0	5/16, 3/8	20		70	55	0
4. 24/0	3/8	24	16	60	45	0
5. 24/0	15/32, 1/2	24	24	60	45	0
6. 32/16	15/32, 1/2, 19/32, 5/8	32	28	55	35[5]	16[6]
7. 40/20	19/32, 5/8, 23/32, 3/4, 7/8	40	32	40[5]	35[5]	20[6] [7]
8. 48/24	23/32, 3/4, 7/8	48	36	40[5]	35[5]	24

[1]These values apply for C-C, C-D, Structural I and II grades only. Spans shall be limited to values shown because of possible effect of concentrated loads.

[2]Uniform load deflection limitations $1/180$ of the span under live load plus dead load, $1/240$ under live load only. Edges may be blocked with lumber or other approved type of edge support.

[3]Span rating appears on all panels in the construction grades listed in Footnote No. 1.

[4]Plywood edges shall have approved tongue-and-groove joints or shall be supported with blocking unless $1/4$-inch minimum thickness underlayment, or $1^1/2$ inches of approved cellular or lightweight concrete is placed over the subfloor, or finish floor is $3/4$-inch wood strip. Allowable uniform load based on deflection of $1/360$ of span is 165 pounds per square foot (psf).

[5]For roof live load of 40 psf or total load of 55 psf, decrease spans by 13 percent or use panel with next greater span rating.

[6]May be 24 inches if $3/4$-inch wood strip flooring is installed at right angles to joists.

[7]May be 24 inches where a minimum of $1^1/2$ inches of approved cellular or lightweight concrete is placed over the subfloor and the plywood sheathing is manufactured with exterior glue.

[8]Floor or roof sheathing conforming with this table shall be deemed to meet the design criteria of Section 2516.

TABLE NO. 25-S-2—ALLOWABLE LOADS FOR PLYWOOD ROOF SHEATHING CONTINUOUS OVER TWO OR MORE SPANS AND FACE GRAIN PARALLEL TO SUPPORTS[1] [2]

	THICKNESS	NO. OF PLIES	SPAN	TOTAL LOAD	LIVE LOAD
STRUCTURAL I	15/32	4	24	30	20
		5	24	45	35
	1/2	4	24	35	25
		5	24	55	40
Other grades covered in U.B.C. Standard No. 25-9	15/32	5	24	25	20
	1/2	5	24	30	25
	19/32	4	24	35	25
		5	24	50	40
	5/8	4	24	40	30
		5	24	55	45

[1]Uniform load deflection limitations: 1/180 of span under live load plus dead load, 1/240 under live load only. Edges shall be blocked with lumber or other approved type of edge supports.

[2]Roof sheathing conforming with this table shall be deemed to meet the design criteria of Section 2516.

TABLE NO. 25-S-3—ALLOWABLE LOADS FOR PARTICLEBOARD ROOF SHEATHING[1] [2] [4]

GRADE	THICKNESS (Inches)	MAXIMUM ON-CENTER SPACING OF SUPPORTS (Inches)	LIVE LOAD (Pounds Per Square Foot)	TOTAL LOAD (Pounds Per Square Foot)
2-M-W	3/8[3]	16	45	65
	7/16	16	105	105
	7/16[3]	24	30	40
	1/2	16	110	150
	1/2	24	40	55

[1]Panels are continuous over two or more spans.

[2]Uniform load deflection limitation: 1/180 of the span under live load plus dead load and 1/240 of the span under live load only.

[3]Edges shall be tongue-and-groove or supported with blocking or edge clips.

[4]Roof sheathing conforming with this table shall be deemed to meet the design criteria of Section 2516.

TABLE NO. 25-T-1—ALLOWABLE SPAN FOR PLYWOOD COMBINATION SUBFLOOR-UNDERLAYMENT[1] [2]
Plywood Continuous over Two or More Spans and Face Grain Perpendicular to Supports

IDENTIFICATION	SPACING OF JOISTS (Inches)			
	16	20	24	48
Species Group[3]	Thickness in inches			
1	$1/2$	$5/8$	$3/4$	—
2, 3	$5/8$	$3/4$	$7/8$	—
4	$3/4$	$7/8$	1	—
Span Rating[4]	16 o.c.	20 o.c.	24 o.c.	48 o.c.

[1]Spans limited to value shown because of possible effect of concentrated loads. Allowable uniform load based on deflection of $1/360$ of span is 125 pounds per square foot (psf), except allowable total uniform load for $1\,1/8$-inch plywood over joists spaced 48 inches on center is 65 psf. Plywood edges shall have approved tongue-and-groove joints or shall be supported with blocking, unless $1/4$-inch minimum thickness underlayment is installed, or finish floor is $3/4$-inch wood strip.

If wood strips are perpendicular to supports, thicknesses shown for 16-inch and 20-inch spans may be used on 24-inch span.

[2]Floor panels conforming with this table shall be deemed to meet the design criteria of Section 2516.

[3]Applicable to all grades of sanded exterior-type plywood. See U.B.C. Standard No. 25-9 for plywood species groups.

[4]Applicable to underlayment grade and C-C (plugged).

TABLE NO. 25-T-2—ALLOWABLE SPANS FOR PARTICLEBOARD SUBFLOOR AND COMBINED SUBFLOOR-UNDERLAYMENT[1] [5]

GRADE	THICKNESS (Inches)	MAXIMUM SPACING OF SUPPORTS[2]	
		Subfloor	Combined Subfloor-Underlayment[3] [4]
2-M-W	$1/2$	16	—
	$5/8$	20	16
	$3/4$	24	24
2-M-3	$3/4$	20	20

[1]All panels are continuous over two or more spans.

[2]Uniform deflection limitation: $1/360$ of the span under 100 psf minimum load.

[3]Edges shall have tongue-and-groove joints or shall be supported with blocking. The tongue-and-groove panels are installed with the long dimension perpendicular to supports.

[4]A finish wearing surface is to be applied to the top of the panel.

[5]Floor sheathing conforming with this table shall be deemed to meet the design criteria of Section 2516.

TABLE NO. 25-U—ALLOWABLE SPANS FOR 2-INCH TONGUE-AND-GROOVE DECKING

SPAN[1] (In Feet)	LIVE LOAD	DEFLECTION LIMIT	f (psi)	E (psi)
		ROOFS		
4	20	1/240 1/360	160	170,000 256,000
	30	1/240 1/360	210	256,000 384,000
	40	1/240 1/360	270	340,000 512,000
4.5	20	1/240 1/360	200	242,000 305,000
	30	1/240 1/360	270	363,000 405,000
	40	1/240 1/360	350	484,000 725,000
5.0	20	1/240 1/360	250	332,000 500,000
	30	1/240 1/360	330	495,000 742,000
	40	1/240 1/360	420	660,000 1,000,000
5.5	20	1/240 1/360	300	442,000 660,000
	30	1/240 1/360	400	662,000 998,000
	40	1/240 1/360	500	884,000 1,330,000
6.0	20	1/240 1/360	360	575,000 862,000
	30	1/240 1/360	480	862,000 1,295,000
	40	1/240 1/360	600	1,150,000 1,730,000
6.5	20	1/240 1/360	420	595,000 892,000
	30	1/240 1/360	560	892,000 1,340,000
	40	1/240 1/360	700	1,190,000 1,730,000

(Continued)

SPAN[1] (In Feet)	LIVE LOAD	DEFLECTION LIMIT	f (psi)	E (psi)
7.0	20	1/240 1/360	490	910,000 1,360,000
	30	1/240 1/360	650	1,370,000 2,000,000
	40	1/240 1/360	810	1,820,000 2,725,000
7.5	20	1/240 1/360	560	1,125,000 1,685,000
	30	1/240 1/360	750	1,685,000 2,530,000
	40	1/240 1/360	930	2,250,000 3,380,000
8.0	20	1/240 1/360	640	1,360,000 2,040,000
	30	1/240 1/360	850	2,040,000 3,060,000
FLOORS				
4 4.5 5.0	40	1/360	840 950 1060	1,000,000 1,300,000 1,600,000

[1]Spans are based on simple beam action with 10 pounds per square foot dead load and provisions for a 300-pound concentrated load on a 12-inch width of floor decking. Random lay-up permitted in accordance with the provisions of Section 2517 (e) 3 or 2517 (h) 8. Lumber thickness assumed at 1½ inches, net.

TABLE NO. 25-V—WALL BRACING

SEISMIC ZONE	CONDITION	TYPE OF BRACE[1]								AMOUNT OF BRACING[2]
		A	B	C	D	E	F	G	H	
0, 1 and 2	One Story Top of Two or Three Story	X	X	X	X	X	X	X	X	Each end and each 25' of wall
	First Story of Two Story or Second Story of Three Story	X	X	X	X	X	X	X	X	
	First Story of Three Story		X	X	X	X[3]	X	X	X	
3 and 4	One Story Top of Two or Three Story	X	X	X	X	X	X	X	X	Each end and each 25' of wall
	First Story of Two Story or Second Story of Three Story		X	X	X	X[3]	X	X	X	Each end. 25% of wall length to be sheathed
	First Story of Three Story		X	X	X	X[3]	X	X	X	Each end. 40% of wall length to be sheathed

[1]See Section 2517 (g) 3 for full description.

[2]Bracing at ends shall be near thereto as possible. Braces shall be installed so that there is no unbraced section along the wall exceeding 25 feet.

[3]Gypsum wallboard applied to supports at 16 inches on center.

TABLE NO. 47-I—ALLOWABLE SHEAR FOR WIND OR SEISMIC FORCES IN POUNDS PER FOOT FOR VERTICAL DIAPHRAGMS OF LATH AND PLASTER OR GYPSUM BOARD FRAME WALL ASSEMBLIES[1]

TYPE OF MATERIAL	THICKNESS OF MATERIAL	WALL CONSTRUCTION	NAIL SPACING[2] MAXIMUM (In Inches)	SHEAR VALUE	MINIMUM NAIL SIZE[3,4]
1. Expanded metal, or woven wire lath and portland-cement plaster	7/8"	Unblocked	6	180	No. 11 gauge, 1½" long, 7/16" head; No. 16 gauge staple, 7/8" legs
2. Gypsum lath	3/8" Lath and ½" Plaster	Unblocked	5	100	No. 13 gauge, 1⅛" long, 19/64" head, plasterboard blued nail
3. Gypsum sheathing board	½" x 2' x 8'	Unblocked	4	75	No. 11 gauge, 1¾" long, 7/16" head, diamond-point, galvanized
	½" x 4'	Blocked	4	175	
	½" x 4'	Unblocked	7	100	
4. Gypsum wallboard or veneer base.	½"	Unblocked	7	100	5d cooler or wallboard
			4	125	
		Blocked	7	125	
			4	150	
	5/8"	Unblocked	7	115	6d cooler or wallboard
			4	145	
		Blocked	7	145	
			4	175	
		Blocked Two ply	Base ply 9 Face ply 7	250	Base ply—6d cooler or wallboard Face ply—8d cooler or wallboard

[1] These vertical diaphragms shall not be used to resist loads imposed by masonry or concrete construction. See Section 4714 (b). Values are for short-term loading due to wind. Values must be reduced 25 percent for normal loading. The values for gypsum products must be reduced 50 percent for dynamic loading due to earthquake in Seismic Zones Nos. 3 and 4.

[2] Applies to nailing at all studs, top and bottom plates and blocking.

[3] Alternate nails may be used if their dimensions are not less than the specified dimensions.

[4] For properties of cooler or wallboard nails, see U.B.C. Standard No. 25-17, Table No. 25-17-H.

TABLE NO. 24-D-1—ALLOWABLE TENSION, B_t, FOR EMBEDDED ANCHOR BOLTS FOR CLAY AND CONCRETE MASONRY, pounds[1,2,3]

f'_m (psi)	EMBEDMENT LENGTH, l_b, or EDGE DISTANCE, l_{be}, inches						
	2	3	4	5	6	8	10
1500	240	550	970	1520	2190	3890	6080
1800	270	600	1070	1670	2400	4260	6660
2000	280	630	1120	1760	2520	4500	7020
2500	310	710	1260	1960	2830	5030	7850
3000	340	770	1380	2150	3100	5510	8600
4000	400	890	1590	2480	3580	6360	9930
5000	440	1000	1780	2780	4000	7110	11,100
6000	480	1090	1950	3040	4380	7790	12,200

[1]The allowable tension values in Table No. 24-D-1 are based on compressive strength of masonry assemblages. Where yield strength of anchor bolt steel governs, the allowable tension in pounds is given in Table No. 24-D-2.

[2]Values are for bolts of at least A 307 quality. Bolts shall be those specified in Section 2406 (h) 1 A.

[3]Values shown are for work with or without special inspection.

TABLE NO. 24-D-2—ALLOWABLE TENSION, B_t, FOR EMBEDDED ANCHOR BOLTS FOR CLAY AND CONCRETE MASONRY, pounds[1,2]

BENT BAR ANCHOR BOLT DIAMETER, inches							
$1/4$	$3/8$	$1/2$	$5/8$	$3/4$	$7/8$	1	$1 1/8$
350	790	1410	2210	3180	4330	5650	7160

[1]Values are for bolts of at least A 307 quality. Bolts shall be those specified in Section 2406 (h) 1 A.

[2]Values shown are for work with or without special inspection.

TABLE NO. 24-E—ALLOWABLE SHEAR, B_v, FOR EMBEDDED ANCHOR BOLTS FOR CLAY AND CONCRETE MASONRY, pounds[1,2]

f'_m (psi)	BENT BAR ANCHOR BOLT DIAMETER, Inches						
	$3/8$	$1/2$	$5/8$	$3/4$	$7/8$	1	$1\,1/8$
1500	480	850	1330	1780	1920	2050	2170
1800	480	850	1330	1860	2010	2150	2280
2000	480	850	1330	1900	2060	2200	2340
2500	480	850	1330	1900	2180	2330	2470
3000	480	850	1330	1900	2280	2440	2590
4000	480	850	1330	1900	2450	2620	2780
5000	480	850	1330	1900	2590	2770	2940
6000	480	850	1330	1900	2600	2900	3080

[1]Values are for bolts of at least A 307 quality. Bolts shall be those specified in Section 2406 (h) 1 A.

[2]Values shown are for work with or without special inspection.

TABLE NO. 26-E—ALLOWABLE SERVICE LOAD ON EMBEDDED BOLTS (Pounds)[1,2]

DIAMETER (In Inches)	MINIMUM[3] EMBEDMENT (In Inches)	MINIMUM CONCRETE STRENGTH (In psi)		
		SHEAR[4]		TENSION[5]
		2000	3000	2000 to 5000
$1/4$	$2 1/2$	500	500	200
$3/8$	3	1100	1100	500
$1/2$	4	2000	2000	950
$5/8$	4	2750	3000	1500
$3/4$	5	2940	3560	2250
$7/8$	6	3580	4150	3200
1	7	3580	4150	3200
$1 1/8$	8	3580	4500	3200
$1 1/4$	9	3580	5300	3200

[1]Values are for natural stone aggregate concrete and bolts of at least A307 quality. Bolts shall have a standard bolt head or an equal deformity in the embedded portion.

[2]Values are based upon a bolt spacing of 12 diameters with a minimum edge distance of 6 diameters. Such spacing and edge distance may be reduced 50 percent with an equal reduction in value. Use linear interpolation for intermediate spacings and edge margins.

[3]An additional 2 inches of embedment shall be provided for anchor bolts located in the top of columns for buildings located in Seismic Zones Nos. 2, 3 and 4.

[4]Values shown are for work with or without special inspection.

[5]Values shown are for work without special inspection. Where special inspection is provided values may be increased 100 percent.

SI Metric Units

Introduction

In 1960 the Eleventh General Conference of Weights and Measures adopted the name International System of Units (accepted abbreviation SI, from Système International d'Unites) for a practical and consistent set of units of measure. Rules for common usage, notation, and abbreviation were adopted. Most industrial nations in the world have adopted and converted to SI. SI is not the old metric system (cgs or MKS).

A large number of code and industry design tables are required to carry out a timber structural design. Until these tables are converted to SI metric units by the appropriate agencies, there will be little practical wood design done in metric units.

However, the future trend will be toward the use of SI units. The following brief introduction to SI is included to aid the structural engineer in conversion between U.S. Customary (USC) units and SI units. Additional information can be found in Ref. 13.10.

Notation

SI is made up of seven base units, two supplementary units, and many consistent derived units. The following units are pertinent to structural design.

	Quantity	Unit	SI symbol
Base unit	Length	meter	m
	Mass	kilogram	kg
	Time	second	s
Supplementary unit	Plane angle	radian	rad
Derived unit	Density (weight)		N/m³
	Density (mass)		kg/m³
	Energy	joule	J (N · m)
	Force	newton	N (kg · m/s²)
	Frequency	hertz	Hz (1/s)
	Moment of force		N · m (kg · m²/s²)
	Moment of inertia		m⁴
	Stress, pressure	pascal	Pa (N/m²)

Prefixes

The following are SI-approved prefixes and their abbreviations used to denote very small or very large quantities.

Multiplication factor	Name	Symbol
$0.000\,000\,001 = 10^{-9}$	nano	n
$0.000\,001 = 10^{-6}$	micro	μ
$0.001 = 10^{-3}$	milli	m
$1000 = 10^{3}$	kilo	k
$1\,000\,000 = 10^{6}$	mega	M
$1000\,000\,000 = 10^{9}$	giga	G

Conversion Factors

The following is a list of structurally pertinent conversions between USC units and SI units.

Area

$$1 \text{ in.}^2 = 645.2 \text{ mm}^2$$

$$1 \text{ ft}^2 = 92.90 \times 10^{-3} \text{ m}^2$$

Bending Moment or Torque

$$1 \text{ in.-lb} = 0.1130 \text{ N} \cdot \text{m}$$

$$1 \text{ ft-lb} = 1.356 \text{ N} \cdot \text{m}$$

$$1 \text{ ft-k} = 1.356 \text{ kN} \cdot \text{m}$$

Lengths or Displacements

$$1 \text{ in.} = 25.40 \text{ mm}$$

$$1 \text{ ft} = 0.3048 \text{ m}$$

Loads

$$1 \text{ lb} = 4.448 \text{ N}$$

$$1 \text{ k} = 4.448 \text{ kN}$$

$$1 \text{ lb/ft} = 14.59 \text{ N/m}$$

$$1 \text{ k/ft} = 14.59 \text{ kN/m}$$

Moment of Inertia

$$1 \text{ in.}^4 = 0.4162 \times 10^6 \text{ mm}^4$$

$$1 \text{ ft}^4 = 8.631 \times 10^{-3} \text{ m}^4$$

Section Modulus or Volume

$$1 \text{ in.}^3 = 16.39 \times 10^3 \text{ mm}^3$$

$$1 \text{ ft}^3 = 28.32 \times 10^{-3} \text{ m}^3$$

Stress and Modulus of Elasticity

$$1 \text{ psi} = 6.895 \text{ kPa}$$

$$1 \text{ ksi} = 6.895 \text{ MPa}$$

$$1 \text{ psf} = 47.88 \text{ Pa}$$

Unit Weight, Density

$$1 \text{ lb/ft}^3 = 0.157 \text{ kN/m}^3$$

Appendix

E

References

1. Publications of the International Conference of Building Officials (ICBO) (5360 South Workman Mill Road, Whittier, CA 90601):
   1.1 *Uniform Building Code,* 1991 ed.
   1.2 *Uniform Building Code Standards,* 1991 ed.
   1.3 Bush, Vincent R.: *Handbook to the Uniform Building Code,* 1991.
   1.4 Articles from *Building Standards* magazine:
      a. Nosse, John: "Anchorage of Concrete or Masonry Walls," November–December 1975.
      b. Sheedy, Paul: "Anchorage of Concrete and Masonry Walls," September–October 1983.*
      c. Letters and responses commenting on Ref. 1.4*b*, March–April 1984.*
      d. Henry, John R.: "Adequate Bracing versus Lateral Design: A New Look at an Old Problem," September–October 1990.
      e. Barbera, Jerry: "How the 1988 Uniform Building Code Regulates Wind Load Design," March–April 1990.
      f. Sheffield, James W., and Jerry J. Barbera: "The 1991 Uniform Building Code Wind Load Provisions, Part I of II," July–August 1991.
      g. Sheffield, James W., and Jerry J. Barbera: "The 1991 Uniform Building Code Wind Load Provisions, Part II of II," September–October 1991.
      h. Barbera, Jerry J.: "The 1991 Uniform Building Code Wind Load Provisions (Part I of II)—Corrections." November–December 1991.
      i. Sheedy, Paul, and Christine Sheedy: "Concrete and Masonry Wall Anchorage," July–August 1992.

2. *National Design Specification for Wood Construction and Supplement,* 1991 ed., National Forest Products Association (1250 Connecticut Avenue NW, Suite 200, Washington, DC 20036).

3. Publications of the American Institute of Timber Construction (11818 S.E. Mill Plain Blvd., Suite 407, Vancouver, WA 98684):
   3.1 *Timber Construction Manual,* 3d ed., Wiley, New York, 1985 (revision in progress).

---

*See Ref. 14.13.

877

3.2 "AITC 117-87 DESIGN, Standard Specifications for Structural Glued Laminated Timber of Softwood Species," 1987.

3.3 "AITC 117-88 MANUFACTURING, Standard Specifications for Structural Glued Laminated Timber of Softwood Species," 1988.

3.4 "AITC 104-84 Typical Construction Details," 1984.

3.5 "AITC 109-90 Standard for Preservative Treatment of Structural Glued Laminated Timber," 1990.

3.6 "AITC 110-84 Standard Appearance Grades for Structural Glued Laminated Timber," 1984.

3.7 "AITC Technical Note 8, Bolts in Glued Laminated Timber," 1986.

3.8 "AITC Technical Note 19, Guidelines for Field Drilling and Notching of Glued Laminated Timber Beams," 1992.

3.9 "AITC Technical Note 20, Guidelines to Minimize Moisture Entrapment in Panelized Wood Roof Systems," 1992.

3.10 "AITC Technical Note 21, Use of a Volume Effect Factor in the Design of Glued Laminated Timber Beams," 1990.

3.11 "AITC 113-86 Standard for Dimensions of Structural Glued Laminated Timber," 1986.

4. Publications of the Forest Products Laboratory (FPL), Forest Service, U.S. Department of Agriculture, One Gifford Pinchot Drive, Madison, WI 53705-2398:

4.1 *Wood Handbook: Wood as an Engineering Material,* Agriculture Handbook 72, 1987.

4.2 *Wood Handbook: Wood as an Engineering Material,* Agriculture Handbook 72, 1974.

4.3 Patton-Mallory, Marcia: "Yield Theory of Bolted Connections Compared with Current U.S. Design Criteria," 1989 (originally published in *Proceedings, 2d. Pacific Timber Engineering Conference,* 1989, 28–31, Auckland, New Zealand. Auckland: Centre for Continuing Education, University of Auckland; 1989, 323–329. Vol. 1. Copies available from FPL.)

4.4 Aune, Peter, and Marcia Patton-Mallory: "Lateral Load-Bearing Capacity of Nailed Joints Based on Yield Theory," Research Papers FPL 469 and 470, 1986.

4.5 Wilkinson, Thomas Lee: "Dowel Bearing Strength," Research Paper FPL-RP-505, 1991.

4.6 Green, David W.: "Moisture Content and the Shrinkage of Lumber," Research Paper FPL-PP-489, 1989.

4.7 Bohnhoff, David R., Russell C. Moody, Steve P. Verrill, and Leo F. Shirek: "Bending Properties of Reinforced and Unreinforced Spliced Nail-Laminated Posts," Research Paper FPL-RP-503, 1991.

5. Publications of the American Society of Civil Engineers (345 East 47th Street, New York, NY 10017):

5.1 ANSI/ASCE 7-88, *Minimum Design Loads for Buildings and Other Structures,* 1990 (formerly ANSI A58.1).

5.2 Zhan, John J.: "Biaxial Beam-Column Equation for Wood Members," *Structures Congress '91 Compact Papers; Congress Proceedings, 1991 April 29–May 1, Indianapolis, IN,* ASCE, pp. 56–59, 1991. Copies available from U.S. Forest Products Laboratory, One Gifford Pinchot Drive, Madison, WI 53705.

5.3 *Evaluation, Maintenance and Upgrading of Wood Structures,* 1982.

5.4 *Structural Wood Research,* 1984.

5.5 Bower, Warren H.: "Lateral Analysis of Plywood Diaphragms," *Journal of the Structural Division,* ASCE, vol. 100, no. ST4, Proc. Paper 10494, April 1974, pp. 759–772.

5.6   *Wood Structures,* 1975.

5.7   "Building Structures," edited by Donald R. Sherman, *Proceedings of the 1987 Structures Congress,* 1987.

    a. Diekmann, Edward F.: "Design of Low-Rise Wood Buildings for Wind Loads."

    b. Meeks, John E.: "Stability of Wood Trusses during Construction."

5.8   *Classic Wood Structures,* 1989.

5.9   Foliente, G. C., and T. E. McLain: "Design of Notched Wood Beams," *Journal of the Structural Division, ASCE* (in progress).

5.10 Zahn, John J.: "Design Equation for Multiple Fastener Wood Connections," *Journal of the Structural Division, ASCE,* vol. 117, no. 11, November 1991. Copies available from U.S. Forest Products Laboratory, One Gifford Pinchot Drive, Madison, WI 53705.

6. Publications of the Structural Engineers Association of California (P.O. Box 1940, Sacramento, CA 95819-0440):

    6.1   *Recommended Lateral Force Requirements and Commentary,* 1990.

    6.2   *Recommended Lateral Force Requirements and Commentary,* 1975.

7. Articles from *Wood Design Focus, A Newsletter of Contemporary Wood Engineering,* Wood Products Information Center/World Forestry Center (4033 SW Canyon Road, Portland OR 97221):

    7.1   Caldwell, R. Michael, Bradford K. Douglas, and David G. Pollock: "Load Duration Factor for Wind and Earthquake," vol. 2, no. 2, summer 1991.

    7.2   Cheung, Kevin C. K., Don E. Wallace, Brad E. Shelley, Lisa A. Johnson, and Eric D. Jones: "Lumber Design Values from In-Grade Testing," vol. 2, no. 2, summer 1991.

    7.3   McLain, Thomas E.: "Engineered Wood Connections and the 1991 National Design Specification," vol. 2, no. 2, summer 1991.

    7.4   Zahn, John J.: "New Column Design Formula," vol. 2, no. 2, summer 1991.

    7.5   Rood, Roy: "Panelized Roof Structures," vol. 2, no. 3, fall 1991.

    7.6   Pneuman, Fredrick C.: "Inspection of a Wood-Framed Warehouse-Type Structure," vol. 2, no. 4, winter 1991.

8. Publications of the Applied Technology Council, 2471 E. Bayshore Road, Suite 512, Palo Alto, CA 94303:

    8.1   Goers, Ralph W., and Associates: ATC-4, *A Methodology for Seismic Design and Construction of Single Family Dwellings,* 1976.

    8.2   H. J. Brunnier Associates: ATC-7, *Guidelines for the Design of Horizontal Wood Diaphragms,* 1981.

    8.3   ATC-7-1, *Proceedings of a Workshop on Design of Horizontal Wood Diaphragms,* 1980.

9. Wood design reference books:

    9.1   *Western Woods Use Book,* Western Woods Products Association (1500 Yeon Building, Portland, OR 97204), 3d ed., 1983 with 1987 update.

    9.2   Gurfinkel, German: *Wood Engineering,* 2d ed., Kendall/Hunt Publishing Company, 1981 (available from Southern Forest Products Association, Box 524468, New Orleans, LA 70152).

    9.3   Hoyle, Robert J., and Frank E. Woeste: *Wood Technology in the Design of Structures,* 5th ed., Iowa State University Press, Ames, 1989.

    9.4   Faherty, Keith F., and Thomas G. Williamson (eds.): *Wood Engineering and Construction Handbook,* McGraw-Hill, New York, 1989.

9.5   *Wood as a Structural Material,* vol. 2, Clark C. Heritage Memorial Series on Wood. The Pennsylvania State University (University Park, PA 16802), 1982.

9.6   *Wood Design Manual,* Canadian Wood Council (55 Metcalfe, Suite 1550, Ottawa, Canada K1P 6L5), 1990.

10. *Seismic Design for Buildings,* Technical Manual 5-809-10, NAV FAC P-355, Air Force Manual No. 88-3, chap. 13, Departments of the Army, Navy, and Air Force, Washington, 1973.

11. Publications of the American Institute of Steel Construction, Inc. (400 North Michigan Avenue, Chicago, IL 60611):
11.1   *Manual of Steel Construction,* 9th ed., 1989.
11.2   *Manual of Steel Construction—Load and Resistance Factor Design,* 1986.

12. Amrhein, James E.: *Reinforced Masonry Engineering Handbook,* 3d ed., Masonry Institute of America (2550 Beverly Boulevard, Los Angeles, CA 90057), 1978.

13. *1991 Annual Book of Standards Volume 04.09 Wood,* 1991, American Society for Testing and Materials (1916 Race Street, Philadelphia, PA 19103):
13.1   ASTM D 9-81, "Definitions of Terms Relating to Wood."
13.2   ASTM D 143-83, "Standard Methods of Testing Small Clear Specimens of Timbers."
13.3   ASTM D 245-81, "Methods for Establishing Structural Grades and Related Allowable Properties for Visually Graded Lumber."
13.4   ASTM D 1760-83b, "Specification for Pressure Treatment of Timber Products."
13.5   ASTM D 1990-91, "Practice for Establishing Allowable Properties for Visually Graded Dimension Lumber from In-Grade Tests of Full-Size Specimens."
13.6   ASTM D 2555-81, "Methods of Establishing Clear-Wood Strength Values."
13.7   ASTM D 3737-85, "Method for Establishing Stresses for Structural Glued-Laminated Timber (Glulam)."
13.8   ASTM D 4761-88, "Standard Test Methods for Mechanical Properties of Lumber and Wood-Based Structural Materials."
13.9   ASTM F 547-77 (1984), "Definitions of Terms Relating to Nails for Use with Wood and Wood-Base Materials."
13.10 ASTM E 380 (1984), "Metric Practice (Excerpts)."

14. Publications of the American Plywood Association and publications of American Wood Systems (P.O. Box 11700, Tacoma, WA 98411-0700):
14.1   *Plywood Design Specification,* 1986.
14.2   *Plywood Design Specification,* Supplements 1–5, 1990.
14.3   *Grades and Specifications,* 1990.
14.4   *Design/Construction Guide—Residential and Commercial,* 1990.
14.5   *Panel Handbook and Grade Glossary,* 1990.
14.6   *APA Research Report 154—Structural Panel Shear Walls,* by John R. Tissell, 1990.
14.7   *APA Laboratory Report 106—Horizontal Plywood Diaphragm Tests,* 1966.
14.8   *U.S. Product Standard PS 1-83 for Construction and Industrial Plywood,* reproduction by APA, 1990.
14.9   *Performance-Rated Panels,* 1990.
14.10 *Technical Note—Load-Span Tables for PS-1 Plywood,* 1989.
14.11 *APA Research Report 138—Plywood Diaphragms,* by John R. Tissell and James R. Elliott, 1990.

14.12 *Application Notes for Calculating Diaphragm Shear ref. Appendices A, B, and C of Plywood Diaphragms—Research Report 138,* by John R. Tissell.

14.13 APA reprint of Refs. 1.4*b* and *c. Note:* This reprint contains an introduction by APA that provides additional information relating to Refs. 1.4*b* and *c.*

14.14 *Design/Construction Guide—Diaphragms,* 1991.

14.15 *APA Research Report 151—Plywood End Shear Walls in Mobile Homes,* by John R. Tissell and John D. Rose, 1988.

14.16 EWS R525, "Moisture Control in Low Slope Roofs," 1992.

14.17 EWS S550, "Glulam Beam Camber," 1992.

14.18 EWS 560, "Field Notching and Drilling of Glued Laminated Timber Beams," 1992.

14.19 EWS R475, "Evaluation of Check Size in Glued Laminated Timber Beams," 1992.

14.20 *APA Technical Note N375, Design Capacities of APA Performance-Rated Structural-Use Panels,* July 1988.

15. Publications of the National Evaluation Service, Secretariat of the Council of American Building Officials (CABO). (The current secretariat of CABO is the International Conference of Building Officials, 5360 South Workman Mill Road, Whittier, CA 90601.)

    15.1 National Evaluation Report, "NER-108 APA Structural-Use Panels," May 1990.

    15.2 National Evaluation Report, "NER-272 Pneumatic or Mechanically Driven Staples, Nails, P-Nails and Allied Fasteners for Use in All Types of Building Construction," February 1989. Reprints also available from The International Staple, Nail, and Tool Association (ISANTA), 435 N. Michigan Avenue, Chicago, IL 60611.

16. Senco Products, Inc. (8485 Broadwell Road, Cincinnati, OH 45244-1699): "Air-Powered Nailers and Staplers and the Fasteners They Drive," 1991.

17. Stern, E. George: "Nails—Definitions and Sizes, a Handbook for Nail Users," No. 61, Virginia Polytechnic Institute, Research Division, Blacksburg, VA, 1967.

18. Federal Specification FF-N-105B, "Nails, Brads, Staples, and Spikes: Wire, Cut, and Wrought" (General Services Administration, Federal Supply Service, Washington, DC 20406).

19. American Iron and Steel Institute (1000 16th Street NW, Washington, DC): "Specification for the Design of Cold-Formed Steel Structural Members," 1987.

20. Rummelhart, Richard, and Jeffrey A. Fantozzi: "Multistory Wood-Frame Structures: Shrinkage Considerations and Calculations," August 1991. *Proceeding of the 1992 ASCE Structures Congress,* San Antonio, TX, April 1992. Copies available from Western Wood Products Association (WWPA).

21. Building Officials and Code Administrators International, Inc. (BOCAI) (4051 W. Flossmoor Road, Country Club Hills, IL 60478-5795): *The BOCA National Building Code/1990,* 11th ed.

22. Southern Building Code Congress International, Inc. (SBCCI) (900 Montclair Road, Birmingham, AL 35213-1206): *Standard Building Code,* 1991 ed.

23. Publications of the Truss Plate Institute, Inc. (583 D'Onofrio Drive, Suite 200, Madison, WI 53719):

    23.1 "Design Specification for Metal Plate Connected Wood Trusses," TPI-85, 1985.

23.2 "Commentary and Recommendations for Bracing Wood Trusses," BWT-76, 1976.

24. National Bureau of Standards (Washington, DC): *The International System of Units (SI)*, NBS Special Publication 330, 1974.

25. Bodig, Jozef, and Benjamin A. Jayne: *Mechanics of Wood and Wood Composites*, Van Nostrand Reinhold, New York, 1982.

26. *Structural Use of Wood in Adverse Environments*, edited by Robert W. Meyer and Robert M. Kellogg, Van Nostrand Reinhold, New York, 1982.

27. Folente, Greg C., Thomas E. McLain, and Fredrick C. Pneuman: "Draft Design Criteria for Notched Wood Beams," February 1992, publication in progress (for information contact Virginia Polytechnic Institute and State University, Blacksburg, VA 24061-0503).

Publications dealing with fabricated wood components

28. Laminated Truss, Inc. (P.O. Box 1056, Tacoma, WA 98401): *Panelized Roof System Design Manual*, 1991.

29. Alpine Engineered Products, Inc. (P.O. Box 2225, Pompano Beach, FL 33061-9990): *Alpine Architectural and Engineering Manual*, 1988.

30. Louisiana-Pacific Corporation (2706 Highway 421 North, Wilmington, NC 28401): *Engineered Products Design Manual*, 1992.

31. Trus Joist MacMillan (9777 West Chinden Blvd., Boise, ID 83714): *Design Manual*, 1991.

Publications (catalogs) dealing with connection hardware

32. Simpson Company (1450 Doolittle Drive, P.O. Box 1568, San Leandro, CA 94577): "Connectors for Wood Construction," Catalog no. C-92H-1, 1992.

33. KC Metal Products, Inc. (1960 Hartog Drive, San Jose, CA 95131): "KC Metals Superspeed Connectors," 1991.

34. Publications of TECO (5530 Wisconsin Avenue, Chevy Chase, MD 20815):
    34.1 "Lumberlok—Structural Framing Connectors," 1988.
    34.2 "Structural Wood Fasteners," 1988.
    34.3 "Design Manual for TECO Timber Connector Construction," 1973.

35. Silver Metal Products (2150 Kitty Hawk Road, Livermore, CA 94550-9611): "Wood Connectors," 1991.

Index

I